IN
TWO MINDS

A Biography of Jonathan Miller

KATE BASSETT

First published in Hardback in 2012 by Oberon Books Ltd

First published in Paperback in 2014 by Oberon Books Ltd

521 Caledonian Road, London N7 9RH

Tel: +44 (0) 20 7607 3637 / Fax: +44 (0) 20 7607 3629

e-mail: info@oberonbooks.com

www.oberonbooks.com

Typeset by Kenneth Burnley & Caroline Waldron, Wirral, Cheshire.

Printed and bound by Replika Press Pvt. Ltd, India.

eBook conversion by CPI Group.

Visit www.oberonbooks.com to read more about all our books and to buy them. You will also find features, author interviews and news of any author events, and you can sign up for e-newsletters so that you're always first to hear about our new releases.

CONTENTS

LIST OF ILLUSTRATIONS

Any unattributed photographs are from Jonathan Miller's private collection.

For Martin,
for my parents,
and in memory of Jeremy Maule

There is no subject on which he has not touched, none on which he has rested. With an understanding fertile, subtle, expansive . . . few traces of it will perhaps remain. He lends himself to all impressions alike; he gives up his mind and liberty of thought to none . . . a general lover of art and science . . . the most impressive talker of his age.

— William Hazlitt on Coleridge, *The Spirit of the Age*

And did you get what
you wanted from this life, even so?
I did.
And what did you want?
To call myself beloved, to feel myself
beloved on the earth.

— Raymond Carver, *Late Fragment*

ACKNOWLEDGEMENTS

To say that this biography has written itself would be a wild exaggeration. It has, of course, involved a mountain of work. However, literally hundreds of people have helped me along the way, making the process not just easier but profoundly enjoyable. First and foremost, Jonathan Miller has been enormously generous with his time, talking me through his life from his very earliest memories to the present day. The interviews he gave me are the most eloquent I have ever encountered, full of vivid images and humorous anecdotes, as well as being intellectually brilliant – ranging across seemingly every subject under the sun. He was terrifically understanding when progress was slow. Furthermore, given his self-confessed sensitivity to criticism, he has been courageously trusting, declining to read and censor what I have written in the manner of an authorized biography. I cannot thank him enough. Researching his life has enriched mine.

I extend my heartfelt gratitude to his family as well, especially to his wife Rachel who has been constantly welcoming and tolerant about recording sessions at the kitchen table – microphones and notepads strewn among the coffee cups. Their son Tom Miller, a photographer, has been extremely kind, supplying some of his own images for the plates sections and pointing me to other sources. His brother William Miller's wit and powers of description have enhanced this book too. He spoke to me about their father with great humour, frankness and affection.

I am also indebted to a huge number of Jonathan Miller's friends, colleagues and other associated professionals – as well as some acknowledged foes – who have all given me insights and stories galore. A few of them, sadly, have now passed on, but I hope that I have not omitted anyone from this list of interviewees: Claudio Abbado; Pippa Ailion; Nelson Aldrich; Antony Armstrong-Jones, 1st Earl of Snowdon; Neil Ascherson, Horace Barlow; Desmond Barrit; John Barton; John Bassett; Ann Beach; Eric Beck; Alan Bennett; Michael Billington; the actor and satirist John Bird; Michael Blakemore; Michael Bogdanov; Sue Bond; Christopher Booker; Willie Botterill of the Michael Palin Centre for Stammering

Children; Melvyn Bragg; Leslie Bricusse; John Bridges; Robert Brustein who was particulary magnanimous, taking a transatlantic phone call at an ungodly hour; John Burgess; Humphrey Burton; A. S. Byatt; Isabella Bywater who supplied me with photographs into the bargain. Likewise, thanks to my further interviewees: Patrick Carnegy for his observations and encouragement; George Christie; Susannah Clapp; John Cleese; Michael Codron; Michael Colgan; the writer Clare Colvin; Stephen Conroy; James Cornford; Michael Coveney who additionally shared illuminating material with me from his own archived files; Julian Crispin; Bernard Culshaw; Tony Cutler who went to the trouble of digging out a charming round-robin from his schooldays with Miller; Peter Davison; Richard Denton; William Donaldson; Freda Dowie; Ronald Dworkin; Mark Elder; Barbara Epstein; Peter Eyre; James Fenton; Carlos Fishman of the Portman Clinic; Renée Fleming; John Fortune; Christopher Foster; Michael Frayn; Clement Freud; Richard Gaddes; Peter Gallagher; Caroline Garland; Nicholas Garland who went out of his way to help, sending me extra material; Patrick Garland; Robert Gillespie; Jack Gold; Jill Gomez for her memories and her enthusiasm; Jack Goody; Robert Gore-Langton; Roger Graef; Richard Gregory; John Gross; Marit Gruson; Peter Hall; Terry Hands; Thomas Hampson; Michael Hastings; Charles Hazlewood; Stephen Hearst; David Heycock; Andrew Hilton; Robert Hinde; David Hinton; Jane Howell; Richard Hudson; Anne-Marie Huxstep (née Mallik); Nicholas Hytner; Eric Idle; Michael Ignatieff; Leon S. Illis; Richard Ingrams; Anne James who has assisted on several fronts with documentary records of BBC programming as well as photographs; Jonathan James-Moore; Terry Johnson; Peter Jonas; Will Kerley; Karl Kirchwey; the splendid Eric Korn; Elisheva Landman; George Lascelles, 7th Earl of Harewood; Roger Law; Tim Leggatt; Andrew Leigh; Anton Lesser; Naomi Lewis; Harvey Lichtenstein; Jean Liddiard; John Lubbock; Alastair Macauley; Charles Mackerras; Brian Marber; Cesare Mazzonis; Ian McDiarmid, Colin McGinn; Keith McNally; Zubin Mehta; Joseph Melillo; Diana and George Melly; Frank Middlemass; Robin Midgley; Jane Miller whose writings on Betty Miller suppled additional insights; Karl Miller; Sarah Miller who had partially investigated the family history and shared her findings with me unstintingly; also Hayley Mills; Rodney Milnes; Lee Minoff; David Mirvish; John Mordler; Elijah Moshinsky; Peter Nichols; Roger Norrington; Nicola Pagett; Tony Palmer; John Pardoe; Nicholas Payne; Norman and Johanna Platt who opened up Kent Opera's archives for me; Piers Plowright who also sent me illuminating background material; Christopher Plummer; David Pountney; Tristram Powell; Enid Presoody; Philip Prowse; Dick Quinnell; Sophie Radice; Ruggero Raimondi; Frederic Raphael; Julian Rees; David Ritch; Nick Rhodes of the Nightingale Project; Patrick Robertson; David Roderick; Anton Rodgers; Ann Romyn, Hans-Dieter Roser who posted me several production videos; Garry Runciman; Barrie Rutter; Oliver Sacks, not only for his perceptiveness but also for his trove of letters; Erich Sergeant; Fiona Shaw; Alan Shotts; John Shrapnel; Robert Silvers; Michael Simmons; Denis Mack Smith; Susan Sontag; Charles Spencer; Julian Spiro; Maggie Stearns who shared her rehearsals diary with me;

Karen Stone; Alan Strachan; Charles Sturridge; the opera critic Tom Sutcliffe; Janet Suzman; Judith Taylor (née Mundlak); Eugene Thaw; Heather Thomas; Jeannie (also known as Haleem) Thomas; Nancy Thomas; Claire Tomalin; John Tomlinson; Patrick Uden who unearthed his production files and photographic records; Rosemary Vercoe; Rudolph Walker; Irving Wardle; Trevor Williams who retrieved vintage photographs too; Penelope Wilton; Lewis Wolpert who sent me additional recorded material; Michael Wood; and Stephen Wright.

In the course of my research, I have constantly benefitted from others' admirable efficiency. I am obliged to countless institutions and individuals who have given me assistance, advice, information and materials, including: Kate Merriam of the ADC in Cambridge; Katalin Mitchell at the American Repertory Theatre, who hunted down lost theatre programmes; Caroline Shepherdson, archivist for Arnold House; Larysa McKenna and Sandy Sowotka at BAM; Beatrice Baumgartner; Katrin Fasel, Carrie Fischer and Juliet Kessler at the Bayerische Staatsoper; Karen White and the quietly superb Erin O'Neill at the BBC Written Archives; Berlin Staatsoper's press officers; Jill Reading and others at the BFI; Pierre Vidal at the Bibliothèque Nationale de France; Kathryn Johnson at the British Library and its map room staff; Joanna Mackle and Kate Eustace at the British Museum; Flora Smith of Broomhill Opera; Buxton Opera House's press office; Wendy Brown at Cambridge University Museum of Archaeology and Anthropology; John Wells and many others at the Cambridge University Library; Richard Clarke as well as Clive Conroy of Celebrity Productions; Chloë Dunbar at Channel 4; Chichester Festival Theatre's press office; Gary Rosen for the magazine *Commentary*; the Community Security Trust; Jack Kennedy at Company Pictures; Maria Yiannikkou of Condé Nast; Ben Chamberlain of The Corner Shop PR; Susan Calvin and Jennifer Hancock at Dallas Opera; Leslie Downie; Kate Edgar; Owen O'Leary in the Edinburgh Fringe Festival press office; Alyson Hall of the Emanuel Miller Clinic; Emma Holland of Emma Holland PR; Jane Livingston at the ENO and the company's archivist Clare Colvin; Brigitta Grabner at Ferrara Musica; the late Harry Porter, archivist for Footlights; Frankfurt Opera press office; the French Institute's librarians; Emma Foote at Dublin's Gate Theatre; Gavin Barker Associates; Glasgow University Library; Michael Willis and others at Glimmerglass Opera; Julia Aries at Glyndebourne; Emma Dunstan at Graeae; Laura Grant; Pia Ehnes at Graz Opera; Will Francis at Greene and Heaton; Christine Groom; the Hackney Empire's press office; Maggie Sedwards, assistant to Peter Hall; Harriet Hall of the Hallé Orchestra; Brian Mitchell, archivist at Houston Grand Opera; Jessica Ford and Ronan Tighe at IMG; Kirsteen Walker of Ingpen and Williams; Avivit Menahem and Rachel Levy of the Israeli Philharmonic Orchestra; the archivists for the publishing house Jonathan Cape; Coddy Granum, assistant to James Earl Jones; KBJ Management; Nancy Miles at King's College, Cambridge; the Lincoln Center's press office; the London Library; John Weller at Los Angeles Opera; Simon Gillis of the Marlowe Society in Cambridge; John Pennino and others at New York's Metropolitan Opera; Bill Morgan; Jenny Lea at the National Gallery; the library staff at the National Institute of Neurology; the National Library of Scotland; Gavin Clarke and others at the National Theatre Archives; Mary Parker in the National Theatre's press office; Susan Woelzl and Megan Hollingshead at New York City Opera; staff at the New York Public Library and Library of Performing Arts; Nathaniel Rich and Darryl Dopwell, as well as Robert Silvers, at the *New York Review of Books*; staff at the library of the *New Yorker*; Ioan Reed-Aspley at Nottinghamshire County Council; Emma Williams at Opera Australia; Eli Stalesen for Opera Island; Stephane Bouteloupe at the Opéra de Monte-Carlo; Jorg Quatran at the Opéra National de Paris; Jane Bonner and Richard Ashton at Opera North; Annick Cebeau at the Opéra de Paris; Lucie Garnett at Opera Theatre of St Louis; Alexander Moore and others at Opernhaus Bühnen; Bonnie Jones at PDF; Judy Sternlight of Random House; Natalia Ritzkowsky; Kirsty Macdiarmid of the Royal Academy of Arts; Ewan Thomson for his help at the Royal Court; Ann Richards, Rita Grudzien and Eleanora Claps at the Royal Opera House; Sue White at the Royal Opera House Archives; the Royal Shakespeare Company; the Royal Society of Medicine; Torbjorn Eriksson at the Royal Swedish Opera; Daniel Bryan, librarian at the Rudolf Steiner School in Kings Langley; Malcolm Underwood, Fiona Colbert and Alistair Brookshaw at St John's College, Cambridge; Sally Kirkham, Alexandra Aslett and the excellent archivist Simon May at St Paul's School, plus Paul Leppard of the *Pauline* magazine; Franziska Lettowskey at the Salzburg Festival; Gaby Berginz at Salzburg Landestheater; Wendy Sanford; Cindy L. Layman at Santa Fe Opera; Laura Valente and Andrea Vitalini at La Scala; Libby Jones at Scottish Opera; staff at the Shakespeare Centre, Stratford-upon-Avon; Manisha Ferdinand at Sky Arts; Sarah Baxter and Lisa Dowdeswell at the Society of Authors; Matthew Bell at the *Spectator*; Ellen Sweeney; Mary Tabbron and others at Talkback; David Bridges at Taunton School; Tina Kelly of Theater Basel; the press office at Teatro Comunale di Bologna; Roberta Scheggi, Susanna Colombo and Silvia Zani at Florence's Teatro del Maggio Musicale; Paola Cappo at Turin's Teatro Regio; Sophie Jerrold, press officer for the Tobacco Factory, and also their programme designer, Alan Coveney; Jane Flaherty of Trust Talk Magazine; Maureen Baker at University College Hospital's Development Office, and UCH's librarians; Brigitte Klein at the University of Frankfurt; everyone at the V&A/Theatre Museum Archive; Karl Lueger-Ring and Silvia Stantejesky at Vienna's Burgtheater; Florence Palomo who delved into *Vogue's* archives for me; Sheona Walker; Watford Central Library; the Wellcome Library; Penny Simpson at Welsh National Opera; Pamela Jordan from the Drama Library of Yale University; Yorkshire Television's production office; Laura Myers, then of the Young Vic; Nadia Stefanizzi, Markus Wyler, Maja Enderlin and Grischa Asagaroff at Zurich Opera; Steve Segal and Janet Polata at the 92nd St Y in Manhattan.

Working with Oberon Books has been a pleasure. Everyone there has been welcoming, encouraging and calming, toiling away at innumerable tasks. So resounding applause for James Hogan and his whole team: his senior editor Andrew Walby; Charles Glanville; Sophie O'Reirdan and Lewis Morgan;

Josephine Dyer and George Spender who has been an absolute trooper. Special credit is also due to Kenneth Burnley and Caroline Waldron, both eagle-eyed copyeditors; and to all the photographers who I've not already mentioned – Sarah Ainslie, Timothy Allen, Simon Annand, Catherine Ashmore, Anders Bach, Clive Bournsnell, Jane Bown, Nobby Clark, Bill Cooper, Tristram Kenton, Geraint Lewis and Alastair Muir.

The acumen and dedication of Kevin Jackson, Alan Franks Michael Arditti, Barbara Bassett and Duncan Bassett has been inestimable. They perused my manuscript closely, giving me judicious and expert advice. Alan has assisted on many other fronts as well, and the television producer David Thompson has been extraordinarily obliging, not least in supplying me with stacks of archival recordings. Many others have alerted me to matters I would otherwise have missed, as well as being heartening and helpful. Great thanks go to Erica Wagner and to her beloved parents, Arthur and Ellen, with whom I stayed when researching in New York; to the superlative Sarah Wallis and Juliet Carey; to Caroline Adams and Pat Aske at Cambridge's outstandingly hospitable Pembroke College, where I regularly holed up to write in peace and quiet. I am additionally grateful to Anne Mayer and her husband, John Bird, to Mabayoje Akin Adekeye, Charlotte Allanby, Janet Anderson, Richard Bassett Snr and Richard Bassett Jnr, Stewart Barling, David Benedict, Emily Campbell, Mel Crowe, Annick Dewald, Will Eaves, Max Eilenberg, Natasha Fairweather, Eleanor Fazan who has allowed me to draw on her forthcoming biography, Craig Fees, John Field, Marcus Field, Francis Gilbert, Jenny Gilbert, Ruth Gledhill, Robert Hewison, Mike Higgins, Henry Hitchings, Chris Horner, Kate Hunter, Sue Hyman, Ian Irvine, Richard Johnson, Phil Jones, Philip Gwyn Jones, Ian Kelly, Lucy Kenwright, Rhoda Koenig, Rob Newman, Maggie Noach, Blanche Marvin, Mike Maskill, Rohan McWilliam, David Miller, Giles Ramsay and his tremendously kind parents Dee and Douglas Ramsay, Christopher Reeves, William Relton, Stuart Rosenblatt, Eleanor Padmore, Arabella Pike, Simon Reynolds, Roy Smiles, Ian Smith, Frances Spalding, Paul Taylor, Djuna Thurley, Ion Trewin, Jill Waters, Graham Whybrow, Andrew Wilson, Susan Woollacott, and Johann F. Zietsman.

Finally, my family has been wonderfully tolerant about me being busy for years, and my partner Martin has been positively heroic, endlessly supportive and astoundingly patient.

INTRODUCTION

To begin with, two snapshots. The first is this: Jonathan Miller, aged thirteen, is impersonating Danny Kaye. He adores the popular comedian. He dreams of being him and launches into impressions of him here, there and everywhere. One day in 1948, the gangly and flame-haired mimic is spotted, by Kaye's manager, outside the London Palladium where the American star is performing. The adolescent has been larking around, entertaining other loitering fans, when suddenly he finds himself being led backstage to repeat his turn.

'I succeeded in getting into Kaye's dressing-room,' Miller recalls, 'and I did my imitation in front of him, rather embarrassingly. He asked me what I wanted to do. I said I wanted to be a doctor and he said: "You'll never do it."'

His teenage crush on the zany celebrity was out of step with his parents' vision. His mother, Betty (née Spiro), was an acclaimed novelist who mingled with Bloomsbury's literary set. Her husband, Dr Emanuel Miller, was a psychiatrist and founding father of child guidance practices in England. Both were intellectuals devoted to the life of the mind, and neither were given to warm demonstrations of affection.

The second snapshot is of the young Miller dangling outside a window: a symbolically prophetic image. As a boy, shortly after World War 2, he used to sneak off to watch films in the West End with coins filched from his mother's purse. On one occasion, he recollects:

I saw *A Matter of Life and Death*, accompanied by an equally delinquent figure who turned out, in the end, to be much more delinquent.[1] I became very friendly with him. He was intriguingly exciting and excitable, with all sorts of fascinating things in his house in Eaton Square – leftover uniforms from his grandparents, from the Light Brigade. I remember sometimes we used to let ourselves out of the sixth-floor window, on these fire-escape ropes that would let you down into Belgrave Place. He was called John Bingham then: now better known as Lord Lucan.

Ironically, Dr Emanuel Miller's area of expertise included forensic psychiatry. He was a co-founder of the *British Journal of Criminology* and a key player in establishing the Portman Clinic, the clinical arm of the Institute for the Study and Treatment of Delinquency, originally known as the Psychopathic Clinic.[2] He was, however, always so busy with work that he failed to spot one of the world's most elusive felons in the making. Had he been less preoccupied, he also might have guessed that his own firstborn – playfully flying between floors – would not grow up to be the dedicated medic he envisaged. Kaye's assessment had been close to the mark. Miller Jnr would not stick to being a doctor, becoming instead a leaper of boundaries, jumping between categories, the best-known polymath of late twentieth-century Britain.[3]

In Two Minds explores how, as a comic prodigy, he split away from his parents' world of scholarly dedication but then became the embodiment of their respective interests in his subsequent career. He has far surpassed their fame: his work encompassing both the sciences and the arts; his thinking, like a Möbius strip, seamlessly linking the two. With age, he has come to loathe the labels 'polymath' and 'Renaissance man' because he thinks, wrongly, that they are always accompanied by a philistine sneer. With a pronounced streak of self-reproach, he sees his life as having been ruinously divided. He is tortured by regrets, forever lamenting that he abandoned serious medical research for the 'frivolous' lure of theatre.

This is a portrait of a complicated, riven, even contradictory man. Nonetheless, the overwhelming truth is that he has been a connector, straddling the arts–science dichotomy with a witty intelligence which has entertained and educated the public. His career has been exceptionally rangy. Having 'a brain the size of a planet' – as one fellow stage director puts it – has enabled him to be a pundit on everything from Mozart to post-mortem examinations, and from anthropology through neuropsychology to pornography.[4]

Obsessive interests and themes can be traced running through his work, binding it together, even as he has changed, chameleon-like, from a medic into a comic, a stage and screen director, TV presenter, executive producer and even a critic, working as the *New Yorker*'s film reviewer in the mid-Sixties. To call him a hyphenate (a person excelling in more than one craft) hardly seems sufficient.

He started young, years before he became a household name in the ground-breaking, satirical sketch show of 1960, *Beyond the Fringe*. He featured on BBC Radio when just eighteen and, on graduating from Cambridge in 1956, he had already starred in two Footlights revues which had become West End hits. Later, having earned transatlantic fame performing with Peter Cook, Dudley Moore and Alan Bennett in *Beyond the Fringe*, he turned to theatre directing.

Among a host of outstanding productions, he staged the National Theatre's *Merchant of Venice* with Laurence Olivier; an award-winning Chekhov's *Three*

Sisters in the West End; and a Broadway production of Eugene O'Neill's *Long Day's Journey into Night* with Jack Lemmon and the young Kevin Spacey – kickstarting the latter's career. Miller then became a pioneering artistic director for London's Old Vic, helping to introduce British audiences to little-known European classics.

A dazzling conversationalist, he appeared on countless television chat-shows and discussion panels. Michael Parkinson still ranks him among his favourite guests and, in the USA, he appeared on Dick Cavett's show for an unprecedented five nights in succession.[5] On becoming a TV presenter himself, he shook up the revered BBC arts programme *Monitor* in the mid-Sixties. As its controversial editor and frontman, he used bleeding-edge camera techniques and introduced many viewers to Susan Sontag, Andy Warhol and the hip New York scene. The shock was too great. The series died of a heart attack. Notwithstanding, the Corporation swiftly re-employed him to direct small-screen films, and his superb *Alice in Wonderland* and *Whistle and I'll Come to You* have now been released, on DVD, as classics by the British Film Institute.

In the Seventies, he presented *The Body in Question*, the BBC's epic series on the history of medicine, which was the next big thing after Kenneth Clark's *Civilisation*, Jacob Bronowski's *The Ascent of Man* and J. K. Galbraith's *The Age of Uncertainty*. A triumphant success, it made him a much-loved popularizer of science, after which he was invited back to save the gargantuan, ailing *BBC Shakespeare Series*. More recently, in 2004, he was writer and frontman for BBC4's high-powered and contentious series on atheism, *A Brief History of Disbelief*. That was, like *The Body in Question* and the *BBC Shakespeare Series*, also shown in the States.

Miller has written and edited various books, from a pop-up bestseller about human reproduction to a scholarly tome on Freud, but he has suffered from crippling writer's block, a condition particularly infuriating for someone begotten of two authors.[6] Vastly more prolific as a director, he expanded from theatre into opera. He helped transform the tiny Kent Opera troupe into a nationally acclaimed company, and created the longest-running hits in the English National Opera repertoire, notably his Mafia *Rigoletto* (set in Fifties America) and his Marx Brothers *Mikado* (transporting Gilbert and Sullivan to a Thirties English seaside hotel). *The Mikado* received its twenty-fifth anniversary revival in 2011, with another run starting in December 2012. His chic Armani *Così fan tutte* has been a repeated hit at the Royal Opera House in Covent Garden (enjoying a revival in 2012 too) and, for the past three decades, his work abroad has taken him to La Scala in Milan, the Maggio Musicale festival in Florence, the New York Met, Tokyo and elsewhere. He has become centrifugal, travelling widely as a world-class and workaholic director.

In Two Minds tells the story of this diverse career, its highs and lows, while placing Miller within the broader framework: the big political changes and societal shake-ups, the new ideas and artistic vogues arising during his life. As regards formative experiences, the impact of World War 2 can be charted from the Blitz – when his family, fleeing London, spent unsettling years on the move – through to his decades of directorial globetrotting, driven by a recurring sense of rootlessness. In the wake of the Nazi Holocaust, being of Jewish lineage, he developed an abiding wariness of persecution, although the more immediate fallout was with his father who, in a post-war gesture of clan solidarity, started insisting on Judaic religious observances. That provoked a parent–child schism, activating resistant atheism and very mixed feelings about being Jewish in Miller.

He was further shaped by stimulating mentors and by the milieux in which he was educated, attending the leading public school, St Paul's – where he was close friends with Oliver Sacks – and then Cambridge University. There he was taught by Nobel Prize-winners and initiated into the Apostles, the secret debating society now associated with the Cambridge spy ring.

Miller quickly became a culturally influential figure. Most famously, *Beyond the Fringe* sparked Britain's Satire Boom and fed into the Sixties' anti-establishmentarian ethos. For his early brilliance in the Footlights hits *Out of the Blue* and *Between the Lines*, he has been dubbed the 'Godfather' of the Oxbridge Mafia in the comedy industry.[7] In stage directing, he established himself as a trailblazer, ingeniously updating the classics: a practice which subsequently became widespread. He was, moreover, a pioneer of understated naturalism in opera, persuading singers to relax, sitting or lying down rather than standing stiffly for their arias, a move which was considered revolutionary by conservative audiences.

This biography also considers how, while he was *ahead* of his time in some respects, he was born *after* it in others. As a boy, he took a fanatical interest in all things Victorian, especially nineteenth-century science. As a director, he is forward- yet backward-looking too. While known for updating operas, he frequently uses his in-depth knowledge of history to create exceptionally accurate period settings, from the Renaissance to the *belle époque*.

He came into his own in the Sixties. At a time when sections of the press and TV were growing more intellectually stimulating, he was perfect material for stardom. With today's dumbing down, by contrast, he is out of step. Many lifelong admirers now regard him as a lone beacon in the encroaching dark ages – one of the few great British intellectuals remaining, a kind of cerebral Last of the Mohicans. Certainly, he has been going down fighting, a fearless combatant in the battle against the lowbrow. While he has remained, into his seventies, a source for journalists who want an expert opinion and trenchant comments, a sting in the tail has emerged as he uses these interviews to berate the media's own prevailing stupidity.

Closely related to his satirical bent, his outspokenness is such a strong trait that it has damaged his career. It embroiled him in several headline-making quarrels, including a spectacularly bitter feud with Sir Peter Hall at the National Theatre and a locking of horns with the diva Cecilia Bartoli at the New York Met. He has not minced his words about reviewers either. Admitting that he likes to stand under an adoring 'Niagara of praise', he is hypersensitive to criticism. His discontent intensified in 1991, under Margaret Thatcher's philistine regime, when he felt insufficiently cherished by the nation. It was then that he let rip with a sweeping condemnation of this whole 'mean, peevish little country' and its drizzling acid rain of criticism.[8] Lancing authority figures, his jibes have been laceratingly funny, but his complaints have become protracted and, in retaliation, sections of the British press have mocked his peevish habit of waving goodbye to England then making comebacks. Clearly, relations have soured.

Today he is a highly paradoxical figure: a one-man British institution and knight of the realm, yet one who – while deriding establishmentarian organizations – feels mournfully outcast. This chimes with his interest, as a director, in characters whom he calls interstitial or liminal: those who stand in a gap between or on the fringe of social groups, with one foot in and one foot out of the circle. Ultimately, his ambiguous insider–outsider status might be seen as a personal variation on those issues of integration which faced his Jewish, immigrant ancestors and his second-generation parents.

He has never actually quit his native land. Although he has been a centrifugal director, going international, his domestic life has centred closely around Regent's Park. That life can be mapped almost entirely – excepting the wartime peregrinations – on one double-page spread of the London A–Z. Rachel, his wife of over 50 years' standing, became a doctor and stuck to it. Likewise, she has been a marital rock of stability in spite of rough patches, a crucial constant. For nigh on half a century, their family home has been in Camden Town's Gloucester Crescent, a hub of left-wing intellectuals and media types which was, for a time, satirized in TV skits and a strip cartoon called *Life and Times in NW1* (originated by their neighbour Alan Bennett).

In taking stock of the private and the public man, *In Two Minds* examines how Miller has managed to stay well known and keep working into the twenty-first century. In parallel, it contemplates how his parents' renown encouraged his initial ambitions, creating role-models and aspirations which he has failed to live up to, in his opinion. Some even call his globetrotting 'his years on the run' as if he were being pursued by his august father's ghost, a paternally indoctrinated sense of guilt. In the next generation, Miller's three children have variously benefited and suffered as the progeny of such a stellar figure: a loving, very liberal father but perhaps unwittingly overbearing, sometimes alarmingly gloomy and maybe addicted to the limelight.

He keeps saying that he is finally going to retire, nevertheless the curriculum vitae has remained ongoing, with, among other projects, two new ENO productions (*La Bohème* and *The Elixir of Love*) in 2009–10; a return to the National Theatre (staging Bach's *St Matthew Passion*) in late 2011; further opera revivals in Valencia, Washington and at Milan's La Scala in 2012; and two UK-touring productions for Barrie Rutter's theatre company Northern Broadsides, namely a 2013 staging of Githa Sowerby's *Rutherford and Son* to be followed by Rutter in *King Lear*.[9] Indeed, he has enthusiastically embraced even more métiers. He curated an exhibition entitled *Mirror Image* at London's National Gallery (contemplating reflective and gleaming surfaces), then another in 2010 for Islington's Estorick Collection called *On the Move* (concerning fast-shutter photography and futurism). Elsewhere, he has enjoyed small exhibitions of his own paper collages and found-object sculptures. His photographs have been published in *Nowhere in Particular*, an absorbing scrapbook of snapshots and of aperçus which he has jotted down over the decades.[10]

Never quite abandoning his medical and academic interests either, he returned to research for brief spells in the Seventies and Eighties. Recently, he contributed to the Imperial War Museum's exhibition on camouflage which incorporated zoology and aesthetics, and he has zigzagged between the sciences and the arts as an interdepartmental visiting professor at various American universities, including Berkeley.

Like his corduroy-clad, lanky limbs, his achievements seem to go on and on. To the last, he will probably be a man in at least two minds. Yet he has been a tireless builder of bridges, an associative thinker whose talk has been rich in vivid similes and metaphors, constantly seeing parallels, throwing suspension cables between normally segregated worlds.

· 1 ·

BIRTH AND PARENTS

An infancy in print

JONATHAN WOLFE MILLER made his first appearance on 21 July 1934. He was born just off Harley Street, the main artery of London's medical mile. His father, Dr Emanuel Miller – as a distinguished psychiatrist – had easily secured a bed for his 24-year-old wife at the Welbeck Nursing Home, a private maternity hospital of some prestige.[1] The National Health Service was, of course, only a twinkle in Aneurin Bevin's eye at this point.

Emanuel had married Betty the previous year and their home was just a short walk from Welbeck Street. The perambulator merely had to trundle three blocks west from the hospital and turn on to Portland Place, by the BBC's new edifice Broadcasting House. There, over the portico, stood Eric Gill's sculpture of Prospero symbolically sending Ariel out into the world. Then three blocks north, where the road branched, was the Millers' home at 23 Park Crescent: a maisonette above Emanuel's consulting room.[2]

Looking over Marylebone Road towards Regent's Park, this is no common or garden address. Although the perfect circle planned by its architect, John Nash, was never completed, the Crescent's graceful neoclassical arc makes it the loveliest of all his stately terraces round the park.[3] It is like a wedding cake turned concave: all white columns and tiers of stucco. This is blue plaque territory as well, with grand previous inhabitants. Betty and Emanuel's infant would have been crawling in the footsteps of Joseph Bonaparte, ex-king of Spain and a fleeting resident of No. 23.

Science and the stage, the two magnetic poles which would proceed to tug at Miller throughout his life, also flanked his childhood abode. On one side had resided Sir Charles Wheatstone, the inventor of the stereoscope, an optical gadget which – using two views to create an illusion of 3-D depth – has always fascinated Miller.[4] On the other side, the dame-next-door was the West End star Marie Tempest. In 1934 she was playing in *Theatre Royal*, Edna Ferber and George S. Kaufman's affectionate send-up of thespian types.

1

Miller has one very early shard of memory: being lifted up to look over the balcony at a gleaming troop of soldiers as they marched along the Crescent. They were on their way to George VI's coronation, which dates it to May 1937. He vividly recollects certain smells and sounds too: the sweet aroma of Bengers milk drink and the peculiar percussive score of Nanny Hogarth's underwear. Sharing his room, as Betty's resident home help, Hogarth always disrobed in the dark after Miller had been put to bed, but her elastic twangs and thwacks only encouraged fantasies about the female body. The small boy wondered if Nanny separated out into an array of blancmanges.[5] His enquiries into this received only the Sibylline reply, 'I'm doing what I'm doing' (a line later immortalized in the play *Forty Years On* by Miller's friend Alan Bennett).[6]

The young boy was not much the wiser, as regards the facts of life, after a brush with some older girls in a privet hedge. This occurred in Park Square Gardens, just opposite the Crescent, where the said girls sought to inspect his personal equipment, tantalizingly holding out the promise of a Hornby train set in return. The deal was halted as Nanny extracted him from the hedge.

Soon afterwards, the Miller family moved to St John's Wood, on the north side of the park's circumferential road, the Outer Circle. With his sister Sarah born in 1937, his parents wanted more room, and 35 Queen's Grove was a large Victorian semi-detached in a leafy street. 'Living in what you might call a grand middle-class house, we never lacked anything,' Miller acknowledges. Yet he adds, with a perplexed frown, 'Those memories I have of childhood are mostly wretched and miserable.' He was something of a 'problem' child, evidently bright and often exasperated, sitting on the lawn and crying, 'I want to be occupied!' That cry, he states, is the only link he can see between his infant and his adult self, because he still suffers from dismal moods when left to kick his heels.

His boredom threshold has always been extremely low and, according to Sarah, he screamed so much, out of acute unhappiness, that Nanny was driven to distraction. Evidently, Hogarth did not share the positive views of today's cognitive neurologists who (opposing the Attention Deficit Disorder label) believe that low boredom thresholds indicate exceptional intelligence and energy, with potential for inventiveness and multi-tasking.

Miller also spoke with a stammer, an astonishingly shaky start for someone who was to be the darling of chat-shows on both sides of the Atlantic. Detractors say the man became logorrhoeic and he has been nicknamed Windy Miller. However, in his prime, his genius was for incisive fluency and the perfectly chosen word. Admirers have declared they would rather hear him talk than listen to Caruso sing, and he has been described by chat-show host Dick Cavett – America's equivalent of Michael Parkinson – as 'one of the most amazing conversationalists the world has ever produced', and of an extremely rare breed 'whose conversation is instantly publishable'.[7] He has sometimes made his interlocutors feel inarticulate, his lexicon being so extensive and his eidetic flair for painting in words being dazzling.

Nonetheless, he suffered for decades from a stutter which was, he says, bad enough to wobble his jaw, deform his face and humiliate him. As a schoolboy using the London Underground, he was given extra money by his parents in case he couldn't say his destination and had to name a station further down the line instead.[8] Nowadays, hitches surface in his speech only occasionally: when he is re-establishing contact after a while on the telephone, or when he has to introduce himself in public. Rather than saying, 'I'm Jonathan Miller', he just takes a longer run-up with 'My name is Jonathan Miller.' He is a patron of the British Stammering Association, and is fascinated by language-related neurological dysfunctions.

As a child, getting stuck on the letter 'm' made him sound like a train being held at a station, 'a sort of Westinghouse stammer,' as he recalls. One cure for that, he discovered, was slipping into a foreign accent: liberation gained through play-acting and adopting a different persona. One pre-school friend, Elishiva Landman, affectionately remembers him, at playgroup, as all red hair and freckles with a loud voice. Plainly, he wanted to make himself heard in spite of his impediment, unless he was having to up the volume just to articulate. Landman believes he stuttered because he thought faster than he could talk, although Miller himself remarks that speaking rapidly helps him whoosh through or ski-jump over obstructions.[9]

Voracious reading and a highly retentive memory soon helped him expand his vocabulary, and he learnt to sidestep his 'speaker's block' with more elegant paraphrases. Even today he may be redesigning a sentence behind what seems like a thoughtful pause. Perhaps the hunt for synonyms underlies his acclaimed propensity for associative thinking and illuminating similes.

His stammer may well have been genetically inherited from Emanuel who had similar trouble as a child, but the young Miller was further afflicted with distressing incontinence.[10] With clinical frankness, as well as a flash of bewilderment, he states: 'I was an anxious child. It just all seemed incoherent and I couldn't make my way and I wet my bed and shat myself and did all sorts of things.' His infantine difficulties tie in, significantly, with a feeling of being underloved. He has spoken most publicly of this on BBC Radio's *In the Psychiatrist's Chair*, in conversation with Dr Anthony Clare.[11] When asked if Betty had been motherly, he replied: 'Not at all, no. I was never kissed by either of my parents as a child, never embraced. Any extravagant display of emotion, indeed any display of emotion was "surplus to requirements".'

A few old acquaintances consider that ungracious. Many parents rationed cuddles in the 1930s and 1940s as a matter of course, and to see Dr and Mrs Miller as purely cerebral cold fish would be wrong. Betty's writing is sensitive and sensuously alert. That said, it rarely conveys open affection, and Sarah's memories support her brother's: 'Ma had a great deal of charm, but not a great deal of warmth. Neither she nor Dad were physically demonstrative.' They were, it seems, semi-detached parents, only half there for their children. One early friend of Miller's adds that Emanuel seemed 'old as Methuselah and completely unapproachable', while Betty was never maternal, wafting around with a faintly ironic air. 'Once Jonathan and I were duelling', he says, 'with sticks: we were sort of Errol Flynn out in the garden. To make it more real, we were making the noise of steel against steel, and Jonathan's mother appeared at the window, just repeating "Tish, tish" – as if it was the most irritating noise in the world.'[12]

Having grown up as an emotional child in a repressed era, Miller wonders if his 'limited capacity' for friendships in adult life stems from those early 'disorders of attachment'. Although Betty and Emanuel are no longer around to contest or assent to that view, they both wrote books that contemplated tricky parent–child relationships. These now create an intriguing kind of perpetuated dialogue with their son's personal memories. A survey of their early lives and writings certainly sheds some light.

*   *   *

Betty's roots were complex. She was born in Ireland in 1910, the second child of four.[13] Her father, Simon Spiro, had emigrated in 1882 from Silauliai (which is officially in Lithuania today, though he described himself as Russian). He joined the mass exodus from the Pale of Settlement, the western flank of Tsar Alexander III's empire which was rife with anti-Semitism. Unjustly blamed for Alexander II's assassination in 1881, the local Jews – known as Litvaks – faced xenophobic assaults; draconian laws limiting where they could live; and the conscription of their sons from the age of twelve.[14] Back home, Simon's family had apparently been innkeepers, but Jews trading in alcohol had become scapegoats, accused of causing the ruin of the local peasants.

In his teens, Simon escaped. He boarded a ship and disembarked on the south coast of Ireland after being assured, by the crew, that the vessel had reached America with quite remarkable speed.[15] It would be 1964 before his grandson, Jonathan, sailed all the way across the Atlantic to perform in the satirical revue *Beyond the Fringe* on Broadway. Meanwhile, Simon settled in Cork and became an exceptionally successful, self-made businessman. Sporting dapper three-piece suits, he managed to be assimilated and still religiously devout. A shopkeeper of standing – owning a cigar store, a jeweller's and other properties – he became the highest ranking member of the town's Jewish community. He was appointed president of the local synagogue. He acted as a grand juror and Justice of the Peace, as a committee member for the Cork Savings Bank, and as the master of a masonic lodge.[16] In his spare time he played the violin in the orchestra at Cork Opera House, and he married, by arrangement, a Swede of Polish stock.

Sara Bergson came from a family of prosperous garment manufacturers in Karlstad. They were Jewish but less strictly orthodox. Having gained a teaching diploma from the esteemed Royal Women's Superior Training Academy in Stockholm, Sara was a confirmed intellectual and the proud possessor of a leather-bound library. She was prone to quote Goethe and Nietzsche. Though gentle in manner, there was a touch of frost about her: a shortcoming that, while being a family trait, was described by her daughter as a 'bit withering'.[17]

Several illustrious relatives figured on Betty's family tree. Through Sara, she was a great-niece of Henri Bergson, the Nobel Prize-winning, Franco–Polish philosopher and polymath. [18] His renown was burgeoning during her childhood, with his works being translated into English. Marcel Proust was, in turn, related (his second cousin marrying Bergson) and *A la Recherche du Temps Perdu* was famously influenced by Bergson's theories about memory. Having met Henri once or twice, Betty would go on to employ the double surname Bergson Spiro when she became a novelist: a smart move in self-promotion, and an indication of how she prized the connection.

Problematically for Simon, Cork was near Clonakilty, the birthplace of the Sinn Fein revolutionary, Michael Collins. The city thus became a seedbed for the militant republican movement, along with Dublin. Within three years of the 1916 Easter Rising, Collins had become the MP for South Cork, scorning Westminster and setting up an alternative Irish parliament with Eamon de Valera. As the War of Independence against the British authorities got under way, Collins was behind the creation of IRA guerilla units and a special assassination squad. Soon Simon's sentencing of criminals, as a JP, led to a death threat from the militarized local Mafia. [19] Though not quite a case of history repeating itself, half a century later Jonathan Miller and a BBC TV crew would have to flee an IRA ultimatum of the homicidal variety when they tried to film a James Joyce drama, in Ireland, during the 1970s Troubles. [20]

Betty and her youthful siblings did not side with their father, identifying instead with the imprisoned Feinians and the protestors whom they could hear singing outside Cork Gaol at night. Simon Spiro could be a crushing patriarch and, in reaction, his offspring turned into what Betty described as infantine 'Fifth Columnists', with impish cries of 'Up de Valera' ringing from the nursery. In a short memoir on the subject (and alluding to later IRA bombings in London), she concluded that 'heresy begins at home . . . with regard to authority . . . and the time-bomb that explodes in a lavatory in Leicester Square station had its fuse set to that purpose twenty years ago on a nursery hearth-rug, under the foot of omnipotent and oblivious adults'. [21]

Surmising that the conflicts in Ireland were going to persist, Sara and her children sailed for Stockholm in 1920. Two years later, seeing the Free State dividing from Ulster and civil war erupting, Simon upped sticks too. He reunited his family on mainland Britain, settling in Notting Hill, west London, where he restarted his business and Sara set about acquiring the best possible English education for her brood.

St Paul's School for Boys opened its doors to Betty's favourite brother, Henry, who went on to be an outstanding Oxford scholar and ministerial private secretary before his life was tragically cut short. As a Pauline, Henry made friends with the budding philosopher and brilliant talker Isaiah Berlin who also became very fond of Betty, having literary conversations with her at Notting Hill dances. 'She used to wander into long rambling modulations which I found totally absorbing,' Berlin later recalled, describing her as 'a pensive, slightly melancholy girl, with the most beautiful manners I have ever known'. [22]

Though her youngest sibling, Julian, was less academic, after St Paul's he landed a job as Alfred Hitchcock's junior assistant on *The Thirty-Nine Steps*, and he made documentaries for the Crown Film Unit. So he may well have introduced Miller to the notion of getting behind a camera.[23]

Betty did not enjoy her brief and interrupted stint at St Paul's School for Girls but she was a born writer. Having produced stories and plays for her siblings from the age of seven, she wrote even more when she was sent away to recuperate from tuberculosis of the neck, staying at a sanatorium near Calais.[24] By the time she returned, she had become a go-getting teenager with fluent French and Swedish, determined to become a professional author. Aged eighteen, she sent a script to the Irish critic and author St John Ervine, with a covering letter alluding to Joycean streams of consciousness. Doubtless she had been encouraged by Henri Bergson winning his Nobel Prize in Literature in 1927, and by Proust's *A la Recherche du Temps Perdu* being published (posthumously) in a full English translation that same year. In his reply to her letter, Ervine admired her ambition to 'be somebody' by the time she was 22, her sauciness and her eager mind.[25]

Her writing was a means of escaping her father's strict regime. He thrashed his sons with a razor strop when they began gadding about town and coming home late. Betty slipped out of the house by studying for a diploma in journalism at University College in Gower Street, Bloomsbury – not far from Regent's Park. Here she met other writers including Montagu Slater, Benjamin Britten's librettist. Moreover, right on cue, when she reached 22, her first novel, *The Mere Living*, was taken up by Victor Gollancz, a publisher in whose Notting Hill garden she had formerly played.[26] Not long after that, she became engaged to Emanuel. Though, at 40, he was almost twice her age, she had attended one of his lectures and instantly declared, 'That's the man I'm going to marry.'

Swiftly befriended by the literati, she was introduced to their social circles in Bloomsbury and Fitzrovia, the neighbouring enclave stretching east from Portland Place where creative types, bluestockings and bohemians congregated in the 1920s. Fellow authors and the press admired her writing for its pin-sharp observations and its 'stereoscopically' clear characterizations.[27] Even if St John Ervine had suggested that her style could be neurotically overblown, the *Observer* newspaper judged her 'exceedingly intelligent', and *Time and Tide* loved her 'super-sensitiveness'. She was deemed to be a worthy successor to Bergson: a bright spark with great promise.[28]

Over time, she wrote six more novels, various short stories and book reviews for intellectual journals such as *Horizon*, the *Cornhill*, *Twentieth Century* and *Times Literary Supplement*.[29] She was celebrated enough to be photographed for *Vogue* by Cecil Beaton who, she dryly observed, made her look like a long-faced horse gazing over a stable door. Moving away from fiction, she turned into an essayist and a biographer, producing a greatly admired book, *Robert Browning: A Portrait*, for which she was elected a fellow of the Royal Society of Literature.[30] Her second-hand Remington typewriter, bought to launch her career, served her for the rest of her life. As her son recalls:

Though she did, indeed, always retain a soft Irish brogue, I remember her strange old-fashioned Englishness: you know, a sleeveless fawn woollen jumper, a pleated tartan skirt, and these rather – for someone who was an intellectual – rather startling, red, varnished fingernails. Rather elegant fingers, nibbling at the typewriter.[31]

In the long run, time proved less kind to Betty. Nobody has ever turned her novels into screen dramas although they are, at their best, comparable with Virginia Woolf or Katherine Mansfield. Her prose runs like a movie in the mind's eye, with close-ups, cutaways, flashbacks and glides down city streets. She died aged just 55, and her writing was forgotten for many decades until Virago and Persephone Books reprinted two works as minor modern classics: *On the Side of the Angels* (in 1985) and *Farewell Leicester Square* (in 2000).

She was painfully timid in some respects, shying away from public performances and seeming prim to certain acquaintances. Yet others say that she was much like her son, charmingly witty. In its humorous eloquence, her prose shows how much he inherited from her. Equally significant is the fact that, on the page, she comes over as an early feminist rather than a shrinking violet. She had been born in the era of militant suffragettes and seen women finally get to vote after World War 1. Her semi-emancipated heroines frequently balk at domestic constraints, and her ambivalence about motherhood stands out sharply.

This is most evident in *Portrait of the Bride* which was published by Gollancz in 1935, when her son was still in his cot. The story centres on Rhoda, a partygoer in north London's bohemian set, who has married Bernard, a surprisingly patriarchal older publisher (like Gollancz crossed with Emanuel). She soon feels underloved and insecure, worrying about his reaction to her ruby-red nail varnish among other matters.[32] After wavering over an affair, she ends up wanting to devote herself to her newborn baby, without a nanny. Bernard sounds jealously sceptical about this.

Since Betty absorbed many Freudian theories about prototypal families from her spouse, it would be unwise to interpret her stories as simply autobiographical. Nonetheless, the passages about childbearing are palpably informed by her own experience. Even if her son is disguised as the fictional Sally, 7lbs 2oz, members of the British public were essentially reading about Miller from the start. He was documented even as a foetus, and it is peculiarly poignant – now that he has lived through his seventies – to read of Betty's pregnant Rhoda lying in bed as the baby kicks.

Now and then a ripple would break through her, an impulse from that oncoming tide . . . She thought of the unknown child sleeping within her. The future itself was there . . . the threescore years and ten of her child, telescoped up within her . . . a personality there, imprisoned, still in some mysterious other-dimension.[33]

Later, when starting to breastfeed, Rhoda experiences a surge of blissful maternal love, sensing that 'The gross commonplace love that passes between man and woman was suddenly . . . distilled.' She felt that 'the very flesh and bone of her child should be composed, built, out of this love-substance'.[34]

That ought to qualify Miller's sense of being uncherished by his mother, as should some vintage snapshots in the family photograph album where Betty looks smilingly pleased, if not quite cuddly with her baby. However, there is a flipside with Rhoda. She is in two minds. She has felt suffocatingly oppressed by the growing foetus and, immediately after the difficult delivery, she is enveloped in a 'hazy indifference', declining to hold the baby.[35] In the months after that, she develops breastfeeding problems, and her unmarried friend Edith sounds like her alter ego or subconscious, sneering:

> I'm afraid it sounds terribly depressing, darling. Tell me: are you going to turn into a Fond Mother and get fat and dowdy and worn out, devoting your time to a brat who'll walk off without a word of thanks one fine day . . . [Or] will you have a full-time nurse for the kid, park it out, and go off and amuse yourself like a rational human being? Which is it to be?[36]

One of Betty's cousins remembers her being proud of her first child yet remaining self-absorbed, 'living only for her writing, in a world of her own'.[37] Given that Miller inherited some of his mother's super-sensitivity, his emotional antennae surely picked up her mixed messages.

His early wretchedness was exacerbated by a pervading atmosphere of unease. These were anxious times for his parents. The Great Depression had made almost everyone feel economically vulnerable. Emanuel perpetually feared penury, besides being prone to deep depressions of the non-financial variety, which made him emotionally unavailable. He was, moreover, a Jew seeing the emergence of anti-Semitic Blackshirts in London. Oswald Mosley founded the British Union of Fascists in 1932, followed by violent clashes at their 1934 Olympia rally; by the Battle of Cable Street; and by an alarming number of BUF votes in East End elections. Continental Jews were beginning to flee Hitler's escalating persecution, and by 1935 Betty was writing, in *Farewell Leicester Square*, about anti-Semitism lurking within England's middle and upper classes.

Farewell Leicester Square dealt with anti-Semitism and complicated forms of internal self-contempt. One character, Alec Bergman, is the son of a Jewish tradesman who breaks away to become a successful film-maker and to marry a non-Jewish woman. However, fearing anti-Semitic bullying and seeing his young son playing with the upper-class Timothy Hope-Sewell, Alec is shocked to realize he wants his child to have Jewish friends. He is culturally torn and he returns to his roots, with his marriage collapsing en route.[38]

Miller's infantine unhappiness further coincided with Betty experiencing professional disappointments. On an artistic high when drafting *Farewell Leicester Square*, she immodestly declared it would be 'one of the best novels Victor

Gollancz Ltd have ever published'.[39] The script was then rejected, seemingly because of its controversial theme. Devastated by the implicit criticism, and privately distressed by the death of her mother in 1936, she did not publish any full-length work until 1941, when the publisher Robert Hale finally championed *Farewell Leicester Square*.[40]

She had not come to a complete halt in the interim. She had been working on another novel called *A Room in Regent's Park*. Published in 1942, this super-imposed elements from her own and from her son's early years. The scenario is as follows. World War 2 is imminent. Judith is attending lectures at University College and living near Harley Street with her father, a doctor whose attention she craves. In spite of her 'father complex', she is dating Robert, a medical student who meets her for kissing sessions opposite Park Crescent, in Park Square Gardens: the same 'oasis guarded by privilege' where Judith frolicked as a toddler, 'under the auspices of a uniformed nanny, frisking decorously'.[41]

Another passage leaps out:

> The children born to medical men living in Harley Street, Wimpole Street, Devonshire Place . . . In their own homes they are treated as a form of contraband; to be smuggled in and out of doors between the exits and entrances of patients; their voices summarily hushed upon the sacred staircase . . . their routine has to be carefully timed, their conduct governed: not only must they not be heard, but, during consulting hours, they must not be seen either. This entails an elaborate system of repression . . . the family perambulator . . . is here subject to the most extraordinary manoeuvres . . . hidden in boot cupboards, hauled up on half-landings . . . stage-managed in accordance with a convention tacitly understood . . . save, perhaps, by the children themselves; who, subjected to these miracles of organisation, the sole aim of which is to keep them as far as possible from the public view, not unnaturally acquire an impression of unworthiness, even of guilt, which may remain with them for the rest of their lives.[42]

In that milieu, the infant Miller's loud voice and frightful screaming may have been an act of defiance, insisting on being seen and heard, on being centre stage rather than remaining stuck in the wings. If so, it could be said that the rebellious spirit of *Beyond the Fringe*, the sketch show which refused to respect the British Establishment, was germinating even then. As Betty herself said, 'heresy begins at home . . . with regard to authority', the time bomb having its explosive fuse set on the nursery hearth rug.

In her account of secreted prams and shushed toddlers, she was palpably criticizing her husband's work/family balance. Still, regarding that imbalance, one needs to understand the course of Emanuel's life.

*   *   *

It began with bearskins. That is to say, *Jonathan Miller's London* (a televisual tour through the city, filmed in 1979) opened with footage of the Queen's guardsmen in their trademark headgear.[43] As the programme's presenter, Miller was outlining his family history, contemplating his Englishness or non-Englishness as he went, and the reference point was Emanuel's father. Abram Miller had supplied the said fur hats to Queen Victoria.

That sounds like an easy life but, far from it, Abram had emigrated from Lithuania to London as an adolescent in the late 1860s. He came from a shtetl called Wigrance, a small Jewish town near the shores of Lake Wigry (an area which is Polish today, due to altered borders).[44] A revolt against imperial Russian rule in 1863 had been crushed by the local governor, Count Muravyov, nicknamed 'the hangman', who sent droves of Lithuanian villagers to Siberia. Like Betty's father, Abram was, moreover, fleeing anti-Semitic persecution. The Jewish Litvaks had been caught in the middle of the uprising: some executed by the rebels who deemed them to be tsarist sympathizers; others viciously attacked by the Cossack retaliation units. Abram is said to have witnessed atrocities, and the situation worsened with an ensuing famine and cholera epidemic.[45]

His mother is thought to have died young and his elder siblings headed for America.[46] His British naturalization papers, where his surname is anglicized (probably just truncating the Lithuanian patronymic 'Milleras'), suggest that his father had been a 'healer'. This struck Sarah Miller as noteworthy in the light of Emanuel's subsequent medical training, and she surmised her great-grandfather was a ritualistic shaman, using cabbalistic names – few Lithuanian Jews having trained as more 'enlightened' doctors. The document probably says 'dealer', though, on closer inspection. [47]

Sheer unremitting toil and a head for business had to sustain Abram when he reached the Dickensian slums of England's metropolis. Having escaped the Pale of Settlement and contrived to board a ship bound for the Port of London, he would have disembarked on a dockside swarming with thieves and swindlers, all ready to pounce on gullible 'greeners' (as the newcomers were called). If lucky, he may have been helped to a soup kitchen or temporary shelter by the charitable Board of Guardians for the Relief of the Jewish Poor.[48]

As the horrified sociologists Charles Booth and Henry Mayhew recorded, the East End was a hellhole of deprivation in the mid-nineteenth century. This was a world of muddy streets teeming with malnourished infants and lurching drunks, lined with squalid overcrowded tenements and workhouses. The air reeked of sewage, offal and dustheaps.[49] Israel Zangwill's more humorous East End chronicle *Children of the Ghetto* observed that Jewish greeners landed, nonetheless, with an inner world of dreams and hopes, 'with a great deal of luggage in the shape of faith in God and in the auriferous character of London pavements'.[50]

Abram found work, and possibly a floor on which to doss, in a sweatshop in Whitechapel, the district increasingly populated by East European and Mittel-European Jews, just north of the wharfs. There he also met his bride-to-be, Rebecca Fingelstein, who hailed from Vilkaviškis, not far from Wigrance (in what is now Lithuania but was then Russian Poland).[51] They married in 1871.

Though over half of London's Jewish immigrants ended up as paupers, Charles Booth's survey observed that others did well. They were, he suggested, highly adaptable and slaved stoically to accrue the wherewithal that they needed to become 'tiny capitalists', moving up the economic ladder to run their own outfits.[52] Abram was one of those. By the mid-1880s, he was his own boss. A merchant fashioning products from skins and furs at the northern tip of Whitechapel, he was resident in a thoroughfare between Spitalfields Market and Brick Lane, with his own small sweatshop in the garret of his house.

No. 5 Fournier Street was where Emanuel was born in 1892, catching the last decade of Victoria's reign. The youngest of nine siblings, he would fall asleep every night listening to the whirr of sewing machines overhead.[53] Today this street is gentrified, a terrace of Queen Anne townhouses looking quintessentially English, yet it has been home to waves of immigrants. On the corner, towering like a white cliff over No. 5, is Nicholas Hawksmoor's Christ Church. Though it was named Church Street for a time, the residents were at least 95 per cent Jewish by 1900. Before the Jews arrived, the street was inhabited by silk-weaving Huguenots, who had fled persecution on the continent. Their French Protestant chapel, on the junction with Brick Lane, serves today as the London Jamme Masjid (Bengali for 'Great Mosque').[54]

The refugees of Abram's generation were regarded by some locals as job-snatching interlopers. Booth's survey was, in fact, pro-native workers, and parliamentary select committees looking into immigration issues particularly scrutinized sweatshop Jews in the East End.[55] The immediate vicinity remained, during Emanuel's childhood, alarmingly rough and racially tense. Just before he came into the world, local prostitutes were being horrifically murdered by Jack the Ripper. Two bodies were discovered within 150 yards of No. 5, and anti-Semitic rumours claimed that the nightmarish slasher was a Jew, dubbed 'Leather Apron'. A scrap of bloodstained evidence was found with graffiti above it reading 'The Juwes are the men That Will not be Blamed for nothing'. The constabulary raced to erase this scrawled incitement to hatred, fearing it would spark a full-scale riot.[56]

Spitalfields was, generally, a byword for criminality and chronic indigence. When Emanuel was ten, the journalist Jack London was slumming it to write *The People of the Abyss*, and standing at the foot of Christ Church. Staring at the homeless men, women and babies huddled in the abutting strip known as Itchy Park, he saw 'a mass of miserable and distorted humanity . . . a welter of rags and filth and loathsome skin diseases'. He further described visiting a nearby sweatshop in Frying Pan Alley. Stepping over a 'spawn of children [who] cluttered the slimy pavement', he glimpsed backyard hovels covered in garbage like a 'human sty', and entered a den where five shoemakers 'sweated' with scarcely room to stand, working fourteen-hour days.[57]

Such scenes and Abram's tough start engendered Emanuel's dread of destitution, always fearing he would lose the roof over his head unless he worked ceaselessly.[58] His professional commitment to healing psychological scars may, likewise, have had its roots here. Abram was not a loving father, except when his children were ill. Then he revealed a desperately concerned side, and rightly so given that 55 per cent of East End children died before they were five.[59] Mostly Abram was strict, religiously devout and domestically violent. He also threw himself into street brawls from which the youngsters had to extract him. Emanuel got off to a shaky start at Parmiter's School in the East End, with one teacher reporting that he stuttered nervously and could not stop chattering in class. Even as an adult he was described, by one family member, as being 'shy and probably fairly traumatized'.

He and his siblings were better off than some. His father wanted, in some ways, to play the English gent, buying a pony and trap which was a sign of respectability, albeit not wholly practical.[60] The pony had to clop to the back yard through the family's front door, blinkered with a shawl to stop it rearing up or just horsing around at the sight of the cut glass in the parlour.

Nor were the streets entirely devoid of fun. There were bustling markets and the organ grinders making music. One of Emanuel's boyhood friends, Hugh Gainsborough, later recalled how they used to laugh and play together outside No. 5.[61] More importantly, Emanuel was extremely bright. Jack London had been too sweeping in his prognosis that youngsters from this quarter were inevitably 'born falling' with 'all the forces of society driv[ing] them downward' to perish 'feeble, besotted and imbecile'.[62] From Parmiter's, Emanuel went on to shine, winning a scholarship to the City of London School (known for being the first in England to use scientific experiments in class). He was, indeed, part of an exceptionally gifted East End generation, along with Hugh Gainsborough – who became an esteemed medic too – and the aspiring artists Isaac Rosenberg, David Bomberg and Mark Gertler. They congregated at the inspirational new Whitechapel Art Gallery and Whitechapel Public Library, discussing culture and aesthetics into the night.[63]

Often the scholarship-winning youngsters of Jewish immigrants hit a glass ceiling when their own parents – though desiring upward mobility – drew the line at higher education, insisting they go into trade.[64] Emanuel was almost forced to join the furrier business, escaping only because his sisters battled on his behalf. After being badgered morning, noon and night, Abram grudgingly let him try for a place at Cambridge University.

The father–son rift never quite healed, a cultural divide opening up as the nineteen-year-old Emanuel departed to become an awarded exhibitioner and prizeman at St John's College.[65] It was a prodigious leap considering that neither Abram nor Rebecca, Jonathan Miller's grandparents, could even read or write. Their marriage certificate had been signed with two circles, and now their *wunderkind* Emanuel was off acquiring top-class learning and the transformative accent of a thoroughly English intellectual.[66] Was it not also a quiet act of rebellion that he joined the university's newly founded Heretics Society, which questioned religious dogmas and traditional authorities?[67]

Cambridge in 1911 opened up a world of groundbreaking ideas. Emanuel plunged into studying natural sciences, botany and zoology, learning about Darwin's still disputed theories of evolution and about Mendel's laws of inheritance. Those laws had just spawned the whole notion of genetics, a term coined by the Johnian professor William Bateson.[68] Enthused by the youthful lecturer Bertrand Russell, Emanuel additionally read moral sciences – embracing philosophy and philosophy of science – for the second part of his Tripos. In later years, very strikingly, his interests would be passed down to his son, with Jonathan Miller loving many of the same subjects as a student.

Alongside Russell, Emanuel's other mentor was W. H. R. Rivers, the extraordinarily pioneering doctor who features in Pat Barker's *Regeneration* trilogy of novels. Shortly before 1911, Rivers had conducted a celebrated neurological experiment at St John's, severing a nerve in his colleague Dr Henry Head's arm, then charting the return of sensation.[69] Prior to that, he had joined the university's seminal research expedition to the Torres Strait and helped to establish both anthropology and experimental psychology as disciplines. Beyond this, he was to be admired for his sympathetic treatment of shell-shocked soldiers during the Great War, with Siegfried Sassoon among his patients. Emanuel was profoundly inspired by Rivers' interests and, ultimately, he gained a DPM (Diploma in Psychological Medicine) from Cambridge, where Britain's first department of psychology had been founded at the turn of the century.[70]

On returning to London, he entered a vibrant social circle of Jewish intellectuals who were engaged with the arts as well as the social sciences and medicine. Emanuel shared digs in Bloomsbury with his friend Jack Isaacs, a literary critic and future London University professor. He attended classical concerts at the Albert Hall with the fast-rising University College and LSE philosopher/sociologist Morris Ginsberg. He fraternized, as well, with those artists who had, by then, become known as the Whitechapel Boys at the Slade, especially Mark Gertler (who was increasingly entangled with the Bloomsbury set) and Isaac Rosenberg (who had also developed into an outstanding poet).

Emanuel himself was an avid reader of literature and an amateur artist, enjoying painting and sculpting. Depressing developments were to come when Rosenberg was killed in World War 1 and when, later, Gertler and another painter friend, Bernard Meninsky, committed suicide. For all that, Emanuel's bachelor life in the Edwardian *belle époque* was often jovial and mildly liberated, at least compared to Victorian strictures. A window opened, albeit briefly. He went on roving trips to Paris, allegedly sowing some wild oats and starting to collect art there.[71] He adventured further afield in Europe, too, with the popular scientist and humanist Julian Huxley – brother of Aldous and grandson of Thomas Henry Huxley (the zoologist and agnostic known as Darwin's Bulldog).

In between, Emanuel was continuing his medical training at the London Hospital, again as a prizeman. Rivers' associate, Henry Head, was a physician there, encouraging intense interest in the nervous system. When World War 1 struck, Emanuel became a captain in the Royal Army Medical Corps, acting as a psychiatrist and neurological adviser to the Ministry of Pensions.[72] Notably, he had connections with Netley, the huge military hospital near Southampton where shell-shock victims started receiving experimental treatment.

Seeing the trauma which the trenches inflicted on soldiers was undoubtedly harrowing for such a young doctor. Nonetheless, his response was dynamic and, after the war, he moved on to become a founder of child psychiatry in Britain. The late 1920s and early 1930s were, for many in England, years of desperation, frustration and anxiety, yet there was also great hope and innovation, the goal being to forge a better world after the traumas of the Great War. Some believed that those with scientific knowledge would be the ones to save society. It was even suggested that Julian Huxley should stand for Parliament.[73]

Determined to help the inhabitants of his impoverished and crime-ridden birthplace, Emanuel returned, in 1927, to work in the East End. Escalating juvenile delinquency was causing alarm. Therefore he set up the East End Child Guidance Clinic – the first of its kind in Europe – and it made his name.[74] Today called the Emanuel Miller Centre, it continues his work on the housing estates overshadowed by Canary Wharf's corporate skyscrapers. Also honouring his memory, there is an annual Emanuel Miller National Conference and an Emanuel Miller Lecture.

Initially, his clinic did not even have a home of its own. It made use of a few bare rooms in the Jewish Free School, off Frying Pan Alley, very near Fournier Street. Keen to catalyze new ideas and generate what would, today, be called 'joined-up thinking', he consulted and brought together a team of specialists from different fields including the high-powered Sybil Clement Brown, then a young social worker, who had visited trial clinics in America.

Entailing constant sallies out to visit 'problem' children in the Isle of Dogs and the East India Docks, the work became especially gruelling when the Great Depression took hold. Unemployment and despair, hunger and squalid housing conditions were endemic. Emanuel, moreover, had to battle with hostile education authorities and public health officials. As he himself observed, the ideal clinic director, if such a species could evolve, had to be of a kind that could survive and thrive 'on land or sea . . . rid[ing] the whirlwind'.[75]

His energy remained remarkable. Colleagues described him, in his thirties, as sparky, eager and boldly 'throwing gauntlets' at everyone.[76] In 1933, while his son was in the womb, he was taking on extra work for the now famous Tavistock Clinic. As the head of its children's department, he was one of the first to import Jean Piaget's developmental ideas, and he promoted family therapy. Indeed, his section was renamed the 'children and parents' department in 1933, emphasizing how adults can impact on their offspring and ought to be part of the remedial process. Helping to establish the Portman Clinic, he acted as its vice-president and appealed for public support alongside Freud, Jung and H. G. Wells.[77] In the year when Betty gave birth, he gained a staff post at the West End Hospital for Nervous Diseases, and somehow found a spare moment to chair the medical section of the British Psychological Society.[78]

He was, furthermore, a popularizer of science: a doctor-journalist penning articles for the *Listener* and *Twentieth Century*; broadcasting as a guest speaker on BBC Radio; and writing accessible psychology books. Those books

14

intertwined Freudian theories and older ideas (such as the four humours). Cross-disciplinary, they also referred to anthropology and the arts (with analyses of literary characters such as Don Quixote).[79] As Sybil Clement Brown observed: 'To work with Emanuel Miller was an education . . . His was a mind and sensibility which widened the vision of us all . . . [with his] refusal to think in terms of any particular school of thought.'[80]

One connection which might cause consternation today was his membership of the Eugenic Society, which debated whether civil ills might be alleviated if the 'right' sort of people were encouraged to breed more than 'undesirables'. The argument was that hereditary flaws created the 'problem group' of feckless, feeble-minded and destitute citizens. Many leading intellectuals in Emanuel's era had discussed and publicly supported eugenics, but the thesis seems disconcertingly at odds with his left-wing leanings, particularly given that he was a member of the society after World War 2, knowing of the Nazis' *Übermensch* policies.[81] He surely did not sign up to the genetic argument in its entirety, given that he devoted his life to helping 'problem' children through psychotherapy and saw the impact of environmental factors in the East End.

He worked assiduously and was finally made an FRCP (Fellow of the Royal College of Physicians) in the mid-1940s, in spite of some institutionalized anti-Semitism within the profession.[82] By the end of his days, he was distinctly clubbable. He was a member (as his son has been too) of the Athenaeum, a meeting place for those who cherish the life of the mind, especially eminent scientists and medics.

In the eyes of many traditional physicians, the study of the psyche, nonetheless, remained peripheral or 'beyond the fringe', pretty much extra-institutional. It was considered borderline science, dealing with the irrational and without foolproof theories. So Emanuel was never comfortably part of the Establishment or fully satisfied with his achievements. He never made it on to the Queen's honours list.

From the age of 50, he was prematurely blighted with rheumatoid arthritis: a doctor gallingly unable to cure himself. His beloved eldest brother, Wolfe – a multi-talented scholar, humanist and champion swimmer – had been horrifically crippled by the same disease in his thirties and died not long after. Wolfe lived on only in Jonathan Miller's middle name.[83] Meanwhile, Emanuel's ill health threatened to realize his nightmare of destitution and caused him physical agonies, with his fingers reduced to gnarled knots and his legs ultimately in metal braces to enable him to walk. 'We lived on a knife-edge for years,' Miller remembers, 'not knowing if my father would be able to continue.'[84]

Emanuel soldiered on, consulting and teaching at St George's Hospital and the Maudsley. He set in motion and headed the ACPP (Association for Child Psychology and Psychiatry) and, at the age of 68, was editing its newly established journal.[85] He went on working into his late seventies, right up to the fortnight before his death. Described as 'one of the best loved figures in psychological medicine', his colleagues cherished him not only for his outstanding scholarship and enthusiastic teaching, but also for his humorous conversation and his modest, gentle manner.[86]

The founding father of England's child guidance practices was not, however, the world's best father. His parenting skills were not as disastrous as those of his contemporary, Melanie Klein. After settling in London in 1926, she quarrelled publicly and irreconcilably with her rivalrous daughter, Melitta Schmideberg, who followed her into the profession. Emanuel's busy schedule did cause problems, though. Devoted to curing others' emotionally damaged children, he left precious little time for his own. In his son's early memories, he is largely an absence. Moreover, his worst behaviour and wretchedness came to the fore when he was home, such that – in Sarah's words – he was 'very much a presence, casting a great pall of gloom, slamming doors and saying nobody cared. He always had to be the centre of attention or there was trouble.' That trait grew worse over the years.

Miller's nascent talent for showmanship helped him to compete for the limelight in a more entertaining manner, and ultimately his Danny Kaye impressions would lead him away from a career paralleling Emanuel's. Dr J. Miller would prove to be a kind of mirror image of Dr E. Miller. He would become the opposite of his father, an inversion in many ways, while being extraordinarily similar as well. Emanuel was a serious, dedicated medic who would never (or would only) have dreamed of taking to the stage. Miller was to follow in his footsteps but he qualified only to jump ship, swiftly heading off to *Beyond the Fringe* and a working life of ever more diversity.

On the other hand, Emanuel was obviously admired by his peers as a wide-ranging polymath with artistic hobbies, and Miller's early scientific passions, so interconnected with his father's, have remained central to his intellectual life, rather than being abandoned. Thus his mournful comments to Anthony Clare, concerning the distance between himself and his parents, were not the whole story.

·2·

THE WAR AND POST-WAR YEARS

Peripatetic and prep-school days

The War Years: On the Road

B RITAIN DECLARED WAR on Hitler's Germany a few weeks after Miller's fifth birthday, causing the family to be uprooted even before they had settled in at 35 Queen's Grove. Emanuel was once again enrolled as an RAMC psychiatrist to treat traumatized soldiers. Dispatched for training at Aldershot, he was subsequently posted – with his wife and two children in tow – to a string of military hospitals, moving 'from one nut house to the next', as Miller recalls.[1]

It was farewell to Leicester Square, as these metropolitans found themselves journeying through the rural heart of England and off to its extremities. Between 1939 and 1945, Miller's path can be charted zigzagging from the south coast to the western border with Wales, from Bishop's Lydeard in deepest Somerset to Abbots Langley, which lies just north of Watford. He attended eight or more schools between Dunkirk and D-Day, and – as he once mentioned, when contributing to a collection of wartime memoirs – the dislocations and restlessness left indelible traces.[2]

The move to No. 35, with its bare rooms undergoing redecoration, had been excitingly novel. After that, though, his father vanished, 'Not with any painful suddenness,' the memoir states. 'But here, there and everywhere, he casually disappeared and the smell of turps and housepaint appeared in his place . . . then everything seemed to fly apart and the travelling began.'

Miller and his sister were never parentless evacuees, labelled with name tags like human luggage and dispatched into the arms of total strangers. As bombing raids were expected in London, with gas masks being distributed and anti-aircraft guns positioned on public buildings, Betty decamped with her children on what she described, reassuringly, as an extended seaside holiday on the south coast.

At first, they stayed with Nanny Hogarth in the village of Felpham, not far from Bognor Regis, between the strand and the Downs' rolling hills. The poet and visionary William Blake once holed up there, calling it a heavenly retreat and being inspired to write his lines about 'England's green and pleasant land', now famous from the hymn 'Jerusalem'. After Felpham, the family became so nomadic that much is blurred. Exactly when Betty took lodgings in Rottingdean, near Brighton, is lost in the sands of time. Hogarth was left behind somewhere en route, being replaced by Nanny Morgan.

What became increasingly clear to Betty was that these beaches on the English Channel were no safe haven, with the Luftwaffe making murderous excursions across the water. She headed inland and north-west with her children before the Battle of Britain went into full throttle. They stayed for a while in the Cotswolds' market town of Fairford with its pretty seventeenth- and eighteenth-century stone houses, and in Worcestershire's Droitwich Spa. They also spent a rustic month at Nanny Morgan's childhood home in the village of Brockweir, on the Monmouthshire–Gloucestershire boundary, walking down the lane to collect the milk churns, and washing in a tin bath. That verdant setting, near the River Wye and Tintern Abbey, was serene in many respects. It seeded, in Miller, a love of nature which he describes as 'an almost Wordsworthian appetite for the English scene'.[3] Only years later did he learn that his mother had been terrified of a Jew-annihilating Nazi invasion, and that her weekend absences had involved frantic house-hunting.

When Emanuel reappeared, he seemed 'mysteriously renovated'. In his son's eyes he looked younger: bushy and spruce in his khaki and Sam Browne belt. 'Even my mother', Miller notes, 'seemed to have been born again by courtesy of this strange political Easter. She sparkled now as an officer's wife . . . sport[ing] an RAMC badge, tricked up into a piece of costume jewellery.' Never quite the conformist, he rebelliously kicked Emanuel in the shins when three privates saluted in the street. After being given a mini soldier suit of his own, both he and his sister dutifully played at standing to attention.

He has one other haunting, almost hallucinatory memory of that summer with its 'drugged rural heat' in which he can still see his father, 'heroically uniformed, standing amongst the harvest sheaves', taking a glass of cider with the local farmer. Although he recollects no open talk about the Führer's persecution of the Jews, an anxiety seeped through, either then or retrospectively, affecting Miller's view of the world. As he explains:

> The memory of that delicious corn-coloured heat is poisoned with suggestions of danger . . . The sweating stillness of that Wye valley . . . There was an air of dreadful pregnancy and I can still hear the cool unhurried morse of a cuckoo hidden in those distant woods spelling out the order for some horrible but as yet unrealised enactment.

The war gripped the national psyche. Adults generally felt more alarm than children, to whom evacuation meant getting the run of the countryside – increased liberty. At the same time, with squadrons zooming overhead, every youngster was aware of epic battles being fought with dauntless resilience. The link may be indirect but a correspondence was to emerge with Miller's long-term sense of being prone to attack and his urge to fight back, resisting dictatorial figures and anybody else who has gained the upper hand.

His family were soon on the move again, he recollects, caught in 'a huge convection current . . . [with everyone now] chronically mobile as if the whole of English society had turned into plankton'. Locomotives became a running theme and, although his parents tried to keep the family unit together, his predominant memory is of feeling lost. On more than one cross-country trek, their train drew into a station, then – while the accompanying grown-up had disembarked for refreshments – reversed away into the middle of nowhere. After a seemingly eternal '*va et vient*', shunting back and forth along sidetracks, the engine would eventually grind back to the platform 'where', he recalls, 'the vanished parent would be waiting to laugh at one's blubbering face pressed to the filthy window'.

Worse confusion was induced by the very first air-raid siren that he heard: this 'raucous unclassifiable ululation [which] burst into the blackness [of the small hours] in such a way that the whole universe seemed to be on the point of breaking up'. It left him feeling desperately disoriented and lonely, as if he were 'hanging in the dark somewhere between Saturn and Betelgeuse'.

That lost feeling explains, in part, why a brood of hens looms peculiarly large in his memories of World War 2, a clutch of Rhode Island Reds to be precise. Fluttering in his parents' trailer when they travelled by car, or ring-fenced at the bottom of various gardens, these feathered friends were one of the few permanent features in his life. They were being kept to supply eggs which were, of course, strictly rationed in the shops, along with meat, cheese, sweets and much else. The birds fascinated him, and he began to study hen lingo. Although he claims, oddly, that he never had a sense of humour, mimicking them was his first comic turn, and he depicts himself, tongue-in-cheek, as a precocious scientific researcher scrutinizing the coops.

> I noticed that some of the cruder impersonators of chickens, and there were competitors at school, never understood that there was a rather subtle variation of 'buk, buk, buk' for every 'bacagh'. They used to think it was absolutely regular. But I noticed, and this was really a big breakthrough in chicken linguistics, that chickens like to lead you up the garden path.[4]

That is a pivotal little snapshot, capturing the moment when Miller first oscillated between mini-scientist and showman, between biological naturalist and theatrical naturalism.

Besides being a pin-sharp observer, like his mother, the infant impressionist must have overcome his stutter to precision-perform these rhythmic (and paradoxically stammer-like) clucks. His repertoire soon extended to include steam trains and, today, he can still cup his hands to his slightly skew-whiff mouth and conjure up poultry and puffing, clanking engines with startling brilliance.

19

He did not get off to a flying start academically. The small boy whom he describes – suffering from feelings of horrible inadequacy because he couldn't understand the lessons – sounds a million miles from the adult who was to become a spokesman of the English intelligentsia. What were précis? He hadn't a clue. Maths (always to be his weak point) made no sense. It was all chaotic and wretched. He couldn't grasp what being clever consisted of, except that other boys seemingly understood the teacher's instructions.[5] Surely this was not a perverse case of refusing to learn, although his mother once wrote of her nursery days: 'I resisted silently and tenaciously the regime of the conqueror [i.e. authority figures]. My resistance took the form of blank stupidity, which, unfortunately . . . outlasted by a number of years its original intention.'[6]

As for the theory that parentally underloved children develop cognitive problems, Miller's struggles were probably more to do with all the swapping of schools.[7] These institutions, with their regimes of corporal punishment, made him constantly nervous and, on one occasion, so terrified him that he wet himself. He talks with loathing of 'that world of Christian sadists where masters beat with one hand in their pocket, getting their jollies'. Memories of the injustice unleash a retributive, verbal whipping for a whole pack of persecutors. He remarks excoriatingly:

> There are all sorts of Tory public school people who look back to their whacking as 'character-building' and as part of what being 'a decent Englishman' was. I just think one of the disadvantages for me – not believing in God or an afterlife – is that I have had to surrender the notion of a cruel hell in which Mr Whitty [Dr Headworth-Whitty, head of Somerset's Thone School], Mr Heaton [of Watford's Shirley House] and others are having their eyelids cut off with red-hot scissors. I regret the fact that they are unconsciously at peace having tormented so many little boys.

Providing intimations of what Miller was like out of school, Betty's novel *On the Side of the Angels* was written in Somerset and featured a protagonist called Honor Carmichael. While akin to Flaubert's Madame Bovary, Honor was distinctly autobiographical: married to an RAMC doctor and stuck in a rural backwater with two small children. The older one, called Peter, often sounds painfully like the author's son.[8] He looks up adoringly to his unresponsive workaholic father, plaintively demands more affectionate attention, and is upbraided by his mother for habitually wetting himself. In one teatime scene, he misbehaves until everyone else leaves, then smiles radiantly at her as he exclaims, 'Now there's only you and me.' His declaration of love is greeted by a stony silence.[9]

If Betty was similarly inattentive, that problem was exacerbated by her contracting near-fatal double pneumonia in Bishop's Lydeard. Miller was rushed away, hidden under a gas cape in an army truck, to join his father, for a while, in London. Having recuperated, his mother was then shattered by the death of her most beloved brother. A handsome and witty young man, as well as a high achiever, Henry Spiro had gallantly joined up to serve King and Country. He was torpedoed aboard HMS *Firedrake*, drowning in the icy North Atlantic in the New Year of 1943.[10] Miller can still picture his mother entering the room, red-eyed and shakily holding the telegram which said Henry was missing, presumed killed. It was an emotional broadside from which she never fully recovered, withdrawing even more into her work.

By the last stretch of the war, while his father was collaborating with the popular scientist Launcelot Hogben in a study of mental instability across the social classes, Miller was starting to enjoy himself in rough-and-tumble battles with other children in Abbots Langley. He points out:

> For someone who has now got a reputation for being a 'Renaissance man', I can't imagine a less 'Renaissance childhood' . . . I just did what little boys did: looked scruffy, scrumped apples, made catapults, had forts and hideaways in which one kept clubs and cudgels. I read the *Just William* books and felt that was my story . . . There were also brick fights: having bricks chucked at one by gangs of boys from up the road, who were possibly slightly lower-class . . . I used to love conkers too. They looked like the eggs from which Sheraton sideboards were hatched, and I loved the glossiness as they first split out of that wonderful, soaked, white felt enclosure. All those things are much more intense memories for me than anything 'artistic'. Artistic memories come from the commonplace experiences of childhood.

Though born into a highbrow family, his home was not a hermetic ivory tower. Popular entertainment was beaming straight into the Millers' living-room thanks to the wireless, around which everyone gathered in this pre-television era. While Emanuel listened avidly to the philosopher C. E. M. Joad and Julian Huxley opining on *The Brains Trust*, and while much of the BBC's mid-century output was stultifyingly anodyne, an exuberant golden age of radio comedy was under way too. The young Miller relished the light entertainment programmes. Along with half the nation, he could reiterate the catchphrases from *ITMA* (or *It's That Man Again*), Tommy Handley's show with a whirling medley of characters including the charwoman Mrs Mopp ('Can I do yer now, Sir?') and soused Colonel Chinstrap ('I don't mind if I do').

As for the brick fights and other outdoor adventures, one Abbots Langley friend, Julian Crispin, recollects how Miller just appeared out of the blue one day, when the local boys were playing on a building site, and effortlessly became part of the gang. On long, hot afternoons, the two of them would roam the countryside, cycling and on foot, or sit on a creosoted fence for hours, train-spotting. Noting down engine numbers and knowing wheel formulae apparently enthralled Miller, combined with the more sensational thrill of 'these huge green and brass locomotives racing by, named after warships and parts of the Empire – *Bihar* and *Orissa* and *Mysore*,' he remembers. Likewise keen on planespotting, along with almost every other boy, he would pride himself on recognizing distant Mosquitoes and whoop formations of Lancaster bombers.

Captivated by all things American, he sought out the GIs stationed in the area, hoping for candy or chewing gum and admiring the guys' cool. Meanwhile, Crispin looked up to his friend as the natural leader when it came to pretending games. As he explains:

> Jonathan seemed very worldly-wise. Possibly he'd had more exposure to adult company. I was totally under his spell. He knew far more about everything than my parents or teachers. He was possessed of great imaginative powers, and the world, for him, was full of things waiting to be discovered. There was buried treasure under every rotting tree stump. The fact that we never found any didn't affect this at all . . . We dug up large parts of the building site . . . We found an old hunting lodge in the woods, on the other side of the valley, hung with animal skulls, and of course it was haunted. There were limits. On one occasion, Jonathan wrote to my parents for permission for us both to go camping on common ground a few miles away, saying, 'My mother has given her consent.'

Crispin's father, having telephoned Betty to verify, found the boy's inventiveness highly amusing.[11]

Sarah occasionally accompanied her brother on his escapades. They used to swing in the trees together and, back at the house, they staged a playlet: a scene from *Alice in Wonderland*. Lewis Carroll's book had become a great favourite after Emanuel entrusted them with his own treasured copy (given to him as a school prize).[12] The playlet was not so much the start of Miller's dramatic career as a hilarious fiasco, or farcical precursor of his superb 1960s film of *Alice*. With Sarah cast as the heroine and Miller making his debut as the Caterpillar, their vignette had barely got started when he was overcome by giggles, resulting in wild squeaks from the recorder which was supposed to be his hookah. The show closed instantly.

The siblings were never really soulmates. Allegedly, infantine rivalries caused him to cry out repeatedly, 'Sarah's the favourite!' The chance of gaining his parents' undivided attention was even smaller with her around, and he rightly felt insecure. According to one confidante, Betty admitted she was fonder of her quiet daughter. She surely tried not to let that show, because she herself had suffered childhood anxieties. 'The damage to my self-esteem brought about by the birth of my young brother', she once recalled, 'was so extensive that I welcomed eagerly any reassurance as to my own value.'[13] The seed of competitive envy was perhaps sown in her son, nonetheless. In later decades he would be accused of professional jealousy and, while denying any autobiographical element in his directorial readings, he would markedly put Iago's envy at the heart of Shakespeare's *Othello* and see Mozart's Don Giovanni as compulsively competing with other men 'like an envious sibling' or spoilt infant subsequently unable to brook competition.[14]

It must, equally, have been difficult for Sarah to follow in her brother's coruscating wake.[15] As personalities, they were very different. She was certainly not dim but, lacking his vivacity, she was increasingly left out of his games and his life. They grew steadily apart.

In neighbours' gardens, one or two other girls popped up, with whom Miller 'played bottoms', a precocious pastime which cannot really be classified as his first medical examination. He ruminates, a mite fetishistically:

> I can remember all sorts of things about knickers and especially the material around the elastic band. I've never lost that. I looked at girls' bottoms wherever I could. I used to like that very much . . . getting Janet H**t to take down her green school knickers . . . knowing that there was some sort of itching excitement between the legs but not quite knowing what you could do. It just was exciting to look at her bottom in the thicket. It still is, you see . . . No, not with Janet H**t, but that has, essentially, remained the same.

Regarding this bending-over fixation – if that's what it is – he adds breezily that he was interested in the bottom long before his neurological fascination with the brain, and that the former obsession will probably outlast the latter.

In another of his short memoirs, entitled 'Led Astray', he describes the Rudolf Steiner school which he attended near Abbots Langley as an oasis of pastoral kindness.[16] It bordered, at the same time, on the loony fringe of education. Based round an old friary, with an attached farm, it was called the Priory, and Miller's account of it blends liberal affection, mild satire and a flicker of serious disapproval. As he recalls, morning prayers were entertaininigly wayward:

> After a formal cough [the headmistress] would lead us off into a sort of Jungian chant to which I never somehow managed to learn the words. There were a lot of hand movements . . . both fists were placed together, side by side over the heart. Then, as the chant grew to a crescendo (something about 'the spirit of the sun within us glows'), the arms reached up and out in an expansive double arc of spiritual ecstasy. This was always the signal for a lot of facetious horseplay; the idea being to fell both neighbours.

Various subjects were quirkily elided, so everyone set about learning their multiplication tables in French, and art lessons in the barn involved more Oriental mythology, with much painting of the legend of Manu on wet paper.

> 'Moisten your papers,' [the art mistress] would cry flutily, and the class would set about the ritual douche . . . the colours running together into a maddening archetypal blur . . . 'Manu leading his peoples out of Atlantis' was hard to distinguish from 'Elijah ascending to heaven in a fiery chariot'. One boy even managed to pass off a detailed representation of 'What he would like to do to Betty Grable' as 'Prince Gautama teaching the Word'.[17]

23

As for the music teacher, one of Ivy Compton-Burnett's sisters, she merrily shunned notation in favour of each child copying her finger movements. The result was 'Lillibulero' reduced to banshee cacophonies as Miller produced 'a hideous mirror image of the tune'. In the end, he suggests, this oddball approach to education was a setback. It temporarily rendered him a misfit, without the proper skills, when he returned to the traditional cap-and-blazer system at Shirley House in Watford. A fellow-pupil from Shirley House confirms that Miller was placed one class down, rather than with his own age group, as he had no Latin and was still struggling with maths.[18]

He had been happy at the Priory, though, and found a good friend there. Nicholas Garland, now the *Daily Telegraph*'s political cartoonist, fondly remembers Miller, aged nine, as a mix of showing-off and nervousness. The newcomer had, Garland agrees, a fantastic imagination, whether he was play-acting Robin Hood in the spinney or organizing a crowd of small children in a bout of *Simon Says*, with them all running after him like the Pied Piper. There, surely, is a glimpse of the future director. Miller further entertained everyone with his air-raid imitation. This was a source of terror transmogrified into a thrilling party trick, as Garland recalls:

> It was definitely a performance and he was going to do it properly. He'd begin with the street sounds, cars honking, the clip-clop of horses. Then it would start, the long, looping sound of the siren, very accurate. Then silence would fall. Nothing would happen . . . until, very very low, you'd hear this 'Grrr' and it was the bombers. He'd make the engines sound nearer and nearer, and then all hell would break loose. There'd be the whistle of the falling bombs, the crump of explosions, the ding-a-ling of ambulances – a tremendous din, all coming up like a volcano from this little boy, rising to a great crescendo. And then it would begin to be quiet once again, and into the quiet came the long, single, sustained note of the all-clear. It was quite extraordinarily dramatic.

When Garland went round to Miller's house, he was invited to view the 'museum', with the entry fee magnanimously waived. The exhibits were set out in the greenhouse: a stash of Dinky aircraft-carriers which were, Miller assured his visitor, incredibly secret models, all entrusted to him by his naval uncle. Alongside was a hoard of bullets, except they were made of wood. 'I remember arguing with him about them,' remarks Garland, 'saying you could squish them with your finger. But he said that was why they were so brilliant: when you shot Germans they splintered into bits and caused terrible injuries . . . That was why he was such a terrific companion: Jonathan could live in his imagination and you could play the game with him of believing all that nonsense.'

*   *   *

The Post-War Years: Back in London

On D-Day, Miller awoke in the small hours. The rumble of RAF planes passing overhead was almost continuous. Unbeknown to the British populace, the biggest combined land, air and sea operation of all time was under way: the Normandy campaign, invading the Nazi-occupied continent at last. On hearing the news announced a few hours later, at school, Miller sensed its momentousness. In the subsequent months, he followed the Allies' progress more closely – the miniature flags, pinned to his father's map of Europe, shifting inch by inch.

Germany's final surrender, in May 1945, was celebrated with huge ruddy bonfires and bunting, in Abbots Langley as across the land. From the capital, Churchill addressed the nation over the airwaves. 'Advance Britannia!' proclaimed the PM before joining in the massive party, stepping out on to a Whitehall balcony to conduct and sing 'Land of Hope and Glory'. Feeling ecstatically liberated, the crowds below hurled confetti, kissed and danced the hokey-cokey up to Buckingham Palace where they hallooed their diffident king, George VI, and the young princesses Elizabeth and Margaret.

With lightning bolts and thunderclaps, nature was spectacularly mimicking the Blitz on the night when the Millers returned to north London to resettle at Queen's Grove. Soon decorators were repainting the house, which had been requisitioned for Polish army officers. Two part-time cooks were also hired because, when it came to anything involving a hot stove, Betty was absolutely hopeless, or resolutely hopeless as part of her covert feminism. Conveniently for her, the remnants of a serving class were still catering to the well-to-do: not so much 'Advance Britannia!' as harking back to the Edwardian era.

Emanuel acquired a chauffeur who, with a wife and child, lived in the basement flat. Not only a status symbol, the chauffeur was a necessary precaution. The eminent doctor, though keen to get motoring, proved a liability behind the wheel, accidentally trundling his shiny new Austin into the wall of the Pakistani Embassy at the end of the street. 'This might', his son wryly suggests, 'have been interpreted as the first Jewish attack on the Muslim world.'[19]

After the glow of VE Day and VJ Day faded, post-war Britain remained grey during years of austerity. Over a million buildings in the capital had been bombed flat or badly damaged. With the economy struggling and severe shortages of food, fuel, newsprint and other raw materials, rationing was to drag on for the best part of a decade. Pollution caused the city to be covered by fog for up to 60 days a year. In the notorious smoggy pea-soupers, Londoners had to grope to find their front gates while the trolley buses nosed past at a crawl. Each breath tasted of pungent sulphur dioxide. The nation was further plagued by floods and crippled by the wintry Big Freeze of 1946–7.

In the international arena, Fascism had been trounced only to be replaced by the Cold War with Stalin's Soviet Union. 'An Iron Curtain has descended . . . The dark ages may return on the gleaming wings of science,' Churchill warned as the nuclear arms race commenced.[20]

Britons' fighting spirit did not wilt. Many coped by grinning and bearing the hardships. After over 2,000 nights of blackout, the West End's lights were switched on once more to resounding cheers.[21] Although the era of affluence was still a long way off, earnings had risen and rationing varied. Yes, they had some bananas at Covent Garden's fruit stalls in 1946, and black-market spivs could slip you some extra chocolate if you had the readies. There was no longer any need for the squirrel pie recipe, hysterically issued by the Food Ministry.[22] The USA's Marshall Plan, announced in 1947, additionally supplied welcome aid. Miller remembers a rusty tin of peaches, sent over by some Californian philanthropist, being opened to reveal its contents: slithering crescents of gold which seemed, to him, like slices of American sunshine.

With the British being hungry for change immediately after the war, the Labour Party had won the General Election in the landslide victory of 1945. Emanuel and many others beamed joyously that day because – inspired by Clement Attlee's manifesto slogan, 'Let us face the future' – they saw the promised Welfare State as a new dawn. This was another chance to construct a better society, a 'new Jerusalem'. The National Health Service was certainly a huge step, aiming to care for everyone from cradle to grave. It was established before the decade was out (and before Churchill was back in).

From a young boy's perspective, the Big Freeze, with its thick snow and candlelit power cuts, was largely an escapade. During the summer, the bomb-blasted streets did not strike Miller as dreary either. Fascinated by Kipling's wolf boy Mowgli and *The Jungle Book*, he saw the wrecked mansions around Queen's Grove as a playground of enticing ruins, like overgrown exotic temples to be explored. A thrilling guest arrived too. Betty's surviving brother, Julian, returned as a war hero, having led a flotilla of barges across the Channel on D-Day. Even if *Beyond the Fringe* would later satirize World War 2's 'Valiant Few', Miller was hugely impressed by his uncle's courage and bravado. Julian shot at the washing on the line in the back garden, with real bullets, while the ration-conscious Betty yelped that pyjamas didn't grow on trees.

The King's Troop, Royal Horse Artillery also had their barracks just around the corner, as Miller vividly recalls:

I have very fond memories of that strange, as yet unfocused susurration at six in the morning, which was the first sound of the troop coming up the road on their morning exercises. It would get louder and louder, then the noise of the hooves would separate, and you'd rush to the window to see these young men with their khaki hats and their khaki capes – as if it were raining – and these uncaparisoned horses. There were 50 or 60 of them. It was as familiar to me as an alarm clock. They'd leave wonderful scuff marks on the road, with cobbled piles of horse shit which my mother once described as looking like Jewish challah bread, varnished and plaited. The old-fashioned uniforms, their gun carriages and limbers somehow pointed back to wars long before the Second World War.

He has always had an ambivalent, love–hate attitude to old-school matters, especially the relics of the Victorian era. On the one hand, he felt a romantic attachment to the past, particularly lapping up nineteenth-century adventure stories and historical yarns.[23] On the other hand, he hated that epoch's lingering proprieties and strictures. Unfortunately, Nanny Morgan was a malign presence of the repressive sort. It seems that she was, by this point, nursing a violent dislike of her ward, menacing him like some Dickensian horror. Her attitudes, he says, were so much a product of the nineteenth century that he didn't realize he was a modern child for years. And this was under the nose of a famously progressive child psychiatrist.

Morgan frequently hit Miller. On one occasion, having raised a purple bruise with a broomstick, she asked him how he got it, then, leaning into the bath, murmured: 'You tell your parents I done that, it'll be your last day on earth.'[24] She was morbid to an almost fetishistic degree, regularly muttering, 'There's an 'earse, there's an 'earse going by', and taking the children to graveyards. Miller was scared rigid by one broken tomb, which looked as if it housed a silhouetted cadaver amid its knotted roots and corms.[25] Nanny liked to dwell on how his mother had been at death's door with her bout of pneumonia. Shrouds were a favourite topic and, for a little light relief, she would read out the newspapers' daily lists of memorial services.

As a consequence, Miller was obsessed with death through most of his childhood, repeating the word under his breath like a funereal drumbeat and sometimes screaming out in the night, panicking that his parents were going to die. Emanuel bizarrely dumping a bear's skull in the garden, among some lilies of the valley, reduced the young Miller to a gibbering wreck, and the flowers' fragrance chilled him for years afterwards. He was frightened whenever he saw adults in a deep sleep, and he thought that the solemn, marmoreal 'unanswering-ness' of a corpse would drive him out of his mind.[26] Perhaps he made an indirect connection between that and his emotionally cold, otherwise engaged parents. When he dared to ask Nanny what exactly death was, she replied with a macabre sibilant hiss: 'The peace which passeth all understanding.' That, he states, was the most threatening thing ever said to him: the idea of this 'impenetrable' thing defying comprehension.

He grew out of his fearful obsession at about twelve, when his mother finally plucked up the courage to dismiss Morgan. He gained further independence, roving off on his own and developing a passion for the movies. When Betty believed he was wholesomely rowing in the park, he was nipping down to Regent Street's filmhouse, the Cameo Polytechnic. Illicit trips to the cinema struck him as exotic beyond belief.

A handful of British pundits complained about Hollywood imports and cultural Coca-Colonization by the USA. That didn't stop hordes of young fans hurrying to watch American flicks as a way of escaping, being transported mentally for an hour or two. In Miller, they generated a wide-eyed longing for 'this wonderful elsewhere' across the ocean, a realm once again (as with the canned peaches) associated with lustrous warm colours and abundance. He saw the States as a Canaan producing golden, billowing harvests of comedy; a Technicolor land of copper-sulphate blue skies, with bright yellow cabs and guys looking fabulous in gabardine.[27] His crush on Danny Kaye sprang from this: the star just seemed luminously brilliant to Miller, up on the big screen, radiating transatlantic glamour.

Another entrancing world was opening up, effulgent and magnified. By 1947, Miller's last year at prep school, he had become intrigued by a brass microscope given to him by his father.[28] As a consequence, he began regularly catching the bus to Hampstead Heath and plundering Viaduct Pond, using jamjars on strings. The dull empty jars, when filled with water, became bewitchingly lucid with a kind of gleaming, enhanced transparency. Within that, the curious movements of minuscule water fleas, or Daphnia, were visible. 'Then at home, on the microscope slide, you could watch this wonderful crustacean with tiny, tiny feet itching along,' Miller explains, imitating the feet with his large hands. He goes on to describe the ciliated movement of paramecia, with their minute beating hairs 'like the wind passing across a cornfield. Yes, that suddenly comes back to me now,' he says, with a visible flush of pleasure. 'That was the excitement . . . these translucent creatures which filled my imagination when I was young.'

Back in the macrocosm, his family ventured abroad together for the first time, to holiday with his jovial uncles, aunts and cousins in Sweden (or more strictly speaking, his first cousins once removed and second cousins). As successful garment manufacturers, the Bergsons divided their time between their factory-side apartment building in Karlstad and hunting lodges on Lake Vänern. Reminiscent of *Fanny and Alexander*, this was an idyllic sojourn for Miller. His young cousins included Marit Gruson, a spectacular beauty who went on to be an actress at Sweden's Royal Dramatic Theatre and one of Ingmar Bergman's circle.[29] At the end of this vacation, he and Sarah were presented with tailor-made coats as mementos. With fabrics being rationed in Britain, that gift was a gorgeous luxury, and it just possibly encouraged Miller's stockpiling of quality clothes in later life.

A few years after Sweden, he was allowed to go on a lone sally to Dieppe. Legend has it that, not being as fluent a polyglot as his mother, he developed a kind of motor-mouthed French gibberish which so bedazzled the locals they mistook him for some strange, provincial prodigy.[30] He himself only remembers preparing one introductory sentence for his landlady: 'O bonjour, Madame du Fleuve, voulez-vous porter mes bagages, s'il vous plaît?' Not exactly Gallic charm. More like sheer gall.

Those two foreign excursions were exceptions to the rule. In spite of her youthful travels, Betty's philosophy of life advocated a kind of societal close reading: one should scrutinize one's immediate surroundings, the undiscovered country of the nearby. She may have overlooked her own small children but, artistically, she had grasped that the essence of life resides in its normally ignored trivia – as had Flaubert in *Madame Bovary*. Her son now recognizes the value of that. 'My mother taught me something of which I was very impatient at the time: the value of monotony,' he says. 'With hindsight I see that the imposition of her routine was in effect a spiritual exercise which has lasted the rest of my life. She saw epiphanies in the mundane.'[31] Heaven in a grain of sand.

Shortly after the war, at Hythe in Kent, there was one other vacation spent away from home and infamously spoilt.[32] This is when the unmarried author and poet Stevie Smith, one of Betty's best friends, joined the family and then wrote *Beside the Seaside: A Holiday with Children*, a short story based on them. Among Betty's circle, you were never too young to be reviewed, and her depiction of Miller amounted to a slating. Worse, in subsequent newspaper features about him, Smith's tale has been cited as evidence of his precocious brattishness.[33]

Beside the Seaside starts off with Helen (the character representing Smith's position) sunbathing on the beach with her dreamy, married friend Margaret Levison (Betty). Helen recites her poems, irked by interruptions from Margaret's gloomy doctor-husband, Henry. Then their skinny and red-haired son, Hughie (all too recognizably Miller), comes racing up with a 'wicked faced' jellyfish in a net. He disobediently tips it out and assails Henry with awkward questions about biological reproduction. He squats by his mother, loudly mimics another little boy, then announces that his sister, Anna, probably has poliomyelitis. We are told (in brackets) that Hughie is going to be a doctor when he grows up.

During his 'famous imitation of a train', Helen reflects that he is devoured by restless energy and, in demanding an audience, makes people want to smack him. Hughie reappears later, moaning that he would rather be back in London's Edgware Road, and the women then abandon him for the afternoon. On their return, he is hysterically upset and accusatory. Sounding like one of Ivy Compton-Burnett's histrionic protagonists, or Konstantin from Chekhov's *The Seagull* in tantrum mode, Hughie screams that Anna is favoured and that he has been maternally crippled. He cries that he will have a permanent inferiority complex and is going mad.

The Levisons (like the Millers) do not favour corporal punishment, nonetheless Helen takes it upon herself to slap Hughie with a rolled-up copy of *Life* magazine. We are told that she found this 'agreeable'.[34] One gets the feeling that if she had seen Hughie – in the words of Smith's best-known poem – not waving but drowning offshore, she would have found that 'agreeable' as well.

In their passing references to this story, journalists have missed a crucial point. While Smith draws a horrible picture of Hughie, she makes Helen look poisonous in the process, and that is a knowingly critical self-portrait. Hughie mirrors Helen. She is a childish, attention-craving, jealous rival for Margaret's affection, so it is the pot calling the kettle black.

The family portrait appalled Betty, especially since Smith had already written a vile (not to mention metrically fifth-rate) poem about Miller. Called 'A Mother's Hearse', it depicted him as not nearly neglected enough, as overindulged rather than underloved.[35] It was recited at a literati bash held in the house of another writer and mutual friend, Inez Holden, and this is how it goes:

The love of a mother for her child
Is not necessarily a beautiful thing
It can be compounded of pride and show
And exalt the self above every thing.

Oh why is that child so spoilt and horrible?
His mother has never neglected the trouble
Of giving him his will at every turn
And that is why his eyes do burn.

His eyes do burn with a hungry fire
His fingers clutch at the air and do not tire
He is a persecuting force
And as he grows older he grows worse.

And for his sake the friends are put down
And the happy people do not come round
In pride and hostility against the world
This family upon itself is now curled.

Oh wretched they and wretched the friend
And this will continue without end
And all for a mother's love it was
I say it were better a mother's hearse.

Another friend, Olivia Manning (author of *The Balkan Trilogy*), described Smith as battening on Miller, and Betty got wind of the poem via a network of gossip.[36] She was apparently upset and mildly annoyed. Smith sending her the script of *Beside the Seaside* was just too much. She wrote a perturbed letter back, saying:

As a story, I enjoyed it enormously – I think it charming – full of nostalgic quality – and I could not but admire it.

What distresses me however is that you have described in it an episode that upset me considerably at the time, and which I myself, as you may remember, told you about – in confidence – next morning.

I did not think that under the circumstance that you would choose to make use of that.

Betty[37]

The two friends did not speak for five years, until Smith sent a missive praising the humour and compassion in Betty's biography of Robert Browning, a book that notably dealt with Elizabeth Barrett's failing marriage and the unsatisfactory rearing of her son.

What is really poignant is that Miller remained blissfully ignorant, for decades, about the sideswipes which he had received in Smith's scenario. He featured her work when he was editor of the BBC arts programme *Monitor*, and he remarks that, as an infant, he liked her, having no inkling of her disapproval. Forgetting his more wretched hours, he even says his childhood seaside vacations are entirely sunlit in his memory, golden days with just the sound of the surf on the sand. Most ironically, he thought of the letters which Betty and her friend exchanged as 'tiny fairy notes', and of Smith herself as an ethereal sprite.[38]

Miller now sees her depiction of him as sad and spiteful, merely serving as ammunition for those who have wanted to damn him down the years. Anyone so prematurely demonized might well consider themselves more persecuted than persecuting and, getting a little of his own back, he says he noticed an uncanny resemblance to Smith when he saw Laurence Olivier's Richard III.

The general picture he paints of Betty's literary circle is of a clever but catty bunch. He speaks of Inez Holden with some affection as a tough, funny, chain-smoking journo, but Marghanita Laski (well known at the time for her novel *Little Boy Lost*) comes out badly. He describes her as an 'awkward, cosmetically done-up intellectual', and Manning (a Queen's Grove neighbour) is dispatched as querulous and self-regarding. They were thwarted, maritally discontented and complaining women, he concludes sharply.[39]

The domestic atmosphere surrounding and inevitably affecting Miller as an adolescent was often sour.[40] Emanuel was a less emancipated husband than Betty had anticipated. He disliked her nights out at meetings of PEN, the society upholding writers' freedoms. On a daily basis, when she heard her husband's key in the lock, she would dash to hide her scripts in the linen cupboard, and this was not purely histrionic. Emanuel was once seen, by a guest, bitterly spooning cat food on to her works. His blackest moods could be fearful, worsened by his arthritis and the side-effects of his medication. In his deepest depressions, he would leave the house and make his way back – as if through time – to his youthful East End haunts, because his later life had not taken the path he had hoped.

Betty acquired a male co-author to dramatize, of all things, a marriage-straining episode in Elizabeth Barrett Browning's life: namely, the period when the poetess became enthralled by the spiritualist David Dunglas Home, after the drowning of her brother. Like Betty's earlier plays, *Shadow on the Window* was never staged, and the writer-photographer Sam Rosenberg afterwards claimed that their collaboration on the script was extremely formal, with a chaperone in the next room.[41] Miller suspects that Emanuel, nonetheless, felt threatened by this roughcast, interesting American who may have made a pass.

The more crucial domestic conflict, between Miller and his father, revolved around Englishness versus Judaism. One of the best-known gags from *Beyond the Fringe* is Miller's line from the sketch *Real Class*: 'I'm not really a *Jew*. Just Jew-*ish*. Not the whole hog, you know.'[42] But behind that jokey hyphen lay a substantial family division.

Exactly how Jew-ish he is (or is not) remains a vexed question. Any answer comes with qualifications and conundrums, and the complexity is increased because, of course, Jewish can refer to the faith or to a racial and broader cultural identity. Those who do not know the *Real Class* routine tend to think of Miller as a tweedy, quintessentially English intellectual, or a British institution in his own right. He grew up feeling and being English, attending Anglican schools and listening to Aunty (as the BBC was affectionately called back then). Regarding his British-Jewish cultural identity, he says the second half of that combination is irrelevant to his daily life, as if the hyphen there were simply a subtraction sign.

Jewishness discernibly is an issue for him, nonetheless. Or, to split hairs, it *isn't* definitely a *non*-issue. For instance, he sometimes conspicuously – and rather sweepingly – tags social groups as Christian or Jewish when mentioning them in passing. Just recently, he was poring over a new book about the Dreyfus Affair, finding it agitating. He once spent an evening calculating the total death count of historical genocides (though, actually, that sprung from a debate about hardwired xenophobia, not the Holocaust alone). Most publicly, he has stated that English anti-Semitism still lurks in crevices of the United Kingdom. He has spoken of its high, almost inaudible bat's squeak, pointing an accusing finger at *Private Eye*, the satirical magazine which poked merciless fun at him for a time.[43]

He has been called paranoid about bad reviews, however he does not consider them Judeophobic, just imbecilic. In the press coverage of him, down the decades, it is not easy to pinpoint any categorically anti-Semitic squeaks. Is the *Daily Mail*'s 1991 cartoon an instance, picturing Miller with a massive nose and a clutched suitcase spewing bank notes, labelled 'MY FEES'? He himself thinks not. Maybe the *Sunday Telegraph* was also entirely innocent in commenting, in 2001, that his repeated directorial farewells were 'as familiar as the chorus of the Hebrew Slaves', adding that 'his readiness to cast himself as the hapless victim' made him an irresistible target for *Private Eye*.[44]

Miller is a scientific rationalist and staunch atheist. He rejects all creeds, has no truck with godheads, dismisses the notion of souls outliving bodies. 'All religions are equally repulsive and, as for their accounts of the universe, they are little different from the *Just So Stories*,' he concludes. His qualifying comments on this are few and far between, though he did once surprisingly acknowledge: 'The coherence of creation is majestic, ineffable. It produces feelings of silence and subjection, religious feelings.'[45]

As an adolescent, he was taken with the 'other world' as envisaged in *A Matter of Life and Death*, where David Niven (playing the critically injured RAF hero) finds himself on a silvery stairway to the beyond. Miller credits Powell and Pressburger's cinematic fantasy with instilling what small quota he has of mystical or vague oceanic feelings (a reference to Freud's *Ozeanisches Gefühl*, the sense of a boundlessness about the universe and of being one with it).[46] He was enchanted by the film's idea of a transcendental world, this immense, 'impenetrable infinity'. Though impenetrability had scared him as a small child – as in Nanny Morgan's 'peace which passeth all understanding' – he had come to find it fascinating. Still, that is not the same as praying to a deity. Powell and Pressburger, in fact, kept one foot in reality with 'the other world' hovering ambiguously between an afterlife and a hallucination. Miller recalls how he yearned to experience Niven's sort of ecstatic trance, yet the scientific interpretation slips back into the scenario. The injured pilot's vision was, after all, sparked by a medical disorder.

More startling, at first glance, is Miller's definition of himself as a prophylactic Jew, in the sense that this prevented him from being a Christian. In his school assemblies, he liked the hymn tunes and the ritualistic phrase that sounded like 'Heer Endzerlessen'. He assumed it was something akin to Hans Andersen. Really, though, his boyhood concept of the joys of Christianity concerned Christmas fun and missing out on that:

> I spent the early part of my life dreaming, not of a white Christmas, but of a White Anglo-Saxon Protestant Christmas. There was this wonderful world of jolly people and Father Christmas in brilliant scarlet, a colour which never figured in Jewish life, with a white beard and jolly red cheeks, and I felt like one of those children in Hans Christian Andersen, with my nose pressed to the frosty pane. In a sense I felt myself neither fish nor fowl nor good red herring. Nor good salt herring, I'm afraid.[47]

Conflicts with his father markedly developed concerning Judaic worship when Emanuel took a religious turn after World War 2. Countering his own past membership of the Heretics Society at Cambridge, Emanuel's return to his ethno-cultural roots was a gesture of post-Holocaust solidarity, reconnecting his dual British-Jewish identity. He had 'a sort of amphibious relationship with his Jewish origins . . . [like] a lungfish, half in and half out of Jewish water', according to his son's zoological simile.[48] The young Miller was taken aback and estranged by the Sabbath rituals suddenly instituted at Queen's Grove. His mother also disliked the enforced regime and she told her son as much, on the side.

It is again worth remembering that Betty prided herself on being an anti-authoritarian spirit. She even half-mocked herself when laying down parental laws, be it merely telling Miller to untie his laces before kicking off his shoes. She noted how her grown-up side could be infuriated 'at the sight of my son J.'s attempts to evade the scheme of petty duties'. Nevertheless, she wrote: 'I listen with mingled awe and astonishment to the sound of my own voice proclaiming, with every appearance of conviction, the validity of principles which I myself have never been known to respect.'[49]

While sympathizing with her son concerning Emanuel's unwelcome Sabbath observances, Betty outwardly conformed, buying a challah loaf, laying out a tablecloth, lighting candles. As Miller recollects:

> Then my father would put on a black Homburg hat and mutter Jewish prayers over the bread. Sometimes her father [by then in his eighties] would also come to Friday night suppers, with a prayer shawl, and they'd go into the next room and mutter and face in one direction or another. I didn't know what was going on. I used to be bullied into going to synagogue too, not on Saturday

mornings – he didn't go as far as that – but certainly on the high festivals. To me it was as odd as going to a mosque.

He detested the whole business. At his most riled, he fumes that he is 'not a self-hating Jew but a Jew-hating Jew', before underlining, 'I am only a Jew for anti-Semites and an anti-Semite for Jews'.

A lasting father–son schism opened up in 1947 when he was required to prepare for his bar mitzvah, the rite of passage instituting the adolescent boy as a fully responsible member of the faith.[50] Mr Gilboa, a woefully plodding Hebrew teacher hauled in by Emanuel, would tramp up the stairs at Queen's Grove every week, knowing that his pupil was going to be thoroughly unco-operative. Saying that he merely pursued his own ends with quiet obstinacy, Miller won't categorize this as a classic teenage rebellion. All the same, some sort of undercover resistance was being orchestrated, and he won the war of attrition when Mr Gilboa, clomping up the front steps, found himself ensnared in a web of invisible trip wires. Here ended the lessons, and that proved to be a serious dividing line because, as Miller puts it:

> What I wanted was not what my father wanted. I did not want to be part of his world. We were not from the same world – apart from [our shared interest in neurological pioneers such as John] Hughlings Jackson.[51] I was just more English than he understood, and I suppose the moment when my father and I really had a long-lasting alienation was when he gave up and I didn't have my bar mitzvah.

Emanuel had tried to introduce him, more caringly, to a different sort of church or school of thought, believing that fellow psychiatrists might cure his firstborn of his stammer and any infantine unhappiness. Miller Snr considered it too awkward to pursue his own creed of family therapy, where both parents see a consultant to assess if they are aggravating the child's problems. From a very young age, though, his son was sent to leading child-development theorists and analysts. Among these were Susan Isaacs and D. W. Winnicott, both renowned for their gentle approach and for experimentally encouraging the expression of emotions through free imaginative play.[52]

The patient himself remains unpersuaded that analysis made any real difference to his life. If it is a creed, he is no devout believer. Winnicott was nice but would keep asking him why, when playing with toy trains, he delighted in seeing them crash. Miller says he mainly just hankered for some proper model engines, not the awful wooden ones of which psychiatrists were so fond. He is, today, not given to self-analysis either, and one relative says he has ever but slenderly known himself. The great thing about his teenage sessions with the psychiatrist Leopold Stein was, in Miller's view, that they simply conversed about philosophy and Hughlings Jackson's early neurological theories. His stutter disappeared during these stimulating conversations.

He regarded his father's unorthodox branch of medicine as some kind of black magic, says one ex-school friend. In later years, notwithstanding, he would give a speech to mark the unveiling of a statue of Freud at the Tavistock Clinic. He quipped that it was a nostalgic trip down memory lane for him, returning to the Avenue of the Unconscious where he had visited so many shrinks. He certainly alludes to psychoanalytic theories in his theatre directing, and he tried the talking cure again in middle age, when suffering from severe writer's block – in spite of suggesting, even then, that psychoanalysis is the latter-day derivative of the séance.[53]

Miller rates some of Freud's essays, especially the one on mourning and melancholia, as great literary works. They describe neurotic behaviour with vivid brilliance, he says. The attention Freud paid to neglected details, such as slips of the tongue, was equally superb, but Sigmund was wrong to consider himself a scientist, being 'absolutely cockeyed' in that respect. Taking issue with other central tenets, Miller has written about how the unconscious mind is more enabling than repressive or custodial. Most of his own sexual and anarchic thoughts are, he suggests, right there in his conscious mind. Rather than acting like some cerebral, censoring Lord Chamberlain, the unconscious helpfully processes stacks of information, allowing one to get on with other things.[54]

As for other authority figures, Miller is often keen to mention inspiring teachers, associates and authors. Though he likes to be thought highly original, especially as a director, his talk is strewn with acknowledgements, and he once intended to pen an autobiography entitled *Influences*. He certainly excels at picking up ideas and passing them on, playing the middle man with enthusiasm when in educator mode.

He acknowledges that he may have inherited his scientific bent from Emanuel who additionally presented him with enticing items, such as the brass microscope. In particular, he recalls how, aged six, he was shown a picture of the brain in *Gray's Anatomy* and instantly responded, 'Where is the mind?' However, he resists any straightforward idea of imitation along the lines of 'like father, like son'. He points out that engaging paternal discussions were rare. Family suppers were not mini salons and, though he has surely glanced, he claims that he has never read his father's works. Instead, other stimulating books sat waiting to be found on shelves, and he says rather vaguely that ideas were 'just in the air' – as if they were some kind of mysterious ether.

His ongoing education created a surrogate or alternative 'family tree': one made up of influential thinkers, spreading out over numerous academic fields, ever more widely. This is his great love. He is always happy dwelling on it: swinging across its connected branches of thought; tracing the ancestry of, and developmental links between people's discoveries. This 'family tree' underlies his work, his conversation, his patterns of thinking. Miller has embraced many of the same intellectual boughs as Emanuel, however. They have favourite sprigs in common. So the son has – abstractly or vaguely 'in the air' – perpetuated a dialogue of sorts with his father.

As with Betty's oeuvre, Dr E. Miller's writings survive him. Slightly ponderous yet eloquent, his medical books, articles and papers are, of course, not highly personal, but his growing family must have been in the back of his mind when, even as Sarah and Miller were in their infancy, he published *The Generations: A Study of the Cycle of Parents and Children*. There he poignantly touched on the stresses of new marriages and parenthood, discouraged domineering patriarchs, and advocated tenderness and 'fixity of domicile' to create emotional stability. He discussed how some children, without enough parental love and attention, cope by regressing into protective narcissism or develop grudges and feelings of persecution.[55]

Obviously, Miller's own comments about feeling underloved do not make him *The Generations'* worst-case scenario. To be sure, he comes with psychological baggage, but it has not grounded the plane. He did not turn into a psychotic juvenile, let alone Lord Lucan; his marriage has stood the test of time; professionally, he has been highly productive; and he has been a popular TV presenter because of a palpable warmth in his personality. How individuals grow up and largely out of their problems is encapsulated in Miller's relationship with repose. He could have served as an infantine case study for Emanuel's book *Insomnia and Other Disturbances of Sleep*, with his bedtime panics and night-sweats.[56] He recalls:

When I was very small, I had bad dreams where I was required to eat something like the sun. It was some sort of enormous thing which I couldn't get into my mouth, with an impenetrable shining surface which resisted my chewing. And I suppose Freudians would say, 'Of course, that is the breast.' But I'm not certain that's right. I just had dreams about impossible simple tasks such as eating the sun, and used to wake up in startled horror.

As an adult he has occasionally had trouble dropping off to sleep and resorted to telling his restless brain, 'I am losing consciousness. I am losing consciousness.' He has suffered the odd nightmare about, say, Spanish radicals being garrotted. However, more often he enjoys eight hours of solid slumber, and he even names sleep as his recreation in *Who's Who*. The strangeness of dreams has enriched his screen and stage work too, his productions often containing oneiric elements.

As Emanuel observed in one of his less anxious moods, writing in the *Twentieth Century* magazine: 'Many child problems are not as acute nor as ominous as they are sometimes thought to be . . . The toddler who pilfers pennies and pastries is not a potential delinquent . . . the seedling forms of future character . . . while vexatious, may be of great promise'.[57]

In the battle over the bar mitzvah, though, he did not exactly practise what he preached. In *The Generations* he had written: 'You cannot foster religious ideas or moral ideas in adolescents without a knowledge of temperamental difference . . . to ask youth . . . to accept stereotyped formulas . . . is to court ridicule where youth in its sceptical mood is prepared . . . to deny and to reject everything.'[58] He would have been wise to have taken that leaf out of his own book.

·3·

1947–53

St Paul's School

MILLER MOVED ON FROM PREP SCHOOL to St Paul's in the autumn of 1947. Barely a teenager, he felt daunted entering the portals of this top-flight public school: a financially exclusive, single-sex establishment in Hammersmith, west London.[1] Its neo-Gothic buildings (which have since been demolished) were designed by Alfred Waterhouse along the lines of his other huge edifice, the city's Natural History Museum.[2]

Complete with soaring spires and lancet windows, the place was the size of a cathedral, constructed in red Victorian brick and terracotta. Inside, seemingly endless corridors stretched away into the distance, lined with Graeco-Roman statues. At the top of the stairs, none too encouragingly, stood the Laocoön: the plaster cast of two sons and their pater being throttled by serpents. Further along, the forbidding office of the headmaster or High Master, R. L. James, lay behind frosted glass.

St Paul's illustrious alumni, who included Milton, Pepys and G. K. Chesterton, encouraged keen aspirations. Field Marshal Montgomery had added a dash of military glamour, having used his alma mater as his wartime HQ. He had delivered his brief for D-Day there, and he returned annually to lecture the new boys on single-mindedness, 'the necessity of deciding what you want to do, what time to get up in the morning and give Gerry a jolly good thrashing'.

That did not become Miller's mantra. He merely parodies Montgomery's punctilious delivery, but he was soon happily ensconced in the First Year Classics form. The Small Lecture Theatre served as their raked classroom. Here he practised his Latin grammar and simply carried on working, along with other Jewish pupils, while everyone else attended school prayers in the barrel-vaulted Great Hall. 'It just seemed very pleasant, doing Latin exercises, getting your conjugations right . . . And those faintly overheard sounds of hymnody', he says with nostalgia, 'are probably one of the reasons I later included "Immortal, Invisible" in my film of *Alice in Wonderland*.'

As he moved up the school, his exam marks improved dramatically, and this won him parental approval. Betty repeated her mother's form of congratulations, 'That shows you can do even better.' He felt that she was right: he could and should do better. 'Yes,' he reflects, 'it was very pleasing that they seemed pleased.' By this time, he had found several benevolent teachers among the staff as well. He pays tribute to his form master, Mr Longland, for being a lovably vibrant man, and to one or two other 'nice, sloppy, Fitzrovian bohemians' in the art department.

When it came to entering the Lower Sixth or Year 12, known as the Lower Eighth at St Paul's, he was all set to specialize further in Classics. He had a role model in that line, his kinsman Henri Bergson having been a professor of Greek and Latin philosophy. In spite of that, one afternoon, loitering outside the biology department, he underwent a crucial change of heart. Pressing his face to the laboratory window, he found himself longing to join the boys on the other side of the glass who were absorbed in the dissection of dogfish. It struck him as a scientific paradise from which he was excluded, 'being condemned, instead,' as he puts it, 'to a prison of the Classics'.[3]

In desperation, he asked for a special audience with the High Master to discuss changing course. Opining with fingertips pressed lightly together, R. L. James proved a frosty classicist. He asserted that Miller should not think of forking away from the pre-arranged path, and concluded with a piece of logic worthy of Lewis Carroll's *Through the Looking-Glass*. 'Has it occurred to you, Miller,' said he, 'that, if you discover a disease (as I'm sure you will), without Latin you won't be able to name it?' Instantly possessed by Montgomery-style decisiveness, Miller exited and signed up for the Lower Biological Eighth – the science course.

At home, his enthusiasm for studying microscopic pond life had already expanded. He had performed primary dissection on frogs and worms from the garden, wielding a scalpel and forceps supplied by his father. Most influentially, he had read the scientist-novelist H. G. Wells' descriptions of turn-of-the-century labs, and had fallen in love with that scene of bearded Victorian savants gathered round darkly gleaming teak benches. Though science is obviously forward-looking, concerned with new revelations, he saw it – courtesy of Wells – in a romantic, retrospective, sepia-tinted light.

In his adult life, Miller has been regarded as a man of the moment and/or the spirit of a long-gone age, as an exemplar of the revolutionary Sixties and/ or a Renaissance Man. His adolescent taste for Wellsian science could be said to encapsulate his Janus-like nature, forward but also backward looking. Certainly, he seemed a teenager born after his time, by 50 years or so, as he became obsessed by Victoriana and hoarded stacks of mildewed, pre-1900 tomes on pathology and microscopy, thrown out by Emanuel.[4]

Regardless of their divergence over religion, Miller was captivated by his father's consulting room, which was in Harley Street by this point. Visits paid there on Saturday mornings felt, he says, like secular communions in a sanctified annexe. There was also a hint of gentleman's club. He was lured by the beautiful antique equipment, heavy ebony rulers and vintage drug jars, all combined with the smell of ink, tobacco and leather upholstery. His novelty-loving side, meanwhile, appreciated the 'spruce novelty' of seeing his father at work, rescued from the erosion of domestic familiarity, and he loved the almost psychedelic effect generated by Emanuel's bright ophthalmoscope.[5] A paternal eye inspection always left an after-image, 'dancing like a lime-coloured sixpence on the floor of the taxi on the way home'.[6]

His boyhood memories are strewn with such jewel-like, magically luminous circles. At Queen's Grove, his microscopy became a passion, and he would regularly burn the midnight oil examining magnified slides. A year-long journal was also kept, recording developments in a jar of rotting hay which served as a thriving habitat for tiny organisms. Like a schoolboy Faust or the student Frankenstein, he would grow sore-eyed as he noted down observations in his desk lamp's 'dedicated circle of light'. As he recalls, he played the scientist with a mix of narcissistic romanticism and genuine interest.[7]

He had additionally embraced chemistry, commandeering the garden shed as his lab. Cadging round-bottomed flasks from industrial suppliers in nearby Kilburn, he cooked up compounds with a methylated spirit lamp. He would spend hours observing catalytic reactions and colour changes. To this day, Pyrex's trademark triangle (embossed on every beaker) is his equivalent of Proust's madeleine cake, precipitating memories. 'I can still', he says, 'feel the greased glass tap of the burette and hear the zizzing of acid jetting into the alkaline solution.'

One of his early friends at St Paul's had an impressively lavish laboratory at his home in Hampstead.[8] They sometimes played a dangerous game, acquiring a hefty lump of solid sodium, hacking it into slices like a swiss roll on the lawn, then firing the garden hose. When water hits sodium, the latter becomes incandescent and explodes: a spectacular DIY bomb.

In preparation for the Lower Biological Eighth, Miller spent a whole vacation reading about organic chemistry. He was intrigued by carbon atoms and molecules. Their architecture was particularly satisfying: long string formations with side shoots called radicals; and the benzene ring (C_6H_6) forming a tight circle with strong internal bonds.

Socially too, even before he entered the Lower Eighth, he became friends with Oliver Sacks and Eric Korn who were both outstanding scientists at the school. They cannot quite go down in history as the phenomenal Class of 1953, because Sacks and Korn were one year ahead.[9] Nevertheless, convening in the science labs during their lunch-hours (a time for extracurricular activities at St Paul's), they swiftly became what R. L. James might have termed a triumpuerate. Sacks and Korn helped trigger Miller's positive use of the term 'Jewish', referring to sparky and cultured kindred spirits, without religion being an issue.

Sacks is now, of course, a world-famous neurologist and author, and, in his autobiography *Uncle Tungsten*, he depicts his first encounter with Miller in the school's Walker Library. He himself was in a nook, reading avidly about electric eggs, when a shadow slipped across the page. 'I looked up,' he records, 'and saw an astonishingly tall, gangling boy with a very mobile face, brilliant, impish eyes, and an exuberant mop of reddish hair. We got talking together, and have been close friends ever since.'[10]

One of Sacks' own areas of neurological expertise, the unreliability of memory, crops up because Miller begs to differ. Having exclaimed that 'Oliver has aspects of a Borgesian fantasist,' he insists that they met on the sidelines of a rugby pitch where Sacks cut a rotund yet elegant figure, swathed in a long tweed overcoat.[11] Wherever the location, they had a considerable amount in common. Besides the fact that Sacks' father had come from the East End's Lithuanian community and trained as a medic with Emanuel, Sacks himself had a stammer, like Miller, and had been distressed by prep-school beatings. He was unwillingly dispatched to child psychiatrists and, at times, felt that his parents were busy absentees. Though Korn was never to attain renown on a par with the other two, he was another extraordinarily intelligent individual. Humorously dubbed the Ink Louse at St Paul's because he was a small, heavily bespectacled creature, permanently blotched with fountain-pen stains, he went on to gain a zoological PhD (specializing in snail brains). He then turned into an antiquarian bookseller, and wrote erudite and entertaining articles for the *Times Literary Supplement* and *Guardian*.[12]

Miller still gives Korn the top rating, describing him as having been brilliant across the board, and Sacks ranks himself third, saying: 'I've always felt that Jonathan and Eric were much more gifted than I was, and Eric was the most precocious and articulate of us.' Korn has modestly pointed out that, somewhere along the line, he lost his scholarship to Miller in a reassessment process.

Whoever was nudging into first place, these whizz-kids were soon conducting further crazy chemical experiments on Hampstead Heath. A staggering three-pound slab of sodium – not your average case of teenage substance abuse – was lobbed into Highgate Ponds where it skated around dementedly, engulfed in flames.[13] When the friends visited each other's houses, Sacks quivered with awe at Emanuel's library of learned monographs (around 10,000 books in all), while Miller adored Sacks' mother, Elsie Landau.[14] She was an eminent, magnificently quirky and enthused gynaecologist, as he explains:

Oh, she was wonderful! She did this extraordinary thing: she totally blurred the distinction between domesticity and surgery. So, for example, you'd go and watch her doing operations and you'd hear her say, 'Oh, Sister, remind me to get some crystallized ginger on the way home, could you hold that protractor still?' Then you'd be having supper with her and she'd say, 'Oh, Jonathan, interesting case, elderly patient, I cut through the acres of fat, opened the peritoneal cavity, it was absolutely full of pus, Sam, pass the mayonnaise.' She was absolutely marvellous!

The schoolboys were in the doghouse at one point, after they were left in charge of Betty's rented summer cottage for a week or two. This was another ill-fated vacation in the cursed town of Hythe. On this occasion, it could have been written up as *Beside the Seaside: A Holiday Without Parents*, or maybe *Bang Goes the Basement*. Innocently thinking it would be nice to come home with some pickled marine specimens, the trio begged a stack of unwanted cuttlefish from a trawler, stowing them in alcohol-filled jars in the cottage's cellar. A few days later, hearing muffled explosions, they tiptoed down to discover lumps of shattered glass and putrid flesh adorning the walls like shrapnel. An intolerable stench rose and mushroomed out across the garden, and their cunning plan to disguise the pong with splooshes of coconut essence backfired horrendously. Greeted by nauseating waves of the twin smells on their return, Miller's grim-faced parents reeled away, returning to London, and the property reportedly remained unfit for habitation months later.[15]

At school, the threesome's motto was manifestly not '*Mens sana in corpore sano*'. Miller's extreme aversion to sports was something of a running joke. He would try to get excused from athletics with mock sicknotes about Jewish plantigrade feet. During cricket matches, the trio would lie low in the long grass, reading books and ducking the malignant whizzing ball which seemingly refused to obey Newtonian laws.[16]

They were, most unwillingly, roped into the annual boxing competition, the Green Cup. A contemporary remembers that Miller and Sacks were, on one occasion, pitted against each other and camped it up hilariously, with much puffing, kangarooing around and pirouetting.[17] Other muscle-bound opponents, however, smashed Miller mercilessly across the nose, releasing a cold smell of aluminium as the blood began to flow. Worse, Sacks suffered a sadistic blow which left him with a traumatic cataract in one eye.

The softer option was referred to as Jewish Gym. There Miller was allegedly so unco-ordinated that his tumbles became a spectator sport, with bets placed on the frequency of him keeling over, as if he were a junior version of Lewis Carroll's White Knight. In the swimming pool, he struggled with the idea of arms and legs pursuing different rhythms. A far cry from his Uncle Wolfe, the swimming champion, he remarks: 'All I could ever do were these rather incompetent breast-strokes, the very fact that they were called breaststrokes seeming to call into question our manliness and suitability for membership of a public school.'

That is not to say that he and his friends were all brain and no brawn. During another holiday, they buckled down to hard manual labour in order to earn some money, smashing and smelting old sparkplugs in an industrial unit under the arches in Battersea, south London. Korn was, by the by, a long-distance runner of surprising stamina, and Sacks, when dropped into water, swam like a seal.[18] They and Miller, nevertheless, still scorned the athletic and military side of St Paul's, especially its Combined Cadet Force where boys volunteered to march around in blancoed gaiters, as if their years doing compulsory National Service were not going to suffice. The geography teacher, an ex-army man, would try to recruit with a threatening sneer thrown in, as Miller recollects:

He would get himself up with a swagger stick under his arm and address the school, then range his eyes over the Jewish intellectuals at the front, adding: 'No doubt, there will be those who choose to grease their way out of their obligations.' We would drop our eyes and undertook to grease our way out of our obligations . . . We secreted a protective shell around us, so that the world of sporting Christians and the CCF simply had no contact.[19]

*   *   *

The biology labs became a key haven. The trio spent more and more lunch-hours there, becoming highly skilled at dissection. They felt jubilantly fulfilled and safe among the sciences, under the aegis of Mr Pask. Affectionally known as Sid, Pask was a quiet, yeomanish fellow with a shredded-wheat moustache and a severe stammer, which did not stop him being a great teacher.[20] It was, quips Miller, rather surprising that any information was exchanged with so many stutterers in one room. However, Sid would fix everyone with his large bulging eyes, while he wrestled with the name of some obscure crustacean, and everyone was hypnotized.

Sacks compares Sid's Bunsen burner to the perpetual flame above the ark in a synagogue, and describes how the boys adored their master:[21]

Our love was intense and comprehensive, sometimes exceeding the love we bore our parents. I well remember how three of us, chatting in the park one day, wondered how we could express our love for him. One of my friends suggested that we kiss him . . . This amazing suggestion was received at first in a thoughtful silence, until we remembered his constant pipe, and fell into helpless laughter at the thought of this troublesome burning thing between us, being thrust down one or another throat.[22]

Drawing a literary parallel with Miss Jean Brodie and her girls, Korn says that they adored and made a kind of fetish of Pask.

Theories about parental and other love substitutes are questionable in Miller's view, but he does make 'Mr Pask's bright boys' sound like a band of intellectual devotees, and he says they were nourished and nursed by this exceptional man.[23] He names Pask as the strongest influence in his life, for igniting a passionate interest in biology and provoking a phenomenal level of scholarship. This teacher brought in scientific experts as guest speakers and stocked the library as if it were a professional research institution, such that his students were, apparently, almost ready to sit their Finals when they arrived at university.[24] The admiration was mutual, for Miller was to be Sid's most warmly remembered pupil.[25]

Scientists were making international headlines in this period. Remarkable advances included Einstein's new generalized theory of gravity; the inauguration of CERN; and Bernard Lovell building the world's biggest radio telescope at Jodrell Bank, in the English county of Cheshire. In medicine, trailblazers came up with the first kidney transplant and artificial heart, not to mention award-winning insights into the immune system, key developments in penicillin, the polio vaccine and TB-fighting antibiotics. Britain was second only to the USA in the number of scientific Nobel Prizes which it was accumulating, so Sid's fledglings certainly had their sights set high.

From Pask, Miller also acquired a teacherly urge to disseminate knowledge. During the eighth form, he became a self-styled proselytizing Darwinian. Even today he clambers up and down a stepladder in his Gloucester Crescent study, eagerly sharing the books he first encountered under Pask's tutelage.[26] He fetches down Kerner and Oliver's *Natural History of Plants*, revealing its beautiful illustrations, like fairytale vegetation alongside no-nonsense facts. He blows a light dust off D'Arcy Thompson's *On Growth and Form*, admitting he struggled with the mathematical graphs about mice, then he plucks down J. Z. Young's *The Life of Vertebrates*. Young became another of his personal heroes, writing about anatomy, psychology and neurology, as well as actually turning up at St Paul's for the boys' viva examination.

Miller's memories are equally lit up by Pask's histology classes when they learned about plant structures: cutting cross-sections of stems; mounting them on slides; and differentially staining the cells blue and pink with exotically named pigments. He reprises those names like an enraptured liturgy – 'eosin, haematoxylin, gentian violet' – and he describes the result as a wonderful, glowing rose window.

The learning extended beyond school hours, with Pask's Field Club expeditions being a source of great delight. On winter weekends, his brainy corps would make a beeline for the Natural History Museum, where Miller became fanatically excited about morphology, spotting likenesses between organic chemistry's formal regularities and animal design.[27] The repeated metameric segmentation of worms and crustaceans became an obsessive interest, and he was riveted by the idea of ancient structural blueprints or baupläne. 'I just loved the idea', he says, 'that nature had already got the basic forms or plans in place, probably shortly after the Cambrian Explosion [around 530 million years ago].' While noticing that segregation was upheld ('no wooing and screwing between species'), he was most intrigued by the deep homologies, the increasing affinities discovered when a line is traced back along the branches of evolution. The splint bones in horses' legs are, for example, the pentadactylic remains of ancestrally separate digits.

During the summer months, the Field Club sallied forth to oak woods, chalk downs and verdant habitats all over south east England. These hikes were at once Elysian and pragmatic, with Sid leading the way in his wellingtons. Frequenting canals, the boys would trawl the waters with delicate nets on brass-hinged poles, and they gathered flowers in the meadows, stowing them in a black tin satchel or vasculum. Their mission was then to identify these plants using Bentham and Hooker's *Handbook of the British Flora*. 'It was all about dual, dichotomous decisions,' Miller elucidates. 'Through a series of forking choices – "It's not that, so it's that" – you would arrive at the genus and finally at the species. *Taraxacum officinale*, the dandelion!'

The schoolboy Miller relished taxonomy's neat classification system, even if his adult career path was to fork and branch out repeatedly rather than narrowing down in a scientific manner. In his youth, he evidently found it soothing to see order imposed, whether that was via Bentham and Hooker's methods or in the form of morphological baupläne. It was the opposite of his own restless sense of being, socially, 'neither fish nor fowl nor . . . good salt herring'. Hard science was like a rock, providing certainties after his rootless, unsettling war years. Sacks observes that he, likewise, adored chemistry's systematic periodic table, partly as a relief from his youthful upheavals.[28]

Miller's characteristic hybrid of humour and erudition also blossomed at St Paul's. What leaps out from the written accounts left by Pask's bright boys, preserved in the school archives, is their comical springiness combined with dedicated learning. The two were absolutely intertwined, like a double helix, whenever Sid's star pupils went on excursions or were offered in-house platforms (presenting lectures and scientific demonstrations of their own). To take one example, the Apposition Exhibition was part of a major open day, and the school magazine, the *Pauline*, records how Pask's Field Club held an excited preliminary meeting. 'Miller volunteered to bring back large sections of the Scottish coast,' it says, 'while the Secretary sought the loan of the School truck in order to obtain a piece of Wimbledon Common.' The fizzy mix of larking and learning is again irrepressible in a reported visit to Kew Gardens where, one reads, 'unfortunately the risk of being arrested stopped even the boldest from collecting specimens but we were nonetheless agreeably surprised by a rare Ginkgo'. Then there was the trip to the canal at Byfleet when, it was noted, 'our Gargantuan Secretary [Sacks] fell through a "bridge of duckweed", but nevertheless we collected . . . a fine Nuphar for the School pond'.[29]

In the event, at the Apposition Exhibition, Miller's display on blood was impressively elaborate and a great success. He answered parents' questions for hours. Meanwhile, his lecture on whales was an astonishing if untamed Leviathan for, the *Pauline* reported, 'In spite of his amazing alacrity, he did not manage to cover the whole subject, even though he gave a second performance the next Friday.' He was willing to give impromptu talks on anything, explaining vertebrate evolution with much dramatic gesticulating from behind a pile of old bones – possibly the hind legs of a donkey?[30] One fellow biologist still remembers him playing the student-teacher in class, hilariously imitating a horse in orgasm 'at the same time as having presentation skills and as much knowledge as any master'.[31]

One cannot leave the Field Club without mentioning Cumbrae, for this was the boys' transcendent adventure. Catching the night train out of London, they headed north, across the Scottish border and all the way out to Millport, a small island town in the Clyde Estuary. This Easter trip began Miller's long love affair with Scotland. 'I have never', he muses, 'really recaptured the . . . idyll of that sun-lit fortnight,' and it remained a joyful memory for Korn and Sacks too.[32] They established their HQ in a professional lab at Cumbrae's marine research station, and glorious spring days were spent down on the beach, scrambling over the rocks to collect specimens. This was in competition with the station's venerable researcher, Lord Victor Rothschild.

Back in the laboratory, they would stay up into the small hours watching the ritual fertilization of the sea urchins. Adding the urchins' male sperm to the eggs with a pipette, they would view, under the microscope, 'this enchanted illuminated disc in which', as Miller puts it, 'you could see the cells developing a waist, as if an elaborate corset had been tightened. Then they each divided into two cells, then into four . . . these sixteen cell stages until you began to discern differentiation and the emergence of destinies.'

The shoreline, so often associated with anthropological rites of passage, was both blissful and formative. It was where Pask's intellectual bequest seemed truly to mature. Miller and Korn so loved Cumbrae that, in their twenties, they would return there with their future wives, simply to go down to the water's edge and collect again. In Miller's photograph album is a snapshot, slightly blurred and fading now, yet somehow iconic and encapsulating: a translucent jar of sea life, held on Rachel's knee, with the stony beach and hills beyond. If Miller believed in ghosts, his eternal haunt of choice might well be this austere littoral.

*　　　*　　　*

On his first expedition to Cumbrae, Miller saw his emerging destiny to be a life in science, but he had, along with Sacks and Korn, become part of a group of eighth-formers at St Paul's whose interests spanned the arts and the sciences. They simply called themselves 'the gang', although they are described by their contemporaries as a sextet of eccentric geniuses.[33] Of the six, Tony Cutler was officially the odd man out, being the only non-biologist. He was classified as 'the arts person' and, indeed, went on to be a professor of art history at America's Penn State University. The other two were Misha Nathani and Dick Lindenbaum who, like Miller and Sacks, were to train as medics.[34] Nonetheless, Lindenbaum yearned to be a poet, Nathani was a keen lover of the arts, Sacks was a talented musician, and Korn was extremely well versed in literature.

The arts were enjoying something of a boom in post-war Britain. This was encouraged by government schemes, especially the creation of the Arts Council which promised state funding. The demand was there, with the nation hankering for more leisure activities as it gradually emerged from the culture of austerity. Cinema-going was massively popular. Even if one-fifth of West End playhouses were bomb damaged, the Old Vic company was rising from the ashes in a pioneering mood, a match for Stratford-upon-Avon's reopened Memorial Theatre.[35] A buzz-creating drama critic, Kenneth Tynan, burst on to the scene in 1951, and the foundation stone (if nothing else) was laid for the National Theatre by the young heir presumptive, Princess Elizabeth.

Orchestras reassembled. Ballerinas pirouetted back into London along with opera productions. Enticing festivals sprang up elsewhere, notably the Edinburgh International Festival of Music and Drama and the Aldeburgh Festival, brainchild of Benjamin Britten. The television industry was still finding its feet, having had its development arrested by the war, but the number of viewers was swelling. In the meantime, BBC Radio's remarkably highbrow strand, the new Third Programme, began broadcasting concerts, plays, poetry and reviews of exhibitions on an unprecedented scale.[36]

For those seeking out the fine arts, the National Gallery was lined with master-pieces once more, having been stripped during the Blitz, and in 1949 the Tate reopened fully for the first time in a decade. Crowds flocked to exhibitions of Van Gogh, Picasso and Matisse. Modern art, moreover, became a national talking point after the Royal Academy's annual dinner (broadcast live) turned into a bunfight. With thrilling irreverence, fusty old Sir Alfred Munnings was heckled during his presidential speech in which he was slating avant-garde 'silly daubs'.

The morale-boosting Festival of Britain, in 1951, symbolized the idea that the country could shine in more than one field. Its purpose was to celebrate the nation's ongoing recovery and promote a bright future in both the sciences and the arts. Everyone, including Miller, went to see the festival's flagship site on the South Bank.[37] A bomb-blasted wasteland beside the Thames, near Waterloo, had been architecturally transformed into an almost space-age realm. The Dome of Discovery housed exhibits demonstrating technological advances. Beams of light gloriously shone from the ground beneath your feet, Miller remembers. Nearby was the rocket-like construction called the Skylon, under which sat the Royal Festival Hall for music and other arts. This was the new venue which would sub-sequently form the core of the South Bank Centre. Over at the festival's affiliated Battersea Park site, a funfair merrily sat alongside sculptures by Henry Moore, Barbara Hepworth and Jacob Epstein.

The marriage of arts and sciences in Miller's schoolboy gang of six was not always so happy. An occasional quarrel erupted when members of the group took up polar positions, arguing over whether to visit the Natural History Museum or the National Gallery. Tony Cutler recollects that he and Nathani thought of Miller and Sacks as barbarians because they knew little of the humanities. 'And Jonathan', he adds, 'would sometimes get very angry and bad-mouth people. He would go off on – not exactly screaming fits, but it was quasi-hysterical.'[38]

More general sparring and teasing arose for, as Korn acknowledges:

> The gang was a sort of society, a group that put an enormous premium on quick responses, on slick answers . . . [and] Jonathan had a terrifically flashy mind at that age . . . The gang could be an arena for testing one's new weapons. Oliver was always gentle, but Jonathan could be cruelly sarcastic and, no doubt, so could I.[39] There was a bit of that. The terms of membership were you gave as good as you got, you didn't complain, you took no prisoners, and I remember being jeered at, from time to time, for some foolish thing I'd said.

Using Robert Louis Stevenson in a memorizing competition, Miller and Sacks recited swathes of his prose, and Sacks won by a narrow margin. That must have been quite a feat, even allowing for an element of exaggeration in the comparisons which some have drawn between Miller's powers of recall and those of Henri Bergson. The latter could reel off France's railway timetables.

One ex-classmate suggests that Sacks felt eclipsed when Miller started to outshine him in other respects, and even that he ultimately quit Britain for America because he felt the stage was not big enough for both of them. This theory is not really confirmed by the protagonists' own accounts. Miller merely recalls that he, Sacks and Korn jockeyed a bit, seeing who could best enumerate and describe the vast variety of polychaetes, cephalopods and holothurians (polychaetes being the bristled worms favoured by Miller, cephalopods encompassing the squid and cuttlefish beloved of Sacks, and holothurians being Korn's speciality, your sea cucumber).[40]

When asked about mutual competitiveness, however, Sacks thoughtfully responds:

> Well, that's an interesting question which Jonathan and I may both underplay because we, neither of us, like the idea. In many ways, we have gone in different directions [since St Paul's] . . . I have intermittent feelings of being a flop, and I've been wistful and envious of Jonathan's success and this and that . . . I wish I had his knowledge of drama . . . But I have always been surprised when – though I don't bring it up – my analyst has wondered whether Jonathan too has envied me . . .
>
> One episode [from St Paul's] comes to mind, although it's not to do with competitiveness. I had just read Maynard Keynes' essay on Newton and talked about it excitedly to Jonathan . . . About three weeks later, he came up to me very excitedly and said, 'I've made an amazing discovery, Maynard Keynes on Newton.' I said, 'Jonathan, how did you get on to this essay?' and he said, 'I don't know.' I was intrigued by this . . . Though he has a prodigious memory, I think he genuinely didn't know . . . The Russian psychologist Vygotsky likes to talk about dialogic memory, and now Jonathan and I have had an intermittent conversation for over 50 years. Often we don't know what emanates from whom, all we know is it came out in the interaction . . . and there are innumerable things in which I, consciously or unconsciously, appropriate what Jonathan says.[41]

*   *   *

Frictions within the group never led to punch-ups. They thought of themselves, collectively, as neurotic Jewish subversives.[42] According to Korn, they all had inferiority complexes, large or small, and the gang offered protection. The group could be divided up in various ways, having close pairs within it, and triplets hooking up, but no leaders: a structure not unlike organic chemistry's benzene ring, in fact, with its six molecules circularly linked by single and double bonds.[43]

The group played a key role in Miller's increasingly enjoyable adolescence, and their assorted interests broadened his intellectual range. So it was a clique, but a cerebrally expansive one, contrasting with the standard notion of a gang mentality. It was a coterie where they were all contributors – synapses firing – to generate constant activity and discussion. As Cutler highlights, at this stage, Miller was terrific fun, if sometimes fiery:

> In this sort of magical way, we struck sparks off each other and ideas would flow, and I have never been able to find that sort of ambience again . . . There was a connective tissue which linked all our interests, and Jonathan was the best connector of all.

Significantly, one of the books they passed round was *The Hedgehog and the Fox*, in which Isaiah Berlin discussed two personality types: your 'hedgehog' who has a centripetal mind, inclined towards concentrated expertise; and your 'fox' with a naturally roving intellect, pursuing many ends. The copy of that essay which the gang shared is still in Cutler's possession, with its flyleaf inscribed by them all, and Miller was to be a fox for the rest of his life.[44]

Under Korn's influence he started absorbing more modern literature, especially James Joyce and T. S. Eliot, whose *Four Quartets* left him 'intrigued', as he puts it, 'by things I only half-understood, and still only half-understand'. In turn, Miller introduced Sacks to the works of Proust and the Swedish novelist Selma Lagerlöf.[45] The whole group headed off to poetry readings at Swiss Cottage's Cosmo café, where cultured émigrés listened to Dannie Abse, the Jewish–Welsh compound of doctor and versifier.

Fired up by this, the boys founded their own Literary Society at school, setting up readings, inviting VIP speakers, and speedily rivalling St Paul's official literary club.[46] Sacks was a charmingly uninformed president, startled to discover that their guest Richmal Crompton (of *Just William* fame) was not a man. He also asked George Bernard Shaw if he would pay them a visit. G. B. S. wrote back very sweetly, in a shaky hand, saying he would love to but he was ninety-three and three-quarters.[47]

Disaster struck when the High Master got wind of *The Prickly Pear*, a journal which the gang started mimeographing under the Literary Society banner. Using the school's Gestetner printer (a forerunner of photocopiers), they churned out reams of articles smudged with its trademark purple ink. *Nota bene*, this was not the St Paul's equivalent of Shrewsbury School's droll journalism, which emerged almost simultaneously and is regarded as a precursor of the Satire Boom.[48] *The Prickly Pear* was more impudently seditious.

Misha Nathani had contributed a steaming, radical piece about Jewish world domination, naively lifted from *The Protocols of the Elders of Zion* (the 1903 tract actually forged as part of a Russian anti-Semitic libel). As Korn explains, Nathani really just liked the prose style, but their big mistake was 'to leave this inflammatory thing to be printed off by the school porter who promised to look at it. He did look at it, and promptly took it to the High Master.'

Not remotely amused by his biologists-turned-bellelettrists, R. L. James appeared to think St Paul's was facing an all-out revolution, as if Miller, Sacks and co. were members of the Stern Gang. That Zionist terrorist group, abhorring the British Mandate in Palestine, were said to have planned a London bombing in 1947, so maybe James was on paranoid red alert.[49] In high-and-mighty mode, he summoned Sacks to his office and decreed that both *The Prickly Pear* and the Literary Society were axed, with no reprieve. 'I don't have to have reasons,' he declared. 'You can go now, Sacks. You don't exist. You don't exist anymore.' He snapped his fingers and Sacks showed himself out.[50] The gang were enraged and shocked by their sudden powerlessness. The High Master was a dictator, a little Hitler, or a small-scale equivalent of Joe McCarthy over in the States where, at this point in time, left-wing artistic types were being hauled up and blacklisted as communists by the House Un-American Activities Committee (in spite of protests by stars including Danny Kaye).

Sacks' literary activities were, obviously, not quelled for ever. Today, his acclaimed books, eloquently describing his neurological research, are defined by the author himself as hovering at the intersection between fact and fable.[51] That is medicine and creative writing rolled into one, his own idiosyncratic brand of science/fiction. The whole gang bounced back swiftly from James' censorship by organizing play readings off the school premises. Miller remembers them selecting James Elroy Flecker's *Hassan* (from 1922), which was hardly cutting-edge but was a steamy saga set in Old Baghdad with luscious dancing girls. He can still quote chunks of it.

The only stage show he recalls having actually seen as a wartime child was *Jack and the Beanstalk*: a phosphorescent pantomime where he fell for the principal girl and, doubtless, relished the audacity of giant-slaying. His adolescent brushes with drama increased when, besides the play readings, he began going to the theatre with his parents. They saw a couple of musicals including *South Pacific*, but mainly went to historic dramas presented by the Old Vic company, which had been refreshing its reputation with star performances by Laurence Olivier and Ralph Richardson. Miller recalls outings to Shakespeare's *Henry V* (with Alec Clunes) and *Love's Labour's Lost*, Ben Jonson's *Bartholomew Fair*, and Oliver Goldsmith's *She Stoops to Conquer*, where the high-born heroine pretends she is of the servant class.

Classic plays were, he points out, the only sort he saw. Though he read T. S. Eliot, his parents did not choose to take him to premieres of *The Cocktail Party* or Christopher Fry's experimental verse dramas which were in vogue. In Miller's own career, he would largely stick to staging the classics too.

It would be some years before he caught up with the director Peter Brook whose groundbreaking, pared-down style would strongly influence him and who was, at that time, cutting his teeth in Stratford-upon-Avon. Melodramatic hamminess and the decorous stuffiness of drawing-room dramas were, in general, persisting in the British theatre. The Old Vic productions were, however, being staged by innovative spirits, notably George Devine and Glen Byam Shaw, with the young Dorothy Tutin, Michael Redgrave and Leo McKern on board.[52]

Miller says that he cannot link these early experiences to his own directing career. He states that, before the eighth form, he had studied Shakespeare's *Twelfth Night*, taking pride in knowing every line but never even envisaging it on the stage. In turn, his Old Vic visits seemed completely unrelated when, years later, he ran that very venue. As a young theatre-goer, it was as if an invisible glass wall divided him from the performers, yet he acknowledges that it was magical and thrilling:

> People wore very bright make-up, with strongly outlined eyes and red cheeks. The actors were like living toys – very large, animated, living toys. It was another world, an alternative world, what the philosopher Saul Kripke called a possible world . . . When I returned to the ordinary world, accommodating my eyes to the evening, I found that the buses were not as brightly coloured as the people on the stage had been. This was very interesting . . . I longed to go and see these things happening.[53]

The glowing stage reminded him of an aquarium, an analogy which suggests that it was as entrancing as the translucent jars and the magnified slides of his biological pursuits.[54] Furthermore, the invisible glass wall, as in *Through the Looking-Glass*, might ultimately be traversed.

He was struck by another image of someone spookily passing through a mirror to 'the other side' when he saw Jean Cocteau's 1950 film, *Orphée*, an updating of the death-conquering myth of Orpheus. Alongside his theatre trips, Miller's taste in films was growing more sophisticated as he now frequented Hampstead's Everyman Cinema, watching what would, today, be called classic and art-house movies. He was still relishing Hollywood comedians: Charlie Chaplin, Laurel and Hardy, and especially the Marx Brothers whose scripts he came to know by heart. At the same time, European cinema was becoming chic, and he and his friends became *au fait* with Marcel Pagnol and René Clair's light satires as well as Cocteau's dreamlike fantasies. He was even more lastingly impressed by the British film-maker Carol Reed's *The Third Man*, starring Orson Welles. 'When I came to direct [for stage and television],' he comments, 'I was also probably very influenced by the films Welles himself made, by the arrangement of space, the deep focus in black-and-white, as well as his overlapping conversations.'

On the gang's trips to the National Gallery, Tony Cutler supplied mini guided tours, teaching the others about paintings. These could never match up to Miller's lectures, though, delivered in front of dusty cases in the Natural History Museum, 'and giving you', as Cutler recalls, 'the whole of evolutionary theory plus the philosophical implications, with this astonishing capacity to start small and elaborate the universe out of that point'. Miller was manifestly learning from Cutler's art history, nonetheless. He started to chip in, discussing how the distorted, anamorphic skull worked as a trompe l'oeil in Holbein's portrait *The Ambassadors*. 'There again', Cutler remarks, 'was the philistine scientist not looking at the brushwork. But that [issue of the trompe l'oeil] added another dimension, of course, and Jonathan was exploring that long before the books on Holbein which have been written since.' Visual teasers are, interestingly, akin to hyphenates: morphing before your eyes, presenting themselves as one thing then another. And such trompe l'oeils were to intrigue Miller down the decades, repeatedly featuring in his own work.

By his own account, he was ignorant about art as a youth, vaguely liking the Impressionists and hardly aware that Jackson Pollock was making a splash. However, he appreciated the relaxed atmosphere of St Paul's art department and he briefly took up painting as a weekend hobby.[55] Archival records of the school's Chesterton Society – a forum for lively debates – additionally reveal that the 'volcanic Mr Miller (flames on top and a crater below)' was turning into a pundit already, defending modern art and reviling the Royal Academy's crustier members with histrionic flair.

Declaring that the RA's president Sir Alfred Munnings (after his 'silly daubs' gripe) was a fogeyish 'fate worse than death', he contended that to be hanged by the neck would be preferable to having your portrait hung in that institution. He went on to challenge aesthetic definitions, 'waving a few pictures of the South Bank, obviously cut from [the magazine] *Picture Post*', and insisting that photographs must be considered artworks because they were good reproductions. He won this debate by a huge majority and *in absentia*. Blithely whisking off to take an exam, he left the room in uproar with his parting comment on Winston Churchill's RA efforts: 'God bless his soul, sir; but God damn his paintings.' Miller's style was mock-archaic, like Samuel Johnson in a coffee house, except with an avant-garde conclusion – verbally giving Churchill a V-sign of the rude variety.

His nascent pedagoguism entailed some overwrought gabbling, at least according to the Chesterton secretary who noted, in the minutes, that this grandstander was 'no doubt of the opinion that a good speech can be appreciated without being understood'. Still, Miller was enjoying himself, 'twist[ing] his mouth into a wondrous sight, a despiteful pout, a chastisement of the small-minded children that sat before him, an apotheosis of the true artistic perception'.[56]

Jazz became his great joy as he revelled in the Dixieland revival. Even though compelled by his parents to be home by 11 p.m., he gained an electrifying sense of independence when he headed off with the gang, on Saturday nights, to catch live bands. This was at the 100 Club, in Oxford Street, and other sweaty basements. 'It was absolutely our Damascus,' Korn says. 'Dancing had been awful ballroom lessons, but this was wonderful!' Exhilarated by the blasting front-line trombones, they saw Humphrey Lyttelton and George Melly live, and they jived to 'Tiger Rag' amidst a sea of duffle coats and Fair Isle jumpers. Apparently, you had to dress as if you were on the bridge in *The Cruel Sea* to have legitimacy. Miller adds that he was good at dancing. When asked for a retrospective review of his friend's moves, Korn exclaims with widening eyes:

Incomparable! Very balletic. I remember a blur of these extraordinary long limbs, like an octopus. I was famous for incorporating a few of the steps of the

Ukrainian gopak: your buttocks five inches off the ground, legs shooting out in all directions. But I had no rhythm nor any sense of melody. Jonathan was kind of body-popping before it had been invented. He was always graceful, certainly enormously gangly, but very much 'in' his body.

Miller hasn't stopped dancing yet. In 2009, the ska group Madness was on a publicity stunt, gigging in an open-topped double-decker bus around Camden Town. Peering into someone's living-room en passant, the lead singer Suggs was pleasantly surprised to see an old geezer skanking to the beat, and positively astounded when he recognized Dr Miller.[57]

*   *   *

Omitting to master any instrument, Miller would never perform music himself, nor did he act in any straight dramas at school. He designed one distinctly spartan set for a production of *Julius Caesar*, his decor amounting to three chairs, two statues and one bench. This sounds intriguingly like his later minimalist aesthetic. Most likely, though, he simply had no budget.[58] Where he really shone was as a leading light in St Paul's regular comedy shows, called the Colet Clubs revues.[59]

Back at Arnold House, his final prep school in St John's Wood, he had already been something of a child star. Admittedly, he was no Julie Andrews. She was playing the London Hippodrome, aged twelve in 1947. Nevertheless Arnold House's staff had drafted Miller in to entertain the whole school with his chicken and train impressions whenever rain cancelled outdoor sports, and he went on to appear in the Colet Clubs revue of 1949, mimicking Danny Kaye.[60] One of his fellow entertainers, Michael Codron – who became a major West End producer – recollects getting meagre applause for his own sketch, only to be followed by this freckled boy with an unruly manner who made the audience scream with laughter.[61]

Incidentally, it is also tickling to find, in the school's records, how the young Miller and Codron twice debated the relative merits of Shakespeare and Woolworth's. Codron switched sides, initially favouring the chain store then plumping for the Bard, while Miller doggedly argued that William S. owed a heck of a lot to Woollies.[62]

In 1951, Miller paired up with Korn as a double act for the Colet Clubs revue, and their skit 'Round the World with Radio' was hailed by the *Pauline* magazine as exceptionally accomplished. They were pre-university wits with imitative powers of 'astonishing range and skill'.[63] This sketch was a collage of soundbites, a boiled-down version of the BBC's output: something like flicking through the *Radio Times*, getting ludicrously bad reception on the wireless, or spinning its dial. In using compaction as its comic principle, 'Round the World with Radio' was also a structural forerunner of Tom Stoppard's speeded-up *Hamlet* and of the Reduced Shakespeare Company's hit format.

By the 1952 show, Miller and Korn were a major high point, performing spoofs of journalistic film reviews. They were merrily, albeit discerningly, praised as:

M. E. Korn and J. W. Miller with their inspired lunacy of the Marxian [i.e. Marx Brothers] variety. Too long – yes; indistinct – yes; ebullient – yes; clever, certainly. Here were two boys completely at home on the stage, able to add impromptu touches at will: they knew they had the audience in the hollow of their hand. A remarkable performance.[64]

Korn narrowly missed going on to become a Satire Boom luminary along with Miller. In a subsequent chapter of his life, he was enrolled in the Joint Services Russian course, which aimed to train conscripts for intelligence work or interpreting. Korn's contemporaries there included Alan Bennett (pre-*Beyond the Fringe*) and Michael Frayn. They created off-duty entertainments and Frayn was seen, by some, as Korn's protégé. In regard to the Colet Clubs revues, Miller plays down his own comic talents, saying that Korn thought up the wittiest lines. His own lack of fecundity, he says, led him to recycle material from St Paul's for years, for the Cambridge Footlights and beyond.

Korn had left St Paul's by 1953, along with Sacks. Both were bound for Oxford. For his last Colet Clubs revue, Miller therefore teamed up with a new partner, Michael Bacharach, whom he warmly describes as a dandy-like genius and a further member of the 'subversive underground resistance'. Bacharach went on to become a decision theorist and Oxbridge academic.[65] Their joint routine was punningly entitled 'Les Enfants du Parodis', and the *Pauline* lauded Miller's growing originality, garnering him with 'the palm for inspired buffoonery and sheer intelligence'.[66]

He had become an adroit physical clown, whirligigging, turning his body into living cartoons, pulling grotesque faces and stretching his limbs as if they were elastic bands. In this regard he was Britain's Marcel Marceau, several years before the Frenchman became internationally famous.[67] The flexibility, by the by, contradicted Henri Bergson's seminal theory of comedy, namely that what provokes laughter is automaton-like rigidity. Still, Miller's style chimed with Bergson's broader belief that life is quintessentially fluid, forever mutating, driven by *élan vital*.[68]

The *Pauline*'s reviewer spotted the young comic's natural (or naturalist's) ability to look amusingly like a whole ark of animals. Describing how he morphed into some fantastically interbred octopus/mosquito/jazzman/terrapin, the commentator wrote, 'I remember best the small gesture . . . the rubberised proboscis and chin, the clever treatment of the Duffle [sic] coat, which at last let me see through the benignly vacuous expression of the captive turtle.'[69] Down the years, Miller would be compared to everything from a stork to a camel that has passed through the eye of the needle, with one reviewer vividly recording, 'At the mere mention of marsh birds, his chin is sucked into his Adam's apple and he is twice round the stage at a high-stepping gait with one arm reared into a majestically elongated neck.'[70]

What Miller mainly recalls from the Colet Clubs revues is the laughter from the other side of the footlights. 'I remember that being very intoxicating,' he says, 'and I remember the thrill, the humming suggestive darkness, and then stepping out into this bright light onstage.' The applause surely made him feel loved and may have been addictive.

Or else it was the experience of standing in the wings that really entranced him. He says:

> It wasn't just a matter of being onstage. It was the backstage hush and – an image which has always stayed with me – the glimpse of people performing, watched from the wings, somehow looking elsewhere or, if they did look at you, looking remarkable because their faces were heavily made-up and they were speaking louder than usual, with special exaggerated gestures. It was this brilliant, illuminated elsewhere, right next to you in the dark . . . I shall always be mystified by the view from the wings.

That specific spot is a kind of shoreline between viewing and participating in the performance. You can stand there as much as you want as a director, and Miller still loves to do so. Given his future career dilemmas as a doctor/comic/director, his conflicting interests were encapsulated, as well, by the very boards he trod at St Paul's. They literally lay over a laboratory bench, the auditorium being a converted lecture theatre for the sciences.[71]

Only eight weeks after Miller and Bacharach's school gig, they became BBC Radio starlets. Having sent up the Corporation, they were sent for and they found themselves on air. If not having your cake and eating it, this was surely the art of biting the hand and being fed. The *Radio Times* listing for *Under-Twenty Parade* (a series which promoted teenage talent on the Light Programme) announced: 'John Miller and Michael Bacharach, in their very first broadcast, take a friendly sideswipe at some of their fellow under-twenties . . . (practically no holds barred).' Clearly a hit, they were invited back several times in 1953–4.[72]

Another glass wall, ultimately penetrable, crops up in these early recording sessions, as described by Miller:

> We'd go downstairs into those airless basement studios, with the enormous cheese-grater microphones they had in those days. It was all basketwork tabletops, and you'd be sitting behind glass, unable to hear what the producers were saying until they'd mouth 'Sorry!' and switch on . . . I've been doing that ever since, in and out of BBC basement studios for more than fifty years.

He denies that he got a taste for it but he enjoyed these early sessions, and being paid a few pounds was another step towards independence.

A fragment of Miller and Bacharach's *Under-Twenty Parade* material has, remarkably, survived in the form of a rough transcript of studio takes.[73] Though only a snippet, it is illuminating as regards Miller's subsequent West End performances and his longer-term creative style. As the transcript records, the double act parodied a panel of critics who were part of the programme. The pair aped the perky 'Hello, listeners', the critics' waffle, every little cough, the bad segues and the indecipherable 'talking together'. Then they joined the panel (for real) to discuss their techniques. During that exchange, the boys said that they generated routines by conversationally ad-libbing and had struggled with the BBC's request for a formal script. An improvisational approach, in the spirit of jazz, was to continue throughout Miller's career. Combining a musical ear with near-scientific observations, his adolescent comedy was serious-minded at root. 'We are interested', he said, 'in the sound pictures that are made by people . . . just the noises and the flux of noises . . . [And] even now', he told the panel, 'exactly the same rises and falls, exactly the same cadences are occurring.' That Miller was to spend his life tuned in to the rhythms of conversation was natural enough, given his upbringing amidst the intelligentsia, the chattering classes.[74] The 'talking together' in this critics skit also interestingly foreshadows Miller's later approach to classic plays, radically overlapping lines of dialogue.

The *Under-Twenty Parade* panel dubbed him a satirist for the first time on record, but then he and Bacharach proved wildly surreal as well. They performed a variation on the Miller-Korn skit 'Round the World with Radio', combining imitation and way-out imagination.[75] Mingling BBC announcers, gale warnings and newsflashes, it ran like this:

> Er, er, that was 'Lift Up Your Socks' . . . Next week, 'A Short Gap' recorded anonymously . . . the South of England is going to move in a westerly direction . . . Now here is a police message, published Methuen at twenty-one shillings. There was an accident last night on the Great North Circular Road, when an elderly chrysanthemum was knocked down by a steamroller and received injuries from which the Chief Constable of Hertfordshire has since died . . . The police are anxious to interview a man with long blue hair – they have never seen a man with long blue hair.[76]

'Round the World with Radio' was also to provide further evidence of dialogic memory at work. It would be refined by Miller into a quirky Cambridge Footlights monologue – renamed 'Radio Page' and applauded by West End crowds – without Korn or Bacharach getting a writing credit.[77]

What is remarkable, more immediately, is this extract's sheer craziness. It is garbled, elided and dreamlike, with slivers of the everyday made strange by being miscategorized, everything playfully grafted into the wrong slots. Miller's own theory of comedy, expounded in later life, would home in on precisely that: laughter aroused by errors of classification.

The boys had clearly been influenced not only by the Marx Brothers but additionally by BBC Radio's own madcap comedy series, such as *Take It From Here*.[78] Fans of *The Goon Show* might see a direct parallel with Spike Milligan's and Peter Sellers' zany style. The Goons indeed penned a comparable newsflash skit and Miller listened to their show in the 1950s, relishing their latently satirical anti-authoritarianism (not least the caricaturing of flatulent old Major Bloodnok). Nevertheless, *The Goon Show* was only part of a broader wave of surrealist comedy and, actually, 'Round the World with Radio' just preceded Milligan and co.'s first broadcast.[79]

Miller and Bacharach probably were not echoing the radical absurdism of Eugène Ionesco's play *La Cantatrice Chauve*, his works not being well known in England at that point.[80] Ionesco, however, admired psychiatry's concept of letting the irrational loose, and the key may be the link between that idea of freeing up – as propounded by Emanuel's profession – and comic performance. Miller Snr may have turned his son into a comedian by dispatching him to all those child psychiatrists who encouraged him to play around or say whatever sprang to mind.

Miller Jnr and Bacharach's turn on *Under-Twenty Parade* was so wacky that, afterwards, they had to reassure the discussion panel they weren't complete nutters with their neurological wires crossed.[81] Likewise, Tony Cutler remembers:

> Most of us, onstage and off [stage in the Colet Clubs revues], just stared in awe at – within a repressed public school society – this incredible liberation of Jonathan's. He could achieve a sort of release, could let the spring go in a way that was quite amazing.

*　　*　　*

Miller's manic glee spilled over from the revues into the school corridors and the Chesterton Society debates. In fact, the society's minutes paint a picture of him as St Paul's anarchic jester, a bit like Hamlet, the Clown-Prince of Denmark, acting crazy. The society was sometimes a kind of mini-House of Lords, soberly discussing the topical issues of the day – the fledgling NHS, sanctioned gambling, sexual equality, racism – and Miller himself could be earnestly incensed.[82] The minutes describe how, opposing the motion 'This House Believes in Ghosts', he 'attacked bitterly' such superstitions as mental aberrations and argued 'through a barrage of criticism' that no reputable scientist would ever associate himself with 'psychic trickery'.[83]

More often, the Chesterton became another comedy show, effervescing with humour. Korn and Sacks, before they left, had contributed to the high spirits. On the topic of better quality BBC programming, Korn had suggested *Mrs Dali's Diary* and *Housewives' Joyce*. In turn, Sacks abandoned his shyness to praise perpetual motion machines in a farcical vein, crying 'Forward the revolution!' while attempting to lift himself up by his own hair.[84] Miller, though, proved the most madcap of all. One comic monologue, tucked away in the minutes, records how he sent a discussion about a new casino in Brighton into free fall. Although this is juvenilia, for sure, the loopiness is extraordinary:

> Mr Miller revealed to us that Brighton was a mystery town. There are only four in Britain – Brighton, Bath, Plymbe-under-Firs and a town which only one man knows and he won't tell. This can now be revealed as Tooting.

The only indication of Brighton being a mystery town is the sudden drop in temperature of 2.5 degrees according to Sir Alexander Plankton or 2.7 degrees according to Andreyovitch Michaelov Trotski, the eminent English nuclear physicist.[85]

Some of Miller's contemporaries from St Paul's suggest that he was an anxious and self-conscious adolescent, one for whom mimicry and fooling served as a shield – another safe haven. Having somewhat envied the mental release that accompanied David Niven's brain disorder in *A Matter of Life and Death*, he had now found his own form of crackpot-style escapism.

The surrealist movement's interest in unfettered, reason-free self-expression originally sprang from André Breton's experience as a World War 1 medic, observing the ravings of shell-shock victims. In the light of that, one might wonder if Miller's comic lunacies were actually imitations of Emanuel's psychiatric patients. They occasionally arrived for consultations at Queen's Grove, and Miller does remember his father speaking of one near-surreal case, a man who wanted his buttocks transplanted onto his shoulders. He never encountered Emanuel's patients at close quarters though, and the schoolboy's humour may well have been homegrown without direct contact with anyone profoundly deranged. Emanuel himself could be hilarious and eruptively absurd when his gloom lifted. Even if Mrs Miller's wit was less delirious, she could be freewheeling too, as in her 'long rambling modulations' so enjoyed by Isaiah Berlin.

What is unmistakable is how Miller's role as 'the Clown-Prince of the Chesterton' (for such he was dubbed) anticipated his adult ambivalence towards institutions.[86] He was a valued member of the society, yet there were rules and he breached them more cheekily than anyone else. He alone had several speeches 'entirely censored', and on two occasions – when he got his hands on the minutes book – he proved an outrageously careless honorary secretary. His was the shortest ever entry, laid out with mock formality:

Here lie the unwritten
minutes of a debate meeting
killed at 1.10 in room 2 by
the inefficiency of the secretary
aided by an uncooperative society.

Summarizing the debate as merely tedious, he concluded with a flourish:

At this point the secretary ceased to take minutes.
Lord preserve us from the plague.
signed
J. W. Miller (Dishon. Sec.)[87]

He got away with this as the society's licensed fool. His second round of note-taking, in January 1953, caused official consternation, however. We are told that his wayward minutes, when read out, prompted roars of laughter 'in all the wrong places'.[88] They were duly covered in stern corrections by another hand, and Miller disappeared under a cloud, never to be mentioned again. As one Old Pauline remembers:

> It was a lot of fun having him around but he just couldn't conform. He stood out so, being tall like a bird, with that red hair, and doing impressions of the masters' walks . . . The thing was to keep on the right side of the line, and Jonathan hadn't developed that protective mechanism.

*   *   *

There was some trouble at home before Miller headed off to university. Although he conversed, now and then, with his father about their shared interests, they had furious rows too, not least when Emanuel accused his son of purloining some curios from his study – a set of glass eyes. Miller's curfew was also enforced with a shocking rigour when he returned home late after celebrating a New Year's Eve in town. Every entrance was bolted and he had to wander the streets all night. The feeling of punitive exclusion must have been genuinely chilling. 'My mother was haggard and worried in the morning,' he says, 'desperately wondering where I'd been. Well, I hadn't been anywhere, except round and round the house.'

He became much closer to Betty during his last years at St Paul's. Even if she and Emanuel were not always on speaking terms, mother and son came to enjoy each other's company. It was as if the infant and the young adult were, for her, two different people, a dull pupa and a brilliant butterfly. Miller does not go so far as to say they developed a warm emotional bond, yet he speaks of their brief meeting of minds with discernible tenderness:

> It was a rather strange companionship, but I had a very good time with her then. I got close to her for two or three years, sitting opposite her at the dining-room table, swotting for my exams [while she was writing] . . . I was beginning to think about zoology and philosophical ideas, and was getting acquainted, through Korn, with some literary notions. I can't remember what we talked about, but we seemed to engage one another. She felt that she was in the presence of an intelligent and interesting colleague. I think, in some ways, I replaced [her brother] Henry when I was eighteen.

Through Betty's connection to Bergson and Proust, he was, moreover, drawn to *A la Recherche du Temps Perdu*, reading the leather-bound copy which Emanuel had given to his wife as a wedding gift.

One family friend suggests that the Millers were a classic Freudian constellation, with the son wanting to please the love-object, his mother, and to slay his father metaphorically, by becoming more celebrated. It is tempting to recall the tea-table scene in Betty's *On the Side of the Angels*, with Honor's little boy beaming and saying, 'Now there's only you and me.' Nonetheless, Miller says he neither competed with, nor emulated Emanuel.[89] As for his mother, parent–teenager relations often happily adjust to incorporate more sibling-style egalitarian elements.

Extant is a humorous letter written by Betty and sent off with a draft of her Robert Browning biography, explaining that the script is 'in folders lent to me by my son' and 'the title "The Invertebrates" does not refer to the Brownings'.[90] Her book enveloped in her child's biology file is a curiously touching image, and Miller was proud of the acclaim which the biography won on publication. He presented copies to his friends.

It was in his very last term at St Paul's, at eighteen going on nineteen, that he met his future wife, Rachel. According to Tony Cutler, Miller was no ladies' man, being a gawky scruff who 'could never look the part . . . [and] was extraordinarily awkward around women'. However, various girls had hooked up with the gang, via the north London Jewish social circuit. This outer circle of 'group girls' expanded through parties where jiving and necking were prevalent, and where Miller's fame spread quickly as a boy-mimic who could go stellar.[91] The group girls included Hannah Horovitz (daughter of Phaidon Press's co-founder Bela Horovitz), Nina Obstfeld (now mother of the film director Beeban Kidron), and Elishiva Landman (Miller's old playgroup friend from Hampstead). A fourth, Judith Mundlak (who was destined to become a neurologist), admits readily that she was 'very taken' with Miller because he was 'wonderful looking and extraordinary fun'.[92] A St Paul's pal remembers him proving that he could chat up an impossibly sophisticated blonde at a jazz club.[93]

Miller himself is fairly sardonic about his limited dating, referring to a 'brief going-out' with Judy Mikardo, daughter of the Labour MP Ian Mikardo. On one cinema trip, he spent an eternity trying to touch her little finger, his hand creeping towards hers like a near-paralyzed spider, only to be left unsure, after all that, if there was any response.[94]

Rachel materialized in the Walker Library, attending a play reading organized in conjunction with St Paul's School for Girls.[95] He may condemn the theatre for diverting him from science but he does not regret Rachel arriving as an added distraction. He set his heart on her almost immediately and with great determination. She struck him as wonderfully alluring and glamorous and, he says, he knew 'something very different had happened' as soon as they began seeing each other.

She was seventeen, and there is a photographic portrait of her from that time. Beautifully dignified, with dark glossy hair and a luminous heart-shaped face, she holds the camera's gaze. It is a look of captivating composure: classy and sweet, with just a hint of astute mockery. Her mother, Ruth Collet, was a Slade-trained artist who came from a wealthy and intellectually well-connected Jewish family, the Salamans.[96] Rachel's father, Robert, was a pianist, a professor at the Guildhall

School of Music, and a polyglot of Anglo-Saxon Unitarian stock (with anti-slavery and Chartist ancestors). Robert impressed Miller by practising a piece and reading a book simultaneously.

The middle child and one of three sisters, Rachel had been a potential star at the Sadler's Wells Ballet School (now the Royal Ballet School), only her planned career went awry at fifteen. She had outgrown the minute dimensions demanded by the profession, and she felt a lingering sense of guilt about not going on the stage – the inverse of Miller today.

He did not exactly charm her at their first encounter, urging her to ditch modern languages (her new focus) in favour of medicine (the only worthwhile pursuit). 'Apparently he was famous, but I hadn't heard of him!' she exclaims, raising an eyebrow. Over 50 years on, their relationship is down to earth and fundamentally rock-solid. She is silver-haired now and stylish in a very casual, unshowy way. She can be judiciously sharp yet always with a robust supportiveness underneath, and he patently adores her, appreciating both her teasing and straight talk.

As he explains, his attempted gallantry in the Walker Library – offering his scholar's gown because she was cold – struck her as dreadful showing-off, and she vowed that she would never see him again.[97] Then he embarrassed her by loitering outside her school gates like a love-struck pest. 'My teachers thought I was just a loose woman, a flibbertigibbet,' she declares, 'with Jonathan hanging around on Brook Green!' She got into further trouble, spotted doing her prep with him in Hyde Park, scandalously not wearing her school hat.

When Sacks – back from Oxford of a weekend – first played the cupid-chauffeur, driving his friend out of London to the Collets' home in Northwood, the romance faced another temporary uphill struggle. Rachel's older sister, Jane Miller (the feminist writer who shares the surname by chance, through marriage), remembers seeing Jonathan coming along the garden path:

> He was bearing this very unfortunate pink cyclamen in his very red hand with a very red face. In those days he stammered a lot and was very nervous. So there was this wonderful sight, really, at the door. My sister Naomi – who's quite a lot younger – looked horrified at the arrival of these boys and said, 'You can't come in. Dad's got eczema.'

Miller's ardour was flattering but overwhelming, causing Rachel to fight shy. 'I didn't know what had hit me quite,' she says. 'Jonathan had this mixture of being very full-on but also being aware that I was rather reserved, and considering it a terrible disaster. This put me in a difficult position.' Her father asked the boy's parents if he could lay off a bit and, when Rachel went to Italy that summer, she had a small fling which caused a temporary parting of ways on her return.

Even at seventeen, she felt very comfortable with him in many ways. 'Knowing what to talk about was never difficult with Jonathan,' she observes. 'He's never been short of something to say!' Moreover, Great-Aunt Brenda thought he was splendid. This was the ancient and august Brenda Seligman, president of the

Royal Anthropological Society. Because Northwood was so far from school, Rachel spent half of every week with her in Kensington. It was an odd existence: living like an only child, surrounded by display cabinets which housed antiquities from China and Benin (now in the British Museum). This aunt was quite a character as well. Ensconced in a wheelchair referred to as 'the chariot', she was autocratic yet also cherished Rachel like a surrogate daughter, having lost her own.

She adored Miller because he knew, from Emanuel, about anthropology, Freudian theories and botany – all her interests. She would, in her last will and testament, leave him many of her books, and his anthropological knowledge, enhanced by her, went on to enrich his theatre productions. Meanwhile, the gang had swiftly decided that Rachel was first-rate and the one for Miller, turfing a rival 'group girl' out of the car on a collective outing. Thus, even with their initial advances and retreats, this young couple soon became a fixture. Sacks fondly recalls how Rachel had a tranquil sanity, unlike the rest of them. She was the magnetic still point of Miller's turning world. Tony Cutler, casting his mind back, believes she was a kind of balm, for he says:

> Rachel was quiet, at least she seemed quiet and calm, and she had an amazing effect. She was the only person who was able to pacify Jonathan. In some way she was able to mollify him and turn him into a functioning human being, instead of a loony genius.

· 4 ·

1953–6

Cambridge

A BREATH OF FRESH AIR, if not a thoroughgoing wind of change, is always blowing across the Fens and into Cambridge. Bidding farewell to London once again and heading across the flats of East Anglia to arrive at this famed, scenic university city, Miller swung into the porter's lodge at St John's College, his new habitation, ready for the Michaelmas term of 1953. Flying the nest was, naturally, a rite of passage, the adolescent moving towards autonomy. At the same time, he was managing to please his father, St John's being Emanuel's alma mater. Miller had won a scholarship and he was now officially on course to become a doctor.[1]

Founded on the site of a medieval hospital, St John's is one of the largest colleges in Cambridge. Stretching through grand quads and cloisters to the Backs, it rounds off with green lawns and white crenellated parapets over the River Cam, pretty as a fairy tale and, of course, academically exclusive. In this era, Cambridge strongly imbued its freshers with hopes of a brilliant future. It was a thriving hive for the intellectual *jeunesse dorée*. One of Miller's contemporaries recollects: 'As a clever boy at Cambridge at that time, you felt you really were among the cleverest anywhere . . . It was the acme of English education and nowhere abroad could really hold a candle.'[2]

The British nation, as a whole, felt itself to be doing well and making progress in the mid-1950s. It had not just won the war but was finally emerging from the austerity era, with rationing drawing to an end. It had seen the youthful Princess Elizabeth crowned in June 1953 amidst glittering splendour and media fanfares about a glorious new Elizabethan age. News headlines announced that Edmund Hillary had planted the Union Flag on Everest's summit that same month, England's cricket team triumphed in the Ashes after twenty years, and Roger Bannister (a medical student at Oxford) was soon to break the four-minute mile.

For Miller's generation, the country's post-war spirit of 'Advance Britannia' had translated into keen personal aspirations and growing self-confidence. A public schoolboy, accustomed to architectural magnificence, might take even St John's in his stride with a sense of entitlement. In decorating his allotted room, over the college's Bridge of Sighs, Miller neither dithered nor displayed a prodigious grasp of aesthetics. He stuck one poster, featuring a wolf, on his wall and headed off to the buttery for a packet of biscuits. For all that, winning a Cambridge place was a heady achievement. Anxiety was inevitably mixed with excitement at the prospect of meeting a new crowd and trying to make one's mark.

Strongly appreciating the history of the place and its overlapping generations of scholarship, he liked residing on the same winding staircase as the acclaimed professor of psychology Sir Frederic Bartlett – formerly a student with Emanuel. Bartlett used to trundle past like Mr Badger from *The Wind in the Willows*, and Miller was soon acquainted with his acclaimed book *Remembering*, on the reconstructive nature of memory.[3] The young man also made friends with the eminent Cambridge anthropologist Meyer Fortes, who had once worked as Emanuel's assistant in his East End clinic.[4]

At the same time, the 1950s were seeing a new, vigorous youth culture. Teenagers were attracting public attention as an emergent social group with less deferential inclinations. During Miller's Cambridge years, rock 'n' roll took the USA and the UK by storm. Elvis Presley and his gyrating pelvis – sneering with his hips, as one critic put it – electrified many youngsters. Bill Haley and the Comets' hit film *Rock Around the Clock* triggered riotous excitement in British cinemas, with seat-ripping teddy boys taken into custody. Angry Young Men proliferated in *Rebel Without a Cause*, Kingsley Amis' novel *Lucky Jim* and John Osborne's play *Look Back in Anger*.

Thanks to the Butler Education Act of 1944, which made free secondary school education available to all, Cambridge University itself was undergoing a change, admitting a growing number of students from less privileged backgrounds. As one college employee remarked to Miller: 'Once they were all gentlemen on this staircase. Now there are more of them up on their brains.' Young women were progressing via this innovative system, which enhanced the sense of a groundbreaking generation soon to become movers and shakers. One of Miller's female contemporaries, the journalist Joan Bakewell, particularly recollects the feeling of incipient liberty, encouraged by Simone de Beauvoir and Sartre's existential ideas about freedom of action.[5]

A whirlwind revolution it was not, however. In many respects the 1950s remained distinctly staid. The Establishment considered a young man racy if his hair touched his collar. Cambridge remained predominantly a convocation of public schoolboys, and all its colleges were still strictly single-sex. A few chaps dared to slip in and out of the ladies' institutions in the small hours, but those were the only overnight changes. With college servants being provided – to help with luggage, serve meals and make the beds each day – the students were undeniably pampered, yet subject to rigorous strictures. Sexual intercourse was an offence for which you could be sent down, as if Cambridge really were the Garden of Eden. Gown-wearing was obligatory after dusk and for all lectures, so everyone cycled around with billowing black wings, like clouds of bats. Proctors patrolled the streets, with constabulary sidekicks, known as bulldogs, detaining any rule-breakers.

Miller emphasizes that he was eager to study hard, feeling that much was expected of him. Living in the fast lane, James Dean-style, was hardly an option anyway. Having an exotic Indian curry at the Taj, opposite St John's, or a cappuccino in one of the cafés with novel Gaggia machines seemed adventurous enough.

Nevertheless, at Cambridge, Miller was starting to be tugged in contrary directions, between science and the stage. In 1953, science was certainly a buzzing field with a surge of Nobel Prize-winners among the university's academics and associates. It was what you might call a Cantabrigian Explosion. That very year, the metabolic chemist Hans Krebs, an affiliate, was awarded his Nobel in medicine for discovering the citric acid cycle and, even more influentially, Crick and Watson determined the double helix structure of DNA. Crick famously burst into the Eagle pub, off King's Parade, to announce that – conducting their research just around the corner in the university's Cavendish Laboratory – they had solved the mystery of life. Their Nobel was to be won in conjunction with Maurice Wilkins, their St John's-trained colleague. That is not to mention Frederick Sanger's insights into insulin – the first full chemical analysis of a protein, completed in 1953 – or the two Johnian physicists Edward Appleton and John Cockcroft winning Nobel Prizes in 1947 and 1951 respectively.[6]

The theatrical scene was also flourishing. Dadie Rylands, a fellow at King's College, was using the university's Marlowe Society to nurture a new school of intelligent Elizabethan verse-speaking.[7] Its student productions were attended by the national press, and Rylands' influence was spreading to reinvigorate British theatre. Peter Hall had just proved himself to be an undergraduate prodigy. In 1953, he was directing *Twelfth Night* at the Cambridge Arts Theatre. Not long after he would be boldly premiering Samuel Beckett's *Waiting for Godot* in London's West End, and then making his Stratford-upon-Avon debut at the Shakespeare Memorial Theatre. Nearly every college had its own drama society and, along with the increasingly lively media industry, the stage was beginning to be seen as a fast route to fame. Here was a viable alternative to the traditional Oxbridge goals of public service and the professions.

Although he would end up starring in two Footlights revues, Miller's anatomy course was a far more immediate and sobering prospect.[8] The *jeunesse dorée* had to buckle down and start dissecting corpses. He stood shivering with apprehension in the stone-flagged antechamber of the 'dead house' where the bodies were laid out, awaiting them, in long rows. Laughing nervously about who would faint first, he and his fellow novices blenched as the clammy odour of formalin leaked under the doors. Paradoxically, he found himself yawning with fear.

When the initiates came face to face with the cadavers, the dead looked strangely unlike flesh and blood. In Miller's words:

> The preservative had bleached them to the colour of dirty clay and they . . .
> [were] frozen in stiff and curious postures like the calcined mummies at

Pompeii. They all shared the same expression. The facial muscles, contracting over the skull, had pulled the mouth into a tense, lipless 'O' of spinsterish surprise. We somehow felt cheated of our ordeal.[9]

Within minutes, he was making his first incision. The texture was akin to vulcanized rubber and the heart looked as if it were choked with red earth, like a flowerpot. Eventually, after methodical procedures, little would remain except 'a few knuckle bones and a heap of giblets which were solemnly bundled into . . . a pine box for Christian burial'.[10] It sounds grisly but he was fascinated by this hands-on work, and by all the related learning in physiology.

His Cambridge mentors manifestly impressed him. Under the guidance of the veteran neurophysiologist and Nobel Prize-winner E. D. Adrian (whom Emanuel had also known at Cambridge), he became enthralled by the all-or-none law, which highlights that nerves respond to stimuli either fully or not at all.[11] Miller was additionally taught by two electrophysiologists and future Nobel-winners, Alan Lloyd Hodgkin and Andrew Huxley (half-brother of Aldous and Julian). Taking Lord Adrian's work further, they had developed the Hodgkin-Huxley model in 1952, essentially making them the first to describe how signals were transmitted by nerve cells.[12]

Equally, Miller was inspired by the retinal physiology experts Richard Gregory and Horace Barlow (a great-grandson of Charles Darwin), who tutored him individually.[13] He willingly played the guinea pig in their vision supervisions, being exposed to blinding flashes of light to test how his sight recovered. Ever since then, he has been intrigued by the psychology of consciousness and seeing. 'It continues to obsess or preoccupy me now,' he says, 'how the proximal stimulus (where light strikes the retina) leads to a subjective experience of a distal world (a world "out there").'

Still researching in Cambridge today, Barlow recalls how his former student mastered large topics amazingly fast yet had a vulnerability as well. Miller very much wanted his ideas to be considered seriously. Perhaps he was not cut out for the confines of specialization though, being more instinctively panoramic in his outlook; more of an Isaiah Berlin-style fox than a hedgehog; 'a bit of everything' rather than 'all or none' in his proclivities. One contemporary stresses that 'Jonathan's genius was clearly for lateral thinking . . . rather than the consistent, long-term concentration which major scientific discoveries require.' Nonetheless Miller still regrets that he did not focus in on advanced physiology in his third year (as most other top medical students did).

He kept his options unusually open, taking on two extra half-subjects, both of which Emanuel had also read: zoology and philosophy of science (the latter embracing the history of science).[14] In zoology, he sought out Robert Hinde for special tutorials, visiting the new experimental Ornithological Field Station in the nearby village of Madingley. This was soon to become the university's internationally reputed Sub-Department of Animal Behaviour.[15] Having grown up doing chicken impressions, Miller spent his Madingley afternoons observing how goslings were 'imprinted'. In experiments which tested Konrad Lorenz's celebrated theories, he watched how the baby birds copied the moves of what they took for parents (actually wastepaper baskets being dragged around an enclosure).

Professor Hinde comments: 'I was primarily interested in the behaviour of human and other species but we talked for hours about everything under the sun. It was extraordinarily stimulating for me . . . An original mind? Good God, yes! – though I was always a bit frightened he might be gathering satirical material.' Miller would remain friends and later hook up professionally with both Barlow and Hinde, for conferences and on television programmes.[16]

He judges philosophy to be the most significant thing he learned at university. Having read Emanuel's sun-bleached volumes of Bertrand Russell before coming up to St John's, he moved on to the works of Ludwig Wittgenstein, Russell's Cambridge colleague who died in 1951. Wittgenstein's landmark *Philosophical Investigations*, published in 1953, aroused intense excitement. Electrified by his analyses of language and volition (intended, voluntary and involuntary actions), Miller felt that they were 'a road to Damascus'. Joan Bakewell recalls Miller screeching to a halt on his bike to regale her with his latest thoughts on this.[17]

He went on to organize late-night confabs that really do sound like a philosophers' salon, if not an alternative séance, discussing the Wittgensteinian difference between 'My arm goes up' and 'I lift my arm'. Even today, he remains enthralled by this debate, keeping the *Blue and Brown Books* (the preliminary studies which fed into *Philosophical Investigations*) beside his bed like a Bible. Such ideas are embedded in his thinking, and he admires analytic philosophers who continue to scrutinize language and the mind, contemplating how we think and have knowledge, and what we mean by certainty.

He found Norwood Russell Hanson's tutorials truly life-changing, for this philosopher of science introduced him to the notion that supposedly objective systems of classification might, in fact, be subjective. That may sound arid or abstract, but Hanson was a hugely vivacious American, an ace trumpeter-turned-pilot-turned-Fulbright scholar. He had a dramatic mane of hair and rubber-soled, springy shoes. In his tiny office, up rickety stairs in the Whipple Museum of the History of Science, Hanson would literally bounce with excitement when demonstrating the principles of thought, and Miller emphasizes that his world was turned upside down by this intoxicating man's ideas.[18]

Hanson's pioneering thesis was that our preconceptions filter the information which our brain receives, therefore all our observations are theory-laden. We interpret what we see, so there is no pure objective truth. He loved to illustrate the distinction between 'seeing that' and 'seeing as' by using entertaining trompe l'oeils. Favourite examples were the duck-rabbit (the psychologist Joseph Jastrow's brain-teasing illustration, where the bunny's ears can be re-viewed as a bird's bill) and the Necker Cube (a line drawing which looks, alternately, like a box seen from below and a box seen from above).[19]

Hanson's argument affected his student's whole approach. It would be wrong to say that Miller's faith in science was destroyed. If not a crisis, however, it was a crossroads. Once taught that science's truths were not written in stone, he took a step back – away from the microscope – and his determination to practise medicine began to dwindle.[20] He became absorbed by the history of scientific concepts, how they mutated and developed over time.

As an atheist rejecting religious dogmas, he had already joined the Humanist Society at Cambridge. Now he additionally became the secretary of the Philosophy of Science Club, keenly discussing Hanson's lessons. Listings in the *Cambridge Review* record that he lectured publicly under the club's auspices, to town and gown.[21]

*   *   *

In spite of these pursuits, the so-called loony genius had not lost all his comic eccentricities in the transition from St Paul's. According to the playwright and novelist Michael Frayn, who was at Cambridge, Miller wandered the streets barefoot.[22] During his first few weeks at university, he was also seen striding around with a massive marrow. This didn't quite amount to an avant-garde 'happening' (a term not coined until 1957), but it wasn't so far off performance art. Certainly, such showy theatrics made him an outstanding student in more ways than one.

Trevor Williams, then a second-year Johnian and later Miller's room-mate, spotted this ectomorphic fresher entering the dining-hall with the said bulbous accessory, like some bizarre animal/vegetable double act. He believes that Miller was, furthermore, determined to liven up St John's hallowed hall by starting outrageous conversations over supper. These were based on Freudian psychiatry and, allegedly, he advocated that everyone should give the rowing team a wide berth because one gent staring at the next gent's back had sexual connotations. This was not the last time that he was to jibe at homosexuals.

Was the marrow itself not looking suggestively phallic though? It was almost certainly ditched before he headed off to visit Girton, the outlying college for female students. There he started 'paying court', as he puts it, to Rachel's sister Jane, perhaps hoping she would act as his go-between and heal the post-Italian rift. There was an added attraction. Jane was part of the circle of bright sparks who produced *Granta*, the witty and literary magazine, now a renowned professional publication.

Some ground was being gained by Britain's quality press during the 1950s, and journalism was certainly a happening scene in Cambridge at this point. The university newspaper *Varsity* (founded in 1947) was winning awards and expanding, almost like a mini-Fleet Street organ, under the editorship of Michael Winner (the future film director and columnist).[23]

Miller knew about the gloriously controversial departure of *Granta*'s editor-illustrator Mark Boxer who, subsequently, became the professional cartoonist

Marc and a leading light in the magazine industry (launching the massively successful *Sunday Times Colour Section* in the early 1960s). Boxer's expulsion by the proctors, for printing an irreligious poem, had stimulated a student protest in the summer of 1953. It was staged on King's Parade as a funeral for free speech with Boxer departing, flamboyantly, on a horse-drawn cortège.[24] Miller had learned of this brilliant young man from Rachel. 'And so,' he explains, 'in a rather desperate attempt to compete with Rachel's admiration for Mark Boxer and the others in Jane's smart set, I submitted a few rather feeble cartoons to the *Gadfly*.'

Jointly edited by Karl Miller and Nick Tomalin (who were destined to be leading journalists too), the *Gadfly* was *Granta* reincarnated during its official suspension. Miller remains a huge admirer of Karl's intellect to this day, and the list of contributors to those twin journals during his three years at Cambridge reads like a *Who's Who* or *Who'd Soon be Who*. The names include the award-winning biographer Claire Tomalin (then Claire Delavenay and Nick Tomalin's girlfriend), the comedian John Bird, the theatre critic and writer Ron Bryden, Michael Frayn, Bamber Gascoigne, Ted Hughes, Sylvia Plath, the architect Cedric Price and Frederic Raphael, author of *The Glittering Prizes*.

Miller was no straightforward networker. Jane points out that he began by chastising her for hobnobbing with certain pals. As she explains:

> I introduced him to everybody and he was very putting-down! In a very puritanical way, he kept telling us that we were snobs and fools and things. He would have these 'seriousnesses', which were little gatherings of people he knew, in front of his gas fire, and I'm not sure that they weren't, in some ways, intended as an alternative to the life he thought I was leading . . . Jonathan was very young compared to most of the others who had been in the army [doing National Service, a delayed requirement for medical students]. So he was slightly taking up a position, that's all . . . Then he became their friend too, very much a friend of Karl's, and he was, in those days, full of life and ideas, and interested in other people.

Karl, who married Jane after graduating, can still picture the first time he saw Miller:

> It was shortly after Jonathan's arrival in Cambridge and I was in a teashop called The Whim talking to Jane, when in came somebody known to her as her sister's admirer. And there was this man who was like a wolf boy or the wild boy of Aveyron.[25] He seemed barely conditioned to the social *va et vient*. He had sneakers and a duffle coat: red hair, looked like a fox, and shy and nervous and stammering a lot. I mean likeable, very brilliant and keyed-up, intense and kind of barely house-trained, you could say. But then he became less of a wild boy, settled into Cambridge, and became known as a wit and a clever fellow and became a star. This was, I think, the passage that he negotiated at Cambridge. So he shed some of that innocence, if that's the

word for it. He entered into the spirit of things at Cambridge and was very successful.

Miller was rapidly absorbed into Jane and Karl's circle, a new gang who are remembered by the Johnian professor of social anthropology, Jack Goody, as tremendously clever. 'I thought they were outstanding and I still do,' Goody says. 'I have never known another group that crosscut fields in the way that they did.'[26]

Getting started as a cartoonist, Miller illustrated one of the *Gadfly*'s front covers in his first term, when there was a printing-works crisis, and his drawings are scattered among many *Gadfly* and *Granta* articles thereafter. His graphics were whimsical, their childish sweetness combined with comparatively sophisticated captions, sending up zoology textbooks and philosophical ruminations. Two wickedly grinning fishes stalk a wary man. Below his feet hover the words: 'APRES MOI LE DELUGE'. Cats and beaky birds became his trademarks, the former often drawn as rectangles with a watchful eye in each top corner. In an issue about past Cantabrigian high achievers, several squat felines look competitively askance at a rival on a pedestal. Boxer and Nelson's column were possibly knocking about in the artist's subconscious.[27]

Elsewhere a pair of elongated cats, in two minds, are seen pulling in opposite directions with their tails knotted together, just signed 'Jonathan Miller'. That is an image that catches the eye given his professionally riven future. In his illustrated send-up of the literary critic William Empson's seven types of ambiguity, visual double takes and mirror images proliferated, including a doodle of identical siblings and of a man staring at his own reflection through binoculars.[28]

At the bottom of another page, he slipped in a more daringly sacrilegious gag. Alongside the hazy claim that 'GOD MOVES IN A MYSTERIOUS WAY' stood a venerably robed and bearded figure, with two ludicrous wheels where his feet should have been. This little joke did not, of course, spark fundamentalist riots in the manner of the 2005 Danish Muhammed cartoons. All the same, Karl remarks: 'This was the mirth of the scientist, for which I marvel that he wasn't sent down.'[29]

Miller dabbled with journalism at Cambridge.[30] He co-edited one issue of *Granta* but was not to emerge as a pundit until much later.[31] His most noteworthy contributions were two delicate short stories depicting London lives. These were akin to his mother's fiction even if underdeveloped. 'Fragment of a Story' portrays a writer who has been sleeping rough in the railway tunnel that cuts through Camden Town. The description starts with this character gazing out along the tracks, another Milleresque case of forking choices.

> The entrance to the tunnel was right round his shoulders and wobbly with rain drops: he stood between the rails and felt his face and body all bright and his upright back all dark. The space in front of him was wide and sunlit and the rails running out of the tunnel . . . gleamed before fading obliquely into the five black tunnel mouths on the other side of the clearing . . . [He] rummaged in his knapsack; he took out his notebook.[32]

Miller's own infantine refrain stands out as an autobiographical detail in this piece. Having broken free of his social bonds, the nameless protagonist yearns for stable routines and for a course of action to be re-imposed upon him, because 'his childhood moan kept coming back to him[:] "I want to be occupied"'.

The other *Granta* story, entitled 'Servant Couple', depicts a well-to-do house near Regent's Park, from the viewpoint of the two servants.[33] They reside in the basement flat, like the chauffeur and his wife at Miller's home in Queen's Grove. Perhaps the insightful glimpses of servants in Betty's novels had caught her son's eye. His stage directing would, later, echo that trait, making normally sidelined domestics into scene-stealers.[34] However, the mood is more dreamily melancholic here. With their employers drifting round art galleries on the continent, the servant couple feel there is something desolate about the grand upstairs rooms, finding that the mirrors there 'reflected the order and the emptiness, enlarged it and extended it'.

In his twenties, Miller would harbour literary ambitions, talking of a full-length work in progress, though nowadays he regretfully says that he lacks a novelist's sustained narrative skills.

*   *   *

His multifarious pursuits, as an undergraduate, might be likened to a Venn diagram of overlapping rings. One important circle, interlinked with the *Granta* crowd, was the Cambridge Conversazione Society, otherwise known as the Apostles. This debating club, though officially secret, is now famously associated with the Cambridge Spy Ring, because Anthony Blunt and Guy Burgess were inducted into the apostolic brotherhood in the 1930s.

Miller says he was never knowingly approached by Soviet agents.[35] A loquacious 6'3" redhead, with a taste for the limelight and with Jewish-Lithuanian roots, probably wasn't an ideal mole from Moscow's viewpoint. In any case, the nature of the Apostles had changed over time. It was still an all-male preserve in the 1950s but, in contrast with the clandestine homosexuality and communism of the Blunt and Burgess era, Miller suggests the brotherhood was going through a heterosexual phase. Being an Apostle in his time was, he says, more likely to 'get a guy into a girl's knickers' than 'in with' the KGB.[36] Earlier Apostles had been politically active, becoming involved in a doomed liberal rebellion in 1830s Spain. Others fought in the Spanish Civil War against Franco, and one of Miller's contemporaries says that the mid-Fifties lot were all republicans. Yet Miller himself recalls no political discussions about that.[37]

The brotherhood had far more literary and Victorian associations for him when he first arrived in Cambridge. At that point, he knew of this historic 'sect' only through his mother's investigations. While he was settling in at St John's, Betty was next door visiting Trinity College, researching what would have been (if illness had not intervened) another major biography, this time on Tennyson. A cryptic allusion to the Apostles had been worked into the poem 'In Memoriam' when

Tennyson wrote about revisiting his old college: 'Where once we had debate, a band /Of youthful friends, on mind and art,/And labour, and the changing mart/. . . The rapt oration flowing free'.[38] Looking along the Cam to the battlements of St John's, Betty further perceived that this was the river from 'The Lady of Shalott', winding down to 'many-towered Camelot', and that the Apostles had been transmuted into the Round Table in Tennyson's 'Idylls of the King'.

Knowing of his mother's detective work but thinking that the Apostles were relatively obscure, Miller was startled when Karl knocked on his door and asked if he had heard of them. Eventually, it dawned on him that he was being inducted into the society then and there. In apostolic argot, he was being 'fathered' as a new 'embryo' by Karl. He had been vetted at several previous tea parties.

An extremely select club, with dons on board and only twelve student members, this group was Cambridge's answer to Plato's *Symposium*: top brains from various disciplines assembled to debate ideas. It required weekly attendance and the presentation of thought-provoking treatises, but it mixed informality with formality, and it favoured egalitarianism in its discussions rather than any pomposity. Its meetings were held in the rooms of E. M. Forster in King's College. The renowned veteran author, a sensitive and ironical humanist, presided quietly amidst his florid William Morris furnishings. He did not, it seems, offer the Apostles' legendary fare of sardines on toast, code name 'whales'. Everyone's papers were, nonetheless, read out from the hearth rug, as was the society's long-standing tradition. Forster provided port and biscuits. If the session went on very late, he would slip off to bed.

The house rule, that one should graciously admit one's errors and be open-minded, was very mature by comparison with the vehement pow-wows of St Paul's Chesterton Society, yet Miller flourished. Even if not innately temperate, he respected the code of practice here. 'The whole point was conviviality,' he underlines. 'You wore your learning lightly. It had to be warm-hearted and witty.' By the mid-twentieth century, having turned away from heavy metaphysics towards language analysis, philosophers liked to intertwine their ideas with jokes. So, you had to be both clever and funny. 'It was', Miller says, 'the humour which made your serious thinking original.'

Forster's novel *The Longest Journey* – with its telling dedication, 'Fratribus' ('For the brothers') – opens with a hearth-rug debate which brings out the comedy. A group of Cambridge chaps are philosophically quibbling over whether things, such as cows, still exist when unobserved: 'Well, if you go, the cow stops; but if I go, the cow goes. Then what will happen if you stop and I go?' and so on.[39] This contrasts with the po-faced grandiosity of the nineteenth-century Apostle Donald MacAlister. He praised the brotherhood as a near-masonic clan of fledgling potentates, claiming: 'The voice that issues from the hearth-rug on a Saturday night has gone through all the earth . . . It speaks in Senates though men know it not, it controls principalities and powers.'[40]

The tone in Miller's era was a delicate balance, all the same. According to one member of the group, Michael Frayn was vetted but never elected because he was 'very amusing but wouldn't be serious'. Moreover, everyone in the society was well aware of their prestigious predecessors, many important alternative thinkers and artists: Bertrand Russell, Wittgenstein and their philosopher-colleague George E. Moore; the poet-physician Erasmus Darwin; the historian G. M. Trevelyan and the economist John Maynard Keynes; Victor Rothschild (the Cumbrae biologist and suspected Fifth Man); Rupert Brooke and Roger Fry; Leonard Woolf and both Lytton and James Strachey (the authority on Freud).

The Conversazione Society was, indeed, a nexus for Britain's so-called 'intellectual aristocracy', and it is said to have raised the calibre of British conversation by nurturing so many of the Bloomsbury Group (with which Forster was closely associated). Both social sets liked to combine the highbrow with argument, gossip and gaiety when they chinwagged.[41] As a great cerebral talker, Miller is a direct descendant of that tradition.

Woolf and James Strachey were still attending the Apostles' annual dinners in the 1950s, and Anthony Blunt was present at one such gathering at Kettner's restaurant in Soho. Everybody headed back to Blunt's rooms at the Courtauld for postprandial drinks, having no idea of what the dark horse with an impeccable cut-glass accent was up to beyond art history.[42]

As well as Forster, senior members attending the society's regular Saturday meetings included Dadie Rylands, the politics don Noel Annan (later a life peer), and the outstanding historians Denis Mack Smith and Eric Hobsbawm. The student contingent of the time, it can also now be revealed, were notable high achievers:[43] not just Miller, Karl, Nick Tomalin and Ron Bryden but also the satirist John Fortune; the award-winning journalist-historian Neal Ascherson; Garry Runciman (sociologist, viscount and British Academy president); James Cornford (political and education expert); the art historians Francis Haskell and Michael Jaffé (who became director of the Fitzwilliam Museum); the economists Christopher Foster (professor, knight and RAC Foundation chairman) and Richard Layard (professor, baron, life peer); Lal Jayawardene (Sri Lanka's High Commissioner in London) and Nicholas Monck (knight and parliamentary permanent secretary).[44]

Miller himself recollects that one of the hearth-rug papers which he read out was a philosophical piece, inspired by Norwood Russell Hanson, concerned with propositional and procedural knowledge (knowing *that* such-and-such is the case, as opposed to knowing *how* to, say, ride a bicycle). What he stresses is the range of the debates:

> It was just extremely varied conversation, with people pursuing interests recognisably different from one's own, introducing one to subjects about which one knew very little, expanding one's field [of interests] . . . They were civilized, articulate and ironic, very entertaining and illuminating. And after each paper was read, you were always expected to say something, to enlarge on its theme. I'd had discussions with other friends, other medical students, about what we called 'important issues', but I'd never had anything quite

like that. I don't think many people have. There was never anything quite so ironically civilized as the Apostles.

Eric Hobsbawm called Miller's contribution one of 'unclassified multiple brilliance', and Denis Mack Smith remembers that 'He was frighteningly good and a very pleasurable character to have around. He was cleverer than anybody and also funnier.'[45] Neal Ascherson, who has now been a friend for half a century, notes that the newcomer provided a vital voice of scientific expertise:

> Jonathan was always very keen to pass on knowledge, medical knowledge. He was really distressed by how we were so ignorant about physiology. He said we had to go to a lecture. It was almost an order and he organized that we could be admitted. I remember a cat . . . with electrodes in its brains, making mews, bicycling its limbs[46] . . . But what I liked best about Jonathan was his physical excitability. He was even longer and thinner then, and I remember his bicycling convulsions as an idea dawned all over him in every joint. Whatever he said had this passionate originality. It was muscular thinking. He never said anything meaningless, polite or *just* convivial . . .
>
> He's a great parallels man, good at that kind of association and at one-liner ideas. For many years, I thought the most important thing anyone said, in all my time at Cambridge, was Jonathan's remark that the main function of the nervous system is to exclude, to filter out the majority of impulses coming into it. The significance was enormous because of the intellectual and aesthetic way things were changing. The Bloomsbury culture – the sensibility cult – was hanging around and, in some ways, the Apostles were backward-looking. But we all needed to escape from that, as a younger generation . . . Though Jonathan might be delighted to feel the Bloomsbury aesthetic was close to him and to touch on the Apostles' enormous ancestry, he was basically saying that the commandment to be sensitive to everything was unnatural and, if you were sensitive to everything, ultimately you'd destroy yourself.

Ascherson dubbed this subversive idea '*Lex Miller*' or 'Miller's Law', and it met resistance from some of their comrades at the time.[47]

Miller points up that other Apostles were far more informed about history and literature than he was as an undergraduate. Some of them, certainly, were surprised when he moved into the arts. They presumed that he would become a neurologist and win a Nobel Prize for solving the great mystery of consciousness. Notwithstanding, Francis Haskell and Michael Jaffé actively encouraged his interest in art history at Cambridge, and that fed into his subsequent stage and screen directing when – in lieu of comic Danny Kaye impersonations – he turned to imitating artworks in his *mise-en-scènes*.

Down the ages, the Apostles' have prized three things: maintaining a tireless spirit of enquiry; friendship, over and above patriotism if necessary; and candour which (even if it seems contrary to their clandestine nature) was fostered by the very confidentiality of their discussions.[48] Although this society was, at the end of the day, merely a debating club, it exerted an extraordinary long-term influence on many of its members. Its tenets became woven into their moral fibre, its ideals permanently lodged in their superegos.[49] Miller's conscience, in the years to come, would nag him regarding not only his limited capacity for friendship, but also his failure to make medical discoveries through constant inquisitiveness. By contrast, candour is a quality he has manifestly cultivated, taking it fearlessly into the public sphere and intensifying his forthrightness with age.

He additionally remembers a key hearth-rug debate centring on the Wilcoxes and the Schlegels, the characters in Forster's novel *Howards End*. The Wilcox family are essentially associated with business, with attaining money and worldly status. To use Kant's philosophical terminology, they live very much in the 'phenomenal' world. The Schlegels are able to pursue the life of the mind, contemplating the so-called 'real' (or 'noumenal') world of ideas.[50] The question being debated by the Apostles was 'Are we Schlegels or Wilcoxes?'

The majority of those present were young men who, being already well-to-do, saw themselves as Schlegels, able to permanently shun the Wilcoxes' moneymaking world. Miller had extra credibility as an 'intellectual aristocrat', being related to Henri Bergson and Proust. Today he says that he bears his shopkeeping ancestors in mind, and the pretentiousness of the discussion makes him shudder. 'It was easy', he remarks, 'to contemptuously claim that [we were Schlegels] when we had no need of Wilcoxian activities to keep the wolf from the door. We had inherited . . . and previous Apostles had never had the wolves even at the garden gate.'[51]

He continues, even so, to admire those of an august intellectual lineage, and he feels that he betrayed the Apostles' ethic when he slipped into the 'phenomenal' world of professional showbusiness.[52] Christopher Foster confirms that the brotherhood was extremely rarified and considered it rather deplorable to go after the bright lights. All the same, he observes:

> Jonathan may be flagellating himself . . . The feeling that we'd be looking down our noses at him is totally unjustified. It seems to me he has been an intensely intellectual producer-director . . . absolutely in the apostolic tradition . . . [even if] he once admitted that his motive was partly financial, which I thought was odd, a very unapostolic reason to give.

*   *   *

Miller had surely crossed the line into showbiz already with his *Under-Twenty Parade* radio stints and with, prior to Cambridge, an enthusiastic bid to appear on BBC TV. Filed away in the Corporation's labyrinthine archives is a letter penned during Miller's last term at school. In neat, still childish handwriting, on his parents' headed notepaper, it reads:

Dear Sir,

My friend Michael Bacharach and I wish to apply for a Television [sic] audition. We have broadcast already three times on Under Twenty Parade and in the final Under 20 review we received very favorable [sic] notice from Dilys Powell and Paul Dehn.

We specialise in parodies of Radio, films and theatre and also 'REAL LIFE.' We like to think we have an original slant and we would be grateful if an audition could be arranged.

yours sincerely,
J. W. Miller

p.s. I am six foot four which might render me unsuitable for small screen television, I could however bend down.[53]

A bureaucratic lady wrote back, saying auditions were confined to those 'likely to find an early place' in the programming.[54] More fool she.

At Cambridge, Miller's reputation as a comedian gained ground, starting from the bike sheds of St John's which were turned into a rough-and-ready theatre for the Poppy Day festivities of 1953 (a charity event). According to the *Cambridge Review*, the city was a carnivalesque riot in the ruthless grip of a good cause, with floats and stalls, tomato hurling and some poor lad rolling round the streets tied to a wheel. Miller was performing alongside Trevor Williams, his future room-mate, in the Johnian revue, wielding a huge aeroplane propellor. A press photograph records how he also managed to sustain a shoulder stand in the finale while booze was poured down his throat.[55]

The best thing about that day, from his perspective, was that it reunited him with Rachel. She was in town visiting Jane. 'When Rachel and I split up, I think she thought that I was rather awful,' he says sheepishly. 'But then we got together again and (I don't know why) I suddenly decided we were going to marry. We just became sort of inevitable.' By the spring of 1954, he had bought her a ring. She wore it on a chain around her neck because she was still at school.

Word of his comic talent, meanwhile, spread fast. Two Footlighters came headhunting on Poppy Day and 'discovered' Miller. They were Frederic Raphael and Brian Marber (who later became a BBC producer). Footlights' president Leslie Bricusse (today known for his hit musicals) bumped into Raphael who immediately eulogized about this fresher impersonating the BBC single-handed. 'So,' Bricusse exclaims, 'Jonathan came over to see us and "boom"!' The ensuing May Week Footlights revue, entitled *Out of the Blue*, was such a success that the whole cast turned semi-professional for the summer.

Along with Trevor Williams, who was also recruited on Poppy Day, Miller did his bit as a Footlights team player. He took a range of cameo roles, from a melancholic village idiot to an overgrown scout, from a gent with a penny-farthing bicycle to a begowned student in a sentimental musical number.[56] That sort of flannels 'n' boaters scene was not his bag. 'God, it was awful!' he comments. 'England was stuck in the 1930s until the 1960s, and those revues could have been done in 1925. The idea of dons and proctors as glamorous, I mean, for fuck's sake!'

He was happier in the skit 'Julius Caesar Goes West', mocking Hollywood's spate of Shakespeare movies.[57] Spinning a pistol as Big Bill Brutus, he told Raphael's Hopalong Cassius, 'Leave the talkin' to me': a line that would have reverberations in their less good-humoured relationship in later life. He appeared in drag as well, looking splendidly ridiculous as Elizabeth I. That was in a sketch entitled 'Glorious Heritage', indirectly alluding to the coronation of 1953 and Britain's new Elizabethan age. Sporting a period frock and dark glasses, his Good Queen Bess yawned with boredom when fawned upon by her court, and s/he bounced her orb like a basketball. Not exactly your Renaissance man or woman, patently just a bloke messing around, Miller contrived to rout Footlights' tradition of titillatingly effete cross-dressing.[58]

On top of that, he worked as an idiosyncratic solo turn.[59] His Beeb-style 'Radio Page' routine had, by now, expanded to include a preposterous bird impression-ist called Ludwig Kock (close to the actual BBC sound recordist and bird-lover Ludwig Koch), and a panel of critics making hideous animal noises as they discussed an exhibition of contemporary digestive biscuits.[60] Appended was a pastiche of the aged Bertrand Russell in anecdotal broadcasting mode, which surely owed something to the Apostles' humorous philosophizing. Miller once confessed that he partly wanted to be what he parodied, and this skit spoofed Russell's quavery Cambridge reminiscences with impish fastidiousness.[61] It ran thus:

One of the advantages of living in Great Court, Trinity, I seem to recall, was the fact that one could pop across, at any time of the day or night, and trap the then young G. E. Moore into a logical falsehood by means of a cunning semantic subterfuge. I recall one occasion with particular vividness. I had popped across and had knocked upon his door. 'Come in,' he said. I decided to wait awhile in order to test the validity of his proposition. 'Come in,' he said once again, a trifle testily I thought. 'Very well,' I replied, 'if that is in fact truly what you wish.' I opened the door accordingly and went in. And there was Moore seated by the fire with a basket upon his knee. 'Moore,' I said, 'have you any apples in that basket?' 'No,' he replied and smiled seraphically, as was his wont. I decided to try a different logical tack. 'Moore,' I said, 'do you then have *some* apples in that basket?' 'No,' he said once again. Now I was in a logical cleft stick, so to speak, and had but one way out. 'Moore,' I said, 'do you then have *apples* in that basket?' 'Yes,' he replied, and from that day forth we remained the very closest of friends.[62]

Although Miller never actually met Russell or Moore via the Apostles, both were apparently chuffed about this young man popularizing their esoteric subject.

Out of the Blue was applauded, by the national press, for its shafts of clever satire, and the production was such a hit at the Cambridge Arts Theatre and the Oxford Playhouse that Miller and co. found themselves catapulted into London's West End. Over the long vacation they played at the Phoenix Theatre, getting quite handsomely paid. They were invited to perform in cabaret slots at balls and to mingle at glitzy nightclubs near Harrods. Big-shot producers, including the powerful impresario Prince Littler, turned up to schmooze the rising stars, Bricusse got a firm foot in the professional door, and Raphael recorded a skit with him for the BBC. Yet it was Miller who drew the most media attention. In the *Evening Standard*, Milton Shulman proclaimed him the find of the evening, with shy charm and limbs-everywhere energy. He was said to be the complete comedian, supple of body and mind, both intellectual and surreally imaginative. The *Spectator* loved his bats-in-the-belfry fooling, infused with tragic melancholy, and he was variously likened to a salamander, a leaping ostrich, and a giraffe blessed with the gift of tongues (presumably again stammer-free). The *Express* reported that London was cheering him and shouting for more.[63]

One or two columnists muttered about an unmerited fuss but the powerful *Sunday Times* critic Harold Hobson filed a rhapsody, devoting most of his review to Miller. He identified a new species, 'a mimic the like of whom has never before been seen in the Charing Cross Road', and he went on to describe 'Down Under', the starlet's mockumentary about colonial industry:

> Nothing in nature is alien to him. One moment he is an explorer labouring up the Murray, at the next the waterfall that brings the exploration to a stop. Then astoundingly, he becomes Australia itself. He is the Thinker and the Thought . . . if the whole world is destroyed, but Mr. Miller preserved, it will be possible . . . to start the entire adventure over again, for Mr. Miller has blue-prints of the complete consort . . . animals and professors and inanimate nature . . . flow together in a vast incredible harmony of nature in his superbly funny philosophic fantasy.[64]

The newcomer was duly pursued by a jostle of agents, lunched by Paramount and offered a part in the West End hit entertainment *Cockles and Champagne*. He turned that down but was swiftly given slots on BBC TV's variety show *In Town Tonight* and the game show *Guess My Story*.[65] Picked up by a major agency, the Music Corporation of America, his Russell 'n' Moore sketch was recorded on vinyl and he performed it (amidst circus acts) for *Sunday Night at the London Palladium*, a hugely popular television programme on the newly established commercial channel, ITV.[66] The cartoonist Ronald Searle drew him prancing on tiptoe for *Punch*. The magazine *Illustrated* ran a double-page spread about Varsity's Danny Kaye, with shots of him pulling faces like a gallery of madhouse tics.[67] The noted photographer Jane Bown also took his picture: a far more poetic portrait with no attempt at funny business. In a moment of stillness, it captures the private Miller in monochrome soft greys. On the cusp between boy and man, he is looking straight into the lens, but with a fawn-like sensitivity about him.

His celebrity was to set a cultural wheel in motion which would run and run. He is now regarded as the forefather or Godfather of the Oxbridge comedy Mafia. The *Monty Python* team, the Goodies, Griff Rhys Jones, Stephen Fry, Hugh Laurie and many more followed his lead, going on to command top billing in British comedy over decades. Maybe the Russell 'n' Moore sketch even seeped into Tom Stoppard's subconscious, as high IQ comedy. After all, in his absurdist farce *Jumpers*, Stoppard's anti-hero is a philosopher teasingly named George Moore (with acrobats on the side).

Footlights' Brian Marber yelps that he was horribly envious during the summer of 1954; some believe Frederic Raphael really was irked; and all the adoration might have gone to Miller's head, for he was only nineteen. He publicly shrugged it off, however. Perhaps having well-known parents had imbued him with expectations of fame. Or did their serious-mindedness, combined with the Apostles' principles, mean he disliked the tag 'Jolly Miller'?[68]

In press interviews, he gave showbiz very short shrift, saying that he found repetitious stage performances hatefully tedious. 'I don't want to do it again ever,' he said, enthusing that his true love was medicine and that, every afternoon, he was busy dissecting a corpse in the basement of University College Hospital. 'They've given me a couple of legs and an abdomen. I'm happy there,' he assured the unnerved reporter from the *Sunday Express*.[69]

He had officially become engaged to Rachel one week before *Out of the Blue*'s London transfer. By going steady with her in the face of the West End social whirl, he was making his private life a bedrock. Of course, his adieux to the theatre – a profession which he likens to a seductive mistress – would turn into one of the longest goodbyes in stage history. He protests, somewhat excessively, that he was never interested in it; that he simply yielded to unsolicited invitations; that his revue phase was just juvenile prancing which he can barely remember; that he wasn't formally a member of Footlights anyway. Not surprisingly, some conclude that he is in denial or trying to redraft that part of his history.[70]

Nevertheless, his Cambridge friends confirm that he appeared unaffected at the time, in spite of being pointed out, like a local landmark, to college visitors and regarded as a university 'superstar' by contemporaries such as Bamber Gascoigne.[71] Trevor Williams, whose background was Baptist, stresses that his room-mate rarely talked of showbiz and was a trustworthy good bloke, 'a Puritan in the original sense of thinking it best for himself and others to lead a pure life and to avoid luxury, display and self-indulgence, which never seemed to tempt him'. Williams' only real complaint concerns the tomes left out for him when Miller sported his oak – i.e. locked the front door of their shared rooms – during Rachel's visits. 'I'd find my law books piled on the landing. I mean not a novel or anything!' Williams exclaims.[72]

Miller says he was, in the main, busy thinking about his next tutorial or paper for the Apostles, not the kind of 'glittering prizes' dangled by the entertainment industry. He sought to be favoured by Norwood Russell Hanson and to be part of an amusing social circle of Karl's sort, he states. On other occasions, he exuberantly launches into old Footlights monologues as if 1954 were yesterday, and he acknowledges more precisely:

> I suppose I was thrilled by the praise, being on the London stage, having a sort of intoxicating celebrity for a few weeks and . . . [at Cambridge] everyone had a vague idea that I'd become visible. Yes, that I knew, but it was just time out for me. It was a relief from dissecting, but there was never any temptation to leave the [medical] profession until *Beyond the Fringe*.

In his Finals, he disappointingly gained a 2:1 instead of a First because he 'diffused' himself too much. He places the blame on his extra intellectual pursuits, rather than any excessive larking around on the stage. After reading so widely, he says, it was impossible to scribble down all his points in the exams.

Even with his workload, his antics had extended to acting in the Marlowe Society's production of *Volpone*, Ben Jonson's black comedy, at the Cambridge Arts Theatre in his second year. He played the English nerd abroad, Sir Politick Would-Be, who finishes up under a giant turtle shell, hiding from taunting bullies. The *Cambridge Daily News* thought he outshone everybody in this smallish part, but *Granta* rebuked him for milking his gags.[73] *The Times* critic reported that Miller had the audience in stitches but was barely audible, breaking the Marlowe Society's rule of lucid verse-speaking.[74]

The director of *Volpone* was John Barton, later to be Peter Hall's right-hand man at the RSC and the presenter of BBC TV's master-class series *Playing Shakespeare*. Barton remembers this Sir Politick being hilarious, but waggling and darting around excessively. In the end, Miller had to be given a cricket bat as a prop, to root him to the spot.

He went on from *Volpone* to a centenary production at the ADC Theatre, for the university's Amateur Dramatic Club. Here he was cast as the warrant-obsessed lunatic, Troubleall, in *Bartholomew Fair*, Jonson's comedy about Puritans who like a bit of entertainment on the side.[75] Rushing around in extremely scant breeches, he shared the stage with John Bird, Daniel Massey, A. S. Byatt (then known as Toni Drabble) and Sylvia Plath who played Alice, the prostitute. He convulsed Byatt in the dressing-rooms with *Goon Show* imitations. Plath's diary entries – describing herself as 'going mad night after night being a screaming whore in a yellow dress' – indicate she was less of a gas.[76] Her characterization struck Miller as merely an incompetent cliché, 'this rather big, blonde girl standing with one hand on her hip in what she thought was a traditionally "whorish" posture'.

He scoffs that his own performance was utterly eighth-rate and he could never have become a proper actor, being unable to sustain a role for more than ten minutes. Ensemble acting was not his forte, nor had he heeded *The Times*' previous criticisms. The publication's reviewer, returning for *Bartholomew Fair*, laughed then huffed: 'Mr Jonathan Miller, miming brilliantly with lips, eyes and bare wiggling toes, spoils it all by giving . . . Troubleall a false voice which allows hardly a single word he utters to be understood.'[77] The *Cambridge Daily News* agreed he was appallingly slipshod, yet it couldn't resist a sort of panegyric. With cutting asides, it admitted that, in drumming lunatic cadenzas with his feet, he was an insanely funny natural comedian, a breed almost as rare as unicorns.[78] Those notices can now be categorized as early examples of British journalists being sharply ambivalent about Miller: simultaneously impressed and irritated by him.

Footlights' new May Week revue, *Between the Lines*, glided from Cambridge into the heart of London in the summer of 1955. Staged by Brian Marber, this one transferred to the Scala in Soho's Charlotte Street. Laurence Olivier had just played there, Prince Littler was now the students' producer, and Miller was along for the ride once more. He was still dismissing the smell of greasepaint, except, in one interview about fame, he confessed: 'I am frightened that you will soon come to need that acclaim, worry if you aren't recognized when you go out, want people to talk about you.'[79] A chink was appearing in his armour.

One of his *Between the Lines* monologues, called 'Our Island Heritage', provoked some outraged harrumphs. It anticipated the spirit of *Beyond the Fringe* in sending up Britishness. Specifically, it ragged national heroes, undermining their legendary status with a touch of mock biography. After marching about to 'Land of Hope and Glory', Miller portrayed Francis Drake responding to news of the approaching Armada with 'Tell them I'm in my hammock and a thousand miles away.' He followed that up with a faintly senile Winston Churchill impersonation, and a historical-fantastical account of the death of Nelson at Trafalgar. The ship's crew, he suggested, saw their commander keel over and initially assumed he was drunk.

Admiral Lord Nelson was only half the man he was. (*Falls, as if having one leg and one arm*) . . . [He was put] out of harm's way on the poop deck – where, being in his right sense and full possession of his faculties, naturally he was bored. (*Displays idle boredom – turns hat to Napoleonic position*) But what were his thoughts when first struck by that fateful musket ball? (*Sound effect of gunshot*) Hardy! And he falls stricken and is taken down between decks. Between decks? Now exactly where *is* between decks? A place so incredibly narrow that it is totally unsuited for the medical examination of admirals – so narrow that even doctors have to crawl to their patients on their bellies. (*Crawls along stage*) 'How are your bowels?' And there, lying between decks, Nelson says his dying words. But what *were* his dying words? There is some historical doubt about this. Some people say that Nelson said, 'Kiss me, Hardy', in which case a young cabin-boy would have been dispatched up on deck to fetch Captain Hardy – 'Admiral's compliments, sir, Captain Hardy, sir, says you're to come below and kiss him'. But perhaps it wasn't quite as easy as that. Hardy might not even have been on the flagship at the time – and would have been called across miles of stormy seas. 'Ahoy there! Do you have Captain Hardy aboard, there? Nelson's gone gaga – wants to kiss him!' When

Captain Hardy arrived, green and grumbling after a bilious trip in a long-boat – and in no condition to kiss anybody – the whole thing may have been a waste of time because some authorities say that Nelson never said 'Kiss me Hardy' in the first place, but 'Kismet, Hardy' – in which case you can imagine Nelson's surprise . . . (*Slumps against rostrum*) 'Kismet, Hardy . . . Hardy . . . get away from me, Hardy, I'm a sick man . . . Hardy . . . what do you think you're doing, Hardy? . . . Hardy . . . aaaaaaaaaahhhhhhhh!'[80]

Miller's humour now seems mild but the Suez Crisis of 1956 had not yet ravaged Britain's imperial pride and staunch conservatives were outraged by 'Our Island Heritage'. The *Daily Sketch* dished out marching orders, snapping: 'Jonathan Miller wants to be a chemist and not a theatrical cult. I back his judgement.'[81] Nevertheless, this skit was in tune with growing rumbles of political discontent. Queen Victoria's old empire was getting a battering abroad during the early 1950s, with anti-colonial uprisings and bloody chaos in Kenya, in Cyprus and in Cairo where rioters wrecked the British elite's Turf Club, destroying its historic paintings of Kitchener and other figureheads.

Almost everyone was tickled by Miller's other monologue, 'Culture'. Homing in on Arthurian legends, this envisaged the mystical, Excalibur-forging Lady of the Lake having to dash up for gulps of air, before diving back down to do a tad more on the hilt.[82]

Some critics loved the lanky redhead even more than they had the year before. They considered him both slicker and more startling in his leaps of thought, with curiouser and curiouser props (this time including a rhino's head). His imaginative world was said to be as 'self-contained as Lewis Carroll's'. The *Manchester Guardian* saw him as a comic colossus, and Bernard Levin went wild, classifying him as a 'genius' and 'a new star – nay, a planet'. Levin declared: 'If the Home Secretary cannot be persuaded to schedule him as a National Monument, then I am prepared to perjure Mr Miller off the [medical] register.'[83] The would-be doctor was, it seems, not curing but rather inspiring unrestrained hysteria, and the readiness of critics to gush in this era surely made him ill-prepared for the cooler reviews which he would receive in later years.

At the time, even Princess Margaret took off her dark glasses and decreed she simply must meet him. That connection was made through Rory McEwen who became Miller's close friend, being *Granta*'s art editor and a topical calypso singer in *Between the Lines*. Miller fondly remembers him as an elegant, Sebastian Flyte-like figure (as in *Brideshead Revisited*). McEwen came from a very grand Scottish family but sang Leadbelly songs – influencing Van Morrison among others.[84] He often escorted Princess Margaret round London and, when she came to see *Between the Lines*, he told Miller that she wanted him to join them afterwards, for dinner. Even though he claims to have been nervous about what courtesies were involved, Miller reportedly flew into a rage in the dressing-room because Rachel had not been invited. His fiancée did, in the end, attend that meal at the ironically named *Belle Manière* restaurant.

As a girl, the princess had been famously smitten by Danny Kaye, and she must have seen *Between the Lines* at least twice because Miller and McEwen featured in the gossip columns after they cheekily asked to leave a post-show party thrown by Margaret at Clarence House. They had to go and earn some pocket money in Sloane Square, being booked as the late-night act at the Royal Court Theatre's top-floor dining club. In response to this announcement, Margaret had everyone chauffeured there and watched the cabaret.[85] That was the making of the restaurateur Clement Freud's enterprise as customers rolled up in droves thereafter, all asking where HRH had sat. In his final year at Cambridge, Miller was again McEwen's companion of choice when Margaret and the Queen Mother dropped in for lunch at Trinity College.

On a more personal level, Miller's own mother would have appreciated how several jokes in *Between the Lines* were informed by her son's family life. His Lady of the Lake sketch specifically spoofed her subject, Tennyson, before flowing into an imitation of her old friend Isaiah Berlin pontificating about Wittgenstein.[86] Miller's chattiest monologue, later broadcast by the BBC and entitled 'Buld Knuk', was even more directly domestic, nattering obsessively about Swiss Cottage bus routes then suddenly mentioning his sister Sarah in a coda:

Oh, hang on, I've thought of something else to say.

Don't you think the ash on a cigarette looks like the grey Astrakhan hat of an Indian frontier tribesman. When I told my sister this she ran away and locked herself in the kitchen but she can't complain because once we were standing at the window at the back of the house looking out over the summer evening on St John's Wood; it was very quiet and suddenly my sister said 'BULD KNUK', just like that, not very loud; and I . . . stood my ground![87]

While not hilarious, this snapshot at the window is surprising. Whenever people recall the two of them together, Sarah tends to fade into the background with Miller very much to the fore. She gained a place at King Alfred's School in Highgate but then flunked academically, as an act of teenage rebellion against her intellectual family.[88] When she visited her brother in Cambridge, she exuded acute unhappiness – hardly speaking during a punting trip with his friends – and her later career path was relatively modest. She worked as a secretary for the playwrights' agent Peggy Ramsay and for the BBC. The sibling relationship did not grow any easier as she became increasingly religious, which was anathema to him.

During his college years, he appeared relatively happy regarding his parents, although behind the scenes some tensions remained. The West End earnings were especially welcome since Emanuel kept his son on a tight budget, either still dreading penury himself or else believing puritanical leanness to be character-building. On one occasion, when his son asked for some more trousers, he angrily riposted: 'What do you think you are, a bloody centipede?'

Rachel had been shocked when Miller contracted glandular fever in his first year and his father quite unnecessarily dispatched him to hospital, rather than personally tending to him. That said, Rachel and Emanuel always got on well. As for Betty, there was one classic moment at Queen's Grove when she guessed what Miller and Rachel were up to on the other side of his bedroom door. Uncertain whether she should be a permissively modern mother or not, she hovered on the landing politely enquiring if they would care for some tea. More generally, she made Rachel feel wary, having disliked previous girlfriends, yet she proved well disposed. As her daughter-in-law reflects:

> Jonathan had had these very happy days with his mother, this kind of love affair when they used to work in the dining-room: an intellectual flirtation, sharing a view on life, a kind of humour, batting off each other. I came in on that in my very early days . . . Was she possessive? No, I felt she probably would have liked to be and it must have been quite hard for her, but she very graciously handed him over.

When Rachel turned up in Cambridge, she was additionally appraised by Miller's circle. One of his apostolic set remembers hailing him in the street one evening and seeing he was with a diminutive schoolgirl:

> Jonathan was about six foot fifteen, so they seemed a very strange couple, very unalike. She seemed quite reticent, undemonstrative but observant, and probably quite purposeful. It must have been incredibly difficult for her, being younger and . . . surrounded by these dazzling, highly intellectual creatures. And, of course, everyone was asking, 'Is she up to him?' But she was always equitable and very composed and, once you got to know her, you realized none of those things were relevant or important at all.

· 5 ·

THE LATE FIFTIES

Marriage and UCH; qualified medic and collagist

'OUR DANNY KAYE TO WED', announced the *Daily Mail* on 27 July 1956. The student-doctor and Footlights star was tying the knot with Miss Rachel Collet that very day. It was just a month after Cambridge's farewell college balls, Rachel was 21 and Miller had reached 22 that week. Bringing the groom back to within a few hundred yards of his birthplace, they were married at Marylebone Town Hall. The guests were close friends and family, no glitz.

Rachel had briefly entertained the idea of a more ceremonial Jewish wedding. Unlike Miller, she had received no irksome religious instruction and she fleetingly wished to identify more with the Jewish side of her roots.[1] A rabbi, however, would have deemed the couple's prenuptial comportment less than impeccable. Rachel's Great-Aunt Brenda, therefore, laid on a wedding reception at her home instead.[2] Someone at the Town Hall presumably had a satiric sense of humour, the marriage ceremony being conducted in a room decorated with prints of *The Rake's Progress* by Hogarth.

Only one aspect of the day was not entirely happy. Emanuel objected to his son taking such a step before securing a professional post. In that era, the medical establishment was sternly possessive, expecting total commitment. It was all or nothing, so umbrage was taken at any trainee who dallied with outside interests, and acquiring a spouse was deemed almost as cavalier as flirting with the West End. Emanuel's own dedication to work was unbending on the appointed Friday. He did not go to Great-Aunt Brenda's house, saying he had patients to see.[3]

The couple's honeymoon trip then proved farcically unromantic, at least in terms of their destination. Miller failed to book anything until the day before, then he raced into a travel agent with the cry, 'Where can we go?' Both of them groan recalling the Bell Inn in the New Forest, right on a main road with a mini golf course.

Rachel further discovered that the man she had married could not abide holidays. 'I don't think he quite admitted that at the time: it would have been a bit rude. But he just can't bear wandering around homeless in that way,' she says. He has gone so far as to describe vacations as an agony of boredom and despair, scarily vacant. 'In fact the only thing that keeps me going through the gay ordeal,' he states, 'is the comforting mirage of home . . . with everything in its place and no sudden shocks.' Destroying even that pleasant image, he has anxious visions of floods and other natural disasters engulfing his abode during his absence.[4]

The Millers settled down much more contentedly after their honeymoon. They rented the basement flat at 68 Regent's Park Road: a house owned by two architects near Camden Town, on the graceful curve down from Primrose Hill. Rachel smoothly managed the household and its finances, even if money was fairly tight. They saved coins in a jam-jar for cinema trips.[5] Though Miller was not exactly a proto-New Man about the house, he showed willing, whizzing the carpet sweeper around after breakfast. He still makes the bed every day but, because of habitual incompetence, he is usually prevented from washing up or preparing coffee. Rachel once asked him to cook supper at Regent's Park Road, when she was studying for exams, only to hear such an atrocious din issuing from the kitchen that she decided, 'Never again!' It was not a divisive issue, however, as she liked being in charge in that quarter.

Since becoming officially conjoined, she and Miller have discovered additional curious intersections between their ancestors and their social circles. These multiple cross-lacings make him feel that their marriage was somehow all the more inevitable.[6] Rachel's best junior-school friend had been Judy Mikardo, Miller's first date. Before that, Rachel's mother had been treated by Emanuel, when suffering from youthful depression, and she had been expected to marry his bachelor flatmate, Jack Isaacs, at one point. Several generations further back, Rachel's family, the Salamans, had made their fortune selling ostrich feathers for fancy hatters, not so different from Abram Miller making bearskins. The Salamans then transformed – to use the Apostles' *Howards End* analogy – from Wilcoxes into non-commercial Schlegels.

Rachel's grandfather, Redcliffe Salaman, had trained as a pathologist at the London Hospital where his great friend was Emanuel's future mentor, Henry Head. Redcliffe contracted TB and retreated to his country house near Cambridge, becoming an author, plant-breeder and philanthropist.[7] He knew Emanuel as an undergraduate and part-funded his East London Child Guidance Clinic. Redcliffe's brother-in-law had been Charles Seligman, Great-Aunt Brenda's husband. He was the pathologist who accompanied Emanuel's Johnian tutor W. H. R. Rivers on his seminal anthropological expedition to the Torres Strait.

In 1956, Miller and Rachel's more obvious professional connection was that she, like him, was studying to be a doctor. He had persuaded her to shift her focus from modern languages. During his time at St John's, she converted into a scientist at a crammer. Then, realizing they would be apart for years if she took the Cambridge route, she started her training at London's Royal Free Hospital.

*   *   *

By the autumn, Miller was steaming ahead with his clinical apprenticeship at University College Hospital.[8] Here his progress was scheduled to follow the standard plan. After an introductory course, he would become (in the terminology of that time) a clerk or dresser, learning the ropes on various 'firms' (small teams) led by different medical consultants and surgeons. Having completed preliminary courses in specialisms such as obstetrics, gynaecology, psychiatry and skin diseases, he was to return to Cambridge in 1959 to sit his exams.

Assuming he passed, he would be a qualified doctor and spend a preregistration year at different hospitals, taking on more responsible house jobs. After that, a variety of senior house officer posts would have led, in the normal course of events, to the MRCP postgraduate diploma exams and membership of the Royal College of Physicians.

While at UCH, he became particularly preoccupied with what the nineteenth-century physiologist Claude Bernard called the body's *milieu intérieur*, its naturally tranquil homeostasis, its steady inner state.[9] That secure environment for life sounds curiously like Miller's new-found domestic stability, with everything in its place and no sudden shocks. He was walking the wards now as well, dealing directly with patients. This was an old-fashioned medical world, low on technology but kept spotlessly clean and warm: beeswaxed floors, junior nurses in striped dresses, ward sisters in crisp bonnets. 'It was like a nursery, with nanny, at around five o'clock in the evening,' he says – with nanny seemingly a positive presence in this instance.

On the ward rounds, he was taught how to examine a patient and take a history, using sequential questions that offered dichotomous, branching choices (as in taxonomy) to reach a diagnosis. He had a sharp eye for the minutiae of symptoms and found certain highly formalized techniques satisfying. He noted how these reflected the organs' near-heraldic arrangement (in quarterings), and how the set procedures (such as the inspection, palpation, percussion and auscultation of the chest) were 'almost like a form of prayer'.[10] He was deft, too, when it came to lumbar punctures and intravenous drips.

At the same time, his bedside manner was informal. He stresses that it was purely intellectual interest which led him into medicine. Sheer 'cold-hearted curiosity' had motivated him, not any humane urge to help others fight off the Grim Reaper, his great childhood fear. For all that, he had a naturally sociable streak and, never just an impersonal scientist, he found that being chatty could sometimes extract a patient's history as well as more systematic methods.

On duty, he had one close shave when he was inexperienced, failing to recognize an intestinal obstruction. Luckily, he was saved from disaster by a senior who spotted that he was in trouble. From then on, he was more vigilant. Dealing with incurable illnesses and injuries was, inevitably, a tough rite of passage. He found the death of children almost unbearable. Also, trainees had to attend autopsies where the pallid bodies, cut open, were disturbingly red as raw beef. These fresh corpses were quite different from the embalmed effigies in the dissecting room at Cambridge. Here the organs, he noted, were wet and vivid, like a windfall of rotten exotic fruit. A horrid mix of slaughterhouse and lavatory, the stench of the guts was so stomach-churning that he took up smoking, which became a lifelong and life-endangering habit.[11]

Seen from the hospital bedside, the moment of death itself struck him as a quiet anticlimax. Life slipped away in 'a whispering glissando', he says.[12] Witnessing how people were simply alive one moment and not the next, he felt mystified by the impenetrable gravity which they gained in that instant. He did not think of himself as prone to mortality at this stage in his life, seeing death as something that happened to 'this natural kind' called patients. Attending births was, unexpectedly, more alarming. Helping with domiciliary deliveries in slum bedrooms around Euston, he saw new life bursting joyously into the world. Yet it simultaneously seemed like some terrible emergency, as if he were a rescue worker in the Blitz, 'bringing out a body covered in blood, screaming – a bloody catastrophe'.

Back at the hospital, he was observing the institutional hierarchy with a mix of dutiful appreciation and satiric humour.[13] Elaborate rituals of deference were enacted, with everyone donning their starched white coats prior to the consultant's squirish visits. Ward rounds were notably theatrical. The consultant would perform for his comet's-tail of attendants and for the patients. The professional demeanour he adopted then percolated down, imitated by those looking to inherit the role.[14]

Miller was not a wildly anarchic jester in this context. Loose cannons would not survive the course, but he did chafe somewhat at the pompous proprieties and he was comically disruptive on occasion. One fellow trainee remembers him, in a viva, winding up a surgeon who was testing their knowledge of medical instruments. Declaring that his specialism was to be psychiatry, Miller cheekily suggested that a sigmoidoscope would be the most useful tool. This steel tube for examining the rectum would, presumably, be handy for identifying anal fixations (with a bonus hint of Sigmund).

Even if slightly maverick, Miller was as sharp as a tack and much liked by his UCH supervisors.[15] The agony aunt Claire Rayner was a young matron at the time and she clearly admired him, whether or not in a strictly professional vein. 'He was a red-headed gangly boy back then but' she confessed, 'I do remember thinking, "Gosh!"'[16] He himself stresses:

> I wasn't chafing at being a doctor and I certainly wasn't thinking, 'God, I'll be out of this in a couple of years and back on the stage where I really belong!' I fully intended to be a doctor, to do it as well as I possibly could, and to be very highly thought of.

His declared specialism in psychiatry was no mere joke. He spoke of that intention in several press interviews during his twenties, only with his emphasis shifting from mind damage to brain damage – that is to neuropsychology.[17] Some snobbish consultants still scorned psychiatry, calling the mentally ill 'the optional cabaret'.[18] However, the UCH neurologist William Gooddy introduced Miller to engrossing anomalies such as phantom limbs and unilateral neglect (when the patient is unaware of one side of their body). This drew him to concentrate on how the brain works, applying his own grey matter to the study of others' malfunctions. He was to focus on high-level cognitive defects: agnosia (failures of recognition), aphasia (the dissolution of language), and apraxia (the inability to do things).

He had no problem accomplishing his first task. He became a qualified doctor, as planned, in 1959.

⋆   ⋆   ⋆

Neither medicine nor married life stopped Miller pursuing numerous extracurricular activities.[19] He had swiftly crossed the road from the hospital to join in University College's philosophy classes, run by A. J. (Freddie) Ayer, Stuart Hampshire and Richard Wollheim. This was when he first read and became an ardent admirer of J. L. Austin's essays, starting with 'A Plea for Excuses' and 'Pretending', which would later inform his stage directing.[20] Wollheim was interested in art and vision (in the sense of how we see). So he furthered the young medic's understanding of art history, linking it in with retinal physiology and neurology. Miller was especially intrigued by Ernst Gombrich's 'either/or' argument and Wollheim's contrasting 'both–and' thesis (i.e. that the viewer appreciates both a painting's brushstrokes and what is depicted). He would reference their theories in his own subsequent writing on the visual arts. Over the next few years, he also became friends with Wollheim, hanging out with him in Soho.[21]

Within University College Hospital, Miller founded the mind-broadening Thomas Browne Society. The TBS set out to discuss art, literature, politics and philosophy, with papers being read and with guest speakers. In other words, it was something like the Chesterton, St Paul's Literary Society and the Apostles.[22] He announced its birth in UCH's in-house magazine, calling for an enlightened spirit of arts–science co-operation, another kind of 'both–and' creed. His finger was on the pulse, picking up on worries about the arts *v.* sciences schism, aka the Two Cultures, before the chemist and novelist C. P. Snow's 1959 Rede Lecture really popularized the issue.[23]

He started working as a professional journalist in 1958 too, spurred on by the fact that the Cambridge prodigy Mark Boxer had become a hotshot art editor, stylishly rejuvenating *Queen* magazine (subsequently *Harper's and Queen*). His own most direct contact within the growing media industry was Karl Miller, who was now Rachel's brother-in-law, having married Jane. Back from an academic stint in the USA, Karl was appointed literary editor at the *Spectator* which had its offices near UCH. Consequently, the hospital trainee was soon writing pieces for him, reviewing medical and zoological books.[24] He contributed to the *New Statesman* as well, when Karl moved there.

As Karl recalls, the 'awful old economist' Thomas Balogh, adviser to the Labour Party, caught sight of them both at the *New Statesman* and damningly called them teddy boys. 'I was doing my best to wear a suit, but it didn't fool Balogh,' muses Karl, 'and Jonathan was dressed in his *dégagé* style, no doubt still wearing his duffle. In any case, that didn't stop Jonathan writing quite a lot for both publications.'

Miller had to apologize in print for one or two careless errors in his early articles, yet he exuded assurance as a cultural arbiter.[25] He notably applauded more than one popular scientist, a role he himself would assume two decades later when presenting *The Body in Question* on BBC TV. He additionally dabbled in amateur editing in 1957–8, briefly taking charge of the *UCH Magazine*. As head of both the Thomas Browne Society and this publication, he was now beginning to play the gang leader, rather than being just a gang member.

Again tackling the Two Cultures issue, he waxed almost rhetorically militant in his first editorial for the *UCH Magazine*, declaring:

> Potentially we are all sitting on a time bomb . . . no effort is made to integrate the young [narrowly specialized] scientist into Society . . . He becomes a passive tool in the hands of the politicians . . . only a stone's throw from a Huxleyan set up, with technical zombies . . . the magazine has a different function to serve.
>
> We must somehow avoid becoming the moral counterparts of those strange patients with parietal lobe lesions, who neglect one side of their body.[26]

In the next edition, he added that the Renaissance ideal of the 'Compleat Man', capering around the academic landscape chubby with omniscience, was no longer feasible. Instead, another breed of go-between was urgently needed, 'to maintain broad channels of communication between the specialities . . . inciting border incidents . . . making sure that the right hands know what the left hands are doing'.[27]

He himself was, naturally, a prime candidate for such boundary skirmishes.[28] His 'Table Talk' column in the *UCH Magazine* was a patchwork of diverse topics, ranging from the American medical syllabus to endangered Nash terraces in Regent's Park. Jazz reviews appeared alongside notes on a film showing patients' neurologically disordered gaits.[29] He penned serious book critiques on the one hand, and ludicrous reports from fictional correspondents on the other. Among those fantasy articles, one concerned a sun-deflecting mirror being carried across the park and causing picnickers to panic about Martian death-rays. Another announced a cod-cure for arthritis (basically breathing). Miller also admits that the following letter was his own concoction: 'DEAR SIR, You can perhaps imagine my surprise the other day on finding that birds do not have to purse their bills at all, in order to whistle . . . Yours T. Y. Freep'.[30]

In a quieter literary vein, he wrote a fine, lightly satirical short story entitled 'A Brief Exposure'. Therein a camera-carrying, expansive American tourist converses with a vicar, thus breaking the silence in a British train compartment: two more disjunct cultures finding common ground.[31] Miller contributed a further miscellany, called 'From a Notebook: Materia Medica'. This contained fragmentary jottings for a hospital novel that he hoped to write but was never completed (unlike the medical/literary works of Oliver Sacks). In 'Materia Medica', he recorded:

> This afternoon I passed the cubicle of a man who will shortly be dead, and found him rehearsing. He was lying on his back, quite still, with the sheet pulled taut over his head, giving him the chilling profile of a covered corpse. As I paused, he lowered the sheet from his face and through the glass gave me a sheepish, hopeless shrug.
>
> In our ward there is an alcove with five or six beds devoted to patients receiving radiotherapy . . . Sometimes at night . . . these men come under some curious euphoric effect of the drugs they are having and lurch cheerily from their beds, to wander, wakeful and bawdy round the darkened ward. Their hospital night-gowns, their cerements, hardly conceal the wasted calves, the dancing ankles, waltzing facetiously off the mortal coil.[32]

Miller additionally introduced stylish front covers to the *UCH Magazine*.[33] These were inspired by Russian constructivism, by Mark Boxer's taste, and by a new friend. An informal collective of architects would gather upstairs at 68 Regent's Park Road on Sundays, and the Millers were invited. One other regular participant was Germano Facetti, the graphic designer who was to make England's image highly fashionable as the art director for Penguin Books.[34] He designed many covers using collage. Miller fondly recalls how Facetti taught him about typography, trained his eye and encouraged him to keep clippings of pictures and other paper ephemera, all stashed in a shoe box. Besides being fashionable in the mid-Fifties, collage has much in common with pastiche, the comic technique used in Miller's earlier spoofs of radio programming. It is not surprising he took to it.[35]

A few years later the apprentice artist got his fingers burnt when – in a little-known addition to his CV – he designed a psychedelic book jacket for Cape, where Rachel's sister, Jane, worked. It was for the publishing house's first edition of *The Kandy-Kolored Tangerine-Flake Streamline Baby* by Tom Wolfe.[36] Having merrily plundered the shoe box, Miller found himself accused of plagiarism by an extremely riled Bridget Riley. With no thought for copyright laws, he had used a slice from one of her Op Art paintings to form the entire cover, bar the lettering. 'I don't believe Bridget Riley sued me in the end but she was', he admits, 'very indignant. Quite rightly. It was probably the last thing she wanted to think of herself as: a contributor to paper ephemera.'[37] His pleasure in creating collages was, in spite of this scare, not extinguished. It would revive in later years.

*   *   *

Miller had not quite kicked the light entertainment habit either. Joining the UCH medics' revue team, the Fallopians, he appeared in several of their shows.

Furthermore, he mutated into a director at University College, five years before his professional Royal Court Theatre debut. In 1957, he took the Foundation Play slot but, instead of a straight drama, staged *Forks and Hopes* (lifting that title from Lewis Carroll's nonsense poem 'The Hunting of the Snark'). The evening was billed as a 'wildly arbitrary' selection of prose, verse, comic sketches and songs – another variegated form of collage.[38]

Moonlighting as a star comic kept earning him extra money too. He and Rory McEwen from Footlights continued to work as a cabaret duo at debutante balls. He would swot at home until 10 o'clock then fling himself on his bike, pedalling to the Dorchester to entertain 'these flamboyant pink creatures', as he describes them. Their paters always got in a flap, unsure whether such classy comedians should be served refreshments with the band or be ushered to the top table. Miller was back with the BBC as well. During his time at UCH, he was performing various radio sketches on *Saturday Night on the Light* and *Monday Night at Home*, and he was appearing on TV. He was on the Corporation's major new magazine programme *Tonight* from its very first broadcast in 1957, making him one of the show's founder members.[39]

The script of one of his rambling, yarn-spinning routines survives, entitled 'The Pied Piper of Hampstead'. It runs thus, as transcribed (with occasionally dodgy punctuation) in the *UCH Magazine*:

When a rat made its third appearance at the back window I decided to contact the Authorities only to receive a heavy municipal rebuke for my frivolous delay in reporting the matter.

'You may have only *seen* one, sir' said the voice reproachfully 'but that *one* may just be the *top* of the iceberg. I shall send round rodent control at once' and he rang off. I was prepared for an almost instantaneous wail of sirens as a fleet of powerful sedans screeched to the gate; a fusillade of car doors and the disembarkation of a tight knot of helmeted marines, carrying bazookas and flame throwers . . .

Two hours later, there came a heavy respectful knock at the door. A rustic figure stood on the step with trousers of ancient tweeds [sic] tucked into the tops of his wellingtons. Through the garden gate his sturdy bike stood propped at the kerb.

'I'm Rodent Control sir' he said and doffed his hat (Could those *really* have been salmon flies in the brim?) . . . He wandered absently about the garden . . .

'What are you going to do?' I asked dubiously. He glanced swiftly up at the eaves and then slowly, as if deliberating, he said.

'I reckon I'll poison 'im.'

'What? Now?' I said eagerly, envisaging a scene of Borgiaesque ferocity. 'Not likely' he smiled sagely. 'You've got to get a rat's confidence. I gives 'im som'at nice to eat first, and *then* I poisons 'im. What I does is, I feeds 'im up Monday, Tuesday, Wednesday, Thursday – kill 'im on Friday. Smashin'!' He opened his knapsack and took out a bag of the smallest sandwiches I had seen in my life . . . 'They're right' I thought. 'The British *are* mad. We're the only people in the world who really think that rabbits live in wall-papered rooms, ironing their suits and eating porridge.' I had grown to accept this as a nursery tradition but now I realised that Beatrix Potter also provided a blue-print [sic] for pest control . . .

For the next few days he came regularly before eight . . . The sandwiches must have been made by his wife, a pert nimble-fingered little woman, who would have been bustling about in the kitchen while he shaved. 'Elfred!' she would call up the stairs. 'Breakfast's ready and I've left Rat's lunch on the fridge; I've given 'im two cucumbers and a cream cheese' . . . Friday drew near. I tried to visualise the climax of the drama . . . the rat would appear, walking on his hind legs, clutching his throat with one hand, a half eaten sandwich in the other. He would stagger forward a few paces, glance upwards with reproachful forgiveness, mutter 'Et tu Brute' and pitch forward on his face with a thin tell-tale trickle of blood oozing from the corner of his mouth.

Friday was a clear bright day and Rodent Control arrived at his usual time. I went upstairs to take a bath before breakfast. Lying in the hot water I was suddenly surprised to hear his voice echoing up the waste pipe . . . At the end of this crazy week I couldn't be sure that there were not occasional falsetto replies. The possibility of this being a sort of farewell dialogue, in the style of the last days of Socrates, no longer seemed absurd . . . It was tea-time when my attention was drawn to his strange behaviour, out there, at the end of the garden. In the middle of a whimsical wisp of forsythia, Rodent Control was rolling about on the ground, a convulsing heap of tweed . . . if this was some strange form of lure, it became apparent after a while that it held no fascination for rats . . .

I decided to probe the situation. When I got to the bottom of the garden Rodent Control was lying on his back in the rich loam of the flower bed, breathing stertorously.

'Everything going O.K.?' I asked with breezy nonchalance. 'Terrible!' I heard him moan weakly. ''orrible gripes.' He rose shakily to his knees and glanced balefully at his tin of sandwiches which stood open on the garden bench, clutched at his throat and pitched forward on his face, a thin tell-tale trickle of blood oozing from the corner of his mouth.

That evening a rat appeared at the back window and although half-light I could have sworn he wore a smile.[40]

Another BBC piece was 'The Biting of the Generals', a mock Richard Dimbleby commentary on a royal ceremony, featuring a raving mad General Wolfe and an equally barking George III. Miller can still recite this, splendidly sending up Dimbleby's *sotto voce* deference.

There, on the far side, I can see the diminutive figure of General Wolfe himself, his teeth gleaming in the evening sun. And, oh look!, he is cleaning his teeth. What a magnificent gesture! And now he is coming up to the line of the generals . . . We are going down to the parade ground to hear at close quarters . . . '

(*Snarling, ripping sounds followed by 'Thank you, Sir!', repeated down the line.*)[41]

Miller's auditions for *Tonight* were always informal. The producer Donald Baverstock would roll up in person at Miller's flat to listen to his latest sketch. Having declared it very funny, he would add that he was still awfully worried about whether 'the man from Wigan' would be amused. A note sent to Regent's Park Road from the BBC in February 1957 shows that it was, however, Miller who became hesitant about committing himself when the senior executive Grace Wyndham Goldie was urging him to sign a contract. A second letter was dispatched that month to keep him on board, apologizing for *Tonight*'s hair-raising first transmission.[42] During that programme, a sign reading 'STOP QUICK' had been frantically waved under his nose while he was in mid-flow, with the cameras rolling and an audience of several million.

Miller was, in any case, not in Goldie's good books for long. That spring he blithely reprised his 'Death of Lord Nelson' routine for the show, only to find himself in deep water because this was the very night when the BBC was commemorating the 1949 Yangtze River battle, where Britain's Lieutenant Commander Skinner was fatally wounded aboard his ship. That was very bad timing. As Miller affirms, he was 'sacked' for inappropriate irreverence. Baverstock's assistant wrote to him afterwards:

I am afraid I really don't know what Donald wants you to do . . . Grace sent us an irate memo saying that the whole thing was in deplorable taste (seeing that there were so many stony-faced sailors present that night, although their wives, at least, were laughing happily away in the viewing room) and that the whole thing – you – would have to be reviewed.[43]

Alasdair Milne (a *Tonight* producer before becoming director-general) admits that the young performer's lack of studio discipline had not helped. In his enthusiasm, Miller had lurched past the cameras and disappeared from view altogether during the show, but that was a purely technical faux pas. Baverstock and Milne almost mutinied in Goldie's office, questioning her moral condemnation of the sketch until, allegedly, she yelled about underlings shutting up and obeying.[44]

*   *   *

The ruckus over Nelson, in fact, gave Miller kudos with the liberal spirits who were gathering as the Sixties came speeding into view. He was increasingly invited to soirées by the radical-chic theatre reviewer Kenneth Tynan. Heaving with famous names, these Mayfair parties in Mount Street involved Princess Margaret behaving badly (after her enforced split from the divorcé Peter Townsend), and Tynan's wife being so drunk that, once, her dress just fell off.[45]

Less enjoyably, Tynan insisted on addressing Rachel as 'Mrs Miller' in a dry tone, and her husband hated being corralled into the impromptu cabarets. He felt exploited, insufficiently funny and not snazzy enough, especially when he had to head home early as a hardworking medic. Describing the critic as a celebrity hound who 'used people like costume jewellery', he is dismissive of Tynan's later *Oh! Calcutta!* proposal: namely, that Miller should have directed that show because they were 'like-minded'. *Oh! Calcutta!* was the avant-garde and erotically outré revue which Tynan conceived and partly scripted.

They were not cut from identical cloth. Ken himself, on occasion, teasingly classified Miller as a serious Cantabrigian 'Roundhead', at odds with his own Oxford-educated 'Cavalier' frivolity, but they became good friends, for all that. They did have a considerable amount in common, being high-profile inhibition busters, and Miller readily admits that he loved the celebrity hound's 'astrakhan vulgarity'.[46] He found himself craving the attention and affection of this flattering, excitingly effervescent man. In spite of professional tensions, their camaraderie was to last until Tynan's death in 1980.[47]

Meanwhile, the double life that Miller was enjoying in his mid-twenties as a 'both–and' personality – both a doctor and a celebrity associated with the arts – was epitomized in a letter he sent to Oliver Sacks, who had a hospital post in Birmingham by this point. The epistle describes an afternoon spent socializing with Colin MacInnes, the acclaimed novelist who wrote about post-war London's youth, its black immigrants and race relations in *City of Spades* (1957) and *Absolute Beginners* (1959). Miller's account runs as follows (with some uncorrected typos):

Dear Ol,

Just a note to tell you that I have been appointed H.P. [house physician] to the Neurological Dept at the Central Middx [the Central Middlesex Hospital in Harrow, north-west London] . . . how damnable your not having applied for your surgical job here . . . I may hitch up to Bmngm for a day . . .

Rachel and I spent a curious Sunday down in the East end with Colin McInnes [sic] who has established a beatnik hideaway . . . a huge single room which is furnished with studied sparseness . . . The man himself is a tall, dysentery ravished queen (I think) with curious obsessional habits like the quarter hourly lubricating of finger tips with a handy tin of Nivea cream. He is a paragon of evil temper and makes no concession to guests in this matter . . . [We] spent a nerve racking afternoon . . . timidly listened to his specialist collection of Jazz, frightened to ask him anything in case it touched some raw surface and sent him off into a homicidal mania. The room was on about the fifth floor and no-one would have heard our screams as a well known writer went to it with pistol and cleaver.

He conducted us morosely around the environs showing us the markets, the Jews and the ambiance, grinding his teeth from time to time at our inane cries of untutored appreciation . . .

I have been reading omnivorously; Wigan pier, Anna Karenin [sic], Arrowsmith, a history of America . . . a huge volume devoted exclusively to the Central Nervous System. I am going to look at [that] tomorrow and I'll let you know something about it later . . . let's see you sometime soon. I hope that the job is not getting on top of you.

yrs
Jonathan[48]

By May 1960, Miller had completed his own first house job, with the professorial unit of surgery at UCH and had arrived at the Central Middlesex with hopes of specializing in neurology.[49] All that was, however, suddenly put on hold, because he was summoned to fulfil his National Service obligations. He wrote again to Sacks, sardonically alluding to the plea for mercy in *The Merchant of Venice*:

It appears that the Kafka organisation at the central medical recruitment office will be considering our cases on the same day. I hope to actually present myself at the hearing and act Portia for myself. If they reject my claim I shall then be able to burst back into the room, run along the table top and urinate on their grey old heads crying 'I am an unstable Jewish enuretic'. Another slogan I had considered went 'I am a Jewish person with unpalatable sexual interests in flogging; enlist me at your peril' . . . anyway at the moment I creep into bed at night and grind my teeth in anticipation of the rough and unsymapthetic [sic] handling by the fuckers at Tavistock Sq.[50]

He escaped by the skin of his teeth. He underwent his military medical check-up (being marched into a WC with running taps when he struggled to provide a urine sample). He was duly told that he had passed muster. Then, just in the nick of time, the government terminated National Service.

· 6 ·

THE START OF THE SIXTIES

Beyond the Fringe; The Establishment; the Royal Court Theatre

WHAT MILLER HAD NOT FORESEEN was a different kind of hidden enemy, about to blow his plans sky high. He has never been able to resist an invitation to 'come out and play', as he puts it. That being the case, he succumbed to the beckoning finger of comedy when it materialized in the casualty department at University College Hospital, shortly before he transferred to the Central Middlesex. In an off-duty moment, the young doctor agreed to see a man called John Bassett who was assistant to Robert Ponsonby, the artistic director of the Edinburgh International Festival.[1] Ponsonby's lofty programming of classical music and drama was being rivalled by the unofficial and more fun Edinburgh Festival Fringe, so he had decided to beat his competitors at their own game by commissioning a late-night Oxbridge revue. This show was to be called *Beyond the Fringe*.

Having studied at Oxford, Bassett already knew Alan Bennett and Dudley Moore from there. Bennett was a witty postgraduate historian who had been in an Edinburgh Fringe revue the previous summer.[2] A former organ scholar, Moore was a fast-rising jazz pianist, a theatre composer and natural comic actor.[3] When invited to be the third man, Miller recommended Footlights' new prodigy, Peter Cook, as the fourth. Though still an undergraduate, Cook was already a professional, penning sketches for the West End revue *Pieces of Eight* (co-written by the young Harold Pinter and starring Kenneth Williams).[4]

On a return visit to Cambridge, Miller had seen Cook performing (trying out the cranky persona E. L. Wisty) and he had been electrified by this weird, glazed, handsome figure producing comedy 'at right angles' to everything that had gone before.[5] At a party afterwards, Miller had eagerly informed the younger man that his routine perfectly reproduced the speech patterns of schizophrenics.

Cook had not welcomed that comparison, apparently forgetting that Wisty was based on a mentally wayward butler at his public school, Radley.[6] Nonetheless, he had the sense to realize that *Beyond the Fringe* could be a winner. He duly ignored his London agent, Donald Langdon, who assumed that appearing with three amateurs in Scotland would be a thorough waste of time. Langdon's misjudgement, akin to Decca's Dick Rowe rejecting the Beatles, was to make him a laughing stock for years. That said, the joke was briefly on Cook when Langdon negotiated his client's Edinburgh wage up from £100 to £110, then pocketed an £11 commission fee.

Langdon was not the sole sceptic either. When the foursome first met up in January 1960 for a lunch with Bassett, everyone was in two minds, except Cook. They gathered at an Italian restaurant near UCH so that Miller, the medic with comedic leanings, could hasten back to his ward rounds.[7] Bennett, the academic/comic, was suffering guilty pangs about sidelining his thesis on Richard II's retinue, and he felt he was there 'under false pretences' – a feeling which, he says, never really left him.

At the outset, the conversation was tentative and latently competitive. Miller was wary of cracking a joke in case it did not raise a laugh, and various social gulfs lay under the surface. Bennett and Moore came from working-class families while Miller and Cook (an urbane diplomat's son, expected to follow in his father's footsteps) were patently upper-middle class. The Yorkshire-born Bennett remained almost mute – only venting a few nervous cries of 'Oh dear me!' – and Moore, at only 5'2", felt small, figuratively and literally.[8] The others were all a foot or more taller than he was.[9]

Competitiveness was to remain corrosively in the mix. Miller has even suggested that they 'instantly disliked each other' but all 'decided that it might be a profitable enterprise', like a cynically manufactured boy band.[10] He discussed the project in markedly pragmatic terms that day. Was his motivation really as Wilcoxian as he makes out, though? He affectionately remembers how Moore broke the ice, doing a Groucho Marx scuttle in and out of the kitchen's swing doors, chasing after attractive waitresses. For all the personal tensions, the four of them were, at points, if not often, going to enjoy themselves in one another's company.

By the time coffee was served, they had agreed to do the show, and Ponsonby saw that they were sparking off one another brilliantly when they met him a few days later.[11] He gave them carte blanche to send up anything they liked. As he later affirmed: 'I always had a naughty corner in my mind.' Thereafter, whenever Miller was on call at the Central Middlesex and thus half-free, the other three would go to meet him there. Sitting in the young doctor's tiny staff bedroom, they began bouncing ideas around and improvising *Beyond the Fringe* into existence: a quirky kind of hospital birth.

Miller was writing two scripts at this time in quite different modes, like Dr Jekyll with a dangerously funny doppelgänger. On the one hand, with Cook and co., he was drafting sketches destined to become applauded classics, not least the mock-heroic World War 2 spoof 'Aftermyth of War'.

PETER: Perkins! Sorry to drag you away from the fun, old boy. War's not going very well, you know.

JON: Oh my God!

PETER: We are two down, and the ball's in the enemy court. War is a psychological thing, Perkins, rather like a game of football. You know how in a game of football ten men often play better than eleven – ?

JON: Yes, sir.

PETER: Perkins, we are asking you to be that man. I want you to lay down your life, Perkins. We need a futile gesture at this stage. It will raise the whole tone of the war. Get up in a crate, Perkins, pop over to Bremen, take a shufti, don't come back. Goodbye, Perkins. God, I wish I was going too.

JON: Goodbye, sir – or is it – *au revoir*?

PETER: *No*, Perkins.[12]

On the other hand, Miller had teamed up with his registrar, A. D. M. Smith, to co-author his first paper for the *Lancet*, appealing to a decidedly specialist audience with the title 'Treatment of Inorganic Mercury Poisoning with N-Acetyl-D L-Penicillamine'.[13] Although this was not a bundle of laughs, a distinct trace of Milleresque humour can be detected in the description of how their patient – a case of Hatter's Shakes – had uncontrollably broken his wife's best china.[14] One Central Middlesex colleague further recalls how Miller enhanced his hospital presentation with unconventional artistry. He made a film of the man with the shakes standing in the dark, holding a lit taper.[15]

Partly because of his busy schedule (not to mention Cook being commissioned to script another Kenneth Williams revue), *Beyond the Fringe* was not shipshape when the quartet set off for Edinburgh in mid-August 1960. Individually, they had monologues and choice bits of old material, but their collective skits were sketchy to say the least. Bennett had felt incompetent when it came to improvising en masse. The future playwright preferred to craft his words scrupulously. Cook was much more productive but had initially balked at Miller and Bennett's satirical audaciousness, wanting to create an unproblematic commercial hit. Moore had protested even more, anxiously imagining they would all be arrested. His timidity and his suggestions were, he stated later, treated with thinly disguised scorn by the others. He felt crushed and intimidated by the verbal pyrotechnics of the two Cambridge boys.[16] Even Miller admits that he was 'enormously impressed and frightened' by Cook's extraordinary fluency and gift for doing routines non-stop.

*　　*　　*

When it came to the crunch at the International Festival, the foursome had just seven days in which to whip the show into shape after arriving in the Scottish capital. As Bassett recollects:

> They all got there on the Monday and hadn't a clue as to what they were going to do. There was no shape, no running order, nothing. The critic Alan Brien, who was writing a piece about the show, came in on the Thursday and was astounded and appalled that they were going to open the following Monday and were still fooling around and saying, 'It'll be all right on the night.' But there is no doubt that Jonathan brought order out of the chaos and if he hadn't, I dare say, it wouldn't have been the success it was. I think they all agree that Peter wrote the most material or came up with the most ideas for sketches, but it was very marked that Jonathan automatically became and was accepted as the director.

The run-through that Ponsonby saw, just before the show opened at the Lyceum, was a shambles. As he watched the foursome fluffing their lines and collapsing in hysterics, he pictured the Festival's formidable board members tearing him to shreds. Yet miraculously, on the night, *Beyond the Fringe* was more than all right. The *Daily Mail*'s young reporter Peter Lewis started the stampede for tickets with his review:

> Behind this unpromising title lies what I believe can be described as the funniest, most intelligent, and most original revue to be staged in Britain in a very long time.
>
> It is the creation of four, mobile, deadpan young men . . . [who] take the stage for 90 minutes with grey sweaters, four chairs, and a piano, and proceed to demolish all that is sacred in the British way of life with glorious and expert precision.
>
> Disregarding all the jaded trimmings of conventional sketches, production numbers, dancing, and girls, they get down to the real business of intimate revue, which is satire and parody . . .
>
> If the show comes to London I doubt if revue will ever be the same again.[17]

The show's almost bare, low-budget set functioned as a great foil, as well as making this revue look trendily minimalist (in line with the spartan aesthetics of Brecht, Samuel Beckett and Brutalist architecture).[18] By offering no distractions, it concentrated all the attention on the cast's physical comedy and linguistic flair.

Their satiric portraits formed a national gallery of fools and bigots, exposed different cross-sections of British society, and cleverly magnified each type's flaws in a way that seemed at once accurate and grotesque. They boldly caricatured floundering ministers of Church and State, reactionaries and racists, dodgy top-level scientists, crass film producers, pedantic philosophers and mindless royalists.[19] Especially startling was the show's direct parodying of Harold

Macmillan, by Cook.[20] Naming and aping the complacent, old Conservative prime minister took *Beyond the Fringe* beyond the existing bounds of British comedy.

It had, ironically, been Macmillan who coined the phrase 'the wind of change' as 1960 dawned, trying to sound as if he were moving with the times. English society, under his government, was still far from liberated. Beckett's play *Endgame*, for instance, was refused a licence in 1958, being deemed blasphemous, and a British Medical Association booklet on marriage was prudishly withdrawn in 1959 as well, merely for discussing whether chastity was outmoded. The rules were, nonetheless, mutating under pressure. The state ban on *Lady Chatterley's Lover* was being fiercely contested in the courts and, just a few months after *Beyond the Fringe* opened, that restraint would finally be lifted.[21]

The Lord Chamberlain, who vetted all scripts, quite possibly decided to be more flexible than of yore, sensing that the said wind of change might soon blow his house down. He cast aside his notorious blue pencil almost entirely when vetting *Beyond the Fringe*. It may have helped that his Lordship was tickled by Miller, who visited him personally. Ultimately, he censored only one sketch, called 'Bollard', in which Cook, Miller and Moore played camp luvvies attempting to act macho during the filming of a cigarette advert. Even there he merely objected to the terms of endearment 'love' and 'darlings' in the dialogue, presumably deeming this flagrantly homosexual.[22] In spite of the Wolfenden Report of 1957 recommending decriminalization, homosexual acts remained illegal until 1967. To get round the censor in 'Bollard', Moore pertly cried 'Hello, men!' instead, and in another vignette, entitled 'Frank Speaking', he actually portrayed a preposterous Lord Chamberlain, exclaiming: 'I don't want to see lust and rape, incest and sodomy [on the stage] – I can get all that at home.'[23]

In Edinburgh, word spread like wildfire about this new revue subverting sacred cows, blitzing the status quo. The city's *Evening News* proclaimed it to be the Festival's hottest show and started printing highlights from the script.[24] After a thinly attended first night, queues formed round the block and each performance was crammed to 140 per cent capacity with feverishly applauding spectators, some jumping on their seats and hurling their coats in the air.[25]

Miller and Cook continued to improvise and make each other corpse with laughter, yet they won all the more fans with their informality. Bennett believes *Beyond the Fringe* was daring and intimate in a new way because, as he says, 'We dealt with things that young people made jokes about in private but never publicly.'[26] It was as if the Fringers – as they came to be known – were almost literally at home onstage, or the theatre was some Oxbridge Junior Common Room suddenly open to all. This made the audience feel simultaneously at ease, privileged and mentally stimulated. The lack of professionalism generated moments of utterly unplanned hilarity as well, not least when Moore was meant to be playing the National Anthem in the opening sketch and didn't realize that the others had got started. He was duly heard, by a hushed full-house, as he wandered around offstage, whistling and flushing the loo.

A letter that Miller wrote in September and posted off to Oliver Sacks (by then in America) conveys what a roller-coaster those festival weeks were, propelling him from nervous pessimism to elated crowing. Apologizing for the delayed correspondence, he explained:

> I have been too jumpy to compose myself enough to write to you . . . It is now a month since I went up to Edinburgh and a lot has happened as a result of that excursion . . . [I] motored up to Scotland with Peter Cook and his funny little mistress [Wendy Snowden, later Mrs Cook] . . . We settled down to a strange week of rehearsal, rewriting and hangdog prognoses of our forthcoming failure. After a few days the atmosphere became entirely 'huis clos' giving the impression that we were the only things that existed: us, that is, and the handful of horrible jokes that were shortly to bring dramatic disaster. We rehearsed in the flat [communally shared and near the Lyceum] since the Old Vic [Company] had monopolised the theatre for their own production and since we were only doing a late night show our needs were cavalierly disregarded in the face of their impending Seagull. This set up of priorities and privileges was soon to be reversed however by the astounding success of our show.
>
> After the first night the critics gave us fantastic notices and shortly the cast of the O.V. were standing at the back of the auditorium to see us. Within a week half a dozen West End managements were after us . . . The fees which we are to be paid [for the London run] are astronomical . . . If the show is successful we shall almost surely come to Broadway some time at the beginning of 1962.[27]

He retrospectively calls the Lyceum run 'a cocaine-like snort of celebrity and approval', and his letter reveals that the whole transfer package, including New York, was being planned much sooner than some accounts of *Beyond the Fringe* suggest. Nevertheless, in the immediate whirl of Edinburgh, the spiralling excitement spelled disaster for his progress as a doctor. Cook and Moore were keen to transfer to London as soon as possible. They regarded any shilly-shallying from their co-stars as ridiculous. Miller, though, was on the horns of a major dilemma.

*　　*　　*

He had managed to take a fortnight's leave to coincide with the Festival, but no hospital was going to employ a house officer who transformed into a revue artist every night. Such an open relationship was unacceptable. He could not both walk the wards and tread the boards. When Rachel came up to Scotland, the two of them ended up pacing round and round Castle Rock until dawn, with Miller in crisis, unable to make up his mind. He calls it 'that fatal night', noting that Rachel rightly foresaw how there would be no return from this runaway hit if he signed up for the West End. 'But', he adds, 'she knew that I wanted, in some ways, to go on with *Beyond the Fringe*.' Perhaps whichever choice he made, he would never forgive himself.

In his September missive to Sacks, he was still clinging to the idea of attaining medical goals, though wishful thinking had begun to creep in as he wrote:

> I was involved in the old dichotomy [as regards the West End deal]. This time however I have decided differently. I have decided to abbreviate my stay in Cambridge [holding down a new post at Addenbrooke's Hospital] to six months. I shall then give up Medicine for a year whilst the show plays in London . . . I shall, in all probability, try and study seriously for the M.R.C.P. during the day . . . [and on Broadway] I shall stay with it for six months and then hop off and resume Pathology in the U.S.A., being by that time extremely affluent and financially well able to stand the privations of a badly paid job in a good centre. At last I am beginning to see the possibilities of what I have always regarded as an ideal situation viz. Medicine as a delightful hobby, as opposed to an irksome breadwinning slavery.

In practice (or rather, out of it), he would never write a second paper for the *Lancet*, let alone win a Nobel Prize for neurology as his university friends had envisaged. At some point, he must have recalled Danny Kaye's galling personal prediction, 'You'll never do it', or indeed Kaye's screen character, Walter Mitty, who merely daydreamed of being a top surgeon. How ironic too that, after converting Rachel, the child ballerina, to medicine, he himself should caper off into what he calls 'this footling flibbertigibbet world of theatre' while she became a long-standing GP.

Far from disgraced, he is part of a historic line of trainee and qualified doctors who have migrated into comedy and drama: Oliver Goldsmith, Schiller, Chekhov, Ibsen, Strindberg, William Carlos Williams (who wrote some plays as well as poetry), Somerset Maugham, Christopher Isherwood, Mikhail Bulgakov, and more recently Michael Crichton (of *ER*). Other physicians-turned-humorists have included *Monty Python*'s Graham Chapman (who went to Cambridge to read medicine because he saw Miller in Footlights), Graeme Garden of the Goodies and Harry Hill.

Regardless of that, Miller views medicine as his lost ideal and sees comedy as his tragic fall, a woeful degeneration, certainly not progressive evolution. Often he talks of his lapsed state as if it resulted from an accident, a stroke of ill fortune. He compares his career change to being 'tripped up' by showbusiness, to suddenly 'falling out of an aeroplane', to 'stepping off the edge of a diving board into this murky swimming pool where my moral fibre rotted irreversibly'. He makes this sound like a Wittgensteinian case of 'My foot went out' as distinct from 'I moved my foot', and his CV looks like a case of Chinese whispers, of unintentional typos or slips of the tongue, recategorizing the medic as comic, the doctor as director, and sliding from the operating theatre to opera and theatre.

He will admit to a degree of self-determination, observing: 'You make a small choice and find it's committed you to a large change of life.'[28] In an upbeat mood, he will confess that he had great fun and remains proud of *Beyond the Fringe*. Even so, that never cancels out the remorse. 'I still', he concludes, 'fiercely regret the distraction. I think that was a bad thing I did.'[29] In spite of his theory of comedy – that laughter is generated by sudden wrong categorizations – his own reclassification, swapping professions, has left him down in the mouth.

The 'irksome breadwinning slavery', alluded to in his letter to Sacks, had also played a part. He was no longer enamoured with the medical profession because he felt it did not embrace its youngsters with any warmth. John Bassett had caught him at a low point, just as he was facing hard graft as a junior doctor: extended periods of separation from Rachel, exhausting working hours, and what he considered an obstructive geriarchy. It was not institutional anti-Semitism, as in his father's era, but it was ageism of the old-school variety, whippersnappers being put through the mill by their elders.[30]

Emanuel's eminence may have exacerbated worries in Miller about falling short, but it did look like a survival-of-the-fittest scenario. He saw a bottleneck of clever registrars who could not all make it to the top due to insufficient consultancy posts. Many trainees felt it necessary to do a stint in the USA, to bolster their CVs with Stateside internships (nicknamed BTA degrees, as in Been To America).

Reforms were coming. The Conservatives had pledged twenty million pounds for new hospitals in 1959. The future Labour prime minister Harold Wilson was simultaneously developing his progressive 'white heat' campaign, to champion science and technology more proactively, including medical research. Some in that line, however, were unconvinced by Macmillan's 'never had it so good' assurances, still considered themselves undervalued, and wanted a speedier boost.[31] During his UCH period, Miller had also talked of the proliferation of medical journals making it ever harder to keep abreast, a neurosis-inducing task, like his childhood nightmare of struggling to eat the sun.[32]

He was enticed by the comparative ease, glamour and adoring applause of a life in the theatre. Sociologists were, moreover, predicting that the future lay in the cultivation of leisure. With more spending power and mod cons in the pipeline, Britain was going to become a Utopia of free time and frivolities, with the arts and entertainment in the ascendant.[33]

After the heady success of Edinburgh, Miller told Sacks: 'I now for the first time in my life actually don't give a fuck for what anyone in the [medical] profession thinks.' Likewise, writing in the press in October 1960, he called its senior figures pompous and philistine, and associated a doctor's career path, rather than showbiz, with a woeful fall. He claimed:

> I cannot remember ever having decided to become a doctor. The process by which I finally did become one was much like the migration of the lemmings: a blind scramble for the sea . . . a falling-off from this original sombre ideal [of becoming a Victorian-style scientific savant] . . . I was [rapidly] on the

look-out for a job which offered status and security . . . I am now somewhat shamed by this graceless combination of pride and caution.[34]

Being turned down for a registrar's post in neuropathology at the National Hospital for Nervous Diseases, in London's Queen's Square, had riled him, no doubt. One of his University College friends was working there and asked the senior neuropathologist why such a superlative graduate had not been appointed. 'No, no, totally out of the question', came the reactionary reply. 'He turned up wearing a sports jacket.'[35]

Miller did go to Addenbrooke's, and he worked at both the London Hospital and the Royal Marsden during the West End run of *Beyond the Fringe*.[36] However, this only intensified his misery because, on bad advice, he chose to study general pathology and neuropathology, before getting down to neurology itself.[37] As a resident assistant pathologist at Addenbrooke's, his dull task was to cross-match blood for transfusions. At the London he did autopsies, and at the Marsden he took a mind-numbing job, freezing cancer cells, unpaid. He was faced with a prospect of exasperating years before he could really investigate how the brain affects behaviour, and he lacked the patience for that. 'It was,' he says, 'a complete cock-up, absolute folly, and I knew I was up a gum tree.'

The only perk regarding Cambridge was that some old associates were still in town and Rachel briefly came to Addenbrooke's to train in obstetrics. In a winter letter to Sacks, he described her as wonderfully replete with domestic comforts – rugs, warm towels, hot baths, smiles and chocolate. That aside, he went on:

> I have now been working for six weeks and am still very uncertain if this is really what I want to do . . . In the evenings I am on call for all emergency work and sit alone in the empty laboratory waiting for haemorrhages. I actually like the isolation of night work in a lab since I have no concessions to make to convention. I can sing and mutter, wear T-shirts and mocassins [sic] and sink deeper each night into an autistic state. I meander around the upper rooms, appearing at the windows like a mad, male Lady of Shallott [sic] . . . I am very relieved that I have the escape clause of the revue in April.[38]

Some weeks later, he added that he had reached the end of his tether regarding all resident work and he now resented the boredom with a keen fury, yearning for the 'daguerreotypic decor' of old-fashioned science.[39] The strip-lit world of modern medicine was not for him, and the shift to the hi-tech was clearly to become more stark, with Addenbrooke's preparing to move from its neo-Gothic building to a brand-new site on the city outskirts.

A follow-up letter, veering between self-rebuke and self-regard, went further:

> Alas, I think it is all a literary illusion . . . The dancing mote under the micrscope [sic] is all very well until you have to sit over it hour after hour . . . Fickle lad. The baleful shade of Sid [Pask] gobbles and stutters his rebukes at another

1 Miller's paternal grandfather,
Abram Miller

2 Miller's maternal grandfather,
Simon Spiro

3 Miller's father, Emanuel Miller,
in his office

4 Miller with his mother,
Betty (née Spiro)

6 Miller's wife, Rachel (née Collet)

5 Miller (back row, centre) in the Colet
Clubs Revue team at St Paul's School

7 Miller on the beach at Cumbrae in Scotland

8 Miller, aged twenty, photographed by
Jane Bown

9 Miller as Elizabeth I in the Footlights
show *Out of the Blue*

10 Miller (seated, centre) playing a village idiot in *Out of the Blue*

11 A signed cartoon by Miller, from *Granta* (briefly renamed the *Gadfly*) in 1953

12 Miller's *Granta* cartoon from 1954, inspired by William Empson's *Seven Types of Ambiguity*

13 Miller, Peter Cook, Alan Bennett and Dudley Moore in *Beyond the Fringe*

14 Cook and Miller, as Perkins, in the *Beyond the Fringe* sketch 'Aftermyth of War'

15 Miller (far left, back) at one of George Plimpton's parties in New York, 1963, with Truman Capote (on sofa, left), Gore Vidal (back, left, hand in pocket), Mario Puzo, author of *The Godfather* (right, leaning against mirror)

16 Cook and Miller in *Beyond the Fringe*'s Shakespeare skit

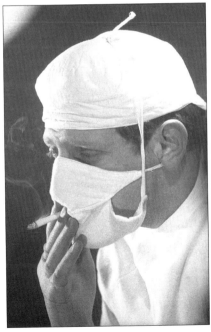

17 Miller in a sketch, shown on film, at The Establishment

18 John Gielgud (the Mock Turtle), Malcolm Muggeridge (the Gryphon) and Anne-Marie Mallik (Alice) filming *Alice in Wonderland*, for BBC TV, 1966

19 Miller taking a break during the filming of *Alice*, with Mallik and with Leo McKern (centre) who played the Ugly Duchess

20 Miller (with watering can) filming *The Drinking Party* for BBC TV, 1965, with (left to right) Roddy Maude-Roxby, Alan Bennett and John Fortune

Not at all, one really should democratise one's talent. In fact I'm planning to write a column about pop music. There's no reason why a new disc shouldn't be treated just as analytically as a pre-audio-tactile artifact like a book.

21 Bernard Goldblatt in *Life and Times in NW1*

22 Miller's Kent Opera staging of *La Traviata*, with Jill Gomez as Violetta

23 Miller on *Parkinson*, BBC TV, in 1975, with Michael Parkinson (left) and Lee Remick (right)

24 Miller on the set of *The Body in Question*, BBC TV, 1978

25 The Torres Strait expedition, with Rivers and Seligman (on the left and the right, second row from back)

failed pupil of astronomical promise. It has happened to all of us [the gang from St Paul's] . . . lured into biology by the [Edmund] Gossian flavours of the subject[40] . . . You . . . Eric [Korn] . . . Our love of science is utterly literary . . . I do not think that I will ever do experimental work of any value, if indeed any at all. Instead, I now feel that I am ready, equipped with an extraordinary biological education, to turn a powerful instrument into a region which I have never dared to imagine myself at home. I imagine that when this theatrical business has burned itself out i.e. in about two years I shall . . . get myself attached to a unit where sociology, psychology and neurology meet. A place which will heat me up to some sort of creative activity: wrting [sic], teaching or even perhaps just talking. The ideas are vague at the moment but the sudden affluence has torn a small rent in the clouds and given me a breathtaking view of some distant intellectual Canaan . . . this is all rather inflated and confused. In a letter to follow . . . I shall try to sketch in a sober factual background to this sententious turmoil.[41]

Incidentally, Sacks' prospects were less rosy than Miller's at this point. He had, as yet, won no public recognition and was living dangerously in a leather-clad biker phase in California, donning a white coat by day but going wild at night, taking what he himself describes as 'a fair sampling' of LSD.[42] Convinced that he would die young, he posted off to Miller, in 1960, a sealed package inside which lay a kind of will and testament in waiting:

Dear Jonathan,

I hope you will never read this note, but if you do you can do me a last favour. This box contains a selection of what I have written over the years, and if I have ever written anything of worth it is likely to be here. I leave it to your good sense and discretion to retrieve anything you think fit, destroy, or keep as a memento.

Love, OLIVER[43]

Among the selected scripts was – crucially, as it turned out – a draft of *Awakenings*. This record of Sacks' extraordinary work with L-DOPA and with patients suffering from post-encephalitic Parkinsonism was, eventually, going to make him world famous.[44]

In the meantime it was Miller who was the obvious success story. At least one publishing house was asking him to write any book he liked and, in early 1961, he became the *Spectator*'s medical correspondent. His column appeared under the pseudonym John Lydgate, although Miller's distinctive seriocomic voice came through, his articles being characteristically strewn with literary, anthropological and philosophical allusions.[45] He ruminated on psychiatry, on rising NHS costs and on cerebral senescence. His piece on the Alice-in-Wonderlandish symptoms of epilepsy, where the patient sees their hand as suddenly huge or the room shrunk to a brilliant miniature, was riveting.[46] John Lydgate was, however, short-lived, peforming a vanishing act in May 1961, when *Beyond the Fringe* opened at the Fortune Theatre.

★　　　★　　　★

The show had been reworked after Edinburgh with director Eleanor Fazan.[47] As she recalls, the Fringers wanted to appear unprofessional yet worked hard, incorporating new material. They fought competitively for solo spots but Miller, she reveals, was the most humane, helping Dudley with his routines. The rewrite included, notably, the nuclear WMD skit *Civil War* with its gallows humour:

> ALAN: Her Britannic Majesty's Government is very anxious to popularize the notion of Civil Defence . . .
>
> JON: [But] if we are lucky enough in any future conflict to be the aggressor, we are in a position to inflict a blow of twenty, thirty, or even forty mega-deaths – or to put that in more human terms, forty million dead bodies strewn all about the place here and there. Jolly good . . . our Sea-Slugs will then come into their own in a second wave and bring our score up into the seventy or even eighty mega-death bracket, which is practically the maximum score permitted by the Geneva Convention . . . Following Armageddon, we do hope to have normal public services working fairly smoothly . . . something in the nature of a skeleton service.[48]

This was considerably sharper than 'Whose Finger on What Button?', the Fringers' earlier routine on the same subject. 'Civil War' was partly fuelled by actual civil defence manuals, such as the one from 1957 (the year of the serious leak at Windscale) which had risibly recommended wearing a hat in the event of radioactive fallout. On top of that, Britain had been testing H-bombs and declared itself a thermonuclear power, such that the new protest group CND drew a record-breaking, 100,000-strong crowd at its 1960 demo against nuclear weapons in Trafalgar Square.

The show's rewrite did not save its pre-West End tour from dramatic ups and downs. The performances in Cambridge were triumphant epics, running on into the small hours as the Fringers tried out virtually all their material on an audience who welcomed them like returning heroes. In Brighton, by contrast, it bombed. The seaside town's war veterans were enraged by the 'Aftermyth of War' vignettes which made fun of the Valiant Few:

> DUDLEY: Please, sir, I want to join the Few.
>
> JON: I'm sorry, there are far too many.[49]

Bennett and Miller still remember the sound of the theatre's flip-seats, angrily vacated, ricocheting like pistol shots. Donald Albery, the major producer who was bringing them into the West End, got cold feet and took against Bennett, decreeing that the blond one must go. Having lost that battle, he refused to transfer the show to Wyndham's, the large Charing Cross Road playhouse which he had previously offered. So, he brought it by default into the Fortune, which is off Drury Lane.

The financial deal was not nearly as generous as Miller had naively supposed either. Albery's young co-producer, William Donaldson (subsequently better known by his nom de plume Henry Root), was outrageously roguish.[50] In his own words:

> My participation was absolutely shameful! I was about the only London manager who didn't even see the show [in Edinburgh] and I knew nothing about anything. All I had ever done was completely screw up a revue by a friend of theirs, John Bird [whose Footlights' 1959 show, *The Last Laugh*, had featured Cook]. And within twenty-four hours Don Langdon [still Cook's agent] had persuaded them this idiot that was me – and that they all hated – was the only person in London qualified to put it on. And they agreed. To this day I don't know what on earth they could have been thinking of. And then we robbed them blind![51]

Langdon's argument had been that Donaldson would be pleasantly hands-off and, for sure, the promised weekly pay of around £75 was huge compared to Miller's earnings as a junior doctor.[52] Nevertheless, the two producers were soon pocketing £2,000 per week, and when the foursome demanded a meeting, having done the maths, they were told that a successful production must, naturally, pay for the investors' flops.[53] According to Donaldson: 'They must have had a combined IQ of about 1,040, with me and Albery in the lower sixties, but we outmanoeuvred them easily. They were dumbstruck and they apologized for wasting our time!'[54] Miller remains, to this day, outraged by the sharp practice, commenting that he and his fellow performers were young innocents and traitorously exploited.

At least they had the satisfaction of seeing Albery look foolish for relegating the show to a small theatre. It rapidly became a West End sensation. Among a chorus of jubilant notices, Milton Shulman in the *Evening Standard* hailed it as uncompromisingly provocative and uproarious. Bernard Levin stumbled away in ecstasies, giving thanks in the *Daily Express* that there should be such men living 'who could come together to provide, for as long as memory holds, an eighth colour to the rainbow'. He moved on to call them 'four immortals' because their wit was so sharp, 'deeply planted and aimed at things and people that need it'. Setting aside a few cavils, Ken Tynan pronounced, in the *Observer*, that English comedy had taken 'its first decisive step into the second half of the twentieth century'.[55] Before long the papers were reporting that tickets were like gold dust, with the demand far outstripping the Fortune's capacities. Even the Queen (allegedly encouraged by the Lord Chamberlain himself) and Macmillan came to see this show. Her Majesty was royally amused by Cook's impersonation of the PM.[56]

The foursome had a phenomenal long-term impact. They sparked off a revolution equivalent to John Osborne's *Look Back in Anger*, the 1956 stage play that shook up British drama. They killed off old-style revue and they kick-started the British Satire Boom which, of course, went on to incorporate Cook's sardonically named Soho comedy club The Establishment, *Private Eye* magazine (of which Cook was to be joint owner), and the hit TV series *That Was The Week That Was*, aka *TW3*. As Michael Frayn puts it, in his introduction to the published text of their sketches: '*Beyond the Fringe* first fell upon London like a sweet, refreshing rain . . . it rained satire thereafter, day and night . . . The demand must have existed, ravenous but unrecognised.'[57]

The show's skits were preserved on vinyl by Parlophone at Abbey Road, the LP being produced by no less than George Martin.[58] He subsequently slipped the recorded buzz of the audience at the Fortune on to the Beatles' album *Sgt. Pepper's Lonely Hearts Club Band*. Comparisons were, indeed, soon being drawn between the Fringers and Liverpool's emergent Fab Four, and their comedy was marketed as a kind of alternative rock 'n' roll. In the black-and-white image used on the *Beyond the Fringe* LP cover – taken by the celebrity photographer Lewis Morley – they are coolly leaning against striped street hoardings, with Miller in a hooded coat, looking more like a juvenile Mod loitering with intent than a married doctor.[59]

The theatre critic Michael Billington was starting out as a student reviewer in 1960. 'My first encounter with Jonathan [chatting after a press conference] was life-enhancing and my generation grew up worshipping him,' he recalls, adding that the record developed a youthful fan club nationwide, who could reprise the sketches with the accuracy of trainspotters. It was their unofficial set text, making *Beyond the Fringe* a real turning point in British culture and a force for social change.[60]

The LP and the live show (on tour and in London) inspired several of the *Monty Python* crew, beyond the aforementioned Graham Chapman. Eric Idle recollects with delight:

> I went with a friend and we could only get standing tickets, but it was just as well because I would never have stayed in a seat. I was rolling around the walls, then I immediately bought the album and learned every single word. It changed my life absolutely and utterly. I never knew you could be funny about those sorts of things before. It was like a liberation, going from a grim boarding school to that world where you could laugh at all the things that were repressing you. I just wanted to make people laugh from then on, and I think, though we tended to be sillier and not quite so smart, it was a direct influence on *Monty Python*.

John Cleese still remembers being reduced to chewing his college scarf in fits of laughter. He observes that Cook's idiosyncratic style influenced up-and-coming Cambridge comics most persistently. 'But I thought then, and I still think that it's the most wonderful show that I ever saw because all four of them were geniuses', he says. 'With *A Fish Called Wanda*, really I was working on exactly the same idea: four characters who are funny in different ways being combined in various permutations.'[61]

Not many stage shows can claim to be genuinely life-changing but Tony Hendra, the humorous writer and star of *This is Spinal Tap*, was going into Benedictine orders until he was converted by *Beyond the Fringe*. The leading TV producer Roger Graef, who became a neighbour and long-term friend of Miller's, also decided to make England his permanent home because, as he says: 'I got off the boat [from America] and, second night I'm here, I see *Beyond the Fringe* and the picture [it paints] of Britain is so wonderfully silly that I think, "I'll stay in this country". I was completely enchanted.'

Paradoxically, therefore, Miller and co. became icons of the iconoclastic Sixties, alternative comedians working like moles from within Oxbridge's old boy network. This was the grown-up version of Jonathan, the small boy who dangled on Lord Lucan's fire-escape rope, well connected yet rule-breaking.

*   *   *

What is hard to determine, categorically, is whether or not Miller and his fellow Fringers consciously set out to create something revolutionary. Bernard Levin retrospectively rued how the group 'suffered the inevitable fate reserved in England . . . for rebels, namely affectionate absorption into the bosom of the Establishment that they are supposed to be out to destroy'.[62] Miller ripostes that none of them ever viewed the world with real spleen because they were all quite comfortably off in the first place, and that having the banner of satire shoved into their hands by Tynan was 'rather like Charlie Chaplin [in *Modern Times*] finding himself at the head of a communist parade'.[63]

He stated, at the time, that the Fringers had adopted no strategic agenda because, whenever they tried that, their scriptwriting ground to a standstill.[64] All the same, Bennett remembers that the fundamental concept was sending up everything they loathed. Moreover, writing in the press about The Establishment's imminent opening in the autumn of 1961, Miller sounded militantly keen on 'the satirical blade'.[65] With the club being technically outside the Lord Chamberlain's jurisdiction, he hoped that the blade could be sharpened to be a match for continental Europe's barbed cabarets and America's new 'buzzing hornets'. By the latter he meant Mort Sahl (whose hard-hitting political comedy he loved), Lenny Bruce, and the Second City group set up by Mike Nichols and Elaine May.[66] In conclusion, he proclaimed:

The Establishment represents a research station in which we might see developed the weapons necessary for the final overthrow of the Neo-Gothic stronghold of Victorian good taste . . . The ranks are drawn up and the air resounds with the armourer's hammer. When battle is joined one can only hope that blood will be drawn.

This was, surely, the closest Jonathan Miller ever came to being England's answer to Che Guevara, the Latin American physician-turned-freedom fighter. Cook did not thank him for the advance publicity, observing afterwards that the only blood drawn resulted from someone whacking him over the head with a handbag.[67]

Miller's level of political engagement offstage was limited. During his third year at Cambridge, and again while at Addenbrooke's, he had lodged out in Newnham village with Rachel's cousin, Nina, and her husband, Bill Wedderburn – today a member of the House of Lords, back then a law don with strong Labour Party connections. Wedderburn fraternized with the future cabinet ministers Denis Healey and Peter Shore, with the lawyer Lee Kuan Yew (soon to be Singapore's prime minister), and with the barrister-going-on-Tanzanian attorney general Mark Bomani (later chief aide to Nelson Mandela on Burundi peace negotiations). Yet the consequent discussions at the house left Miller only mildly politicized.[68]

Along with masses of others, he participated in one or two of CND's Aldermaston marches, a commitment reflected in *Beyond the Fringe*'s anti-nuclear gags. He has also signed a range of high-profile petitions over the years. In the 1960s, among other issues, his name appeared on the British Artists' Protest against the continuing Vietnam War.[69] In the 1970s, he would become a pundit in the heated debate about state censorship. He signed another British Artists' Protest against Kenya's repressive regime, joined George Melly and others calling for the legalization of cannabis, and contributed to an Amnesty International conference on torture.[70] His excoriating quips regarding Margaret Thatcher were warmly appreciated by many in the 1980s. In 1991, when the USSR was disintegrating, he co-signed a letter to the Soviet Embassy – together with Harold Pinter, Michael Frayn, Claire Tomalin and others – protesting at the coup in Moscow and supporting the right to free speech. And so on into the twenty-first century when he joined London's huge protest marches against the Iraq War in 2003, and signed a letter of protest at the Pope's state visit to Britain in 2010.[71]

He was and remains, he says, merely a reflex Old Labour type, not an active socialist or party member. Often tagged as a trendy lefty, in fact he is a more complicated political animal than that suggests. Today, in unguarded conversation, he can tilt breathtakingly to the right on occasion. He alludes to one fellow director as a 'little guttersnipe' and another as a 'slag of a dyke', throwing political correctness to the wind.

Even his 1961 Lydgate articles for the *Spectator* reveal subtle oscillations. In one piece he describes 'the organic charter', metaphorically comparing the inner workings of the body to an orderly republic. That makes nature sound pleasantly democratic. Almost in the same breath, though, he unsettlingly alludes to the body's spontaneous 'xenophobic' reaction to skin grafts. In another piece, he likens low-skilled workers' health complaints, ones which vanish after legal compensation, to 'an insidious form of wildcat strike'. He is hardly taking their side with 'insidious', though his argument then switches, saying those complaints express the patients' sense of exploitation.[72] That shifting perspective – in two minds, half left-wing, half right-wing – owed something to the pre-PC era in which Miller was writing, as well as his own socially complex roots. *Beyond the Fringe*'s satirical gun certainly swivelled in many directions, taking pops at anyone foolish, smug or dishonest, whether they were a Tory leader, a union chief, a racist British landlady (of the 'No Irish, no blacks, no dogs' ilk) or a black African leader.

Racism had, of course, become a highly charged issue since the mid-1950s with the African-American civil rights movement, headed by Martin Luther King, and with London's 1958 Notting Hill riots. Prejudiced white Brits were repeatedly satirized in *Beyond the Fringe*, but Miller also played Mr Akiboto Nobitsu in the slippery, target-shifting sketch 'Black Equals White'. This dodgy post-colonial leader – head of the fictional Pan-African Federal Party, being interviewed in London – declared that 'one man, one vote' was God's law and that it applied to everyone, 'especially the nine million black idiots who vote for me'. Miller's Nobitsu admitted he appeared to be white but he had, he explained, recently undergone an op to remove his skin pigment in the interests of his people, the better to speak to the white man on his own ground. 'Besides,' he said, 'it is the only way I can get lodgings.'

In any overarching analysis of Miller's brand of comedy, *Beyond the Fringe* was his most obviously political, besides being his last major turn. Yet the personal was never far away. As the show continued its run, he slipped in more monologues of the semi-autobiographical variety, teasingly hovering between a cranky comic persona and himself.[73] 'Porn Shop', for instance, described a medical student's research into seedy Soho outlets and their sales of unusual books, trusses and similar 'surgical apparatus'. Even if he was less inspired than Cook and sometimes prolix, such digressive chats made Miller the forefather of today's intimate, observational stand-ups.[74] Consider 'The Heat-Death of the Universe', which Michael Frayn cites as evidence that Miller was not so much a satirist as a humorist of the whimsical-fantastical school:[75]

Some years ago, when I was rather hard up, I wanted to buy myself a new pair of trousers – but, being rather hard up, I was quite unable to buy myself a *new* pair. Until some very kind friend whispered into my earhole that if I looked sharp about it I could get myself quite a nice secondhand pair from the sales department of the London Passenger Transport Board Lost Property . . .

[So,] after a great deal of moral contortion, I steeled myself to the alien crutch, and made my way towards the London Passenger Transport Board Lost Property Sales Department in Portman Square, praying as I did so, 'Oh God, let them be dry-cleaned when I get there.' And when I arrived there, you can imagine my pleasure and surprise when I found, instead of a tumbled heap of lunatics' trousers, a very neat heap of brand new, bright blue corduroy trousers. There were *400* of them! How can anyone lose four hundred pairs of trousers on a train? I mean, it's hard enough to lose a brown paper bag full of old orange peel when you really want to . . . No, it's clearly part of a complex economic scheme . . . along Galbraithian or Keynesian lines, presumably. So over now to the Economics Planning Division of the London Passenger Transport Board Ops room:

'All right, men. Operation Cerulean Trouser . . .'

And they disperse to places far out on the reaches of the Central Line – places with unlikely names like Chipping Ongar – places presumably out in the Essex marshes, totally uninhabited except for a few rather rangy marsh birds mournfully pacing the primeval slime.

And there in the empty railway carriages . . . before they commit the final existential act of detrouserment, they do those little personal things which people sometimes do when they think they're alone in railway carriages. Things like . . . things like smelling their own armpits.

It's all part of the human condition, I suppose. Anyway, it's quite possible they didn't even take their trousers off in the compartments but made their way along the narrow corridor towards the lavatory at the end – that wonderful little room, where there's that marvellous unpunctuated motto over the lavatory saying, 'Gentlemen lift the seat'. What exactly does this mean? Is is a sociological description – a definition of a gentleman which I can either take or leave? Or perhaps it's a Loyal Toast? It could be a blunt military order . . . or an invitation to upper-class larceny . . . but anyway, willy-nilly, they strip stark naked; and then, nude – entirely nude – nude that is except for cellular underwear (for man is born free but everywhere is in cellular underwear) they make their way back to Headquarters through the chilly nocturnal streets of sleeping Whitechapel – 400 fleet white figures in the night – their 800 horny feet pattering on the pavements and arousing small children from their slumbers in upstairs bedrooms. Children who are soothed back into their sleep by their parents with the ancient words: 'Turn your face to the wall, my darling, while the gentlemen trot by.'[76]

Fantastical worlds are not, of course, simply apolitical and almost all Miller's humour is laced with allusions to authorities or institutions. Indeed, the imaginative/realistic mix is a continuity in his comedy. In its merging of fact and fancy, of dull-sounding English outposts and near-magical or fairytale strangeness, 'The Heat-Death of the Universe' is akin to the mock conspiracy theory that he cooked up back at school – the one about the meteorologically weird mystery towns of Tooting and Brighton. It also constitutes a prime example of him weaving small private memories into public entertainment. On receiving no trouser-buying money from Emanuel, he had actually resorted to the LTB's cast-offs. Meanwhile, those marsh birds materialize as in a dream of his past

Field Club expeditions, and the trotting gentlemen subliminally echo the troop of uncaparisoned horses that used to wake him at dawn as a boy – all superimposed on his father's old haunt of Whitechapel.

He himself linked dreaming and laughing when he wrote in the *Twentieth Century* magazine in 1961:

> Some years ago I woke in the middle of the night and found to my astonishment that I was shaking with laughter . . . as I lay there in the darkness giggling foolishly I experienced a curious sense of guilt. For in broad daylight, in the usual run of things, laughter comes attached to circumstances . . . issued by quota to sweeten the rigours of reality . . .
>
> Humour, even when legitimate, fastened to a joke, has something of the naughty about it . . . [it] must have been stolen, like fire, by Prometheus from the gods.[77]

Did the link he sensed between reprehensibility and laughter relate to Emanuel's disapproving view of his comic antics? The son may have projected his own guilty feelings on to his father, or vice versa, suggests Oliver Sacks:

> I think Jonathan's father had a feeling that he [himself] had been undervalued and had not achieved all the professional status he perhaps wanted. There was a real conflict in him between a warm, funny, rather brilliant and artistically talented, Jonathan-like man and this inhibiting and censorious quality. He would intimate to Jonathan that theatre and other things were levity, and that intellectual virtue lay in concentrating and producing a shelf of heavy, learned books. I think the accusing and censorious aspect of the father has been interjected by Jonathan and has haunted him for much of his life, introducing a note of guilt or ambivalence so that his own brilliant and various achievements are, maybe, undervalued by him because of this paternal admonition.

Emanuel obviously did not turn up at the Fortune Theatre like Mozart's Commendatore in *Don Giovanni*, damning Miller's larks in baleful, melodramatic tones. He may, after all, have recognized an integrated outsider's perspective in his son's satirical viewpoint, or been amused by the caricature of a hip vicar preaching about juvenile delinquents. ('It is my aim to get the violence off the streets and into the churches where it belongs.')[78] Nevertheless, he does seem to have cast a long, sombre shadow. Emanuel regarded any sidelining of medicine as an act of treachery, according to Miller. Nor did he laugh heartily at his offspring's gag, 'I'm not really a *Jew*. Just Jew-*ish*.' Although he never spoke of it to his son, he discussed that joke with the rabbi Hugo Gryn, fearing it was anti-Semitic.

On Jews and comedy more generally, Miller has remarked that the Judaic religious practices of exegesis, argument and debate naturally led to comedy being embraced, the disputant's protest being tactically articulated with a smile. Comedians with Jewish roots have included his hero Danny Kaye and the Marx

Brothers, as well as Mort Sahl. Jews make their greatest contribution to contemporary culture, Miller argues, when their intellectual energy, long compressed by the practice of exegesis, is suddenly released like an aerosol spray into 'this huge world of liberty'.

In the process they are assimilated, and that is, he believes, for the best. If orthodox practices are maintained, he says, 'for the sole purpose of making sure that in the future you'll be able to say the prayers for the dead when the Holocaust is finally inflicted again, then I think it's a damnable device'. He has been charmed by ethnic customs – beyond just Jewish ones – when encountering indigenous peoples in, for example, the Atlas Mountains. However, he finds such practices somewhat disturbing when he sees them 'maintained defensively' in modern American or European cities. 'I feel', he says, 'that the Jew must constantly readventure and reventure [sic] himself into assimilation. He owes it to himself and to humanity.'[79]

Whilst shrugging off Judaism, Miller has felt pangs of self-reproach about his decision to abandon medicine, most strongly when discussing cases with his wife, reading professional journals or simply passing hospitals. He strikingly compares the guilt to that of a lapsed Catholic. It is as if he regarded himself as an infidel in the sense of being unfaithful to his father's profession.[80]

Betty surely sympathized with her son's 'Jew-ish' pun, and given that she harboured play-writing ambitions, she doubtless enjoyed seeing him on the stage, but he believes she regarded the comedian's art as second-rate compared to writing novels.[81] Furthermore, she must have flinched at 'Aftermyth of War'. Miller's dialogue with Cook remains droll, yet also terribly painful if one remembers the death of Betty's beloved brother, Henry, in military service.

> PETER: I want you to lay down your life, Perkins. We need a futile gesture at this stage. It will raise the whole tone of the war . . .
>
> JON: Goodbye, sir – or is it – *au revoir*?
>
> PETER: *No*, Perkins.[82]

Retrospectively, Miller himself is appalled by 'Aftermyth', stressing that he now feels ashamed of having made an insouciant joke of those men who risked death to save him and others. He recently spent a day watching *In Which We Serve* and other vintage war movies which moved him to tears. At the time, the Fringers insisted they were not directly mocking World War 2 servicemen, but rather propagandistic or sentimental films such as *The Dambusters* and *A Diary for Timothy*. If that was the case, Miller still risked causing offence because *A Diary for Timothy* was made by the Crown Film Unit where Betty's other brother, Julian, worked.[83] Julian did not object because he remembered his nephew hero-worshipping his D-Day bravery and also David Niven on-screen in RAF mode.

In fact, a close look at 'Aftermyth', on the BBC TV recording of *Beyond the Fringe*, reveals four young men (none of whom did front-line service) playing at soldiers, smirking but also looking as if they were acting out a fantasy or a fear that they have not completely outgrown. That chimes with Miller's statement that he had, as a boy, been 'absolutely fascinated by the mystery, excitement and dread of being aircrew', and with his confession that, at university, he felt slightly envious of those in his generation who had done National Service and seen some 'maturing and possibly rather exciting' action in Malaya or Korea.[84] Alan Bennett did National Service on the language-learning Joint Services Russian course, thus being spared military manoeuvres. Cook had declared himself unfit for enrolment because of an allergy to feathers, and Moore had been exempt because of his club foot.

★　　★　　★

Beyond the Fringe made the group into major celebrities, if not national heroes, as 1960s London began to get swinging. Besides being screened on TV, the show won an *Evening Standard* Award, and Miller was nominated for the title of 'Man of the Year' in 1961.[85] Soon the Goons invited him and Cook to join them on the LP recording of Spike Milligan's lampoon *Bridge on the River Wye*.[86] While Peter Sellers parodied Alec Guinness' Colonel Nicholson, Miller exuberantly spoofed Commander Shears. He was asked to play Fagin – a role he turned down – in Lionel Bart's Dickensian musical *Oliver!*[87] There was also talk of him starring as the oldster-mocking hero, a subversive young lecturer, in a movie version of Kingsley Amis' *Lucky Jim*. In the end, that came to nothing.

He took on one big-screen role, cast as Kirby Groomkirby, the mad genius who teaches weighing machines to sing, in the film version of N. F. Simpson's absurdist comedy *One Way Pendulum*.[88] His performance wasn't dazzling, so a Danny Kaye-style career as a movie star remained a pipe dream.

He was often out on the town, part of the increasingly trendy scene in Soho. As Rachel was busy doing her medical house jobs, he dined with Cook, Moore or Bennett after their evening performances at the Fortune, and he hung around at The Establishment which was buzzing. On its opening night, the club's new members turned up in their thousands. Five hundred packed into a space made for 90, and one critic, who needed to leave early, was entertainingly passed over the heads of the crowd. Miller was part of the first-night bill and he made occasional appearances thereafter. Most memorable was the spoof tobacco commercial, shot on film and shown between live sketches, where he played a surgeon operating on a patient with lung cancer while chain-smoking through his mask. Mainly, though, he was watching the acts and rubbing shoulders at the bar with cabinet ministers, fashion models and the likes of Michael Caine and Terence Stamp.

He became good friends with the regular performers John Bird and John Fortune, Jeremy Geidt and Eleanor Bron.[89] His childhood friend Nicholas Garland turned

115

up again as the venue's theatrical director, while the burly cartoonist Roger Law (now celebrated for *Spitting Image*) contributed comic material and beat up Soho gangsters who demanded protection money.[90]

What of the burgeoning culture of sex, drugs and rock 'n' roll? How did Miller fit into that? 'Well, not at all,' he says. He was certainly not averse to laddish banter. He once declared his vice was lust, and he remarked on Moore's leggy lady-friends: 'I think he found them very fuckable. He liked that size girl. A lot of us do'.[91] One actor-friend similarly remembers Miller's conversational ice-breaker: 'Seen any good plays lately? . . . Oh, yes, I'd like to fuck Judi Dench.' This was, surely, far from high-minded. In the Sixties, though, the term 'fuck' was seen as expressing a positive, liberated spirit of sexual revolution.[92] Or Miller may simply have been all talk, words not necessarily tallying with actions.

It is a truism, universally acknowledged, that a life in the theatre offers ample temptations, and fame bestows extra pulling power. However, he has fended off nosey queries, riposting that stage work probably entails no more sexual temptations than, say, a job in the Stock Exchange where one might, equally, be surrounded by people with whom one might want to experiment. One persistent journalist was told: 'I'm not going to talk about that [question of unfaithfulness] . . . not because I am embarrassed about what I have or have not done but I owe it to my family. I hate it when people boast about their families or their intimacies or whatever'.[93] The man will talk about almost anything, except marital unfaithfulness.

According to one associate's claim, he was once tempted by the possibility of a fling as British society became increasingly permissive, but he backed away, conscience-stricken. In that case, he didn't literally acquire a mistress but just, as aforementioned, regularly compared his two occupations, medicine and the theatre, to a wife and a seductress (an analogy he may have picked up from Chekhov, incidentally).

Even if he did have an eye for a nice pair of femurs and knew – in a purely clinical capacity – how to test a knee, he underlines that he was married. The Sixties were good fun, he says, but he was never into rock 'n' roll; what 'swinging' he had done had been in jazz clubs at sixteen; and it was Moore who was the man of the moment, surrounded by Courrèges-booted dolly birds. Cuddly Dudley himself recalled: 'Jonathan was married, as I think Peter was. Alan didn't seem that interested in girls at that time, so that left only me. I had a marvellous time.'[94] On one occasion at the Fortune, Moore was having such lusty fun in his dressing-room that he again missed his cue, finally dashing on to the stage drenched in sweat. Knowing fine well what he had been up to, the others responded in unison to his 'Oh, hi!' with a pointedly suggestive 'H*ello*!'

Among Miller's stash of personal notebooks, which he has kept since 1961, one entry ruminates on Moore, sounding admiring though not really envious:

> There is a persistence of myth in modern life . . . there are [certain] people who are inheritors of mythical roles . . . They seem almost oversimplified . . . strange immortal, separate and almost vulnerable in their immortality. Like

the Gods in disguise. D.M. is one of these. Libidinous and musical, an Orphic cupid. His club foot in someone ordinary would just be a fault. In him it is an insignia of this hidden divinity . . . The Gods are human species written in an upper case while the rest of us are in lower case.[95]

Moore was not quite superhuman and he eventually keeled over from exhaustion. Consulted as the doctor in the house, Miller told him he was suffering from a liver complaint and had to take several weeks respite.

No screaming groupies ever pursued the Fringers en masse. The only stage-door devotees they attracted were, apparently, two forlorn schoolgirls and their little brother. The small boy expressed his admiration by evacuating his bowels. Miller was sent billets-doux on scented notepaper by one other woeful admirer who used to sit under his nose in the stalls, staring up like a puffer fish in shallow water.[96] The nearest he came to going boho in Soho was, he says, taking to the floor at The Establishment on New Year's Eve, merrily dancing with the colourful antiques dealer and transvestite Geoffrey Bennison in his Big Carol outfit.[97]

Another walk on the wild side had rapidly degenerated into a bedroom farce: this was the private cast party organized to celebrate *Beyond the Fringe*'s London run. Using his seedy underworld connections, William Donaldson arranged for the Fringers to see some blue movies, an activity which, being thoroughly illegal, was regarded as more hip and risqué then than it would be today.[98] They all met, along with Rachel and John Bassett, in a pub off Berkeley Square before tipsily following Donaldson to an address in Bond Street (now the Burberry store). 'There,' as John Bassett humorously relates, 'after much ringing on the bell, an old fat French slattern came down . . . and everyone had to watch [the porn] reclining on a double bed in the hostess' boudoir, surrounded by framed photos of her poodles. Oh, it was terrible!'

Miller was apparently the first to start howling with mirth as the movie proved to be some stuttering 1930s film, shot in Havana, featuring sexual congress in socks and dark glasses. He and Rachel then supplied a medical commentary while the shy and somewhat prim Bennett was, according to Bassett, hiding under the bed, groaning in horror. Bennett himself wryly remembers that the films still managed, somehow, to be exciting and that he wandered away at the end, 'wondering if this at last was "living"'.[99] Cook regularly amused himself thereafter by scandalizing Bennett who, when nervous, had a rewarding habit of stuffing his hanky in his mouth or, better still, chomping on his tie.

As for drugs, it seems they were all innocent on that score in the early 1960s. When the heroin-addicted comedian Lenny Bruce flew in from the States to perform at The Establishment, he sent Cook off into the night armed with some ridiculous phoney prescription signed 'Dr Ziglovitz'. Turned away by every pharmacist, Cook surmised that Moore, the jazzman, must be the right contact for narcotics, only to be offered half a junior aspirin.[100] Miller became pals with Bruce as well, before the controversially foul-mouthed American was deported amidst a public furore. '[Lenny] was actually', he reminisces, 'rather enchantingly nice and easy-going, though there was this row concerning his hotel in Piccadilly where he'd got caught with syringes or something.[101] I can remember winding a sock round his arm once [for an injection]. He said it was because he was diabetic.'

The only problem Miller has ever had with drink and drugs is that he doesn't care for either. He generally prefers Coca-Cola to wine. Some have misconstrued his support for legalizing cannabis. Drug-taking was, he states, out of the question when he was a medical student, and he only tried pot twice after that. It sent him reeling to the toilet with nausea. He has referred to himself as a sleep- and a clothes-junkie, but he is scared of illegal substances which could unhinge his mental faculties. This is not a man who needed his mind to be expanded.

At the height of the Sixties, he wrote a specifically anti-psychedelic article in *Vogue*, entitled 'I Won't Pay for the Trip', which dismissed artificially produced, gaudy visions. What he advocated was acquiring just a sharper sense of how odd it is to be here, and he went on:

> One method which I find works like a charm is to take a trip to a foreign city . . . The dizzying, ecstatic mystery of the experience comes from simply dislocating one's self from the familiar . . . the sense of civic otherness . . . All this scores over drugs in achieving its effect by the unaided activity of the mind alone . . . [and] the dosage works in reverse. Simply with practice, you can get the same effects with smaller and smaller bits of travel . . . a sense of *jamais vu*.[102]

His personal notebooks suggest he was never hugely interested in glitz or celebrity gossip either, for they offer no anecdotes in that line. They are more like so-called commonplace books, collecting thoughts and ideas. Beside the aperçu about Moore, Miller's other entries from 1961–2 typically record quotations from the literary, philosophical and scientific works which he was reading, along with short descriptive passages of his own, inspired by quietly wandering around London. These jottings almost have the feel of a reflective intellectual retreat, escaping the hustle and bustle of fame.

Nov 10 [1961]
This morning woke to the sound of gulls outside. Seagulls squealing with cold in the blenched November sky.

Dickens on childhood vision – from David Copperfield
'. . . Indeed I think most grown men who are remarkable in this respect may be said . . . to retain a certain freshness and gentleness and capacity of being pleased, which are an inheritance they have preserved from childhood . . .'

Dec 7th. Montaigne, 'Of Inconstancy'
'We are all lumps, and of so various and inform a contexture that every piece

plays every moment its own game and there is as much difference betwixt us and ourselves as betwixt us and others.'

Montaigne. 'Of Solitude'
'Wives, children and goods, must be had, and especially health, by him that can get it. But we . . . must reserve a back-shop, wholly our own, and entirely free wherein to settle our true liberty, our principle solitude, our retreat['] . . .

[Feb 1962]
A small moment. Blousy port drinker in a Mayfair bar. While talking, eyes wandering coldly to the legs of a young girl on the bar stool . . . A gap in the conversation – her eyes glance down to her own knees; this sets her hand brushing and fluttering at her dress, flicking and whisking with the little finger edge of her hand. This tiny tornado subsides with a puff or two at some ash on her shoulder. Calm returns . . .

Mar 10
Visited Apsley house [sic] in the afternoon, playing truant in the muggy spring sunshine. The stone pillars of the portico were warm as cider in the sunlight. Then wandering through the deserted galleries. The dull grandeur of a military residence. Windows and mirrors side by side, sliced and pleated time with the mirrors['] sallow reflections of the past hinged beside the windows which transmitted the buses and the sunlight. A puzzling diptych with panels of different period hinged together.

★   ★   ★

In July 1962, when *Beyond the Fringe* had a summer break, he made another notebook entry, marking his debut as a professional director of stage plays. London's Royal Court Theatre had been famously cutting-edge since premiering *Look Back in Anger*, and now its head, George Devine, invited Miller to mount *Under Plain Cover*, also by John Osborne. In fact, this was to be half of an Osborne double bill entitled *Plays for England*. Bennett was portraying an archbishop in the second piece, *The Blood of the Bambergs*, which was a royal wedding satire alluding to Princess Margaret's marriage to Antony Armstrong-Jones, Lord Snowdon.

Under Plain Cover was a pointedly non-judgemental drama about a devoted suburban couple obsessed with sadomasochistic fetishes and knickers. The pair were portrayed swapping doctors' and nurses' outfits, in far from clinical circumstances, then being exposed and persecuted by the press. Miller says he has no idea why Devine asked him to direct this, but suggests it may have been on account of Osborne's subversive tone or because no one else would touch the piece.[103] Ken Tynan, a devotee of S&M spanking, was excited and declared this premiere – six years before the end of British stage censorship – to be 'perhaps the most audacious statement ever made on the English stage'. He did not specifically praise the directing. Inversely, the *Daily Mail* said Osborne vainly tried to shock while Miller displayed diligence and invention.[104]

Even if he had seen *Look Back in Anger* and some other Court productions, Miller emphasizes that he knew little of the theatre scene and harboured no ambition to direct. He had always assumed that the job just involved sitting in the stalls, shouting out from time to time. Reportedly, he jumped at Devine's offer, nevertheless. He was bored with repeating the same lines nightly in *Beyond the Fringe*, and had begun to scorn his own comic monologues, especially compared to Cook's.[105] At the very acme of his success as a West End comic, he was becoming less and less assured about his onstage skills.

Self-doubt had, in fact, struck earlier. His Bertrand Russell skit had gone down like a lead balloon in his spot on *Sunday Night at the London Palladium*, the very venue where he had watched Danny Kaye raise the roof.[106] The rot of insecurity then became pervasive at the Fortune where, paradoxically, the rave reviews made him wary. He now felt overloved, suspecting the adoration was excessive and only temporary. On The Establishment's opening night, he realized he must stop playing the fool soon because he was, in his own eyes, so agonizingly unfunny. He did not perform there much after that.

He was not nervous about directing, except when his seasoned Royal Court colleague, John Dexter, announced that he had finished blocking *The Blood of the Bambergs*. Unaware that this was just the technical term for organizing the actors' positions on the stage, the rookie had a moment of blind panic, envisaging his own production being mauled by the critics for dire blockinglessness. Having got over that blip, he confidently believed that he knew how conversations should sound and, he says, he simply had the actors moving around naturally. What he primarily enjoyed was the 'nursery pleasure' of a group being allowed to continue 'pretending "I'm the king of the castle!"' in grown-up life. The child psychiatrists of his infancy, by strongly encouraging imaginative free play, had indeed had an unexpected long-term effect.

He also became fascinated by 'getting things right', just as his mother had always advocated, shunning sentimental clichés in favour of accuracy, even if that entailed offending people. Directing is, in his view, 'nothing more than reminding people of what they've known all along about being alive, but have forgotten, overlooked or repressed', and 'getting them to forget what they ought never to have "known" in the first place' (i.e. the artificial mannerisms employed by hackneyed theatremakers).

Roger Graef, who was also a Court director, remembers Miller being shyly exhilarated about assembling this new kit of parts – actors, script, lighting and so on. '*Under Plain Cover* had', he says, 'a fresh simplicity, if you like, compared to the more sophisticated conceits Jonathan would do later. Actually, it was closer to the way he now makes his art [his found-object sculptures].'[107] Devine helped Miller as well, solving problems that had developed with the set design, a house that was supposed to open like a clam shell.

When outraged audience members stomped out of the previews, Devine further reassured the company and rightly predicted that eager punters would flood in after press night. His protégé has nothing but praise for the legendary artistic director, describing him as an extremely supportive paternal figure, not an irritable man as some claimed.

The actors who played Osborne's couple, Ann Beach and Anton Rodgers, were in turn impressed by Miller. 'He understood the psychology underlying the piece,' Beach says. 'All his doctor's tact, diplomacy, care and deep insights into the human mind work wonderfully for directing.' Rodgers added:

> He took to directing like a duck to water and what was so marvellous was – and this is an experience I never had before or since – I didn't have to learn the lines at all, because he rehearsed it so well in terms of the reasons behind what we were saying. It was an extraordinary, terribly exciting show to be in because he had this ability to enthuse the cast. There was a tremendous enjoyment factor.

Rodgers further appreciated the Millers' medical skills when he sliced through his thumb, to the bone, on his way to the show's first night. He rang his director's home number, got Rachel's advice on staunching the blood, and was met at the stage door by her other half, who bandaged the wound with sticky tape until there was time for stitches.

Giving himself a pat on the back, Miller thought that Osborne was very approving during rehearsals, whispering with admiration about the production's insights.[108] He further reckoned he had avoided a conflict. When the writer spotted that he had surreptitiously pared some verbose speeches, he acted the innocent and exclaimed that everybody really *must* learn their lines. Little did he know what bile Osborne was pouring into his diary, namely:

> I'm glad I've kept away from J. Miller . . . The striving fluency of the Hampstead nanny's boy is deceptive and occasionally plausible. With its cultural allusions and cross-references to other disciplines, it is the gab-gift of someone to whom English is an adoptive tongue. Intellect does terrible things to the mind. As a director, he's an Armenian carpet-seller.

There is more than a whiff of anti-Semitism or sheer xenophobia there.[109] The dramatist seemed like a spirited dandy but was already turning into a grumpy old snob, observes Miller, who further underlines that 'For someone who'd set so much store by a perfectly ordinary person ranting on the stage [*Look Back in Anger*'s working-class Jimmy Porter], he had very rapidly furnished himself with a Rolls Royce.' Years later, the two men were to meet again for an interview marking Osborne's sixtieth birthday. The playwright insisted this was done at the Garrick Club with champagne at his side. 'He sat there in a cravat and elaborate five-piece suit,' Miller remembers, 'and I asked him about his drift to the right, at which point he said, "I thought this was going to be a celebration. Well, many fucking happy returns!"' It all came to an ill-natured conclusion and was never broadcast.

Whatever Osborne thought, Miller was starting to enjoy directing in 1962, and his July notebook entry shows him grappling with the practicalities, philosophizing about this new craft, and connecting it up with his knowledge of science and Facetti-style collages:

Directing a play
As we go on the actors keep pleading for props . . . we begin to realise how much objects occupy the performer's hands and direct his performance . . . one sees that we are nothing without objects. We are continually looting the tangible world for artificial limbs – anything will do – pencils, hankies, cups and matchboxes. We are like voracious amoebae, gliding about and engulfing things in our pseudopodia, holding them, warming them and rejecting them before we pass on and take up something else. It is as if our body image itself was vague and protean, pouring itself down our hands and into the objects . . .

The James-Lange theory holds to some extent in acting . . . performing unlocks the meaning . . . Direction consists here in persuading them, for a moment, to adopt the James-Lange approach and to discover grief *through* weeping. Performance is . . . the Prince Charming kiss with which the actor stirs the sleeping line . . .

Acting is, at least in rehearsal, collage. Fragments and replicas of the actor's own life, taken from memory and pasted into a new pattern. Then we spin the wheel of the play and the patches and fragments fuse into a luminous blur, like Newton's wheel.[110]

He came to apply J. L. Austin's philosophical essay 'Pretending' humorously too, with the following example:

There are complicated philosophical questions about what it is to pretend to be angry onstage or in life. If you are playing a game, pretending to be a hyena, and you go down on all fours, make a few essays at hideous laughter, then bite a mouthful out of my calf, in what sense has your pretence failed? . . . If I am a burglar on a ladder pretending to polish the windows, and I am polishing them rather well, in what sense am I pretending? . . . If you ask someone to pretend to be Othello . . . It doesn't make him a better Othello if he actually suffocates Desdemona.[111]

As a sideline, Miller was commissioned by Schweppes, in 1962, to co-create posters for a major advertising campaign, a series of cod-Schweppeshire Foundation Reports. The rough drafts survive:

DRAMA AND THE PUBLIC SCENE
The Schweppeshire Foundation has an important part to play in the development of the new National Theatre project. The plan involves a complete revolution in theatrical design. 'Drama,' says Sir Hugo Prompt-Corner, co-ordinator of the scheme, 'must break away from its conventional setting' . . . plans include a daring production of *The Cherry Orchard*, to be staged on the Down Line of the middle span of the Forth Bridge. In this scheme, passengers on the 3.45 to Edinburgh will get a brief but invigorating dose of Chekhov as the train ploughs its way through the assembled actors . . .

THE CHANGING FACE OF BRITAIN
They [the Schweppeshire Foundation's Social Psychology Team] have commissioned Raymond Bulge, Professor of Violence in the London School of Bodily Harm, to conduct a survey of Riots and the Performing Arts . . . a programme of Stravinsky was slipped into the Glyndebourne season, 400 dinner jacketed aristocrats went berserk, slashed seat covers and paraded around the ornamental gardens chanting, 'We want Trad, Dad!' The police of three counties and four fire hoses failed to quell the turbulent 'toffs' and order was only restored when the orchestra, who had fortunately kept their heads, struck up with the overture to *Il Seraglio*.[112]

It was probably for the best that these satirical skits did not make it to the billboards. They sent up top arts institutions which later would employ him as a director.

*   *   *

Miller's income from *Beyond the Fringe* had enabled him and Rachel to leap up the property ladder. They left the rented basement flat in Regent's Park Road and bought a tall, early-Victorian, terraced house in nearby Gloucester Crescent, where they still live. His rise in fortunes was dramatic yet also mirrored the upswing in the nation's finances. The British economy was back on its feet, relatively firmly, for the Sixties. Wages rose and mortgage rates fell, with expansive affluence replacing the age of austerity.

The geometry was peculiarly neat, for Miller's Camden Town property and his two childhood abodes form an almost perfect, right-angled, isosceles triangle on a map of London. Its three points all sit on the edge of the circle that is Regent's Park, with Miller having settled directly north of Park Crescent and due east from Queen's Grove.

Gloucester Crescent itself is a lovely secluded niche, which is simultaneously within earshot of the exotic bellows of London Zoo. It is just off Camden Market which, in the early Sixties, was full of fruit and veg, cheese, poultry and antiques stalls. The market would rapidly turn into a Mecca for hippy and grungy street gear. In the meantime, however, the Crescent was to become a celebrated nerve centre of liberal intellectuals, press and TV stars, so much so that the media was said to be run by an Oxbridge Mafia encamped in NW1 (the North West One postcode).

This area had a history of being inhabited by freethinkers, artists and academics because nearby are the British Museum, Bloomsbury and UCL. More notoriously, Dickens had stowed his wife at 70 Gloucester Crescent when he left her in the 1850s, after she had born him ten children. When the Millers arrived, the author Louis MacNeice was already living in their street. Essentially, though, they helped start an extraordinary trend. Alan Bennett became their lodger during the London run of *Beyond the Fringe*, residing in the basement flat (now the kitchen). This made home life highly entertaining, Rachel confirms, and Bennett shared intellectual interests with her husband, in history, art and literature.

Before many years had passed, other neighbours in the Crescent were to include Miller's Cambridge friends Claire and Nick Tomalin (and later her second husband, Michael Frayn); George Melly and his writer-wife Diana; Max Stafford-Clark (of Joint Stock Theatre Company and then the Royal Court); Stevie Smith's biographer Frances Spalding; the artist David Gentleman; Mary-Kay Wilmers (who took over the editorship of the *London Review of Books* from its founder, Karl Miller); Susannah Clapp (another *LRB* co-founder); Ursula Vaughan Williams (widow of Ralph); the Labour MP Giles Radice; the novelist Alice Thomas Ellis (real name Anna) and her husband Colin Haycraft (whose party-throwing publishing house, Duckworth, was based at No. 43, an old piano factory).

In nearby streets were Joan Bakewell; the philosopher A. J. (Freddie) Ayer and his journalist wife Dee Wells; the writers V. S. Pritchett, Angus Wilson and Julia O'Faolain; and *Private Eye*'s John Wells. That is not to mention Jill Tweedie, Kingsley Amis, Sylvia Plath, Roger Graef, Beryl Bainbridge or Jenni Murray of *Woman's Hour*. The sculptor Anthony Caro has his studio round the corner, and Bennett himself bought a house virtually opposite his co-star's in 1969.

When the Millers moved in the area was not gentrified. Their new home had previously been a cheap boarding house, and an entry in Miller's notebook shows him appreciating the shabbier aspects of his environs. Riding on his Lambretta past the deep cutting at one end of the Crescent, he endowed it with a mythical, almost Orphean status, writing:

> The railway exists at another level . . . a supernatural world hidden behind the houses . . . the shunt, grunt, rattle and shackle of goods yards behind the stucco terraces . . . an industrial spirit world, a plutonic [sic] reality under the surface of things. (There are occasional elegiac cries from the engines) . . . the strangeness of all this . . . that Hell, a supernatural place, should have an entrance geographically located in the ordinary physical world.[113]

Simply putting down permanent roots made Miller feel secure. He called his earnings 'fuck-off money' and, having inherited Emanuel's dread of impoverished eviction, he bought the freehold.[114] That way he could shake off the nightmare vision of being dragged down his front steps, as an old man, by some cruel landlord. He was certainly delighted to be a house-owner, albeit with some professional anxieties, as he typed the following and sent it off to Sacks in San Franciso:

Gloucester crescent, n.w.1 [sic]

My Dear Ol, another sluggishly belated letter. As you can see from the address I . . . am now comfortably set-up . . . My whole purpose, I think, in taking up this review [sic] has been to get enough money to buy a place like this . . . Having a place like this takes all the edge off one's ambition . . . I am writing this from my study which is right at the top of the house looking down onto an enormous rock pool of tree filled gardens swimming with cats and children. Rachel is away doing her house jobs so that I am alone in the place luxuriating in the private emptiness; standing in the basement, shouting yoo-hoo and listening to the sound loose itself into the upstairs emptiness of my own property . . .

We [the *Beyond the Fringe* quartet] have been an astounding and resounding success and have become the theatrical gold standard by which practically everything else is calibrated. The curious and disturbing thing about all this is the fact that there is, implicit in it, a fair ration of resentment all ready to swing in the other direction whenever the climate changes. The whole system of critical praise and contempt seems capricious.[115]

Signing off, he added that he was now being asked to write a great deal for the papers, was still working for his MRCP (the postgraduate medical diploma), and would be coming to the States with *Beyond the Fringe* in September 1962.[116] They were, he said, to play Washington before the big challenge, sinking or swimming on Broadway.

· 7 ·

1962–4

New York

THE MILLERS' FIRST CHILD, Tom, was born on 20 August 1962. Rachel had just managed to complete her registration year at the Royal Free and the London Jewish Hospital. Then, only four days after she gave birth, her husband was obliged to be on the high seas, sailing with Bennett, Cook and Moore for North America. The Fringers were to play Toronto and Boston, as well as Washington, before their opening night in New York. A substitute cast took over in London.[1]

As with household chores, so with fatherhood, Miller was not what we would, today, call a New Man. He admits, with a frown, that he absented himself during the birth and was insensitively casual about it. However, he soon became enchanted by his son, discovering a kind of free-flowing family love which, he says, he never experienced with his own parents. Tom, now a photographer with a flat not too far away, regularly calls in at Gloucester Crescent. Miller Snr's memories of bouncing his first infant on his knee, in a tiny cotton nightgown, provoke satirical exclamations from Tom who claims that early snapshots exist of his dad, virtually in a rubber apron and gloves, holding him at arm's length. Besides inheriting the tall, thin build, he has a vigorous line in ribbing his father.

Back in 1962, parent and child were separated by an ocean for several weeks, during which time Miller's Atlantic crossing, on a luxury liner, was a surprise lesson in humility. Contrary to the Fringers' expectations, star treatment aboard the SS *France* did not even stretch to *egalité*. Having envisaged a magnificent reception and having planned to decline all invitations to join the Captain's table, the four celebs were unceremoniously directed to their cabins and relegated to dining in the nursery because of overcrowding. Later, when a talent competition was announced and they offered themselves for appraisal, they were instantly rejected in favour of a Monsieur Bundy singing 'O, moon of Alabama'.[2]

Miller was also becoming ludicrously anxious about muggers. The boat was heading for the Big Apple where the crime rate was notorious, so he spent sleepless

126

nights imagining the assaults in store. Getting 'jumped' sounded sinisterly sexual, he thought, perhaps entailing being mauled and kissed on the quayside while being relieved of one's bankroll. In the event, the nearest he came to GBH was when a Manhattan drunk was hurled out of a bar, like a javelin, and landed at his feet on the sidewalk, requiring immediate medical attention.

Left in England, Rachel felt somewhat tearful. Being self-sufficient by nature, she rallied pretty swiftly though, and then set off across the Pond with the baby. She fondly recalls her first night reunited with her husband and how he paced round their hotel room, holding Tom and asking with naive anxiety: 'Why is he crying?' On another night in Boston, she watched the show from the wings and Tom became an involuntary child star. This was when Cook, in one of his most startling improvisations, entered Miller and Bennett's skit about philosophy dons, in the role of college porter. Brandishing the squirming infant, he announced: 'It's your wife, Professor. She's had a baby. What shall I do with it?' Bennett luckily had the presence of mind to reply, 'Go away and put it in the fridge, Jarvis.' Backstage that night, the new father's sense of humour failed him and he yelled, 'You might have dropped it!' To this, Cook petulantly replied that he wasn't the one who was clumsy with props.[3]

When they were in Washington, Miller was further enraged by Cook's magazine *Private Eye*, a copy of which had arrived from London. Assuming anonymity, he had contributed a mock medical article headed 'The Hounding of the Pooves'. Therein the correspondent – parodying the furore provoked by the Wolfenden Report – veered ludicrously between homophobic and distinctly liberal directives:[4]

Pouves, pouves! Que pouvez-vous dire? Sont-ils ils ou elles? Not even Montaigne himself, the balding sage of old Dordogne, could fathom the ways of the crafty poove . . .

Doctors have realised, in recent years, that there are many more pooves in society than meet the eye at first glance, many of them running the country . . . More than four out of every twenty men you meet on the top of a bus . . .

After intensive research, both in this country and in America, we know that your average poove is a sick man. He should be treated as such by society – with aspirin or whatever comes to hand. It is simply ridiculous to say that he is abnormal . . . .

There has been considerable agitation in recent years by irresponsible left-wing elements, pooves etc., for a reform of the so-called Labouchere Amendment which makes the filthy and depraved practices of the poove a criminal offence etc.

The trouble was that this was all attributed, in large bold type, to 'DR J Miller', alongside a photograph of him. His primary concern was not what four out of every twenty pals of his would think. Indeed, in later years he would gripe in press interviews about 'disgusting old opera queens' and their 'rampant heterophobia'.[5] Now a happily out-of-the-closet bisexual, Bennett has even dryly described him as the 'Enoch Powell of the sexual world', a dauntingly unambivalent straight man. So it is anyone's guess how Miller managed, somewhere in between, to be appointed a vice president of the Campaign for Homosexual Equality (a post which he holds still).

His immediate worry regarding the 'Hounding of the Pooves' was his professional good name as a doctor.[6] He grabbed a sheet of hotel notepaper and wrote to the magazine:

> You stupid, bloody, irresponsible <u>cunts</u>!! You had no permission and therefore no right to use my medical title as a heading to the article. Are you all so completely frivolous and insensitive as not to be able to understand that such a fucking stupid blunder could well mean my being struck off the register. God rot the lot of you!

> Jonathan Miller

The editor Christopher Booker and his crew found this so funny that the letter remains pinned to *Private Eye*'s notice-board to this day.[7] In time, there would be further enmity.

*　　*　　*

That autumn, Khrushchev and President John F. Kennedy's hostilities appeared to be seriously heading towards nuclear war. The Cuban Missile Crisis reached its climax on 27 October, precisely as *Beyond the Fringe* opened in New York at the John Golden Theater. The comedians felt an acute sense of unreality, rehearsing and previewing in a city paralyzed with fear and facing possible annihilation. It was almost a case of fiddling while Manhattan burned. On his way to work, Miller imagined nuclear gales scorching down the avenues and the steel bridges melting. Bennett was so scared on his own that he went to stay in Moore and John Bassett's apartment.

Amazingly in the circumstances, they did not adjust their material, eliciting desperately twisted grins with their civil defence 'skeleton service' gag and the closing sketch 'The End of the World', where they pretended to be an apocalyptic sect. Armed with a placard saying 'The End is Nigh', they intoned:

Jon: When will it be, this end of which you have spoken?

All: Aye, when will it be, when will it be? . . .

PETER: In about thirty seconds time, according to the ancient pyramidic scrolls and my Ingersoll watch . . . Fifteen seconds . . . Ten seconds . . . Five – four – three – two – one – zero!

ALL (*chanting*): Now is the end – perish the world!

Pause.

PETER: It was G.M.T., wasn't it?

JON: Yes.

PETER: Well, it's not quite the conflagration I'd been banking on. Never mind, lads, same time tomorrow – we must get a winner one day.[8]

Because the preview audiences were sitting in stunned silence, the group presumed they were going to be butchered by the critics if not burned to cinders by the USSR. Then, on 28 October, the Cuban Missile Crisis abated. The reviews materialized, a mood of euphoric relief took hold, and the Broadway impresario Alexander H. Cohen (who had previously produced Nichols and May at the same theatre) had another hit on his hands. The *New York Times* hailed *Beyond the Fringe* as a hilarious antidote to terror. The *Herald Tribune* called the show ruthlessly funny, and the *New York Post* deemed it immense and ingenious. Writing from America for the *Guardian*, Alistair Cooke was sniffier but reported that hardly any reviews were less than delirious.[9]

The quartet were soon guests on *The Jack Paar Show* and other popular TV programmes.[10] Cohen extended the run, as well as duplicating the production in Los Angeles with a second cast. The Fringers won a Tony and a special citation in the New York Drama Critics' Circle Awards. Miller was also shortlisted for the Variety Awards. Having cost $62,000 to stage, *Beyond the Fringe* ultimately made a profit of over $350,000. Its stars had wised up as well, striking a decidedly better deal in the USA than in the UK. Roughly speaking, they had added a nought to their weekly pay cheque, plus a box-office percentage, meaning that Miller was pumping money into his savings account.[11]

Brits were all the rage on the Great White Way around this time, with Peter Hall's recently founded RSC pitching up; John Gielgud and Ralph Richardson in *The School for Scandal*; *Oliver!* going transatlantic; Albert Finney in John Osborne's *Luther*; Pinter's plays off-Broadway; and Cook's Establishment team rolling into town. After the show, Miller would hang out at the thesps' favoured restaurant Jim Downey's or catch the hottest comics' late-night gigs, not least Woody Allen and the Second City troupe. They were raising the roof at Square East in Greenwich Village, near Gerde's Folk City where Bob Dylan often played. Allegedly, Miller steamed with jealousy whenever Mike Nichols' satirical genius was praised, yet he made several other Second

City friends including Alan Arkin, and he warmly lauds the troupe's sassy spontaneity.[12]

Everybody who was 'anybody' flocked to see *Beyond the Fringe*, not least John F. Kennedy who – while hailed as embodying youthful progressiveness, post-Eisenhower – turned up accompanied by the notorious nuclear red button.[13] It was installed in the box office, just in case, and Secret Service personnel sat in the wings, eyeing the toy swords on the props table as highly suspect. The president further honoured the Golden by urinating in its broom cupboard. Bennett scribbled 'John F. Kennedy pee'd here' on the wall for want of a plaque.[14] Once Cook had set up The Establishment with Eleanor Bron, John Bird and co. over at the refurbished Strollers Theatre Club on East 54th Street, America's first lady became so frequent a guest there that Bennett thought Peter and Jackie might be having a closet affair.[15]

The group were lionized in New York, being invited to extraordinarily lavish parties in the Dakota and other apartments buildings, all overflowing with food, drink and artworks. It was like something from the late Roman empire, only with Judy Garland and Steve McQueen milling around alongside Henry Fonda and Lauren Bacall. Bennett says that he has 'never since been in rooms so stiff with celebrity'. The lionizing made the Fringers charmingly and almost unrecognizably confident, says director Eleanor Fazan, who caught up with them in Manhattan. Nervously overawed, however, Bennett turned down several VIP dinners for fear of being sick over the silver platters.[16]

Miller was impressed as well, yet he took it in his stride, even when one or two gatherings turned into classic Sixties orgies. When the lights were switched off at one bash, followed by much heavy breathing, he perched in a state of polite expectation but, he says, his hopes of being seriously interfered with came to nothing.[17] In a similar vein, he had a risible brush with a bunny girl, when he took a trip out to Hugh Hefner's Chicago mansion to discuss contributing an article (of the higher brow sort) to *Playboy*. Crossing the threshold, past the doorbell with the Latin inscription '*Si Non Oscillas, Noli Tintinnare*' ('If you don't swing, don't ring'), he found the magazine magnate lolling in state, proclaiming: 'Well, Jonathan, we'd better make sure you get laid.' At the obligatory poolside party, the designated bit of fluff was ushered over, apparently took one look at the new arrival and turned to Hefner, shrieking, 'You must be joking!'

Back on the Manhattan social circuit, Miller made one top-level gaffe. This occurred when Jackie Kennedy invited him to an extremely select dinner party with her brother-in-law and the Russian ambassador to the UN. As the conversation turned to politics, Miller chipped in with a comment, only for Bobby Kennedy to whip round and snarl that this was neither the time nor the place for *his* contribution. The dinner was, Miller concludes, just a cover for the two politicos to debate what RFK might do in Vietnam, were he to become president post-JFK.[18] Bobby was, of course, shot before he got that far.

*   *   *

The Fringers never had a collective terminal quarrel. Miller, though, officially broke up the quartet when he quit the show in late 1963, saying he had wearied of it.[19] A second reason was his resurgent stammer. He had begun to see the consonants in certain sketches looming up like rocks in the rapids. Playing the vicar in the skit 'Man Bites God', he found he could not say 'God' and endlessly had to get around this glottal monosyllable in a sweat-drenched panic. He wasn't bothered about taking the Lord's name in vain, he underlines. It was surely a form of stage fright or the outward manifestation of his mind balking – almost as if he were gagging at being a gagman. He went to a doctor about the problem to no avail, and he had a recurrent nightmare for years afterwards, a dream of standing isolated under the lights, aware of the waiting audience yet unable to utter a word.[20]

Before the group broke up, they had clearly bonded to varying degrees, more than any simplistic notion of mutual envy would allow. As Bennett remembers, there had been countless shared laughs. Even the four's prickliest recollections of each other tend to contain traces of affection suppressed or sorely disappointed To this day, Miller acknowledges his fellow Fringers' outstanding talents. He pays tribute to Moore as a supremely gifted musician and to Bennett as a brilliant literary miniaturist of unflinching accuracy. He rates Cook as a kind of genius, the most brilliant improvisational comic he has ever seen. He does not mince his words about any of that.[21]

Nonetheless, frictions had worn the bonhomie very thin during *Beyond the Fringe*'s long run. Bennett and Moore were close buddies for a while in Manhattan, regularly dining together as the two bachelors. Dudley, however, was growing increasingly impish during performances. Their friendship ended abruptly when he adorned Miller and Bennett's philosophers sketch, 'Words . . . and Things', from just out of view. Loud fart noises and cries of 'Nurse! Nurse!' were followed by a rubber penis winging its way across the stage, fired from a bow. The perfectionist Bennett was not remotely amused.'We didn't have an argument, *he* did,' Moore recalled, explaining that they never really spoke again.[22]

Having become exasperated by the others messing around, Bennett considered Miller slack as well. '[Jonathan] would often throw the whole performance away,' he says, 'because the audience had failed to respond to some remark.'[23] The two of them had an explosive row backstage, also concerning 'Words . . . and Things', after Miller added touches that Bennett considered attention-seeking. 'Alan was obviously very annoyed,' says the accused, '*I* had actually met these philosophers, but *he* had written the damn sketch. Anyway, I thought he was very priggishly dismissive and, during the interval, in the green room, I got so irritated with him I simply kicked the table over.' Bennett's angle is: 'Once, when Jonathan was being more than usually grandiloquent, and I was being particularly sour, he, with characteristic extravagance, threw a tea service at me. Though, again characteristically, it missed.'[24] Miller remembers immediately racing out in a high dudgeon, 'or trying to race out in a high dudgeon, because what happens is you always forget that the door opens the opposite way . . . which punctures the dudgeon'.[25]

The way Miller effortlessly gained the media limelight was particularly galling for the others. He shone on America's chat-shows and was featured most prestigiously – and solo – in *Life* magazine.[26] Cook jealously viewed him as a fantastic manipulator of journalists and Bennett felt that he was in his shadow too, unfairly undervalued by the press. He has declared that he could understand Kenneth Halliwell battering Joe Orton's brains out because 'There were times in those years 1961–4 when I felt like that myself'.[27]

Miller exaggerates in claiming, somewhat tetchily, that he never hung out with the others in New York, yet his social circle did slide apart from Moore's and from Cook's to form a Venn diagram with decreasing common ground. Bennett was, meanwhile, often holed up due to shyness. Cook's comic genius doubtless ruffled feathers in terms of onstage rivalries, and Miller sounds mildly irritated by the glam lifestyles with which Peter and Dudley were increasingly preoccupied and which he dismisses as shallow. Moore started dabbling with Hollywood starlets including Tuesday Weld who, as Miller pointed out, sounded like a mid-week programme about iron casting. Cook was off fraternizing with members of the Rat Pack who, even if they held a certain fascination, were never going to be the intellectual medic's clique of choice.

House-sharing in Connecticut did not help the four performers patch up their differences. As an escape from the sweltering city in mid-1963, Alexander Cohen lent them his country home. Being the producer, he wanted things to keep running smoothly. Unfortunately, with tempers frayed, the long drive every night after the show seemed interminable. They lived very uneasily under the same roof through that summer, with the weekends swamped by Peter and Wendy's social life, and with Miller and Bennett mutually nettled.[28]

The addition of David Frost as an unwelcome guest was the last straw, though his arrival at least stopped them throttling one another. Having landed the presenter's job on TV's *TW3* series back in the UK, Cook's ex-sidekick from Footlights was regarded by them all – unfairly or not – as a Satire Boom parasite. Miller mockingly dubbed him 'the bubonic plagiarist' and, when Frost nearly drowned in Cohen's swimming pool, it became a long-standing joke that Cook's only regret in life was that he unthinkingly saved him.[29]

After their years in *Beyond the Fringe*, the co-stars went their separate ways, loosely reconfigured as two pairs. Pete and Dud would both pursue more celebrity glitz, wedding and shedding a string of wives in the process, and becoming a legendary double act for a time, aka the foul-mouthed Derek and Clive.[30] By contrast, not being enamoured of showbiz's 'silly paraphernalia', Miller and Bennett would return to a more highbrow life, remaining part of the industry but refashioning themselves as director and playwright.[31] They never formally teamed up again on a production but lived as Gloucester Crescent neighbours for almost four decades. These pairs would continue to blow hot and cold over the years, with Pete and Dud's partnership featuring notoriously messy bust-ups, like a bad marriage. Becoming an abusive drunk, Cook apparently festered with jealousy over Moore's subsequent Hollywood stardom while tragically squandering his own talent.

The Fringers re-formed, only partially and fleetingly, in the late 1970s when Miller, Bennett and Cook made cameo appearances in Amnesty International's West End charity shows *A Poke in the Eye with a Sharp Stick* (working title *An Evening without David Frost*) and *The Secret Policeman's Ball*. Those shows were big televised hits (with Miller helping in a directorial capacity too), and they are said to have inspired Bob Geldolf's 1980s benefit gig *Live Aid*.[32] Still, treading the boards to replay *Beyond the Fringe*'s vintage sketches merely made Miller feel inept and amazed that he had ever done it in the first place.

*　　*　　*

The great thing about Manhattan was that he found his own new social circle and had a wonderful time overall. 'I was absolutely intoxicated by the United States!' he exclaims.[33] On arrival, he and Rachel had been looked after by a set of families who spanned medicine and showbusiness. They stayed with the English actor-turned-diplomat Peter Haden-Guest. His teenage son Christopher Guest (now of *Spinal Tap* fame) counts Miller among his formative comic influences.[34] Other welcoming friends in the Haden-Guests' crowd included Eli Wallach (from *The Magnificent Seven*), the clinical psychiatrist Harvey Corman and his wife Cis (a mother figure for the young Barbra Streisand).

The Millers subsequently found an apartment on the Upper West Side: 10th floor, 310 West End Avenue. He loved the shabby marginal feel which the district still had back then, though the Lincoln Center was already under construction. Rachel occasionally felt isolated and, with her trying to keep her career ticking over, they hired a nanny who proved regrettable, making Tom distressed.[35] It was as if Nanny Morgan had contrived to reincarnate herself for the next generation. In spite of this, family life together was joyful as the young father wrote to Sacks (in San Francisco): 'Tom is a darling and a delight . . . with soprano cries of startled triumph at his own sudden abilities . . . He laughs a great deal and is the main pleasure in our life now.'[36]

Miller found the vivacity of 24/7 New York exhilarating as well. His enthusiastic side was more in tune with America than with British reserve. Post-World War 2, Jewish intellectuals had begun to flourish, playing a leading role in the country's cultural life. 'It was a sort of Promised Land,' he says. 'I just felt it to be a place where intelligence was at a premium and I was swept away by the intellectual ferment.'

Conscious of how easily his Lithuanian ancestors could have sailed on past Cork, he felt that within him was a phantom version of the American he might have been. He started reading as much as he could about the States' literature and history: Alfred Kazin's *On Native Grounds*, Lionel Trilling's *The Middle of the Journey*, and records of the American Civil War. At the same time, he met a whole clutch of New York intellectuals, several of whom remain a cherished part of his life. He stresses:

The things that turned me on, which made me feel I'd made it in New York were nothing to do with showbiz. They were meeting with [the editor] Bob Silvers and becoming part of the *New York Review of Books*' circle and other overlapping [literary circles] . . . To me, these people were the epitome of New York . . . You were just talking to the brightest and cleverest people with that range of cross-disciplinary interests which Americans have and which American Jews have more than anyone else. I felt Jewish without having to be Jewish there. It was smart to be Jewish. It wasn't apologetic.[37]

An outstanding entrepreneurial journalist, Robert Silvers co-founded the *NYRB* in 1963, seizing readers while the *New York Times*' presses were frozen by strikes.[38] Fed up with the middlebrow hacks of the Fifties, he was determined to brighten up the media – the antithesis of dumbing down. In appearance he was terrifically shambolic, covered in a dusting of cigarette ash. He could, nonetheless, convene a lunch with any brilliant mind you wished to meet.

Miller was born to be part of this smart set, the emergent cerebral celebrities of the Sixties. In the style of Viennese society on the Ringstrasse in the 1900s, he was soon hooking up with Silvers and his circle several times a week, conversing for hours in the Russian Tea Rooms near Carnegie Hall. Silvers served as another tutorial presence in his life, introducing him to stacks more books. Colleagues heartily embraced the English newcomer too. Chief among these were the author and essayist Elizabeth Hardwick; her spouse, the celebrated poet Robert Lowell; Silvers' associate editor Barbara Epstein; and the *Paris Review* editors, Nelson Aldrich and George Plimpton.[39] A photograph of one of Plimpton's legendary parties, reprinted in the *New York Times* in 2003, captures Miller amid the elegant throng with Truman Capote and Gore Vidal.[40]

Other literary acquaintances soon included Trilling and Kazin, whose works he was so avidly reading, Norman Mailer, Joseph Heller, Edmund Wilson, and Philip Roth. He became very good friends with Susan Sontag, and his company was certainly enjoyed a great deal by Frances FitzGerald (the journalist and author of *Fire in the Lake: The Vietnamese and the Americans in Vietnam*). Sontag would come round to 310 West End Avenue for breakfast every Saturday, with her young son in tow.[41] Miller frequently headed off to the movies with her and Silvers. He escorted them to neurology lectures at Mount Sinai Hospital, and he sat in on sociology classes at Columbia University. He never, though, took up a medical post in the US as he had planned. In the social whirl, he let slip the opportunity to acquire one of those BTA (Been To America) degrees in clinical research.

Sontag was not best pleased when he categorized her, by gender, as the cleverest woman in America. She was enormously fond of him nonetheless, referring to him as the first person she ever met who was truly at home in the Two Cultures. She stated that he helped her to unify all her diverse interests.[42]

He attended one decidedly private film screening at Plimpton's place with reels of porn supplied by the writer-next-door, Terry Southern of *Dr Strangelove* fame. One can only imagine the post-show discussion by the assembled fine minds.

Miller was not, it seems, entirely sated. He has commented, more generally, on New York's late-night porn cinemas and on the strange reassurance felt by a clientele who cannot sink any further, 'sit[ting] like strange molluscan sea creatures at the bottom of the sea: awful sessile anemones just gulping down this peculiar visual food'.[43]

Surfacing, he was taken for an unforgettable walk across the Brooklyn Bridge one January morning by Kazin. Sounding rather like an aesthetically sensitive Sam Spade, his notebook entry describes Kazin arriving to whisk him downtown:[44]

> With A.K. to the South end of the island . . . He'd taken off his rubbers [that is galoshes] before he rang and when I answered the door they were lying at his feet like snake casts. Thick tweed raglan and an unexpectedly perky little snap-brim felt hat.[45] He was nervously apologetic about getting us up and sat uneasily on the couch talking in eager jerks, turning his head suddenly when small sounds came from the next room. We took a cab and roared down the cobbles of the Westside [sic] Highway. A cold Sunday mist, unheated by weekday activity, hung over the silent docks. Past the Cunard sheds . . . Down at 14th Street and below came the older piers. Erie and Pennsylvania Railroad [sheds]. Green and brick red, timber facades . . . classical stage proscenia with crudely elegant lettering in fading gold along the pediments. Print everywhere – on windows, fading in plastery palimpsests on huge side walls. Hoardings held up by big skeletal scaffolds. Printed roadway signs, arrows, indications. The taxi took a dip of[f] the highway, down into the long foggy vaults of the dockside. We got out . . . [and from] somewhere came the distant thunderous groans of fog-bound shipping . . . Then across the bridge with K now slightly out of breath with exertion and perhaps excitement at the approach of Brooklyn, still invisible . . . A timber catwalk runs down the centre of the bridge, raised above the traffic which howls on either side. You seem to enter a huge cat's cradle of steel [suspension cables] . . . swing[ing] up behind, as you cross, in vertiginous crescents [and] swooping down to run before you . . . To the north is . . . the Manhattan bridge printed lightly on the blotting-paper of the fog.[46]

Miller also started to be categorized as a comic-turned-critic in Manhattan, because he not only socialized with, but also appeared in print alongside the New York intellectuals. He and Sontag often sat typing together as he wrote for the smart Jewish magazines *Commentary* and *Partisan Review*, and occasionally for the *Herald Tribune*. He contributed to the very first issue of the *NYRB*, flaying John Updike's novel *The Centaur* for being pretentious and lacking narrative drive, 'a poor novel irritatingly marred by good features'. He went on to be equally bruising about the grandiose, middlebrow theatrics at the Lincoln Center when it opened, especially regarding the psychodrama *After the Fall* by Arthur Miller, 'the owner of a sound, but essentially minor, talent'.[47]

As Nelson Aldrich humorously remarks, 'Jonathan can certainly dish criticism out, though he can't take it! He's got the thinnest of skins and, at the same time, the most devastating of fists.' On top of this, Miller was slating several of those big-name authors with whom he was mingling. Assessing *The Presidential Papers* by Mailer, he blithely wrote that 'there is a certain ludicrous magnificence in coming on like a pompous bloody fool in the service of a passionate evangelical commitment'. Then he had a run-in with Trilling. This involved an exchange of letters in the *NYRB* where his comments were rebuffed as inaccurate. Mourning the death of Lenny Bruce, he had suggested that Trilling indirectly encouraged the comedian to run fatally wild.[48]

Miller could also be upbraided for not explaining the basic facts in his reviews, but he was essentially just what the *NYRB* needed, combining brains and punchy opinions, encyclopaedic cross-references and a springy style. His articles remain highly rated by Silvers, particularly his sharp account of *The Centaur* and his longer piece about the wolf boy of Aveyron (a feral child found in France around 1800). That article was a prime example of Miller's expansive and educative style, becoming a subsequent reference point for scholarly debate.[49]

He did a further stint as a movie reviewer and a TV columnist at the *New Yorker*, where he was given his own office.[50] His declared agenda, regarding television, was to discuss not just individual programmes but wider social issues too.[51] Analyzing the coverage of JFK's assassination, he observed how the endlessly repeated footage had proved unexpectedly valuable, almost ritualistic, constituting a new form of national mourning, a crash course in grief.[52] Conversely, he slated the nature of small-screen broadcasting as a whole, noting:

> The shuddering fluorescent jelly of which it's made seems to corrode the eye of the spectator and soften his brain . . . It's like ectoplasm, in fact, which makes the term 'medium' doubly appropriate. Television is a low grade domestic séance in endless session . . . small and stingy [compared to the dreamy and oceanic big screen] . . . Not to mention the commercials which inhabit the crevices of the programs like vile, raucous parasites.[53]

He was not alone in his condemnations. Addressing America's National Association of Broadcasters in 1961, Newton N. Minow of the Federal Communications Commission had censured the output, particularly on commercial channels, as a 'vast wasteland' of formulaic junk.[54]

Following Minow's call for more 'blue ribbon' programmes, Miller crossed over from reviewing to working in US TV, in a scriptwriting and directorial capacity. His aim was to run against the canonical grain, try out new techniques, positively explore the medium's intimacy.[55] His initial efforts fell far short of the exemplary, nevertheless. Prompted by the frontier-pushing space race of the Sixties, he co-wrote an adaptation of Jules Verne's Victorian fantasy *From the Earth to the Moon*, together with the CBS producer Robert Goldman. Renamed *A Trip to the Moon*, this starred the Fringers in top hats and mustachios, portraying the members of a gun club who, none too scientifically, fired themselves skywards in a rocket resembling a Pullman carriage.[56] Supposed to be hilarious, with historically informative content, the programme was immediately shot down by the *New York Times* as a stilted, inconsistent assemblage of movie snippets and cartoons, 'without a hint of wit'.[57] So Miller, the TV critic, received a dose of his own medicine. To his credit, he himself pans it as rubbish, 'just boring and no bloody good'.

This was something of a low point since, without the anchor of *Beyond the Fringe*, he needed to fill his time. The foursome were all waiting for the spring of 1964, in order to avoid huge British tax bills. He had already written to Sacks about his distrust of journalism, its capriciousness and transience. He added: 'There are moments when I long for the clouds to open and flights of angels in rather tight formation to come at me shouting through megaphones, "Everything's going to be all right".'[58]

Life in America was losing its gloss, with JFK gone and with racial tensions rising even in the Northern cities, soon to explode in the Harlem riots of 1964. Furthermore, in February, just when *A Trip to the Moon* bombed, the Beatles became America's new darlings, greeted by screaming crowds on tour. On top of this, a theatre directing job went belly up for Miller. He was invited by Alexander Cohen to stage *World War Two and a Half*, a Broadway-bound entertainment about the battle of the sexes, perhaps prompted by Betty Friedan's 1963 book, *The Feminine Mystique*, which kickstarted second-wave feminism in the USA. Miller ended up in a terminal conflict with his leading lady, Barbara Bel Geddes (who went on to play Miss Ellie in *Dallas*). The show was costing $75,000 but their 'artistic differences' could not be resolved.[59] As payback, Miller was subsequently described, by Cohen, as uncommitted, pretentious, aggressive and condescending.[60]

By March, luckily, he had been commissioned to script a drama for the TV series *Profiles in Courage*, which was based on President Kennedy's Pulitzer Prize-winning book of role models. Miller chose the life story of Anne Hutchinson, an outspoken Puritan (played by Wendy Hiller) who was banished from seventeenth-century Massachusetts for heresy.[61] Again, he dismisses the end result, saying his script was poor. He is prouder of, and more defensive about *What's Going On Here?* In this comedy series, he got to direct the performers for the first time, though not the cameras. As an experimental satire show, it was groundbreaking stuff for America's national network, and it has since been referred to as a precursor of *Saturday Night Live*.

The writers and performers were an Anglo-American team including several from The Establishment and the Second City troupe. It was tried out on New York's WNEW TV channel, and it made headlines when CBS' *The Ed Sullivan Show* – which had a colossal audience, coast to coast – decided to incorporate its sketches on a weekly basis.[62] Sullivan apparently commissioned it on hearsay, without watching it, and was then appalled to see such anarchic irreverence. As John Bird, who was on board, explains:

Sullivan was a complete dinosaur really, mainstream America was not ready by any stretch of the imagination, and a huge amount of money was tied up in the show's sponsorship. I said to Jonathan, 'We can't do very strong stuff,' then we discovered we couldn't do anything at all! Jonathan kept walking out of meetings saying, 'This is ludicrous!'

What's Going On Here? was ditched, yet in the greater scheme of things that was a blip. Miller now looks back on his work in American television studios as a useful apprenticeship, because he had the opportunity to watch what the cameramen and technical crew were doing. He was, moreover, pleasantly distracted from the professional downers by William, his second child, coming into the world.[63] The births of his two sons neatly framed his time in America. Six weeks after William's arrival the family were heading back to Camden Town, and the BBC was waiting to offer Miller a plum job.

·8·

THE MID-SIXTIES

Back in the UK and shaking up the BBC, from *Monitor* to *Alice in Wonderland*

THE BBC'S EXECUTIVE GODDESS OF FORTUNE, Grace Wyndham Goldie, was giving her wheel a spin. She was, once more, disposed to look benignly on Miller. Her wrath concerning his Nelson skit on BBC TV's *Tonight* had, in fact, abated as early as 1962, when he was setting out for the States. One of her internal memos from that August is revealing about his long-term plans and about her foresight regarding his potential. She wrote:

> In the course of talking to Jonathan Miller today . . . I found out . . . he does not propose to continue working in medicine, but hopes (and he says this was his original intention) to use his medical training as a deepening of his ability in the sociological field . . . [Therefore] we are trying to arrange that he should consider what he would like to do in the way of longer and different programmes for television, on the sociological/medical front when he comes back . . . [Moreover] he would be very interested, if we are interested . . . in trying his hand at some drama production in television.[1]

On his return to the UK in April 1964, he was immediately back on *Tonight*, chatting about his time abroad. Then in June, in one giant leap of faith, the BBC announced his appointment as the new editor of *Monitor*.[2]

In the history of British televeision, *Monitor* stands as the seminal arts magazine programme. Established in the 1950s by the presenter and former war hero Huw Wheldon (OBE, MC), it was a revered national institution.[3] That said, by 1964 some TV columnists considered Wheldon old-fashioned, and he had become extremely busy, running the documentary and music department. Humphrey Burton had briefly taken over the fortnightly *Monitor* slot but was, in turn, needed to help manage the new channel, BBC2. So both of them were racking their brains for a talented replacement when a knock was heard at the door. Although Miller portrays his life story as just succumbing to invitations to 'come out and play', he can be far more proactive. As he neared his thirtieth year, he was seeking out Wheldon to enquire about preliminary training as a TV director.

He was extremely fortunate to be forging his career in an era when the media were expanding and the BBC was becoming more experimentally adventurous, valuing the highbrow. Television was, at this point, the industry to be in if you wanted to become a household name, with British viewing figures having rocketed since the late 1950s (while radio and cinema audiences declined). Moreover, the first Telstar communication satellites had just been launched, capable of relaying TV images across the world.

So, having knocked at Wheldon's door, Miller suddenly found himself being asked to run the show, as *Monitor*'s anchorman and content-determining editor. Since he had barely even watched the programme, he was amazed. Nevertheless, remembering how he had learned on the job for his directing debut at the Royal Court Theatre, he paused only momentarily before accepting the challenge.[4]

The following months were hectic to the point of hair-raising. He needed to be up to speed, planning and producing the new autumn–winter series, however, he had already promised, to return to New York for two months that summer, in order to stage *The Old Glory*, a trilogy of plays by Robert Lowell. Becoming jumpy, Wheldon insisted that the newcomer make a trial programme before vanishing to the USA. Unscheduled access to studios and cutting rooms had to be sought in a race against the clock and, in this brief interim, Miller became extremely anxious about his stammer.[5] He asked for an alternative presenter to be hired but that didn't work out, so a fortnight's delay in transmission was negotiated while he readied himself and found a way to address the camera without stuttering – squeezing a friendly-faced assistant in beside the lens.[6]

His appointment caused a flurry of excitement in the press. Writing in the *Spectator* (and happily letting the *Private Eye* spat lie), Christopher Booker welcomed him as a bubbling spring of innovation, perfect for the director-general Hugh Carleton Greene, who wanted less stuffy programming.[7] While laced with a kind of nervous laughter, Miller's own public pronouncements had the cheeky, combative arrogance typical of the era's Young Turks. 'Après Huw le deluge,' he declared, noting that it was like taking over from General de Gaulle, except he was only competing with himself, 'because', he said, 'I'm the only person worth competing with. All I can do is hope people like my *Monitor*. If they don't, tough on them.'[8]

His *Monitor* was no longer to be a staid 'cultural Fortnum and Masons', he said. It was going to take a broader and less reverential view, consider the arts sociologically, connect up with science, embrace trendier topics. This was not unlike his boundary-crossing *UCH Magazine*, from his student days, only writ large now, and with a hip Sixties spin. In his first year, he would rove widely abroad, as well as around the UK, covering the work of Samuel Beckett, Magritte, William Empson and the northern working-class playwright Henry Livings, to name but a few. Stevie Smith managed to feature in the mix, Miller still being blissfully unaware of her sniping short story *Beside the Seaside*.[9] A piece about the Royal College of Physicians was aired alongside Ken Russell's boho *Debussy Film*, a documentary-going-on-arthouse biopic. Art historians and contemporary architects gained a high profile, and Miller was particularly fervent about introducing viewers to the happening New York scene. Robert Lowell enjoyed a special feature and Susan Sontag was drafted in as both interviewee and interviewer, hanging out and acting cool with Andy Warhol in Manhattan.

Cutting-edge film techniques were combined with a more casual-looking studio set, featuring sofas and nibbles. The young production crew acquired several handheld Eclair cameras, so technically avant-garde that they had barely been tested.[10] The industrial workings of the studio were deliberately shown too, with the cameramen panning out to catch each other in frame. Even noddies (the traditional, cut-away reaction shots) were shunned by Miller, though that risked monotony. By way of a solution, he placed a TV monitor behind the guest. This showed the interviewer's face, sometimes with that image infinitely multiplied as if in parallel mirrors.

One of his production team, Anne James, recalls: 'Jonathan wanted to toss the camera in the air and do amazing things. I mean if he'd been a musician he would have been one of the Rolling Stones.'[11] In his editorial role, he certainly proved that he could be an inspiring gang leader within an institutional framework, and the spirit of intrepid camaraderie was further encouraged by his office being almost beyond the official, a hut perched on the roof of Lime Grove Studios. With retrospective pride and some defensiveness, he argues that everything about the new *Monitor* was different, right from the opening credits where Wheldon's ponderous signature tune was subversively jazzed up and hummed by Dudley Moore.

The idea that the series was wholly groundbreaking under his editorship needs some qualification. Wheldon had not been entirely averse to trendy topics, and the young Ken Russell had already made a controversially way-out *Monitor* feature, *Pop Goes the Easel*, about Peter Blake and other pop artists.[12] Handheld cameras were being used by French *ciné-vérité* film directors in the early Sixties. In 1962, *That Was the Week That Was* had incorporated shots exposing the mechanics of its TV studio, and *Ready, Steady, Go!* introduced radically jerky camera angles in 1963. That was a youngsters' pop music show on independent television though, not a highly prestigious BBC arts programme.[13] As Miller underlines:

> I sat down on a couch with Susan Sontag, a Jewish woman no-one had ever heard of in England, and we discussed kitsch in the very first programme . . . I shot [the programme] in a way that had never been done before and that got taken up afterwards by all sorts of people – even soaps now. Of course, the shit hit the fan. Bernard Levin came down on me like an ounce of bricks. He got into a tremendous transport of rage, and others attacked it for its pretentiousness.

There were some approving reviews. *The Times* discerned fine astringent irony in the debate on kitsch; the Robert Lowell interview was admired, and a panel of BBC Radio critics thought Peter Brook and Miller were fantastically astute when discussing the portrayal of madness onstage in Brook's boldly experimental Theatre of Cruelty season.[14] The short film about Magritte, shot at his home in suburban Belgium, was quirkily delightful too, tongue-in-cheek with a touch of Monsieur Hulot.

The ex-Fringer was, nonetheless, instantly targeted by his old pals. He was now the satirist satirized, the born-mimic being mimicked. Spouting Millerese, John Bird lampooned him – with Eleanor Bron impersonating Sontag – on Ned Sherrin's BBC show, *Not So Much a Programme, More a Way of Life*.[15] Moore and Cook spoofed *Monitor*'s handheld cameras in their new series *Not Only . . . But Also*, with their guest star John Lennon lurching around in ludicrous, arty slo-mo on a kid's swing.[16] Even Bennett seemed to be laughing up his sleeve a little. After contributing to Miller's series (on the subject of Virginia Woolf), his own hit sketch show *On the Margin* was launched, featuring a faintly *Monitor*esque mockumentary about northern working-class artists with a deadpan commentary:

> We were all miners in our family. My father was a miner. My mother is a miner . . . I suppose in a very real sense, I'm a miner writer.[17]

That was only a glancing blow, and Miller happily participated in *On the Margin*, showing off his beaky profile in a Roman skit, playing a centurion named Copius Mucus, opposite Bennett's laurel-garlanded Spurious Umbilicus. The trouble was that the parodies of *Monitor* were only the tip of the iceberg. The debate on kitsch caused blazing rows among BBC executives and, over the ensuing months, the TV critics became increasingly incensed. The camerawork was judged distracting and Sontag was derided for posing and spouting banalities. She was, indeed, appallingly pretentious, lolling around in dark glasses in the Warhol feature.

Some thought Miller had been Americanized and now wanted to import the USA's culture wholesale. By January 1965, the *Sunday Times* had declared his editorial style, at best, schizophrenic: beatnik one moment, old-school the next.[18] A former colleague from the *Spectator*, Alan Brien, condemned the interviews for their 'egg-head back-scratching', and Christopher Booker retracted all his anticipatory praise, slating the incomer's 'own fevered brand of uncritical cultural sycophancy' as worse than Wheldon's. Booker has gone so far as to say that it was as if England were going out if its mind, now seeking novelty in an excessive frenzy, a welter of nervous energy and handheld cameras behind which, in all directions, lay nothing but dust.[19]

Miller's pre-publicity drive had been asking for trouble, sounding arrogant to some while raising others' hopes too high. Unable to resist talking up his big ideas in advance, he had (not for the last time) prompted reviewers to compare and contrast the theory with the end product. He evidently found the critical shelling traumatic, for he comments:

I think most of my sort of paranoid suspicion about what the English think of me was generated by the response to *Monitor*. I could do no wrong during *Beyond the Fringe* . . . Then I did *Monitor* and the house fell down around my ears . . . Around me was secreted this reputation of being a blabbering 'pseud'. That was the first time I came up against 'too clever by half'. I've never been able to eliminate that, and I'm now endlessly suspicious.

One of the talented documentary-makers on *Monitor*, Patrick Garland, remembers his boss feeling persecuted, being terribly upset and 'crushed like a schoolboy'. The simile is pertinent, for Miller had, as it happens, been woundingly criticized as a prep-school boy by two supposed friends. He himself recalls how:

Standing on a chilly corner of Queen's Grove, they told me what a rotten egg I was . . . perhaps for being noticeable or drawing attention to myself, I don't know, but I took it very badly . . . So it has been there all my life, and the awful thing is it makes you wonder, 'Well, hang on, am I hateful?' . . . It develops like an allergy. Each small, subsequent hurt causes a much greater reaction so that, in a way, my skin gets thinner rather than thicker as time goes on.

Eventually, in the first week of July 1965, he retaliated furiously to *Monitor*'s detractors, dispatching the following letter to the editor of the *Listener*:

Dear Sir,

It has become fashionable . . . to take indiscriminate pot shots at MONITOR . . . Mr J. B. Priestley writing last week in your columns . . . [says it] has got bogged down on the corner of Madison Avenue and 57th Street. This is the sort of rash half-truth which passes for criticism which we have been forced to grin and bear for the last year. Now the grinning has to stop.[20]

What was, in fact, abruptly curtailed was his own two-year contract, and *Monitor* itself. Even as his letter was going to print, the programme was terminated, officially being absorbed into BBC1's new arts slot, *Sunday Night*.[21]

He acknowledges that he made mistakes, having to take many decisions in a rush. Humphrey Burton remarks dryly: 'Jonathan helped to close it down – "scuppered" is another word for it.'[22] Nevertheless, he concludes, 'Doing Andy Warhol was very adventurous . . . and, with hindsight, I don't think of [that final leg] as a failure at all. I think of it as a noble and very exciting experiment.' Melvyn Bragg, who was a relative fledgling on the production team, thinks Miller was tremendous, just badly placed by the Corporation. '*Monitor* was very formal. Jonathan was rangy and omnivorous,' he observes. 'His utter, undoubted, original brilliance was a shot in the arm which television needed . . . but he needed a looser format.'[23]

Patrick Garland, who became a good friend, adds that everyone could see *Monitor* was going off the rails, nonetheless Miller was a crusader, his team were all devoted to him and he was the funniest man in England. The crew had spent most of their time in stitches as he kept slipping into irrepressible impersonations of Wheldon's clipped gravitas.[24] Kicking his heels in the cutting room, with his very low boredom threshold, he would invent hilarious, wildly scatological monologues over footage of po-faced artists such as Henry Moore. He and Garland also saw the funny side when their privileged meeting with Samuel Beckett, in a Paris restaurant, turned into a minor farce. As Garland explains:

> Jackie MacGowran [the participating Irish actor] told us that Beckett had loved Jonathan Miller in *Beyond the Fringe*, never missed *Monitor*, and would love to be on the programme . . . and when the bill [for the meal] came you weren't to put your hand in your pocket, for God's sake, because Sam was the soul of generosity . . . So when the bill came, we all waited and waited, and Beckett was, like all artists, totally tight-fisted, he hated what we were doing and had never heard of Jonathan! . . . We nearly killed Jackie MacGowran.[25]

Memorably too, Anthony Burgess came into the studio to contribute to a strand of prerecorded interviews on provocative subjects. He chose to talk (as you do) about sexual neuroses in Malay, not least the primitive fear of one's penis vanishing up one's anus. Everybody on set treated this with complete seriousness and thanked the great man politely as he departed. Very businesslike, Miller stepped back in front of the cameras, just to round off, saying: 'Well, that's all from *Monitor* tonight. Next week – '. Then with a demure 'Would you excuse me', he launched into an explosive parody, pretending to madly hammer his penis to his thigh and imitating Burgess remorselessly until the cameramen were shaking and howling with laughter. 'We actually had to stop recording and come back another day,' says Garland. So, on one level at least, *Monitor* died laughing.

*   *   *

To its great credit, the BBC immediately opened another door to Miller, engaging him as a producer-director of screenplays for the *Sunday Night* slot. He was transported straight from recording *Monitor*'s final programme to arrive in the village of Wicken, on the border of Buckinghamshire, at midnight on 11 July. At nine the next morning he began filming *The Drinking Party*, a dramatization of Plato's *The Symposium*, in the nearby grounds of Stowe public school. Shifting away from the avant-garde and going to work on a canonical (though not well-known) text in the Arcadian English countryside was a wise move, one likely to soothe most conservative viewers.

Several of his old satirical colleagues were among his cast, most of them lodging with him at the Old Rectory, a bed-and-breakfast run by Wicken's Reverend Hoskins. Alan Bennett, John Fortune, the sketch-writing actor Robert Gillespie and the ex-Footlighter Julian Jebb were on board, along with Michael Gough and Leo McKern.[26] Thus, to an extent, *The Drinking Party* was to continue Miller the comedian's slant on philosophers, investing dusty passages with sly humour.[27] He was, however, making a thinking man's film here, not a skit, and his fellow wits from Oxbridge were proving their credentials as serious actors.

The Drinking Party additionally saw Miller, the emergent director, developing two strategies that were to become recurrent trademarks. First, he chose to convert a non-dramatic script (*The Symposium* being a philosophical dialogue but not a play in any full sense).[28] Second, he changed the setting to an unexpected point in time. Ditching the togas was a stroke of genius (perhaps subconsciously inspired by Ken Russell's *Debussy Film*, which set its historic subject in a Sixties frame). Miller knew that *The Symposium* had been recited informally in Renaissance intellectual circles, and he wanted to have it spoken and discussed in a comparable modern-day setting. The solution was to have a reunion of public school scholars, honouring their Greek and Latin master at a black-tie dinner. By way of postprandial entertainment, they would all take on the roles of Plato's characters – who variously define the nature of love – with their teacher (McKern) playing the sage Socrates.

Miller's old headmaster, R. L. James, must have rejoiced at his star pupil's return to the classics, though *The Drinking Party* actually looks more like a nostalgic nod to the Cambridge Apostles, or to St Paul's Mr Pask and his set of bright boys.[29] Certainly, Miller united the academic and the pastoral with exquisite elegance, filming the dinner al fresco on the portico of the Queen's Temple, a neoclassical folly in one of Stowe School's leafy glades.

His years of avid cinema-going stood him in good stead, with discernible influences including Alain Resnais' art-house movie *Last Year at Marienbad* (from 1961).[30] Having not been a director on *Monitor* however, he was again having to learn on the job. His cameraman, Charles Parnall, was a superb guiding light and Miller soon picked up the jargon, happily mucking in with the technical crew in a manner that was to become characteristic. He may have been raised in a household with a cook, nanny and chauffeur, yet he is never sniffy about craftsmanlike practicalities, in fact decidedly relishing the idea of such hands-on work.

The weather was harder to deal with, as he faced six rainy days out of ten. Resourcefully, he embraced the added naturalism, recording one downpour and creating continuity by spattering his actors with a watering can when the afternoon turned out dry.

Filmed in monochrome with very long uninterrupted shots, his debut proved remarkably serene and assured. As well as Renais' *Marienbad* he evoked Renaissance paintings with his beautiful close-up portraits and his still-lifes of the banqueting table, laid with gleaming glass and silverware. Maybe the sustained focus on monologuists subconsciously influenced Bennett's later *Talking Heads*. Life had imitated art a little, in terms of the personal tensions within the group, as Fortune and Bennett had snickered together about Jebb hanging on Miller's every word and taking notes, like Boswell with Samuel Johnson. That aside, Robert Gillespie remembers the long July days at Stowe as a delight. 'The thing about Jonathan,' he says, 'is he's an entertainer even when he's directing, so there was all this brilliant juvenilia – racy bits of doggerel about vicars – as well as a tremendously sharp sense of getting to the essence of the piece.'[31]

The TV critics were highly impressed when the film was broadcast in November 1965, putting Miller back in their good books. The *Sunday Times* said there had never been a programme more likely to start a philosophy boom. The *FT* applauded his directorial imagination and dexterity, and even the tabloids loved how Socrates' ruminations sounded new-minted.[32] Jubilant viewers called for more, declaring it one of the finest things they had seen on television. One letter particularly catches the eye in the BBC's archives:

Dear Jonathan Miller,

The Drinking Party was wonderful. Wonderfully conceived, organised, directed, played. And that text! I have to tell you it was a triumph. Thank you.

Harold Pinter

Malcolm Muggeridge sent a telegram saying 'UTTERLY ENCHANTED', and the in-house congrats from Wheldon read: 'At long last, I really feel that things are going to work. I was delighted with the symposium [sic].' What was truly remarkable, the executive producer Stephen Hearst noted, was that film directing normally took years to learn, but this was masterly.[33]

*   *   *

On the night *The Drinking Party* was transmitted, Miller was in another BBC studio, helping out as a panellist on *Call My Bluff*. He soon became a regular on the dictionary-definition game show, smoking like a chimney alongside Frank Muir. The accounts department was dreadfully confused, not knowing how to categorize this celebrity guest/on-staff director – fish and fowl. That winter he also appeared, half portraying himself and half caricaturing a Gloucester Crescent champagne socialist, in a TV sketch called 'Camden Town Tramp', written by Bennett. This was based on an actual incident when an aged down-and-out had knocked at the Millers' door, thinking it was still a rooming-house. In the fictional version, Miller and his chum were seen inviting the tramp in for a superficially humane chat then bundling him into their Rolls, saying they were off to the starry Caprice restaurant but could easily drop him at a doss house. In real life, Miller and Bennett – feeling rather more guilty about the district's gentrification – had driven the old man around in Bennett's Mini searching for cheap lodgings before trying to deposit him at a hostel. Presuming to jump the queue, they nearly got themselves lynched, eventually leaving the poor geezer at the police station.[34] Bennett would, of course, later surrender his front drive in the Crescent to Miss Shepherd, the batty bag lady who became famous via his autobiographical play *The Lady in the Van*.

From the seed of 'Camden Town Tramp', Bennett developed *Life and Times in NW1* in the form of sketches for his TV series *On the Margin*. The neighbourhood's chatterati were depicted as poseurs, addicted to casual-chic dinner parties and stripped-pine floors, adopting left-wing stances while owning weekend cottages or getting black home-helps to do their chores. Bennett's characters were rapidly turned into a strip cartoon in the *Listener*. Drawn by Marc (aka Mark Boxer), Bernard Goldblatt was NW1's academic TV presenter and looked distinctly like Miller: a lanky, curly-haired fellow with a pointy nose who subjected soccer matches to anthropological analyses and got critically panned for his hip arts programme.[35] The Millers, furthermore, were the model, at least in part, for the *Life and Times* couple called Nigel and Jane Knocker-Threw, having converted their basement flat into an open-plan kitchen.

Karl Miller, as Rachel's brother-in-law, naturally appreciated the send-up when he took over the *Listener's* editorship in the mid-1960s.[36] Another neighbour, Nick Tomalin, wrote humorously about the street's inhabitants in his *Sunday Times* 'Atticus' column, and there was even a short-lived soap opera called *The Cres*, like some upper-middle-class *Brookside* or *North-WestEnders*.[37]

The Millers enjoyed the collective joke, but bleak news arrived on the November day in 1965 when 'Camden Town Tramp' was being filmed in the street. Rachel received a phone call which informed her of Betty Miller's death, then she had to bear those tidings, interrupting the jocular proceedings out in the Rolls. The bereaved son's reaction was simply to go on working. Refusing to stop may have been his way of suppressing the shock, or a cold response to the demise of a parent whom he had long regarded as insufficiently loving. He says that he never really grieved for her.

It should be explained that he had already, in a way, lost the sparky mother with whom he had bonded as a teenager because Betty had succumbed to early-onset Alzheimer's disease, or presenile dementia, which was little understood and more commonly just called 'senility' at the time. She only lived to the age of 55. Her biographies of Tennyson and Kipling were left unfinished.

The first indication of her illness, which Rachel had noticed, was when she almost dropped the newborn Tom, as if she had forgotten she was holding him. Thereafter, the disintegration was horrendously fast. While Miller was in the States, he relayed to Sacks – in a letter expressing sympathy for the arthritically crippled Emanuel – how his mother was already 'living in a fly-swarm of fantasy' and 'had become floridly deluded and unmanageable at home, assaulting my reasonable, rabbinical old father in the middle of the night like a demented incubus'.[38] In these near-surreal incidents, she would enter Emanuel's room, 'fully clothed and with hat and umbrella and lie down full length on him while he feebly fought off her dotty advances', as Miller's letter explained. He described his father as being 'in a transport of guilt and grief', but by the time he and Rachel returned to England,

Betty was incarcerated in Friern Mental Hospital, a vast mental institution in north London, formerly known as Colney Hatch Lunatic Asylum.

She did not even recognize her son when he visited and – her life of the mind being over – he felt that she was somehow 'the living dead', not his mother anymore. This was a chilling cycle: the parent who had seemed emotionally unresponsive in his childhood now being completely disconnected. He had previously written articles about geriatric wards, noting the admirable authority with which youth handles age in such situations.[39] Far less positively, he says of himself: 'I just – I didn't see the point in it [i.e. further visits], because our connection was intellectual. There was no fondness at all. I didn't feel that I had lost a beloved person.' His sister Sarah and family friends have intimated that he actually found the final phase of maternal estrangement unbearable and annihilating, and later did some weeping about her with an analyst.

Publicly, he responded by working as the president of the Alzheimer's Society from the age of 54, fronting their public appeals. He is, today, their president emeritus. He has presented two television series, *Who Cares?* and *Who Cares Now?*, and has talked on many other programmes about the disease, about social service provisions, the strains placed on home life, and how families can cope. This has been partially driven by self-reproach because, as he acknowledges, he was 'not very caring at all' during his mother's degeneration.[40]

*   *   *

The television films he made in 1966 were also, perhaps, an oblique form of grieving. Having been invited to direct for the BBC's *Sunday Night*, he came up with *Mr Sludge the Medium*, a drama documentary about Elizabeth Barrett and Robert Browning. Specifically, it portrayed the couple's interactions with the medium Daniel Dunglas Home, when they were struggling with bereavement. That was the very subject which Betty had tried to turn into a stage play entitled *Shadow on the Window*. *Mr Sludge* was recorded just two months after her funeral and Miller admitted that his erstwhile obsession with mortality had returned.[41]

He was, of course, not cherishing notions of personally communing with the dead via séances. He openly scorned the resurgent spiritualism of the Sixties as bosh, just as he had ridiculed the idea of ghosts in the schoolboy debates at St Paul's.[42] What he was interested in, he said, was the history of ideas. An opening commentary was attached to *Mr Sludge* explaining why the bereaved in Victorian Britain, where the death rate remained high, sought comfort from mediums. Christian beliefs had fundamentally been eroded by Darwinism.

For a staunch rationalist, Miller has directed some remarkably spooky dramas. *Mr Sludge* made television the medium of the medium. In its account of Home's séances, disembodied 'spirit hands' were seen creeping around Barrett Browning (played by Eleanor Bron).[43] The director remained in a morbid vein for his next BBC TV drama, *The Death of Socrates* (which was based on two Platonic dialogues, *The Crito* and *Phaedo*). In this sequel to *The Drinking Party*, Leo McKern's Socrates lived out his last few days awaiting execution in a cell, like a modern-day political prisoner. It was an early and exceptionally gloomy instance of Miller's taste for bare dilapidated settings, and shots of a coffin loomed large (filmed in a Camden undertakers).[44]

Not long after that came *Whistle and I'll Come to You*, made for BBC1 and extremely spooky. Now classified by the British Film Institute as a masterpiece of economical horror, this short drama was stunningly shot, in black-and-white, around an isolated English seaside hotel and on windswept shores, under lowering clouds. There were shades of Hitchcock here, of Orson Welles and of Bill Brandt's sinister, dream-tinged photographs.[45] Coincidentally, Miller was one of Brandt's subjects in 1966: pictured at home in Gloucester Crescent with a Gothic, morbid slant, a huge gramophone horn snaking out of the shadows behind him and a pickled brain, in a jar, on a bookshelf.

Whistle and I'll Come to You was Miller's own comical and menacing adaptation of M. R. James' short story. A Cambridge professor (played by Michael Hordern) takes a lonely holiday. Conversing briefly with one gentleman in the hotel dining-room, he dismisses the idea of ghosts with smug scepticism. However, having discovered a bone whistle in an overgrown graveyard (cryptically inscribed, in Latin, with 'Who is this who is coming?'), he blows it and finds himself hounded by a spectre.

Miller's adaptation was daringly free compared to other TV dramatizations of James' works in the Sixties and Seventies. Picking up on the author's comment that Professor Parkins was 'something of an old woman', the director altered the character from a precisely spoken young man into a fussy, aged bachelor. He wrote the dialogue himself, departing from James' original exchanges and adding droll philosophical pedantry, a little like his old Bertrand Russell skit.[46]

Generated without luxurious special effects, the phantom in *Whistle* is shroud-like and peculiarly terrifying. For its first appearance, on a deserted beach, the technical crew hung a soaked, tattered cloth from an invisible string. Keeping themselves out of shot, they brought it swooping towards the camera as it twisted in a gale. Combined with a magnified soundtrack, the footage was stretched out by printing every frame twice. This created a slowed-down and simultaneously jerky effect: a blurred image of turmoil that was disturbing, glutinous and aggressive.

The ghost ultimately sends the professor demented. In the closing shots, we see him lurching from his bed in the small hours, aghast and staring as a sheet rises up and takes on a violent, writhing life of its own, like a half-waking nightmare. Parkins loses the power of speech, regressively sucking his thumb as he lets out a wordless wail, like a patient in a mental hospital ward.[47] The *Sunday Times* called the climax 'as powerful as anything Hitchcock ever did'. Many years later, viewers would rank it among the 100 most petrifying moments ever shown on screen.[48]

Like Cocteau in *Orphée* and like Powell and Pressburger in *A Matter of Life and Death*, Miller knows how to create an eerie frisson while keeping one foot in the real world. He has laced his spine-chilling dramas with the psychological possibility that spectres are in people's minds. Hordern's bachelor-professor was, perhaps, being ambushed by his own bottled-up impulses in *Whistle*. Parkins can be viewed as a severe case of sexual repression, suffering from bad dreams and delusions. Reviewing the original broadcast in the *Observer*, George Melly expressed his Freudian interpretation bluntly, describing the writhing bed-sheets as a masturbation fantasy.[49] Or Parkins might be a case for neurologists interested in 'the sense of a presence', a phenomenon associated with disturbances of sleep, epilepsy and subordinate parietal lobe lesions, as well as with extreme stress and solitude. Sufferers think someone – usually sinister – is at their shoulder or has entered their room at night.[50]

Whistle functions as a more straightforward ghost story too, portraying an intellectual sceptic shattered by a paranormal experience. When pushed, Miller admits that the supernatural has always drawn him. He does not believe in it, he says, yet is scared by the idea of it, by its incomprehensibility, by the notion that ghosts hover unclassifiably between life and death. As with Parkins, there are parts of his mind which his reasoning cannot reach for he would, he confesses, be afraid to spend the night in a reportedly haunted room.[51]

What the psychosexual and supernatural readings of *Whistle* have crucially overlooked is that Hordern is being symbolically haunted by death. The ghoul on the beach resembles a cowled Grim Reaper, suddenly coming for Parkins like the wind: an image surely charged with some personal horror for the director, given his recent experience of Betty's galloping dementia and early grave.

As for the practicalities of making *Whistle* and *Mr Sludge the Medium*, the recording sessions for both had become somewhat fraught. Miller had prepared no shooting script for *Whistle*: a hair-raising approach that demanded improvisation then major structural work in the cutting room. Meanwhile, Kenneth Haigh (who famously portrayed John Osborne's angry young Jimmy Porter) was playing Daniel Dunglas Home in *Mr Sludge* and fuming because this required single takes of impossibly long monologues.[52]

The audience response to *Mr Sludge* was uneven, with some viewers enthralled and others complaining about prolix lectures in period costume.[53] Truth be told, the real drama had occurred prior to filming when Sam Rosenberg – the original co-author of Betty's play, *Shadow on the Window* – more or less accused Miller of plagiarism and threatened legal action (alarmingly like Bridget Riley before). Writing to Huw Wheldon, Rosenberg warned that the BBC would proceed at its peril and explained how, having become friendly with Miller in the USA, he was shocked to drop in at Gloucester Crescent and learn, from a fellow guest, that their host was now working on his own TV drama about Daniel Dunglas Home. He suspected this would crib its characters, milieu and much more from *Shadow on the Window* which he and Miller had previously discussed with a plan to see it belatedly produced.[54]

Miller defended himself saying that his interest in the subject had, doubtless, been rekindled by Rosenberg but that his memory of the play was now very vague. His focus was different and *Mr Sludge* used no dramatic dialogue as such, being composed of recited historic documents, letters and so on. Referring to Betty's recent death, he concluded: 'I feel my obligation if it exists at all must commit to her memory and her alone.'[55] His argument won the day because, under English law, you cannot copyright an idea.[56] His resurrection of Betty's subject matter could, therefore, be regarded as a creative form of commemoration, generating an intellectual continuum.

★   ★   ★

Miller almost had to bring Alan Bennett home in a coffin, racing out to Sardinia to help save his life just when *The Death of Socrates* was going through its final edit. 'Fringe Boy in Deathbed Drama', shrieked the *Daily Mirror*.[57] Bennett had been holidaying with Rachel and another friend when, suffering from internal bleeding, he had been rushed to a hospital in Olbia. This institution, Rachel soon discovered, was run by staggeringly incompetent monks who appeared to think blood-loss meant the patient had a surfeit. When Miller arrived to support his beleaguered wife, he dashed off a letter to the *Death of Socrates* team from the inappropriately named Jolly Hotel. Dated 'Friday the God knows what', it concluded, 'Alan remains in jeopardy though the language, the facilities and so on make it almost impossible to know how ill he is . . . I suspect very.'[58]

Whether or not he got on his old co-star's nerves was irrelevant for the time being, though he is notably absent from Bennett's account of this episode in *Untold Stories* (2005).[59] Miller just recalls that he stayed up all night, frantically cross-matching blood. At least his boring stint at Addenbrooke's, specializing in that, proved invaluable.

He and Rachel insisted on setting up a bed alongside the patient so they could provide round-the-clock supervision of the *Fate Bene Fratelli*, the brethren whom, with gallows humour, they rechristened the *Fate Male* for being so deleterious. Bennett's depiction of clueless quacks, in *The Madness of George III*, may well have germinated in Olbia. Luckily, the invalid survived and returned to England to be in Miller's absolutely superb *Alice in Wonderland*.

★   ★   ★

'Wanted: one girl with no stage experience, not very pretty but curiously plain, sallow and a bit priggish, Rossetti-like rather than Tenniel.' A nationwide search was on for Alice, and the BBC was placing other quirky adverts in the British press.[60] They were seeking a mildewed vicarage (for scenes of Alice at home), an incredibly long corridor and freelance hedgehogs.

Wonderland was to be unorthodox, though Miller surely did not expect it to cause even more of a rumpus than his *Monitor*. At this time, Lewis Carroll's fantasia from the 1860s was generally regarded as a bedtime story swaddled in sweetness. It was often staged as pantomime with actors skipping around in funny

151

animal masks. Miller's approach was far more sophisticated, not aimed at entertaining tots, albeit that he had two of his own. He saw the story, psychologically and in its socio-historical context, as an extraordinarily dreamlike and somewhat dark vision, translating elements from the daily life of Carroll's child-friend, Alice Liddell. Those elements included domineering and eccentric relatives, servants and dons because Liddell had been daughter to the dean of Oxford's Christ Church, where Carroll (aka Charles Dodgson) held a lectureship post.

Miller considered the book 'the best description of dreams perhaps ever done', capturing the mercuriality and strange jump cuts, or what he termed 'the fabulous fickleness of dreaming'. He argued that the story was also a Bildungsroman which might be subtitled *Growing Pains*, shot through with the Victorians' ambivalent attitudes to childhood.[61] On the one hand, they stifled it with proprieties and, on the other, they feared and mourned its passing. Its ephemerality was contemplated in Wordsworth's 'Intimations of Immortality':

There was a time when meadow, grove and stream
The earth, and every common sight, to me did seem apparelled in
    celestial light
The glory and the freshness of a dream . . .

It is not now as it hath been of yore . . .
The things which I have seen I now can see no more.[62]

That poem consequently formed the prologue and epilogue in Miller's *Alice*.

No commercial film companies were brave enough to run with the director's vision, but the BBC rose to the occasion and backed it to the hilt, providing a production budget of £25,000, an unheard-of amount for a single drama at that time. This was peanuts, all the same, for what Miller envisaged, which was as good as a movie. After the spartan *Death of Socrates*, his *Alice* was to evoke what he termed the hallucinatory realism and bursting, fatal ripeness of the Pre-Raphaelites. It was to be 'sunlit' and simultaneously 'stuffed', as if containing the entire visual contents of the child's mind, every object and surface she had ever seen and forgotten.[63]

The BBC's head of scenery sent an incredulous query to Humphrey Burton asking what on earth would be left for Ken Russell's film on the Pre-Raphaelites, given the props request from Miller's designer.[64] Julia Trevelyan Oman asked for around 5,000 items – cheval mirrors, glass-domed clocks, Arum lilies, prams, Bath chairs, butterfly nets, taxidermically preserved animals – and she went on to build wonderful sets at the Ealing Studios. Giant and tiny versions were constructed of the passageway where Alice grows and shrinks as she tries to get through the door to the rose garden. A vast tiered courtroom began to materialize as well – merging elements of a chapel, playhouse and hotel – for the climactic trial scene, when the heroine faces the death penalty for growing up(wards).

Miller travelled thousands of miles, crisscrossing rural England with his producer Tony Palmer, seeking the perfect locations for the Queen of Hearts' croquet lawns, the Mad Hatter's tea party and many another curious scene.[65] In one of his less scientific moments, he remarked that this epic journey imbued him with a close-up sense of the magic lurking beneath the vegetation, a feeling for the mystery of English nature, 'its terrible, damp, mossy fecundity with hobbits and angels ripening like dragonfly larvae in the ooze'. While his Wonderland was England, he was also bringing out the exotic otherness of the creatures inhabiting it. He filled the movie with troops of dwarf actors in costumes redolent of Velasquez, 'so as to get Empire of Hapsburg insects', he said.

With his fame and eloquent charm, he persuaded a stack of star players to appear in *Alice* for diminutive pay packets (£500 tops): Peter Sellers was the King of Hearts, Michael Redgrave the Caterpillar, and Wilfrid Brambell (from *Steptoe and Son*) a darting White Rabbit. As the Mock Turtle, John Gielgud danced the Lobster Quadrille at the seaside – on Winchelsea's Camber Sands – with Malcolm Muggeridge's Gryphon (a remarkable debut for the sexagenarian journalist). Alison Leggatt played the axe-happy Queen like a snappy, tyrannical Victoria.[66] Signing up again were Leo McKern (bizarrely perfect as the Ugly Duchess), Peter Cook (the Mad Hatter), plus Michael Gough, John Bird, Julian Jebb and Alan Bennett with side-whiskers (respectively cast as the March Hare, Frog Footman, Young Crab and pedantic Mouse). Close scrutiny of the caucus race even reveals the young Eric Idle – subsequently of *Monty Python* fame – cavorting like a loon around the choir stalls of a bare, ruined chapel.

Having Carroll's characters played in period costume but without animal masks, Miller was analytically decoding the author's dreamwork, exposing what Oxford types the fantastical creatures really represented. At the same time, bringing out Gielgud's inherent turtlishness or how John Bird had a frog in his face had a peculiarly oneiric effect. After all, a dreamer can see a person and be aware that this individual is somehow, simultaneously, a white rabbit or a playing card.[67]

Alice was portrayed by the unknown Anne-Marie Mallik, a dignified schoolgirl of Indian-French stock with a mane of dark hair. Miller knew she was perfect as soon as he spotted her photograph in a pile of 700 others, almost all of them hopelessly jolly would-be starlets. Having her own growing pains, Mallik was unhappy in her remarried father's household (run by Victorian-style staff) and was suffering from a frosty housemistress at school. However, she flourished that summer with Miller and his troupe of actors. He was gently amicable with her and generous with his time, as her chaperone recalls.[68] The verbal pyrotechnics he saved for the grown-ups.

Mallik herself, who went on to become a barrister, says it was marvellous to be treated like a young adult by everybody. The director cherished her flat-toned voice and encouraged her to sustain an air of expressionless indifference, envisaging a solemn infanta in a stiff silk frock. He was influenced by European cinema's penchant for radically low-key acting and non-professional performers (as in Pasolini's *Gospel According to St Matthew* from 1964).[69] He emphasized that Alice's detachment – looking on from the periphery of the action – specifically captured the trance-like serenity of a dreamer.

A few offscreen panics occurred during filming. The Cheshire Cat (an actual tabby, not an actor) ran away, and an off-duty dwarf sustained injuries falling down some steps.[70] Peter Eyre, who played the Knave of Hearts and went on to become one of Miller's favourite actors, passed out when a make-up artist poured a noxious chemical over his head, rather than shampoo. Bobbing around in the Pool of Tears, Bennett probably wondered if he was going to die after all – of cold. He says his view of *Alice* was 'fairly disenchanted through having to stand up to my neck in water for an hour or two!'[71]

Peter Sellers could be a pain in the neck. He improvised absurd Carrollian lines for the dim-witted King superbly, but then delayed the shoot with starry sulks and baloney about his astrological signs being inauspicious. Planes from a nearby air base disrupted the recording of the meadow scenes for the start of the film, where Alice is seen lying down and drowsing. The whole production briefly ground to a halt, moreover, when Tony Palmer got excited about emergent colour TV technology, forcefully arguing that all the black-and-white footage should be reshot.[72] With Sellers being unavailable for a remake, they stuck to monochrome, and Miller took the other snags in his stride.

The noisy planes were obliterated with a spellbinding tabla and sitar score composed by Ravi Shankar, who was just emerging as an international star and influencing the Beatle, George Harrison.[73] Miller handled Sellers so well that he was rewarded with a top-of-the-range camera, a token of appreciation from the moody luminary.[74] The ex-Fringer appeared to be getting on with Peter Cook as well. During breaks, they concocted comic fantasies about a preposterous English scientist named Geoffrey Hovercraft.[75] Eric Idle remembers Miller and Bennett being, likewise, on good form. 'That was one of the best times I ever had!' he exclaims. 'Suddenly there I was filming with my hero [as my director] . . . on this Magical Mystery Tour of country houses, and I went bowling with Jonathan and Alan Bennett which was hilarious . . . They'd do these great [jokey] grumbles, you know, with Alan saying, "You're only winning because you're Jewish!"'[76]

Freda Dowie, having played Alice's nursemaid in an early scene, even enjoyed splashing around up to her neck in the Pool of Tears. Miller crouched at the edge, dispensing slugs of brandy and encouraging everyone to look daft while they swam round and round in Victorian garb. Dowie reminisces: 'I got drunker and drunker and was the last one in because I did look very dotty. Then I was bundled out – because I was starting to shiver – into a hot mustard bath and wrapped in huge towels, and Jonathan came rushing in and gave me a huge hug. That was giddy and super. One would', she says, 'have done anything for him because of his enthusiasm.'

Muggeridge noted afterwards that, rather than giving detailed guidance, this director exuded a 'creative glow' in which everyone basked, 'a bit unearthly if you like, even eerie'.[77] For Miller himself, the nine weeks of filming became almost dreamy. 'We forgot', he says, 'where we had come from and when the end came someone suggested that we just carry on. No film in the camera . . . sinking deeper and deeper into the somnolent magic of Alice's last summer as a child.'[78]

The pre-publicity was flying high with Lord Snowdon taking photographs on location for *Vogue*, and with *Life* magazine making *Alice* its cover story.[79] Even the Swedish, French, Italian and Yugoslavian press were writing about the production. Described by one colleague as 'not shy about putting himself forward', Palmer was marketing the film like crazy, in a manner not to everybody's taste. He had visions of BBC merchandise ranging from Mad Hatter tea-sets to a pop version of the soundtrack's hymn, 'Immortal, Invisible'. He also, as Burton wryly recollects, kept plastering BBC Television Centre with enormous promotional photographs and removing all other productions' pictures in the middle of the night, a tactic that was creating 'something of a sensation'.

Perhaps aggravated by the colour-film crisis, Miller had a bust-up with him at the editorial stage. Harbouring mixed feelings about his ex-boss, Palmer says Miller convinced himself, with 'a demented sense of insecurity', that his junior had a better degree than his own. 'It became a complete obsession, as well as the fact that it's always the assistant director who gets the girls,' Palmer remarks, and he adds:

> I finally got demoted to production assistant after I shouted at him . . . I really harangued him about just giving the film to an editor [Pam Bosworth] . . . I kept saying, 'You know there's wonderful material going straight down the tubes and you really shouldn't allow that to happen.' It was my attempt really to boost his confidence, but he took this as criticism . . .
>
> I was told by Huw Wheldon that, later on, Jonathan had to write a report on me and it was the funniest thing he had ever read . . . Apparently I was someone who had lashed out with criticism at every conceivable opportunity. I was completely irresponsible in my use of criticism and so on . . . I actually did confront Jonathan with that at one point [and he said]: 'Oh no, I didn't mean it as badly as that!'

Palmer relates how he introduced Miller to Shankar's music as well, driving him to a concert and noting, en route, how he sank into his seat at every traffic light to avoid recognition.[80] He continues:

> So we arrive at the Festival Hall, and Jonathan sits at the back of the box, I thought rather ostentatiously reading a book. In a sitar concert they tune up for an age . . . Jonathan couldn't see. All he could hear was this tuning-up noise. And he leaned forward to me and said: 'That's it. That's the music we need.'

A score is settled. In reply, Miller says of Palmer:

> He was very energetic and enthusiastic, then when I edited the film and gave my first private showing of it, he was discovered sloping around the

corridors of the East Tower [at the Television Centre] telling people it was an unmitigated disaster . . . I had a row with him about it. He seemed rather shamefaced but was already on the edge of realising his own ambitions and he became a rather successful film director.[81]

He goes on to recount, with amusement, how Wheldon responded to the rough cut, first nodding with appreciative gravitas and calling it magisterial. When its creator contended that it was still a bit too long, Wheldon sagely shook his head. 'No, no, it's not a bit too long,' he opined. 'It's DISASTROUSLY too long!' Miller took that criticism in good heart as he went back to work and completed the final cut.[82] *Alice in Wonderland* was then all set, scheduled for broadcast, in an afternoon slot, on Christmas Day.

⋆ ⋆ ⋆

In the interim, jumping continents, Miller turned up in the US to have another stab at staging a lucrative show in the commercial theatre, undeterred by the previous meltdown of *World War Two and a Half*. The sex comedy *Come Live with Me*, by Lee Minoff and Stanley Price, was big news for it was to mark the Broadway debut of Soupy Sales, a hugely popular TV comic. There was even a televised press conference when Sales signed his contract under a barrage of flash-bulbs, declaring that this collaboration with Miller would be a blast.[83]

By the time the show was due to come into town, feature writers who had sneaked a glimpse of rehearsals were reporting a chalk-and-cheese calamity. The pairing was surely a bad joke, the equivalent of Peter Brook directing the Three Stooges. Sales was out of his depth and floundering wildly, streaming sweat, forgetting his blocking and asking endless questions. The esoteric answers which he received from Miller – referring to emotional tropism and the stereo-scopic merging of actor and character – were as obscure as a Delphic oracle to the slapstick clown. 'This rehearsing is driving me nuts!' he howled. Miller maintained a remarkably diplomatic front, insisting this was not complete hell or intellectual slumming. He really appreciated Minoff and Price's unpreten-tiousness, or so he told the press. By opening night he had bolted nevertheless, saying that his wife was expecting another baby and it was arriving sooner than planned.[84]

This was a fib. His departure was premature rather than his daughter Kate's arrival in February 1967, albeit that the pregnant Rachel had needed some nursing to get over bronchitis. The papers quoted one of Miller's Manhattan associates saying his professional fickleness might relate to his excessive juvenility or 'the very confused little boy in Jonathan'.[85] He himself now freely acknowledges this project was not his bag and was a complete catastrophe: a classic case of a disastrous try-out in New Haven followed by frenzied rewrites in Philadelphia, with people pacing round smoke-filled rooms at 4 a.m., trying to invent new characters and muttering, 'I mean, Christ, she's got to have a mother!'

It closed in New York after two days. Minoff underlines that, the summer before, *Come Live With Me* had been a big Connecticut hit, under another director. 'It was terrible to see it all go down the drain', he says. 'I'd get calls from [Jonathan's] cast telling me, "He is ruining the play. You must come!" . . . [but] he banned me from rehearsals.' Minoff further condemns Miller, stating:

> His narcissism bled all over the play . . . and he was, certainly, very unpleasant to me, as if he was mad at me because I was a playwright . . . [or] was envious because I was younger or better looking . . . Jonathan ruined the play and, when he saw it was ruined, he wanted out, and took his name off it.[86] He was so terrible. During one of the performances, he was sitting on the stairs of the theatre in Philadelphia. I came in and he said 'What's going to happen to me? Nobody knows *you*, but the whole world knows *me*' – and he was practically weeping. It was a huge mistake for me to approve him and to allow Soupy Sales to be in it . . . It is one of the biggest regrets of my life. I have never been able to get over it.

Minoff, who later became a psychotherapist, may have felt slightly better after he slipped a satirical portrait of Miller into the Beatles' animated film *Yellow Submarine*, which he co-scripted. The hyper-intellectual cartoon character Jeremy Hillary Boob, Ph.D. (or Nowhere Man) blathers away in Latin-strewn gibberish, boasting of his learned multi-tasking and manically typing his own reviews, but fundamentally being a sad nobody. 'Yes,' says Minoff, 'I based Jeremy Hillary Boob on Miller, an intellectualizer who knocks people left and right . . . a great talker who says nothing.'

*   *   *

Back in England, *Alice* had been rescheduled. That may sound inconsequential but the adjustment sparked an amazing outcry, with the furore spreading as far as Parliament. Wheldon had simply decided this was a grown-up take on Carroll's book and shunted the broadcast to after 9 p.m. on 28 December. Immediately, aggressive traditionalists of the Mary Whitehouse brigade were up in arms, supporting her adamant new Clean Up TV campaign. They assumed, before seeing the film, that Miller must have sacrilegiously tampered with this little national treasure, turning it into some kind of Freudian nightmare, especially since Dennis Potter's BBC biodrama *Alice*, shown the previous year, highlighted the original author's unsettling obsession with Alice Liddell. Peter Cook probably didn't help, quipping on *The World at One* that Miller's piece had been renamed *Analysis in Wonderland*.[87]

Not amused, the Conservative MP James Dance raised a hopping-mad motion in the Commons, deploring the perversion and violence being imposed on nice children's stories by the Corporation. Labour's William Hamling cried that he wanted to be left with his illusions. The *Daily Mail*'s front-page headline screamed that Miller's *Alice* was X-rated.[88] It was as if he were being subjected to a surreal judicial system inherited from the Queen of Hearts: sentence first, verdict afterwards.[89]

The matter was so avidly debated that, when it came to the critics' preview, a capacious West End cinema had to be booked to cope with the demand for seats. When broadcast, the film drew twelve and a half million viewers. Some members of the public rang the BBC to insist that it was a blasphemous travesty, the worst programme ever aired.[90] One spluttered that Mr Miller should be committed to Broadmoor. For the young star, Mallik, there was a particularly bitter twist. Her old-fashioned stepmother, having submitted Anne-Marie's photograph in the first place, joined the ranks of the outraged. 'It was very difficult and upsetting. She hated the film,' Mallik recalls, 'and was determined all contact was going to be broken with everybody . . . although Jonathan wrote to me for a while at school.'

Miller remembers the press reaction being dreadful, but most reports indicated, positively, that the previous uproar had been insane. If there was sexual symbolism or menace, it was hardly obtrusive: a man sitting in a bath by a path, completely ignored by Alice; a hole in a window pane; a drag Duchess. A few TV critics declared the production plain dreary. Others realized that the former Fringer and TV presenter had morphed into an astoundingly assured art-house film-maker. In the *Sun*, Nancy Banks-Smith described the production as 'fascinating and fearful, beautiful and mad', while the *Guardian* and *Observer* hailed it as Miller's apotheosis, in a class by itself, and a likely festival prize-winner were it on the big screen.[91]

Viewers also phoned the BBC, praising it as sheer genius, the best thing it had ever broadcast. A 1970s poll, ascertaining the most authentically dreamlike films of all time, would place Miller's *Alice* in the top five along with works by Ingmar Bergman and Fellini, and its influence was to seep, later, into Peter Greenaway's films.[92]

At the time, Gielgud sent a letter of warm congratulations, saying it was 'an enormously bold thing to have conceived and carried through' and some shots were 'as beautiful as the best of Resnais and Antonioni – only really English . . . I am very proud to be in a corner of it.' For its imagery, its sinister undertow and dreamlike disjunctiveness, Miller's film might be compared to other classics, from Cocteau's *Orphée* to Orson Welles' *The Trial* or Bergman's *Through a Glass Darkly* (those last two both being from 1962). The BBC's director-general, Hugh Carleton Greene, instantly deemed it a near-masterpiece, and his colleague Stephen Hearst, looking back four decades later, said: 'It now strikes me as a total masterpiece.'[93] It truly is one of the best things Miller has ever done and, being on film, it will probably stand as his chef-d'oeuvre for perpetuity. Even Tony Palmer underlines, 'Many of the things about *Alice in Wonderland* – including the things that he and I argued about furiously – are absolutely wonderful.'[94]

Regarding autobiographical elements, the *Financial Times* critic T. C. Worsley, while admiring the piece, contended that it should have been called *Miller in Wonderland* because 'the dream is not Alice's but his. It is his relationship to grown-ups that he is remembering.' According to that argument, Mallik's Alice was exclusively a child of the director's era, manifesting the auteur's (rather than the original author's) divided personality and ambivalence towards authority figures. Worsley was on to something. He was simplistic, however, in segregating the two men's visions. He took into account neither the Victoriana that had pervaded Miller's boyhood nor Charles Dodgson's complex relationship with the conservative patriarchy.[95]

Fundamentally, Dodgson's 1860s satire – for such it was, amusing youngsters by sending up old, sententious types – tallied with the spirit of the 1960s. Thus the perceptive viewer of the film was able to see double: the two decades translucently overlaid, though a century apart, as if there were a pleat in time. Redgrave's Caterpillar is, for instance, an aged scholarly fellow of Alice Liddell's epoch, in pince-nez and embroidered smoking-cap. Simultaneously, as Mallik tosses her head, challenging his authority and sanctimonious dictums, one senses that he represents the establishment geriarchy at which the young Miller bridled. Fingertips pressed lightly together, he momentarily evokes St Paul's High Master. Perhaps this Caterpillar's book-lined study even has a touch of Emanuel's consultation room, as Redgrave puts Mallik under his magnifying glass but fails to solve her growing pains.[96]

The extremely long corridor down which Miller's Alice runs may have harked back to St Paul's, together with the reverberations of the school hymn 'Immortal, Invisible'. Alongside that, Nanny Morgan surely surfaces, transformed into Dowie's sinisterly whispering servant and McKern's infant-thwacking Ugly Duchess, who wears a nursemaid's uniform.[97] By the director's own admission, the long Chekhovian silences at the Mad Hatter's tea party were based on his childhood memories, 'those hot summer afternoons when people were sitting around in the garden . . . conversation just simply seemed to seep away into the grass and there was nothing left to do at all'.[98]

His location-seeking treks across England, envisaging angels ripening like dragonfly larvae under the vegetation, sound like a trip back to his wartime years as an imaginative little boy in the countryside. The summer meadow scenes, when permeated with an urgent tabla beat, are not so far off the Wye Valley with its 'drugged' heat and the cuckoo's 'morse', pregnant with menace during World War 2. Also, as Mallik walks more serenely though leafy woods and beside pastoral streams, Sid Pask's rural Field Club expeditions spring to mind.

This is a biologist's *Alice*, its mise-en-scène scattered with stuffed animals, some in glass cases, like the Natural History Museum or Great-Aunt Brenda's house with its display cabinets.[99] Anatomical drawings are strewn around, and the trial scene's crazy zoological soundtrack has Miller reverting (not for the last time) to his childhood chicken impersonations.

In terms of Wonderland's non-British elements, he argues that Shankar's Indian score was used simply to evoke a dreamy other world, and the colonial subcontinent would have been just that in a Victorian child's imagination. Yet his choice of Mallik as an ethnically complex heroine might be compared to the cultural diversity of his own roots. A balalaika band features on the soundtrack, and an orthodox Jew makes a cameo appearance in the crackpot caucus race, along with a lory resembling an Anglican priest.

Although Miller now insists his vision was not meant to evoke an asylum, he stated in 1966 that he was constantly thinking of drama in terms of psychiatry and – sparking an article in the *Lancet* – he applied his neuropsychological expertise to the Mad Hatter (with Cook portraying a case of chronic low-level mania), the March Hare (involutional melancholia), and the Dormouse (a forgetful confabulist with Korsakoff's syndrome, or else senile).[100] As for Emanuel's psychiatric work, the endless corridor down which Alice runs, following the White Rabbit, was actually in Netley, the mental hospital to which Miller's father had been affiliated.[101]

This film may, moreover, be haunted by memories of Betty, indirectly. Friern Mental Hospital, where she ended her days, was a mid-Victorian edifice like Netley, known for having Britain's longest corridor. Stepping away from the pool of tears, Mallik is suddenly surrounded by a menagerie of muttering, squawking and cackling characters, as if she were paying a visit to a dementia ward.[102] Or is she herself losing her mind? When she first slips into the dreamworld – drifting off in the meadows – loud insects buzz on the soundtrack, like that 'fly-swarm of fantasy' which Miller said engulfed his mother. In Wonderland, Mallik's Alice seems to hear voices in her head and, while maintaining a phlegmatic air, combs her hair over her face like a mad woman. She keeps sensing she has changed, says that she's not sure who she is anymore, cannot remember verses she once knew, muddles them up when the Caterpillar tests her recall.

For sure, those mix-ups may be regarded as oneiric, garbling everyday matters as dreams do. Or Mallik's Alice can be seen as becoming wayward because she is hitting adolescence. However, the confusions are accentuated in Miller's adaptation and they start to resonate with the symptoms of Alzheimer's disease when you consider that Betty died, non compos mentis, only the winter before this film was made.

The director might well resist any such reading. If this film is *Miller in Wonderland*, the elements of his own life have been encrypted in the creative and, no doubt, often subconscious process. He underlines that his script (apart from small ad-libs) was faithfully drawn from Carroll's words, the period detailing was scrupulous, and the elegiac slant ('It is not now as it hath been of yore . . . / The things which I have seen I now can see no more') was a quintessentially Victorian lament for childhood's ephemerality. A parallel can, nonetheless, be inferred between Carroll's Alice growing up disconcertingly fast and Betty's almost surreally accelerated senescence. Miller would later compare *Alice* and *King Lear*, as two curiously dishevelled odysseys about growing older, and he was already, at this point, sharply aware of life's transience and the pains of growing old.[103] Aged just 29, he had written to Sacks about being in 'transports of despair' over his own ageing, lamenting his own sagging and stooping frame even as he celebrated Tom's infantine joys. That was in the very letter which dwelt on Betty's chronic deterioration – the fleeting ages of man in a nutshell.[104]

Picking up on the hint of morbidity in Carroll's original title, *Alice's Adventures Underground*, the film's sets are suffused with intimations of mortality. They show signs of decay or are crammed with Gothic furnishings and macabre trinkets (not least an animal skull strung from a dressing-table mirror, like a memento mori). Mallik's flat voice and expressionless face are ghostly, drained of life, in these faintly sepulchral interiors. Or one might perceive another oblique analogy for the limbo of Alzheimer's disease, which Miller has described as a living death. The passageway where Alice finds herself trapped, unable to squeeze through the tiny door to the rose garden, feels like a funeral parlour's waiting room.[105]

Less morbidly and more nostalgically, with Dick Bush's superlative camerawork evoking early photography, Alice is a vision of daguerreotypic loveliness as she glides down other airier corridors. As she wanders through English summer landscapes too, this film cherishes the fading memories of a sunlit childhood and a girl from a past age.[106] If that, in any way, reflects private mournfulness concerning Betty, the emotion is very restrained. It adopts an air, like Alice, of cool detachment.

Many fans, meanwhile, have assumed that Miller's vision was a Sixties psychedelic trip, inspired by LSD or puffing on joints. The Cheshire Cat's head floating in the sky looks as if it might be drug-influenced. However, the Caterpillar doesn't even have a hookah or mushroom in this version. Essentially, Miller's adaptation sprang from his relish of three phenomena which mess up the normal orderliness of life: the nexus of laughter-inducing comedy, psychological disorders and dreams.[107]

Finally, by way of a coda, Miller once had a vision, in his sleep, of Alan Bennett transmogrified into something like Carroll's ungainly White Knight. The playwright Peter Nichols recalls a dinner party at Michael Frayn's house, in the late 1960s, where Miller recounted this dream. The two ex-Fringers were descending a staircase on high-horseback when Bennett became hopelessly entangled with the banister and calmly bid adieu. Miller then found himself riding the actor Patrick Wymark down a grassy slope, discussing whether he had the quintessential Cromwell stoop for his forthcoming interregnum movie.[108]

Nichols exclaims that he wishes Frayn's guests had included a Freudian. Miller, by contrast, dismisses the notion that dreams symbolically express suppressed thoughts, saying:

> My interest in dreams has nothing to do with Freud. I just don't think they work in that way, as desires in disguise. I think they are sort of computational consequences of having a consciousness momentarily denied access to current experiences. What has always struck me is the rich combinatorial character of

dreams . . . the new and strange, composed of elements drawn from reality . . . Though I have never fully dreamed about a place that I haven't seen . . . all my dreams are unvisited elsewheres.

In other words, sleep is not just his favourite recreation, logged as such under his entry in *Who's Who*. Dreaming is, for him, a recycling, creative process.

· 9 ·

LATE SIXTIES TO EARLY SEVENTIES

NW1; extended families; back to the theatre
(Nottingham Playhouse, the Oxford and Cambridge
Shakespeare Company, the Mermaid and
Olivier's National Theatre)

IN GLOUCESTER CRESCENT, other gatherings with the neighbours generated hallucinatory moments of their own. At somewhat bohemian parties, George Melly's favourite trick was doing an impression of a bulldog that entailed a stark-naked moonie and satirically rearranged genitalia. In-depth research reveals that the whole tripartite routine was man, woman, bulldog: that's (a) full frontal; (b) genitals tucked between legs; and (c) the rear view for the grand finale. A witty journalist and expert on surrealist art, as well as a flamboyant jazzman, Melly became great friends with Miller.[1] When Ken Tynan broke television's big taboo, saying 'fuck' on air in the mid-1960s, they jointly fired off a congratulatory telegram from the Crescent.[2]

When the Mellys threw parties, Miller's humorous conversation usually made the shyer guests relax, though the Belgian surrealist E. L. T. Mesens ended up so confident at one bash that he had to be dragged out of the house, drunkenly yelling that he wanted to box Mark Boxer.[3] Conversely, the Beatles' manager, Brian Epstein, was horrified by the informality. He fled in horror when Miller turned up for supper at the Mellys' having just visited Scotland Yard's grisly Black Museum.[4] As the host himself fondly recalled:

> Jonathan came back and launched into a hysterical description of the exhibits, you know, as the policeman. [*Plodding copper's voice*] 'Now this pair of knickers is – as you can see – torn in two, but there is an identical sperm pattern . . .' He was very funny, but Epstein was appalled at the rudery and became more and more nervous . . . [until eventually] he said, 'I've just remembered I've got an appointment!' and hurried out to his waiting Rolls.[5]

To many bright sparks the Crescent seemed like the quintessential des. res., for others it was a competitive, survival-of-the-cleverest environment. Bennett called it a sack of fighting ferrets. Peter Nichols was glad he did not live there and compares Frayn's aforementioned dinner party, with Miller as guest, to fencing with Errol Flynn: '[Jonathan] taking us all on our own ground and sending us each in turn toppling downstairs, careering backwards through a window, disappearing headfirst down a well.'[6] Rachel's visiting sister, Jane, felt that the Crescent residents were constantly on show, with people popping champagne in their gardens, hoping to inspire envy.

It was a fabulous place in which to grow up, according to Sophie Radice (daughter of the MP Giles Radice), but some of the dopier adults dreaded early-morning encounters with Miller's ever-bounding mind.[7] His lack of small talk struck some as almost antisocial. Radice remembers returning, as a youngster, from a trip to the cinema and, agonizingly, being required to analyze the film in depth. Max Stafford-Clark was more appreciatively stunned by chats on the street corner. While he cleaned his car, his fellow director would come up with several brilliant ways of staging *King Lear* and recommend lists of research books, heading off to fetch them like a fabulous librarian.[8]

Rachel's work took her to the rougher side of the tracks in Camden as she was, by this time, working as a GP. During her very first night on call, she had to visit a semi-derelict block of flats, carrying her doctor's bag of drugs, to attend to a patient who introduced himself as the Birdman of Pentonville. 'I think Jonathan did worry about me a little bit and, just once, I made him come in the car but only once ever', she says. 'I just kind of got on with it and didn't talk about it very much.'

In a more gently eccentric vein, back in the Crescent, Miss Shepherd (the Lady in the Van) was parked up for so long outside the Millers' house that Camden Council slapped an obstruction order on her rusting, litter-filled Bedford, labelling it a danger to public health.[9] That was the day when she hatched her master plan of camouflaging the vehicle and emerged, artistically swathed in long scarves and a straw hat, armed with a tiny pot of primrose-yellow paint for model cars. She often knocked at the Millers' door if she wanted a natter or help, usually standing with one leg out at a balletic angle, sometimes complaining about the children being too tall and, on one occasion, initiating the conversation with: 'Sorry to disturb but I just met a snake coming down Parkway. I wouldn't have bothered you but I've had some very close shaves with snakes.'[10] Another time, she wrote to Edward Heath about Britain's unpardonable entry into the Common Market, then asked Miller to arrange a TV interview, adding warily, 'I don't want to attract any publickity [sic] because you know what happened to JFK, so I would give an interview behind a curtain. The programme would be called *Lady Behind Curtain*.'[11]

Life in the Crescent was, of course, more run-of-the-mill than the anecdotal highlights suggest. On a weekly basis, the most obvious competition was a race round the corner to Reg's rag-and-bone stall in Inverness Street. Here Miller and Bennett both bought oddments of antique china and collected vintage group photographs, drawn by the poignancy of sepia perhaps, or by a humorous fascination with institutional formalities, or by the frozen drama of the tableau.

Most of the dinner parties at the Millers' home were just sociable suppers, with neighbours popping round, virtually like members of the family. One child or more would always be ensconced in the kitchen, declining to go to bed. The theatre critic Susannah Clapp (who lodged with Mary-Kay Wilmers while working at the publishers Jonathan Cape) remembers those meals being 'proper family gatherings, not at all dressed up. There would be a mix of Rachel's colleagues and some people from Jonathan's old life, as it were, like Eric Korn, Nicholas Garland . . . Some people', she says, 'get famous and suddenly have a series of new friends but it was never deracinated in that way.' The Millers also hosted gregarious Sunday breakfasts, and Bennett, Tom's secular godfather, was like some Chekhovian adopted uncle. Frequently round for two or three meals a day, he had a house key of his own. The family photo albums confirm the casual domesticity, epitomized by a snapshot of the kitchen complete with homely clutter, with Bennett wandering in a blur across the background and with one child grinning in joke-shop Dracula fangs, seated between contented parents. The street was written up by journalists as if it were a celebrity venue. Its inhabitants simply nicknamed it the Fertile Crescent because it was filled with kids running around and skateboarding.[12] Socially, the connective tissue centred on picking them up from school, says Miller.

His offspring have all discernibly inherited his irreverent sense of humour and his frankness. Too bright and British to be gushing about what the famed polymath was like as a father, they are wryly satirical in their anecdotes while being palpably fond of him. His son William was not born to be boho and has since gone on to cut multi-million pound deals, as Nigella Lawson's business partner in the company Pabulum and in other posts. He is particularly entertaining about the school run:

> My parents were wonderful and Gloucester Crescent was too in many ways, but, when you look back at the photographs, you think, 'My God, we were gypsy children!' . . . And there was this rota. A sort of hippy Dormobile would take half the kids off to one school and a lot of cars would head off to the other. Then, of course, there was a minicab to take a number of the children off to the Tavistock [Clinic] as one or two always needed a bit of counselling to get through this bohemian idyll . . .
>
> I remember when it was my father's turn in the rota, he always used to swear because he'd forgotten he had to do it. So he'd get into the car, still in his dressing-gown, and drive far too fast. He was a terrible driver! Then someone would cut him up and he would wind down his window, shouting abuse and shaking his fist. His favourite was 'I'll rip your fucking thyroid out!' sometimes followed by 'And I bet you don't fucking know where that is!' It used to amuse my friends, but actually it terrified me because I always thought someone was going to kill him, not understanding that he's not a violent man at all and the outspoken rage is sort of drama or theatre.[13]

The motor show aside, this Sixties father was evidently warmer and more physically affectionate than his own parents had been. According to one associate, he never quite knew how to be a standard dad, yet he himself remembers endless playfulness, hugging and tumbling. He enjoys the fact that his children (and now his grandchildren) say what they please, free of dutiful respect. By all accounts, he was non-authoritarian and spoke merrily of being twisted round his daughter's little finger. William could be manipulative, sending his father to Coventry if they had a disagreement. 'It was an awful thing to do,' he confesses, 'because my father is a terribly loving, kind person and he would always break first.' Miller's old friend Nicholas Garland recalls him being protectively tender with Tom as well, when the toddler's kite blew away in the park on Primrose Hill:

> I have this tiny memory [of how] Jonathan began running after it, then Tom suddenly burst into tears because his father – his one life-support system – was disappearing. I picked Tom up and called, 'You get the kite,' but he simply couldn't do it and I remember thinking how touching that he came back to comfort the child and the kite was lost for ever.

Over the years, he has weathered some surly and tempestuous days with his family. One episode was a notable variation on the incident from his own boyhood when Emanuel frostily locked him out of Queen's Grove. As a friend recollects, Tom had been banished to the garden by his father, after throwing a tantrum, and was screaming through the glass. However, rather than coolly continue the adult conversation inside, Miller became distraught about the child's grief and was unsure what to do, eventually letting him in again. Again, when one of his youngsters hit a rough patch in adolescence, he evidently wanted to help. He took part in family therapy sessions (the very practice his father pioneered at the Tavistock Clinic), setting aside his own doubts and his earlier resistance to Rachel's phase of professional interest in psychiatry.[14]

In no uncertain terms, Tom, William and Kate declined to follow in his academic footsteps. The children of this immensely clever man all failed to excel at school, in spite of being manifestly bright. William describes them as the stubborn illiterati, a small resistance movement:

> My father used to read to us, *Emil and the Detectives* with all the accents, which was a kind of transcendental experience, but he was sometimes a bully about reading. When we were small and bored, his favourite expression was 'Have you tried prising open the covers of a book?' and, because we endlessly had these books thrust in front of us, of course we never read ... We had a very strange relationship with television too. My first memory of my father and television was staying up very late, on the sofa with a duvet, just to see his name on the credits ... However, coming home and finding us watching the television – sitting round like zombies – used to deeply depress him. I mean, I

don't blame him . . . In the end he just lost it and said, 'That's it!' He picked it up and took it to the junk store. So we had no television for a couple of years.

Undefeated, the two boys used to clamber over the garden wall to watch *Grandstand* with the soccer-loving philosopher Freddie Ayer and his son Nicholas (Nigella Lawson's half-brother).

Tom says that neither he nor his siblings are bothered about their lack of A-levels though, at one point, their father was envious about others' kids going to Cambridge and wished, unwittingly within his eldest's hearing, that he had children he could converse with properly.[15] As an undergraduate, Miller had pictured himself working at the university for ever and having descendants who married into dynasties of the intellectual aristocracy.[16] If he remains at all disappointed, he now chastises himself for not doing better in the paternal league tables. He recognizes that his growing children were what he lived for, but he was nervously fraught in some respects and culpably careless in others. He had educational goals similar to his own parents', yet he relied on comprehensive schools which he condemns, retrospectively, as multi-storey child parks. Both he and his wife were committed to that egalitarian system. However, this ideology, he now says, justified his parsimony.

Neither he nor Rachel even realized that Kate was playing truant. His daughter was the most obvious rebel of the three in her adolescence, sporting rockabilly hairstyles and not seeing eye to eye with her father. An amused admiration now infuses his account of how she managed to live a secret double life, working as a café manageress in nearby Kentish Town when she was meant to be at school. She was to meet her future husband, a managing director of a chain store, in her late teens, and she worked her way up from television company receptionist to production manager. In that capacity, she was to organize the TV film of her father's staging of Bach's *St Matthew Passion* before she took some years off to be a full-time mother.[17]

Her brothers both suffered from bullying at school and Miller felt that he let them down when a belated transfer to private education neither suited Tom nor saved William's grades. Although the family stammer was not passed down, Tom struggled with dyslexia which went undiagnosed until he was seventeen. Being Jonathan Miller's son made matters worse. 'I was ridiculed by my teachers,' he exclaims, 'mostly because of Dad! . . . You know, "I'm surprised you're so bad at maths, considering who your father is".' Still, he discovered his talent for photography at thirteen, thanks to the school darkroom, and his parents installed one at home, encouraging his interest.

The public school Bedales was William's idea of bliss.[18] It seemed to him like a confidence-reviving convalescent home after the comprehensive which he had attended, and his growing independence took a startling form. He is not sure whether his father was more appalled by Kate becoming a rockabilly or by him turning into a roaring Sloane. The divergence between his and the other Millers' lifestyle choices started with his covert house-tidying, after everyone was in bed. They were to climax some years later when Tom turned up to his brother's wedding in motorbike gear, leading to a petulant tiff over proper dress codes.[19] 'Dad laughed,' William remarks, 'but then *he* came in dirty old corduroys and a tweed jacket!' In a mocking vein, Tom declares that his younger brother practically skipped childhood, seeming thirty at the age of ten. 'I was in my teens getting rat-arsed smoking dope. The parents were the original Stringalong Sixties liberals [as in the caricatured couple of that name in *Life and Times in NW1*] so they didn't object', he says. 'Meanwhile William was [next door] having tea and muffins with A. J. Ayer's wife . . . and Shirley Conran.' The latter was the ex-wife of Habitat-founder Terence Conran and the mother of Sebastian Conran, another future business partner in Pabulum, though at that point roving around the Crescent as a teenage punk.

Even as an infant, Miller's middle child had a kind of alternative, out-of-town family because he adored his father's researcher and secretary, Sue Rogers (now Sue Bond as she married the creator of Paddington Bear). She became part of the family, typing in the living-room, sometimes alongside Bennett. The little boy took a shine to her and she took him to stay at Stanage, her parents' Victorian castle in Wales. Her mother, the ex-West End actress Stella Moore, became William's unofficial godparent and, for him, spending holidays there was like escaping to a completely different, enchanted life.[20]

On the religious front, Miller ignored Emanuel's continued digs about 'striking Anglo-Saxon attitudes' and actively countered his own Santa-free childhood with stacks of Christmas glitter. The doctrine which he disseminated at home was atheism, as he makes clear, though William went through an adolescent phase of churchgoing at Stanage, which shocked both parents. Similarly, Rachel bought the Bible just as a cultural keystone and was horrified by its violent tales, only to find this was the one book that Tom would read avidly.

Shedding additional light on his own and Miller's ethics, William points out that he is not just some inexplicably conservative changeling:

> My father is actually a very moral man, with views based on religious morals . . . For someone who's always so critical of formal society, he is a real old English gentleman with traditional beliefs about courtesy and common decencies. I used to get the most appalling ticking-off for not having said 'Thank you' and he taught me, 'If you're arrogant or rude, you'll never be forgiven for it. People remember you for that for ever.'

This is followed by a stupendous story, from some years on, of his father hotly pursuing criminals:

> We'd just come out of some unbelievably turgid French film at the Renoir Cinema, and this woman along the street screamed 'I've been mugged' . . . By the time I'd turned back round there was no sign of my father. Then I saw him, in the distance, down that concrete precinct, chasing these two really

violent-looking kids. I thought, 'Oh my God, he's going to get murdered' . . . Then the rest of this Bloomsbury cinema-going set decided, 'Oh right, we ought to have a go too!' So there was this posse of tweed jackets and corduroys running down this concourse . . .

We eventually caught up with my father who was, by now, waving a bread palette over his head and shouting, 'I'll fucking kill you! Stop, you little shits!' And as we're running along with my father absolutely leader of the pack, screaming abuse, I overhear this man huffing and puffing and saying to my father, 'We once met at Susan Sontag's,' and my father having to break his anger to say, 'Oh really, how fascinating . . . You fucking cunts, stop!'

Eventually, they actually did stop. These boys turned round and took out a baseball bat. Suddenly, there was this look of complete fear on everybody's face, apart from my father who started doing all this 'Come on, then!' I had to grab him by the collar and drag him back, and he didn't forgive me for a week. He accused me of being a coward. I said, 'I'm not. They would have killed you!' and he said, 'No, that's not the way to behave.' I was quite shocked.

As a young father, Miller had worried that he would pass on physical cowardice to his children.[21]

As for his progeny being little philistines, that was not really the case. Tom was a gifted youth-orchestra cellist and his brother won a school scholarship as a singer and oboist. William wanted to become a medic as well, having already declared as a toddler that he was going to pursue his father's other professions, namely 'readin', writin', smokin' and the postin' of letters'.[22]

Miller bought a holiday home, an old manse in the Scottish Highlands, with the proceeds of an advert-cum-documentary about whisky-making, which he directed for Johnnie Walker, arthouse-style.[23] When staying there with his children, he would take them on wonderful forays into the hills, giving them biology field kits, helping them to collect samples of bog water, then revealing its thriving life forms under the microscope. He once screeched to a halt in the car, leaped out and slung a dead hare in the back, promptly pinning it to the breadboard at home and giving a master class in dissection. It was, William acknowledges, hugely inspiring and, when he duly went on to do biology 'A' level, he could at least dissect the hind legs off a rabbit with panache.

He believes his father perceived that he was more ambitious than his siblings and, sensing this could be harnessed, hoped he would become a doctor. 'I was definitely influenced by my father and very keen to do the things that he wanted me to do, for him to be impressed. Even as a child, one was competing with him,' he states. 'But I realized eventually that it was absolutely pointless trying to compete.' In short, Miller was a pushover emotionally but was intellectually dominant, even unintentionally domineering. The praise he bestowed did not always seem lavish enough either. While thrilled to be shown a school project, he would urge further reading or launch into an expert lecture. This took the fun out of the parent–child relationship and made the work achieved seem woefully insufficient. In a later incident, as a young adult, William gained a pilot's licence and, as he recounts, took his father flying:

> Though [the episode] was amusing, more than anything else . . . I so wanted him to say, 'This is just extraordinary. I never thought I'd have a son who could do this!' . . . We got airborne and he did not say a word . . . and then over Canary Wharf, there was this incredible hazy sunset and the Thames like this sort of silver snake. I tilted the wings so he could look straight down at it and I said, 'That's Canary Wharf. Isn't it beautiful?' And he just went: 'That's where the cunts from the *Telegraph* are.'

Both of them share a desperate craving for approval, William suggests, even as he laughs about their divergent characteristics:

> From when I was very small, I've always wanted to run things and been frightfully organized . . . That's the complete opposite to my father who's like W. C. Fields. He's got all these bank accounts and doesn't know where they are or what's in them, or how to use a credit card! He has taken massive creative risks in his career but never dreamed of taking financial ones. He has a complete panic attack when I say I'm borrowing a million pounds from the bank. And the funny thing is that Nigella [Lawson], who has absolutely no understanding of business, is the daughter of a Chancellor of the Exchequer. I think, actually, we both wanted to do something totally different from our fathers.

Maybe William's marketing nous was inherited from his shopkeeping ancestors.

Opinions differ on whether the youngsters had to compete with their father for the domestic limelight or whether they felt that he was a busy absentee, as Miller had regarding Emanuel. Maybe the more obvious rivalry was just between Tom and William who admit that they 'wind each other up spectacularly'.[24] However, Miller is like an eternal little boy as well, always demanding attention, according to one frequenter of the Crescent. Regarding his absenteeism, his children recall that he would vanish from their Scottish holiday home because of supposed work crises. They suspect he was plain bored. He insists that he was there much of the time in Scotland. He has photographs of days at the seaside to prove it.

More shamefacedly, he admits that they once left the infant Kate at the beach, assuming she was in their companions' car. He also confesses that he scared her stiff by – of all things, given his infantine fears – pretending to be dead. He was not always up for larking around either. The flip-side of this celebrated entertainer is that, though not suffering from severe manic depression, he is prone to what he describes as waves of overriding despondency and acute self-doubt. At odds with his CV, which gives the impression of endless energy, he states that active stints, inducing euphoria, are interspersed with long stretches of lassitude and hopeless indecisiveness. Maybe this is why melancholic figures have featured so often in his productions, adopting the stance of the downcast angel in Dürer's allegorical picture *Melencolia* (aka *Melencolia I*) – seated with head leaning on hand.[25]

His depressive tendency might be traced back to the previous generation. Genetically, he could have inherited it from Emanuel. Psychoanalysts additionally link some adult depression to an early deficit of parental love. According to Freud, melancholia is a 'disorder of self-esteem'. When a love-object is denied or lost, the love is redirected in a complex way, turning inwards, like narcissism but mixed with feelings of reproach which, consequently, can emerge as intense self-condemnation (as well as condemnation of the other).[26] Perhaps Miller's pronounced confidence is, in fact, defensive, creating a sense of elation that drowns out his inner critic most of the time, but not always.

Depressions have stopped him working. They have slowed the hand in writing, like a kind of psychological arthritis, and made him dread the possibility of complete paralysis – a vivacious personality reduced to the living dead. He likens the mood-swing to a bright, expanding star suddenly shrinking to a high-density white dwarf with no source of energy.[27] He prefers to sit out the bad days than to seek any medicated fix.

One friend, keen enough on his Tiggerish aspects but with no time for his Eeyorish alter ego, suggests the man's bouts of protracted dejection would make even his nearest and dearest think of nudging him under a bus. Miller states that he has never been truly suicidal or deeply destructive. From his family's point of view, one of Tom's youthful attempts to please him – returning from a paper round and piling the reviews of his latest production on the bed – provoked a day of frightful moroseness. Emanuel's 'great pall of gloom' comes to mind when William remarks:

> If you were to talk about the downside, the hardest thing of my childhood was that I found his depressions worrying, not because they were going to come in white coats and take him away, but because I felt I couldn't do anything . . . I'd try and amuse him but it wouldn't work. It was so irrational. I was confused and upset by it. When he'd say 'Life's not worth living', I just remember being terrified and taking it seriously . . .
>
> But, though my mother says her biggest regret was she went straight back to work after having us, I don't remember feeling neglected or that my parents were absent . . . I hated my father going away for long periods of time when I was young but I only recall a couple of occasions when that happened. Actually, we were surrounded by people.

That statement qualifies another simplistic view of the informally extended family, viz. that the avuncular Bennett assumed some kind of gap-filling, substitute-father role. Miller did return from some out-of-town projects to find his brood chattering about doing this and that with Alan. Often, though, his directing work and home life overlapped because he invited his casts round to rehearse at his house.

The Millers, furthermore, became an extended family with extra children. Besides the secretarial Sue Rogers, they had a home-help called Beatrice Thomas, a Jamaican émigré whom Rachel knew from her days at the Royal Free Hospital. Beatrice had been a successful shop owner in the West Indies, yet found herself working as an ill-paid NHS cleaner in the so-called mother country. She was facing eviction in the mid-1960s when the Millers suggested that she could help look after their toddlers. She moved in to live on their top floor with her two daughters, Esther and Haleem, who was known as Jeannie.

When Beatrice and Esther moved on again some years later, the adolescent Jeannie said she wanted to stay and she became – like Rachel with Great-Aunt Brenda – an unofficial ward. According to Jeannie's own account, reminiscing three decades on:

> My mother was happy with Jonathan and Rachel because they were very respectful to her, but my relationship with her was fraught . . . [Coming to England] I was in a daze and couldn't understand things, and my mother was very impatient so I got more and more traumatized . . . The first moving thing she ever said to me – which made me weep later – was when she consented and said, 'Go to them, because they'll probably give you what I can't' . . .
>
> I am known as their daughter, and I called them 'Mummy' and 'Daddy' so much in the first few weeks that I must have driven them up the wall. But it was so nice. I'd never had a daddy before and it was like saying 'Father Christmas', and I didn't get shouted at! As a mum and dad, they were extremely patient with me and the nurturing was emotionally and intellectually very stimulating . . . The house was always buzzing [with visitors]. Lots of books and plays and journalistic articles have started as ideas discussed at Jonathan's kitchen table and I was there! The house was like a museum too, with a skeleton in the attic, old Victorian stuff, costumes and stereoscopes, and Jonathan just bubbled 24/7 . . . so I was flying and bubbling too.
>
> He always bought me books whenever he went abroad, the most incredible rare books on black people. He got me interested in black history, so I never had a loss of identity with him . . . George Melly took me over to his house and put on Bessie Smith, jazz and blues . . . [while] Jonathan played lots of classical music and bought me my first records, starting with Vaughan Williams. He was a very good father . . . His kids, who are extremely clever, probably did resist it, but he made me love learning and I was in heaven.

There was only one piece of paternal advice which she found bemusingly metaphorical, when Miller told her that, with boys, she just had to make sure she didn't get a bun in the oven. 'I spent weeks wondering what would happen to the bun,' she says, 'and that was my dad's sex education lesson!'[28] She went on to work with children in care and then in alternative healing.

Keith McNally, the son of an East End cabbie and now one of Manhattan's best-known restaurateurs, also became a kind of family friend/surrogate son.

This was after he left school to act, at sixteen, and quickly landed a part in Bennett's first West End hit, *Forty Years On* (1968). After that he lodged for a while at the playwright's house and would be round at the Millers' home three or four times a week, sometimes staying over and looking after the children, but mostly being inspired by their father's conversation. He spent time at the holiday home in Scotland as well.

Miller was, he notes, a great teacher, never condescending but eager to engage, enthusing him about films, art, Dickens. Indeed, the man's powers of description invited comparison with that supremely eloquent author, suggests McNally, who goes on to underline how generous Miller was with his time and money – always paying for everything and even offering to fund him through college.

Watching Miller's productions, McNally likewise absorbed his taste for beautifully worn decor and for understated performances. After he quit acting, he went on to make two feature films himself, *End of the Night* and *Far from Berlin*, besides establishing New York's Odeon, Balthazar and other acclaimed bistros.[29] When he is building a new restaurant, he always thinks about how Miller (though clueless about cooking) would see it, design-wise. Seeking to imitate his relaxed egalitarianism, McNally says he has no truck with prejudice, snobbery or pretension when managing his employees. The two of them still chat, too, about art exhibitions and films.

*   *   *

To return to Miller's stage directing, in the late 1960s he made swift progress – via London's Mermaid Theatre and Nottingham Playhouse – to become one of Laurence Olivier's hottest protégés in the National Theatre company. This raft of work drew him away, on a rip current, from television dramas.[30]

The British theatre was undergoing remarkable developments, encouraged by more funding from Harold Wilson's government. The decade has indeed been described as the most amazing in this art form since Shakespeare's 1590s.[31] Peter Hall had not only established the RSC in 1960, he had further secured a West End base for the company at the Aldwych. Along with Peter Brook's aforementioned Theatre of Cruelty productions for the RSC (influenced by France's radical Antonin Artaud), the Aldwych hosted seasons that showcased top international troupes from 1964 onwards. Word of Jacques Lecoq's brilliant mime and physical theatre school, in Paris, had also reached Britain.

Under Olivier, meanwhile, the NT corps had been founded at Chichester's brand new Festival Theatre in 1962, with the Old Vic in Waterloo becoming its London residence (until its permanent home was built on the South Bank). Other vibrant regional theatres sprang up in Liverpool, Bolton and Stoke-on-Trent, as well as in Nottingham. Edinburgh's Traverse, a pioneering studio space in a former doss house, opened in 1963 to perpetuate the spirit of the fringe all year round, and the Edinburgh Festival influentially brought Grotowski's raw, intense company from Poland to the West in 1968. Experimental approaches were, thus, gaining ground, and the Open Space Theatre, set up by Charles Marowitz and Thelma Holt on Tottenham Court Road, served as a forerunner of the London fringe.

As for the Mermaid, that was a thriving Thames-side venue, in situ since 1959 among the wharfs and warehouses of Puddle Dock, Blackfriars (just across the river from where Shakespeare's reconstructed Globe now stands). The theatre was run by Bernard Miles who launched his seasons, like a salty sea captain, with the clanging of a ship's bell. Miller's first production here was *Benito Cereno*, a sinister drama that unfolds on a dilapidated slave-trading vessel. It is boarded by a Yankee captain who fails to discern that the underdogs have mutinied.

Adapted from Herman Melville's novella, this was the strongest play from Robert Lowell's highly poetic trilogy *The Old Glory*, which Miller had premiered in Manhattan in 1964 – impressively managing a 40-strong cast and generating menace with a languorous, hypnotic pace.[32] The *New York Times*' reviewer, Walter Kerr, had been dismissive about this production, which inaugurated the American Place Theater (a newly converted, off-Broadway church). A critical battle began when the poet Randall Jarrell wrote a letter to the *NYT*'s editor, declaring it be the best American drama he had ever seen and superbly directed.[33] Robert Brustein of the *New Republic* magazine backed Jarrell up, greeting *The Old Glory* as not only an allegory about the States' foreign policies and race relations but also a theatrical renaissance, far superior to Broadway's pulp.[34] Miller once dryly remarked that his productions always split critical opinion and something would be wrong if they didn't.[35]

Starring Roscoe Lee Browne and Frank Langella (aged just 24), *The Old Glory* went on to become a long-running hit for the burgeoning fringe. It transferred to the Theater de Lys, won five Obies and was recorded for television.[36] In terms of Miller's artistic development, it was part of an extended phase of dreamlike, highly stylized productions. Even if he now sees tiny naturalistic gestures as his trademark, he is no simple realist and his declared aim, in this piece, was to escape the 'dead hand' of naturalism.[37] His use of long silences, almost ritualistic slow movements and puppet-like gestures is seen, today, as having influenced the top American experimentalists Robert Wilson and Andrei Serban.[38]

Arguments had arisen in rehearsals. Playing the leading slave-mutineer, Browne was allegedly infuriated by what he saw as 'typical white directing'. He and Miller talked it through in the end. For Langella, the production exerted such a grip that, after the run, he slept for three whole days. He was, at the same time, impressed by the director's light touch and divergence from Lee Strasberg's Method.[39] Miller scorns that revered school's practice of discussing characters' inner lives at length, slating it as 'sentimental balderdash infected with American psychoanalytical bullshit'.[40]

He was far more sympathetic about Lowell really needing psychiatric care. The writer suffered from manic depression or bipolar disorder, veering between extreme lows and hyperactive mania. Staying in the studio flat above the Lowells' apartment, Miller handled those psychotic phases with medical understanding, affection and humour. Nonetheless, his host did become alarmingly cranky, dressing in peculiar clothes and insistently staying up all night.[41] On one occasion, the director found himself at 4 a.m. in a downtown laundromat, trying to talk his febrile, sweating dramatist out of wildly extravagant schemes.

The Old Glory's cast doubtless realized something was awry when Lowell dashed in, two days before opening night, announcing he had penned a whole extra play, featuring Walter Raleigh's decapitated head. The streaming blood, he assured them, could be done very nicely with ribbons. The poet's wife and Miller managed to get him into a quiet unit in the Columbia Presbyterian Hospital, though the patient was on the phone within half an hour, eagerly continuing the conversation with, 'Oh Jonathan, you must come and see me . . . No, no, I'm allowed any visitors I like. Use the service elevator and say you're Stanley Kunitz.' Recovering from the Raleigh episode, he was manifestly grateful, describing the staging of *The Old Glory* as little short of miraculous.[42]

Miller directed *Benito Cereno* again at the Mermaid in 1967, with Peter Eyre as the beleaguered slave-ship's captain, with Rudolph Walker (today of *EastEnders* fame) in Browne's role, and with Alan Dobie as the Yankee. *Punch* magazine championed the production as a near-masterpiece, with the disquieting clarity of a nightmare. By contrast, it bombed with the Sunday papers' critics who condemned it for soporific mumblings and scant dramatic action.[43] That did not stop Miller heading straight back to the USA to premiere Lowell's very free adaptation of Aeschylus' *Prometheus Bound*, with Kenneth Haigh in the title role and Irene Worth playing Io (who passes by, gadfly-plagued, having been seduced by Zeus). *Prometheus Bound* was the climax of the first season at Yale Repertory Theatre, which had just been established by Robert Brustein (the *New Republic* critic-turned-dean of Yale Drama School, programming professional productions).

Back once more in a university community, Miller gave lectures when he wasn't rehearsing and had a splendidly sociable time. He dined with the students regularly and became good friends with Ronald Dworkin, the professor of law and philosophy.[44] Dworkin affirms that this visitor was a joy to have around and says that, with such imagination, erudition and uniquely connective thinking, 'Jonathan is so good a philosopher that it's easy for me to forget that that's just one of the amazingly diverse worlds in which he's a star.' On the same campus, a small but farcical misunderstanding arose when Miller was introduced to the Polish-born literary critic Jan Kott (of *Shakespeare Our Contemporary* fame). Startled by Kott's inquiry, ''Ave you zeen ze erse of Peter Brook?', the Englishman replied with abstemious politeness that he admired the man and his work but, no, he had not seen his arse. Only then did he realize the point of reference was Brook's latest production, *US*.[45]

Miller was the darling of Yale, Brustein confirms, and dozens of American universities were to follow suit over the years, inviting him in to serve as an inspiring live-wire. Giving lectures satisfies his lingering urge to perform. He has befriended many fine minds by enthusiastically knocking on campus doors, and he has felt useful as an informative 'welcome gadfly', darting between the humanities and science departments. These residencies have been a cherished part of his career, outside the limelight.[46]

Prometheus Bound was, admittedly, hard to bring to dramatic life with its mythological protagonist, chained to a rock, orating at personifications of Force and Power. This was another case of Haigh having to tackle long monologues. Still, this rebel Titan with a cause, shackled for enlightening mankind with fire and knowledge, was clearly an Angry Young God.[47] Lowell pointedly departed from Aeschylus' original to weave in his own concerns about contemporary dictators and repressed progressive thinkers. This attracted the ire of President Johnson, no less. Brustein has since learned that LBJ covertly demanded that the production's grant be axed when he heard that Lowell was making Zeus' aggressive policies sound like his own. With Promethean valour, the National Endowment for the Arts ignored the order.[48]

For his staging, Miller spurned the 'aspic of classical decor', plumping instead for a seventeenth-century prison setting.[49] That, he argued, brought out extra historical correlatives (such as Cromwell's regime) and helped the message come through to a modern audience – working like a hilltop transmitter, part-way between ancient times and the present.[50] Not all the critics were won over by this idea, or by the cast's conversational style. Several objected that Miller, the satirist and scientist, had erased the work's grand poetic dimensions.[51]

Similar complaints were to recur down the years. In other words, this director – who, as a child, had wanted more emotionally demonstrative parents – was chided as an adult for damping down dramatic interactions. Still, *Prometheus Bound*'s dreamlike episodes and mordant wit were appreciated, and Walter Kerr amazed everyone by writing a largely glowing *New York Times* notice.[52] As a consequence, it was officially a big hit. Writing to Sacks, Miller was on a high after this 'smash success . . . one of the best things I have ever done'.[53]

Moreover, his notion of creating that hilltop transmitter by translating the action to another century was the germ of his whole theory about historical transpositions, about plays having 'afterlives' thanks to what he terms '*renovatio*'. At its most straightforward, the *renovatio* thesis is that vintage dramas, instead of dying, can be refreshed via a change of setting. By being played out in a different time or place – artistically emigrating – a work enjoys its own kind of renaissance or rebirth.

Those key ideas would grow more subtle and form a central tenet of Miller's book *Subsequent Performances* two decades later. The concepts of renewal and inventive translation actually extend right back as well, into his memories of childhood. Take, for instance, the way he recalls his parents being 'mysteriously renovated' by their World War 2 outfits. Or, in terms of linguistic translations, there were all those alternative paraphrases needed to circumvent his stammer. However, *Prometheus Bound* was the first significant instance of him practising *renovatio* theatrically.

He linked up again with Haigh and Worth in the UK, making a BBC Radio recording of *Prometheus Bound*, then he moved on to the play's British stage premiere at the Mermaid, this time with Haigh and Angela Thorne.[54] Amidst divergent opinions, the *London Evening News* sang the praises of that 'austere and superb production . . . the epitome of theatrical discipline'.[55]

By this point, he was officially one of Bernard Miles' jovial crew, joining the governors' board and directing *The Tempest* at the same address in 1970.[56] That staging was a prime example of his enriching, widely informed outlook, for he drew on an anthropological and psychoanalytical analysis (by Dr Octave Mannoni). This discerned colonial relationships in Shakespeare's late romance.[57] So, Renaissance costumes were retained but the long-established depictions of Caliban and Ariel, as base monster and ethereal sprite, were jettisoned. Instead. Rudolph Walker and Norman Beaton (who would later star in *Desmond's*) played them as indigenous black islanders from two tribes, responding differently to the white paternalism of Prospero. Walker's more naive, sometimes chortling Caliban contrasted with Beaton's smart Ariel, who was more like a sophisticated butler-going-on-civil servant. In turn, Graham Crowden's Prospero had gone semi-native, wearing a witch doctor's robe over his Puritan garb. Inviting comparisons with twentieth-century conflicts in Nigeria and the Madagascar Revolt, Ariel ultimately picked up Prospero's discarded staff as if to keep Caliban in the post-colonial underclass.

The duo also behaved like rebellious, stroppy little boys, growing up as time passed, and Miller highlighted how Prospero behaved curiously like an analyst in his first scene with Miranda, encouraging his daughter to become a liberated adult via an act of creative reminiscence. ('What seest thou else/In the dark backward and abysm of time? If thou remember'st aught ere thou camest here . . .')[58]

Even if this staging implied all the magic was in the characters' minds, it entranced most reviewers. *The Times* described the production as in a class by itself, even by Miller's standards, and it was to prove seminal.[59] His anthropological interpretation was, for instance, essentially being replayed by the RSC director Michael Boyd in 2002, and it was taken as read by the company Tara Arts in their colonial West End production of 2007.[60]

Beaton retrospectively described Miller's *Tempest* as one of the most pleasurable projects in his career, and the single most important one. Parts for black actors were thin on the ground then, and it was his first major classical role. Somewhat ironically perhaps, given the colonial relations issue, he described the audition as 'virtually like going to meet God'. As an inexperienced young actor, Walker had initially been nervous as well, due to the reputational clouds of glory surrounding Miller. To their relief, he proved charmingly genial. 'Jonathan soon put me at ease,' Walker says. 'We had a very good relationship, working together more than once. He made *The Tempest* very real, Caliban very human. I liked that he gave you several options, three ways you could do [a scene], allowing the actor to choose.' In rehearsals, Beaton recalled, each speech was closely examined like the entrails of a fascinating new specimen, and Miller's textual explanations were like dazzlingly witty dissertations, similes pouring from his lips 'like pearls'.[61]

*   *   *

The Tempest was not, in fact, Miller's first Shakespeare production. Shortly before that, he had looped back to Cambridge University, responding to an invitation from a new troupe of students called the Oxford and Cambridge Shakespeare Company. They could not believe their luck when he agreed to direct their US-touring production of *Twelfth Night*. The next year, he asked if he could come back and stage *Hamlet*, making it a hat-trick with *Julius Caesar* in 1971. Regardless of being a big name, he loves a small-scale enterprise and the OCSC were an outstanding bunch. Even those playing bit parts were to become famous.

His Rozencrantz was Charles Sturridge (subsequently the director of *Brideshead Revisited*), Guildernstern was Nicholas Evans (author of *The Horse Whisperer*), and John Madden (director of *Shakespeare in Love*) portrayed Osric as a sinister henchman, with Sarah Dunant (the novelist) as a lady-in-waiting. The young Michael Wood (presenter of the BBC's *In Search of Shakespeare* and other series) was Orsino, writhing on his daybed in a leather codpiece. Donald Macintyre (now a top political correspondent for the *Independent*) played the fool, Feste, while Sir Toby Belch and Andrew Aguecheek were Jonathan James-Moore (later head of BBC Radio's light entertainment) and Mark Wing-Davey (the actor-director best known as Zaphod Beeblebrox in *The Hitchhiker's Guide to the Galaxy*). Miller's assistant was Michael Coveney (future theatre critic), and Oxford post-graduate Elijah Moshinsky (another top director in the making) watched these OCSC productions avidly, taking the helm thereafter.

Virtually everyone remembers Miller's rehearsals as a golden time. Sturridge comments:

> It was enormously enjoyable. Jonathan creates a gang that you are in twenty-four hours a day, having long arguments into the night . . . He perhaps preaches in a way, but it's with a fervour that is very exciting. You can definitely trace, in our group, this habit which people caught from him of Milleresque [persuasively accelerating] rapid speech . . . If Jonathan influenced me as a director, it is in his very characteristic accumulation of disparate sources.

Coveney agrees:

> It was like the most stimulating tutorial company you'd ever had . . . and he was superb at finding things these young students could relate to in their roles. Then he went round [touring America] with us on a Greyhound bus for about five weeks and became our sort of elder brother or uncle. He entertained everyone, just sort of chatting up the girls and pulling funny faces – those

beaky things he used to do in *Beyond the Fringe*. He was just this brilliant figure in our lives . . . I still think he is the most brilliant person I've ever met.

Wood adds:

I remember I was reading a new book on the philosopher Plotinus on the bus, and he immediately borrowed it . . . He had a wonderful, wonderful enquiring mind and was always reading fifteen things at the same time . . . He was just fantastically inspiring, and he had made it in the media which, at that time, was an incredibly exciting world – before television had gone up its own arse . . . [As a director], he had a very exciting and different way of looking. He was trying to disrupt clichéd ways of playing Shakespeare. I mean he chose Don Macintyre to be this snarling Feste who couldn't sing.

In terms of his directorial theory of *renovatio*, *Twelfth Night* saw Miller increasingly looking two ways, both ahead and backwards in time. If he was forward-looking in disrupting theatrical clichés, he was equally reinstating more authentic details from past times.[62] He was still learning, at this stage, how to use the history of ideas and the art history, which he had been absorbing since his own undergraduate days at Cambridge. Not all the Renaissance iconography that he brought in worked smoothly. He envisaged Shakespeare's Illyria, where the shipwrecked Viola comes ashore, strewn with symbolic Platonic forms (dodecahedrons, cones and cubes) as seen in Dürer's *Melencolia*.[63] The snag was his young cast kept tripping over the esoteric furniture.[64] In the end he simply jettisoned it, displaying more pragmatism than intellectual pedantry. What remained were visually breathtaking allusions to Botticelli. Viola emerged from the waves like Venus, seemingly naked, and the closing union of the lovers echoed, most beautifully, the dancing Graces in *Primavera*.

Once again, discordant reactions erupted in the press. On the initial British leg of the tour, the *Listener*'s critic D. A. N. Jones wrote off the production as dismally gloomy, having recklessly left before the end of the performance. This led to a barrage of irate readers' letters, including a cutting missive from the playwright Simon Gray who likened Jones to a colour-blind man in an art gallery. In his own review in the *New Statesman*, Gray said this *Twelfth Night* outshone even the RSC's excellent staging (by Miller's old university director, John Barton). It was the most subtly funny, forlorn and penetrating rendition he had ever seen.[65] After trekking around America and featuring on James Mossman's BBC TV arts programme *Review*, the OCSC went on to perform at the play's original Elizabethan venue, London's Middle Temple Hall.[66] That idea was picked up in 2002, when Mark Rylance took his Globe Theatre production of *Twelfth Night* there. 'Jonathan brings all the ideas to the table,' Elijah Moshinsky observes. 'He has done a lot of thinking for other directors . . . and certainly no-one, at that time, was using analysis and literary criticism imaginatively as he was.'

Miller's first *Hamlet*, a play he has staged four times in all, was strikingly full of personal reverberations. That is to say the reviewers saw his highly intelligent Prince of Denmark (played by the OCSC's Hugh Thomas) as a love-deprived child.[67] His own programme notes quoted from a biography of Proust, focusing on the abiding hunger for unconditional affection caused by maternal embraces being denied during childhood. Those who think this director has tricky relationships with father figures might point to his other programme note, on Freud's theories about patricidal urges. This discussed how a son's mixed feelings – competitive animosity plus suppressed sympathy – can lead to a search for 'convenient surrogates' to hate (such as Hamlet's step-father Claudius).[68] Moshinsky believes Old Hamlet's ghost related to Miller's own father. 'He really had a thing about the ghost. It was terribly important he should talk to Hamlet as a father to a son and, by talking to him, drive him mad,' he recollects. 'Jonathan may say he doesn't use his own experience but he does, all the time.[69] I think he doesn't know himself. He is a personal director but rationalizes it, lets his emotion into productions via scientific facts.'

Still, Freud was talking about primal father–son relationships and Miller says that he merely wanted an anti-melodramatic spectre, very commonplace, no special effects. 'People seem to think ghosts should be wreathed in smoke and ten feet tall, with incurable hoarse bronchitis, but', he explains humorously, 'I've never understood why death should bring about those changes.'[70] Again, it should be underlined that creative output cannot always be mapped closely onto the life of the individual producing it. To claim that Miller uses directing as a substitute for psychotherapy – expressing his emotions through others' plays and playacting – would be crazily reductive. Actors who have worked with him confirm that he rarely refers to his own emotional experiences, being more likely to correlate characters with people at one remove from himself, with medical cases, with someone he has just seen on the bus. As a doctor and director, he has mainly attended to others, not introspectively to himself.

Whatever inspired his staging, *Hamlet* transferred to the Fortune Theatre, *Beyond the Fringe*'s former West End haunt. Then he became challengingly avant-garde with *Julius Caesar*. Spurred on by the stunning boldness of Peter Brook's white-box-and-trapezes *Midsummer Night's Dream*, Miller presented Shakespeare's Roman tragedy like a phantasmagoric nightmare, in a setting akin to Giorgio de Chirico's paintings.[71] This was a long way from the toga-wearing St Paul's production of his adolescence. On an orange ramp against a stark sky, his crowd choreography – with a masked mob in body stockings moving in the style of zombie-mannequins – came close to mime or modern dance. Jonathan James-Moore's Caesar was a white-suited, arrogant, Edwardian patriarch, strung upside down like the murdered Mussolini or a toppled statue.

Miller's affiliation with theatrical iconoclasts was, seemingly, confirmed here (albeit the Mussolini allusion was not groundbreaking, having been used in Olivier's *Coriolanus* in 1959). A disapproving John Mortimer (he who created *Rumpole*) accused him, in the *Observer*, of vandalizing a lofty classic because he had, for starters, lopped off the opening scene.[72] Even the Marlowe Society veteran Dadie Rylands sighed, 'Oh dear, what have you done with Mr Shakespeare this time?' when he met the director in Cambridge. Those claiming that Miller imposed outlandish conceits were countered by Michael Billington who described him as a careful paleontologist or 'one-man X-ray unit exposing the structure and sinew [of a play]'.[73]

Such divergent portrayals of Miller can themselves create an impression similar to an X-rayed painting, the different views of him generating a multi-layered, ghosting effect. He has contributed to that himself. On the one hand, he has forcefully stated that a director has no obligations whatsoever to the playwright.[74] The absent progenitor has inevitably surrendered control. On the other hand, he has tersely distinguished himself from directors who brashly modernize vintage dramas with no sensitivity to the past's cultural differences.[75] Somewhere in the middle ground, he has explained that he does not *abuse* classical texts but that such scripts, coming with few performance instructions, are fundamentally ambiguous and hence open to interpretation.[76]

Loved or loathed, his *Julius Caesar* made it to the West End and several members of the OCSC were nurtured by Miller beyond that.[77] Besides helping Donald Macintyre find a journalistic job in the USA, he ensured James-Moore was hired as a manager at the Mermaid and Alan Strachan (who claims to have been the worst Fabian ever in *Twelfth Night*) became assistant director there, before going on to run Greenwich Theatre and become a West End director. Strachan holds that Miller taught both him and John Madden the crucial importance of creating a relaxed rehearsal-room atmosphere. As for Andrew Hilton (who played Old Hamlet's ghost), he now runs Bristol's acclaimed company, Shakespeare at the Tobacco Factory, and he concludes:

> Jonathan certainly sowed the seed of what I am doing now. He said to me once that he'd love to assemble a Shakespeare ensemble in a cockpit, to do high-definition productions with virtually nothing but the actors and the words. I thought, 'Yes, I'd like to be part of that.' Of course, he never did it, but here I am decades later [doing just that].

*　　*　　*

While collaborating happily with students, Miller was increasingly in demand as a headline-making professional director, in Nottingham as well as at the Mermaid. In a letter to Oliver Sacks, he wrote, 'The psychic energy required for these enterprises is so large that at the end of the day there is really nothing left.'[78] White as a sheet with dark rings under his eyes, he looked like exhaustion incarnate, yet he was thriving in perpetual motion too. Repeatedly zooming up to the Midlands, he was personally benefiting from this paradisal era in provincial theatre and, in turn, helping to boost the Playhouse's national standing. To Sacks he explained:

I went to Nottingham in the first place out of desperation since none of the big institutions here in London or Stratford were willing to employ me. However, it turns out to have been the best thing I ever did. It publicly demonstrated the satisfactory completion of my apprenticeship . . . I now feel ready to tackle almost anything.[79]

He greatly enjoyed the company of the Playhouse's artistic director, Stuart Burge, who had a touch of *Great Escape* glamour about him, having been captured during World War 2's Italian Campaign. Miller counts him among a handful of ADs for whom he has felt unconditional affection.[80]

Working for Burge, he also broadened his repertoire, enhancing his reputation as an anti-romantic and blackly humorous director of classic plays, beginning with Sheridan's comedy of manners, *The School for Scandal*. Stripping away the layers of varnish – the encrusted theatrical conventions of chocolate-box prettiness and fluttering lace – he pictured Georgian minor gentry living in dank, flea-ridden squalor.[81] He simultaneously intensified the satire by aping William Hogarth and James Gillray's grotesque caricatures.

Thereafter, he resurrected *The Malcontent*, John Marston's long-forgotten gem from 1603 wherein a deposed duke, adopting another identity, bitterly lampoons a decadent court. Seeing it as a surreal, seventeenth-century *Goon Show* but more ghoulish, Miller had white-faced, black-lipped courtiers capering around amidst trompe l'oeil colonnades, at once carnivalesque and macabre. This production went from the Playhouse to London, opening Sam Wanamaker's festive Globe season, which was staged in a tent by the Thames as part of the campaign to get Shakespeare's wooden 'O' reconstructed on its original site.[82]

Miller staged his first play by Anton Chekhov, *The Seagull*, at Nottingham. Just prior to that, he had won relevant credentials when John Gielgud invited him to direct *From Chekhov with Love*, a star-studded biodrama for commercial TV, which used letters to tell the playwright's life story. Gielgud played Anton Chekhov with Peggy Ashcroft and Dorothy Tutin as his wife and sister. Wendy Hiller was his would-be mistress, a character added in the course of Miller's production. Technical problems were still being caused by colour film at this time and the production's 24 backdrops, intended to be in the style of Sickert paintings, were so demanding that they almost sparked trade union action.[83] By comparison, the dramatization was very simply managed, with the cast mainly stationary, turned away from each other as they spoke their epistolary exchanges.[84]

As for *The Seagull*, his Nottingham production was rated as surpassing anything in London, a delicate study of human disappointments with Peter Eyre as Konstantin, the underloved son of the theatrical diva Madame Arkadina.[85] The country estate by the lake was beautifully evoked with gauzes and projected images which created translucent, deep perspectives. Hereafter, Miller would often employ such techniques, fusing his love of film and photography with his stage work, nudging towards what is now called multimedia theatre.

He was pursuing a bold line in casting as well, giving substantial classical roles to performers generally categorized as comedians or character actors, a trend that many of today's star comics wish to perpetuate. Fenella Fielding, from revue and the *Carry On* films, was his Arkadina. *The Times* took exception, declaring that the cast went for laughs and were far too British.[86] Yet actors who have worked with Miller believe he and Chekhov are soulmates, not just as a doctor-director and a doctor-dramatist. They feel the former is at home among the samovars, having the dark and absurdist side and all the intelligence vital to such plays, perhaps because of his family's roots in the Russian Pale of Settlement.[87]

Personally, he identifies with Chekhov as a medically trained, unsentimental observer of life, with an eye for behavioural nuances.[88] As for being Russian at heart, he emphasizes, first, that any British production will inevitably reflect British society and, second, that his ancestry has no bearing. His grandparents, from poor Jewish shtetls, had nothing to do with the world of Arkadina. All the same, he was reacting against Chekhov productions of the English school which he terms 'Keats Grove genteel'.[89] He wanted to inject more Slavic eruptive gaiety and shabbiness. Indeed, he sought out authentic advice from an expert, Tania Alexander, who was born in St Petersburg just before the Bolshevik Revolution. The daughter of Moura Budberg – Russian aristocrat, writer and quondam lover of Maxim Gorky – Alexander would continue to work with Miller for many years, whenever he directed Chekhov or other East European dramas and operas.[90]

As for his Nottingham Playhouse *King Lear*, Michael Hordern took the title role, following his turn as the muttering professor in *Whistle and I'll Come to You* and giving what is now regarded as the performance of a lifetime.[91] His royal patriarch was a comical old codger and ferociously ratty geriatric, slipping into senility and abdicating as a crisis gesture when feeling undervalued. Miller saw Lear as a paranoiac depressive, insatiably wanting love yet practically inviting Cordelia's rejection of him by setting up the praise-game in the first place.[92] She declines to give him, so to speak, a filial rave review.

As with *Prometheus Bound*, certain critics cried out for more heightened passion and cosmic reverberations, saying this was *Lear* seen through the wrong end of a telescope. The director's riposte is that people get ridiculously carried away by the thundering storm scene. He mocks 'Wagnerian Stonehenge' productions, regarding them as the relics of nineteenth-century, grandiose traditions.[93] His love of Victorian scientists contrasts with his scorn for that era's ham-dram. His staging centred on very real family relationships, with neither Lear nor Cordelia being romanticized.[94] No idealized pre-Raphaelite heroine, he had the young princess played with a cold, stubborn streak by Penelope Wilton (in her first major role).

He transposed the action from Ancient Britain to the century of authorship because, as he saw it, Shakespeare's play (from circa 1603) foreshadowed imminent political upheavals, rather like Chekhov's pre-revolutionary dramas. Written just 40 years before the English kingdom collapsed in the Civil War, the play seems to anticipate Thomas Hobbes' *Leviathan* which was written during that conflict. Out on the heath, Lear has regressed into the pre-civilized state of nature where, as Hobbes put it, life is nasty, brutish and short.

The polity, Miller underlines, was beginning to appear unstable in the early seventeenth century, so people were starting to cast doubt on the status quo where monarchs were traditionally ranked not far below God, above lesser mortals as well as animals.[95] Written into medieval jurisprudence was the notion of the king's two bodies: namely, that the monarch was a flesh-and-blood human being, but with the authority of the (more abstract) body politic vested in him by divine right. What if the man and his status were separable, though? That had become the question.

For Miller, *Lear* portrays an overturning of the hierarchy on the family level and the state level, the junior subordinates disrespecting their father and sovereign simultaneously. The subject of undermined authority had likewise, of course, become a contentious topic in the countercultural late 1960s and early 1970s. With civil unrest turning violent (notably in Northern Ireland's 1969 Battle of Bogside, as well as in America and in Paris in 1968), with proliferating wildcat strikes and with rising crime at home, crackdowns were being prescribed by some. Others cheered the era's rebels, only to wax ambivalent on seeing certain of them turn into terrorists or despots (such as the Baader-Meinhof gang and the 'Brotherly Leader' of the 1969 Libyan Revolution, Muammar Gaddafi).[96]

In the rehearsal room, meanwhile, Miller's cast loved his egalitarian style. 'He's not worried about his status,' says Wilton, 'therefore you're all in it together.' Frank Middlemass (who played Lear's Fool) likewise commented: 'He's formidably intelligent but as silly as anybody, daft as a brush and great company.' In this context then, he was a kind of Leveller with a common touch or – to use the popular Seventies jargon – an easygoing Type B personality rather than a competitive, ambitious Type A.

Middlemass' Fool was wonderfully tragicomic and superannuated, with a touch of battered cockney vaudevillian about him. Implicitly Lear's companion from boyhood, he looked curiously like Hordern's double, smeared with a clown's white make-up, functioning as the king's cautionary mirror image. Additionally, Miller was interested in the Fool and Gloucester's disruptive bastard son, Edmund, as two jokers in the pack, as interstitial or marginalized characters who look askance from the boundaries, not quite socially integrated, sardonically mocking.[97]

The director acknowledges a personal analogy, remarking on his later revivals of this same play: 'Perhaps I've seen my own grumpiness, vis-à-vis my own children, in Lear and perhaps that has enriched some of the quarrels with the daughters. "Daughter, do not make me mad!"'

Regarding his parents, he emphasizes, 'It didn't relate to my father at all. No, never, never in any way.' Even if he had been distressed by his mother's dementia, he insists his professional experience of senile lunatics, as a medic, was the key.[98] Wilton remembers him telling them about one old gent in a geriatric ward, being visited by his daughter and politely getting out of bed to walk her to the door at the end, unaware that he was naked. His productions have a wonderful immediacy, Wilton says, because he supplies his actors with such graphic details.

Miller stresses that, among the many books which have fed into his work, he is absolutely beholden to the writings of Erving Goffman.[99] The American ethologist studied the tiny idiosyncrasies of people's social, non-verbal behaviour, and those, Miller contends, are precisely what most theatre productions lack. He elucidates:

> It led on from my interest in [J. L.] Austin's 'Plea for Excuses', because Goffman drew particular attention to apologies and remedial behaviour in public places: someone tripping in the street and going back to inspect the pavement in order to deflect the accusation that he is a fool; people going down to the last possible point to wave departing guests goodbye to avoid seeming rude, or disappearing under a smokescreen of mimed future engagements (*He comically puts an imaginary phone to his ear, followed by a thumbs-up.*) . . .
>
> There's also a vast fringe or penumbra of behaviour called 'subintentional actions', seemingly negligible actions, like now: someone will be talking and absent-mindedly twiddling their ear lobe . . .[100] People don't normally pay attention to these things and don't miss them if they are not in a performance but, when they are, the audience has a sense that five staves of the behavioural score have been filled. It's like an orchestral score: you may not notice the woodwind's note under the strings' melody but it enriches the harmonic structure.

Hordern's performance as Lear was full of tiny Goffmanesque touches and it matured too, for he was to reprise the role for Miller in two subsequent versions filmed for television.[101] In the meantime, the Nottingham Playhouse production transferred, at Laurence Olivier's special invitation, to the Old Vic. Here the drama pundit Martin Esslin judged it the most lucid rendition of the play in living memory.[102]

Ken Tynan had been recruited from the critics' ranks to join the National Theatre team, working as Olivier's literary adviser and right-hand man. As soon as he had seen *Lear* in Nottingham, he proposed Miller as the perfect director for *The Merchant of Venice*, because Sir Laurence's wife, Joan Plowright, was wanting to play Portia. Her husband might well have dismissed Tynan's idea, for he had been unamused by *Beyond the Fringe*'s spoof of enervating Old Vic productions of Shakespeare.

JON: So even now while we to the wanton lute do strut
Is brutish Bolingbroke bent fair upon
Some fickle circumstance . . .
Get thee to Gloucester, Essex. Do thee to Wessex, Exeter.
Fair Albany to Somerset must eke his route
And Scroop do you to Westmoreland, where shall bold York
Enrouted now for Lancaster with forces of our Uncle Rutland
Enjoin his standard with sweet Norfolk's host . . .
I most royally shall now to bed
To sleep off all the nonsense I've just said.[103]

Olivier had further been exasperated by the Fringers' uncontrollable giggles when they were guests together on the ITV arts programme *Tempo*.[104] Worse still, Miller's unflattering comments about his blacked-up Othello, casually confided in a journalist, had appeared in print.[105]

Consequently, when the phone rang and the caller at the other end of the line claimed to be the great man, Miller assumed it was a joke. As he explains: 'I heard this voice saying, "Dear boy, I would like you to do *The Merchant of Venice* for Joanie" and I thought it was Alan Bennett or Peter Cook pulling my leg. Well, he grew rather impatient and said, "No, no, it *is* Laurence Olivier!" . . . I managed to say, "I'd love to do it".'

Soon the veteran star announced that he was going to join Plowright, taking the part of Shylock. This scotched the rumour that he was retiring after his battle with cancer, and he turned up at the first read-through already word-perfect.[106] Unfortunately, he came bearing a bag of facial appendages that appalled Miller: the stock-in-trade hooked nose, orthodox ringlets, and a costly set of jutting teeth which were apparently based on a Jewish member of the NT board.[107] The duo, as a result, got off to a sticky start, but Miller managed to wean Olivier off his worst accessories, with the actor enthusiastically concurring: 'In this play, dear boy, we must at all costs avoid offending the Hebrews. God, I love them so!'[108] He was allowed to keep the teeth, which were not especially Jewish in any case. Sir Laurence loved his dentures so, he used to wander around the corridors and give press interviews with them in, to see if people noticed.

He was very taken with the idea of an 1890s Shylock who would appear assimilated at first glance, and who could have a hint of Disraeli or of the emergent Rothschild dynasty about him. In his dapperness, this Shylock was also like Miller's own grandfather, the smart-suited merchant and bank man Simon Spiro.[109] Thus, the director's ancestral backstory of complex assimilation fed into this staging, alongside his broader historical allusions to the anti-Semitic Dreyfus Affair; to the Count de Primoli's vintage photographs of Venice; and to Hannah Arendt's thesis that modern anti-Semitism grew out of nineteenth-century capitalism.[110]

The production essentially made Shylock and his child, Jessica, 'Jew-ish' in different and conflicting ways. Having read William Empson's literary criticism and absorbed – via John Barton and Karl Miller – some of the close-reading skills associated with F. R. Leavis at Cambridge, Miller was now bringing those to bear on his Shakespeare productions. His *Merchant of Venice* implied that 'Jewish' or 'Jew-ish' was a complex word, almost in the Empsonian sense. Explicitly, when working on the script, he discussed the ambiguities of the term 'kind' (sometimes meaning 'kin', sometimes meaning 'compassionate', but often barbed in context).[111]

Olivier's Shylock was a clean-shaven man, with a morning coat, wing collar and attaché case, barely distinguishable from Antonio's fraternity of mercenary Christian gentlemen. At the same time he was, as one critic noted, a divided self.[112] He was seen donning a prayer shawl at home – not so far from Spiro and

Emanuel Miller on the Sabbath. In turn, Jane Lapotaire's Jessica, having shown signs of an anti-father complex and having rejected Shylock's world, was not absorbed into a happy-ever-after fairytale ending in Belmont.[113] Becoming the focus of the final scene, she was visibly shocked to hear of her parent's ruination and was left ambivalently hovering outside Portia's mansion, distantly hearing a sung kaddish (the Jewish prayer for the dead) and perhaps regretting the frivolous life she had chosen.[114] Presumably Miller thought Emanuel would draw his own parallels. In a letter to Sacks, he exclaimed: 'Thank God my father is too lame to get into the theatre!'[115]

The general public flocked to see the production and, having been tentatively scheduled for just seven performances, it was soon being debated keenly and called the most important theatrical event of the year.[116] Besides transferring for an extended run to the NT's newly-acquired, second auditorium in the West End, the Cambridge Theatre, *The Merchant* was filmed, broadcast on television and sold in the new format of video.[117]

Olivier was delighted. He adored the electrifying bits of stage business which his director had suggested, not least the gleeful jig into which Shylock launched on hearing of Antonio's wrecked fleet. That was loosely based on Hitler's stomp of triumph at France's defeat, recorded on a wartime newsreel. Olivier conversely let out an unforgettable, desolate wail after his final exit from the trial scene, defeated.[118] He wrote in his memoirs, a decade later: 'Jonathan excited us beyond measure by the limitless variety, the originality, and the fascinating colour in the expression of his ideas. He was the only man; we were thrilled by him and remain so.'[119]

The actor further revealed that working on *The Merchant* had helped him recover from five years of crippling stage fright. There were hairy moments during the initial performances as the sweat-drenched luminary downed tranquillizers to stop himself leaping on the first bus home. He begged his fellow actors not to look directly at him and, on one occasion, he almost forgot what a Jew hath. Miller recalls standing in the wings and glimpsing his terrified eyes staring out as if from behind a mask.[120]

Having got through that, Olivier recognized that this young director had given him a new lease of life, reinvigorating his reputation as a great Shakespearean actor by daring to show the king of British theatre some healthy disrespect. 'I remember Jonathan', he said, 'being ruthless in his criticism of some of my [characteristically inflected] line readings. It came as quite a shock to begin with, until I slowly began to realise . . . I'd made a mountain out of mannerisms . . . and ended up impersonating myself . . . Miller opened my eyes and made me look in the mirror again.'[121]

This was a complex kind of paternal-filial relationship. Sir Laurence noted that the ticking-off made him feel like the junior player or an embarrassed schoolboy, while Miller has inversely remarked: 'He was a father to the company in every sense of the word – positive and negative. In the years I worked for the National,

I had all those complicated, equivocal feelings that sons have for their fathers.'[122] He goes on to say:

> He was not a father figure exactly, but he had a paternal intimacy with everyone. There was, of course, a remoteness and competitiveness and there may well have been Machiavellian scheming with regard to others . . . in his own generation. But he was encouraging, amiable and extremely convivial, drifting into the canteen with his saucer over his coffee-cup to keep it warm, sitting down for a chat. He didn't lock himself away. I tell you what it was like: it was like a small bomber command squadron in those Nissen huts [the company's makeshift offices] at the back of Aquinas Street . . . The chaps were ready to scramble for this 'ere Flight Commander Olivier . . .
>
> I had a very good time with him and Joan Plowright too, going down with the family to stay at the weekend in Brighton [their country home]. I remember Tom, who must have been eight or nine, saying this wonderful thing on the phone to a friend, having to put off a sleepover and muddling up the name Sir Laurence Olivier. He said, 'I can't come because Dad's taking us down to meet his friend Roland Saliva' . . . They were very hospitable. He had this sort of patrician hospitality and a real interest in all his staff's welfare which, in turn, generated enormous filial affection and admiration.

·10·

EARLY TO MID-SEVENTIES

Returning to medical matters in academia;
Peter Hall's NT; *Private Eye*; Greenwich Theatre
and a West End Chekhov

T HE KADDISH WAS SUNG for Emanuel even as *The Merchant of Venice*'s
run was drawing to a close. During his seventies, he had been at death's
door on several occasions. In the obituaries, his medical colleagues wrote of his
pioneering achievements, polymathic erudition and gracious manners.[1] However,
he had never accepted that his son was an established director, persistently asking
Miller when he would determine properly on a profession. Maybe this was due to
his own deep sense of underachievement. His last words, as he reared up on his
deathbed, were 'I'm a flop! I'm a flop!'

His daughter Sarah, who never married and administered most of the home care,
believed that he felt both proud and jealous of his firstborn, yet was too inhibited
to admit this.[2] To his son, he sounded like a perpetually nagging conscience: 'Well,
have you decided what you are going to do?' Emanuel's disapproval and his final,
vehement self-reproach caused Miller to have a mid-life crisis and make a U-turn. Or
that is what it looked like, for he abruptly went back to work on medical matters.

He had been on a terrific roll. The year 1970 had been the busiest of his
theatrical career. Just to clarify the sequence of events as he zigzagged between
venues, *King Lear* had transferred from Nottingham to the Old Vic in February,
The Merchant opened in April and transferred to the Cambridge Theatre,
while he was staging his Mermaid *Tempest* for June. His father died in July. By
October, as the startled press reported, he was holed up researching the history
of medicine, back at University College.[3] It was as if he had been immediately
haunted by guilt, a feeling perhaps exacerbated by having to rehearse *Hamlet*
with the Oxford and Cambridge Shakespeare Company in September – those
scenes with Old Hamlet's ghost which he pored over so obsessively.[4]

Ensconced at UC with a three-year fellowship, he planned to use this time to
write a book about mesmerism, the spiritualist movement and the associated
development of neuropsychological theories.[5] He also intended to author an
account of his father's mentors W. H. R. Rivers and Henry Head, and another of

Sir Charles Sherrington, the Darwin of neurology who did groundbreaking work on reflex actions. Emanuel had known him too.

It was not, though, purely his father's death that effected Miller's return to science.[6] He was commissioned by the Fontana Modern Masters series to pen the Sherrington monograph; the mesmerism book had long been on the back burner; and the UCL post was set up, on hold, some months before he was bereaved. Nevertheless, the impression remains that he was suddenly spurred, with a sharpened awareness of his own mortality.[7]

His period as a researcher produced a body of scholarly work. Setting aside mesmerism, Rivers, Head and Sherrington for a moment, he first completed another Fontana Modern Masters volume. This one was about Marshall McLuhan, who had been regarded by many in the 1960s as a bleeding-edge academic guru, having famously proclaimed 'the medium is the message'.[8] Miller's book, *McLuhan*, acknowledged that this analyst of the electronic media boom had been eye-opening, but then it examined his hyperboles and traced the roots of his ideas, exposing him as a personally slanted and less than original thinker. Turning his hand to biographical investigation, the craft in which Betty had excelled, Miller discussed McLuhan's Canadian roots, his Catholic faith and the influence of his Cambridge mentors from the 1930s.[9] The *New York Review of Books* judged this demolition of the man's repute to be more important than anything he himself ever wrote.[10] What is most surprising is that Miller and his subject had been friends. Seeing the publication as a betrayal, McLuhan never spoke to him again.

Moving on to act as commissioning editor on another book, *Freud: The Man, His World, His Influence*, Miller gathered together a collection of expert essays. Offering breadth of perspective and background detailing, they investigated Sigmund's Vienna, the strict physiological training from which he departed, and his connections with philosophers, surrealists and Marx.[11] While Freud's massive impact was collectively recognized, one trenchant contribution from Dr Henry Miller (no relation) was soon being referred to as the strongest succinct case ever made against his theories – another reputation crushed.[12] Well reviewed, *Freud: The Man, His World, His Influence* elicited only a few digs about how Dr J. Miller's introduction sounded subconsciously anxious and how his self-styled 'careless flamboyance', as commissioner, came with inattentive proofreading.[13]

His truly angst-ridden tussle was with the Sherrington monograph, a commission that brought on dreadful writer's block, a kind of literary stammer. Oliver Sacks' memories of this time are poignant, for he himself became a bestselling doctor-author thanks to Miller. Speaking about his own shaky period as a young medical researcher, he recalls:

> I sent this box of my writings to Jonathan [in 1960], asking him to do the right thing if I died . . . I was not only self-destructive but negligent or destructive of many of my manuscripts. I think the original manuscript of *Awakenings* got destroyed in 1969. I had mercifully given a carbon copy to Jonathan

but forgotten this. In 1972, he took it over the road to his neighbour, the publisher Colin Haycraft. Then Colin said he loved it . . . and this becomes my own story now. However, it was Jonathan who, in fact, saved my writings.[14]

Awakenings became an international hit and was turned into a Hollywood movie starring Robert De Niro and Robin Williams. Sacks thereby bridged the science/drama divide in his own way, later progressing to his stage collaborations with Peter Brook.[15]

To return to Miller's writer's block, Sacks describes staying with him in Scotland in the early 1970s. As he recollects:

> In the mornings Jonathan would work on Sherrington. One would hear sheets of paper being torn out of the typewriter, crumpled and flung on the ground. Then he would come down at lunchtime, scarlet in the face with his blood pressure, one felt, sky-high . . . [as if] he was somehow beating up Sherrington, beating up the typewriter. It seems that major ambivalences were involved . . . I don't think Jonathan likes the idea of 'masters' very much.

The revered neurologist proved just too nerve-wracking and the monograph was eventually abandoned.[16] Miller is still kicking himself, exclaiming that he is 'a total chaos' at writing.

Many lectures given during his UC fellowship years and thereafter have, similarly, not materialized in print because he could not commit them to paper. Speaking extempore, he is often scintillating on the rostrum though only half-finished when it is time to stop, having got so carried away at finding himself 'unblocked'.[17] Rachel humorously recalls one august institution attempting, hopelessly, to make a cassette-recording as Miller darted out from behind the lectern, fizzing with ideas.

He confesses that he nearly broke down trying to prepare for the high-powered Cambridge Clark Lectures. Similar agonies preceded his 1971 address, given to the British Academy, on the subject of censorship, which had become controversial again, being linked to law-and-order concerns and the new libertinism.[18] Miller's argument was lucid enough, concluding that excessive images of permissive behaviour, and indeed satire, could have a corrosive effect but that society should not be paranoid. He, nevertheless, endured 'sleepless and desperate nights' in the run-up to the talk. As he recorded in a letter to Sacks, the panic gave way to 'a hanged man's indifference [on the day itself] . . . a state of mesmerised tranquillity. The lecture', he explained, 'then flowed out of me like a venous haemorrhage and I recovered consciousness precisely sixty minutes after I had started'.[19]

As with the Sherrington script, his book on mesmerism was never completed, and he partly blames University College for that. He complains that he was ill-nurtured, insufficiently encouraged and wretched. This sounds almost like a reprise of his infant-school days. In any case, being stuck in a windowless study only proved to him that he was a roving intellectual by nature, not a nose-to-the-grindstone academic.[20]

Even if his academic oeuvre failed to materialize as planned, this period of study fed into *The Body in Question* in the long run, and it produced a few lectures on mesmerism and on Rivers and Head which did make it onto the page. Moreover, that small trove proves biographically fascinating. If McLuhan's writings were personally slanted, so were Miller's specialist papers, between the lines.

'Going Unconscious' and 'A Gower Street Scandal' are transcripts of two lectures depicting Franz Mesmer and University College's first professor of medicine, John Elliotson.[21] Miller related how Mesmer, circa 1767, qualified as a physician and then took up unorthodox experimental practices, claiming he could curatively affect patients' mysterious inner ether by moving magnets across their bodies or, indeed, by just passing his hands over them. Derided by establishment colleagues and censored by France's Academy of Sciences, Mesmer became a celebrity nonetheless. Avid crowds flocked to his 'séances' where, 'in a robe embroidered with Rosicrucian alchemical symbols,' as Miller colourfully put it, 'he stalked the darkened rooms to the accompaniment of a glass harmonica and actively encouraged his clients to luxuriate in their convulsive *crises* [i.e. fits and trances]'. Mesmer's cult grew, we are told, 'precisely because it was the subject of official criticism . . . [as] fringe remedies are today'.[22]

Elliotson was at the centre of a comparable scandal in the 1830s. The eminent physician was, according to Miller, a volatile divided man, attracted to subversive causes and 'in at least two states of mind', being a rational materialist with spiritual yearnings.[23] Taking to mesmerism after his mother's death, with a proselytizing verve, he held his 'séances' in UCH's lecture theatre and opened them to the public. Being subsequently mocked in the *Lancet* and condemned by the outraged Royal Society of Physicians, he was forced to resign.

What catches the eye is that Miller, the showbiz renegade/reformed scientist, should choose to research these shockingly theatrical medics. This is not to say that his lectures are, any more than his productions, heavily autobiographical. However, his accounts of Mesmer and Elliotson's activities are lightly strewn with words that echo his own career path: 'establishment' and 'fringe', 'unorthodox' and 'subversive', 'frivolous' and 'incontinent festivities' (referring to the séances). His tone, regarding their work, is mercurial, repeatedly shifting between disparagement, amusement and appreciative sympathy.[24]

The other key lecture is *Man: The Double Animal* or *The Dog Beneath the Skin*.[25] There Miller described Head and Rivers' great nerve-severing experiment which, conducted at St John's College, tested the sensitivity of Head's deliberately wounded arm with pins and cotton-wool wisps. The duo believed that their results revealed two evolutionary tiers, with the injury seeming to expose a normally buried, primitive, 'protopathic' nervous system. They compared this to some uncouth 'dog beneath the skin', almost like a wolf within. The healing process, they said, reinstated more discerning and superior 'epicratic' responses which once again sealed in and restrained that savage dog. Miller's core argument was that Rivers and Head had been influenced by Victorian political anxieties, as well as by the evolutionary theories of John Hughlings Jackson (the recognized father of clinical neurology, who himself drew inspiration from the biologist Herbert Spencer). Many people had been alarmed by a surge in mob anarchy, after the 1886 riots in Hyde Park, Trafalgar Square and Belfast. Colonial uprisings kept erupting as well (the Zulus, the Ashanti, and then the Boxer Rebellion at the turn of the century). Rivers and Head suggested a neurological analogy: a nervous system where the governing top level could be overridden, for a while, by the suppressed underdog.[26]

The lurking autobiographical element here is that *Man: The Double Animal* sees Miller, in the wake of Emanuel's death, contemplating fathers on multiple levels, with a critical and an admiring eye.[27] Neurologically, he was discussing how traces of our ancestors have been detected in our bodies (rightly or wrongly). As an academic historian, he was uncovering chains of intellectual forefathers. More personally – carrying on the line, in a way – he was teaching his audience about Dr E. Miller's tutors.

That said, this lecture did not dwell on Emanuel at all. It did not directly discuss his connection with Rivers and Head.[28] If anything, Miller's time studying the history of medicine at UC served as a remote filial salutation, one at several removes from his father's work. Today he states that he was not really affected by the death of either of his parents and that he was, in a sense, relieved of a burden because of Emanuel's rheumatic suffering. Nonetheless, he admits to having cried occasionally about things that could have been articulated, 'if only we'd had this talk, or something of that sort'.[29] He recollects:

> I had one dream of my father. Some years after he died, Rachel and I went to Pompeii. We walked around this deserted city of the dead in this bright, cold, winter sunshine . . . and that night I suddenly dreamed and woke crying . . . I was at a kerbside café [in the dream], just outside Central Hall, opposite Westminster Abbey and – through the passing traffic – I saw my father in his Royal Army Medical Corps uniform, a Sam Browne belt and a peaked cap partly shadowing his face. He had a leather swagger stick in his hand with which he lightly tipped the rim of his cap and sort of saluted me across the street . . . I tried to cross the road, to speak to him, but the crowd bore him away . . .
>
> Something to do with having not had a connection with him, I suppose, and wishing for a reconciliation. I don't know. But it came unexpectedly, as a result of these other dead people – as if he had come back with that multitude of the dead – and he never returned again.

*   *   *

Miller could not be trapped in his windowless study for long, certainly not the allotted three years. He was soon springing out of there and directing plays again. He had never said that he was categorically quitting the picaresque theatrical life.[30] Besides keeping his hand in at the Mermaid, at the Nottingham Playhouse and with the OCSC, he returned to Olivier's National Theatre corps in the summer of 1971. There he won acclaim for his revival of *Danton's Death* by Georg Büchner (another lapsed medic). This French Revolution drama helped pull the company out of a slump, and it formed a twin set of stylized, political nightmares with his OCSC staging of *Julius Caesar*. Büchner's guillotined characters appeared in cases resembling museum cabinets. When executed, the actors simply jerked their heads to one side, and Miller used menacing buzzing again, to symbolize the angry mob.[31]

Ronald Pickup, who played Saint-Just opposite Christopher Plummer's dissipated Danton, remembers Miller's rehearsals being like highly entertaining seminars, so brilliant that the play almost got in the way.[32] Plummer explains further:

> What is so fabulous is how Jonathan deals with the work from an oblique angle. He would tell stories or talk anthropology or medicine . . . but it was always applicable. He never interfered in your world, the matter of acting . . . You took from his world.

John Shrapnel, who was to appear in a string of Miller productions, adds a point about academic ideas and humorous demonstrations, observing that some actors can get slightly intimidated because this director is a polymorphous mimic and will act out, say, 'a Jonathan cartoon version' of remedial behaviour from Erving Goffman's books. 'But he does this', says Shrapnel, 'to the point where everybody is in hysterics . . . Then later, when your performance needs something completely off the loop, you realize he's given it to you.'

Watching Miller in rehearsals somewhat disproves the claim that he dispenses no instructions.[33] His enactments of bits of business get imitated, such that some performers' moves and gestures end up looking discernibly Milleresque. Even so, as Shrapnel observes, he mostly directs indirectly, through the medium of the joke and the roundabout chat.[34]

After *Danton's Death*, he restaged *The School for Scandal* for the NT company, with Denis Quilley modelling his manners on Ned Sherrin as Benjamin Backbite. That character and his uncle were cheekily turned into a camp couple. In spite of that, the critic from the *Observer* dismissed the production as the National in its respectable, dour middle period.[35] Miller replied with a personal missive about the dreary, middle-aged Helen Dawson. That was needless really, since others' glowing reviews ensured the show was a hit.[36] In any case, he was palpably delighted to be back, like the scholastic Hamlet fraternizing once more with Wittenberg's travelling players. As Shrapnel remarks: 'Sometimes you read articles where Jonathan seems to be looking down his nose at theatre . . . but that's *never* what you perceive in rehearsal.[37] He's like a rat up an alley – he *loves* it!'

On top of the NT work, Miller headed out to Los Angeles to direct Richard Chamberlain in *Richard II*, an amusing turn of events given *Beyond the Fringe's* send-up of the Bard's history plays, brutish Bolingbroke, Essex, Wessex and all that. He was charmed by Chamberlain and unexpectedly adored the Californian laid-back lifestyle: just driving around on the freeway and lolling in bars with the cast. Though he had missed the Summer of Love by several years, perhaps this was the alternative West Coast life he might have led, had his émigré forefathers made it to America. He returned home wearing hippie beads.[38] They were ditched after about two days as Rachel and the snickering kids alerted him to the possibility that he looked absurd.

Soon after, he was invited to work on *The Taming of the Shrew* with Joan Plowright, for the NT's summer season in Chichester. The character of Kate is ferocious, of course, and British second-wave feminism had just been revved up by the publication of Germaine Greer's *The Female Eunuch*.[39] Plowright was a relative pussycat. Apparently it was Anthony Hopkins, playing Petruchio, who seemed to be wildly neurotic, pacing round the theatre for hours before each performance.[40] Miller also remounted *The Seagull* at this venue, with Peter Eyre and Penelope Wilton joined by Irene Worth as a frisky Arkadina, and with Robert Stephens as her lover. It was so successful that in 1973, when the Festival Theatre was seeking a new artistic director, Miller was rumoured to be on the short list. That came to nothing.[41]

The same year, Peter Hall moved from his reign at the RSC to run the National Theatre Company, sharing power with and then succeeding the displeased, ailing Olivier. As artistic director, Hall dispensed with Tynan but promoted Miller to the rank of associate director. When this was announced, Miller jubilantly predicted a more vibrant and less autocratic theatre world. He publicly rejoiced that the NT's new team members, including associates Michael Blakemore, Harold Pinter and John Schlesinger, were an exciting prospect, much younger and very close.[42]

Yet Miller v. Hall was to become one of the most notorious feuds in recent British theatre history.[43] Sir Peter thinks his antagonist, together with Blakemore, took on the role of a conspirator and a ringleader for the 'enemies within', encouraging hostility to his leadership through backbiting and nostalgia for Olivier's era.[44] It is as if Hall were Julius Caesar, or the loathed stepfather, Claudius, usurping Sir Laurence's Old Hamlet. Miller referred to his takeover as a putsch.[45] Sir Peter has compared the situation to scurrilous dogs snapping round his ankles.[46] While underlining that he has 'always liked Jonathan' and bears no grudge, he says:

> I made a great mistake thinking he was a friend . . . Both of them [Miller and Blakemore] had absolutely hysterical and vitriolic opposition to my appointment . . . And they did very little except try and mess up whatever I was trying to do, frankly. Of all the people that I've known, Jonathan has done me more public damage in terms of the media than anybody else. I mean, he's been obsessive . . . I think he is so brilliant that he has great difficulty in accepting any form of authority or criticism or influence over him, always finding authority to be stupid or ridiculous. There's a kind of hysterical contempt.

Hall was to publish his own side of the story in diary format, in 1983, and in his 1993 autobiography.

Maybe the alliance was doomed from the start. His early diary entries show that he did not wholly adore Miller's work. He told him at the outset, quite bluntly, to stop imposing reductive academic conceits on plays.[47] He also jotted down how this team-mate was delightfully ebullient but 'alarmingly full of confidence . . . the only director I know who always likes his own work'.[48] That confidence would soon be shaken, for Miller was to stage only three more NT productions: *Measure for Measure*, Beaumarchais' *The Marriage of Figaro*, and Peter Nichols' *The Freeway*. It was a steep downward curve.

Measure was a very happy experience, a touring production with no superiors peering over his shoulder. He relished the offbeat venues, not least one civic hall where the manager greeted him with, 'Will you need the microphone to introduce your acts, Mr Miller?'[49] He was positively inspired by the small budget. For the set, he lugged old doors off a building site with his designer Bernard Culshaw, and updating the action to Freud's interwar Vienna made ingenious sense. The Duke, watching from corners, was like an analyst sitting back and putting Vienna on the couch.[50]

Miller's 'knee scene' was electrifying too. Instead of a blatant attempt at sexual assault in the governor's office, Julian Currie's Angelo was creepily repressed, just fingering the hem of Isabella's skirt as she (played by Gillian Barge) sat frozen rigid with horror. Hall agreed, in his diary, that this was a very good production, the best he had seen by Miller, and an extended run was duly planned at the Old Vic.[51]

The Marriage of Figaro, penned by the French playwright Beaumarchais before Mozart's opera version, did not turn out so well. Some reviewers were appreciative. They found Gawn Grainger a convincing pre-French Revolutionary member of the Angry Brigade, playing the titular manservant who is irked by his master.[52] Many complained, though, of longueurs, insufficiently grand aristos, stylistic inconsistencies and weird bagpipes (actually period instruments). Harold Hobson was baying for blood in the *Sunday Times*, calling the director a mediocrity who should be sacked.[53] Miller's fortieth birthday, that same month, must have been pretty glum, especially as his employers had not supportively leaped to the production's defence as expected.[54]

After this, he and the National (which was under fire for other poor shows) failed miserably with its premiere of *The Freeway*. Peter Nichols remembers being blindly convinced that his futuristic comedy, depicting Brits in a traffic jam, was going to be great. It was, unfortunately, inert. He suspects that the director swiftly realized the situation was hopeless and lost his nerve, or lost interest. Miller kept vanishing from the rehearsal room, only to be found, after a hunt, chatting in the NT offices. This is not, by the way, the only instance in his career when he has skipped or cut short rehearsals. His reasoning is that he works fast, but he sometimes describes himself as lazy.

He was particularly avoiding confrontation with the comedienne Irene Handl who kept paraphrasing her lines and was pushing to play Joan Hickson's larger role.[55] When Hall saw the dress rehearsal, he immediately insisted on drastic surgery and cut out large chunks. This came too late and the production died on its feet. Reeling from the terrible reviews, Nichols fled to America. 'I couldn't take it,' he says.

Miller was to avoid new plays almost entirely after this, even though they were a significant part of the British Theatre scene in the Seventies, with active dramatists including David Hare, Edward Bond, Tom Stoppard, David Storey and David Edgar, alongside Bennett and Pinter.[56] Actually, Sarah Miller did more for that particular cause. Her jokey claim to fame, at least, was that she talent-spotted Joe Orton back in 1963 when – ignoring the instructions of her boss, the agent Peggy Ramsay – she accepted an unsolicited script from this curious young man in a plastic mac who walked in one lunchtime. Inside the unmarked envelope which he gave her was *Entertaining Mr Sloane*.

Nichols is retrospectively humorous about *The Freeway* bombing, yet still blames Hall, in part, for persuading him and Miller to pair up in the first place, by assuring each of them that the other was eager to collaborate.[57] Miller vaguely recollects it was, in fact, Olivier who first urged him to do *The Freeway*. Nevertheless, he believes that Sir Peter then used it as a second elephant trap to drag him down, along with the *Figaro*. 'Hall had known perfectly well', he surmises, 'that the *Figaro* would completely fuck me up, and it did. I wrecked myself. He had known that all the audience hear [with Beaumarchais' play] is the absence of Mozart's music. And *he* had just had a huge success with the opera at Glyndebourne.'

Even if some accuse Hall of having been a power-loving Machiavellian, he sounds staggered at the elephant-trapping charge, exclaiming:

> That is completely unfair! He *wanted* to do the Beaumarchais.[58] And if you think Jonathan Miller would ever do anything because somebody asked him to, think again! . . . I think that's advanced paranoia. These strange conspiracy theories that he has . . . I don't know what it comes from. I mean, he *needs* to be persecuted, he really does . . . No, he did a very bad production of the Beaumarchais: [that] is the truth. Both Blakemore and Jonathan did very unsuccessful work and there's nothing to breed discontent like failure, and they couldn't bear it, actually, and they wanted to blame me, I think, for their own failures. But I would say that!

He goes on to highlight that it was not just the productions spiralling downwards. The crucial offstage problem was that Miller could not endure the new style of open government that required him to sit down and collectively discuss his ideas with Harold Pinter and John Schlesinger. Miller ripostes that Sir Peter, whom he nicknamed Genghis Khan, did not institute open government at all.

Actually, the reviling and distrust of Hall's regime at the National might have had more to do with Richard Nixon than with Khan. Faith in leaders was at rock-bottom in precisely these years, 1973–4, because of the Watergate scandal's revelations of top-level shenanigans. Anyway, besides complaining that the NT boardroom meetings were a bore, Miller believes that the artistic director was managing things to his own advantage. Pinter and Schlesinger, he says, became the inner cabal, being allowed more intimate private exchanges because they were a famous writer and film-maker. 'I think Peter Hall only took me on', he continues, 'as a token to show he was not usurping Olivier. I think it gave a false impression of his hospitality to the old regime and was carefully calculated.'

Miller did not like giants, and Hall's NT struck him as a deadly bureaucracy developing Brobdingnagian delusions of grandeur. As the South Bank edifice neared completion, he began objecting to any such monumental institution. He states:

> Peter Hall wanted big, with all this rhetoric about 'centres of excellence', but it seemed to me this great National Theatre, with all its multiple facilities and lobby events, was like a Brent Cross Shopping Centre for the arts. Centres of excellence are not created by fiat. I thought the National Theatre should no more be located on the South Bank than the National Health should be located in St Thomas' Hospital. I said that, rather than dramatic cathedrals, there should be a Congregationalist movement in which we have theatrical chapels. In other words, 'The National Theatre' is the name that should be given to twenty or thirty theatres throughout the country, because you never know where excellence is going to erupt.[59]

Today Miller's vision has, to an extent, been realized by the National Theatre of Scotland and National Theatre Wales, neither of which occupy a grand theatre building, instead staging productions countrywide. At the time, the divergence of his values from Hall's led to intensifying dislike. He used to allude to the high-rise apartment where Sir Peter lived, in the newly built Barbican complex, as 'Satan Towers'.[60] Describing a dinner party for NT associates there, he recalls that everyone had to lunge for their supper, swinging around in those trendy, Seventies, hanging chairs. He adds:

> This sort of cordon bleu deb cooked the meal, then he took us out on to the balcony from where we could see the McAlpine [construction company's] sign haemorrhaging rhythmically in the fog, over the South Bank. We had these big whisky glasses and he raised his towards the sign, saying, 'Gentlemen, that's what we're all about!' And I realized then that he was full of bullshit.

Miller's critics point out that he was a shamelessly snooty, intellectual aristocrat – born to the purple, as it were – referring to Hall (the son of a station master) as a cultural arriviste. He himself acknowledges that he is an old Bloomsbury snob. He believes in the aristocracy of excellence, he says, and Hall struck him as a vulgar mediocrity with whom he just couldn't work.[61] Miller the Leveller is meshed with Miller the elitist.

He was, moreover, acting like the court jester at the NT, taking the king of the castle down a peg or two. Theatrical colleagues, including Blakemore, roared with laughter at his barbed comments and, in a discussion about possible names for various spaces within the new building, they relished his suggestion that, alongside the Kenneth Tynan Bookshop, they could have the *Pierre Foyer*.

He was playing a dangerous game, being breathtakingly free with his tongue. Even Blakemore says it wasn't surprising that Hall became suspicious of him. No one can forget Miller's verbal cartoon, of Gillray-like ferocity, physically comparing Sir Peter to 'a ball of rancid pig's fat rolled around the floor of a barber's shop'. One actor even recalls him launching into a riffing, blistering diatribe while on public transport, such that an American tourist, sitting opposite, bid them adieu as he got out, saying: 'Jeez, I don't know who this Peter Hall is, but I'm sure glad I ain't him!'

Miller's own comments on the Fool in *King Lear* might have given him pause for thought. He was redirecting Shakespeare's tragedy for TV during his showdown with Hall and, most strikingly, remarked that Lear's ragged joker had nothing to lose, whereas 'the fatal place to speak the truth is in the middle of the [social] pyramid where you can tumble'.[62] Hall himself calls Miller 'a genius and a fool': a man born brilliant, therefore scoffing at authority, but thereby making himself unemployable.

Shifting the focus back to the boardroom issue, Hall stresses that what really damaged Miller was a pivotal clash in 1974, not with him but with Harold Pinter. In spite of the playwright's past admiration for *The Drinking Party*, he and the loquacious director proved to be antipathetic. The renowned master of the threatening pause took particular umbrage at Miller's plan for an all-male production of *The Importance of Being Earnest* and interrogated him. What was this casting trying to prove? Was it implying that, secretly, Wilde wished he could write a homosexual play?[63] These days such a reading would hardly be questioned, but Pinter deemed it disrespectful to the text.[64] His censorship must have been particularly frustrating given that Miller had been a laddy drag act himself, back in Footlights, and McKern had been so wonderful as *Alice*'s Ugly Duchess.

No minutes of the fractious meeting are to be found. However, several letters in the NT's archive of internal documents are now open to scrutiny, three decades having passed. An enthusiastic early missive sent from Hall to Miller refers to production ideas and says, 'I loved your experimental IMPORTANCE.'[65] In a further message, dispatched shortly before the crucial meeting, Hall informed Miller that certain associates were expressing some anxiety – 'worry which I do not share'.[66] This somewhat qualifies his memoirs where he records that the all-male idea was 'firmly squashed' in the meeting because it 'seemed to me, and to all those present, a touch mad'.[67] Correspondence from Pinter to Hall indicates that the issue was, in fact, still dragging on approximately a fortnight later. His letter said:

I was very relieved to hear that Jonathan had concluded that there was no justification for an all male *Importance*, but was amazed to hear last night [in a theatre bar] that Michael Jayston is still going to play Lady Bracknell. I suggest that this is no more than a silly gimmick and that in a National Theatre production it is nothing less than disreputable . . . [I] do not understand how [the production] could be set [on these lines] without further discussion between the associates.[68]

The whole thing was subsequently shelved, and that, says Hall, incurably bruised Miller's ego. His conciliatory letter did not work.[69] It read:

I hope you weren't too hurt over THE IMPORTANCE happenings. There is only one person to blame over the whole mess and that is me. I did not think that the Associates' feelings would be so strong . . . Anyway, it is over and I hope with no hard feelings . . . I should think you will be glad of a slight rest.

Miller became seriously unreliable and fraught after Pinter was allowed to get the upper hand. Visibly stressed, he developed rashes and swollen glands.[70] He started skipping certain meetings and, according to Hall's diaries, oscillated between shunning the boss and apologizing in a distraught way for his bad behaviour, saying he was shattered.

By late 1974, he was considered such an alarming loose cannon that Hall got tough and axed the long-promised transfer of *Measure for Measure*, blaming the chaotic South Bank building delays.[71] The construction work would not be complete until 1976, and it looked as if Miller had been made redundant for the foreseeable future. A whole raft of other productions that he had planned – including Etherege's *She Would If She Could* – were stymied too.[72] That is according to Blakemore, who still feels passionately and says:

It was a disgraceful way to behave. It would have been much more honourable to say, 'Look, we are not getting on.' . . . It was an absolutely devastating blow to Jonathan's belief in himself . . . He went into a kind of great gloom. He was so angry and destroyed, for about two years. It was appalling, an appalling thing.

Hall records a climactic 'complete breast-beating scene'. This was after he had accused Miller of 'behaving in a Coriolanus-like way', booking himself up with work elsewhere and openly threatening to resign. Apparently, the despairing Miller then admitted that 'he always loudmouthed against authority, was always against the father figure'.[73] His letter of resignation came not long after, in early 1975.[74]

There is a coda on the subject of father figures. Though very convivial by comparison, the course of Miller and Olivier's relationship had not run altogether smoothly. Sir Laurence and Tynan had considered the staging of *Danton's Death* to have been so disastrously arid that they denied Miller *The Bacchae*.[75] He directed *The Malcontent* at Nottingham, not the NT, because Olivier shilly-shallied.[76] Moreover, Plowright had been horrified when she saw that the final proofs of Logan Gourlay's book *Olivier* included a Miller interview which mixed warm praise with comment on the great man's stubborn ego. The culprit ended up frantically handing over £700 to censor himself, paying for a reprint with his contribution excised.[77] One colleague recalls him saying he ought to kill himself, and Miller confirms:

> I was extremely upset that I'd allowed myself to speak unkindly. I owed everything to him really, and he was always kind and decent and supportive to me. I would have done anything to have it taken out because I think it was ungracious and ungrateful – in a way I don't feel about whatever I've said regarding Peter Hall, because he was never kind.

Olivier forgave Miller. Contrastingly, Sir Peter concludes: 'I can't remember, quite honestly, but if I didn't sack him, I wish I had.' Neither side in that dispute has ever felt he should say sorry, and the reprisals seemed to carry on for years, like some endless revenge drama.[78] Hall's diary entries started to sound a touch paranoid, repeatedly plagued by news of his foe's determination to carry on a guerilla campaign, using the press.[79]

Blakemore laments what the NT lost. 'I thought that Jonathan was', he says, 'worth his weight in gold, with this quite dazzling cross-referential mind, his ideas coming from outside the theatre. It jostled the pack. It was energising. That was Jonathan's function.' He sighs with reference to the power of the NT press office concluding: 'Once I'd resigned we – both Jonathan and myself – were absolutely demonized . . . I found myself bad-mouthed in theatre boards and so forth, and I think Jonathan did too. Both of us paid a heavy price for disagreeing with Peter Hall.' Having felt unloved at the NT, Miller would end up seeing himself as unjustifiably discarded by the British theatrical establishment as a whole.

*   *   *

Britain was going through a bleak spell in 1974, slipping into an economic malaise with high unemployment. Industries and homes were, furthermore, obliged to go dark due to energy shortages, an oil crisis and industrial action by miners having led to government-enforced power cuts. Miller had also been personally disappointed in the early 1970s, failing to break into the big-screen film industry. Various ideas had been floated and he had pencilled in a movie, to be made in India, adapting one of the Inspector Ghote series of detective stories. The furthest he got was talking to Marlon Brando about it in a Calais hotel.[80] He flew out to Hollywood to discuss another project with Peter Sellers, only to receive no word from him for a week. When he finally went in search, to the studios where Sellers was working, the star squinted from the set and hollered: 'Jonathan, long time no see! What are you doing here?'[81] Wasting his time, evidently.

One film did get made, which he directed under the aegis of Columbia Pictures. *Take a Girl Like You* was adapted by George Melly from Kingsley Amis' novel about a northern lass and predatory males. It starred Hayley Mills and Oliver Reed but was a resounding flop.[82] The film-making had degenerated into a ghastly farce. The bustling producer Hal E. Chester – or Hal E. Tosis as he was soon renamed – was constantly breathing down Miller's neck and undermining his directorial authority.[83] Allegedly, Hal E. was so determined to sex up the footage that he slipped close-ups of groping into a deliberately distant sex scene, without so much as a by-your-leave.[84] He kept shamelessly interfering with the props too, surreptitiously turning brand labels towards the camera. Miller's old *Beyond the Fringe* skits about fantastically crass film execs and product placement (performed at the initial Edinburgh International Festival run, though dropped later) now looked like premonitions.[85]

Mills enjoyed the director's idiosyncratic approach: namely, never preparing in advance. It caused major continuity problems, though, so John Bird (who played her father) had to be called back to do a bunch of completely meaningless things, such as taking three steps from the dresser to the door. Miller goes further in his own self-condemnation, saying this was just like his commercial theatre venture with Soupy Sales, an absolute nightmare and a shambles.[86] He is right. The end result was third rate. His primary motivation, to make some money, had cost him dear. He never directed another movie.[87] Melly bewailed that fact, blaming Chester's insensitivity.

At least Miller managed to laugh with Melly about the whole fiasco. By contrast, he failed to see the funny side of 'The Life of Dr. Jonathan', a send-up that began to appear in *Private Eye* under the nom de plume John Boswells. Aping James Boswell's biography of Samuel Johnson, this long-running column portrayed 'the great Doctor' pontificating 'with his customary vigour' at 'his lodgings in Glos. Crescent', surrounded by fawning 'importunate savants'.

He was depicted as the supreme deipnosophist (a table-talker) holding forth over supper, with disciples including 'Prof. Dworkin, the learned jurisprudent from the plantations' and 'Mr Geo. Melly, the critick'. This brought out how a top conversationalist like Miller, rather than truly engaging in an egalitarian two-way exchange, can reduce his interlocutors to kowtowing feeds, the unspoken rule being that they should play second fiddle. The ex-satirist was now being lampooned and perpetuating the art of British comedy by serving as the butt of the magazine's jokes as during his *Monitor* stint, but more persistently. The column was, in some ways, *Life and Times in NW1* rejigged.[88] Here, though, the satire was specifically targeted. It was personal.

The more prolific Miller became, the more he was derided. Doctor Jonathan ('surely an eighth Wonder of the Age') was depicted pompously encouraging panegyrics and lapping up eulogies about his lectures, about his TV appearances, about his long-awaited tomes ('concerning divers topicks too awful and profound to bear thinking of'), and about his theatrical ventures such as *Measure for Measure* (aka *Mesmer for Mesmer*) and *Danton's Death* ('never before performed on account of its extreme length and tedium but . . . rescued from oblivion solely by the operation of my own genius', as Doctor Jonathan put it).[89]

This chimes, discomfortingly, with that sketch of the schoolboy buried in the Chesterton Society minutes book at St Paul's: the passage where Miller was described pontificating about art, 'twist[ing] his mouth into a wondrous sight, a despiteful pout, a chastisement of the small-minded children that sat before him, an apotheosis of the true artistic perception'. Back then, his fellow pupils were palpably enjoying his highly theatrical arrogance. Even so, the amused tone was veined with aggravation.

The painful truth is that 'The Life of Dr. Jonathan' was very droll, and some old friends thought *Private Eye* had rightly spotted full-blown self-importance in Miller, sticking a needle straight in there. Yet rather than being lanced and purged, or just shrugging it off, he was openly hurt and furious. He states that it was, in fact, this relentless ragging which made him feel really depressed and outcast by English society.[90] He saw it as a surreptitiously xenophobic hate campaign. In his opinion, the *Private Eye* gang are taunting, philistine, Christian bullies:

> It's like a prefects' room at Shrewsbury, full of rancid jockstraps and canes, where swots and Jews are put down for being 'pseudo-intellectuals'. It would be interesting to know what they would count as a genuine one . . . I suppose I am answerable to the accusation that I'm a Jack of all trades, but I'm usually called that by people who are scarcely Jacks of one. Being constantly tormented for simply expressing opinions or interests that seem too plural . . . it's what makes England rather second-rate, and it gets you down in the end.

Whether unwisely or bravely, he has never heeded the precept that, if you must be clever in Britain, it is expedient to conceal it behind feigned modesty.[91]

The send-up was uncomfortably close to home as well given that Peter Cook still owned the publication. Miller assumed that he contributed substantially to the articles, and it seemed like a stab in the back 'because', he explains, 'though I saw little of Peter (and he began to sort of deliquesce as he became drunk), I thought – you know – we were friends'.[92] In the years after *Beyond the Fringe*, Cook had sporadically kept in touch. The Millers would occasionally have supper at his house in Hampstead, and he sometimes rang for a chat. This suggests a fondness, deep down, even if irritation and envy were in the mix. Cook's habit of incessantly playing the joker and putting on voices warded off intimacy, but Miller remembers this with some sadness, as he does the most alcohol-sodden phone calls (one of which was vitriolic concerning his and Rachel's 'condescending' visits).

He could never bring himself to rebuke Cook about the 'Dr. Jonathan' articles. It also looked as if another acquaintance had a treacherous hand in them, 'John

Boswells' suggesting the magazine's regular contributor John Wells, who had penned the translations for Miller's staging of *Danton's Death*.

Christopher Booker clarifies that it was actually he, not Wells, who compiled the column, in league with Richard Ingrams and Barry Fantoni.[93] It was a wind-up of Wells, for being pally. Booker goes on to mention that he himself had once been friends with Miller, in New York, fraternizing with the scholarly Robert Silvers and Susan Sontag. That friendship bit the dust when Booker savaged *Monitor* in print. Hearing of the pique caused, he could not resist pushing it further. '[It just] shows', he remarks, 'how malicious and sad I was in those days.' Revealing that traces of admiration lay behind the lampoon, he concedes that the McLuhan volume was 'awfully interesting' and that he meant to write an appreciative footnote about Miller in his own book, *The Seven Basic Plots: Why We Tell Stories*.[94] He recalls that, when they were friendly:

> Jonathan reminded me vaguely of my ancestor, Coleridge. You remember the famous description, in Carlyle's *Life of Sterling*, of Coleridge sitting on Highgate Hill as a sage . . . holding forth for five hours and everyone sitting around in amazement.

The column was 'only really a tease' and Miller should not have been so touchy. After all, he formerly called for satirists to draw blood.

The cruellest cut was that Doctor Jonathan was caricatured flying into hysterical distempers precisely about being teased, hands waving 'like some oriental dervish', mouth venting 'squeaks, groans and cries of torment . . . as fine a display of "non-verbal communication" as one could hope to find'.[95] Many of Miller's colleagues think he should have been above this schoolyard stuff, or positively flattered by the attention. Others still share his strong sense of injustice. Eric Idle argues that it was hypocrisy, not comedy: 'They just shat on him, abused him for years and made his life miserable. It's that English . . . [crushing] of intellectuals by people who pretend they haven't got degrees from Cambridge. And behind it all was the envy of Peter [Cook].'[96]

On the subject of proliferating, fictionalized versions of Gloucester Crescent life, Alan Bennett's *Getting On* borrowed certain elements from the Millers. As a neighbour, Bennett has not merely nipped round for some sugar. He has taken occasional glimpses from life there, anecdotal snapshots and lines spoken around the kitchen table, unobtrusively preserving them in his plays. *Getting On*, a subtle seriocomedy from the 1970s, is set in Highgate rather than Camden and depicts a snooty socialist MP called George, whose wife is attracted to an odd-job man. Nevertheless, Highgate is obviously near NW1; George's eccentric in-law is a Slade-trained artist, just like Rachel's mother; and George laments his ageing body in a monologue which is noticeably akin to a depressed diary piece written by Miller that same year, for *Vogue*. In that article, he described staring in the looking-glass every morning at his 'accelerating senescence', seeing 'a ghastly grey face . . . as I might be when dead', merely shaving off the grave-mould and sluicing out the rotting mouth. It might be sheer coincidence or just similar lines of thought, but Bennett's George, likewise, stares glumly into the mirror, lamenting: 'This sagging cistern, lagged with an overcoat of flesh that gets thicker and thicker every year. The skin sags, the veins break down . . . This is the body I live with and hoist into bed every night.'[97]

Miller sounded pretty grim in his *Desert Island Discs* interview, again around this time, with his chosen luxury being a sharpened razor, 'either for shaving or suicide'. That so horrified the presenter, Roy Plomley, that he stopped the recording, wanting something more comforting.[98] Miller headed off to New York as well, revisiting his old haunts for a documentary called *West Side Stories*, made by the BBC TV producer Tristram Powell. Without the boost of *Beyond the Fringe*, Manhattan made Miller feel he was sinking fast. An alarming bass line of despair is discernible under his rapid-fire commentary for this programme, talking of how he smelled of failure, felt shrunken and invisible. He saw the city's decay as an oppressive, 'larger metaphor of something that's going on inside oneself'. One old family friend thinks the marriage might have hit a rocky patch, and Rachel says there have been ups and downs over the decades. Miller simply remembers he was extremely low: 'I broke down in the middle [of *West Side Stories*]. I just couldn't do it.' Powell had to draft in Patti Smith as a second voice, just to complete the assignment. Still, he emphasizes, Miller had a tremendous sense of responsibility, struggling to fulfill the job.[99]

His sense of humour never completely deserted him either, mercifully. Many of his reminiscences in *West Side Stories* were hilarious and, when he resorted to psychiatry, he ended up entertaining the analyst John Padel. At one session, the shrink took an urgent telephone call, leaped up exclaiming that he was meant to be giving a lecture, and was instantly waved on his way with the quip, 'Good thing you answered, or they'd have been up shit creek without a Padel.'

★   ★   ★

Miller was not a complete outcast when he left the NT. Even before he had quit the battlefield in Waterloo, he had found an alternative shelter out towards Blackheath, in south east London. Greenwich Theatre was a smaller venue, while being far from constrictive artistically. Its founding director, Ewan Hooper, happily allowed his new guest to stage a trio of classics. Ibsen's *Ghosts*, *The Seagull* and (again) *Hamlet* opened in quick succession, then played in repertory.[100] Miller's leading actors busily switched roles because he was exploring how the first two dramas mapped on to the scenario in Shakespeare's saga. In all three tragedies, the son (played, in each case, by Peter Eyre) suffers from an absent father and, arguably, harbours an Oedipal attachment to his mother (Irene Worth every time). He therefore resents her new companion (Robert Stephens, repeatedly).

Besides being collectively entitled *Family Romances* with reference to Freud, Miller's triptych has been described as one of the first instances of a director employing structuralism. His investigation of the underlying dramatic parallels tied in with his avid reading of Chomsky and others, who were studying the 'deep structures' common to different languages and different stories.

Greenwich Theatre's box office was besieged with West End audiences heading out to see the great Ibsen/Chekhov/Shakespeare experiment, performed on a near-bare stage. His *Seagull* was hailed, this time round, as a masterpiece, and many found *Ghosts* phenomenally riveting, with not a second wasted.[101] Humour flickered amidst the Scandinavian gloom, with the added surprise of Worth's Mrs Alving breaking into terrifying manic laughter as the orphanage, commemorating her husband, went up in flames.[102]

Eyre remembers how the cast had huddled around a gas stove in a freezing rehearsal room, reading and re-reading Ibsen's script for a fortnight before they even moved. It generated a thrillingly intense atmosphere, even as Miller led his actors gently towards filling out their characters. He would find correspondences between their own personalities and the dramatis personae, so that the performers could be themselves onstage. Eyre is not alone in considering this skill to be Miller's true gift. 'It was a very subtle and painless transformation,' he remarks. 'When we finally performed the play it was as natural for us as breathing . . . [meaning] a slightly creaking melodrama became a modern and powerful tragedy.'[103]

Hamlet was less impressive. Miller has discussed how varied the interpretations of the Danish prince can be, alluding to Olivier's 'rabbit' and Eyre's radically different 'duck'. This was, of course, a reference to the duck-rabbit trompe l'oeil beloved of his former Cambridge tutor Norwood Russell Hanson. Eyre, however, thinks 'turkey' might have been more apt in his case. The triple whammy was, doubtless, taking its toll. Sometimes the company worked on *Hamlet* during the day, performed *The Seagull* at night, and crammed in a harrowing matinée of *Ghosts* en route. Stephens and Eyre indulged in a spot of hysterical laughter themselves, renaming the Ibsen after the farcical romp *Rookery Nook*, because at least it was shorter – the light relief.

The actors were grateful for the *Sunday Times*' rave, which said that *Hamlet* moved with the lightness of a gazelle, especially since most reviewers saw it as a gabbled, confused blur.[104] It was lucky the critics were not in when Stephens went round the bend. He suffered from the same manic psychosis as Lowell, and drank heavily. Miller knew trouble was brewing when the actor started hiding behind doors backstage and leaping out in a Borsalino hat, pretending to be a gangster. Then, in a wildly alternative performance, his Claudius chose to remain offstage and simply yell his first speech from the dressing-room. The whole court, having already assembled in front of the audience, stood frozen with horror. Stephens did eventually wander in, only to start merrily paraphrasing: 'Well, I've written to Norway and told him this sort of thing simply won't do.'

Ghosts took a staggeringly radical turn into the bargain. At one matinee, Eyre made his usual entrance as Oswald, only to find himself in an instant clinch. Stephens' Manders, a supposedly disapproving character, was kissing him

ardently on the lips. Although Miller had encouraged an unusually warm interpretation of the pastor, this was something else. By the end of the run, Worth and
Stephens were having stand-up rows in the wings, and she became petulantly
difficult with her director as well. They did not speak again for several years.

Somehow none of these hiccups stopped the season being a big hit overall. It
was the top event of the year for Irving Wardle of *The Times*, and the theatrical
highlight of the decade for others. Miller was congratulated for reasserting the
value of directorial concepts at a time of backlash, and he was compared to
great talents like Tyrone Guthrie and Peter Brook, who were similarly forced into
nomadic rootlessness by English discouragement.[105]

He enjoyed working at Greenwich Theatre and was made an associate there.
He returned for a double bill called *Bed Tricks* in mid-1975, combining Shakespeare's problem plays *Measure for Measure* and *All's Well That Ends Well*. He
staged other thwarted NT projects too: *The Importance of Being Earnest* and
the Restoration comedy *She Would If She Could*.[106] His most creatively playful
actors loved the way he kept everything open-ended, even daring them to swap
parts midway through runs.[107] Others were unhappy with his extremely improvisational style.

She Would may have been a forgotten gem but, without fixed blocking,
Margaret Courtenay could not memorize her lines as lustful old Lady Cockwood.
In a decidedly unscheduled move, she walked out just before press night.[108] A
stand-in was found. Also Paul Eddington, playing Cockwood's lugubrious
spouse, kept the audiences laughing. Nevertheless, he condemned the director
as disastrously irresponsible.[109] As for *The Importance of Being Earnest*, Miller
did not resurrect his scorned cross-dressing idea. Irene Handl was cast as Lady
Bracknell, having clearly been forgiven for her bad-mannered pushiness on *The
Freeway*. Unfortunately, she couldn't remember her lines either, until messing
around amazingly saved the day. At the final run-through, Miller told everyone
to try another accent, just to relax. Handl reverted to her continental roots and,
as if by magic, was word-perfect.

The critics' jaws hit the floor when the dowager's legendary plummy lines
were delivered with Mittel-European vowels, accompanied by Yiddish Momma
mannerisms. ('A hendtbeg?' was followed by a non-verbal scoff, 'Phugh!') They
would probably have been less shocked by a drag act. Notwithstanding, Nicholas
de Jongh from the *Guardian* cheered this Lady B. as a breathtaking change from
the norm, and *Punch*'s Sheridan Morley liked the way that Algernon (David
Horovitch) sounded less arch than usual, more like a natural wit from some
predecessor of the Bloomsbury Set.[110]

The critics' ratings certainly veered up and down. Miller's take on *All's Well*
was too bitter-tasting and dour for many. It offered oddly compelling moments
all the same, with Helena's absconding fiancé, Bertram, and his reprobate chum,
Parolles, played like Just William and Ginger with a nasty edge.[111] Miller also
became intrigued by Helena's role as an upwardly mobile doctor's daughter.
Beginning to see her as a tuitional heroine, he would go on to discern deep

affinities with Viola in *Twelfth Night*, Cordelia in *Lear* and Portia in *The Merchant of Venice*: all women who try to teach foolish men to love better.[112] He had now gained an overarching grasp of these plays, which would make him a prime candidate when, in 1980, British television urgently needed someone to take the epic *BBC Shakespeare Series* in hand.

His Greenwich revival of *Measure for Measure*, in the meantime, ended the *Bed Tricks* season on a high. Penelope Wilton's Isabella was a spinster-nun in the making, defensively clutching a large handbag.[113] Horovitch was her worldly brother. Rather than happily reunited, he and his devout sibling remained unreconciled at the close. This edgy staging was fanfared as surpassing all the director's previous Shakespeare productions.[114] Consternation therefore greeted the news that he was again threatening to quit the theatre, because of the roller-coaster of reviews and because freelance work was so penniless. He could not possibly go now, the *Evening Standard* cried.[115]

*　　*　　*

So, before long, he was staging Chekhov's *Three Sisters* in the West End. He took a bit of persuading. Having been invited to direct by Janet Suzman, he had responded with a postcard, saying, 'I will never, never, never do another production!' However, he was soon in rehearsals with a superb cast, including Suzman, Susan Engel, Angela Down, Peter Eyre and John Shrapnel.[116] They bonded like a family and the pre-West End tour opened a whole week earlier than scheduled, an outstanding example of Miller working fast.[117]

Suzman recollects that this staging was delightfully un-English, slightly rumbustious:

> It was the hot summer of '76 and we were a bit like those Toulouse Lautrec cancan dancers in our petticoats – with rivulets of perspiration running from behind your ear and down your cleavage – sitting in this unspeakable heat, longing for Moscow. The temperature under the lights rose to 102 degrees. We put a barometer onstage to make sure our suffering was real.

Miller wanted the production to be astringent, for he saw the play as a sharply focused snapshot, a still that reveals details of pain and decay normally escaping notice.[118] The lapsed and ageing doctor, Chebutykin, was tragicomical, feeling like a renegade flop. Miller had him – presumably with no razor to hand – drunkenly trying to drown himself in the washbasin, panting hopelessly as he resurfaced, as if to say, 'Oh God, I can't even manage that!'[119] Forever mourning that he left high-powered science, this director surely also identified with the Prosorov siblings, yearning for their lost idyll of intellectual sophistication – 'Moscow, Moscow.' He is, in that sense, profoundly Chekhovian.

Members of the press were more than satisfied with the show. It was hailed as a truly great production, one that recognized the playwright's objective balance for the first time. It deromanticized the sisters, exposed their snobbishness, and discovered pathos in the very triviality of their lives. Suzman's Masha was marvellously witty and tough, tense as a coiled spring, like a Mensa veteran hungering for a challenge, and Down's youthful Irena soured shockingly. Rather than lamenting her fiancé's fatal duel in the usual lyrical style, she bitterly rasped out 'I knew it!' between gritted teeth.[120]

The *New Statesman* declared that Miller's near-definitive staging should have opened at the National.[121] Moreover, this production earned him an Olivier Award for Best Director, the first one ever given.[122] This was a pinnacle in his theatre career in terms of industry recognition, and *Three Sisters* proved that he could shine in the commercial sector (at least in the UK). The bookings were extended to 100 performances and, though risky box-office fare, it broke the record for London's longest-running Chekhov.

What did he say in his acceptance speech, trophy in hand? He said farewell to the theatre, again. This time it was official, a high-profile adieu with the cameras rolling, broadcast on *Nationwide*. Or was it just a histrionic gesture, even if sincerely meant? Many in the business and the media had a sneaking feeling this was Jonathan 'Crying "Wolf"' Miller at it once more. Goodbye – or was it just *au revoir*? Very probably.

⋆   ⋆   ⋆

It was to be a perpetual *va et vient*. Nevertheless, his intimate relationship with the British theatre did, essentially, come to a halt here, with the exception of one concentrated spurt of renewed activity when he briefly took over the Old Vic. Setting aside the six plays which he directed as the artistic director there in 1988–9, his theatre productions originating in the UK in the quarter-century ensuing from 1976 can be counted on the fingers of one hand, followed by a scattering thereafter.[123]

The drama critics stood accused, along with Peter Hall and *Private Eye*, of making him feel so undervalued that he withdrew. Therefore an overview, weighing up their remarks, is called for here. They had said he manhandled texts as carelessly as medical students (supposedly) treated corpses. He butchered them like a demon-surgeon. He anaesthetized comic plays as if solemnly trying to live down his early career as an entertainer. Or else he was too comical, too gimmicky. He was over-cerebral, under-dramatic, better at having theories than at theatre practice.

What should be pointed up is that some of those excoriating comments were expressed by reviewers as a preamble to them reassessing such stances, and even declaring there were 'two Jonathan Millers'. There was a Miller whom they loved. He was an enticingly experimental director who injected new life into time-worn classics and long-forgotten works. He refreshingly pared away dramatic excesses. Rather than gimmicky or over-cerebral, he would often be sensitive, imaginative and superlatively intelligent.[124]

Qualified praise was not enough for him, though. These notices blowing hot and cold felt like a harsh climate. It was the opposite of that medically healthy ideal, the notion of the steadily temperate *milieu intérieur* which had so appealed to him when he was a young doctor. Directing was a naive career choice if Miller wanted constant love and admiration. One colleague observing that, adds: 'In some ways Jonathan is still a bright Jewish child trying to impress. He has put the critics where his parents should be.' Another states, more impatiently, that his complaints about being unappreciated are 'impossibly childish' and 'complete rubbish'. Rachel suggests a different slant, one that relates to melancholia. He is 'too self-critical,' she says, 'always afraid other people will see him as badly as he sees himself'.[125]

He has been very affable with certain reviewers. Robert Gore-Langton, for example, remembers an interview when his back pain was cured by the ex-medic who (benignly) told him to hang from a beam. The poet and theatre critic James Fenton has sustained a friendship with him for many years. In the early 1970s, Michael Billington and Irving Wardle had been on amicable terms with him as well, until they found fault in their professional capacity. Billington recounts how he and the director enjoyably discussed theatrical matters on arts programmes such as *Kaleidoscope*. Then, one day he penned a *Guardian* opinion piece saying that the relentless criticisms of Hall's NT regime had to stop. He says:

> I shall never forget Jonathan coming into the [recording] studio, unshaven and looking rather grey and shocked. His tone to me that morning was obviously, radically different . . . It was as if I had betrayed him. That's what I most vividly remember. It was as if he saw me as a sort of friend who had turned into an enemy.

Maybe Miller had a gang mentality regarding arts journalists: they were either with or against him, onside or excommunicate.

Before long he was so galled that he began retaliating. His pique was not quite on a par with John Osborne, who famously sent out hate mail, threatening to duff up and do in critics, all in the name of his fantasy gang, the Playwrights' Mafia. Still, when a panel gathered for a platform discussion at the Theatre Royal Stratford East, Miller chipped in from the audience specifically mortifying Wardle and Billington with the slight: 'After six months you become like the Wizard of Oz, booming through the public address system of your paper.'[126] Assuming that his fellow directors would be judicious, he contested that peer review, as in the world of science, would be far better.

Increasingly, he used the loud-hailer of the media in return, giving vituperative interviews about the 'poisonous venom' of these opinion-formers, and the 'peculiar sort of shrieking hatred which the totally non-creative [meaning critics] have for the half-creative [directors] . . . who interpret the fully great'.[127] With more than a hint of the schoolyard, he invented bogeyman nicknames, such as Jack Stinker (for the now late Jack Tinker). He has caricatured one or other reviewer as a 'greasy old porker with a biro stuck in the cleft of his trotter' or a 'snaggle-toothed intestinal parasite'. Offering up one's work to such people is, he proclaims, 'like rolling a Fabergé egg under a pigsty door'. Reading bad notices is like being a seagull, getting covered by oil-slicks of crude ideas. And if they're good reviews, it's like being interfered with in the back row of the cinema. He has further claimed that criticism is often driven by macho competitiveness, saying, 'the whiff of testosterone, as they go in for the kill, is unmistakable'. The best aesthetic analysts are, he concludes, those with 'less of an axe to grind and less of their own ego involved'.[128] It is not clear whether giving his perceived enemies a verbal thrashing momentarily relieves his irritation or only exacerbates it.

The *Daily Telegraph*'s Charles Spencer humorously confesses that the mere thought of Miller hospitalized him at one point when he was working, unhappily, at another paper and was sent off to interview the great mind. Unable to face an intellectual harangue, he went doolally, boarded a random train to Dawlish and checked in for a six-week stint of (Miller-free) medical help on arrival. Wardle rolls with the punches, just very reasonably protesting, 'Jonathan is unfair to say that no critics are thoughtful.' Miller continues, regardless, to bombard the 'whinging fraternity' with retaliatory flak. He writes them off as ignoramuses 'farting in public', as 'worse than leukemia', and no better than kerb-crawlers looking to be 'sucked off in an interesting way'.[129]

It is somewhat perverse, perhaps, that the author of this biography is a theatre critic, and that's not to mention Miller's own past phase as a book, screen and stage reviewer. One journalist even dared to suggest that, as a director with great exegeses, he was fundamentally a critic.[130] How he relates to the profession has been mind-bendingly complicated ever since, as a schoolboy, he played the satirist-critic to criticize the critics on the BBC's *Under-Twenty Parade*.

In the mid-1970s, whether it was a self-destructive or a reconstructive urge, he stated that he was knowingly burning his boats. He intended to return to neurology, to study serious brain damage. The critics probably just hoped they weren't going to end up under the knife.

What actually happened was that he sidestepped into opera.

·11·

MID-SEVENTIES ONWARDS

Operatic beginnings and *The Body in Question*

THIS WAS NEVER SUPPOSED TO HAPPEN. Miller had said, 'I want to try a bit of everything – except opera. I'm frightened of my ignorance of music.'[1] Unbeknownst to most of the press and in between NT productions, he made his operatic debut nonetheless. Slipping under the radar as a local Christmas romp, Benjamin Britten's one-act ark lark *Noye's Fludde* was performed by a horde of 200 primary schoolchildren at the Roundhouse, NW1's Victorian engine shed which had been converted into an adventurous venue in the 1960s.[2]

The children swarmed around in T-shirts printed with the names of the animals they were meant to be, like a swirl of alphabet soup. Kate Miller (aged five) was unofficially assistant director, surveying the scene from her father's lap. He loved the playful atmosphere and, more seriously, believes that *Noye's Fludde* laid the foundation for his later, internationally celebrated production of Bach's *St Matthew Passion*. There he would return to the idea of an extremely informal performance, in ordinary clothes, without scenery.

Somewhere among Noah's creatures were the offspring of Roger Norrington who was a fast-rising conductor from round the corner in Primrose Hill. Norrington hatched a plan to work with this director in the near future. Miller, meanwhile, headed off to stage his first professional opera production. The UK premiere of Alexander Goehr's *Arden Must Die* was experimental fare, playing for three nights at Sadler's Wells.[3] The New Opera Company, who brought him on board, was a small troupe backed by the English National Opera and devoted to modern composers. They reckoned his satiric roots were apt for Goehr's dark comedy about murderous avarice (based on the Tudor play *Arden of Faversham*).[4]

He felt horribly anxious at the initial rehearsal, having to confess that he could not read music. Nor did he find the score easy listening. The orchestra, he says, sounded like a blind burglar blundering into a hardware store. This was an extremely difficult opera for a debut and he would, subsequently, steer away from cutting-edge, contemporary composers.[5] 'But', he remarks, 'I thought I could hear what people *meant* by what they were singing.' Nipping out of the stage door on opening night, suffering from nerves, he was given a scathing earful by John Dexter, his old Royal Court rival. In the pub opposite, whither he had stomped, Dexter pronounced the staging insufferable.[6] He must have been puce with rage when the recipient of his scorn shot up the operatic ladder, swiftly receiving an invitation to direct Janáček's *The Cunning Little Vixen* at Glyndebourne.[7]

Miller was more musical than his stated anxieties suggest. He had, for sure, never been a keen opera-goer, telling his old friend Roger Graef, a fan of the art form, that it was a waste of time. Indeed, according to the mischievous Peter Cook, he had regarded all classical music as aural wallpaper before his career move.[8] He himself describes having once gone, unaccountably, to see Verdi's *Falstaff* at Covent Garden and been bored stiff, saved only by the cry of 'Is there a doctor in the house?' At this he catapulted from his seat to attend to an ailing singer and accompany him to the hospital. 'The illness came as a huge relief!' he maintains. In spite of his maternal grandfather's talents as a Cork Opera House violinist, he had never been able to follow explanations of harmony. In Gloucester Crescent, it was the rest of the family who performed small concerts. Following Rachel's lead as a flautist and cellist, Kate took up the flute, playing alongside Tom on the cello and Jeannie on piano, with William juggling violin and oboe.[9]

Sarah Miller affirmed that classical composers had been her area of expertise, in the main, when she and her brother were teenagers.[10] Be that as it may, Emanuel had turned both his children into music-lovers in the 1950s, taking them to classical concerts. The Royal Albert Hall and the Royal Festival Hall had become familiar haunts, and Miller recalls two opera outings. Alongside a West End *Barber of Seville*, he was taken to see *Rigoletto* because he had been singing the aria 'La donna è mobile' after hearing it on the radio. Betty was tone deaf, banned from the choir by Gustav Holst when at St Paul's School for Girls, and she wrote off most opera as caterwauling. Emanuel, though, installed a radiogram at 35 Queen's Grove and his son raced off to Marylebone Public Library to borrow records, eagerly lugging home 78s of all Beethoven's sonatas and symphonies. Introduced to further recordings by his schoolfriend Michael Bacharach, and becoming highly informed about jazz, he gave a presentation for St Paul's Gramophone Society. That mini-lecture was praised for its 'most interesting' hybrid look at popular and classical works.[11] There was the earlier evidence, too, that he was aurally acute if not intrinsically musical: all those infantine imitations, the rhythmically precise chicken clucks, the crescendoing air-raid impressions.[12]

When he began theatre directing, music was woven in from the start. He remembered hearing Gluck's 'Dance of the Blessed Spirits' (from *Orfeo ed Euridice*) issuing from a wireless in Cocteau's haunting film *Orphée*, and he echoed that in his first production, *Under Plain Cover*.[13] His OCSC *Twelfth Night* had been laced with Monteverdi madrigals, exploring ideas of human and divine harmony. He had worked repeatedly with the composer-conductor Carl Davis, notably turning *The Tempest*'s masque scene into a cross-cultural Monteverdi pastiche, sung by black opera singers in tribal/baroque gear. In the opening café scenes of his NT *Merchant of Venice*, a medley of tunes from *Rigoletto* played in the background, hinting at parallels between Shylock's trouble with Jessica and Verdi's titular father and his daughter.[14] In *Danton's Death*, he had Saint-Just's great speech rising in pitch, semitone by semitone, and his *Measure for Measure* was formalized according to the rhythm of a Schoenberg sonata, with doors opening and closing to coincide with notes played on a twelve-tone scale.[15] This was not a man who knew nothing about music.

The reviews of *Arden Must Die* concurred that he was sensitive to Goehr's score.[16] The now world-famous bass John Tomlinson, who was in the company, recalls how Miller was feeling his way but absolutely on the music's wavelength, so it never mattered that he could not read the dots on the stave.[17] As for Glyndebourne, the immediate technical challenge was how to stage *The Vixen* because this Czech fable about a forester and lady-fox was told in peculiarly short scenes and usually entailed twee animal outfits.[18] The *Noye's Fludde* T-shirt trick was not going to satisfy the black-tie audience at this glamorous manor house in England's home counties. This was the very crowd Miller had envisaged, in his Schweppeshire Foundation skits, going berserk about anything unorthodox. Adding to the pressure, *The Vixen* was the season's opening production and the venue's first ever Janáček.

Miller was daunted and, for a while, could not think what approach to take. At last it clicked when he and his designers realized that animal skins and birds' feathers – with their symmetrical patterns and chevron markings – tallied with folk costumes and vintage military uniforms. In the title role, the soprano Norma Burrowes looked like a peasant girl in a fur toque with pointedly feral ear-flaps.[19] The scintillating dragonfly became a sabre-flashing dragoon and the hens, gossiping and bobbing with knitting needles, wore rustic frocks exactly matching the hue of Rhode Island Reds.[20] The woods were evoked with fluid photographic projections on a wide cyclorama. Here Miller was re-exploring the effects of magic lanterns and the magnifying lenses which entranced him as a child, with the scale of the projected foliage changing, looming large around the tiniest animals.

Lord Harewood, the ENO chief, came to see the production and said it knocked Walter Felsenstein's East Berlin staging – formerly considered definitive – off its perch. Sir George Christie, who was Glyndebourne's helmsman, agrees it was a great success. In spite of that, Miller's idyllic stint at the Sussex mansion, with hospitality extended to his small brood, was short-lived. It was not just that Peter Hall was to become artistic director there in the 1980s. Christie had not relished Miller's initial indecisiveness and numerous alternative concepts. 'Jonathan was . . . trying desperately to find some solution which was not going to be just one of conventional wisdom,' he comments dryly, adding that the kibosh had to be put on some 'completely potty' ideas.[21]

Miller staged this *Vixen* again in 1976, for Opera Australia, who performed at the recently built Sydney Opera House, and then for Frankfurt Opera.[22] Though not yet ready to launch out full tilt on the international circuit, he dipped a toe in the waters. He was unavailable, in 1977, for Glyndebourne's UK-touring revival. He suggests that may have caused 'slight resentment', though Christie states that it was the director who 'rather resented' them, for not running with an idea he proposed about Rossini's *Ermione*.[23] 'Once Jonathan is upset, he gets a bee in his bonnet,' Sir George observes. 'I think we are on speaking terms now and I actually adore the guy. I would love to have his friendship, but we haven't used him since *The Vixen*.'

⋆   ⋆   ⋆

Roger Norrington had moved fast, introducing himself at the post-show party for *Noye's Fludde* with the salutation: 'Hallo, and will you work for us?' The conductor was the music director at Kent Opera, a bold young touring company founded by baritone Norman Platt, which was determined to bring low-budget yet high-calibre operas to England's regional towns.[24] As Norrington recounts:

> Very soon Jonathan and I were working together and it was magic. One critic described the productions we did as 'levitating'. They were sort of off the ground. We worked absolutely as a team, with an extraordinary intensity and trust and, of course, an element of fun. Jonathan is very like [W. S.] Gilbert: he has that wonderful witty turn of phrase . . . as well as being incredibly musical. It was serious fun. It was like you fed in sugar and out came some steel. It was like those bread-makers where you just turn the handle. It shouldn't be so easy.

They were to sustain this teamwork, hooking up on an annual production for the next eight years and having a significant impact on how the art form was seen.[25]

With a family atmosphere and no top-heavy management, Kent Opera was the opposite of Hall's National Theatre and just what Miller needed. Once again joining a brilliant and dedicated fringe gang, he did not mind roughing it, regularly squeezing up dustbin-filled alleyways to rehearse in community centres. He loved journeying out to wintry seaside towns where he would wander along the empty promenade then sip ginger wine back at the hotel, spinning comic fantasies into the small hours with Platt and Norrington.

Some of the venues were stupendously down-at-heel. In Southsea's leaky King's Theatre, during a performance of Miller's *Eugene Onegin* by Tchaikovsky, it didn't just rain in the garden scene, it poured in Tatiana's bedroom. His Bruegel-inspired, earthy staging of Verdi's *Falstaff*, with Thomas Hemsley as the Fat Knight and a hefty lighting rig, literally brought the house down at Bath's Theatre Royal.[26] Chunks of the roof started landing on the stage. Unvanquished, the cast improvised a slimline version in front of the curtain, taking the risk of toppling into the pit and being impaled on a double bass. Jonathan Summers (who played

Ford) says Miller's talent-nurturing approach made everyone so confident that they would have tried anything for him.[27]

The Miller-Norrington double act was also a marriage of minds because of their shared interest in history. The MD was a pioneer in period music, rediscovering how it was originally played and, like Miller, he stripped away sentimental accretions.[28] During this partnership, Miller's reputation for vandalizing all things old-fashioned was increasingly supplanted by the view that he was highly informed about how a work springs from ideas in circulation during the original artist's lifetime.

For Mozart and Da Ponte's *Così fan tutte*, dispensing with the standard Rococo fripperies, he homed in on the 1790s' plainer neoclassical style, observing that it was more analogous with the elegant symmetries in this partner-switching comedy.[29] Likewise, he appraised the characters in terms of key Enlightenment notions. Within the drama's moral diagram, he saw Don Alfonso (who bets that the ladies will betray their sweethearts) and the maid Despina (who encourages them to do so) as the representatives of Reason and instinct-led Nature. Instead of a cynical wag, his Alfonso was, moreover, a *philosophe* conducting a proto-psychoanalytic experiment with profound consequences. The scene featuring a Mesmeresque doctor – normally seen as a parody – was played remarkably seriously, the apparently suicidal lovers miraculously resurrected by magnet therapy as if it were some renovating, secular baptism.[30] In spite of his own attitude to bigwigs, Miller argued that Wolfgang would not have simply laughed at Mesmer, the latter having acted as patron for the composer's first opera.[31]

After despairing over Beaumarchais' tune-free *Figaro* at the NT, he found himself blissfully uplifted by Mozart's music.[32] This was the composer with whom he was to be, for the rest of his life, most closely associated.[33] Mozart's operas, Miller explains, have the most sublime moments of transcendence, when it seems as if an aria 'consumes the bodies of the singers and when it's over you sense this wafting, invisible breeze'. He compares it to the candle, blown out by the angel passing, in Annunciation paintings.[34] Mozart's genius also lay in bringing out the libretto's subtext, illuminating the intentions underneath people's words. Two of Miller's favourite philosophers, J. L. Austin and John Searle, had delved into such 'speech acts' (to use their terminology), and here was an equivalent, exquisitely expressed in music.[35]

Norrington and Miller went on to breathe life into *L'Orfeo, favola in musica*, Monteverdi's early opera (from 1607) which depicts Orpheus' journey through loss and mourning.[36] Kent Opera's budget could not stretch to reconstructing elaborate masque machinery, so Miller alighted on Poussin's seventeenth-century paintings instead. The artist's pastoral scenes, depicting the world of classical myths, became *L'Orfeo*'s backdrop. The singers learnt to imitate contrapposto stances, bodies turning in complementary directions as they recreated Poussin's *A Dance to the Music of Time* with light-footed grace.[37] The movement and music seemed beautifully suited, and Rosalind Plowright, who played the Messenger, recalls that contrapposto became second nature to the company. They even caught themselves hailing each other in the street in postures *après* Poussin.[38]

Miller explains that the painter was an exceptionally good match for Monteverdi because Poussin aimed to make his art accord with the rules of harmony underlying music. Neoclassicists of that era believed that universal laws of harmony ought to exist across the arts.[39] Miller helped audiences sense the *simile*, as it were, by uniting the pictures and the opera, showing how *like* they were.

While recreating the art and the mentality of past epochs, Miller's Kent productions were influencing the future of opera by rejecting the grandiose in both stage design and acting styles. Helping to stimulate a new interest in chamber productions, the set which he requested for *Così* was groundbreakingly economical: just two doors, two chairs and one Récamier couch on a shallow frieze-like stage.[40] The long-overblown *Onegin* he scaled back to the intimate drama that Tchaikovsky had wanted.

Simultaneously, he assured his performers that big singing voices could be accompanied by unmelodramatic, naturalistic acting. The results were often poignant, not least the duel scene in *Onegin* where Lensky – instead of being histrionically dashing – was a bespectacled, clerk-like figure. He died fumbling on the ground, trying to find his glasses.[41] Miller's approach was, evidently, an extension of his understated theatre directing, as well as creating a close-up feel akin to his television dramas.[42] It was startlingly novel for many opera-goers. 'Jonathan', as Norman Platt underlined, 'brought truth to Kent.'

In particular, he instigated a small revolution by having far more arias sung in a seated or prone position. The soprano Jill Gomez, who was his Tatiana in *Onegin* and Violetta in his unfrilly, Flaubert-influenced *La Traviata*, affirms that his style was electrifyingly fresh.[43] She still recalls Violetta's encounter with Germont *père* who, as played by Thomas Hemsley, found himself attracted to her, even while he was censuring her affair with his son. As she explains:

> We sat in two chairs, almost facing but hardly daring to look at each other for the entire scene – so much more intense than two singers pacing the stage. I think Verdi would have loved it as he, like Wagner, longed for the *chantacteur* who was prepared to risk everything in pursuit of dramatic truth.

When it came to Violetta's tubercular death scene, Dr Miller firmly told her to stay in bed, pointing out that the traditional prima donna's lap of honour, running round in a stream of chiffon, was medically ridiculous because dying was a full-time business. 'I swear', laughs Gomez, 'that this was an excuse so he'd have the stage to himself, to hilariously imitate an NHS matron with bedpan . . . [but] he talked very movingly about the things dying people do with their hands, that plucking of the sheets with nervous restless fingers.'[44] Even if it was difficult to sing propped up on pillows, his behavioural truth carried her through, right to the scene's conclusion when she pulled herself up feverishly before crumpling beside the bed. 'My sense of relief, at finally getting up,' she explains, 'then matched Violetta's own sudden, transfixing desire to leave, with the intensity of blood and energy flowing again being almost unbearable.'

Miller had not, of course, passed over into some wonderful, criticism-free realm with Kent Opera. Isaiah Berlin raged about liberties being taken with these canonical operas. Gomez had to defend her director's ideas vigorously at a lunch party where Berlin decried the 'degraded laundry scene' in *Onegin* – Miller having set Onegin's rejection of Tatiana's love in a garden among shroud-like, drying sheets.[45]

The opera critic Tom Sutcliffe was regarded, by Miller, as another foe because he disliked various productions, finding them flat, fundamentally conventional and pointlessly clever in their medical realism.[46] In retaliation, Miller gave him several verbal duffings, not least yelling at him in the middle of the National Gallery, where everyone in the room slowly turned to gaze at this uncatalogued display of fury. Rachel attempted to blend with the wallpaper while he explained to Sutcliffe's remonstrating wife that he wanted her husband dead. This was in the John Osborne league of enmity. 'I think I phoned later to apologize,' he says.

On the subject of criticism, Norrington comments:

> It isn't so much that Jonathan wants to be loved. I think that, being intelligent, he expects to be understood . . . [Artistically,] you're trying to make a point – 'It's not really like *that*, it's like *this*' – then somebody just slams it for not being like *that*. Ignorance is a very frightening thing. I mean, he's an elf and we're all hobbits . . . and sometimes he feels totally without armour.

The majority of the reviewers cheered his Kent Opera work. *Falstaff*'s liveliness and wit were said to have knocked Covent Garden's high-tech version into a cocked hat.[47] *La Traviata* had never been played with such heartrending truthfulness, or such a strong father–son conflict.[48] Rodney Milnes of *The Times*, briefly apoplectic about the spartan *Così*, was soon celebrating Miller's 'flower[ing] into one of the most remarkable opera producers of the day', ('producer' being a synonym for 'director' in the opera world).[49]

Milnes pays especial tribute to the Kent production of *Rigoletto*, updated from its faux-1550s setting to Verdi's own 1850s.[50] That has been largely forgotten in the wake of Miller's later ENO hit, his famous Mafia *Rigoletto* set in the 1950s. Platt missed a trick because he turned down the Mafia concept, hatched during one of those late-night ginger wine sessions. He thought Miller was joking or completely mad. In any case, Norrington still holds that Kent's production was more extraordinary and touching than the ENO's. It was, Milnes confirms, an indisputably great staging, conjuring up a very dark, almost Dickensian world of sinister streets and cruel poverty, with Jonathan Summers as an emotionally blazing Rigoletto and Meryl Drower as his daughter, the most vulnerable Gilda imaginable.[51]

Kent Opera and Miller went from strength to strength together. The troupe gained an illustrious place at the Edinburgh International Festival: a return for Miller but in a new métier.[52] The company was to gain further renown, in the late

1970s and early 1980s, as Miller's fame and camera-friendly exuberance drew TV documentary crews. Various Kent Opera productions were filmed, including a six-part documentary tracking the rehearsals for his *Fidelio*, a staging which evoked the prison etchings of Goya, Beethoven's contemporary.[53] Norrington jovially admits that they both loved being in front of the cameras. 'When the film crew left,' he exclaims, 'we hardly knew what to do with ourselves!' These broadcasts would also help establish Miller, for the decades to come, as a leading popularizer of opera on the box. He demystified the director's art by presenting himself as a journeyman, showing how it was done.[54]

None of that would stop the demise of Kent Opera in the late 1980s, when grant-slashing by Margaret Thatcher's Conservative government was to lacerate Britain's performing arts. It remains one of the most notorious decisions ever taken concerning arts funding in the UK.[55] At a commemorative concert in Canterbury Cathedral, Miller returned to speak in praise of the company. He had never, he said, been happier than with Kent where the work had become indistinguishable from the companionship and where they had, in some sense, redefined what opera might be. 'Although I have', he attested, 'done bigger things since, with splashier names and more critical attention, I have never been involved with anything better. And I have a constant nagging suspicion that, as a producer, I was probably at my best.'[56]

Concentrating his expertise on the concert circuit, Norrington largely ceased to conduct operas after this. 'I was spoiled', he says, 'working with Kent and with Jonathan, because his were genuine productions. When I think of doing, say, *Fidelio* again, I just remember the one we did together and I think, "Who, as it were, needs the film version when you've read the book?"' Fortunately, Miller had found another congenial home at the Coliseum, with Lord Harewood's English National Opera. He started there in 1978.

*   *   *

That was something of an *annus mirabilis* for him. While the country was heading towards its strike-bound Winter of Discontent – under Thatcher's predecessor, James Callaghan – Miller was, most gratifyingly, fully occupied. Besides his ENO debut, this was a twelve-month in which he became the nation's favourite doctor.

It had been sixteen years since the BBC's Grace Wyndham Goldie wrote her internal memo about luring him back to make sociological/scientific TV programmes. Now a second note had circulated, from the science department, proposing that he should present the Corporation's next educative megaseries. This dispatch from the executive Karl Sabbagh catalogued the previous epics and ended with a tantalizing question mark.

1969: Kenneth Clark's *Civilisation*, 1973: Jacob Bronowski's *The Ascent of Man*, 1977: J. K. Galbraith's *The Age of Uncertainty*, 1978: Jonathan Miller?

In spite of his shift away from television drama to stage directing, Miller had never really been out of the BBC loop. He had featured regularly as a pundit, as well as a subject, on its arts programmes (*Arena*, *Omnibus* and so on). He had continued to be a superb chat-show guest, with Parkinson repeatedly inviting him back, right through the 1970s. He featured on discussion programmes including *Any Questions?* and on comedy quizzes such as *Quote . . . Unquote* and Ned Sherrin's *Who Said That?* as well as *Call My Bluff*.[57] Claire Tomalin remembers being a fellow guest on one discussion show where Miller was momentarily floored by a question, 'before just taking off like a balloon filling with air, with this stream of wit and fluency that was magical to watch'.

He had kept his hand in as an occasional presenter too. *The Zoo in Winter* was a stroll round the aquaria and enclosures of Regent's Park with Miller launching into hilarious, imagined monologues on behalf of languidly aristocratic giraffes, 'too clever by half' chattering monkeys, and a whole raft of other animals. This was a sophisticated variation on Johnny Morris' series *Animal Magic*, but it was also a comic spin-off linking back to the more literary, non-jokey ruminations on the zoo, jotted down in Miller's private notebooks during the early 1960s. There he anthropomorphically described the antelopes, with their large eyes permanently darkened with fear, as the 'ceremonial Jews of nature', having 'the sombre, sacerdotal dignity of their ancient role as victims'. He also vividly observed how pacing tigers 'swim rather than stride, turning like fish . . . wreath[ing] their cage in an endless feline film strip'.[58] When the BBC came to celebrate 40 years of broadcasting, *The Zoo in Winter* would be picked out as one of its highlights, and it was shown again in 2012.[59]

Miller had fronted one serious science documentary, *Charles Darwin Lived Here*, where he roamed round the evolutionist's historic home, Down House.[60] Sabbagh produced that and saw it was time to get this natural teacher on board in a much bigger way. 'One of my prime aims was', he declared, 'to share with the public this remarkable man – the way he talks, the way he thinks – and to share his excitement'.[61]

So, the answer to that open invitation, '1978: Jonathan Miller?', was *The Body in Question*, a massive, thirteen-part, landmark series on medicine.[62] Made for BBC2, it was to combine an introductory course on how the body works with a history of our progressive understanding of human biology down the ages.[63] Thus it was to range from ancient theories (such as the four humours) to modern-day discoveries, paying tribute to famous trailblazers and the undeservedly forgotten. A huge budget was swiftly raised with international funding from American, Canadian and Australian TV companies. They were all keen to export this production round the world, so everything was ready to roll.[64]

Two alarming hitches occurred. Commissioned to script the whole series and pen an accompanying book, Miller once more suffered crippling writer's block. 'I had to have it dragged out of me,' he admits. According to Gloucester Crescent rumours, at one point he was curled in a ball of despair in his study. A note he sent during this period, apologetically turning down other work, made no bones about the fact that he was 'many *months* behind' his schedule and 'running the risk of a crack-up!'[65] Eventually his neighbour Susannah Clapp, who worked for the publishers Jonathan Cape, was to come to the rescue, spending every spare evening talking the book through with him and transcribing what he dictated. He gratefully gave her a generous cut of his advance. 'Not everybody would have done that, and it was probably more than half as much as I earned in a year, so it made a huge difference to my life,' says Clapp.

The filming hit a rocky patch, early on, too. The producer-director Patrick Uden, who was a young maverick in the BBC science department, remembers hearing that a crisis meeting was being held for collective brainstorming.[66] As Uden explains, Sabbagh was an excellent executive producer. However, visual imagination was not his forte and he was attempting to direct this series. He had shot some footage that was distinctly awkward, with Miller looking uncomfortable. Money had been spent and the Corporation was now in this right up to its neck. Uden went along to this meeting where various producers were pushing their own agendas while Miller kept talking about how the world of mechanics provided metaphors for how the human body works. As the son of an automotive engineer, Uden loved machines and chipped in, remarking that the steam engine had always struck him as a good comparison. He noticed that the writer-presenter perked up at this, but the meeting was going nowhere so he ambled back to his office.

An hour or so later Miller peered round the door. 'How would you feel about directing the series for me?' he asked. Uden replied that he was, regrettably, neither senior enough nor the type to be trusted with such a large project.[67] 'Well, leave that bit to me,' the other replied and whisked off to talk to the boss. Apparently, he made it clear that if the series wasn't given to Uden then it wasn't happening. The comparative novice was duly summoned, stubbornly dug in his heels about directing solo, and won. From there on, the visuals took off as he pursued two ideas: first, the interior of Miller's head and, second, the use of metaphors.

Gathering an adventurous team around him, he told his designer Colin Lowrey to, as it were, bring him the brain of Jonathan Miller. Instead of endless globetrotting in the style of Galbraith (though there was certainly some of that), *The Body in Question* was to feel like a tour through the doctor-presenter's eclectic mind, even as the topic being discussed was mankind's innards. As a result, Lowrey's rolling circular set, built at the Ealing Studios, was epic yet intimate, gargantuan yet snug. It housed multiple niches stuffed with knick-knacks. Medical instruments were hoarded alongside, say, a chicken skeleton, Russian dolls, an African pot and a phrenologist's ceramic head. The effect was, simultaneously, like a consulting room, a museum and Gloucester Crescent. Miller felt at home.[68]

The medley of props served to illuminate obscure medical notions, by serving as parallels. For instance, in the programme about reproduction, the nest of Russian dolls provided an analogy for the seventeenth-century idea that a sperm housed a tiny person who, in turn, contained an even more minuscule homunculus of the next generation etc. Miller had hosts of such comparisons at his fingertips. 'From the moment we lit that blue touch-paper,' says Uden, 'each programme became a mass of metaphorical examples, an absolute festival of visuals.'

Moreover, all this tied in with Miller's thesis that advances in scientific understanding emerged from thinking associatively, from drawing parallels, spotting similes, grasping that one thing might serve as metaphor for another.[69] When fire pumps, for example, began to be widely used, William Harvey realized the heart might work in that way. When gun turrets were developed in the mid-twentieth century, using predictive generalizations to aim automatically, it dawned on cognitive psychologists that the brain might, similarly, have in-built conjectural models to facilitate anticipatory action. 'That was', Miller stresses, 'the series' absolutely key idea: the heuristic value of metaphorical thought in the course of medical history.'

Making *The Body in Question*, says Uden, became riotous fun. Calling off a strike, the BBC's notoriously militant unionized electricians were kept happy with Miller's running gags and free tutorials, and the whole team became like a productive band of guerillas within the pernickety bureaucracy.[70] Most astoundingly, they completely bypassed the authorities to film a gory post-mortem examination without any departmental permission. In a culture where staff had to fill in quadruple forms just to request an extension cable, this was (metaphorically) getting away with murder. Shown in the programme about death called *Perishable Goods*, the footage is still breathtaking. The corpse of a vagrant (attained from a hospital) was arched back and split open like a banana skin, while Miller laid out the inner organs on a slab, like a display in a butcher's shop. It was the first ever autopsy on public television, well over twenty years before Gunther von Hagens' broadcast autopsies caused shocked cries from amnesiac members of the British press.[71]

In spite of his own past TV directing, Miller never trod on Uden's toes, nor was he high-maintenance. He required careful handling only when anxious about his stammer. Some words became the equivalent of fences in the Grand National, so Uden developed ploys, having casual 'rehearsals' where Miller did not know that the cameras were running. Having to write further chunks of script could also produce kerfuffles because, as Uden recalls:

> Jonathan would put it off to the last minute, then there'd be, you know, boxes and boxes of cigarettes smoked and sleepless nights . . . But I'd always have a fallback sequence we could shoot, and the Autocue girl was there, so he could dictate a piece right before we shot it. He was really very good at busking it, and the minute I said, 'Great, that's a take,' he'd rush to the Autocue machine, rip the paper out and send it to his publisher, saying, 'That's the next chapter!'[72]

As the BBC publicity machine whirred into top gear, the hardback was serialized in the *Guardian* and became an instant bestseller.[73] The author was dispatched to sign copies everywhere from Regent Street to Israel (since someone obligingly translated it into Hebrew). A fever of excitement duly broke out in the British press when the broadcasts started. *The Times* declared that it was impossible to go out on Monday nights for the next three months. Miller was nicknamed the Beeb's Dissector-General by the *Telegraph* – doing for the cadaver what Clark and Bronowski had done for culture – and newspaper cartoonists began cracking jokes like medical students.[74]

In his mid-forties now, Miller had really come of age as a presenter. His *beau laid* face had grown warmly photogenic, framed with reddish-brown curls. His manner was on a perfect cusp as well, combining still boyish excitement with mellowness. The vast majority of reviewers loved the way in which he was informed and informal, intellectual yet democratically popularizing. Jonathan Miller was, in fact, the walking, talking embodiment of those famous goals established by the BBC's first director-general, John Reith. He educated and entertained. One of his specialities was leavening the grisly bits with comical-poetical flourishes. He declared he was succumbing to 'incipient hepatic rhapsody' when contemplating a fresh human liver. He likened the glistening intestine to a 'huge unconscious Amazon', and he beautifully envisaged the nerve endings as 'millions of seed pearls embroidered throughout the fabric of the body'.

A handful of columnists, including Clive James, felt that Miller's mind leaped about excessively. A few others refused to be impressed and noted small factual errors.[75] Heartily appreciative feedback included specialist reviewers. The polymathic cardiologist David Mendel in the *Observer* called the book a fascinating *Michelin Green Guide to Man*.[76] As regards the great British public, the programmes created a whole new fan base, the next generation, one down from those who had known Miller since *Beyond the Fringe*. He only had to wander along the street to be regaled with greetings: 'That was a lovely spleen!' and the like.[77]

A particular source of fascination for everyone was this frontman putting his own body under scrutiny. Far from offering just a tour through his mind, he played the guinea pig in his own medical trials, in the stoical tradition of Henry Head. He twitched through an unsuccessful acupuncture session, hooked himself up to electrodes, jumped out of a hot bath in front of thermal cameras, and made himself feel extremely ill swooping and looping in a biplane.[78] He tried dancing with the locals in the Andes before acclimatizing. He also slipped into unconsciousness by donning breathing apparatus and depleting his supply of O_2. This was suffering for your science. Indeed, the final oxygen-deprivation episode might have been subtitled *His Life in His Hands*. 'I only discovered afterwards that people had died from that experiment,' he remarks. On another day, during the Andes stint, he and the film crew nearly drowned on Lake Titicaca because hostile locals put sand in the engine of their boat.[79]

Miller was, furthermore, seen as if under the microscope. That is to say, wide-angle prime lenses were used when he was addressing the camera. These magnified his ever-mobile 'body language' which Uden realized was an endearing and distinctive trait.[80] With the mild fish-eye effect, his limbs loomed amusingly large as he sat in an armchair on set. When he reclined with his hands behind his head, his elbows jutted into the corners of the frame. At other times he would lean forward, hunkering over with eager gesticulations. His outsize hands emphatically conducted what he was saying, twirling in the foreground and almost protruding into your living-room.[81] It was as if his adolescent letter to the BBC auditions department had finally won approval: 'I am six foot four which might render me unsuitable for small screen television, I could however bend down.'[82]

Taking the longer biographical perspective, *The Body in Question* was the point where his lifelong love of science came to high-profile fruition. This was not only a history of medicine but also a personal treasure chest crammed with subjects which had fascinated him from boyhood. It was not just *an* education but, in many respects, *his* education compacted. So much was enthusiastically revisited: metameric segmentation and deep morphological homologies; the fertilization of sea urchins' eggs (for which he went back to film in Cumbrae); the neurological all-or-none law and Claude Bernard's *milieu intérieur*; close diagnostic observations (focusing on patients' tiny hand gestures); Hughlings Jackson and Rivers and Head (with footage of St John's College); the strange phenomena of unilateral neglect, phantom limbs and more. Thus he passed on to TV viewers, worldwide, what he had learned from his father's library, from Sid Pask, Norwood Russell Hanson and the rest.

The cross-disciplinary nature of *The Body in Question* was akin to Emanuel's popular psychology books with their anthropological and literary allusions.[83] His son comparably fused the sciences and humanities, bringing together medicine, anthropology, philosophy, paintings, music and drama. The illustrations in Miller's bestseller, in fact, made it look like a physiology and a fine art book rolled into one. Microscope slides and the *Mona Lisa* were juxtaposed. Magnified cilia were pictured alongside a Van Gogh cornfield. Even the distortedly anamorphic skull in Holbein's *The Ambassadors*, once discussed by Miller and his school friends, resurfaced here. Now it served as a metaphor for the divergence between a person's 'seen' and 'felt' body images: that is, your 'seen' self, as viewed in an everyday looking-glass, versus your 'felt' self-image. In the latter, painful or sensitive parts (such as the tongue) feel disproportionately large, more like a funhouse-mirror effect.[84] As for theatrical moments, Miller slipped in a kooky reconstruction of Mesmer's Paris salon and extracts from his Kent Opera *Così* and *L'Orfeo*, which rounded off the last programme.[85]

All in all, the *Sunday Times* declared the series a masterly exploration in which Miller's diverse skills had climactically combined, and Britain's TV critics bestowed their Best On-Screen Performance of the Year Award upon him.[86] In the following decade, he would write three more immensely popular science books, for a younger audience. He would front further TV series and – with a medical bent – several fascinating, single-episode documentaries. In terms of profile, however, *The Body in Question* was the acme of his presenting career.

He remains rightly proud of it, though his children did not care for his overwhelming workload at the time. Kate asked, during filming, when they were going to get him back, and William wryly recalls the day when the household reacquired a television, via a shameless paternal *volte-face*. 'I remember', he exclaims, 'catching sight of my father walking up the street with this huge TV in his arms . . . He'd just bought it so he could watch *The Body in Question*, so we could *all* watch *The Body in Question*!' In anecdotal mode, William describes a more irksome incident from a few years later, after the programmes had been shown in the USA. He was doing his first job, after leaving school, as a Manhattan office dogsbody, only to be accosted by a female staff member who declared that she adored his father. As he recounts:

> I replied, 'Oh, that's lovely for you.' Then she pursued me down the corridor repeating, 'I am such an admirer, he's so wonderful, I've been in love with him and everything.' I got to the lift, standing there waiting for it to turn up, and she wouldn't stop going on . . . Finally she just said, 'I am so in love with him!' and I said, 'Sorry, he's married to my mother,' and the doors closed.

More beneficially, his children were to find jobs in the TV industry via Uden's independent company, Uden Associates. Kate gained work experience, assisting there. William, who began as a runner, rose to be Uden's managing director and, subsequently, a director of brand ventures. He now markets the BBC worldwide.[87]

As the *annus mirabilis* of 1978 drew to a close, Miller switched once more between the Two Cultures – like that visual teaser, the duck-rabbit – proceeding to make his Coliseum debut with *The Marriage of Figaro*. In the week before Christmas, and within 24 hours of appearing in *The Body in Question*, he was featuring on Melvyn Bragg's arts programme *The South Bank Show*. The ITV special was devoted to his *Figaro*, and that ENO production essentially began Act II in his tripartite operatic career.[88] It saw him progressing from Kent Opera and moving a step nearer the international circuit of directors considered world-class.

·12·

ON INTO THE EIGHTIES

The ENO and the *BBC Shakespeare Series*; science in Sussex, *Ivan* and *Prisoner of Consciousness*

*T*HE SOUTH BANK SHOW augured well for Miller's new phase at the English National Opera. No one could have predicted how phenomenally successful his subsequent *Rigoletto* and *Mikado* would be, but company members relished his *Marriage of Figaro* rehearsals. John Tomlinson, who portrayed the titular manservant, recalls how exceptional naturalism migrated from Kent Opera to the Coliseum, London's largest drama auditorium. 'Taking away all the overblown acting, accepted in singing circuses elsewhere, Jonathan created genuine and convincing music theatre which – as a house that sings in the vernacular – is the ENO's raison d'être,' he states. Equally, Miller's historical expertise inspired a great sense of security. It extended to the details of what people would have been eating in a specific era, and even to their facial expressions. His aim, with *Figaro*, was to capture what life in a country house would truly have been like, with the servants slogging away for this rather spoilt aristocratic couple.[1]

He declined to link the opera back to the Beaumarchais *Figaro*, his bugbear at the NT. Mozart's brilliant creation about the vicissitudes of love was, he preferred to think, 'an orphan with no parents', or was more like Chekhov and Shakespeare's high comedies in its subtle depiction of relationships.[2] One of his innovations was, nevertheless, inspired by Beaumarchais' sequel, *La Mère Coupable*, for Miller had the Countess depicted as a mother. The soprano Valerie Masterson, taking that role, had two infants fleetingly brought to her by a nursemaid. Love-deprived in her marriage, this Countess was acutely melancholy, though cheering up in the company of the page Cherubino (played by Sally Burgess).[3]

Miller suggested that the amorous youth was a womanizing Don Giovanni in the making, a boy-man with 'what Freud called polymorphous perversity'. The frock-donning scene, where Cherubino dresses as a woman, was unusually frisky, involving some research into eighteenth-century pornography and whipping with ribbons. Miller had specially requested a Cherubino with a small bottom.[4] In the garden tryst scene, Burgess also hummed the tune of Mozart's 'Champagne' aria from *Don Giovanni*: a witty symmetry since Mozart himself slipped a musical quotation from *Figaro* into *Don Giovanni*.[5]

The production was regarded by the *Daily Telegraph* as decidedly 'controversial'. Its reviewer took exception to the director cutting out the more 'traditional horseplay', not staging individual arias 'as is the custom', and having the Countess sit in a chair while singing.[6] If British theatre critics had slowly become less conservative, some of their opera colleagues still had a long way to go.[7] Miller sighs about some aficionados in this field having stereotyped ideas. 'They're like Konrad Lorenz's geese,' he says, 'who are reared in isolation with only a wastepaper basket dragged around their enclosure, and who woo the wastepaper basket thenceforth. I think opera-goers become imprinted, clinging desperately to the first version of *Figaro* they've seen at an impressionable age.' He suggests a Platonic analogy, where any new variation is viewed as 'a failed version', falling short of the supposed ideal.[8]

For sure, not all critics are so narrow-minded. The *Sunday Times* applauded the freshness of Masterson's performance and a second *Telegraph* reviewer rejoiced at the stock comic business being junked and at the audience being trusted to notice tiny smiles and frowns.[9] *Figaro* was a resounding hit in-house as well. Nicholas Hytner (now artistic director of the NT) comments: 'When I was at the ENO [as an assistant and staff director], that production was a revelation. It was beautiful, wonderfully acted, done in a big theatre with fantastic simplicity.' It formed part of the repertoire for twelve years, receiving generally warmer and warmer reviews.[10]

Lord Harewood, as head of the company, wasted no time. At the first cast party for *Figaro*, he invited Miller to direct *The Turn of the Screw*. Based on Henry James' novella, Benjamin Britten's chamber piece centres on a Victorian governess, possibly a fantasizing neurotic, who strives to save her young wards from the menacing and perhaps sexually corrupting ghosts of her predecessor (Miss Jessel) and the ex-valet (Quint). It was reported that, mid-way through rehearsing this intense piece, Miller was 'almost theologically obsessed' by the ghosts, insisting they had to appear real.[11] He had it both ways, though.[12] Some saw his ghouls as excessively palpable. Graham Clark's threatening Quint strode right up to the little boy, Miles, on an extended stage jutting over the pit – almost into the audience's laps. Conversely, the opera's neo-Gothic mansion, with forbidding facades and crenellated towers, was conjured up using phantasmagorical, multi-layered projections. This meant that the characters could glide past each other in a kind of intermediate transit zone that blurred the real and the imagined.[13]

On the question of the governess hallucinating, Miller knew that Henry James had consulted the neurologist Hughlings Jackson and discussed the deathly foreboding silence of the aura phase which precedes epileptic fits. There is a silence, in both the novella and the opera, just before the governess sees the ghosts. 'I wasn't claiming she had epilepsy, but there are intimations of a hysterical mental state. There were lots of these neurasthenics,' he says, referring to nineteenth-century records of hysteria which described thwarted and isolated women who, with no sexual life of their own, became obsessed with elaborate fantasies.[14] Jill Gomez, who took over the role of the governess, says that she was so spooked by James' characters and Britten's music – let alone Miller's eerie set – that she woke up screaming in the night.[15]

Miller says that he did not regard her ward, Miles, as a wicked, dirty-minded or sexually abused delinquent, but as running messages between Jessel and Quint, like the boy in *The Go-Between*.[16] 'Miles has probably', he remarks, 'just blundered into the attic and overheard sounds of intercourse, the snapping of suspenders, and been intrigued by these games of bottoms, you know.' Some reviewers, nonetheless, discerned signs of sexual corruption in the children's games, and Britten's partner, Peter Pears, wrote an enraged letter to Harewood declaring that Benjamin would be turning in his grave.[17] It was the startlingly physical struggle over the boy which, Miller believes, touched a raw nerve and caused Pears' 'Niagara of petulant, violent, contemptuous disagreement'.[18] Or maybe there was some irritation going right back to *Beyond the Fringe*. Miller had, after all, played the MC in Moore's *Little Miss Britten* skit, a hilariously precious rendition of 'Little Miss Muffet'.

The production was acclaimed as powerful, ingenious and 'nightmarishly unnerving', with its minimalism reflecting the music's economy of means and its restrained performances conveying darkly twisted psyches. Nicknamed *The Return of the Screw*, it continued to be revived into the 1990s.[19]

Legend has it that Miller arrived at the start of rehearsals for his next ENO project, Richard Strauss' Viennese confection *Arabella*, exclaiming, 'I've just heard the music. Not very good is it!'[20] Though he had been called in late, at the leading soprano Josephine Barstow's special request, this is not the only tale of him barely studying the score beforehand.[21] Ever keen on improvisation, he favours listening and responding on the spot, not swotting up on others' recordings (even if many of his singers, inevitably, know previous versions).

The real problem, as Nicholas Hytner recollects, was that *Arabella*'s romantic storyline was unreconstructed hokum and everyone involved eventually realized this.[22] The piece was, as a result, not programmed for long.[23] Still, Miller's staging was reviewed quite amiably. He came to appreciate Strauss' ability to capture conversational rhythms and intonations in musical phrasing, and he would later direct four more of the composer's operas.[24]

His value to the ENO had already been recognized, with Harewood making him an associate director not long after *Figaro*.[25] Having signed up to stage a new opera every year, Miller was scheduled to follow *Arabella* with *Rigoletto*, but he obligingly squeezed in another of Verdi's tragedies, *Otello*, when the veteran tenor Charles Craig decided he wished to sing at the Coliseum. This show nearly didn't happen because of industrial action. Only last-minute negotiations ensured the curtain was raised, late, on press night. John Tomlinson raced to the rescue as well when the cast member playing Lodovico fell ill. Already engaged at the Royal Opera House, Tomlinson had to scoot from the show there (where he was handily killed off in Act One) to rematerialize on the Coliseum stage as the Venetian emissary in the second half of *Otello*.

Performed in Elizabethan costume on a wooden arched set, loosely based on Shakespeare's Globe, *Otello* was hailed as one of the venue's greatest successes, 'a triumph in almost every way'.[26] Finding the production sold out, would-be punters were seen waving banknotes outside the venue in St Martin's Lane.[27] Miller was praised for improving Craig's acting and adding psychological nuances to the opera's simplified characters. Horribly plausible, Neil Howlett's Iago was coldly manipulative, behind his bluff manner, as he seeded jealous thoughts in his newly-married general's mind.[28] Miller, in turn, encouraged Rosalind Plowright to play Desdemona as a vivacious woman defying her father and, when attacked by her husband, putting up a fight. Instead of unliberated saintliness and a limply accepted suffocation, her final scene was ferocious, with legs kicking and sheets flying.

In spite of the plaudits, Miller dismisses this production as utterly unmemorable, saying the music is wonderful but the drama is sentimentalized drivel. Opera directors, he observes, have to spend much of their time performing reconstructive surgery. Moreover, he did not much rate *Otello* because he had been filming Shakespeare's far subtler play for the BBC. His *Othello* was broadcast just ten days after *Otello*'s opening night.

⋆   ⋆   ⋆

Miller was making the news not only at the ENO but also as the flying doctor-director brought in to save television's ailing *BBC Shakespeare Series*.[29] He took charge of this venture in 1980, being entrusted with the top post of executive producer. The series had been introduced two years earlier as the greatest drama project that the Corporation had ever undertaken. A co-production with the American media company Time-Life, it boasted a mammoth £7 million budget, and its mission was to work through the Bard's entire dramatic oeuvre of 37 plays over six years.[30] However, the initial output, with Cedric Messina at the helm, had been unimpressive. An inept *Much Ado* had been shelved and other dull productions were panned.[31]

In some respects, the new recruit was a risky appointment. Time-Life and their corporate backers had insisted on 'classic interpretations' which could be sold as a definitive video collection and, supposedly, never age. The contract therefore stipulated that every play must be done in traditional costume, with no monkey tricks. Even as he donned the executive mantle, Miller openly argued that the master plan was naive, almost any recording would soon look dated, and monkey tricks could be enlivening. 'I hope', one executive sniped, 'he's not going to do them underwater.'[32]

In fact, Miller was ideal for the series, having a strong interest in the Renaissance combined with zing. His popularity in America was also refreshed by the Stateside broadcasting of *The Body in Question* and by Dick Cavett's chat-show on which he appeared for an unprecedented five nights in a row.[33]

He had already proved he could televise Shakespeare in period dress, having turned his Michael Hordern *Lear* into a BBC *Play of the Month*. That had been produced under trying circumstances during 1974, when the British government was enforcing not just frequent power cuts, but also three-day weeks and reduced TV broadcasting hours. He had managed to cope with a drastic slash in the programme's length and a consequently miffed cast.

For all that, he was astounded when the Bardathon landed in his lap, because the job offer came just as he was making a hash of *A Midsummer Night's Dream* at Vienna's Burgtheater.[34] Exacerbated by his lack of German, an excruciating impasse had been reached as the performers, including the star Klaus Maria Brandauer, wanted decisive instructions and as the Englishman waited, in vain, for spontaneity from them. One afternoon, half-way through the rehearsals, their acting had suddenly improved. Miller had hastened over to his assistant and whispered, 'They're finally getting it. Tell them that's exactly what I want them to do', only to be told they were not doing it at all. They were discussing it.

He says that he was, justifiably, fired in the end, because he was floundering and despairing. Hans-Dieter Roser, the theatre's general secretary at the time, clearly liked him and now sees the funny side, even as he confirms:

> Yes, it became a real disaster! Jonathan came to the office and said, 'How much did the production cost? I want to pay it back and go.' We talked him into staying but then Brandauer left. He got a doctor to write a note: 'The right ankle of Brandauer is not suitable for the part of Puck.' The artistic director read this out at a press conference and the journalists just laughed and laughed, then the doctor called and said he would take us to court . . . Yes, yes, it was terrible!

Apparently Miller was in such a stew that, having invited a friend to come and stay, he returned from the theatre one afternoon and literally sent her packing, saying he could not imagine what she was doing there. The astonishing peripeteia occurred soon after that, when his son William had turned up for a visit. As Miller explains:

> We were sitting in a cafe and suddenly I saw these two unmistakably English figures from BBC management, in nylon shirts with their jackets over their arms, making their way across the Ringstrasse. They were waving and calling 'Hello, Jonno!' and asking me whether I would take over the series.

He had been seeking a niche on the continent precisely because he had no foothold at the National Theatre or at Trevor Nunn's RSC, therefore he leaped at this opportunity to return to spoken drama and a cornucopia of Shakespeare in the UK. He knew that dramas written for the Globe's wooden 'O' might not adapt perfectly to the electronic square of a TV screen, but television was Britain's real national theatre, playing in everyone's home, countrywide.

Over the next couple of years, before passing on the executive baton as arranged, he oversaw eleven Bardathon productions along with his continuing ENO and Kent Opera engagements. Besides co-ordinating the series, he directed six works himself: *Othello*, *The Taming of the Shrew*, *Antony and Cleopatra*, *Timon of Athens*, *Troilus and Cressida* and (for his successor, Shaun Sutton) another *King Lear*.[35]

Bringing a new buzz to the proceedings, Miller pulled the series out of a nosedive.[36] His casting had appeal, a combination of the populist and the adventurous. Bob Hoskins, who had played the gangster in the BBC's *Pennies from Heaven*, transmogrified into Iago, opposite Anthony Hopkins' Othello. John Cleese, from *Monty Python's Flying Circus* and *Fawlty Towers*, was to take his first classical role as Petruchio in *The Taming of the Shrew*. With *Antony and Cleopatra*, Miller decided to counter the cliché of glamorous sexiness, having Colin Blakely portray the Roman soldier like a battered, ageing rugby star alongside the unvoluptuous but vivacious Jane Lapotaire, whom the director describes as an 'interestingly sluttish Cleopatra'. The Egyptian queen was irresistible, he says, 'not because she sucked Antony off in some spectacular way, but because – unlike the awful twin-set-and-pearls Octavia [his wife] – she was prepared to stay up till four in the morning and go out in disguise to the bazaars'.[37]

He also caused a stir within the BBC's Television Centre by shaking up the status quo there. He turned his executive office suite into a humming communal HQ, like a brains trust.[38] His technical staff, designers and other bright sparks piled in together. Michael Wood (formerly of the Oxford and Cambridge Shakespeare Company) worked on the series' appended educational programmes, and a small corps of imaginative directors was gathered: crucially Elijah Moshinsky (who had become a fast-rising opera and theatre director after the OCSC), Jane Howell and Jack Gold.[39]

Looking back, Gold believes that Miller was brave to offer him *The Merchant of Venice* since he had done no Shakespeare before and very little studio work.[40] 'Jonathan let you get on with it,' he says, 'so it was wonderful, and kind of frightening.' Actually, Miller avoided sitting in on others' rehearsals because he found it hard to keep his lips sealed. As Jane Howell remembers it, he made the whole venture artistically liberating because, while offering support at just the right moment, he was never interfering or daunted.

When he did watch his recruits at work and was pleased, he would bound out from his viewing booth to congratulate everyone. At one point, when Howell did not have enough room to mock up a set for large-scale battle scenes, he stormed into the offices of the managerial big guns to ensure the problem was solved. Howell recalls that he would pick up on the slightest hint of interest which she showed in any topic. A pile of books would magically appear on her desk the next morning.[41] 'That was tremendous. We were all part of Jonathan's gang really,' she says.

She and Miller both saw the series as a chance to test how Elizabethan and Jacobean dramas might adapt to TV.[42] While exploring a mix of approaches, they each tried retaining elements of bare-boards theatricality. In *Troilus*, Troy's colonnades were abstracted to their simplest architectural outlines and visibly constructed out of raw plywood.[43] Elsewhere the camera roved around a simple, raised stage. Howell shot her *Henry VI* trilogy on a single-unit set: a scaffold evoking a playground fortress.

For Moshinsky, there was a backstory. Some years before, he had turned up at the NT for a job interview with Peter Hall and, as he explains:

> I was sitting around waiting and I saw a file on the table – about me – so I looked in it and there was a note in which Jonathan had spoken against me, saying I had a very peculiar personality. I'm afraid he was right! . . . But his description desperately hurt me. He couldn't take the competition at that time, when he was being crushed by Peter Hall, and he can't control it . . . Jonathan has always had a problem with jealousy. It's a small problem but it's a major part of his personality. I learned at an early stage never to compete with him . . . The thing is, though, that Peter Hall never said a cross word against me and I can't bear him, whereas I admire Jonathan greatly. He is up and down, but he's the real thing.

Miller proved a generous boss on the Shakespeare series, offering *All's Well* to this Young Turk with no TV experience and alleviating his fears.[44] As Moshinsky explains: 'Jonathan said, "Just follow me", so I got a kind of apprenticeship on *Antony and Cleopatra*. Everyone helped everyone else.' He goes on to praise how innovative the productions were with Shakespeare's verse, making the metre sound conversational for the small screen. That was in direct opposition to the RSC 'where', he says, 'it was all leather and opera, people speaking in a meaningless singsong way'. Miller's ENO *Otello* and near-simultaneous BBC *Othello* were especially fascinating because the TV play was deliberately anti-operatic and *sotto voce*. Penelope Wilton's Desdemona barely even sang 'The Willow Song' under her breath, being too dazed with grief for anything more.[45]

Moshinsky and his executive producer were united in their desire to explore the small screen as a picture frame. They introduced numerous allusions to period paintings, with chiaroscuro lighting effects and with rich palettes of reds and golds – or, in the tragedies, bleaker greys and blacks.[46] By this point in his career, Miller believed a director should be like the head of an art history faculty, educating his designers and introducing a wealth of visual references. In *The Taming of the Shrew*, the family home was a Vermeer-style interior with a servant serenely cleaning the tiled floor, unfazed by the sound of Kate scuffling furiously in the room beyond.[47] In *Antony and Cleopatra*, he drew on Veronese's depiction of classical heroes and heroines who sported half-Roman and half-Renaissance garb. Artists of Veronese's era, he suggested, had stereoscopic vision in that sense.

Rule-teasing modern allusions also sneaked under the radar, together with a drag act. The Greek army's costumes in *Troilus* were based on Cranach, yet they evoked *M.A.S.H.* with shades of khaki. The subversive character Thersites was

26 Michael Hordern in Miller's *King Lear*, BBC TV's *Play for Today*, 1975

27 John Cleese, *Taming of the Shrew*, *BBC TV Shakespeare Series*, 1980

28 Richard Angas (centre) as the Mikado in Miller's Grand Hotel *Mikado*, first staged in 1986 for English National Opera

29 Miller getting into the seaside-holiday spirit, rehearsing *The Mikado*

30 *The Tempest*, Old Vic, 1988. Max von Sydow (Prospero), Cyril Nri (Ariel)

31 Miller's Mafia *Rigoletto*, for the ENO, with John Rawnsley (in the title role) and Arthur Davies (as 'the Duke', to his right)

32 *The Liar*, Old Vic, 1989. Alex Jennings (left), Desmond Barrit (centre)

33 *Andromache*, Old Vic, 1988. Kevin McNally and Penelope Wilton (centre)

34 *The Emperor*, staged by Miller at the Royal Court in 1987, with Nabil Shaban (right) in the title role

35 Miller in rehearsals, restaging his Vienna Staatsoper production of
The Marriage of Figaro at Ferrara's Teatro Comunale in 1994

36 *Così fan tutte* at the Royal Opera House in 1995, with Amanda Roocroft (Fiordiligi)
and Susan Graham (Dorabella). Costumes by Armani

37 Miller's *Don Pasquale* at the Royal Opera House in 2004, a production originally staged at Florence's Maggio Musicale in 2001

38 *The Elixir of Love*, ENO, 2011, with Andrew Shore (in the car, as Dulcamara) and (directly behind him) Sarah Tynan (Adina) and Ben Johnson (Nemorino)

39 *Dance to the Music of Time* by Nicolas
Poussin, an inspiration for Miller's
stagings of *L'Orfeo*

40 *Fidelio*, staged by Miller for the Danish
National Opera,
in Aarhus, in 2007

41 Miller in the garden at Gloucester Crescent, with one of his sculptures
in the background

42 Miller in rehearsals for the ENO production of *Don Giovanni*, 1985.
Contact sheet by photographer Clive Boursnell

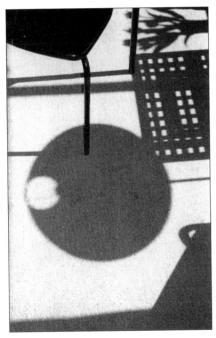

43 Photograph by Miller, reflecting his interest in abstract forms and geometry

44 Miller rehearsing *Così fan tutte* at the Royal Opera House

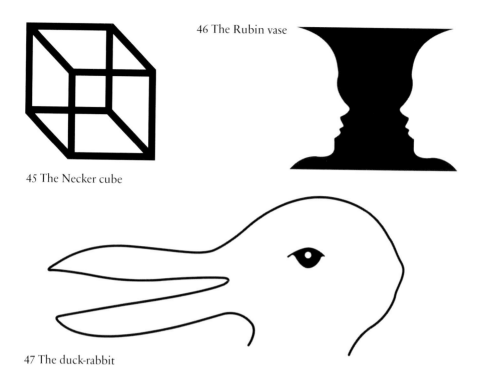

46 The Rubin vase

45 The Necker cube

47 The duck-rabbit

48 *Melencolia* by Albrecht Dürer

49 Stephen Conroy's portrait of Miller, National Portrait Gallery

specifically played like the cross-dresser Corporal Klinger, in a period frock.[48] Courtesy of Miller's designer, Colin Lowrey (formerly of *The Body in Question*), Ajax had Cranach's Eve as a pin-up by his camp-bed, and in the generals' tent were flip-chart sketches of a horse (glanced at, with bemusement, by the Trojan emissary). A touch of more personally informed satire kicked off *Timon*.[49] In the opening scene, John Bird and John Fortune played the socialite aesthetes at the Athenian equivalent of a chatterati party, impersonating Huw Weldon and Isaiah Berlin.[50]

Miller took a strictly historical line on *The Taming of the Shrew* regarding Kate's final speech, in praise of female obedience. It would originally have been delivered without any rebellious twist, he said. That reading raised a few feminist hackles, and eyebrows may, indeed, have been arched in Gloucester Crescent at the notion of an authoritative *pater familias*. Nevertheless, Michael Walzer's social history book *The Revolution of the Saints* backed up Miller's idea that Petruchio – rather than an unacceptable bully – was a Tudor Puritan squire who would have believed, in line with his times, that the male head of the household must be obeyed.[51]

John Cleese points out that a secondary, psychoanalytical reading lay behind the production. As played by Sarah Badel, Kate's anxiety-driven tantrums were aggravated by her family's panicky responses, and by her sibling being favoured. She was soothed by the unflappable manner of Cleese's Petruchio.[52] Besides being a mature suitor, he captured the slightly aloof yet gentle demeanor of a consultant child psychiatrist, subtly making their relationship a game. Though he was in doublet and hose, you could almost see a medic's white coat, or vestiges of the Tavistock Clinic through the veneer of Vermeer. Later, his Petruchio moved on to different role-play, acting barmy so Kate could see the effects of her delinquent behaviour as in a looking-glass.

Tempered thus, *The Shrew* did not cause a huge furore. It was, in general, warmly received.[53] However, being executive producer on this series certainly was not a breeze for Miller. The rule about using traditional costumes was unacceptable to many of the world-class directors whom he wanted on board, including Ingmar Bergman and Peter Brook. In a brief fracas, Michael Bogdanov threatened court action after being sacked for not abiding by the brief. 'I engaged him', Miller recalls, 'to do *Timon of Athens*, then the costume designer rang up and said, "I'm up to my arse in kimonos. He's doing it all Japanese!"' Bogdanov now accepts that it was not the cleverest episode in his life. At the time, he testily called the BBC project the greatest disservice to Shakespeare in years.[54]

Tight schedules were another tricky factor, with just six days to tape each play.[55] The productions' exceptionally long, single-camera shots were soon being analyzed at Shakespeare conferences, hailed as bold artistic choices, but some resulted from sheer pragmatism – five shots frantically replaced by one, because there was no more studio time.[56] A few old hands in the technical crew grumbled that Miller was insufficiently trained and did not plan ahead enough. Trying to splice *Troilus* together in the editing suite proved hellish. At WNET (the New

York TV company collaborating with Time-Life), staff were driven mad because they needed to axe passages to fit their time slots, but could find scarcely any suitable points for cutaways. Due to divergences in tape size, their equipment munched sections of *Lear* as well, so the woebegone king arrived at the heath at an incredible lick.

Furthermore, after a relatively smooth ride with *The Shrew*, the series faced American protest groups who objected to *The Merchant of Venice*. They considered the play intrinsically anti-Semitic and were not placated by Warren Mitchell (best known as the bigot Alf Garnett in *Till Death Us Do Part*) being cast as Shylock. Some sent letters to the *New York Times* and to WNET, saying that the broadcast should be cancelled because it could arouse racial hatred. One of Time-Life's corporate backers, Exxon, nervously distanced itself, stating that it was the BBC's product, not theirs. WNET was not cowed, but Miller appeared in an introductory programme and follow-up discussion to stress that he himself, Jack Gold and Mitchell were all Jewish. The play, he added, was symmetrical in its prejudices.[57]

Another row blew up regarding *Othello*. This had started during Cedric Messina's tenure. The UK actors' union, Equity, was so annoyed by the American star James Earl Jones (aka the voice of Darth Vader) being cast in the title role that the whole production had been put on ice. Miller did not entirely calm the waters by replacing him with Anthony Hopkins, the UK's last major blacked-up Othello.[58] He says this got him into terrible trouble and was embarrassing:

> Of course, it was put down as racist on my part and you certainly wouldn't do it with a white actor now, or need to . . . But it was on the edge of that moment of political correctness, and I didn't think that James Earl Jones was right, not because he was black but because I didn't want an American in the middle of a British cast . . . I have some misgivings about it, but at the time I wanted the best actor and I wasn't interested in whether he was black.

The Brixton, Toxteth and other riots of 1981, sparked by perceived white racism, broke out between the filming and the transmission of *Othello*, which must have made it more prickly. Miller's opinion is, still, that skin colour is not the play's main issue. In his view, Othello is an assimilated foreigner who is not expecting Iago's hate campaign, having largely forgotten his racial difference. 'Moor' denotes someone of Arab or Berber descent, and Hopkins' Othello (like Charles Craig's Otello at the ENO) was only slightly darker skinned than his ensign.[59] For a model, Miller had King Hussein of Jordan in mind, a Hashemite warrior drilled in Sandhurst manners.

According to Hopkins, the directorial reading was that Othello had long been susceptible to jealousy because he was emotionally insecure, his mother having been taken from him at an early age.[60] Miller regarded Iago's envy as the truly crucial driving force in the play, and strikingly suggested that the ensign's mother might have failed at breastfeeding. According to Melanie Klein's psychoanalytic theories, that would have led to pessimistic dissatisfaction and envious destructiveness in later life.[61] Like Edmund in *King Lear*, Iago was portrayed as an interstitial mischief-maker too, disgruntled at not being fully welcomed into the elite ranks. Bob Hoskins played him like a cockney sergeant-cum-psychotic Rumpelstiltskin, seemingly the salt of the earth, covertly a wicked practical joker.

That said, it was Hopkins (not Hoskins) who put a spanner in the works, during rehearsals and on set. As Miller recollects, one run-through was being performed in modern army kit, just for fun, with an audience of school kids. It was going perfectly well until the tragic hero suddenly walked off in a huff. Then the last two days of filming were abominable, he says:

> When we came to the murder of Desdemona, he [Hopkins] obviously got pretty anxious about it. I began giving him some notes, then he stormed off saying, 'It's all directing, directing, directing.' He sulked in a corner and refused to come back . . . almost jeopardiz[ing] the production. Many years later, he wrote a letter apologising to me, but I still don't understand what went wrong, or whether he really understood the bloody-mindedness. I think he would withdraw from things I suggested out of cowardice and panic.

He did not reply to Hopkins' letter but acknowledges that the actor was, in spite of everything, brilliant.

More large egos had been at loggerheads in *Troilus and Cressida*, especially in the Greek army camp where Kenneth Haigh, as the testy Achilles, appeared to be in character round the clock. He moaned about crushed toes whenever a tight group shot was required, and he wanted to throttle the squawking chickens which Miller had caged outside the mess tent.[62]

Struggles aside, many actors had a great time on the series. John Shrapnel may have met a gruesome end as Hector in *Troilus* – jammed face-down in a puddle, spattered with lumps of fake cerebral cortex – yet he would race to rehearsals every day buoyed up by Miller's sense of adventure. John Cleese came away from *The Shrew* with a new-found admiration for Shakespeare, and he still wishes he could have worked with Miller again. He observes:

> The sense of confidence, working with him, was extraordinary. There is someone in charge who knows what they want but, at the same time, creates an atmosphere where you can try anything . . . I think he liked operating from the parental position. Actors feel he's a good father, he'll look after them. I don't think he's after equal relationships but, in that parental situation, he's about as good as you get.[63]

Miller really did look after Bob Hoskins who, after the launch of *The Long Good Friday*, had swung from a divorce and breakdown into a crazy, partying high. Insisting that he come to stay at Gloucester Crescent, the director calmed him down considerably. This house guest only got up to a few impish pranks, being dared by Tom to break into William's assiduously locked cupboard. As Hoskins recalled: 'He kidnapped me, basically. It was wonderful . . . Jonathan got hold of me and started teasing me about psychopaths and [then] I was OK.'[64]

The public reaction to the Bardathon, undeniably, kept veering up and down during Miller's tenure. Complainants called the productions either too conservative or too disrespectful, either reductive or excessively sumptuous – looking like a National Gallery calendar. Some said that his new *Lear*, again starring Hordern and Middlemass, was little more than a repeat of his BBC *Play of the Month* version, though for Hordern it was definitley the best.[65] Several other splenetic attacks were launched from academic institutions in America. H. R. Coursen, who co-edited the book *Shakespeare on Television*, decried *Antony and Cleopatra* as an unmitigated disaster and steamed with indignation about Miller's patronizing insistence on introductory programmes (though WNET had asked him to do those).[66]

The director himself says, with a shrug, that his productions were largely dismissed and only Moshinsky was lauded. However, alongside the applause for *The Shrew*, the *New York Times* praised *Timon* for its uniformly splendid cast (with Jonathan Pryce in the title role), and the *Los Angeles Times* found *Lear* utterly compelling. Countering H. R. Coursen, the *Washington Post* deemed *Antony and Cleopatra* gorgeous, and Michael Ratcliffe of *The* (London) *Times* hailed it as a triumph of unaffected verse-speaking and vibrancy.[67] Surveying Miller's contribution, Ratcliffe saw the enterprise setting new standards and displaying a rare jubilant faith in TV.[68] Retrospectively, the series has been described as a defining moment in British television, with one of the greatest companies of actors ever assembled. The DVD box set was finally released in 2005.[69]

At the time, the chief cameraman took home a BAFTA, and Miller won the Royal Television Society's silver medal for 1981.[70] In the following few years, various institutions jostled to recognize his achievements. The National Film Theatre held a retrospective dedicated to his screen work. He was made a fellow of UCL and an honorary fellow of St John's, Cambridge, and he was awarded a CBE by the Queen in 1983.[71] Bogdanov still claims that the BBC project was a terrible flop and that the shelves of TV companies worldwide remain stacked with the tapes, pre-bought, not broadcast. Yet by 1983 it had been seen by millions of viewers across 37 countries, from China and Iraq to Poland and Peru.[72]

*   *   *

Even as *Lear*, Miller's final contribution to the series, was being broadcast throughout the UK, he was back in the West End with two productions.[73] His new staging of *Hamlet* opened at the Warehouse Theatre, today known as the Donmar. He had so relished working with John Shrapnel and Anton Lesser (his Troilus) at the BBC that he recast them as King Claudius and the Prince of Denmark.[74] Miller's close-up TV and his cockpit-style theatre almost seemed to merge in this pocket-sized production in Elizabethan dress.

Finding Lesser unpoetic and puny, a few critics jibed that it was *Hamlet* without the princeliness, but Miller's intent was to create a less hero-centred piece. He was pursuing the idea of Hamlet as a problem child, 'a tiresome, clever, destructive boy who is very intelligent but volatile, dirty-minded and immature'.[75] Lesser blubbed, sniggered and could not shoulder the strain of his late father's expectations. In the closet scene, he curled up in his mother's arms like an infant.[76] In the later scenes, he grew up bit by bit, and Lesser speaks of a maturation process in his own relationship with Miller.

Troilus had been a challenging role, though a thrilling one. Lesser had found himself awed and intimidated by the director's flood of eloquent ideas, sometimes wondering if the cast would ever get up on their feet and just do it. He began to fear that he could not act anymore and, he says, 'Jonathan would be hugely entertaining [acting bits himself], but then I'd try to replicate . . . erroneously thinking that was what he wanted.' Lesser got through *Troilus* on sheer adrenalin and Miller instantly offered him Edgar in the BBC *Lear*. 'By that time, I felt more confident,' the performer states, 'and I had got the measure of him. I was going through this process of learning to listen but not necessarily replicate . . . By *Hamlet*, I felt I'd really found the way to do justice to his brilliance and enjoy the relationship creatively.'

Kathryn Pogson's Ophelia was a second problem child, regressing into infantile madness, playing with dolls rather than with flowers. Her insanity was distressingly unprettified, pushing further than Miller's previous stagings. Based on clinical cases which he delineated to Pogson and on a schizophrenic girl she saw on a train, this Ophelia drooled, scratched at her lips, retched with her fingers down her throat and gradually faded out, becoming emotionally absent to the point of catatonia. 'It stunned the audience,' Shrapnel says, 'and it was quite terrifying to behold, almost unwatchable.'

Comic relief came in Hamlet's advice to the players on holding the mirror up to nature. Lesser delivered this like a know-it-all undergraduate hanging around at the Cambridge Arts Theatre, precociously lecturing a visiting company while they slapped on the greasepaint and exchanged glances. A real-life graduate, from Swaziland, was loitering at the Warehouse rehearsals, incidentally. Having gained permission to sit in and watch, he appeared to be living out of a suitcase and wishing he was in the show. That student was Richard E. Grant, later to star as the grungy thespian and Hamlet manqué in *Withnail and I*.

Miller's *Rigoletto* opened at the ENO on the very same night that *Hamlet* transferred, as a hit, from the Warehouse to the Piccadilly Theatre. The omens for the opera were bad. On hearing of Miller's concept, several critics had blanched and declared he was reverting to shocking monkey tricks if he was going to drag Verdi's classic out of its sixteenth-century setting, at the ducal court of Mantua, into the Mafia underworld of 1950s New York.[77] Conservative aficionados started cancelling their tickets in droves.

Miller was not a lone groundbreaker and, by the mid-1980s, he would be seen as part of a growing international breed of revisionist opera directors along with

Peter Brook, Patrice Chéreau, Andrei Serban and Peter Sellars.[78] Nevertheless, he has been dubbed the inventor of the time-shift opera and, certainly, members of the ENO chorus were obstreperously sceptical at first, having never seen a canonical work given such unorthodox treatment.[79] Miller and Mark Elder, who was conducting, had certain disagreements about James Fenton's libretto translation, with Elder resisting American idioms in case they were seen as merely guying the piece.[80] Elder readily admits:

> I got tense because I was very young and conscious of my responsibilities as [the Coliseum's] music director, and Jonathan directs with the loosest rein of anybody I've ever worked with . . . The rehearsals [with the principals] often degenerated into tears of laughter as if we were doing the Christmas pantomime, not one of the greatest tragedies in the repertoire! But that is Jonathan's way, engendering a relaxed atmosphere . . . Also, everything changed with the chorus the first time they put on their costumes, those 1950's suits, with Brilliantine in their hair. They all looked in the mirror and recognized themselves – 'Hey, Charlie, you looked like that when you got married!' – and they all started to play the game.

Some took such a shine to their mobster outfits that the wardrobe department had to padlock its doors.[81]

On opening night, the company was excited and petrified, dreading that the audience would be too conventional and the fur would fly. 'Well,' says Elder, 'if anything deserves the phrase "The rest is history", that does! At the end of the first scene, the applause was huge and I remember thinking, "Goodness, perhaps we've done it! Perhaps it's going to be all right!"' The performance was punctuated, thereafter, with cheers and gasps of delighted surprise. The almighty gamble had paid off and it was soon global news, with *Time* magazine calling the production the talk of London.[82] It drew new crowds, including many who usually went to musicals, so Miller was now categorically playing a vital role in popularizing live opera – the 'pop op' revolution.[83]

He points out it was his wife who had started the ball rolling by reminding him of *Some Like It Hot*. In that movie, when the chief gangster needs a St Valentine's Day Massacre alibi, he claims to have been at *Rigoletto*, and his cronies meet under the guise of a Friends of Italian Opera convention. When Miller began to map Verdi's scenario on to the Mafia world, he found an extraordinary correspondence, 'like two hands, right and left'. The Duke simply became a gangland leader or *capo*, keeping his title as an underworld nickname and having the same power of life or death over those who irked him. His court became a Cosa Nostra-owned hotel, and Rigoletto, the court jester who pushes his luck, morphed into its barman.

The art deco cocktail lounge, in the first Act, was partly inspired by Keith McNally's Odeon restaurant in New York, where William Miller was waiting tables around this time.[84] For other scenes, the set designs gave a nod to *West*

Side Story, Leonard Bernstein's update of *Romeo and Juliet* where Verona had, of course, become Manhattan. Rigoletto's daughter, Gilda, was seduced by the Duke in a wire-fenced backyard and abducted down a fire escape. Most dazzlingly, in the final Act, the riverside tavern run by Rigoletto's hired assassin was transformed into a bar by the docks, glass-fronted and glowing in the dark like the one in Edward Hopper's painting *Nighthawks*. It came complete with a poster trailing *From Here to Eternity*.

The jukebox moment in the bar, when the Duke puts a dime in the slot then sings along to '*La donna è mobile*', is now world famous. Miller says that he had the idea on the spur of the moment, wondering why there was a pause in the score before Verdi's hit song. Two memories from his formative years may have linked up in the back of his mind. He had witnessed Gluck's music issuing from a wireless in Jean Cocteau's 1950s film *Orphée*, and Miller had also heard the Duke's aria on the radio before his eager childhood outing to *Rigoletto*. The director was even more in tune with his period setting than he realized, for he has since discovered that '*La donna è mobile*' was No. 3 in the list of hit records played on America's jukeboxes in 1954.

His *Rigoletto* went on to be one of the English National Opera's greatest ever hits, with only a few hiccups. Although superb in the title role, John Rawnsley lost his voice during one performance and had to mime while someone else sang his words, then he accidentally smashed his hand on a glass and left the blood-spattered scene for hospital.[85] A bigger snag presented itself when the ENO company was booked to make its New York Met debut and a feud developed. The Order Sons of Italy in America, angrily protested that this gangland *Rigoletto* would be a slur on their community. The congressman Mario Biaggi additionally pressed the National Endowment for the Arts to cut all financial support to the Met. Even after President Reagan stepped in, defending the programming, the ENO still had to remove all direct references to the Mafia and Little Italy from its libretto. Far from terminally damaged, the show broke the Met's box-office records.[86]

That same summer, the Greater London Council threatened to withdraw the ENO's grant when Miller objected to the black singer Willard White joining a second cast, which was being assembled to keep *Rigoletto* in rep at the Coliseum.[87] Rather than accept White as colour-blind casting, the director said it contradicted his otherwise accurate social realism, because the Italian-American underworld would have been too racist to incorporate black people in the Fifties.[88] He was completely happy to cast the black soprano Dana Hanchard in the title role of another opera some years later, and White would eventually work with him on another production.[89]

Rigoletto continued to pull crowds for well over quarter of a century, in spite of the management flagging up several revivals as 'Positively the Last'. It was broadcast on television in the UK and internationally. It came out on video in the 1980s and, in 2003, featured in the reality TV talent show Operatunity. In 2014, one critic called it, 'as close to cult status as opera gets,' even as the ENO replaced it with Christopher Alden's alternative staging.[90]

Even at its premiere, in the autumn of 1982, the press recognized Miller's concept as a milestone for the ENO and the most electrifying production they had seen for ages – or ever.[91] The director was presented with an *Evening Standard* Award and a second Olivier Award, this time for Outstanding Achievement in Opera. With that and his Piccadilly *Hamlet*, he was on another career high, and yet he was, once more, going to bid the stage goodbye in order to return to medicine. *Rigoletto* was to be his ENO *canto del cigno*.

Might he mean it this time? Was he, the media asked, quitting permanently now? For sure, he said. His guilty conscience was pricking him and, if he was to make a solid contribution in the field of neurology, it was now or never. Stage creations were simultaneously hard work and mere shimmering bubbles, melting into thin air. He had ticked off everything that he wanted to do as a director, and completing a trio of *Lears* and a trio of *Hamlets* had brought that home. Suffering a burn-out from years of hectic work was, perhaps, inevitable as well. He was approaching 50 years of age.

Furthermore, the future looked bleak for the subsidized arts. Miller would have loved a cockpit theatre of his own, but the chance of gaining state funding for that seemed slim. Even within the first year of Margaret Thatcher's regime, the Arts Council's budget had been cut by around eight per cent, and the number of RFOs (Regularly Funded Organizations) was being drastically reduced. Unsure if his disaffection was predominantly personal or political, he ruminated:

> Whatever is making me change my life is a mixture of disappointment, exhaustion and something which I can't quite put my finger on which makes me wish to be elsewhere. I have a growing inner feeling I am no longer at home.[92]

He was not eager to tour England's regional towns anymore, to create his notion of a Congregationalist national theatre, nor was he keen to become an operatic globetrotter. 'I just feel I've come to the end of it . . . like one of those bomber pilots. I've been out over the target too often now,' he said. 'Roger, so to speak, and out.'[93]

★   ★   ★

Before he went, he had to tie up several loose ends in terms of stage and screen. For his last fling with TV directing, he filmed a BBC version of John Gay's satirical *Beggar's Opera*. This yoked Roger Daltrey, from The Who and the rock opera *Tommy*, together with the classical conductor John Eliot Gardiner. Relieved to find that Miller wanted a gritty rendition, Daltrey sang Gay's musical interludes – ballads from the eighteenth-century's Top Ten – in a rough-and-ready manner. As the womanizing highwayman Macheath, he was like an East End gangster in Hogarthian garb, sexually hands-on and ferociously self-centred.

In a licentious humour, Miller announced that he was green with envy at his star's pulling power and the copious amount of groping that he was allowed. All the director got to tweak was Gay's ending, so that the fun-loving criminal was accidentally terminated at the gallows rather than enjoying a reprieve. Though throwaway in tone, this was a remarkably punitive conclusion: *la commedia è finita*, in no uncertain terms.

Besides being cast as one of Macheath's nemeses, the actress Patricia Routledge was taking no prisoners when, afterwards, she condemned Miller's relaxed style, snapping: 'I tend to look at my watch and think, "Come on, never mind that joke."'[94] *The Times* was not overly impressed by the end result either, observing that some of the acting, not just the singing, lacked finesse. Still, the *Telegraph* deemed it the best TV-studio opera in a decade, enough to restore viewers' faith in the medium.[95] The director was manifestly sorry to leave the scene, shedding a tear as he called it a wrap.

He then gave a valedictory and foreboding address on the subject of TV to key players in the business. In his MacTaggart Lecture at the Edinburgh International Television Festival, he described the small screen as an endoscope which lets people peruse otherwise inaccessible worlds, but he expressed grave concerns about the imminent growth of a multi-channel industry with a potentially 'insatiable appetite and chronic incontinence'.[96] At this point, in 1983, Britain's fourth TV service, Channel 4, was less than a year old and was winning praise for its high-calibre arts programmes, being a commercial station with a public service remit. Miller's own opera productions had featured.[97] The government, though, was about to change the law on cable transmissions, making numerous commercial channels viable.[98] Anticipating a slew of trashy TV stations, Miller's speech was prescient.

For his adieu to staging opera outside the ENO, he directed Mozart's *Magic Flute* as a UK-touring production for Scottish Opera. Rather than a fairytale pantomime, his setting was an Age of Reason library where the young hero, Tamino, fell asleep over his books and began dreaming.[99] Miller saw this piece, from 1791, as an Enlightenment fantasy, with the Queen of the Night and Sarastro respectively representing the era's opposed camps – Jesuitical Catholics and progressive, rationalist freemasons (with whom Mozart had connections).[100] Several critics wrote off his notion as over-intellectualized, though this *Flute* went from strength to strength in subsequent revivals.[101]

Finally, he signed off in terms of stage plays with a reprise of his seedy and, again, Hogarthian *School for Scandal*. That was in the States, reuniting the director with Robert Brustein, who had moved from Yale to run Harvard's American Repertory Theatre. The cast, though featuring the future Broadway star Cherry Jones, won only patchy applause.[102]

Anyway, Miller was now en route to take up his post as Visiting Professor of Medicine for a semester at Canada's McMaster University in Ontario. Here he taught philosophical classes on the language of complaint (focusing on sickly patients, rather than on theatre and opera critics). He was taking an unofficial refresher course too, joining neurological ward rounds and conferring with cognitive psychologists. One journalist noted that he looked like the eternal student, on campus with a book sticking out of his coat pocket. 'That's what I want to be. There's no reason ever to stop,' Miller beamed, evidently feeling rejuvenated.[103]

He had been beginning to get back up to speed over the previous few years. *The Body in Question* made him realize how much he missed medicine, and from that he had gone on to present *States of Mind*.[104] This was an astoundingly high-powered BBC chat-show: a fifteen-part series of tête-à-têtes where the workings of the brain and the mind were discussed by psychiatrists, psychologists and neuropsychologists, by behavioural and social scientists, philosophers and scientifically-inclined art historians. The assembled company included Rom Harré, Hanna Segal and Ernst Gombrich, Harvard's Jerome Bruner and Daniel Dennett, as well as Miller's former UCL and Cambridge mentors Stuart Hampshire, Richard Gregory and Robert Hinde.

Making these programmes and having in-depth, six-hour conversations before the cameras rolled, Miller felt thrilled to be grappling once more with what mattered to him. It was as if he were thawing out after years of being frozen. 'You can feel the blood racing through the fingers that have been numbed,' he enthused. 'They suddenly feel nimble and sensitive again . . . coming back to life.'[105] He was keen to examine the background to, and developments in psychology's cognitive revolution. Ranging from Locke and Descartes to artificial intelligence, he and his interviewees elaborated on a central idea: namely, that the brain attempts to match its own conjectural models with the sensory information it is receiving from the outside world. That is to say, in trying to categorize, we actively interpret what we see (or think we see).

Gregory, in particular, expanded on how the mind can flip between different possible readings of the world, the idea which Miller's old tutor Norwood Russell Hanson had inculcated back at Cambridge. This capacity to flip was illustrated using several of Hanson and Miller's favourite trompe l'oeils: along with the Necker Cube, the Rubin Vase (where the pot's outline suddenly looks like two faces pointing inwards).

In a somewhat different vein, Hanna Segal alluded to Miller's childhood psychiatrist, D. W. Winnicott. She was discussing Kleinian theories, sexual symbols (such as trains supposedly representing parental intercourse), and infants' ambivalent feelings towards their mothers (centring on breastfeeding). The presenter politely declined to swallow whole her suggestion that an adult's curiosity about the world necessarily springs from early Oedipal cravings.

Anthony Clare of *In the Psychiatrist's Chair* wrote a hostile review of *States of Mind* for the magazine *New Society*. Questioning who watched these talking heads on a Sunday afternoon, he scorned Segal and judged the accompanying book of edited dialogues to be a slog.[106] Other ambivalent peer reviews, including Stuart Sutherland's in the *TLS*, wished that Miller had taken issue with his interlocutors more often, and had not subjectively omitted core academic psychologists in favour of those with heterogeneous fringe interests. Still, most acknowledged the series to be interesting and winningly convivial in manner.[107] As a participant, Gregory had been especially delighted to encounter a knowledgeable TV personality.[108] 'Jonathan's neurological programmes are extremely good and I rate him incredibly highly as an expositor,' he says. The *States of Mind* book went on to be used as a standard text in American universities, so it clearly was not over everyone's head.

Rather than becoming part of the UK's academic brain drain, Miller returned to England after his McMaster semester and began a three-year research fellowship in the University of Sussex's cognitive sciences department. This was with a grant from the Leverhulme Trust of over £88,000. He underlines that he never made huge amounts of money from his hit operas, being paid only an initial fee and then royalties in the case of international transfers.

Joining the team at Sussex's experimental psychology lab, he pursued connected clinical work, studying local hospital patients with brain damage and consequent disorders. He wanted to investigate questions relating to memory, perception and processes of knowing. These subjects, close to philosophy, had been considered illicit when he was a trainee.[109]

His research did not turn out well. As with his University College fellowship, he did not last the course and he blames himself:

It was my last fling at trying to escape [from directing], but I just didn't have the stamina to go through with it. Maybe I'd lost the verve. I'd lost the plot because I'd been rotted by showbiz . . . Even the journey [back and forth to Brighton] just wore me out . . . It was very bad and sad.

Some years later he was able to comment jokily that a cross-disciplinary post, holding 'the Askance Chair', would have been nice, or just a La-Z-boy recliner might have been apt in his case.[110] At the time, he was dog-tired and sorely disappointed in himself, finding he was unfit for the marathon of catching up with modern medicine.

He also reproaches some Sussex colleagues. As at UC, he craved more encouragement. Although willing to function as a junior assistant, he could not find an individual prepared to act as his superior. There was insufficient money to conduct the desired experiments, and more clinical work was required. He did conduct tests relating to perception. These were inspired by the Swedish psychophysicist Gunnar Johansson who discovered that people, when shown footage of points of light moving in the dark, swiftly distinguish between random shifting dots and human beings in motion (with lights attached to their joints).[111] Miller's experiments were preliminary, though, and by no means publishable. He spent weeks struggling to get to grips with computers and the fiendish mathematics involved in modern psychophysics.[112]

In his hospital work, he collaborated with Sussex's Professor Alan Parkin, a formal experimental psychologist who showed signs of exasperation at the newcomer's casual technique of just chatting to the patients with brain damage.

Miller had intimated, prior to taking up his post, that he believed many of the perceptual skills he had developed as a director would be swiftly translatable into the clinical situation, and he stuck to his opinion that patients' incapacities became more fully apparent if one engaged them in everyday conversation.[113] Parkin, however, wanted more rigorous statistical tests. Miller now concedes that a quantitative approach was necessary, only he found it boring.

He and Parkin co-wrote one article for the specialist journal *Cortex*, concisely entitled 'Multiple Neuropsychological Deficits Due to Anoxic Encephalopathy: a Case Study'.[114] After a dry statistical start, this paper becomes unexpectedly fascinating and tragicomic. It recounts how one patient – a Mrs T, brain-damaged after a cardiac arrest – could no longer fully control her lower limbs or eye movements, was disoriented and severely amnesiac. The article specifically reports that she often bore an expression of glum vacancy yet could become distressed like a child. She would greet her husband very emotionally before turning to stare again at the TV. Miller's personal style comes through there, in the attention drawn to Mrs T's retained sense of humour and in several descriptions of touchingly idiosyncratic, painfully funny test results. On one occasion, the patient identified Princess Diana, photographed in a white and yellow hat, as a poached egg. On another, she saw only one of the two examiners in front of her and was visibly startled when the other said, 'What about me?' – as if he had sprung out of nowhere.

Miller remembers Mrs T with warm affection and he concludes that, in the long run, his treks up and down the Brighton line were worthwhile as he learned a great deal from Stuart Sutherland, a leading cognitive psychologist and engaging colleague. His scientific stint, moreover, led him to present *Ivan* and *Prisoner of Consciousness*, two outstanding medical documentaries, produced by Patrick Uden of *The Body in Question*, this time for BBC TV's *Horizon* and for Channel 4's *Equinox* series.[115]

Ivan Vaughan, a Cambridge lecturer who had developed Parkinson's disease, suggested that Miller should pay him a home visit. The resultant film showed Vaughan brushing his teeth with terrible shakes, struggling to play billiards, and being able to start but not stop jogging. It was an unforgettably intimate study of determination and frustration, with the doctor being fascinated and gently humorous, learning about the condition rather than cosseting or offering miracle cures. Reviewing *Ivan* in the *Observer*, Julian Barnes thought it one of the most original and compelling medical documentaries ever shown.[116]

Prisoner of Consciousness then dealt with the agonies of Clive Wearing, a musician with a devastated short-term memory. Wearing remained a fluent pianist yet was amazed every time he discovered that he could play, having forgotten the fact and forgetting it over and over again. His love for his wife persisted but he was harrowingly incapable of understanding that she, when absent, was not dead or lost for ever. *The Times*' reviewer called this a superlatively intelligent, bizarre and disturbing medi-doc. He lauded Miller for expanding a case history, via conversations with Wearing's wife, into a philosophical discussion about consciousness and a person's essential character.[117] Oliver Sacks still rates the programme as superb. It shared some ground with his own book *The Man Who Mistook his Wife for a Hat*, which came out the year before, and the overlap of interests was to carry on with Sacks visiting Wearing two decades later, writing about him in his 2007 book *Musicophilia*.[118] 'I wish Jonathan would make more programmes like that,' Sacks muses, and Miller himself says that he would like to be remembered long-term for those films.

In spite of his difficulties at Sussex, he worked Gunnar Johansson's experiments with lights into *Moving Pictures*, another Miller–Uden documentary for *Equinox*. This combined the presenter's childhood passion for cinema and for stereoscopes with neurology, contemplating the nitty-gritty of film editing and how the eye and brain register movement.[119]

He may well curse the fact that he abandoned Sussex with only one *Cortex* article to his name but, in the early 1980s, he wrote three immensely popular science books for the layman, or for what would now, hideously, be termed the kidult and edutainment market. *Darwin for Beginners*, with cartoon illustrations by Boris Van Loon, is still in print today around the globe, recently rebranded as 'a graphic guide'.[120] In the *New York Review of Books*, the evolutionary biologist Richard Lewontin called it a superbly informative introduction, scientifically impeccable.[121] Then there were the pop-up books *The Human Body* and *The Facts of Life*. In these Miller's mini biology lessons appeared alongside fabulously intricate origami designs by David Pelham, all suitable for family viewing even if some wags had hoped for a pop-up penis.

Miles Kington thoroughly enjoyed himself in *The Times*, devoting his column to a satire conflating *The Human Body* and *Peter Hall's Diaries*, which came out simultaneously:

Jonathan Miller's Diaries.
'Jan 19. I have been asked to produce another 49 operas for television. God, how I hate television. I will just do these 49 operas and then go back to life as an ordinary GP, with just one hand-held camera and a sound recordist. Who knows – perhaps one day Peter Hall will come in complaining of a runny nose.

'Jan 20. Why have we got a nose? I mean, why not two noses? To sniff in stereo would be to give us directional location of the thing we were sniffing. On the other hand, a double nose would be very difficult to do in a pop-up book.

'Jan 21. My hands have received a very lucrative TV offer. They have been asked to demonstrate the history of theatre today. On the other hand, the rest of me will not be involved at all. God, how I hate television. Recorded three operas this morning. Must try to do better tomorrow.'[122]

Private Eye slipped in a dig, alleging that private parts were omitted from the first book to keep the cheap female labour, in Columbia, folding the pages without protest.[123] Both pop-up publications received squeamish and stinking reviews in the *Spectator*, for being repulsive, textually negligible and appealing to no one.[124] Begging to differ, the public dashed out and bought the first print run – all 100,000 copies of *The Human Body* – in ten days. The TV ad campaign had to be cancelled until a further 125,000 were rushed through the presses.[125]

A few years later, both the Miller–Pelham collaborations were being seen as artworks, displayed in a New York exhibition of books with moving parts and picked out by the *New York Times* as the most spectacular items on show.[126] Though they were not going to win any Nobel Prizes, they were very popular in doctors' waiting-rooms and were used, in America, to explain diagnoses to patients. Ultimately, nearly one and a half million of these pop-ups were sold worldwide, though Miller says he again failed to make a fortune because of the deal cut with the publishers.

A third book, on the brain, did not materialize, and a playful medical software program called *Body Works*, on which Miller collaborated, was a flop. The CD-ROM market had not taken off at that point and he did not help, blithely belittling computers in what was meant to be a promotional interview – causing his agent to look bug-eyed.[127] He remains, to this day, rather hilariously incompetent regarding electronic gadgets. According to his children, he once accidentally junked a whole bunch of work on his PC because he did not know how to save files, and he has often called them to ask how his video recorder works.

Off the back of *Darwin for Beginners*, he planned to write a major TV series on evolution. This fell through, possibly because a rival science presenter, James Burke, was then in the ascendant. Miller had to make do with being the link man for *Origins*, a one-off programme telling the story of the Earth and homo sapiens through documentary video snippets. The press coverage focused humorously on him as a super-sophisticated specimen, shaped like a gangly question mark to epitomize mankind's intellectual quest.[128] Compared to *The Body in Question*, however, this was science programming on the slide, padded out with second-hand scraps.

In the second half of the Eighties, when proposing other scientific series, he was to be frustrated by unreceptive management strata.[129] He spoke out about the BBC succumbing to a lowbrow, ratings-based agenda, linking that to Thatcher's market-led philistinism. It was to little avail.[130] Dumbing down had begun.

⋆   ⋆   ⋆

Sussex had proved, once and for all, that a brilliant career in science was no longer attainable and had been naively idealized in the first place. In his disappointed state, what Miller caught himself pining for were the dramatic arts. Now he was suffering pangs having relinquished *them*. As early as June 1984, less than eight months into his Leverhulme fellowship, he had started publicly upbraiding academic backbiters, contrasting their viciousness with the herbivorous decency of actors.[131] He had found many university scientists to be, in his own words, uncultured jerks, not least one eminent professor who was ignorant of, and then sniffy about, Orson Welles.[132]

Miller longed, too, for the knockabout affection of the rehearsal room, the designer's charmingly untidy workshops, and, as he put it, 'all that intense activity dedicated to the realisation of a beautiful object'.[133] In truth, no one had fully suspended their disbelief in 1983. He was called the retiree in question and, with hindsight, he agrees that he was a fool to have proclaimed that he was quitting.

Soon he was rubbing shoulders once more with those in the performing arts, because he was named as the new chairman of the Edinburgh Fringe Festival in 1984. Holding this post (which did not entail any hard work) for the next decade, he served as a jovial figurehead. His most vivid memory is of a none-too-aesthetic, but hilariously anti-hierarchical incident at one of the festival's annual cavalcades. He was waving to the crowds from an open-top vintage car, as in a royal progress, only to be hailed at a pelican crossing by a raggedy drunk. The latter, leaning into the vehicle for a wee chat, noted the occupant's eye dropping to his urine-soaked trousers and quipped, quick as a flash, 'Oh ay, I've bin havin' some problems wi' ya toilet facilities.'

In 1985 Miller was back directing, with his *Don Giovanni* opening at the English National Opera.[134] If it was ironic that his not-so-final West End play had been *Hamlet* – the tragedy of a man who could not make up his mind – then the same went for this Mozart. The tale of a playboy who failed to renounce frivolity marked Miller's return to his so-called mistress, showbiz. His vision was a gloomy one, evoking the eighteenth-century Gothic murk of Goya and Fuseli's nightmares. William Shimmell, playing the eponymous philanderer, was pursued by Lesley Garrett, Felicity Lott and Josephine Barstow around a looming brick tower which split and revolved to create multiple locations: a piece of architecture as changeful as the man himself.[135]

One surprise for traditionalists was the Commendatore's arrival at supper. The statue of the late patriarch, coming to life to chastise Giovanni, was far less marmoreally stiff than usual, sitting down at the table without any supernatural effort.[136] The finale did not entail Giovanni falling through a trapdoor into hellfire either. Inspired by the historian Richard Cobb's writings on dishonoured ladies who were found drowned in the Seine, this staging had the Don climactically dragged off by the spectres of bedraggled women he had driven to abortions and suicide – his psychological demons. Some even brandished their gory foetuses and slit wrists. 'I thought, "What is hell?"' says Miller. '"Hell is the harm we have done by our actions . . . come back to haunt us".'[137]

In fact, he pictured this Lothario as a bored aristocrat doomed from the start, relentlessly doing the rounds in his personal hell of compulsive seducing, weary but never satisfied.[138] Thus the 'Catalogue' aria enumerating Giovanni's conquests – normally played as a lengthy laugh – grew arid and desperate. Miller saw him as almost vampiric, and as less interested in possessing females than in dispossessing male competitors.

Most reviewers were not allured, unfavourably comparing this production to Peter Hall's at Glyndebourne.[139] The staging, nevertheless, became a central pillar of the ENO's repertoire for seven years, and an increasing number of critics came to appreciate its relative traditionalism, compared to, say, Peter Sellars' superhip Spanish Harlem version, featuring a Big Mac supper and heroines on heroin.[140]

Opera houses in Italy, America, Finland and New Zealand imported Miller's *Giovanni*, and his assistant Karen Stone (later head of Graz Opera) felt that he thoroughly understood the tragicomic mix. 'That's why his production', she says, 'could grow over the years, get a good patina and be hugely successful . . . For the last ENO revival, people were queuing outside.'[141]

Miller's next production at the Coliseum, his Grand Hotel *Mikado*, was a huge immediate hit, starring Eric Idle as Ko-Ko, the Lord High Executioner.[142] Harewood's successor, Peter Jonas, had been wondering how the company could survive the ongoing diminution of government funding, and on the day he met Miller for a brainstorming session he returned to work beaming.[143] Miller instantly developed the joyous idea of taking Gilbert and Sullivan's well-known operetta and tossing out all the old Japanese nonsense. He would wittily anglicize the piece or, to be more precise, bring out its true nationality.[144]

Though he had always associated G&S with fusty revues and ossified D'Oyly Carte productions, he grasped – as had G. K. Chesterton – that the jokes were all about English life. The cod-Asian names were from Nanny's potty-training and nursery talk: Nanki-Poo, Peep-Boo and Yum-Yum. Moreover, Gilbert was satirizing Britannia's institutions: the class system, royals, the Cabinet. 'It's as English as Buckingham Palace garden parties and the Eton-Harrow match,' Miller announced.

The joke-Oriental town of Titipu was transformed, by set designer Stefanos Lazaridis, into a dazzling, white Grand Hotel somewhere on the UK's south coast, a 1930s establishment with surreal touches.[145] Everyone was dapper in monochrome, with hilariously pukka accents based on Noël Coward's *Brief Encounter*. 'I'm to be *merried* today to the *men* I love best,' exclaimed Lesley Garrett's Yum-Yum. Bonaventura Bottone's Nanki-Poo resembled Jack Buchanan or a P. G. Wodehouse type in blazer and boater. Garrett and the other little maids from school sported gymslips, like caricatures out of an old Footlights skit or St Trinian's.

Observing that the Thirties' silver-screen musicals and the Marx Brothers' nuttiness had been influenced by Gilbert and Sullivan, Miller extended the filmic references to Hollywood. His vision was culturally Anglo-American in that regard. A chorus line of chambermaids, bellboys and wacky headless waiters imitated Busby Berkeley dance routines.[146] Eric Idle was having a ball as a would-be clubbable Ko-Ko, being a medley of Groucho Marx and Max Wall in an 'Anyone for tennis?' mode. Maybe there was, additionally, a hint of Hitler about his moustache. The autocratic Mikado, with a goatee and near-planetary girth, was a cartoon colonialist, resembling Oliver Hardy crossed with Sidney Greenstreet in *Casablanca* (or, some said, Sir Peter Hall).[147]

The country's Savoyards could have been up in arms because Miller had provocatively alluded, in the planning stages, to an 'Entebbe raid' on those who had assumed custody of G&S. That had only encouraged the likes of I. E. Snellgrove of East Grinstead to fume, on the *Sunday Telegraph* letters page, about the imminent costly wrecking of a classic.[148]

Previous adaptations had, in fact, been more radical: the rescored jazz version *The Hot Mikado*, from 1939; Michael Winner's 1963 film *The Cool Mikado*, with re-orchestrations incorporating the cha-cha-cha; and the reggae *Black Mikado* of 1975.[149] In the end, Miller's production did not outrage the conservative contingent because it was frightfully British and not aggressively satirical. It repatriated the work in a teasing yet pleasing way.

His 1930s vision created a feel-good bubble, permitting escapism. Even Ko-Ko's 'Little List', which slipped in up-to-the-minute digs about politicos and celebs, was delivered in a cheeky rather than a caustic humour. Sounding more high camp than highbrow, the director gayly described the show as an enormous 'meringue' of an entertainment – Miller light?[150]

Jonas knew that the company was on to a winner even before opening night. As he recalls:

> In rehearsals, everyone sensed that this was something extraordinary. I used to go and sit in endless performances just for the fun of it, and to recover – [feeling] the layers of damage which the Arts Council had done to me during the day peeling off like a rotten artichoke . . . It was absolutely magnificent and it became a hit such as the ENO has never known since.[151]

Miller's Grand Hotel is now iconic, one of the most instantly recognized settings in the business. Along with *Rigoletto*, it made him Britain's best-known opera director.[152] The production became Christmas viewing on ITV in 1987, with an audience of three million. In the accompanying documentary, entitled *An Innocent Source of Merriment*, the director was filmed having such a good time that he rolled around on the floor laughing at Idle's shoe-licking scene. 'It was one of the greatest moments in my life, getting Jonathan Miller in hysterics!' Idle exclaims. The Public Broadcasting Service, PBS, telecast the opera across the States as part of its *Great Performances* series.[153] Today it is on DVD and, with a longevity to rival Andrew Lloyd Webber's megamusical *Phantom of the Opera*, it remains in the Coliseum's repertoire, drawing fans aged eight to eighty.[154]

To a degree, this directorial vision was personal as well as popular. Most evidently, it drew on Miller's avid boyhood cinema-going, and maybe there was a trace of his 1939 sojourn on the south coast: that extended holiday with Nanny in Rottingdean, away from wartime London. Emanuel, in his old age, sometimes stayed at Brighton's Grand Hotel, and his son had recently returned to the seaside with his scientific sallies to the same town.[155] More fundamentally, the Thirties constituted Miller's earliest memories of Englishness and, as he has pointed out, that decade's influence ran on through the Forties and Fifties. Having scoffed, as a young man, at the period's protracted fustiness and sentimentality – those awful Footlights flannels and boaters – he was now looking back with a mix of satire and nostalgia, mocking those old-school chaps in blazers, yet celebrating the era's breezy side, its zany humour and chic style.[156]

What, though, of his growing inner feeling that, in Britain in the Eighties, he was no longer at home?

·13·

THE MID-EIGHTIES

Going international; *Subsequent Performances*;
finito at the ENO (for now)

EVEN AS HE WAS STAGING *The Mikado*, Miller told one journalist that Britain
now seemed 'an ugly, racist, rancorous little place' from which the kindness
had evaporated.[1] To put that in context, the UK was socially and economically
riven in the mid-Eighties. Brash yuppies were making stacks of money in the
City while other citizens struggled to make ends meet. Unemployment figures
surpassed even the Great Depression. Bitter disputes between unions and bosses
led, during 1984–6, to violent clashes in the miners' strike and in the Wapping
dispute (at the plant owned by media mogul Rupert Murdoch). By then ensconced
for her second term in office, Thatcher had also tightened immigration controls,
and another spate of race-related riots had broken out in Brixton, Tottenham and
Birmingham in 1985.[2]

England now struck Miller as 'drudging and grudging', with his aversion to
British reviewers remaining unabated. Globetrotting was starting to seem like the
best option. 'I'm not a fugitive from an oppressive regime, but I feel myself a
fugitive from a regime I don't like very much,' he told *Marxism Today*.[3] Thus the
centrifugal phase of his career really got going on the continent in the Eighties.
His failed Viennese *Midsummer Night's Dream* was soon forgotten, and his
reputation enjoyed a boost after Frankfurt Opera invited him to stage *The Flying
Dutchman*.[4] Though repelled by Wagner's notorious anti-Semitism, he accepted
this invitation because racism was not a major issue in *Der fliegende Holländer*
where the gloomy hero sails the seas, seeking someone wholly adoring.[5]

Miller loved the music's fantastic, deep, oceanic orchestrations and he did not
recoil from the plot's Romantic supernaturalism. He echoed the painter Caspar
David Friedrich's seascapes, with mist-shrouded ships and silhouetted crags,
to create a sense of metaphysical mystery hanging over nature and penetrating
people's minds. He made the heroine, Senta, into a visionary artist. Not just
gazing at a portrait of the famed Dutchman, she was surrounded by canvases
which uncannily anticipated his arrival and final destiny.[6]

251

Miller headed off to the States too, staging *Così fan tutte* at St Louis' pioneering Opera Theatre, in a leafy corner of Missouri.[7] There he instantly bonded with a delightful new colleague, a brilliant young conductor called Calvin Simmons who was considered to be America's answer to Simon Rattle at that time. Still only 32, he was already musical director of the Oakland Symphony Orchestra – the first African-American to hold such a post – and everything he touched was turning to gold.

A flamboyant San Franciscan, he would regularly burst into 'You are My Sunshine' to announce tea breaks in rehearsals, and Miller adored him. Both were bright, entertaining showmen, without any competitiveness in this case. The *New York Times* correspondent Linda Blandford came to watch them at work and wrote of an amazing harmony between the two. Soon she was reporting, 'Miller looks positively angelic. It has been blissful. He and Simmons have become inseparable.' Most importantly, they were kindred spirits in their artistic aims. 'Jonathan and I are both classicists,' Simmons remarked. 'His approach is my approach.'[8]

Miller recalls with unstinting warmth:

> Calvin was just wonderful. I don't think I've ever worked so intimately and so easily with someone as I did with him . . . and it was just the most wonderfully convivial time. We used to have breakfast together every morning and buy each other books – he was fantastically well-read – and, you know, we'd go out with the girls, go out with the chaps.

Miller organized a jitterbug expedition to the Casa Loma Ballroom and the conductor encouraged shopping-mall sprees during which the director happily stocked up on shirts at Brooks Brothers.[9] The Opera Theatre's chief, Richard Gaddes, hosted homely supper parties too, dishing out lasagne and ice-cream while Miller zoomed through *Beyond the Fringe* sketches and Simmons launched into *Mikado* numbers.[10]

In the rehearsals for *Così*, Blandford thought the singers looked intellectually shell-shocked at Miller's erudite references. Among the company were the soon-to-be-star tenor Jerry Hadley and baritone Thomas Hampson. The latter begs to differ, saying:

> It was at the very beginning of my career and it was a big deal for me, and for Jerry. I was absorbing everything – buying books and getting into the science of the mind – and Jonathan also had a pivotal impact on how I developed as an artist, saying 'Go with the flow' . . . [encouraging me] to instinctually convey character without posturing . . . He was my mentor. He's my hero really, and he seemed extraordinarily happy at St Louis. Halcyon days.

Miller's staging evolved from his Kent Opera *Così*. The action was now set in a revolving wooden box, with Don Alfonso more clearly conducting a kind of lab experiment on the paired lovers. He was seen in his study surrounded by microscopes and eighteenth-century chemistry equipment.[11] If some feminists had been annoyed by his BBC *Taming of the Shrew,* the director was now redressing the balance regarding sexual equality. Qualifying *Così*'s traditionally misogynistic message – that all women prove fickle – Miller had the partner-switching become a lesson in life where both sexes saw their weaknesses exposed.

The production was a triumph. It is still talked about on the international circuit, along with Alfred Lunt's renowned *Così* at the Met. The *New York Times* critic, Donal Henahan, declared that Miller, if not already the world's best opera director, was thinking more incisively than anyone else about how to stage classics for modern audiences. 'A more intellectually provocative and internally consistent *Così* you are not likely to come across in a lifetime,' he stated.[12] The American TV network PBS booked in to film a documentary series about Miller and Simmons' *Don Giovanni*, scheduled for the following summer, and the duo decided they were going to wrap up Mozart's operas, do the lot.

Then, tragically, just a few weeks after *Così*'s last night, Simmons drowned. He had been canoeing on a lake and was caught in a storm. Miller was devastated by the news, heartbroken to have lost such a joyful friend. He surely felt something akin, now, to the deep shock his mother had experienced on hearing that her brother had been torpedoed at sea. For a while, he lost the will to work at all, and he would never set foot in St Louis again because, as he says, he could not bear to go back there.[13]

Eventually he did recover enough to work on *Così* again. Three years later, he filmed a television version as a USA–UK collaboration with an accompanying documentary, *Miller on Mozart*.[14] Thomas Hampson and Ashley Putnam, from his St Louis cast, were joined by an ENO favourite, Jean Rigby.

As with *King Lear* and *Hamlet, Così* illustrates Miller's marked habit of creating multiple productions of a single work, reiterating core aspects but with modifications over time. Compared to his Kent Opera and St Louis stagings, this version was set in a more naturalistic Neapolitan villa, with sunlight pouring through drawing-room windows and a view of Vesuvius.[15] In a subsequent production (in Italy), his setting would be inspired by the eighteenth-century canvases of Thomas Jones, who painted views of Naples' higgledy-piggledy rooftops.[16] Finally and most radically, he would update this piece in the 1990s, with modern-day Armani outfits and mobile phones.

⋆   ⋆   ⋆

In 1986, the same year in which he completed his TV version of *Così*, he was busy with the launch of *Subsequent Performances*.[17] This fascinating book – his key text about the art of theatre-making and his own productions – explained why he found such repeat-plays engrossing. As he underlined, when performed live on stage, dramatic works can never be identically reiterated, even from one night to the next. Their significance, moreover, changes for audience members, from place to place, from epoch to epoch (and that would apply to a filmed version as well). The notion of an objective, definitive reading is, therefore, a nonsense.

Rather, Miller argued, dramas are 'renovated' or gain 'afterlives' through ever-modulating productions and subjective re-viewings.[18]

This thesis implies that an innovative director, such as himself, is in tune with the vital, protean nature of such works. At the same time, he emphasized that those works, and hence their stagings, had inherent deep structures, persistent elements. To help illuminate his theory, *Subsequent Performances* drew the biological analogy:

> As Darwin pointed out, careful analysis shows that the fin of a porpoise, the paw of a lion, the hoof of a horse . . . are all related to one another by their common descent from a prototypical vertebrate limb. The successive performances of a play or an opera can be compared to this process.[19]

That correlation highlights how consistently Miller had been engaged by the whole notion of reproductions and variations, ever since Sid Pask's school lessons about baupläne and evolution. It also serves to demonstrate how *Subsequent Performances* and *The Body in Question* were like mirror images in terms of the Two Cultures. Intellectual and lavishly illustrated, both were coffee-table publications with brains: the volume on medicine enriched by plentiful metaphors from the arts; the one on theatre packed with scientific similes.

Further leitmotifs were shared with not only *The Body in Question* but also *States of Mind*, especially regarding *Subsequent Performances*' interest in the visual teasers beloved of neurologists. The previously mentioned Necker Cube, for instance, now served as a neat comparison for how a dramatic character can spring into three-dimensional life in alternative ways, if their lines are read differently.[20] So, even as Miller was discussing the innovations and changes entailed in restagings, he was revisiting *recurrent* ideas such as the Necker Cube from *changing* and *innovative* angles.

While expounding on the ephemeral nature of dramatic renditions, maybe he wanted to counter that as well. The nearest he ever came to a professional autobiography, *Subsequent Performances* committed his own account of his productions to paper, thereby giving them a more permanent kind of afterlife – in print.

Again, he had found it difficult to write down his ideas, and some book reviewers pointed out that his line of argument might have been tidier, but the vitality of *Subsequent Performances* came from the author thinking on his feet, having subsequent thoughts.[21] Overall, his contentions were hailed as fantastically stimulating. Michael Billington called it a brilliant book (which immediately went on the cover of the paperback) and the *Evening Standard* proclaimed: 'On the evidence of this, [Miller] could give us a new manual of Shakespearean production to sit beside the great preface of Harley Granville Barker.' When the book was launched in America, one dazzled columnist even surmised: 'Leaving Da Vinci out of it, on the grounds that he wrote backwards and almost never finished anything, there has probably been nobody like Miller since Aristotle.'[22]

*　　　*　　　*

As time passed, Miller found himself working more frequently in the USA. He dismisses his first production for LA Opera, Wagner's *Tristan und Isolde*, as an unwise brush with David Hockney.[23] It was meant to be a glorious big-name event, with the California-based painter designing the show. However, the composer's *Gesamtkunstwerk* theories, about synthesizing music with drama and the visual arts, did nothing to make Miller and Hockney see eye to eye. As the artist drew disproportionate press attention, the director observed that his own role was being reduced to that of a docile traffic cop or real-estate agent, 'showing people around the set'.[24] Some who witnessed the end result strained to see any input from him at all.[25]

The conductor Zubin Mehta, who was caught in the middle, recollects: 'It was a tug of war! They didn't get along . . . At one rehearsal [where Hockney was trying out myriad-hued lighting], I suddenly heard Jonathan saying, "That looks like a nightclub in Beirut!"' Afterwards Miller trounced the gigantic, cut-out designs, commenting that they resembled a pop-up book, thunderously over-coloured.[26] Obviously, there was a time and a place for pop-up books and, in his opinion, recreating paintings by old masters was more fitting for the stage. Hockney has since riposted that Miller was not interested in the metaphysical aspects of the piece and declined to listen to the score with him, during a seemingly endless car journey to Santa Barbara.[27] The director never worked with Hockney again, or with Wagner.[28]

He had miles more fun restaging *The Mikado* for the same LA company. On that occasion, he reunited with Dudley Moore who, having split from Peter Cook, had been starring in Hollywood movies including *Arthur*.[29] Moore was nervous about returning to the stage, but he agreed to take the Eric Idle role of Ko-Ko after he met Miller for lunch and they instantly slipped into larky mode.[30]

Moore relaxed slightly too much. His mind was not entirely on the matter in hand when rehearsals began. That was on a Monday after he had spent the weekend celebrating his latest marriage (number three). He reported to work with his bride, the towering model Brogan Lane, still on his arm. He further frustrated other cast members by not bothering – or not being able – to learn his lines.[31] At one point, the script-bound celebrity was heard to wail: 'I love Jonathan. All I wanted was to have lunch with him, and now I'm doing Ko-Ko!'[32] In the end his performance was charming, though never word-perfect, and the show was a box-office hit. Miller recalls:

> We had a good time together in Los Angeles. We saw a great deal of each other, went out to dinner and laughed a lot. It was easy, it was nice . . . but we were never really intimate friends. I suppose I had a certain sort of culpably condescending view towards the life that he led in California. It seemed to me sort of fatuously New Age, 'finding himself' . . . psychoanalytic groups and . . . lots of West Coast friends who were, you know, these rather bosomy girls.

A decade later, when Moore was diagnosed with progressive supranuclear palsy (a brain-destroying neurological disease related to Parkinson's), Miller was horrified and desperately sympathetic. He tried to re-establish contact, wanting to offer some comfort, but never managed to penetrate the superprotective shield of Moore's musician-friends.

When *The Mikado* was restaged at Houston Grand Opera, Eric Idle rejoined the cast.[33] He had a joyful time with Miller, going out to eat tapas, discussing everything from philosophy to baseball. 'Jonathan's just the finest company in the world – him and Mike Nichols,' Idle declares, and he adds a coda to that episode. It had occurred to him that Mel Brooks' film *The Producers* would make a great musical, so he asked Brooks if Miller could stage it in London. The idea was that the comic duo, Bialystock and Bloom, could be played by Brooks and Idle. The former turned down the idea, only to take it up later and see it become a massive hit, without Miller or Idle on board. The ex-Python struck gold with the song-and-dance version of *Spamalot* instead, but he plumped for Nichols as his director that time round. Miller thus missed out on two Broadway and West End musicals, which would have made him a fortune.

★   ★   ★

During the Eighties, Miller became an increasingly celebrated director in Italy as well as in the States. Learning to cope with Shakespeare in a foreign language, he reworked his *Measure for Measure* for a production that toured to Rome and Verona. He was delighted by his Isabella, the admired actress Elisabetta Pozzi, even if the dress rehearsal in Verona's alfresco amphitheatre turned into a hair-raising disaster when a mighty storm whipped off the Alps along the River Adige. The wind lifted the whole set into the air, then smashed it to the ground. Luckily, no one was killed.[34]

A big political risk was taken when he made his Italian operatic debut at Florence's prestigious, annual Maggio Musicale festival.[35] Miller's take on *Tosca* generated startled headlines as the news spread that this visiting director was to touch the still raw nerve of Italy's wartime memories, a subject charged with suppressed guilt and grief. Puccini's revered classic was to be updated from the Napoleonic era to 1943, the final year of Mussolini's regime, when the Allies were moving in to liberate Rome. The police chief, Scarpia, would be played as a Fascist, with a troop of OVRA henchmen – Italy's equivalent of Hitler's Gestapo. This meant that Scarpia's tortured prisoner, the artist Cavaradossi (beloved of the diva-heroine, Tosca), was a resistance sympathizer. The set was, moreover, to be a vast bomb-damaged church, framing Scarpia's offices and symbolically leaning to the right, as if morally skewed.[36]

Before opening night, a Christian Democrat member of Florence's City Council denounced the production as a publicly funded scandal and 'true infamy', if it was going to associate the Church with Fascist atrocities. A wild conspiracy theory was aired, furthermore. The English director and Zubin Mehta – the Maggio

Musicale's Indian-born conductor, who also ran the Israel Philharmonic – might be part of a Semitic plot to tar the Vatican, it was suggested.[37] This was starting to sound like *The Protocols of the Elders of Zion, Mark II.*

The ENO, co-producing the piece, was taken aback. 'We had no idea', exclaims Peter Jonas, 'that it would become this huge, political hot potato, with fraught newspaper articles saying, "Ah God, we are going to be confronted with our collaborative past!"' Miller and his singers braced themselves for picketing and barracking. As Mehta reveals, religious right-wingers had telephoned the opera house making darker threats. 'We didn't tell Jonathan half of it,' he says. 'We even had calls from the mayor's office saying, "Are you sure you know what you're doing?"' On opening night, a contingent of armed police (of a protective, rather than a menacing variety) surrounded the Teatro Comunale, fearing that it would be attacked. Inside, the capacity audience waited on tenterhooks.

In the run-up to all this, the cantilevered church had also been enormously troublesome, just technically. In his desire to show the international world that he was the greatest designer on earth, Stefanos Lazaridis had produced a monstrosity of weight and size. The stagehands could not hoist it, leading to a rash of crisis meetings. Jonas had to fly out from London to pour oil on the troubled waters, having two lunches a day to calm people down, and when the careening house of God was finally erected, it proved a health hazard, unsettling the eye and brain. Miller's assistant, Karen Stone, recalls working onstage into the small hours with the lighting crew:

> It looked fabulous but suddenly everything started to spin around me. I looked at this wire hanging down and it appeared to be hanging at an angle. [With its sloping floor and walls] the set created this optical illusion. You didn't know what was the horizontal anymore.

At the technical rehearsal, one of the children in the cast was sick and a chorister fell off the stairs, breaking a shoulder blade. The lack of a handrail sparked another blazing stage-management row.

For all that, on opening night, this seemingly fated show performed a volte-face. As Miller describes it:

> I was fully expecting shouting, booing and showers of missiles, but I stood in the wings and there was this tidal wave of almost hysterical enthusiasm. I have never had such an overwhelming response. I mean, little old men and women came up to me afterwards, backstage, saying, 'Thank you, for remembering our dead,' and stuffing these pieces of paper in my pockets with the names of their fathers and sons who had been killed by the Fascists. I was in tears and Rachel was overcome . . . And it had the most astounding reviews.

The audience had flooded down to the orchestra rail, like a rock-concert crowd, and cheered for fifteen minutes. Miller's fellow director Elijah Moshinsky was there and confirms: 'It was amazing, a very brave and shocking production, and half the audience virtually carried Jonathan off on their shoulders.' The tenting of Italy's wounds had been therapeutic.

The run's sensational success led to a long and fruitful partnership between Miller and the Maggio Musicale. He is likened, by Mehta, to Italy's great director Giorgio Strehler, having a comparable sense of inventiveness and humour. Even Miller's supposed foe, Tom Sutcliffe from the *Guardian*, reported from Florence that this *Tosca* was astonishingly good and chilling in its understated, bureaucratic horrors. A typist sat tapping away by a side-room routinely used for torture. Caravadossi was shot unceremoniously, seated backwards, straddling a chair.[38] Scarpia quietly toyed with Tosca's neckline then crawled at her feet, beside his filing cabinet (with echoes of *Measure for Measure*'s Angelo, but more sadomasochistic). Ultimately, Eva Marton's Tosca – the diva-turned-politicized assassin – strewed shredded death warrants over Scarpia's corpse, rather than piously lighting candles.[39]

*　　*　　*

Back in England in 1987, when Miller's Fascist *Tosca* was remounted by the ENO, the euphoric bubble burst. In the first place, more snags arose with the set. Refusing to fit inside the Coliseum, the church had to be hacked down to size. Even then, performances were delayed as the sweating stage crew forced the darned thing into place. Further horrible accidents followed. The tenor Eduardo Alvares, playing Caravadossi, fell on to sharp wire-mesh when rehearsing the execution scene. He needed over 70 stitches and skin grafts on his nose and lip. It had been his own decision to have his hands tied behind his back for authenticity, and Miller helped his swift recovery by racing to the hospital with him and insisting that a plastic surgeon was found at top speed. Alvares coped heroically, staggering back to sing at press night, but the director still partly blames himself for the calamity. On top of that, the soprano Janice Cairns suffered spinal injuries in a subsequent revival, when performing Tosca's suicidal jump through a window. She was laid up for months.

Miller's concept met with a British critical backlash too. By the late 1980s, operatic updates had become a widespread fad, with many gimmicky directors jumping on the bandwagon. The ENO was, at this point, being run by the so-called Power House triumvirate: Jonas, Mark Elder (as music director) and David Pountney (as director of productions).[40] They were being accused of pursuing the modernizing trend ad nauseam, and because of Miller's landmark *Rigoletto*, he was unfairly branded as a directorial Dr Who, as if he were habitually time-travelling. His *Tosca* was dismissed all the more readily because the British critics had already seen a Mussolini-era *Tosca*, several years earlier, courtesy of Scottish Opera.[41]

Although usually appreciative, Rodney Milnes loathed Miller's version, and this had repercussions, as he remembers:

I think it was at the time of *Tosca* . . . I admired Jonathan very much, and we had planned to do a popular book about opera – with him talking into a tape recorder . . . I was really looking forward to it and we made the first date, but he didn't turn up. So I rang and he said, 'Oh, something else turned up.' We set a date for the next week and he didn't turn up and not a word ever. Never referred to again! It's things like that make it hard to love Jonathan as much as one does. Stuff happens.

The director remains galled, even now, about *Tosca*'s reception in London.

Jonas still sings the production's praises, emphasizing that it became a box-office hit with a concept no less ingenious than the Mafia *Rigoletto*. 'Though the press', he says, 'were somewhat grudging, Jonathan's transposition was a perfect fit.' Even so, opening in the winter of 1987, Miller's *Barber of Seville* was to be his last for the ENO under Jonas' regime. Rather than time-travelling with this popular comedy from 1816, he took it on a short trek across continental Europe. In spite of Rossini's title, Miller argued that the piece was not really Spanish at all, being far more influenced by Goldoni and Italian *commedia dell'arte* traditions.[42] In his staging, therefore, masked Punchinellos gathered in a shadowy alley to help serenade Dr Bartolo's jealously guarded ward, Rosina. Other visitors to the old medic's abode resembled antique Venetian marionettes or clockwork automata, and he had a faintly kinky cabinet of curiosities. This featured wax-model body parts, based on a historic Bolognese collection.[43]

Once again, press night unleashed lacerating criticisms. Tom Sutcliffe concluded that if the director didn't want this *Barber* to be funny, then he had succeeded brilliantly.[44] Nonetheless, when it came to be revived, some papers began to acknowledge that it was delighting the public, and by 1995 (with Jane Glover conducting a vibrant cast) the show was being praised as yet another hit.[45] In 2005, it was trumpeted as a joyous farce, advertised all over town as a highlight of the ENO's crowd-pulling season co-sponsored by Sky. It was back again in 2008, marking its twenty-first anniversary, and it is scheduled for another run in 2013.

There is a thorny debate about Miller's long-running productions. One camp argues that the revivals – the subsequent performances – are tightened up by the staff directors whenever he is not there in person. This remains disputed, however. Several critics from 1995 onwards thought that coarsened panto-style comedy was creeping into *The Barber*, without him on board.[46] He speaks of the piece being messed around, sometimes, by young men who think they can do better than him, producing a kind of polystyrene version of the original, without weight or sharpness. He reserves his admiration for two deft deputies, David Ritch and Karen Stone. She remarks:

It's a legitimate criticism [that] . . . many directors who've come from theatre or film are used to working with highly creative actors who don't need instructing on every move [as some opera singers do]. When Jonathan works well, it is with talented actor-singers and with an assistant director who sorts out the [other stage] business . . . So, some productions do benefit from revivals . . .

But Jonathan also leaves you with a wealth of detail and information so, if you are on track and you understand the basic tenets, you can enrich it every time . . . He absolutely understands that, with a different cast, you're going to do it differently. You can be terrified when other directors come in for the last three days [of revival rehearsals], but with Jonathan it's tremendously pleasurable collaborative work. He'll have half a dozen fabulous ideas, be gorgeously amusing, and just energize everyone around him.

In any case, Miller says that it was *The Barber*'s scorned premiere which caused the Power House troika to dismiss him as passé. At the time, he complained that if it wasn't one thing, it was the other. Either he was being called a vandal by the conservative clique, whom he called 'disgusting old opera queens', or else he was being shunned as a fossil by the new order's avant-gardists who were churning out deconstructionist bosh.[47]

By 1988, a Rossini cycle that he was supposed to direct for the ENO had been shelved, and the schism was official when he ceased to be billed as the company's associate director.[48] Asked about the parting of ways, Pountney retrospectively comments (in writing):

Jonathan is a brilliant person and perhaps above all a brilliant conversationalist – it always seemed to me he belonged in some 18th century salon . . . When [however] we got going at the Coli, Mark and I and later Peter Jonas were very keen to break new ground and to take a generally more radical stance. Jonathan's work sometimes has the 'appearance' of being radical, but for many of the reasons I give above [e.g. his productions' reliance on inspired moments, with dull, undetailed stretches in between] it rarely is [radical] in substance . . . [So] it was for that – no doubt slightly puritanical point of view that we deliberately turned away from him. That was, quite naturally when he started criticising US – (I think we were known as the Ceaucescus – or something like that).[49]

The hostilities were muted by comparison with Miller's rift with Peter Hall at the NT, post-Olivier. Yet this was, once again, a regime change issue and it was Lord Harewood, the previous boss, who was to retain Miller's affection. In contrast to 'the Ceaucescus', he likens Harewood to a 'wonderful, gracious Whig grandee'.[50]

Though Pountney says that he and Miller always got on well, certain insiders allege that the ousting push mainly came from him, with complex reasons behind it.[51] One colleague says that Pountney (who was, of course, a director himself) put excessive emphasis on sleek choreography. Instead of valuing Miller's brilliant ideas, he kept complaining that his blocking was incompetent. The colleague states: 'Jonathan was the real auteur-director, the only one we had. He created an identity for the ENO, but the jealousy it created was extraordinary.' Jonas comments on the issue of personal frictions:

Jonathan did get on with everybody, except I don't think he got on very well with my friend David Pountney . . . That wasn't a marriage made particularly in heaven, though they're much more similar than they probably think . . . [They] certainly didn't have rows but Jonathan would bitch about David to me and David would bitch about Jonathan to me, and I told them both that they were taking each other too seriously . . . Maybe Jonathan sometimes felt he should have been director of productions.

Jonas emphasizes that such an eclectic intellect deserved to be treasured, and he even speaks with nostalgic amusement of the man's 'glorious talent to insult'. This is with reference not to the Ceaucescus jibe, but rather to a VIP reception at the Coliseum where Mrs Thatcher was spouting about the arts. Miller promptly declared that her grating opinions were like fingernails being drawn across a blackboard, and he went on to publicly savage 'her odious suburban gentility' and 'sentimental saccharine patriotism, catering to the worst elements of commuter idiocy'. Not surprisingly, some journalists damned his snobbishness, and his further aperçus hardly cleared the air. He observed, unforgettably, that she sounded like a 'perfumed fart', and he called her the loathsome, culture-killing equivalent of typhoid.[52] It was, Jonas believes, damaging for the ENO. But it was exhilarating.

Miller's craving for praise struck the triumvirate as harder to handle, though Pountney points out that the trait was, 'considering his enormous abilities, quite touching really'. Another insider highlights the dilemma:

Jonathan is very, very critical. He gets a quick swish in about his colleagues' shows but, because of his own paranoia and insecurities, you can't say [in rehearsals]: 'Jonathan, I don't think this scene is working.' Before you draw breath, he says: 'I think it's one of the best things I've ever done!' This is when someone is giving a quite ordinary performance . . . It inhibits creative criticism. One felt part of him couldn't cope with hearing it wasn't perfect.

Like Jonas, Elder expresses lasting fondness for Miller, whatever his foibles. He underlines:

Jonathan is an extraordinary, incredibly compassionate and wonderful man, and it is very important to stress that he gave the company a bushel of productions that earned it thousands and thousands of pounds. They've been the company's lifeblood because they have enough that's eccentric and enough that's traditional . . . [But] then it was a question of us, as a team, deciding to what extent we wanted the style of Jonathan's productions to dominate and, because several operas he'd done were central pillars of the repertoire, there began to be a feeling that we shouldn't overburden it with his view of things.

On the one hand, his directing was considered too hit and miss. On the other, it seems, he was a victim of his own success.

·14·

NEARING THE NINETIES

Long Day's Journey; the RSC;
a return to the Royal Court; running the Old Vic

WHILE THE POWER HOUSE TRIUMVIRATE was holding sway at the Coliseum, Miller had, wisely, not relinquished the theatre. He staged a major Broadway show, *Long Day's Journey into Night*, starring Jack Lemmon, which swiftly transferred to the West End, and that helped him leap from his terminated ENO contract to running the Old Vic.

Quite by chance, he had bumped into a Broadway producer in a hotel lobby and got chatting about who, in an ideal world, would play James Tyrone Snr, the father in Eugene O'Neill's famed tragedy. The play was venerated as American drama's answer to Aeschylus and Sophocles, but Miller contended that it had more in common with Neil Simon's drunken showbiz characters in *Broadway Bound*. He suggested that Lemmon, known for comic movies such as *Some Like It Hot*, would be terrifically demythologizing, because he could portray Tyrone as a barnstorming thespian who had dwindled into a mere sour old ham, a tight-fisted dad with two recriminating sons. Becoming excited as he hatched this concept, he ended up declaring he would like to direct the piece himself.

Rehearsals speedily got under way, with the production to open at New York's Broadhurst Theater.[1] Lemmon had accepted the part instantly. 'If Jonathan thought that I could [do it], then that was all I needed,' he explained afterwards.[2] The pair worked harmoniously together, the director loving his star's amenable modesty. Bethel Leslie, an old friend of Lemmon's, was cast as his morphine-addicted wife, and the fast-rising Peter Gallagher was enrolled as Edmund, the Tyrones' tubercular writer-son.

Gallagher nearly missed his chance. He failed to attend his first audition because he was having a crisis of confidence, thinking he should become a cab driver. A phone call from the big-shot producer Emanuel Azenberg brought him to his senses.[3] He picked up the receiver to be greeted by, 'Hey, Peter, Manny here. Listen, you know I'm Jewish? Uhuh. Well, I'm also half-Italian and, if you don't come into this next audition, I'm going to break your fucking legs.'

That was, Gallagher says, the most flabbergasting act of generosity he had ever encountered, and working with Miller was a tremendously uplifting experience (followed by roles in Steven Soderbergh's film *Sex, Lies and Videotape* and Tim Robbins' *The Player*).

A relative unknown at the time, Kevin Spacey was ready to beg, borrow or steal his way into playing Lemmon's bitter actor-son, James Tyrone Jnr.[4] Attending a lecture which the director was giving at the Lincoln Center's Julliard School, he filched an invite to the ensuing drinks party, out of someone's handbag. Nervously downing cocktails, waiting for a window of opportunity, the gatecrasher then slipped into Kurt Vonnegut's vacated chair abutting the guest of honour. As Miller recalls:

> This rather truculent young man accosted me and said I ought to audition him. He was very insistent and something about him made me think, 'Oh, I'll have to concede' . . . He came along first thing the next morning and, within five minutes, I said, 'Well, it seems you've got the part.' He was so outstanding.

Somewhat exaggeratedly, Miller has complained that the actor never looked back with even a wave of gratitude, which makes the show sound rather like a Broadway hit-and-run. Spacey has, on more than one occasion, spoken of *Long Day's Journey* as his breakthrough and a cherished achievement, describing Lemmon as the encouraging father figure in his career.[5] When the BBC was filming its *Arena* documentary about Miller in 2012, he and Spacey amicably met up to reminisce on camera (at the Old Vic, which Spacey now runs).[6]

Though O'Neill's family portrait is bleak, Miller characteristically brought much comic relief into the rehearsal process, and that laughter even leaked into a preview performance, when Lemmon was not yet word-perfect. Entering a festering filial scene where he should have ominously pronounced, 'There's a gloom in the air you could cut with a knife,' he ad-libbed bathetically, 'There's a gloom in this room you could shake a stick at.' Seized by a fit of giggles, Gallagher made full use of Edmund Tyrone's tubercular cough, turning his back on the audience in convulsions. Sprawling on the couch, Spacey rolled over too, desperately trying to look moody while stuffing half a cushion in his mouth.

The director's radical handling of the canonical dialogue, meanwhile, proved seriously controversial. He scorned grandiose stagings of *Long Day's Journey* which lasted four hours and indulged in *largo* intoning, as if the running time had to live up to the title. His production came in at under three hours, because he made the repetitiously grouching Tyrones talk right *over* each other. A few years earlier, in the field of British new playwriting, Caryl Churchill had experimentally meshed characters' words (notably in *Top Girls* at the Royal Court in 1982), but Miller could, equally, have been influenced by operatic arias for two or more voices singing at once.[7] The musical analogy which he drew was, in fact, with the *Grosse Fuge*, Beethoven's composition for string quartet. He played the cast a recording, and he almost conducted the play text like a score, rearranging everyone's cues very precisely, marking their overlaid speeches with bar lines.[8]

The goal, though, was to recreate truly naturalistic conversations and quarrels. His Overlapped O'Neill, as it came to be called, essentially emerged from his abiding interest in the rhythms, structures and rules (or broken rules) of conversation; in what he had, even as a schoolboy comedian, referred to as the 'sound pictures' or 'flux of noises' created in verbal exchanges. He had tentatively tried overlapping lines at Nottingham Playhouse.[9] With his West End *Three Sisters*, he had taken that further, remarking that Chekhov had an exceptional ear for real talk even while structuring his plays like sonatas.[10] Conversational turn-taking had been a topic of discussion in *States of Mind* as well.[11] He himself stresses:

> Linguistics has been a major concern of mine . . . The overlapping [in *Long Day's Journey*] was a small part of a much larger enterprise which was to restore the actual surface texture of ordinary speaking. When you restore the linguistic rubbish which gets written out by most playwrights in a process called rectification – the 'um's and 'er's, the half-finished sentences, ungrammatical structures and interruptions – people are shocked by the naturalism.

His wife comments, in passing, that this production sounded remarkably close to home in capturing the way families talk. 'I don't know if it's worse in this household than in some, but that idea of everyone speaking at once, it certainly happens a lot here,' she says. 'There's quite a fight to be heard.'

Miller predicted that his overlapping would be decried by O'Neill custodians as violent irreverence inflicted upon the master.[12] The *New York Times*' critic, Frank Rich, felt that the accelerated tempo spoiled the play's slow-building power, and a Professor B. F. Dick penned an irate letter to the same publication, to which the director riposted that only a fool would estimate a drama's greatness by its duration.[13] The British press reported a flop, too controversial for mainstream American crowds, as the run ended somewhat earlier than planned.[14]

This was no reprise of Miller's previous Broadway-bound fiascos, however. The Broadhurst went dark on what was termed Black Sunday, in a New York box-office slump that shut down five other straight plays.[15] *Long Day's Journey* ultimately received four Tony Award nominations (for the director, Lemmon, Leslie and Gallagher), and it was filmed for TV broadcast and video release. In spite of his criticisms, Frank Rich had called this *Shorter Day's Journey* fascinatingly bold and fresh. Clive Barnes of the *New York Post* saluted it as thrillingly close to life, 'one of the landmark productions of our time'.[16]

The show transferred to the West End and enjoyed high-profile coverage by Joan Bakewell on BBC TV's *Newsnight*. Some reviewers harked back to Olivier's grander portrayal of Tyrone Snr, and Miller was riled by Michael Billington who mildly questioned the tubercular Edmund's look of rude health.[17] Nonetheless, this production was hailed as magnificent, and the announcement that Miller was to become artistic director at the Old Vic was duly cheered as splendid news.[18] It was time he had a place of his own.

Before he took up the post, he gained bonus points by slipping in two further hits, for the RSC and the Royal Court. His strictly Tudor *Taming of the Shrew*, reworked in Stratford-upon-Avon, was his overdue Royal Shakespeare Company debut at the age of 53.[19] Things did not go entirely smoothly. Indeed, he nearly walked out, due to frictions with the young hotshot Fiona Shaw (his Kate).[20] 'Though we got on quite well at first,' he says, 'I found her argumentative feminism really too much . . . God, it was awful!' In his view, he had to 'take note of feminism and repudiate it' out of respect for history. 'The past is a foreign country,' he underlines, 'where they do things differently and, as I kept saying, one reason we do these plays is to visit the past.'

Barrie Rutter, who played the jocular manservant Grumio, recalls that Miller was being driven up the wall yet somehow managed to remain diplomatic. While not enamoured of the play, Shaw herself sounds surprisingly nostalgic. She speaks of relaxed rehearsals and praises Miller's notion of Kate as a Tavistock Clinic child, behaving unlovably because unloved.

Terry Hands, who was running the RSC after Trevor Nunn's departure, says the sparring matches between actress and director were inevitable and worked a treat, feeding into the play. The press applauded Miller for rescuing the company's waning reputation with a *Shrew* that was funny, truthful and moving. Though he never worked for the company again, the show transferred to London for a lengthy run.[21]

As for the Royal Court, Miller had kept the artistic director Max Stafford-Clark waiting for ages, having been appointed as an associate a decade earlier.[22] Finally, all was forgiven when he staged *The Emperor* in 1987. This dreamlike, darkly satirical chamber piece was his adaptation – co-scripted with the writer Michael Hastings – of Ryszard Kapuściński's 1978 book of the same name. The storytelling was hypnotic, with former palace attendants recalling the last days of Haile Selassie's autocratic reign in Ethiopia, and conjuring up a decaying hermetic world of Byzantine protocols.[23] Eschewing dialogue, Miller interwove monologues with fluid role-swapping and quirky, mimed episodes.[24]

He enjoyed being back in cockpit conditions in the theatre's upstairs studio, working with actors of African, Caribbean and Jordanian origins. The disabled, diminutive performer Nabil Shaban was fantastic as the beady-eyed sovereign. Gliding around in a wheelchair, he impishly bumped into the front row when imitating one of the country's dilapidated, stalling tractors, and he waved his tiny limbs with crazed glee during a bout of collective callisthenics. The director donated his fee to the fledgling designer Richard Hudson, for the set: a dusty chamber of numerous doors and spyholes, some of which opened behind the audience's heads or by their ankles, to reveal snooping ears and muttering lips.[25] With everyone dressed in anonymous suits, it had a touch of Kafka's Eastern Europe. The novel was, after all, a veiled analogy for Edward Gierek's ruinous, Seventies regime in Kapuściński's native Poland.

Fired up about Ethiopian politics, pro-Selassie demonstrators gathered outside the Royal Court, and their shouts of protest about grotesque fictions were audible throughout the press performance. Far from vitiated, the production thrilled Kapuściński, sold out in two days and was granted an extended run in the main house.[26] It toured to Poland and was filmed, by Miller, for a BBC broadcast, with his trademark wide-angle distortions and deep-focus shots used to enthralling effect.[27]

One regrettable offstage incident had occurred, as a company member recalls:

> Jonathan has these huge long arms and will occasionally wrap his arms round a person very heartily. He did that to the casting director who, ridiculously, panicked and thought he was trying to seduce her in broad daylight in her little office. There were lots of hysterical shouts of 'Jonathan! Jonathan!' and he came out looking absolutely sheepish. People do misunderstand him sometimes.

Some minor tensions simmered during the creative process too, with Hastings billed as Miller's co-director but mainly just sitting at the back and observing. Hastings suggested this was a diplomatic policy:

> Make no mistake, Jonathan is very edgy and competitive . . . and finds writers intrusive, but we did have a wonderful exchange of ideas. Max [Stafford-Clark] clearly knew he would have a strong affinity or interest in Eastern Europe . . . Jonathan identifies with other cultures as well as other times. I told him my family [ancestors] sailed to England from Amsterdam, coming from some unknown area in deeper Eastern Europe and just choosing the name of the town they landed in. He grinned and said, 'Supposing it had been Bognor!' Then his eyes lit up and he said, 'Well, we all come from somewhere, don't we.' He feels that there are long distances and travels and journeys inside people . . . and, if you went that far back, they would go through Europe to, maybe, an Oriental world or Turkey or Lebanon.

*　　*　　*

Staying in London for the moment, Miller presented his first season at the Old Vic in 1988. Taking the helm as artistic director, he made everyone on board feel as if they were 'part of one journey, one ship and one style', according to his protégé, the now renowned director Richard Jones.[28] The beautiful Victorian theatre in Waterloo, vacated by the NT company, had been bought by the Canadian father-and-son team, Ed and David Mirvish. These arts-loving businessmen (whose fortune was made through a Toronto department store) were looking for an artistic director with enough daring and flair to rival the National and draw audiences across the Thames from the hub of Theatreland.

Announcing his opening programme on a day when all Shaftesbury Avenue's playhouses had gone dark, Miller proclaimed that his hope was to light a beacon, as it were, on a promontory above the ruthless demands of normal commercial theatre. That was possible thanks to the Mirvishes' philanthropy, he said. It might have struck his old Apostolic associates from Cambridge as a curious venture: Schlegel-meets-Wilcox, the intellectual teaming up with trade. However, Miller's artistic vision was financially backed without pressure to make a large profit. The Mirvishes' intention was to break even, aiming for box-office sales of around 60 per cent.

Principally, their artistic director's adventurousness lay in embracing European classics which, at this time, were not frequently seen in London and were regarded with some trepidation. Miller was not the first pioneer in this vein but he was Waterloo's theatrical match for the Channel Tunnel, the digging of which coincided with his directorship. Influenced by his work on the international opera scene, he particularly concentrated on bringing stunning, continental-style set designs to the British theatre. So his Old Vic productions indeed vied with the strongly architectonic work of Germany's Peter Stein and France's Patrice Chéreau, as well as that of Giorgio Strehler.[29]

To further reinvigorate the Old Vic with a clear identity, the AD was to direct no fewer than five of the seven shows in his opening season. This generated much excitement. Box-office subscriptions rocketed and arts journalists saluted him for creating London's most cosmopolitan and lively new repertory theatre in years. He was helping to generate a backlash against the rot which had generally invaded the West End.[30]

In the two and three-quarter years during which he ran the building, his audiences saw a clutch of works from the French school in English translations: Racine's tragedy *Andromache*, Corneille's metatheatrical teaser *The Illusion*, and the same author's little-known comedy of mistaken identities, *The Liar*. Feydeau's farce *A Flea in Her Ear* contributed to a strong vein of humour, together with *Candide*, Bernstein's musical *après* Voltaire (a Scottish Opera co-production). From Eastern Europe came Brecht's adaptation of Reinhold Lenz's sardonic *The Tutor*, along with Alexander Ostrovsky's social satire *Too Clever by Half* and a revolutionary drama, *Marya*, by the Russian–Jewish writer Isaac Babel. Visiting companies included Yuri Lyubimov's ensemble, and Hungary's renowned Katona József Theatre troupe, the latter with its stagings of *Three Sisters* and Gogol's *Government Inspector*.[31]

In terms of neglected English dramas, George Chapman's Jacobean tragedy *Bussy D'Ambois* was reclaimed. Continuing the Old Vic's tradition of Shakespearean productions, Miller returned once more to *King Lear* (this time with Eric Porter in the title role). He also reworked his colonial *Tempest* (with the Swedish star Max von Sydow as Prospero). Lyubimov, meanwhile, brought his Russian *Hamlet*.[32] Evidently not holding a grudge, the AD employed Fiona Shaw in *As You Like It* (directed by Tim Albery), and played host to Michael Bogdanov's English Shakespeare Company with their great *War of the Roses* cycle.

Behind the scenes, he turned one of the Old Vic's attic rooms into his office, with utter informality. He had no desk, just a shabby armchair, a phone and piles of books – like another home from home. As with the *BBC Shakespeare Series*, his designers and assistants shared the space, and it functioned as a green room. Actors and stage crew wandered in and out, with coffee permanently on the go. The office was likened, at the time, to a tutor's study-cum-common room.[33] Having no closed door or appointment system was, he says, in deliberate contrast to the bureaucratic style which Peter Hall had imposed during his NT years in the Old Vic building. Instead, Miller aimed to rekindle the warmer feel of Laurence Olivier and Ken Tynan's tenure.

After a long battle with illness, Tynan had sadly been defeated by emphysema. Miller had visited him in his last days in California, finding him fighting for breath and feeling exiled from London.[34] Unable to offer any cure, he determined that Ken's spirit of raffish humour must live on in the playhouse in SE1, and he simultaneously accentuated the family atmosphere once fostered there by Olivier (who died in 1989).[35] His set designer Richard Hudson, who joined the Old Vic team after working on *The Emperor*, remembers Miller being immensely kind beyond the call of duty. 'When I split up from a relationship and was wondering where I could move to,' he says, 'Jonathan put me in the car and drove me all over the place, saying, "What about here? What about there?" That's the kind of thing he is brilliant at, generosity and openness.'

Miller's regime helped advance the careers of new and up-and-coming artists, from the actors Alex Jennings and Alex Kingston (later of *ER* fame) to the sparky translator Ranjit Bolt and the Polish poster designer Andrzej Krauze (soon snapped up by the *Guardian* as a political cartoonist).[36] Formerly Miller's assistant at Scottish Opera, Richard Jones was given a big break, entrusted with *Too Clever By Half* and further productions. Another bright young director, Roger Michell, was brought in from the RSC (several years before his TV *Buddha of Suburbia* and film *Notting Hill*).[37] With only a slim portfolio of set designs to his name, Hudson could not believe his luck either, being hired for the whole first season:

> Jonathan just said, 'Oh well, why don't you do them all,' and my jaw hit the floor. We had a ball. He introduced me to all sorts of things: painters, photographers, buildings. He would drive me all the way out to the East End to look at an abandoned shop window – filthy glass with old fittings behind it. And the inspiration for [the towering kiltered palace in] Andromache was the Coronet Cinema in Notting Hill which, at night, was lit from below with all the window frames casting these deep, odd shadows . . . The things that inspired him were wonderful.

The critics did not unanimously love *Andromache*, the first production which Miller himself directed. 'It was an uphill struggle,' he sighs, and that was literally true for his cast. This was very much his tilt-the-stage phase, and he had Racine's neoclassical, doomed House of Atreus on a precipitous incline.[38] Playing the titular stoical Trojan, Janet Suzman relished the production's strange hieratic gestures and surprising passion, but her royal sufferings on the slope soon included housemaid's knee.[39] Cast as the rival princess Hermione, Penelope

Wilton loved the visually austere look and her Fortuny-style, pleated, silk dress, except when she whisked round to exit from one scene and accidentally climbed up her own skirt, collapsing in a tangle on the floor.

A few reviewers took issue with the translation by Miller's old school friend, Eric Korn, questioning its sporadically slangy idioms. Only weeks before rehearsals started, the AD had decided that Craig Raine's commissioned adaptation – envisaging a 1950s, Nazi royal family – would not work. Korn obligingly penned the substitute at top speed. Miller still prizes it as superbly vibrant, reviling the critics' 'lordly condescension'.[40] Korn shrugged, saying he had fun indulging his suppressed yearning for glitter and greasepaint.[41]

A fair number of the press were, in fact, encouraging. 'If the rest of [Miller's] season at the Old Vic is as powerful as this [*Andromache*] . . . attendance will be compulsory,' declared the *Independent*, and the first year of programming netted five Olivier Awards.[42] The AD's own staging of *Candide*, with Patricia Routledge on board, won the Best Musical category, for striking just the right balance between the work's American writers and its European source.[43] The famously picky Bernstein flew over, apparently loved it, and was filmed backstage for its BBC telecast. Ebulliently pinching Miller on the cheek, he exclaimed, 'Hey, I think we've got it for the first time!'[44]

Two Olivier Awards went to Jones' *Too Clever by Half* which was a huge hit: Jennings won Best Comedy Performance and the director was named Most Promising Newcomer, while Hudson was chosen as Best Designer of the Year for his whole residency.[45] Miller confesses that, as with Moshinsky on the *BBC Shakespeare Series*, he felt a bit irked about Jones being so very dazzling when, as he remembers it, 'most of my productions did rather badly'.

In its entirety, his tenure was chequered. Eric Porter's Lear was much admired. *As You Like It* was not. Miller's comically sparkling *The Liar* was adored (with Jennings and Desmond Barrit as a master-servant double act), and he was proud of his *Bussy d'Ambois* (with David Threlfall as the Machiavellian court's malcontent), yet Chapman's knotty poetry was slated as dull and arcane.[46] He freely admits that his programming misfired with *The Tutor*.[47] Directed by a veteran colleague of Brecht's, it bombed, and his own staging of N. F. Simpson's absurdist *One Way Pendulum* looked more dated than he expected. Two decades had passed since he had starred in the film version.[48] Though the piece was strongly cast (with John Fortune and John Bird), it played to frighteningly small houses, the nadir being 65 bums on 1,000 seats.

Economically, this was a disaster even if other productions such as *Candide* and the Max von Sydow *Tempest* played to full capacity.[49] The proprietors had miscalculated at the outset, according to the Old Vic's financial manager, Andrew Leigh. He suggests that, driven by a zeal to realize their dream, the Mirvishes had been Panglossian optimists. Most West End investors aim to be breaking even when their ticket sales reach around 30 per cent. To hope for 60 per cent to cover one's costs was dangerous. 'We never overspent by a penny,' Leigh emphasizes. 'The income target was unrealistic.' The theatre lost money, averaging 50 per cent at the box office in the first year. Try as he might by upping the quota of Shakespeare – familiar name, safer bet – Miller could not get out of the woods.

Clinging on to his sense of humour, David Mirvish recounts how, on his initial trips to London, he would stay at the Savoy but, as the Old Vic consumed his cash, he ended up at the unbelievably seedy Jubilee Hotel, next to Stringfellows strip club.[50] Summoned to the Jubilee for a meeting, Miller rushed in yelping that he hadn't, surely, lost so much money that it had come to this! Mirvish may have been making a point, yet he is only half-joking when he says: 'We stopped before I had to sell my art collection.' Feeling the pinch was not painless. Still, Mirvish adds, 'It's not Jonathan's fault. That I would never say.'

Miller recognizes that the Mirvishes were extremely generous, but he was livid at the time when the cash flow stopped in medias res. This was in October 1990. Leigh was on holiday in Greece when he picked up an English newspaper and reeled with shock, seeing the headline, 'Miller Quits Old Vic'. Two complementary productions – *A Midsummer Night's Dream* and Botho Strauss's modern variation, *The Park* – had been in rehearsal when Mirvish suddenly pulled the plug, announcing they were not viable. Miller walked out almost instantly, leaving instructions that his wages should be distributed among the actors. Though Mirvish expressed regrets about the exigency and paid the actors more compensation than anticipated, he was vilified.[51]

That is not, however, quite the whole story. Even if the artistic director had been in his element at the Old Vic, he privately veered between elation and despair in his first year, depressed by the negative reviews. It was rumoured, in 1989, that he was tempted to move to California, with the offer of a professorial chair at UCLA.[52] He did not opt for that but he had, actually, tendered his resignation a couple of months before *The Park* and *The Dream* were summarily axed. He was due to leave in March 1991.[53] Leigh ruminates: 'David would never in a million years have got rid of Jonathan. He said he was terribly sorry [about his imminent departure] . . . though I think he was slightly relieved.'

Other associates question if Miller honoured the vow he made when appointed as artistic director. 'If I work there, I work there,' he had promised, with reference to Trevor Nunn and Peter Hall's much criticized absenteeism from the RSC and NT. Apart from one or two prior engagements, he said, it would be 'total commitment'.[54] In practice, he was not wholly devoted. His attention was never undivided.

Truth be told, there was a great deal of absenteeism when he was artistic director. In 1988, his schedule included the pre-booked *Mikado* in LA with Dudley Moore and two TV series. *My God*, on ITV, saw him presenting and discussing questions of faith with Iris Murdoch, Don Cupitt and others. Fronting Channel 4's *Four Virtuosos*, he interviewed great musicians including the pianists Murray Perahia and Vladimir Ashkenazy.[55] In the next year and nine months, before Mirvish's shutdown, he directed only *Lear* and *The Liar* at the Old Vic, while the number of projects elsewhere was fairly staggering.

Whether he was itching to be free of bureaucratic responsibilities or was simply responding to invitations, several trips abroad occurred in 1989–90. He revived *The Mikado* in Houston and tackled *Rise and Fall of the City of Mahagonny* for LA Opera, making Brecht and Weill's satire of capitalist greed distinctly local, placing it on what looked like the Hollywood set of Charlie Chaplin's *The Gold Rush*.[56]

Heading out to Florence, he reworked *Don Giovanni*, and he edited a book of fine scholarly essays on the roving playboy, entitled *The Don Giovanni Book: Myths of Seduction and Betrayal*.[57] During this stretch, he returned to directing for BBC Television's drama department, in a philosophical vein. *Dialogue in the Dark*, by Michael Ignatieff, featured the death-obsessed James Boswell (David Rintoul) encountering the sagely atheistic, ailing David Hume (Alec McCowen).[58] Again for the BBC and almost concurrently, he was fronting the medical five-parter *Who Cares?*, about coping with illness and ageing.[59]

Also broadcast during his Old Vic tenure, Channel 4's profile, *Jonathan Miller: A Full Life*, could not have been more aptly named, especially as he had managed to land two more BBC TV series.[60] In *Born Talking* he explored language and the brain.[61] Ensconced in a book-lined den, he grappled with the theories of Chomsky (one of his top interviewees) and revisited his beloved topics of neurological dysfunction, conversational turn-taking and non-verbal communication – mimicking a buzzing Jewish bee for light relief.[62] The press humorously surmised that this presenter had, in all probability, been talking eruditely when still in the womb. His handling of complex topics mightily impressed them, even if Chomsky made Nancy Banks-Smith's brain hurt.[63]

The other series was *Madness*. This was a history of the subject, looking into the rise and fall of asylums, Hitler's gassing of the mentally ill, psychoanalysis, drug therapies, and shifting definitions of madness (with the final episode called 'In Two Minds'). The reviews picked up on how Miller, even more directly than in his book on Freud, cast trenchant doubts on his father's profession.[64]

On top of all this, he was to be seen expounding his theory of comedy in *What's So Funny About That?*, a special made for the BBC science documentary strand *Q.E.D.* Here he offered a perceptive alternative to his famous relative Henri Bergson's seminal ideas on the subject. Rather than pursuing Bergsonian ideas about automata-like behaviour, he expanded on his own observation that, fundamentally, what makes us laugh is the assigning of things to wrong slots – unexpected errors of categorization or classification.[65]

It is a persuasive thesis, better than Bergson's. However, the Mirvishes were probably not amused by the professional category-jumping that kept dislodging their artistic director from his Waterloo pigeonhole. Of course, Miller's television appearances, extending to chat-shows and arts programmes, provided free extra publicity for the Old Vic.[66] Even his clash on *The Late Show* with the anti-abortionist Victoria Gillick, when she called him a mouth-on-legs, became an instant *cause célèbre*.[67] To his credit, too, many of those whom he directed between 1988 and 1990 found him perfectly concentrated, in spite of his multitasking.[68]

Nevertheless, the notion that his Old Vic post required more hard graft was voiced by his former Footlights friend, Frederic Raphael. He called Miller's programming 'a repertory season of his old ideas', meaning that the erstwhile groundbreaker was now going over old ground.[69] John Fortune, in turn, described being in *One Way Pendulum*:

> As far as I remember, we rehearsed for three weeks and Jonathan never stopped us once! . . . It was either that he thought it was perfect or he was thinking about something entirely different. It was very odd. There was this scene and Jonathan never decided whether or not it was going to be cut. On the day that the play was to open in Toronto [at the Mirvishes' Royal Alexandra Theatre, prior to its Old Vic run], Jonathan was in Los Angeles [working on *The Mikado*], and we were all standing round saying, 'Well, are we doing this scene or not?' John Bird came out with the wonderful line: 'This is direction by rumour!'

One journalist who attended a *Candide* rehearsal, when Miller was not present, recorded more ferocious mutterings. The piece was co-adapted by John Wells and he was trying to co-stage it. Cast members were calling him 'bloody amateurish' and saying the absentee was an addict, hooked on making public appearances.[70] Another colleague, with hindsight, comments: 'I think Jonathan is a workaholic . . . of the sort who abuses work by making sure he's got so much of it that there's a really good excuse for not doing it properly.'

Finally, the hitherto unmentioned factor, which immediately preceded Miller and David Mirvish's split, was the latter having to go to another venue with Stephen Sondheim's musical *Into the Woods*. The theatre owner wished to produce its London premiere and wooed the composer, but Miller resisted. With exasperation mounting on both sides, Mirvish ended up realizing his ambition, in September 1990, at the West End's Phoenix Theatre. The staging was directed by Richard Jones and designed by Hudson, with Leigh moonlighting as executive producer. It won multiple awards.[71]

After that glittering triumph, Mirvish sharply refocused his attention on the Old Vic and reassessed the fact that, having unwisely agreed to a huge set, he stood to lose half a million pounds on the Botho Strauss/*Midsummer Night's Dream* bill. Moreover, that was assuming 60 per cent ticket sales. So, he cut his losses.[72]

Inevitably, there was bitterness during the bust-up, and yet that is largely forgotten now. It is also worth pointing up, by way of financial comparisons, that London saw the Barbican go dark in 1990, due to an RSC deficit of £4 million pounds, and Covent Garden was £3 million in the red, having to cancel its new productions. Today, Mirvish prizes Miller's artistic achievement and long-term cultural influence, stating:

> Many people said Jonathan wouldn't stick it out for even one year, but we did it for nearly three . . . and I think they were the best of all our years at the Old

273

Vic [which was sold on in 1998]. Jonathan had the most compelling vision . . . and I believe he achieved that. I think he had a profound impact on English theatre that still echoes. It was a gift, a gift worth receiving, and I'm proud to have been part of it. That's the bottom line . . . When I went to see shows in other theatres, I could see the impact, visually. People also said very nice things at the end of our tenure and probably the best compliment I had was [the director] Stephen Daldry saying how much the Miller years affected the way younger professionals looked at theatre.

Before going on to run the Royal Court and direct *Billy Elliot*, Daldry started out at Notting Hill's tiny Gate Theatre in 1990. There he staged thrilling foreign classics, continuing Miller's legacy, with fewer seats to sell. In the same year, Ian McDiarmid teamed up with Jonathan Kent and took over the now renowned Almeida Theatre in Islington, north London. McDiarmid states: 'Yes, those pioneering seasons at the Old Vic were an inspiration . . . We weren't particularly looking for models, but we kept saying, 'The sort of thing Jonathan was doing.'[73]

Miller has never run another building. He could have sought out an alternative space in London, the ideal cockpit theatre of which he had once spoken.[74] Or he might have followed in Peter Brook's footsteps, settling on the arts-cherishing continent with something comparable to Brook's Parisian Bouffes du Nord playhouse. He chose not to be tied to any single institution. What he did, instead, was accelerate away and take off, in top gear now, as a stellar freelancing director on the international opera circuit. This is the final large-scale movement of his career: staging productions at many of the world's leading opera houses including La Scala, working everywhere from New Mexico to Tokyo, and eventually circling back to the homelands of his grandparents, Sweden and Lithuania.

·15·

THE NINETIES

Damning England; round the world and back again;
ENO II and the ROH; Broomhill, the Almeida and
Dublin's Gate Theatre

W AS MILLER AIMING FOR A PLACE in the *Guinness Book of Records?*
Opera Now magazine thought he must be, surveying his phenomenal
global schedule for 1991.[1] He was to work on six new international productions
in the first seven months, as if he were determined, after the halting of *A
Midsummer Night's Dream* at the Old Vic, to put a girdle round about the earth
at an astounding speed almost on a par with Puck. He heard the clock ticking
ever more loudly after he reached 55, the age at which his mother died, but other
impulses were driving this intense second phase of working abroad, one which
saw him nicknamed opera's lone ranger.[2]

Going by his sons' sparring comments, it might be tempting to think he was
running away from home to get a bit of peace and quiet. The *Sunday Times*
interviewed William and Tom in the early 1990s, and the former exclaimed
about his older brother still hanging around at home.[3] Tom admitted he would
often quarrel with his father, testily attacking Miller Snr for holding intolerably
right-wing attitudes and for leaving crates of books in the hall. Their rows would
be followed by muttering sulks, with Rachel as the intermediary.

Familial tiffs were never going to make Miller fly the nest, though. Tom
acknowledged that their arguments were ridiculous because they really loved each
other. They enjoyed vibrant conversations and they had a great deal in common,
as he underlined. Miller speaks of readily taking criticism, in the context of home
life. 'I would never', he says, 'have felt free to insult my father . . . in the way that
my children freely do . . . without jeopardizing my affection for them in any
way.'[4]

Rachel had found it difficult in earlier decades when her husband had been
away from home (working in Nottingham, filming *Alice*, heading off to St Louis
and so on). By 1991, a happier solution was emerging. A couple of years earlier,
she had taken a sabbatical in India, and that, along with a brief illness, had
altered her attitude to the hard grind of being a GP. She took early retirement and

was then free to join Miller in those destinations which she particularly liked.[5] 'In a way, Jonathan and I get on best when I can give myself a hundred per cent,' she says, 'so, since I gave up work, we've had really nice times together . . . Abroad [without so many household ties], we behave like adults more.' Professionally, however, her husband was still looking for a world elsewhere in a disaffected mood. As Thatcher's regime dovetailed into John Major's dull, grey Conservatism, he had a resurgent sense of being sick of England.

In 1989, he had gone to Lithuania, with his childhood friend Nicholas Garland, to see communism in its last throes and to trace his ancestral roots.[6] This was, perhaps, more unsettling than he had expected. As Garland explains:

> The absence of Jews was very noticeable. It was on his mind. Sometimes in the street he would say, 'There's one.' When we went to a small town (little more than a village) where I think Jonathan's family came from, we met this Jewish guy who said, 'I'll take you to the Jewish cemetery.' So we arranged to go the next day. He led us to the outskirts and finally – in a street giving way to almost open countryside – he said, 'It was here.' Jonathan said, 'Where?' and [the guy] said, 'The Germans bulldozed it and flattened it and it's all gone now. But this is where it was.' We were standing on the site, only there was no site at all . . .
>
> Later we went to Paneriai, just outside Vilnius, walking down a track into these pine woods, these killing fields – the place where they [the Nazis and their Lithuanian collaborators] murdered thousands of Jews . . . There's a museum with lists of people's names, huge bookfuls of names, and Jonathan found the name 'Milleras'.

It was going to be another decade and a half before he would go back there, in a directorial capacity. In the meantime, other countries were keen to employ him, and that widening escape route encouraged him to launch into a major attack on England's defects, embellishing on his mid-Eighties remonstrances. In short, he felt that there had been a national failure of recognition – if not mass agnosia – regarding his worth. In a 1991 *Opera Now* interview, with reference to British critics, he announced:

> I'm fed up with the steady drizzle of acid rain that falls all the time. After a while you find your branches are falling off. I've decided now I'll work here as little as possible. I get paid more for working abroad. I'm better received there . . . This is a mean, peevish little country.[7]

He continued in the same vein on the BBC's *Today* programme, and in a further *Daily Telegraph* piece where he rebuked the nation's rancid, depressing minginess and niggling anti-intellectualism. By way of contrast, he praised Italy.[8]

Exit pursued by a baiting. With patriotic pride insistently wounded, various bulldogs in the press snapped at Miller's heels, with a vengeance. Between the lines, he was represented as not just peevish but disgracefully unBritish, almost traitorous, a double-dealer. A *Daily Telegraph* editorial stated that 'Nothing so enrages the British people as the spectacle of their own kind expressing a preference for foreigners and especially foreign pay slips.' How different from the welcome which *Beyond the Fringe* had received for skewering Englishness with a sense of humour, back in 1960. Another *Telegraph* article sniped:

> [O]ne cannot honestly pretend the 'good doctor' has really lived up to his early promise . . . He has not produced any creative work . . . All his opinions are fatuous . . . [not to mention] his impertinence in borrowing and ruining the work of greater artists. Perhaps he should stay in Italy.[9]

Besides comparisons being drawn with John Osborne's notorious 'Damn you, England' rants, the *Daily Mail* listed a derogatory catalogue of forerunners who had expressed a preference for other climes: W. H. Auden and Christopher Isherwood who 'slunk off' to escape war service; Byron lording it in Italy after his 'unmentionable practices'; Robert Browning 'always coming back or moaning from abroad, "Oh to be in England, now that April's there" [sic].'[10] The *Evening Standard* joined the fray, saying that every charlatan gets revered across the Channel and concluding:

> It is just possible that Dr Jonathan deserves the critical displeasure he has sometimes incurred, that the critics are right in not universally sharing his own high regard for his work . . . [Although unquestionably gifted,] he was never a first-rate original creator, not in the way his fellow fringer, Mr Alan Bennett, has proved to be.[11]

The contrast with Bennett was, obviously, intended to sting. A decade before, Miller had been riding high at the ENO and the BBC, while his former colleague was in the doldrums, slated for his play unwisely entitled *Enjoy*. Reportedly, the insecurity and jealousy which Bennett had felt in the Sixties had resurfaced around that time and caused a rift.[12] It seems the writer simply stopped visiting the house for several years, withdrawal allegedly being his 'nuclear weapon' in relationships.[13] Miller says that they have never discussed that, and Bennett politely fends off further enquiries with the general comment: 'We've always gone on the assumption that the less I said about him and the less he said about me the better. We know each other too well.'[14]

The dramatist's popularity had rocketed by 1991, with his NT *Wind in the Willows* and *The Lady in the Van*, and he was happily back visiting Rachel and Jonathan's house.[15] He acknowledges, moreover, that it was Miller who suggested the subject of his next triumph, *The Madness of George III*.[16] What seems somewhat unfair is that the media were now regularly awarding the playwright 'national treasure' status while vilifying his old friend for being unpatriotic.[17] In the process, they overlooked the fact that Bennett could be pungently anti-nationalistic himself. Disturbed by British jingoism, he had written the following in the 1989 preface to *An Englishman Abroad*, his play about the ex-pat spy Guy Burgess: 'The trouble with treachery nowadays is that . . . there is no one satisfactory to betray [one's country] to. If there were, more people would be doing it.'[18] He even implicitly toyed with a Burgess-Fringers comparison, arguing that a sceptical attitude to one's country was part of one's heritage and, by extension, betraying one's country was 'irony activated'.

The difference was that Bennett avoided talking directly to journalists and thus his remarks passed largely unnoticed, whereas Miller had aired his grievances with maximum publicity.

*   *   *

Other aspects of Miller's life, some from long before *Beyond the Fringe*, invite comparisons with the roaming nature of his late career. The man who, as a child, had felt deprived of parental affection was now seeking to put a distance between himself and a whole under-appreciative nation. His motherland did not love him enough. He was peripatetic once again, as during his wartime youth, and he spoke of himself as a *Gastarbeiter* or wandering tinker – thereby establishing a further, century-spanning connection with his continent-crossing grandfathers and the whole history of nomadic souls plying a trade.[19]

His itineracy was like his rangy cross-disciplinary thinking, except now he was literally traversing borders. As for life and art reflecting each other, while at the Old Vic he had talked of his increasing interest in the *Sprecher* in painting.[20] That is the figure, depicted in a crowd, who looks outwards, at the viewer. Miller started incorporating such figures in his Old Vic productions, and he spoke about the proscenium arch as a frame, saying 'I'm always wanting to violate it in some way, push stuff through it.'[21] Likewise, geographically, he stepped out of the English bracket.

*   *   *

The idea that he was unloved in Britain must be qualified. In 1990, the Duke of Edinburgh presented him with the Royal Society of Arts' Albert Medal, an honour previously bestowed upon Winston Churchill, Laurence Olivier and Lord Sainsbury. In 1991, he was made an honorary fellow of the Royal Academy. He was also, incidentally, voted the nation's sexiest man by high-earning executive women in their thirties, responding to a marriage-bureau survey. This fact titillated the *Daily Mail*.[22]

On the other hand, he was receiving a satirical pasting from ITV's *Spitting Image*.[23] This hugely popular comedy show ran a string of skits entitled 'Jonathan Miller Talks Bollocks', where his puppet-caricature gabbled fantastically esoteric nonsense.[24] In other sketches, he was portrayed as hilariously category-defying and hyperactive, performing a liver transplant while simultaneously making calls to the 'National Opera' and managing a mini-cab service on the side. ('Terry 2, Terry 2, come in, come in.')[25]

Unlike many of those caricatured by Peter Fluck and Roger Law, he was not fond of his foam-latex incarnation. He only occasionally asked his children what it was getting up to because they watched the show. As with *Private Eye*, some admiration was mixed in with the mockery, even if the ex-Fringer did not appreciate that fact. Law rumbustiously embraces the complexities, remarking:

It was Miller's way of popping up everywhere [which became the puppet's comic tic] . . . then you'd get this convoluted crap [in 'Jonathan Miller Talks Bollocks'] and there was a lot of truth in it. I met him in Cambridge once and we were talking bollocks about [artistic] fakes. I'm interested in whether things are fake or not . . . I like intellectuals. They're very stimulating, and if you're interested in his latest obsession, you'll get your money's worth . . . Obviously, I can't think he's a wanker, 'cause I actually sent him a letter once [after working on a *Peter and the Wolf* video with Claudio Abbado] . . . I wrote and said, 'Why don't we do something like that on stage?' He probably thought, 'What a wanker *he* is, popping up in *my* area!'

At one point, both men contributed to an *Omnibus* TV documentary on Degas, but when they bumped into each other at the related exhibition, Law merrily interjected, 'I don't know why you have to talk bollocks about it.'[26] He was taken aback by the irate response.

Miller argues that the real motivation for his 1991 whirlwind of work outside Britain was sheer pragmatism, not petulance. Being a freelance director necessitates careering around, like some Wall-of-Death biker. You turn jobs down, you fall out of the loop.

*　　*　　*

The marathon of six international shows in seven months began with his debut at Milan's world-renowned opera house, La Scala, that January. In brief, he staged Puccini's *La Fanciulla del West*, starring Plácido Domingo, and immediately afterwards started work on *Katya Kabanova*, his first in-house production for the New York Met. That opened in February, conducted by the great Janáček pioneer Charles Mackerras. The following month, he squeezed in a lecture tour of US colleges. By April, he was busy working on *Figaro* for the Vienna Staatsoper. Three days after that was up and running, he was back at Florence's Maggio Musicale staging *Così* for mid-June. Then it was *The Magic Flute* in Israel, with just two days to jet back to America for *Fidelio* rehearsals at Glimmerglass Opera.[27]

The results were impressive. Featuring a singularly gritty Gold Rush saloon bar, *La Fanciulla del West* was a commendable hit, transferring to Japan and being filmed for television.[28] 'Take the romance and make it a bit more rough and realistic and you see it's a movie really. Puccini is the first writer of movie music,' he says.

Next his stark and sensitive staging of the small-town Russian tragedy, *Katya*, helped the Met recover its ailing reputation and look like an important opera house once more. Most of New York's reviewers admired this '*Madame Bovary* on the Volga' with its lonesome scattering of clapboard houses evoking both the Russian steppes and American prairies.[29] 'There were no gimmicks. The characterizations were absolutely splendid . . . I'm a great admirer,' said Mackerras.

Moving on, Miller's *Figaro* in Austria built on the historical realism of his ENO staging and was a triumph.[30] He had a delightful time with the bass Ruggero Raimondi, who played the Count, and with the highly cultured conductor Claudio Abbado.[31] 'That *Figaro*', Abbado affirms, 'remains one of the best I have ever seen.'

Così continued his run of success in Florence where he received the city's Lion's Club Award for directing, succeeding Zeffirelli. He returned the following summer and every year or two over the next decade to stage further productions.[32] His speciality there was Mozart, but his updated *La Bohème* was also applauded, starring Roberto Alagna. It resembled a 1930s French film, in the style of his old cinematic favourites, René Clair and Marcel Pagnol.[33] The sets were by Fellini's designer, Dante Ferretti. His *Don Pasquale*, which premiered in Florence, was even more visually stunning, played out in a gigantic, antique doll's house, three storeys high. This angle on Donizetti's opera buffa allowed the upper-crust characters' shenanigans to be accompanied by constant comic business below stairs.[34]

A rare achievement for an English director, he became a core part of the Florentine company, almost one of the family, along with Zubin Mehta as chief conductor. Italian opera-goers clearly shared Miller's love of artworks and period chic. 'His productions have been hits, always,' Mehta attests. 'He is rated very highly here.'[35] Essentially, the Maggio Musicale took the place of the ENO in his life, and Florence was his European home from home, with Rachel frequently joining him there.[36] In spite of his workload, he found time to potter. Residing on the Piazza Santo Spirito, he could be spotted ambling round the market, or heading off to the Palazzo Pitti on a sit-up-and-beg bicycle. There he would scrutinize the paintings for hours, at a non-touristic pace, coming to know them like the back of his hand.

Miller's partnership with Mehta extended to Tel Aviv for *The Magic Flute*, which he completely re-envisaged on this occasion. Instead of an Age of Reason library, his new setting was a 1920s conference hotel (far more sober than the seaside hotel in *The Mikado*). The point was that Mozart's parable about the resolution of conflicts could be translated to the post-World War 1 era, when idealistic statesmen gathered together to establish the League of Nations, hoping to eradicate war and tyranny.[37] The production garnered warm applause and, while in Israel, Miller enjoyed visiting old-fashioned, left-wing kibbutzim. 'But I didn't feel I'd come home,' he says. 'Nothing like that.'

*　　　*　　　*

Across the Atlantic, Glimmerglass was becoming another regular base camp. He staged five productions in six years at this pastoral opera house which stands, like a Shaker clapboard barn, on the shores of Otsego Lake, near Cooperstown, in Upstate New York.[38] This enterprise, with relatively modest budgets, was his cherished substitute for Kent Opera. His arrival really put the company on the map. He was soon regarded as a sort of local hero, for using his influence to get better facilities for the technical crew.[39] Lodged in a cottage in the nearby eighteenth-century town of Cherry Valley, he was quietly content, watching the Fourth of July parades and inviting Mr Rury, the grocer, to his opening nights. Again, Rachel came to stay there, and house guests included their old American friends Nelson Aldrich and Robert Silvers from the *New York Review of Books*.[40]

For his Glimmerglass productions, he first reworked two of his Kent Opera stagings, *La Traviata* and *Fidelio*, before expanding his range with more recherché curios, including baroque operas and Domenico Cimarosa's eighteenth-century entertainment *Il Matrimonio Segreto* (or *The Secret Marriage*).[41] Some expressed surprise at the high-powered doctor taking on Cimarosa's piece of fluff about farcically confused couples, yet the result was a delight, abounding in Goffman-esque gestures of social embarrassment. Miller threw in an extra joke, having Count Robinson, Cimarosa's flailing Englishman abroad, crane out to read the surtitles when struggling to understand his Italian sweetheart.[42]

As for the baroque operas, Miller did not consider them hugely problematic, though they are notoriously stationary. In Monteverdi's *L'Incoronazione di Poppea*, he discerned interesting parallels between *da capo* arias and the way in which repetitions serve in the verbal art of persuasion. Combining slow-motion gestures and sumptuous seventeenth-century costumes, he produced a dark, scintillating depiction of Nero and amoral love affairs.[43] His approach to stasis was witty as well, for he had the presiding deities, Amore, Fortuna and Virtù, sardonically pose as marble statues. Besides being recorded for television, this Glimmerglass production transferred to the world-class Brooklyn Academy of Music, and the *New York Times* called it sublime.[44] 'It was stunning,' says BAM's former president, Harvey Lichtenstein.

Miller again used movement very sparingly when he came to direct Donizetti and Bellini's *bel canto* operas in Monaco and Munich. Though his own career has been one of perpetual motion, stillness can play an important part in his productions. Just as he had favoured exceptionally long, single takes in his TV dramas, so on stage he could appreciate the intensity of a frozen moment. At Monte Carlo's glittering Salle Garnier opera house, he staged the Tudor Queens trilogy over three consecutive years: first *Roberto Devereux* (with Roberto Alagna), then *Maria Stuarda* and *Anna Bolena*.[45] Donizetti's protagonists are, of course, tragically for the chop, but the shows had extended lives touring to Italy then Spain.[46] Monte Carlo revived them as a big triple-bill as well, to mark the composer's bicentenary. It was a technical nightmare, with frighteningly overloaded rigging, but this event drew fans from all over the world, packing the place to the rafters.[47]

Munich's grand Bayerische Staatsoper (or Bavarian State Opera) invited him to stage a larger-scale *Anna Bolena* and Bellini's Roundhead and Cavalier romance, *I Puritani*, with the star soprano Edita Gruberova playing the grief-crazed heroine in both.[48] Even though he scoffed at the fanciful storylines, Miller was delighted with Gruberova's convincing mad scenes, where she gibbered melodiously on the floor. Highly successful, *Anna Bolena* continued to be revived for a decade, and *I Puritani* is still in the repertoire. These productions were commissioned by the former ENO boss Peter Jonas, who had moved on to Munich. Obviously not as hostile as Miller had thought him to be back in Britain, Jonas remarks: 'I loved both those shows . . . Like historical tableaux with minimal movement, they were extraordinarily beautiful.'

On top of this, Miller's *Il Matrimonio Segreto*, scaled up for Zurich Opera, proved to be a hit, and this distinguished institution became his other main buttress on the continent, to match Florence.[49] He dismisses his least successful production there, *Die Gezeichneten* by Franz Schreker, who was a product of Freud's Vienna. 'It's an unbelievably silly piece. I can't even remember what it's about,' he says hastily, committing to oblivion Schreker's heroine who, poor thing, dies of pleasure after her first orgasm. He went on to clock up eight productions, and Zurich's reviewers particularly relished his psychological insights. They referred to him as 'der britische Psychiater', and they embraced him as if he were one of their own when lauding his 'Swiss precision' in comedies.[50] His *Magic Flute* was stunningly monumental, developing his Age of Reason library setting.[51] This production became a staple in the repertoire, and his vision of *Falstaff* matured at the same venue, migrating in its allusions from Bruegel towards seventeenth-century Dutch paintings.[52]

It seems astonishing that he had any truck with *Nabucco*, Verdi's religious saga where Nebuchadnezzar, King of Babylon, is struck by a thunderbolt then penitently converts to Judaism. In the wake of the Gulf War in Iraq (present-day Babylon), Miller additionally feared that the piece could seem anti-Islamic. He rendered the setting semi-abstract, and the result has been frequently revived.[53] He has, in fact, tackled an assortment of Muslim- and Ottoman-related works, with *Il Seraglio* opening in Switzerland.[54] For this Mozart opera, he had the European heroine being half in love with the Pasha Selim who holds her captive.[55] That staging saw a rapprochement, as well, between the director and Klaus Maria Brandauer. The latter's 'ill-disposed' ankle and mood had clearly improved since 1979. 'We got on fantastically well,' says Miller.

⋆   ⋆   ⋆

Other megastars on the international circuit began to frustrate Miller. He increasingly referred to them as Jurassic Park singers, indicating they were inflexible monsters who stupidly regarded rehearsals as an intrusion on their time.[56] They are often, he says, merely transported like '200 cwt of condemned veal' and lowered into position by stage management, just two or three days before opening night.[57] Of Domingo, he comments that it was 'like working with King Kong'.[58] He remains mild about José Carreras, calling him a sweet man though no great actor. They worked together on *Fedora*, Umberto Giordano's third-rate Romanov romance, for the Bregenz Festival, famed for its floating stage on Lake Constance. It was the tenor's co-star, Agnes Baltsa, who was the annoyance, apparently insisting on wearing her own anachronistic evening dress. The production sank without trace, metaphorically speaking.[59]

Miller felt that Roberto Alagna's ego had become inflated too, when they met in Paris for the transfer of *La Bohème* from Florence.[60] The director confided to a passing journalist that he was having 'terrible trouble' and was dreading his next production at the Bastille Opera. That was *La Traviata* with Angela Gheorghiu, who was soon to wed Alagna. Unwisely, Miller contrasted her with Cecilia Bartoli, the hitherto unspoilt 'shining gem' whom he was booked to direct later, in a *Figaro* at the Met.[61]

La Traviata was duly hellish. First there was trouble from an unexpected quarter when Miller's designer, Peter Davison – in a surprise variation on the French Revolution – stormed *out* of the Bastille after a tiff. Then there was Gheorghiu crying 'I die alone!', objecting to Miller's hospital ward setting. He adds that the prima donna has since abused him publicly, though it is his satirical name for her and Alagna which has stuck: 'the Bonnie and Clyde of opera'.[62] He predominantly blames the music industry for deforming rising stars, giving them 'the bends' by turning them into overnight sensations.[63] Presumably, he views this process as more intensive than his own youthful fast-track to fame in the entertainment business.

His bust-up with Bartoli would rapidly become international news. He had liked working at the New York Met, going on from *Katya* to stage Debussy's *Pelléas et Mélisande* with Frederica von Stade, whom he describes as 'the most noble, gracious woman'. She said his interpretation exquisitely complemented the music.[64] Seeing analogies with Proust, he envisaged Debussy's quasi-incestuous lovers not as medieval characters, but as the vestiges of an aristocratic family circa 1895, paralyzed by neurotic fantasies in a decaying chateau.[65] The reviewer John Simon was allegedly heard growling in the interval, 'Where's the fucking forest?' The director called him Simple Simon, for his literal-mindedness. Others hailed the production as both erotically intense and a masterpiece of understatement, 'like a prism transmitting rays of illumination' while having a brooding, Bergmanesque quality.[66]

After that, Miller was entrusted with *The Rake's Progress*, Stravinsky and W. H. Auden's opera based on Hogarth. While certainly not winning all-round raves, the humanizing of this chilly moral tale was applauded. Its setting was updated to Auden's own decadent pre-World War 2 Berlin, and Jerry Hadley's Rakewell ended up as a touchingly childlike madman.[67]

So Miller had no serious complaints regarding the Met, apart from criticizing its glitz-loving audiences and observing that the management was very hands-off, 'a bit like the *Marie Celeste* . . . [making it] difficult to know if there's anybody on the bridge'.[68] That was to change when Bartoli turned up to play Figaro's fiancée, Susanna. Having become the world's hottest mezzo, she insisted on singing two long-sidelined arias (variants on those normally performed). Overriding the director's objections, she was endorsed by the conductor and reigning music director, James Levine. In protest, Miller left her to her own devices when it came to the dramatically redundant inserts.[69]

Word of the dispute leaked to the press shortly after opening night. That led Joseph Volpe, the head of the opera house, to declare that the New York Times had unjustly questioned Bartoli's professionalism, and the story swiftly went global.[70] Miller was interviewed, back in Europe, saying it was a mere blip, but he had been disappointed and disturbed. Bartoli retaliated that he had been ungentlemanly, disdaining the arias. 'I felt like Caesar with Brutus,' she avowed.[71] He sighed that she was a 'rather silly, selfish girl – wilful, wayward and determined to have her own way'.[72]

After a hiatus, he became more forthright. He alleged that Levine and Bartoli's agent had acted like a cabal, and that Volpe was confrontational, jabbing a finger in his face.[73] Cheekily likening the boss to Tony from The Sopranos (as in the TV series), he said that Volpe snarled, 'Don't fuck with me' and then fired him.[74]

This caused the Met major embarrassment. Volpe affirmed that Miller was 'a wonderful stage director' whose work was loved by the whole company. Unconvinced, the press delved and discovered that his board members were riven over the matter. Volpe's own statement had been barbed: 'a wonderful stage director, with a vivid imagination'.[75]

Today Volpe is openly caustic, thumbing his nose at Miller's Cambridge education, calling him the real prima donna in this wrangle. He describes how the virtuoso talker – 'lov[ing] the sound of his own voice more than most opera singers' – complained to everyone within earshot about his and Levine's cowardice, then invented the 'Don't fuck with me' dialogue. The sacking accusation was also baloney, says Volpe, because Miller 'fired himself'.[76]

Leery of American litigiousness, Miller refrains from any further comment, but the flames of controversy have never been quite extinguished. His old colleague Nicholas Hytner appends a scathing coda, remarking: 'I happened to see that Figaro which was – and I'm prepared to be quoted on this – hijacked by the most disgustingly plush, scandalously self-absorbed conducting I have ever heard . . . [from that] fat monster in the pit, James Levine, one of the great musical villains of our time.'

The production was a magnificent hit, regardless. The cast were vivacious with Bryn Terfel in the title role. Declared a timeless 'Figaro for the ages' and 'as close to perfection as is imaginable', the first run generated a queue for returns long enough to fill a second house. The Met have repeatedly presented revivals, without Miller on board.[77]

*   *   *

Regarding the reviews which he received on the international circuit, he says that he blissfully could not decipher the ones in foreign languages, but, certainly, they weren't all paeans. Some critics were bored stiff by the stillness of his baroque and *bel canto* pieces.[78] Moreover, the *New Yorker*, far from cosseting him as one of its own former columnists, circulated the idea that his stagings were becoming 'weak and pallid'.[79] British journalists kept flying out to report on his work abroad as well, and Peter Conrad let rip with a philippic in *Opera Now*. He asserted that Manhattan was just 'enviably underexposed' to this director, and that *Katya* only demonstrated the repetitiveness of his tricks, the talented mimic now merely imitating his own previous works.[80]

On the road in the Nineties, Miller also came to dislike certain grand opera houses. He decided La Scala was horrid, with claques who would boo unless bribed. Puccini's *Manon Lescaut*, his second production there, was an uninspired flop, lumbered with someone else's leftover set.[81] While delighting in Florence, in Berlin (where he restaged *Falstaff*), and in Bologna (which imported his Donizettis), he decided that Monte Carlo was 'an arsehole', populated by tax-dodging, fur-coated fools, and he reckoned you had to be positively heroic to make much of Zurich.[82]

Relenting somewhat on the latter, he jovially recounts how Alexander Pereira, the silver-tongued intendant (the administrative head) of Zurich Opera, wooed him back after one particularly fractious rehearsal. Fuming, the director had whirled off to his hotel room to hurl his belongings in a suitcase and quit Switzerland instantly, only to realize that half his clothes were at the cleaners, and it was shut. Reduced to merely leaving town for the weekend, he returned to find the phone ringing. It was Pereira murmuring in dulcet tones, 'Jonathan, do you like caviar?' – a bribe so amusingly preposterous that it led to concord.

There was no such peacemaking with Salzburg. Reunited with the conductor Roger Norrington for the city's famed arts festival, Miller happily staged *Mitridate, re di Ponto*, Mozart's youthful opera seria set in Asia Minor. He declined, however, to endear himself to the Austrian locals, reminding them of Salzburg's proximity to Berchtesgaden, Hitler's former mountain retreat. Breathtakingly, he told the press that a disturbing fragrance lingered in the air, a mixture of incense and Zyklon B.[83] He did not work there again.

Moreover, while he had complained about deconstructionist bosh gaining ground at the ENO, the deconstructionist creed ruled supreme in many German-speaking opera houses. He ridicules their admiration for '*konzept regie*' or 'concept directing', which allows directors to impose any idea they like, as long as it is novel.[84] That may bemuse those who categorize Miller himself as a seminal concept director or, indeed, accuse him of suffering from conceptitis.[85] Nonetheless, the distinction he draws is between other directors' crass, ill-fitting concepts and his own apt, historically informed and sensitive responses to scripts and scores.[86]

Peter Jonas confirms that some German reviewers deemed Miller's Munich productions controversially classical. Nor were they comfortable with his 'konzept' for *Capriccio* at Berlin's Deutsche Staatsoper, since it seemed more politically accusatory than avant-garde.[87] With echoes of his Fascist *Tosca*, he appended an outer frame to Richard Strauss' frivolously hermetic costume drama about periwigged aesthetes.[88] Pointing up the grim World War 2 situation which surrounded the original premiere, the cast were shown arriving to rehearse as if it were 1942, with Nazi boyfriends in tow. The walls of the set ultimately split open to reveal a bomb-cratered city beyond.[89] The Staatsoper's administrator, Hans-Dieter Roser, remembers:

> Yvonne Kenny was perfect as the Countess and the servant scenes were so funny – absolute show-stoppers. Working with Jonathan was a real pleasure after all those directors in Germany with very crazy concepts, and it was revived very, very well. But I think it was the confrontation with the war: the newspapers hated it.[90]

*   *   *

Miller began to miss home intensely. Even if he savoured the perks of international travel, especially the superb art galleries, he was wearied by the endless airports. At night, he would find himself in the no-man's-land of an anonymous hotel, longing to see his family and spending huge amounts on phoning England.

He returned, inevitably, to direct in Britain, though he would never again become truly wedded to the idea of working there, instead constantly coming and going. He was back as early as 1993 with a wave of productions. His undercast *Maria Stuarda* was frostily received at the Buxton Festival in the Peak District.[91] The *Observer* jeered that the moaning doctor was now working the chocolate box circuit. The *Sun* announced his return with the headline, 'Not welcome', and the conclusion, 'Just when we were getting on so well without him.'[92] In spite of this, *The Secret Marriage* won over virtually everyone, co-produced by Opera North and featuring the comic baritone Andrew Shore, whom Miller treasures.[93] This piece was said to mark the director's 'rehabilitation', easing him back into the opera scene in the UK, six years after his last ENO production.[94]

That same season, he had a fine time back in rural Kent, now with the small, enterprising Broomhill Opera group. They had discovered a lovely, panelled auditorium at the country house Broomhill.[95] Their summer course for young singers culminated in a showcase festival, a kind of mini Glyndebourne, and its centrepiece was *Ariadne auf Naxos*. This Richard Strauss *divertissement* (first conceived in 1912) was very suitable, its setting being a private theatre where troupes of comedians and tragedians collide.[96]

Reflecting the period of composition, Miller had the commedia characters resemble silent-movie stars while Ariadne languished on a couch like a mournful aristocrat in a sanatorium.[97] Even as he spoke of his own star waning and as the twentieth century neared its close, the director's productions featured more than one such figure, wan with end-of-the-Hapsburg-Empire melancholy.[98]

Nevertheless, at Broomhill he was celebrating. 'I feel like the scientist in *Jurassic Park*,' he said (now using the comparison positively), 'watching the eggs hatch and seeing these amazing talents emerge. I'm having the time of my life.'[99]

Back in London, a glowing critical reception greeted his experimental *St Matthew Passion* at Sloane Square's Holy Trinity Church.[100] Freeing Bach's oratorio from its concert-hall format (usually featuring lectern-bound soloists), he animated the piece discreetly, in a style often referred to as semi-staged. Contemplating the events surrounding Christ's crucifixion, this *Passion* was performed in the round, with little more than bread, wine and an apple on the props list. The singers and instrumentalists encircled the playing area in everyday clothes (Milleresque plaid shirts and jeans), and they wandered around, mingling with one another. An *obbligato* oboist might join a meditative singer, and the pair would breathe together, like alter egos, as their poignant countermelodies intertwined.[101]

What was striking, in the interviews which Miller gave, was how his bridge-building instincts resurfaced here, in contrast to his confrontational side.[102] As when dramatizing ghost stories, being a non-believer did not stop him being sensitive to the spiritual. 'Never underestimate the piety of atheists,' he said, and he brought to the fore aspects of Jesus' story which inspired sympathy beyond religious sects, essentially depicting a virtuous man who endured agonies, doubts and betrayals.[103] The reviewers adored how he drew the audience in, creating a true sense of communion. 'It was', reminisces Rodney Milnes, 'one of my great evenings and, in the broadest sense, a profoundly religious experience – from Jonathan! In every way extraordinary.' Tom Sutcliffe, a Christian, was equally moved and judged it exemplary.[104] Other top directors took to dramatizing Bach's oratorios thereafter.[105]

This staging inspired increased familial harmony too. The director's father-in-law had always been a little contemptuous of Miller's inability to read music, but, right at the end of his life, he attended that *Passion* and thought it wonderful. As well as being filmed for an Easter BBC broadcast, with Kate Miller working as TV production manager, it went on to be restaged all over the world, from Barcelona to BAM.[106] There, the *New York Observer* called it the most exhilarating and important musical-dramatic event in years.[107]

★   ★   ★

The Power House triumvirate had all moved on from the English National Opera by mid-1993. The BBC veteran Dennis Marks took the helm and, by December, Miller was having a second lease of life there, rehearsing Richard Strauss' greatest hit *Der Rosenkavalier*. This was to be followed by Bizet's crowd-puller, *Carmen*, and *La Traviata*. All were eagerly awaited big nights.[108]

Once more updating to the era of composition, Miller shifted Strauss' frilly eighteenth-century setting to a darkly autumnal Vienna in 1911. If you see it played that way, he points out:

You suddenly realize it's an opera about the end of the Hapsburg Empire. When the Marschallin talks about stopping the clocks, she's not just talking about her age. She's talking about her Age, because in some strange way she knows that it's coming to an end, the jig is up. And there's that wonderful dramatic irony – as with Chekhov – that the audience, with hindsight, knows exactly what happened soon after. The shot rang out from Sarajevo . . . You just know that Octavian [the Marschallin's young lover] will die on the Eastern front, and Faninal [an arriviste moving into a mansion] will perhaps become an armaments merchant . . . Strauss' music, filled with Viennese waltzes, suddenly delivers this sense of wistfulness and pathos.[109]

Many cheered his sugar-free *Rosenkavalier* for being extraordinarily astute.[110] Rescuing the ENO from declining popularity, it became the hottest opera ticket in town and another international export, so the pendulum had swung once more.[111] Realizing that the ultra-hip directors, previously favoured, had only short-term appeal, Marks signed up Miller as a safe pair of hands, to create productions of the classics with a long shelf life.[112]

The director's comeback was not as glorious as his 1980s heyday. Some called for more romance and passion. In *Carmen*, they did not care for the traditional gypsy sexpot being played as a tarty, defiant factory girl.[113] With *La Traviata*, they found the Parisian demimonde dreary, with a spartan set which the director himself had helped to paint.[114] Others, nevertheless, loved *Carmen*'s relocation, which was inspired by Cartier-Bresson: a sun-scorched industrial suburb in 1930s (rather than 1830s) Seville.[115] One technical hitch also proved felicitous. When Louise Winter (playing Carmen) lost her voice halfway through a performance, the popular mezzo Sally Burgess was spotted in the audience and was rushed into the wings to sing, while Winter lip-synched onstage. Burgess went on to play the role in subsequent revivals.[116] The *Guardian* rated Miller's *Traviata* as top-notch at its third reprise, perceiving how his dispassionate approach preserved the work's emotional power, stripped of sentimentality. 'Its flaws', the paper concluded, 'are few.'[117]

*   *   *

More momentously, the Royal Opera House had got him on board, late in the day.[118] Brought into the fold by Nicholas Payne (who had previously run Opera North), Miller made his debut at Covent Garden in 1995, aged 60, staging *Così* amidst huge media excitement. This is when he put Mozart into modern dress for the first time in his career, with outfits supplied by Giorgio Armani.[119] High security in the dressing-rooms ensured the haute couture did not walk, and fashion journalists piled into the stalls alongside the music critics.

Così went on to become a frequently revived, five-star production.[120] With a cast incorporating Thomas Allen and Amanda Roocroft, its premiere was exalted as an absolute joy, subtle and penetratingly bittersweet (there being no easy final reconciliation for the unfaithful lovers).[121] The *Wall Street Journal* whooped that the magus of Maggio Musicale, maven of the Met, and guru of Glimmerglass had, herewith, shown himself to be 'peerless among British opera directors . . . in almost every way, the best'.[122] A profile in London's *Evening Standard* suddenly remembered Susan Sontag's description of Miller as one of the United Kingdom's most valuable people. The time was now ripe, the publication declared, to honour him in his own land. He was, after all, king of both London opera houses, with *Rigoletto* simultaneously playing at the ENO.[123]

Doing himself no favours, Miller publicly contrasted his own ROH handiwork with their normal 'plush nonsense'. Sometimes it is as if he has some anti-estab-lishmentarian form of Tourette's syndrome. Several years later, just as Covent Garden were importing his Doll's House *Don Pasquale* from Florence, he threw PR to the dogs in a fabulously dyspeptic interview. He recounted how he had been insultingly offered a second-hand set for *Così*, how he had designed a new one gratis and had suggested off-the-peg Armani, only to see the avidly marketed label steal the limelight. In addition, he lampooned the venue's wealthy patrons with the appallingly funny slur, 'Harrods Food Hall yields up its dead.'[124]

Don Pasquale received some tart appraisals, being condemned as cold and excessively busy, and with digs being made about its curmudgeonly old protagonist.[125] Revivals have since played to packed houses, and Payne is good-humoured about Miller's anti-institutional jibes. He emphasizes that the director was exceptionally unmercenary and a charming collaborator on *Così*, unlike Armani's brigade who were, he says, 'a complete bloody nightmare' – stopping the costumes being reused because they were *so* last year.[126]

All the same, Miller received no further ROH commissions and he fell out with Payne when the latter took over the Coliseum.[127] Another younger cadre caused him, he believes, to be dropped from the ENO books.[128] Payne admits that is partially true, but he abruptly cancelled Miller's scheduled *Cav and Pag* because this double bill risked overshooting its budget in lean times.[129] The two men had discussions thereafter, trying to agree on new projects. For Payne, the one that got away was *My Fair Lady* with the director himself playing Professor Higgins.[130] This musical was supposed to be part of a package with a more serious piece, but no consensus could be reached, ending in a horribly fractious meeting where Payne did not share Miller's enthusiasm for translating Janáček's *Jenůfa* to a Czech émigré community in small-town America. Payne felt that his colleague was no longer in touch with the company's Englishness. 'I was right,' he says. 'Still, as a producer it's your task to get the best people and, in the case of Jonathan at the ENO, I regret that I didn't.'

When BBC TV enrolled Miller once again, in 1997, for its master-class series *Opera Works*, he chose the music director from Broomhill to be his co-star, rather than any big-shot conductor.[131] The series launched Charles Hazlewood's career as a music presenter. He remains amazed by Miller's 'nose for horseflesh' and his ability to draw emotional truth from very young singers. BBC2's controller Mark Thompson regarded the series as the channel's jewel in the crown that year.[132]

Miller helped Broomhill Opera further when they moved into Wilton's Music Hall, a wonderful Victorian edifice going to rack and ruin in London's East End. As Hazlewood underlines:

> If you need a letter from someone of Jonathan's stature, it's there by return and, at one performance, he even volunteered to sell the programmes when some ushers hadn't turned up. Very, very good value! He was also absolutely instrumental in creating Wilton's look, because he had the vision . . . creating these amazing textures and layers of paint, suggesting ways of distressing it, scraping a bit here, scratching a bit there. He got his hands dirty right from the start and he was a great friend to the company.

Indeed, in creating that look, Miller turned Wilton's into the London Fringe's beautifully dilapidated answer to Peter Brook's Bouffes du Nord.[133]

To fit the venue, his staging of *The Beggar's Opera* had Gay's seedy crooks and whores in nineteenth-century garb, with the actor Michael Feast as a rough-voiced, East End Macheath. This was a world that would have been familiar to Miller's grandfather, Abram, with the director drawing on both Dickens and another favourite of his, the Victorian sociologist Henry Mayhew.[134] Hazlewood observes that it could, however, be frustrating when Miller was not firing on all cylinders:

> Maybe, in a way, Jonathan thinks Jonathan isn't very good, or has a lot of flukes. You know, he has this mantra whenever a show opens. He paces around outside, saying to virtually anybody, 'I think it's really rather good,' again and again . . . *Ariadne* was a blue-ribbon piece of work . . . but I think he relies on the flash of genius that catalyses a production and, with *The Beggar's Opera*, it never happened. It was just a duff month for him. From my point of view too, the whole thing was ghastly.[135]

*   *   *

That was his last collaboration with Broomhill Opera. He returned to theatre directing, to reappraise *A Midsummer Night's Dream*.[136] All those years ago, when his Burgtheater staging of *The Dream* was in meltdown, he had wandered into the mirror maze in Vienna's old fairground and realized that he was staring at the set which he ought to have had.[137] Finally, at the Almeida Theatre, in north London, he saw the opportunity to redeem himself, bringing in the esteemed Quay Brothers to design Shakespeare's forest of confused identities as a mildewed hall of mirrors, a labyrinth of refracted images.

He remains fiercely proud of this production, and his sexagenarian angle on the play was remarkable. The surprise was not so much that he set Theseus' court in stuffy, pre-Sixties England, all smoking jackets and evening gowns. Beyond that, he presented, as one colleague put it, *The Geriatric Dream*. Peter Bayliss'

Bottom was doddery if not senile, and Oberon and Titania were exceptionally long in the tooth: a silver-haired Norman Rodway and a still slinky but bony Angela Thorne.[138]

What this produced was a striking paradox: an innovatively weary reading of Shakespeare's youthful play, a wintry revision of this midsummer romance. The cast radically infused the play's poetical speeches – about love, musk roses and eglantine – with tones of cynicism and melancholy. A few reviewers were thrilled, one calling it 'as bracingly controversial as Peter Brook's white-box *Dream*'.[139] Puck attracted comment, played like a below-stairs chauffeur with attitude, and so did Angus Wright's 'Millerish', gawky Lysander, who transmogrified into a smoothie in the dream wood.[140] Even if this director has never gone in for Hitchcockian cameo appearances, he has permitted a brace of actors to imitate his gangly style.

Most of the notices, however, were damning. Miller says that they were some of the most wounding of his life.[141] His *Dream* was judged to be unpleasantly sour, laboured, unfunny, woefully lacking in passion and magic. Michael Billington concluded that it was 'desperately underpowered' and patronizingly reductive.[142] He named it as a nadir when he came to write his annual overview. Miller is still seething about that.

Speaking in measured tones, Billington retraces how he and Miller have crossed paths through the decades:

> For many moons [after we fell out over the business of Peter Hall's NT], I hardly saw him or spoke to him. Then, when he was working at the University of Sussex, we were both involved in another [BBC] programme, and it was as if he was desperately trying to renew the acquaintance, this sort of lost relationship. We went for a drink afterwards and he said, 'I wish you could come and see the work down there [in Sussex]' . . . I don't know why he was doing that. Because, I suppose, he doesn't like to have too many breaches. But what finally caused the definitive rupture between us, I think, was my review of his *Midsummer Night's Dream* . . . and the fact that I singled it out in the Christmas round-up as one of the worst productions of the year. Shortly after that I got a postcard from him. It was crisp and abusive. It was a New Year's card, actually: my first card on January 1st. There was an exquisite art[work on the front] . . . but on the back something, you know, about 'your foul pork scratchings'. It just shows the strange zigzag, in the course of a life, that you go through with someone like Jonathan . . . I feel very ambivalent because I still have a great admiration for him.

Ian McDiarmid, who was co-running the Almeida, prized both Miller's offbeat concept and the upbeat side of his personality. He avers:

> Jonathan is endlessly funny and ludic. Play comes as second nature to him . . . so I knew that, in the building, his spirit would cheer up everybody, not just the actors. The bar staff couldn't wait for him to come in . . . All that made

us very happy. The only sad thing was that he was so upset by the reviews. I sometimes wondered if this wasn't a sort of role – the misanthropic clown – but I don't think it was. It genuinely depressed him and it rankled. I think critics are often surprised by what they seem to have torn within people.

Miller was adamant that he would never stage another play in England.

Straddling *The Dream*, fore and aft, was a small clutch of dramas in Ireland. His roving in 1992 had led him back to his mother's homeland to put on *The Double Dealer* at the Gate Theatre in Dublin. That created, long-distance, a suite of more or less Hogarthian productions, connecting back to his *School for Scandal* and *She Would If She Could*.[143] He managed to capture both the nastiness and humour in Congreve's adulterous post-Restoration comedy, winning hurrahs from the Irish press and, incidentally, from Billington. One of the few English critics who headed out to greet this 'welcome return to drama', he described the show as near-perfect and impenitently sexy, with bitingly sharp character studies.[144]

Miller felt very at home in easy-going Dublin, with the Gate's affable ensemble, and the artistic director Michael Colgan confirms that their visitor was charm itself. 'One of the things that Jonathan's best at', he observes, 'is being good company. He loves talk and he loves company: very Irish!' There was one disastrous dinner date with Jean Ann Kennedy. She was the US ambassador to Ireland, sister of JFK and Bobby, and a devout Catholic. Having invited the ex-Fringer to join her at a swish restaurant, she iced over when she learned he was less than awed by the Lord. She then, reportedly, ignored the bill until he and his fellow guest – the renowned novelist Peter Matthiessen – were forced to split the cost. JAK immediately became *persona non grata* at the Gate, while hearty applause was soon greeting Miller's second venture there, Goldsmith's comedy of hierarchical inversions, *She Stoops to Conquer*.[145]

Unfortunately, as with his three Nineties ENO shows, the critical reaction took a downward turn. His third and final Gate production, *As You Like It*, was much less fun, staged after *The Dream*, in 2000. 'I don't think it was very good. I was tired,' he recollects, 'and ill with a bad back . . . and I found I didn't like the play as I went on.'[146] This staging was generally considered pretty straight and conventional without much searching ambivalence in the cross-dressing: sporadically perky, for sure, but flagging towards the end.[147]

·16·

INTO THE NEW MILLENNIUM

The ongoing international roundabout; art and
curating; a knighthood; a BBC comeback and home

HOW IS A BIOGRAPHY OF A LIFE – when that life is still in progress – meant
to finish? With a dot, dot, dot, or a series of question marks? There
are numerous threads that cannot be tied up neatly. As the twentieth century
has rolled on into the twenty-first, Miller has continued to jet around the
world, well beyond the official age of retirement, making acclaimed returns to
Florence and Munich in 2001, popping up in Zurich every other year between
1999 and 2005, and returning to La Scala to stage his *Don Pasquale* there in
2012.[1]

The range of opera houses has expanded during this period. Along with treks
out to Tokyo, his European work has stretched from Graz, Venice and Valencia
to a nexus of Scandinavian and Baltic companies, including the Royal Swedish
Opera in Stockholm.[2] Over in the States, he directed a spate of productions for
Santa Fe's extraordinary open-sided amphitheatre, out in the New Mexico desert,
as well as becoming a favourite of the New York City Opera company – for many
years the Lincoln Center's alternative to the Met.[3]

It must be said, though, Miller's operatic destinations have generally become
less prestigious than of yore. Though several of his productions remain in rep at
the Met, he has not been there – or at Berlin or the Bastille – for a decade. Nor
has he staged a new Florence production since 2001. That is not necessarily a
problem, because he has never stopped cherishing fringe enterprises. In 2002, he
was in seventh heaven, lodging with Rachel in a forest hut on the Danish isle of
Bornholm, for a summer academy with fledgling singers.

That project, in fact, contrived to be off the beaten track but also the subject
of a TV documentary, seen across Scandinavia and Poland. He hooked up with
the same company again for a *Traviata* in Norway, with two of his grandchildren spending their holiday with him by the sea. Coming almost full circle in
terms of Miller's Scandinavian ancestry, his son William is now married to a half-
Norwegian interior designer. The Millers spent another week or two at her

family's summer retreat, a traditional group of turf-roofed huts, a variation on the idyllic Swedish vacation of Miller's childhood.

What he is unhappy about is the offers of work dwindling, really tailing off now. He may be in his seventies yet he still wants to be occupied, and he has taken the prospect of involuntary retirement hard. He has grown bitterly depressed about it, accusing the industry of ageism.[4] This has been his late-life crisis. The withdrawal symptoms were bound to be severe for such a habitually energetic mind, and for a showman who, according to one rehearsal-room colleague, 'seems compelled to hold court'.[5] He himself admits to revisiting his long-running hits for a top-up of applause. It is, he says, like 'a continuation of when you are five and call out, "Mummy, mummy, look at me! You're not looking! Look!"'[6]

He wants to wean himself off this. A kind of directorial Flying Dutchman or Don Giovanni, he has done the incessant rounds with a restlessness perpetuated by his own celebrity, but also with an increasingly deep-seated weariness. Maybe half of him dreads being laid off, while half of him devoutly wishes for that end. In press interviews, he has harped on about quitting to the point of making others (if not himself) believe it is a *fait accompli*. 'I'm disappointed', laments Zubin Mehta, 'when I hear Jonathan doesn't want to do any more.' Miller's explosive satirical jibes have been even more professionally suicidal, making intendants flinch from inviting him under their roofs. He might, rather, have learned the lesson which he taught his son William, that, 'If you're arrogant or rude, you'll never be forgiven for it. People remember you for that for ever.'[7]

A far more cheering reason for minimizing the peregrinations is that he is devoted to his grandchildren, four girls in all now, with the first having been born in 1995 and preparing to start training as a doctor in 2014. When Miller is away he misses them acutely. When he is home it is a joy twice over, he says, to watch them growing up and feel none of the worries which he went through as a parent. So, he explains:

> The travelling has lost its charm. As time has gone on, I've found that the labour of just moving around the world, in these vast luggage-hauling crowds, gets more and more burdensome and I hate it. I'm whittling away my life when really I'd rather be at home. I don't like being away from the grandchildren, from Gloucester Crescent, or from Rachel's garden.

*   *   *

While the opera productions started thinning out, another fertile branch of creativity burgeoned. His artworks of a non-dramatic variety have enjoyed several small-scale London exhibitions since 2000, causing one broadsheet to ask if he was due a second coming as an artist.[8] This line of interest can be traced back to his schooldays and his father's drawing and sculpting, or, certainly, to his Germano Facetti-inspired fondness for paper ephemera. Privately, he always kept tinkering: learning the ropes of photography from Betty's old admirer, Sam Rosenberg, in Sixties Manhattan (before their bust-up over *Mr Sludge*), trying screen printing when he had a spare minute in the Seventies, and amassing artistic scrapbooks through the Eighties and beyond.

A key development occurred in the Nineties, when he was at a loose end in Florence and, as he puts it, he turned into 'Jack the Stripper'. Prowling the streets every night with a Stanley knife, he would loiter by billboards, slashing titbits off ragged posters and stuffing them into plastic bags. He was once approached in mid-dissection by a policeman who, wondering if this was a superannuated vandal or some sort of mad anti-publicity campaign, questioned him: 'Che fai?' On hearing the explanation, the strong arm of the law soon shrugged appreciatively: 'O arte! OK!' This left the exonerated miscreant to tiptoe back to his hotel room and arrange his hoard into a new series of paper collages. Overlapping torn slivers of typography with strips of pure scarlet, mustard yellow or rain-washed blue, he reconfigured the accrued snippets with a fragmented yet formal beauty, adding an occasional trickle of paint or a skeletal grid of pencil lines.

Then in New Mexico he was taught how to weld. The art dealer-turned-benefactor Eugene Thaw and his wife, who knew Miller from Glimmerglass, provided accommodation on their Santa Fe estate. One afternoon, their guest got talking to their handyman, Jim Johnson, who suggested that Miller should try working in metal, and promptly showed him how to join girders. After that they drove around in a pick-up truck once a week, scavenging for cast-offs in scrapyards. An element of male bonding was involved as Miller declared that the joy of stripping to the waist, donning a visor and letting the sparks fly was undeniably a macho thing.[9] There was a distant echo, perhaps, of that teenage summer job, smelting sparking-plugs under the arches in Battersea.

His roughest constructions in iron and steel, while bringing Anthony Caro's sculptures to mind, can look like artistic accidents, as if a bunch of sawn-off pipes and RSJs happened to have become magnetized in some corner of a building site. Other pieces have a very fine tranquil composure, strong yet delicate, using sheet metal to build up abstract shields or friezes, with overlaid rectangles, triangles, discs and crescents.

When not in New Mexico with the welding gear, he has carried on making his bricolage, or *assemblages* as he calls them, by employing other found materials. This has produced some particularly satisfying works in wood, combining chunky cubes and cylinders, the perpendicular and the sharply slanted, subtly varied grains, sometimes with a bright dash of paint on one plane. In tandem, his photography has become more abstract. There are close-ups of tattered billboards (like instant collages in their own right), of crumpled cardboard boxes, peeling walls, rust-blistered skips.

If his collages are partly inspired by the artist Kurt Schwitters, and if his sculptures are influenced by the Russian Constructivists, those photographs have affinities with Aaron Siskind and Bruce Chatwin. More in line with Thomas

Jones' offbeat paintings, his snapshots of rooftops are architectonic while being framed off-centre. They offer deliberately atypical views, with the subject slipping off the fringe of the picture, and with expanses of sky above.[10]

A handful of his images had a preliminary airing in the *Observer* magazine in the mid-Nineties. That was followed by his quietly beautiful book entitled *Nowhere in Particular*.[11] Published in 1999, it united many of his best photographs with a loose patchwork of aperçus from his personal notebooks. The eclecticism is quintessentially Millerish. His jottings range from literary descriptive prose to hypotheses about theatre and art criticism. Comic exchanges overheard on planes, like nuggets from an Alan Bennett play, lie alongside neurological and philosophical pensées, with nods to Wittgenstein and Bertrand Russell. Here are a few examples:

Dreaming
It's possible to wake quite slowly from a nasty dream and it may take some time to recognise the fact that one has been unhappily awake for several minutes. You can roll gently in and out of restless sleep, imperceptibly passing from the imagery of dream to the train of wakeful thought, like a half-drowned sailor washed backwards and forwards in the shallow breakers at the low-tide line – gradually and unnoticeably left high and dry [etc.]

Overheard
'I think television is the curse of the age. I used to think it was the aeroplane.'
'I travelled on an American boat – though, speaking personally, I've never had any faith in American seamanship.'
'I've never been much good at looking down steep ravines. How about you?'
'I can remember the time when you couldn't give snooker tables away.'

Air miles
Striding along the moving walkway at Frankfurt airport I get the enigmatic impression of weightlessness. Presumably this is because the speed at which visual images stream across my retina is much greater than it would be if I were walking unaided. It's as if one weighs oneself by comparing the muscular effort that one puts into an action with the visual displacement that results.

More about seeing in
Wollheim talks about seeing apples *in* the paintwork (as opposed to the traditional expression of seeing the paintwork *as* apples). It may seem obvious and trivial but there are all sorts of 'seeings in' and it would be nice to be clear about the differences.

1 Seeing apples *in* the foliage . . .
2 Seeing something in a container. Apples *in* a bowl or *in* a box or indeed *in* a bowl *in* a room.
3 Seeing faces in leaves [etc.][12]

Soon after *Nowhere in Particular*, more of his photographs and collages were exhibited under the auspices of an art-in-hospitals scheme called the Nightingale Project. Dr Miller thus improved the quality of patients' lives by unexpected means at the South Kensington and Chelsea Mental Health Centre. Since then his wood, paper and metal works have been shown at two fringe galleries in London and at the Daniel Katz Gallery in Old Bond Street (normally dedicated to Renaissance works).[13]

He has toyed with the idea of bringing out a second photography book (working title, *Considerable Detail*) and, in the last few years, he has befriended Anthony Caro, spending several days working at the sculptor's studio. In this progression from objets trouvés to moulding from scratch, he has sculpted a human body with the torso opened up, as in an autopsy.[14] Encouraged by Caro to do more, he has started spending afternoons at the Royal College of Art as a kind of unofficial, mature student.[15] He would like to attempt large-scale works in metal. He fancies having one standing outside Waterloo Station. One of his arc-welded sculptures was scaled up massively, to form a stage set of angular, rusty towers in his production of Stravinsky's *Oedipus Rex* in Graz. That was a first for him: recreating his own, not just others' artworks on the stage.

If asked to analyze his artworks, he points up, first, that he has a predilection for formal geometric arrangements.[16] On the simplest level, he just has an eye for pleasing shapes. Biology's symmetrical baupläne and metameric segmentations, of course, entranced him long ago and – though his mature artworks embrace jagged asymmetries – his sheet-metal pieces faintly recall his youthful fascination with the human body's 'heraldic . . . almost armorial arrangement'.[17] Maybe his brain was imprinted, even before that, with the highly geometric London map of his infancy: the John Nash crescents and verdant squares, the Inner and Outer Circles of Regent's Park.

Second, he stresses that the found objects in his sculptures are detached from their original location and without personal associations. In other words, these inanimate émigrés are non-autobiographical.[18] Third, however, he speaks of appreciating the overlooked, those things sidelined or considered past their sell-by date. He says that he believes, almost religiously, that it is in 'the negligible or the neglected' that the 'considerable' is to be found. That sounds like a link between his art and his life. 'Could he by any chance be talking about himself?' asked the *Sunday Telegraph*, only too aware of his complaints about being undervalued in Britain.[19]

His policy of salvage, and the torn or corroded surfaces in his artworks might serve as an analogue, a metaphor for his personal sense of being damagingly exposed to critics and undeservedly trashed. Nonetheless, it is wrong to assume that encroaching obsolescence has instigated his creed about the negligible and the neglected. Digging around in the archives reveals that he was incubating his tenet over 50 years ago, writing admiringly about Paolozzi's junk sculptures in a *UCH Magazine* article headlined 'Throw Away Line: Towards a Definition of Rubbish'.[20] The creed has well-established parallels in his theatre work as well, most evidently in his liking for 'negligible' gestures and his principle of *renovatio*.[21]

In an ironic twist on the theme of neglect, less attention has been paid to his art than he would like. Showing me his stash of photographic scrapbooks, he exclaims with frustrated eagerness, undisguised pride and some habituated need for public validation: 'This is what I do. This is ninety per cent of my life but, oh, it's hopeless! I'll die without these things being known!' Without much of a PR drive, *Nowhere in Particular* passed virtually unnoticed and, even when his son William became the Saatchi Gallery's communications director during 2003 (via the Nigella Lawson connection), Miller was never going to become a big fish in that Britpack collection.[22] Few critics have reviewed his exhibitions, some gallery owners have reportedly dismissed his *assemblages* as sheer garbage, and, adding insult to injury in 2007, a passing scrap metal merchant gaily carted off two outsize pieces from the front garden in Gloucester Crescent. At least their creator had sufficient humour to remark that they had been returned to the tip whence they came.[23]

At root, his art has been scorned by certain sections of the press because of the continuing Renaissance Man issue and the idea that he is a one-man show-off. The *Sunday Telegraph*'s opinion piece said it all with its headline, 'The polymath as irritant . . . now he's become an artist'.[24] This was the last straw: the theatrical exhibitionist now dabbling in exhibitions. Still, he has not done badly for a rookie. The *Independent*'s Kevin Jackson championed his new talent; *The Times*' art critic John Russell Taylor contributed an appreciative essay to Miller's Boundary Gallery catalogue; and a TV documentary, sportively entitled *Absolute Rubbish*, followed him out to Santa Fe.[25] In that programme, it was a joy to watch Miller being, in the main, forgivably boastful and full of sunny bounce as he hunted for scrap with Johnson and jubilantly applauded passing freight trains.[26] His childhood love of locomotives is unabated, though, as a traveller, he now discerningly loves branch lines for the generally ignored viewpoints they offer on the world.[27]

He has turned curator too. The launch pad was a series of lectures, named *From the Look of Things*, which he gave at London's National Gallery in the mid-Nineties.[28] The four topics he examined were the gaze in art; how movement is visualized in a static medium; the difference between pictures and mental images; and the nature of reflection. Out of that final talk sprang *Mirror Image*, his major National Gallery exhibition.[29] It was part of a novel wave of shows curated by intellectuals, not just rounding up works by one artist or school. Miller was investigating both paintings and the science of perception. He set out to explore how our eyes and brains see or interpret mirror images; precisely how reflective surfaces are imitated on canvas; and what visual games are played with virtual realities-within-virtual realities (the equivalent, in art, of plays-within-plays in the theatre).

He definitely shook up conservative aesthetes with his category-defying medley. Renowned paintings such as Van Eyck's *Arnolfini Marriage* were displayed alongside visual teasers by lower-ranked artists such as Escher. In the mix were physics diagrams, cheeky zoological photos (chimps eyeing their reflected private parts), and entertaining installations (such as a corridor of mirrors). Worried that great art was getting confused with chaff, those critics who took umbrage felt that the exhibition – and Miller's handsome accompanying book, *On Reflection* – overplayed the science, just using the paintings to demonstrate sometimes obvious points. The *Evening Standard*'s pundit, Brian Sewell, impetuously pronounced that the curator knew nothing of the history of art and, by way of a coda, he cast a peculiarly off-putting aspersion. 'I just wanted to get out my penis and flash it at all those mirrors,' Sewell declared.[30]

The public flooded in regardless, and other reviewers praised the show for managing to be intellectually stimulating and unsnobbish.[31] Miller was especially sharp on the phenomenon of apparent sheen. By zooming in on reflections, he revealed that the gleam does not actually exist. When the mind surmises that a particular surface is reflective, it conjures up the glint. This is, presumably, to distinguish the potentially treacherous zone.

Having been accused, already, of stripping plays of their magic, now the rationalist Miller was explaining away lovely shimmers. Yet, when he presented the viewer with a cropped close-up, the effect was of a wizard trick. Hey presto! The gleam disappeared. Writing in *The Times*, the media don Lisa Jardine cheered him for, once again, triumphantly spanning the Two Cultures, and the Science Museum's head of exhibitions, Graham Farmelo, rebuked Sewell's condescension. 'I believe [*Mirror Image*] will', he wrote, 'be remembered as a landmark in innovative art interpretation.'[32]

Behind the whole enterprise lay Miller's perennial infatuation with glass and glimmer, luminosity and trompe l'oeils. With hindsight, aficionados could also mull on the myriad looking-glasses which have featured in his productions down the years – a phenomenally long mirror phase, so to speak. They have glistened quietly in everything from *Alice* to his Almeida *Midsummer Night's Dream*, from his *Così* to his *Carmen* where the heroine dies still checking her face in a compact.[33]

Cutting from the science to the symbolism of mirrors in art, *On Reflection* helped to illustrate why they have been such richly suggestive props. They variously denote vain self-regard, wise self-knowledge, and the mercurial question of alter egos. That's not to mention passages into other worlds, as in Lewis Carroll. Miller's own professional plurality chimed with the thoughts that he had about mirror-gazing during his National Gallery venture:

> We are always intrigued by the idea that we may contain at least one other personality that is in an ambiguous subversive partnership with ourselves . . . Are we in fact one thing or are we a loosely organized confederation of separate independent personalities who are operating under one business heading?[34]

In 2007, Miller went on to work as the specialist adviser on the Imperial War Museum's major exhibition *Camouflage* (uniting zoological trompe l'oeils and cubism with military history). He then curated *On the Move* at London's Estorick Gallery.[35] *On the Move* may sound like a portrait of his own restless career, but his subject was the fast-shutter photography of Eadweard Muybridge and Etienne-Jules Marey, showing how their multiple, sequential images of people and animals in motion influenced the futurists and the depiction of movement in painting. This illuminating exhibition pipped Tate Britain's 2011 Muybridge exhibition to the post.[36]

Lastly, from curator to artist's model. In the National Portrait Gallery's permanent display, a large canvas now hangs depicting Miller.[37] In Stephen Conroy's oil painting, he has adopted the pose of the angel in Dürer's *Melencolia* and Rodin's *The Thinker*, leaning hand on chin. He often falls into that position during everyday conversation – as Conroy observes, 'a natural Rodin' – but the subject himself concedes that he was probably eschewing any suggestion of showbiz frivolity.[38] Since then, another haunting picture of him has become the iconic front cover of a book on portrait photography. Mark Guthrie's close-up of his pale weathered face, half turned away with eyes almost closed, captures intense sensitivity while looking eerily frozen, like a death mask. The brow is furrowed with pain or concentrated ecstasy, as if listening to music.[39]

⋆   ⋆   ⋆

While art has occupied more of Miller's time, the invitations to direct have not dried up, so a small fleet of stage productions is always taxiing to take-off. He entirely rethought *Fidelio* for the Danish National Opera in 2007, crisply translating it to Pinochet's dictatorship. This staging deserves a wider audience.[40] Grappling with *Don Giovanni* in Valencia, conducted by Lorin Maazel, he impressively worked round the hair-raising collapse of the stage floor, which left his set in smithereens at the bottom of a crevasse, just before opening night.[41]

He has lost footholds due to regime changes, for example at Santa Fe.[42] Nevertheless, more than a decade after his last Glimmerglass production, he returned to the rolling hills of Upstate New York to realize his American take on *Jenufa*, the one which the ENO rejected.[43] His portrait of Czech émigrés, in the Northern plains during the Great Depression, received standing ovations, as did his stagings of *La Traviata* and of Purcell's *Dido and Aeneas* when, in 2009, Glimmerglass celebrated his twenty-year association with them.[44] He has, meanwhile, continued to be a favourite at the Brooklyn Academy of Music, with his *St Matthew Passion* enjoying its fourth BAM revival at Easter in 2009, and with his Glimmerglass' *Traviata* recreated there in 2012.[45]

Back in Britain, Miller fetched up at Sheffield's high-ranking regional theatre, the Crucible, to direct Joanna Lumley in Chekhov's *The Cherry Orchard*. So much for all his oaths of 'Never again' regarding theatre productions. The *Sunday Times*, most gratifyingly, declared that this intelligent staging showed British audiences what they had been missing during the hiatus.[46] It was essentially a classic production in period costume, certainly a far cry from his Sixties satirical notion of a lethally avant-garde staging on the tracks of the downline from Edinburgh.

Soon after the Chekhov, Miller moved on to his fourth production of *Hamlet*.[47] This was at Bristol's Tobacco Factory, with the cockpit theatre company established by Andrew Hilton, formerly of the Oxford and Cambridge Shakespeare Company. Before the show even opened, its run was extended because of unprecedented box-office demand. Its gripping lucidity won accolades, with a fine central performance from the little-known Jamie Ballard, who was a weeping and sardonic Prince of Denmark.[48] Hilton himself, now white-bearded, reprised the role of Old Hamlet's ghost. This was, again for the *Sunday Times*, 'the best and the most thrilling production of this great play . . . in years', although not everyone would appreciate Miller's proclaimed aim of radically naturalistic speech, 'taking the poetry out of Shakespeare' in opposition to the verse-speaking style long associated with Cambridge's Dadie Rylands and Peter Hall.[49]

Late in the day, he has also enjoyed a septuagenarian comeback at the English National Opera. After Nicholas Payne's departure, the ENO spent some time in disarray. A bevy of arts journalists kept asking why on earth Miller was not being brought back into the fold, given that his golden oldies were, alone, sustaining the company's reputation. The ENO eventually listened to this.[50] As well as presenting more revivals – *The Mikado*, *Rigoletto*, and the twenty-first anniversary staging of *The Barber of Seville* – the company finally invited him back to create two new productions, after thirteen years. These were *La Bohème* in 2009 and *The Elixir of Love* the following year.[51]

In line with his previous stagings of *La Bohème* on the continent, Miller updated Puccini's tragedy, about doomed love and cash-strapped bohemians, to Paris in the Great Depression. This was achieved by evoking the monochrome, shadowy, period photographs of Brassaï and André Kertész, as well as the films of René Clair and Pagnol. Miller was extremely happy working with his young cast, including the rising star Alfie Boe who played the romantic hero, Rudolfo.[52] The production was additionally picked to popularize opera by new means. Sky Arts televised the opening night live and, for the first time in the medium's history, the hectic backstage activity was broadcast in synch, being shown on a second channel. This simulcast (after a 48-hour delay due to London being engulfed in snow) went off pretty well.[53] The production quickly secured a successful international transfer to Cincinnati Opera. Some of the British critics expressed serious disappointment, declaring the evening dull and unengaging. A handful, by contrast, found the acting intelligently low-key and predicted that it would become another long-lasting classic. Revived the following year, it would gain more acclaim.[54]

As for *The Elixir of Love*, Donizetti's folksy Basque Country comedy centres around a mountebank's love potion, but Miller and his designer Isabella Bywater wittily transposed all that to a roadside eatery in 1950s Texas. Working together and being firm friends for over a decade, Miller and Bywater, in fact, first collaborated on this Texan *Elixir* for its Royal Swedish Opera premiere, in Stockholm in 2003, followed by a New York City Opera transfer in 2006.[55] Audiences at London's Coliseum were treated to stylish visuals and a cheekily idiomatic American translation. The red neon signs of Adina's peppermint-green diner glowed against a desert backdrop, and the elixir-hawking snake-oil salesman, Andrew Shore's Dr Dulcamara, rolled up in a Chevy convertible.[56]

This generally went down a treat.[57] The trouble was that Miller had, meanwhile, misfired by publicly grumbling about how his Bristol *Hamlet* had not been snapped up for a West End transfer. He complained of Theatreland's celebrity obsession, making reference to the RSC's London-bound *Hamlet* starring 'the man from *Dr Who*' – namely, the much-loved actor David Tennant. He was instantly shot down for this, with many retaliating that he was behaving like an anti-popularizing snob and was foolishly ignorant of Tennant's substantial career in classical theatre.[58] Michael Billington had manifestly had enough. He alluded, in his *Guardian* blog, to Miller's whingeing and 'the boiling oil of sour grapes'.[59] Tennant himself was relatively mild in his response, saying that he had always been a Miller fan and to be 'slagged off by someone you've never met but always rather liked is a bit crushing'.[60]

None too wisely, Miller made further headlines in mid-2010. This was the month in which he dismissed the Edinburgh Fringe Festival; scorned Gilbert and Sullivan as simply 'boring self-satisfied English drivel' and as 'UKIP set to music'; reiterated his generalized West End celebrity-casting complaint; and added that he had not been to a play in nearly ten years (a comment sweeping aside his occasional attendances at the Donmar and National Theatre). He stated, slightly bizarrely, that he'd rather stay home or just go to Marks & Spencer.[61]

Commercial Theatreland producers had expressed a preliminary interest in a transfer of *The Cherry Orchard*, and in half a dozen other schemes, including a Haymarket Theatre Royal residency. However, no contracts have been signed there to date.[62] Nor have Miller's hopes that Riverside Studios, in west London, might become his UK equivalent of BAM come to anything, in spite of discussions about him staging an Ibsen there, or a Beckett, or a docudrama about Raphael Lemkin (the Nuremberg Trials adviser who coined the term 'genocide').[63] Likewise, still to bear fruit is the 2010 declaration by Islington's King's Head pub theatre-turned-opera house that Miller would be directing there.[64]

Far more productive was the sudden invitation from Nicholas Hytner to discuss a National Theatre project. Having risen from his stripling days at Kent Opera to run the NT, Hytner clearly still rated Miller and scheduled a staging of his *St Matthew Passion* for the Olivier auditorium in September 2011.[65] Half a lifetime after Miller's feud with Peter Hall, this marked his directorial debut in the South Bank building. That month was a professional Indian summer to a modest degree, as the NT simultaneously presented *One Thing and Another*, a foyer exhibition of his artworks, and as the ENO followed up a triumphant twenty-fifth anniversary production of *The Mikado* with a warmly received *Elixir of Love* revival.[66]

Miller is now scheduled to direct another play, *Rutherford and Son*, Githa Sowerby's drama about a Victorian industrialist and overbearing patriarch who, intent on preserving the family business, clashes with his rebellious children. This is being staged, in early 2013, in a converted mill in Yorkshire, by Barrie Rutter's company Northern Broadsides. Miller is planning to experiment with overlapping dialogue again.[67]

Over in the US in the Noughties, he also pulled off a prestigious Broadway transfer with his fifth *Lear*, starring Christopher Plummer as the outcast king. Starting at the Stratford Festival of Canada (North America's largest classical rep programme), this staging went on to the Lincoln Center.[68] The *New York Times* adored Miller's intimate, 'deeply personal' vision and Plummer's subtle mapping of encroaching senility. It was 'the performance of a lifetime', the critic Ben Brantley proclaimed, adding that he had 'never seen an audience so saturated in tears'.[69] The *New York Review of Books* further analyzed the remarkable use of space and pace: having Lear on a narrow thrust stage, visibly 'taking up too much room [so] he needs to be thrust out', with entrances and exits winding round staircases, like the merciless action of a grinder.[70] In the final race against time, the director increased the momentum by splicing scenes into each other, with one transcendent minute of contrasting stillness when Lear – reunited with Cordelia – envisages their imprisonment together being blissfully serene.

This didn't stop other New York columnists praising Plummer but throwing the director to the dogs.[71] Miller was, once again, verbally whipped for denying the play its majesty, together with accusations of leaden staidness. An *Observer* report, back in the UK, even suggested he was to blame 'in no small part' for a slump in British prowess on Broadway. His direction, it suggested, was 'the stuff of bog-standard provincial repertory', without any detectable interpretation whatsoever.[72] Plummer begs to differ:

> I had no intention of playing King Lear. I'd always thought he was a terrible old boring kvetcher . . . and I'd just got out of Peter Hall's production [in LA]. Then I found that Jonathan had such a wonderful take on him [Lear] and on the play . . . 'If you take care of the comedy, the tragedy will take care of itself.' There is a lot of unbelievably ironic humour in the play which one doesn't often see when it's performed. That was the great value of his concept, and its simplicity – no gimmicks, just total starkness, the absence of music which was absolutely right, just the sound of the wind and dogs barking . . . nothing to lean against or hide behind. That's the way you should tackle these great plays.

The production ultimately landed two Tony nominations: Best Revival and Best Actor for Plummer. The star now longs to persuade his director back to screen drama, to film an *Alice Through the Looking-Glass*, but that is probably a pipe dream.

★   ★   ★

Miller's long-term contribution to British culture has earned further public recognition, including an honorary doctorate from Cambridge University and fellowship of the Royal College of Physicians, matching his father's FRCP of 50 years earlier.[73] In 1999, he attended the Queen's Lunch of the Century for the country's top achievers, an honour of which his bearskin-making grandfather, Abram, could only have dreamed. In 2002 he was knighted.

That elicited a few snipes about the former anti-establishmentarian satirist taking a grand title. Some muttered that it tallied with his imperious habit of denouncing 'impudent' critics, as if he now deemed himself a sacred cow.[74] Miller may well have found it pleasant to be graciously thanked for a lifetime's work. Friends say it mellowed his feelings for Britain somewhat, but his left-wing leanings still make him squirm about having accepted the KBE, and he never wants to be called Sir Jonathan.[75] Nor has being titled deactivated his satiric impulses vis-à-vis royal ceremonies. He humorously mimics how Her Majesty did an alarmed double take, whipping round as the palace band started playing 'If I Were a Rich Man'. He further recalls how he saw Mrs Thatcher, in a suspiciously crown-like hat, rubbing shoulders with the monarch, 'like the Red and White Queen in *Alice*'.[76]

He respects Elizabeth II. She is 'fine,' he says, 'nice, clever, knows what's going on'. He and the heir apparent hit it off as well at the Investiture when Prince Charles quipped: 'I hear you are out of the country a great deal nowadays. I wish I were in your shoes!'[77] When asked if he is a royalist, he hesitates and says:

> I suppose I am a republican in my heart, but not an enthusiastic one. It might have been better if we had gotten to be one in 1649 and stayed one after the Commonwealth was established . . . I go along with what we've got, in spite of all the absurdities . . . I have a feeling it's one of the things which gives England a sheet anchor and a keel.

*   *   *

A classic case of seeing the glass half-empty, he was miffed that his knighthood only 'worthlessly' acknowledged his services to the arts. The resulting upside is that he has increased his services to science, latterly making yet another comeback, as a presenter of BBC documentaries. He says he is not such a polymath that he could leap back into the saddle as a practising medic. Not so long ago, he found himself in a hair-raising crisis on a plane, when the steward put out an emergency call for any doctor on board to make their presence known. Several passengers pointedly turned to stare at him until he found himself propelled into action, diagnosing a case of acute retention then desperately trying to think how to pass a catheter without any anaesthetic or lubricant. Mercifully, the aircraft managed to land in the nick of time.

Humorous rumour has it that, if friends are off-colour, he anxiously speculates on appalling illnesses while Rachel calmly diagnoses nothing serious. Or else he comforts the prospective invalid with the reckoning that he himself may have something far worse.[78]

In 2005, he finally became a Harley Street consultant, in the BBC2 drama *Sensitive Skin*.[79] This was entertaining casting: Miller in a cameo role as Dr Cass, a seemingly impeccable specialist, with a shameless habit of looking over his half-glasses and inspiring lucrative hypochondria. Perhaps there was something tragicomic about that: Miller just playing at being a medic, like Danny Kaye's Walter Mitty performing fantasy surgery. In real life, he remains formidably conversant with developments in neuroscience. He contributed, with noted brilliance, to the Q&A in V. S. Ramachandran's Reith Lectures and, during his academic residencies, he still goes on ward rounds and watches neurosurgery. 'I can't pretend it's any more than tourism, but at least I know exactly what's going on and can talk intelligently to the consultants about it. I'm not just like Danny Kaye,' he says.[80]

His mini-renaissance as a presenter of BBC science programmes began with *The Nation's Health*.[81] Here he was back on the radio with gravitas, almost 50 years after he first kidded around on the Light Programme. An intelligent person's guide to the modern history of British medicine, his Radio 4 series delved into the founding of the NHS. It tracked down extraordinary forgotten pioneers, and it came up to date, tackling the contentious issue of immunization.[82] These programmes were regularly in the *Guardian*'s 'Pick of the Day' listings.[83] He returned to present a further one-off, entitled *Flu: A Medical Mystery*.[84] With timely reference to fears about bird flu, he investigated the terrifying pandemic of 1918 which killed more people than World War 1 and which saw people dropping dead in the streets of London's East End. Miller's own paternal grandmother had been one of its victims.

His next Radio 4 series, *Self-Made Things*, took over Andrew Marr's *Start the Week* slot for a month in the summer of 2005.[85] This history of ideas traced how, via Darwin and the discovery of DNA, scientists have progressively come to understand reproduction and heredity, life's ongoing patterns of consistency and variation. Miller covered vintage ground here: Aristotle, Galen, William Harvey, and later theories which ranged from the Spemann Organizer (a command centre which tells cells what course of development to take) to extended phenotypes.[86] Featuring interviews with acclaimed professors such as Richard Dawkins, Simon Schaffer and the Nobel Prize-winner Aaron Klug, *Self-Made Things* was the equivalent of *States of Mind* for biologists.[87] It was also a variation on Emanuel's book *The Generations*, taking a genetic rather than a psychiatric angle. Some layfolks who tuned in expecting easy listening didn't know what had hit them. Others revelled in trying to keep up, if not cerebrally evolve on the spot.

Today's IT advances, with listen-again podcasts, should theoretically encourage more high-IQ programming. Moreover, BBC4 provides a small haven for such fare. In 2004, Miller had appeared on TV again, fronting *A Brief History of Disbelief* for that digital channel.[88] His mission was to recount the unsung story of godless thinkers, to 'make clear what our pedigree is', he said. The resultant three-part documentary dug up a startling cache of anti-theistical comments, not only from Ancient Greek philosophers, but also from American presidents.[89] En route, he revisited the Reformation and the Renaissance, Hobbes and Hume. He ferreted out accounts of eighteenth-century Paris' outspoken Baron D'Holbach, leading on to Thomas Paine, Darwin again, and Freud.

A Brief History was the culmination of his lifelong opposition to religion.[90] In essence, it was his mature reworking of that Chesterton Society debate at St Paul's when, aged fifteen, he attacked all superstitions as mental aberrations. He grants that some great scientists have been devout. Still, believing in supernatural myths is just hard-wired in the brain, he propounds, or else it is indoctrinated before a child's cognitive immune systems really start working.

The series brought in scholarly talking heads: the Nobel-winning physicist Steven Weinberg; Dawkins once more; Miller's professorial philosopher-friends Daniel Dennett and Colin McGinn; and, from the opposing camp, the theologian Denys Turner.[91] Arthur Miller made one of his last screen appearances here. His interlocutor's past assessment of him as 'a sound but essentially minor talent' had clearly been forgiven or forgotten.[92]

A flash of satire livened up the programmes' learnedness, when the presenter incorrigibly called the Holy Land 'the largest outdoor lunatic asylum in the world'.[93] In poking fun at the frightening sacred cow of fundamentalism, post-9/11, the ex-Fringer proved himself still controversial and, surely, more high-risk than ever before. The jokes were, however, wisely kept within bounds. Only weeks after A Brief History was aired, Birmingham Rep Theatre had its windows smashed by protesting Sikhs enraged at its supposedly sacrilegious new play, Behzti.[94] That brought stage censorship back in an alarming new form, and clamorous Christian demonstrators tried to stop the BBC broadcasting the irreligious spoof Jerry Springer: The Opera.[95] Before long Denmark's cartoons of the Prophet Muhammad had literally drawn blood, sparking international riots and attacks on embassies.[96] Some BBC4 staff, doubtless, thanked their lucky stars that A Brief History did not come under such fire.

A few jests came zinging back at Miller. Private Eye resurrected its 'Dr Jonathan' column with Boswell enquiring if the good doctor really disputed the existence of a superior all-knowing being, to which the smiling reply came: 'Indeed, sir, 'tis myself.'[97] Miles Kington, meanwhile, imagined United Deities as an ecumenical all-god forum who cast doubt on the existence of Miller, because being asked to believe in a transmogrifying medic-comic-director and career atheist was, frankly, pushing it.[98]

One incensed remonstration issued from A. A. Gill in the Sunday Times. The frontman's 'whiff of brimstone', his 'fog of reason' and the 'smugness of his brilliance' were all fierily condemned by Gill.[99] Christian websites picked up and ran with his complaint about Miller's sort who, in appreciating religious art, wanted to have their cake and eat it.

When aired in George Bush's Bible-bashing USA, the series caused rather more controversy. Rigorously conservative groups accused it of being demagogic propaganda, while the American Humanist Association sang its praises. Other progressives protested, via the web, about regional PBS TV stations which had failed to schedule it, or had allotted it only graveyard slots.[100] Back in Britain, Miller became a rallying point for atheists, and he was appointed president of the country's Rationalist Association.[101] Equally, he was held up as a shining example of old-fashioned public service broadcasting. The BBC received near-ecstatic feedback from viewers lauding *A Brief History* as a return to standards of excellence.[102] The *Guardian* found it exhilaratingly high-powered as well as urgently relevant, and Howard Jacobson in the *Independent* cheered, 'Give me wall to wall Jonathan Miller on telly and I would never leave the house.'[103]

Regardless, this comeback may have been a mere flash in the pan. Admiring columnists refer to him, regretfully, as a kind of cerebral last of the Mohicans, for he no longer embodies the spirit of the age.[104] If he was felicitous in the Sixties and Seventies – being clever and funny when bright young things were giving a sharp boost to Reithian values – a gulf is widening between him and today's so-called 'idiocracy'. Even *Top Gear*'s presenter Jeremy Clarkson (writing in the *Sunday Times* in 2009, under the heading 'Cleverness is No More'), bewailed the dumbing down of British television. Stating that producers assume that their viewers 'know how to breathe and that's about it', Clarkson added that the only intelligent comedy sketch show was *Harry & Paul* (starring Harry Enfield and Paul Whitehouse) which had just been shunted from BBC1 to BBC2. 'And you get the impression,' he concluded, 'it'll be gone completely unless they stop using Jonathan Miller as a butt for their wit. Today you are not allowed to know about Jonathan Miller because if you do, you are a snob.'[105]

In his time, Miller was a kind of expansionist empire in his own right, steaming into many cultural fields with enormous energy. Now, with his standing diminished, he wants the new superpower, Dumbing Down, to have no dominion. In my book, he is on the side of the angels in that respect. Though he might sound haughty or excessively insulting, his criticisms have usually pinpointed fundamental flaws in contemporary society. Crusading against the rise of the 'morons', he vigorously condemns BBC commissioners' numerous peabrained shows about home makeovers and how to chop up vegetables.[106] Refusing to scrunch down for the small screen's shrinking IQ, he stormed out of BBC2's lightweight discussion programme *What the World Thinks of God*, calling it (with reference to the channel's then controller) 'real Jane Root shit'.[107]

Patently, he exaggerates when he says that nobody cares, that it's as if his TV career never happened, or as if he has merely spent his time 'shouting down an empty drainpipe'. *A Brief History* was given a second airing in 2005, on BBC2, and several of his screen dramas have surfaced again and been remarketed on DVD.[108] All the same, it took the BFI to push through the release of his BBC *Alice* and *Whistle and I'll Come to You* on disc, ranking them alongside works by Visconti and Godard.[109]

The Corporation has reacted minimally to the fan mail about Miller, declining to bring out the requested DVD of *A Brief History* and scarcely responding to the pleas for more presenting by him.[110] He has put forward several new series ideas, all turned down, and an in-house proposal to mark his seventieth birthday with a retrospective of his greatest TV work was rejected.[111] His seventy-fifth was celebrated, not by the BBC, but by BSkyB, which presented a mini Miller season in July 2009. Still, maybe the tide is turning again given that producer David Thompson's BBC *Arena* documentary about the doctor-director was aired and very enthusiastically received in 2012, followed by a showing of *The Zoo in Winter*.[112]

Miller has become history in another curious way, with his early career as a comic now being treated as part of showbiz legend. In recent years, he has been impersonated in several dramas about the Fringers.[113] The actor Jonathan Aris offered a somewhat arid impression of him as perpetually analytical in *Not Only But Always*, Terry Johnson's TV biopic which primarily focused on the volatile friendship between Moore (who died in 2002) and Cook (who preceded him in 1995).[114] An Edinburgh Fringe hit called *Pete and Dud: Come Again* also transferred to London in 2006.[115] It tinkered with the past, misrepresenting Miller as hostile to improvisation. In other words, his own life is now being rewritten with – depending on how you look at it – a lack of historical accuracy, or the inevitable inventiveness of a subsequent performance.

*   *   *

As regards rocky friendships, Miller continues to worry that, socially, he is not good at sustaining relationships. Rather than pointing the finger at his years of peripatetic work, he blames a mix of personal anxiety and laziness, as well as the long-term impact of feeling underloved in his infancy. His capacity also strikes him as meagre because friendship was so prized, as a core value, by the Apostles.

He can turn on a sixpence, very unsettlingly, if displeased, vituperating about someone for whom he has previously expressed fondness and admiration. His love, outside his immediate domestic circle, is conditional, not to say fickle. A few old acquaintances say the bigger problem is that his egocentric trait has become more marked, tiring or positively tedious. They suggest the great mind has turned into a bore, his expansive thinking shrunk to self-regard. This has been a big disappointment to them, if not Miller's personal tragedy. Garry Runciman from the Cambridge Apostles indicates that he largely stopped seeing Miller because:

> I (like others among his friends) later found difficult his extreme sensitivity to what he regarded as criticism of any kind. Since he was by far the most original and talented of my contemporaries, I always found this rather puzzling.

Runciman recounts one incident from as early as the 1970s. He recalls having made some mildly unflattering comment to Miller. One evening, soon afterwards, his personal secretary chanced to be at the theatre and she spotted the director in the stalls. She introduced herself, saying, 'You know my boss, Garry', to which came the reply, 'Would you please tell him that I don't criticize the books he writes, and he is not to criticize what I do.' Runciman got a second snappy response at a dinner party, having quoted to Miller Goethe's dictum, 'If you dislike being mobbed by the crows, don't climb to the top of the tower.' Miller retorted that Runciman couldn't know how nasty it was at the top.

By implication, this is why Gloucester Crescent is less frequented than of yore. As with the small boy in Betty's *On the Side of the Angels*, ill manners at the tea table have contrived to clear the room. Those lines from Stevie Smith's old poem, damning the brattish infant, suddenly echo uncomfortably down the years: 'the friends are put down/And the happy people do not come round'.

Miller and the ex-Footlighter Frederic Raphael notably had a rift which grew into a public feud. Raphael had, long ago, slipped a satirical dig into *The Glittering Prizes*, his novel which was turned into a TV drama in the mid-Seventies. In the book, the protagonist's chums titter about a Cambridge May ball cabaret, saying: 'They've got this brilliant young man who does Bertrand Russell singing *La Traviata* . . . He also impersonates the days of the week. I'm dying to see his Friday.'[116] Then in 1989, Miller slaughtered the author in a widely reported Folio Society debate on adapting novels for the screen.[117] As Miller's domineering Big Bill Brutus had told Raphael's Hopalong Cassius, all those years ago in Footlights: 'Leave the talkin' to me.'

Worse, Miller went on to have a furious altercation with Raphael's son, Paul, not realizing who he was.[118] Reportedly, he enraged the latter by repeatedly making comments during a screening of one of the *Godfather* movies in a Chelsea cinema. When rebuked on the way out for 'Renaissance yob behaviour' by Raphael Jnr, Miller charged up the street in pursuit, shoving a £20 note at the complainant, by way of a refund, and shouting, 'Take it, you cunt!'

Raphael Snr was not going to let Miller have that sort of last word. He promptly published an account of the fracas in *Prospect* magazine.[119] He followed that up eight months later with a satirical short story called *Son of Enoch* (an allusion to a comparable tale by Max Beerbohm).[120] The main character was a certain Methuselah Soames, who was stammering, skittish and unstoppably high-flying. Soames appeared in a Cambridge revue alongside the narrator, but was privy to a far more exalted Apostolic world. He was 'the unmistakable comet; the rest of us [being] . . . but a train of concomitant dross, sparkling with reflected glory'. The tale continues: 'Methuselah had so many gifts . . . such oscillating purposes, that his genius lay precisely in his lack of precision . . . Parody and paradox marched in step for him.' Going on to soaring renown in mid-century London, Methuselah meets up with the novelist-narrator once more, only to boast of producing a book of his own. This he has done ingeniously, 'By not writing it . . . a masterpiece which cannot ever be criticised.' Stepping into the future, the unlaurelled storyteller sees that the blank-paged novel by his former friend – entitled *Nothing* – has sold millions of copies and gained awestruck reviews. He himself has one paltry entry in literary history, for having been at university with Soames.

Raphael provoked an extra flurry of media gossip by slipping in an insinuation that Miller once had a fling with Princess Margaret:

> By night, [Methuselah] often dined, candle-lit, with a scandal-hit princess who, the toadies croaked, solicited from him an insolence of style which would have led her to banish another from her table. Who has not heard the story that when she proposed marriage, he told her that she was beneath him? Some even say that, at the time, it was literally true.

This story is an elegantly written and lacerating match for *Beside the Seaside*, Stevie Smith's portrait of Miller's childhood precocity. The two sit like a pair of corrosive bookends to his life amidst the literati. Once again, though, the satire is complicated in *Son of Enoch*. Besides its palpable envy, a strange undertow of elegiac yearning and bruised adoration runs through it, as when Raphael writes:

> If I imagined, with silly sentimentality, that Methuselah might, from time to time, or decade to decade, renew contact with me, I underrated his economy of style. His absence from my life was the contact he had with me. Damn him to hell, he knew it.

In responding to Raphael's grievances, Miller was apologetic, to a certain extent. He said that he was ashamed of having lost his temper in the post-*Godfather* chase, only he did not retract the four-letter word. He conceded that the short story was virtuosic (as Betty had with *Beside the Seaside*). At the same time, he judged its vitriol to be battily obsessive, and he underlined that he had never disparaged his ex-buddy's considerable achievements. The Millers suggest that their real faux pas was donkeys' years ago, when they forgot to go to one of Raphael's dinner parties. They look sheepish recalling this, and then start giggling. Actually, it was two of his dinner parties, they say.

As for the royal affair, Miller comments that he often bumped up against Princess Margaret – socially, along with other showbiz folk – but he was never eligible material, being Jewish and married.[121] Having had a crush on Danny Kaye, though, she surely might have taken a shine to his comedic successor. 'Didn't she once', prompts Rachel, 'try to get you to take her home [from a society bash], and you didn't?' 'Oh, that's right!' Miller responds, adding hastily, 'Oh, not "*take her home*"! It wasn't a seduction.' 'I thought it was,' says Rachel. 'No, I don't think so,' says he. When I inquire if he liked the party-loving princess, he does not sound too enamoured.

> She was all right. She was awfully silly. She wanted to play both sides of the fence, to be part of the bohemian life, but at the same time let it be known that she was, after all, the Queen's sister. She had this mixture of imperiousness and intimacy, alternating between these freezings (if she felt that things had gone too far) and wanting to be totally informal . . .
>
> I remember once being invited to dinner by [the conductor] Raymond Leppard . . . just Raymond, me, some minor Rothschild and her . . . She would take out a reticule and reconstruct her face between mouthfuls with

this very elaborate nuclear silo of lipstick. Then, after dinner, she screwed her cigarette into her jewelled holder and stood beside the piano, in a high wavering voice going through a vast repertoire of famous musicals: [*Sings flutingly*] 'I could have danced all night!' Wonderful! . . .

As time went on, as her life disintegrated and she became more and more broken down, people became less and less respectful, huddling in the kitchen at parties refusing to talk to her. I remember Gore Vidal having a birthday party where he took Rachel and I by the elbows, saying, 'You must come over here and help me entertain the Hanoverian.'

Nor had Margaret exactly endeared herself to him when they first met. She chattered about morning prayers and the conversion of the Jews, before exclaiming, with the following peculiar turn of phrase, 'Oh, I didn't know Rachel was Jew!'

Perhaps more love was ultimately lost between Miller and Raphael who, in 2003, sent me this discernibly pained, though still pugnacious email:

I rather dread talking about ephemeral matters . . . Jonathan is an interesting man whom I have wished might have been my friend. It ain't worked out like that, as much (maybe) because we have our similarities as because we have (had) our differences . . . I have admired a number of things which Jonathan has done . . . and I remember our little number together in the 1954 Footlights, even if he doesn't. I wish our relationship had worked out otherwise than it did, but I don't propose to argue the toss about it.

Miller's childhood playmate, Nicholas Garland, sounds more quietly heartbroken and bewildered – not acerbic – about losing his friend's companionship in later life. He says:

I have no idea why, you know: I've never understood why we stopped seeing each other because there's no – He was my closest and dearest friend. It was to do with the break-up of my marriage [to Caroline] and I was – I was very sad. I really loved him.

Forgiving reunions are not on the horizon regarding Peter Hall, Joseph Volpe or Michael Billington. Hall concludes: 'A reconciliation? No, no, no. I think it's quite important to know who your enemies are, and I don't think you usually help yourself by trying to make up to them – certainly not Jonathan.'

For all these rifts, Miller has had lifelong loyal friends, especially in Eric Korn and Oliver Sacks. He affably keeps in touch with others: Penelope Wilton, Colin McGinn, Keith McNally. His peacemaking side has not been inactive either. Not so long ago, he accepted an invitation to lunch with the old gang from *Private Eye*. 'He went down rather well,' says Christopher Booker, sounding slightly wolfish, but acknowledging, 'He was thought a very genial fellow.' The opera critic Tom Sutcliffe has, likewise, enjoyed an entente cordiale. 'Jonathan called me up on Christmas Day,' he recalls. 'I was absolutely astonished. I'm not sure why he rang, except to have a long chat . . . a lovely chat. We've been talking about having lunch.' Garry Runciman's story ends with a rapprochement too, at least 'back on terms', he says, 'and out to dinner a couple of times'.

According to Cecilia Bartoli, the row over *Figaro* is now *finito*: 'I saw Jonathan recently,' she stated in 2005. 'It was all fine. I think this story is over.'[122] Having fallen out of favour, Peter Eyre was even happier to find himself playing the lead when Miller had one more theatrical fling at the Almeida, after *A Midsummer Night's Dream*. Eyre was creepily fascinating in *Camera Obscura*, a darkly comic, diary-based drama about Arthur Crew Inman – a kind of hermetic, hypochondriacal, Yankee Proust who shot himself in 1963.[123] The actor conjectures:

> Jonathan must have forgotten that I drive him mad when I work with him . . . I offended him once, saying something critical about a scene. He was hurt. He was very angry . . . We had several years when we didn't really speak, but we got on incredibly well [doing *Camera Obscura*]. It's all water under the bridge.[124]

Finally, some associates remark that Bennett does not frequent Miller's house as he once did, and that the ex-Fringers have drifted apart again. The duo, they observe, used to make each other laugh like eternal schoolboys, but that was always interspersed with 'non-speaks'. According to Peter Nichols, the Yorkshireman once wryly cried, 'Oh dear, I see Jonathan coming across the road and I just hide behind the furniture!' It is said that, when dramatizing *The Wind in the Willows*, he may have heard a surfeit of Miller's views on the book.

Another Gloucester Crescent rumour is that Bennett knew that his neighbour would always dash to take a phone call. Therefore, just for a prank, he would wait for Miller to emerge from his house. Having seen him secure all the locks and head down the front steps, Bennett would then dial his number and watch him going frantically into reverse. When the playwright was filmed for *The South Bank Show* in 2005, despite his ever-burgeoning acclaim, his last word was a regretful comparison with Miller. Seeming to think the cameras had stopped rolling, he sighed that his first experience of interviews had meant 'being in the shadow of Jonathan', witnessing his articulacy 'and never being able to do it'.[125]

A parallel might certainly be drawn with Bennett's recent National Theatre play, *The Habit of Art*. In this partly fictional work about W. H. Auden and Benjamin Britten, the latter visits his old friend and ex-collaborator after years of estrangement. Struggling to write an opera (*Death in Venice*) which is a veiled autobiography, Britten craves reassurance and encouragement, but he dislikes the dominant role Auden has always assumed in their relationship. Both men are portrayed as being anxious, in their last years, about professionally atrophying, and Bennett suggests that, fundamentally, what drives them is a desire for love or – in the case of Auden – just continued public attention, even if he merely achieves that by rankling.

Markedly, Britten finds himself suffering from a persistent sense of inferiority and expresses his frustration, recalling how, as a young man, he was overwhelmed by the torrent of magnificent words that would pour out of Auden. Though not devoid of tenderness, Auden seems selectively deaf, due to self-absorption, in his response:

> BRITTEN: I have not been alone with you in thirty years, but five minutes and I slide effortlessly back into the same groove, as tongue-tied as ever I was. I tell myself I am not the twenty-three year-old prodigy . . . I am Benjamin Britten, CH.

> AUDEN: CH! I do the occasional reading, mostly in America, where they always love me. The English are more . . . wary.[126]

Bennett declines to name names in his introduction to *The Habit of Art*, but he states:

> Thinking of *Beyond the Fringe*, now nearly half a century ago, makes me realise how I have projected onto Britten particularly some of the feelings I had when I was a young man . . . thrust into collaboration (which was also competition) with colleagues every bit as daunting as Auden.

He goes on to quote a passage cut from the final NT script, where Britten reminisces:

> In those days I used to bring along a few carefully worked out notions I'd had for the film shots and sequences, but it was no good. Wystan, you see, could never admit that I'd thought of anything first.
> 'Oh yes,' he'd say, as if I was just reminding him of something he'd thought of earlier . . . Either that or he'd scamper off with your idea and make it his own.

This is, clearly, an unhappy case of dialogic memory. While stating that he cannot sympathize with Britten's notorious habit of suddenly cutting friends out of his life, Bennett acknowledges that he identifies with the composer more than with the character of Auden.[127]

In the end, even with its ups and downs, Miller and Bennett's relationship has been less turbulent than Pete and Dud's. The dramatist is good friends with both Tom and Kate (who introduced Bennett to his long-term partner) and he has, now and then, been glimpsed nipping in for a cup of tea with their parents. Though they didn't catch *The _____* _____ _____ _____ went to see his NT _____ *story Boy* _____ key to their _____

What of more long-distance emotional reconciliations? What are Miller's feelings now when he recalls his late parents? He still sees them as having been insufficiently loving, and perhaps he will never forgive them for that. Yet he does speak tenderly of his teenage years with his mother, and he occasionally refers to his father as 'my dear old dad'. In 1998, he spoke warmly, on camera, of Emanuel's connections with W. H. R. Rivers. That was when he and a BBC TV crew journeyed to the Torres Strait to make a *Horizon* documentary, commemorating Rivers' anthropological expedition of exactly a century earlier.

More recently, he headed out to Dr E. Miller's child guidance clinic in the East End, as a guest speaker, to celebrate its seventy-fifth anniversary, declaring that he had not appreciated how cutting-edge Emanuel was professionally. In 2008, for a lecture at Liverpool University, he took along a volume of Sir Charles Sherrington's writings to highlight the interests which he had inherited, its opening leaves being inscribed: 'Emanuel Miller, St John's' and 'Jonathan Miller, St John's'.[128]

With the passage of time, it certainly seems that he has grown more understanding, for he confirms:

> It was useful [during the therapy sessions for writer's block] . . . to discuss things which were still painful, to make them explicit and then perhaps objectify them, put them at a distance from you . . . You become adjusted to it and think more generously about them [your parents] . . . Looking backwards, I see a landscape of pain that they were travelling through which made them perhaps less than competent.[129]

His sister Sarah died in 2006, having fallen into a coma after a car accident. He was away working abroad and did not fly back to be at her hospital bedside. She was an intelligent woman, loved classical concerts, knew her literary references. She used to join the family at Gloucester Crescent during Yuletide, and William believes that his father felt anxiously responsible for her. Her style of life out in suburban Hendon, however, seemed a million miles from her brother's world. Moreover, like Claudio and Isabella at the end of Miller's *Measure for Measure*, the siblings were never reconciled concerning her religious piety.

As regards his children, the worst clashes are probably past. Friends say that he mainly just worries, as do many of his class and age, about needing to remain a financial buttress. He has been alarmed by the recent stockmarket crashes and comparisons with the Great Depression, and he says that he keeps working principally to ensure that there is enough money in the bank.

Whenever I have seen a family gathering, it has been rumbustious and happy. *Long Day's Journey into Night* it most certainly isn't. Miller does not always resist the urge to assume centre stage. Nonetheless, if he launches into a woebegone monologue, he is often howled down and laughed out of it. Like Lear's Fool, his ̶ pectful. 'What are goin filial exasperation.[130] When he voices mixed feelings about his knighthood, the cry goes up that they only told him to accept it because they thought it might shut him up at last. On hearing yet another retirement speech, Tom recites the *Spitting Image* skit about him unstoppably juggling surgery with directing and a mini-cab service. Miller Snr looks momentarily mortified before conceding with an amused grimace, 'That really is quite good.'

On another occasion Tom arrives, solo, in the middle of an interview and perhaps wishes that his father wasn't preoccupied with that in the communal kitchen. He wanders off to Alan Bennett's house. It has been surmised that the father risked treading on the son's toes with the publication of *Nowhere in Particular*. Photography is, after all, Tom's job. In fact, Tom took that in his stride. After all, he hasn't done so badly himself, having had specially commissioned works exhibited at the National Portrait Gallery. Its archives house about 30 of his pictures.

One afternoon, I go round to Miller's house after he has been away for a long stint, and I find him sitting quietly at the kitchen table with Rachel and Tom. He is palpably enchanted to see his eldest child, giving his ear a stroke. It is a sweet, funny little gesture that, just for a second, feels like the Act V reunion in a Shakespearean late romance with everything forgiven – a sort of familial state of grace. Another day, Tom is heading out. His father asks him a parentally caring question, then, having not listened properly, repeats it. Tom rags him and they wave each other off with a round of mocking, vigorous insults. Miller himself later comments:

> The only thing which has actually given me a sense of security and continuity has been this household and these children. They may have suffered all sorts of things from me, [my] being famous and clever (as I seem to have become) probably being an ordeal to them all. But, nevertheless, I think they are fond of me, and the continuity provided by Rachel, and the spontaneous natural affection, created a world that has been a very good, alternative substitute for what I missed as a child. We are all banteringly at ease with one another and see more of each other than almost anyone else.

The American journalist Nelson Aldrich, a friend since the Millers' New York years, underlines the marital brilliance of Rachel. 'Jonathan has a wife who understands him, both his faults and his favours,' he says. 'She doesn't let him get away with much, but couches her discipline with good humour and affection. She's unbeatable. And I've rarely seen a more devoted husband, more respectful, more loving or more grateful.' She herself is not given to gushing and does not pretend that being wedded to such a famous man and big personality has been a bed of roses. 'But', as she puts it, 'that didn't really matter, because "he was it".'

All three of their children have now settled in north London, so they and the grandchildren can visit easily. Having once seemed the keenest to have a life elsewhere, William has bought a house just up the road, in Gloucester Crescent.

His relationship with his father may have been put under some strain by this fairly recent move. While refurbishments were in progress, he and his young family camped out for several months in the parental home, residing on the top floor, and William certainly sounded riled when Miller publicly lamented, in the *Sunday Times*, that his kids could have done better, made more of a living, got more satisfaction if only they had gone to university. The son retorted the following week, in the same publication, that he was surprised and that his father ought to feel guilty for naively packing them off to state schools.[131]

Still, when in a more appreciative mood, William remarks:

In spite of the fact that he was overbearing intellectually . . . I don't think I ever stopped, throughout my childhood, being deeply proud of him, of what he has achieved. I'm very, very proud to be his son. He was an incredibly loving and kind father. He's probably the most compassionate person I know . . . Many of our peers [from boho, Seventies NW1] died of drugs, became alcoholics, were deeply disturbed, but the three of us now, you know, we're fine . . .

My mother is the absolute pillar of the family, she created this incredible home which is probably the most important thing in my father's life . . . They've gone to hell and back. He's not the easiest person to live with and she's been a saint really. But for a theatre couple to have survived this long and to still be in love with each other as much as they are is staggering. And actually as they get older, it gets stronger . . . [When I was staying at their house recently], you would hear her giggling helplessly downstairs. He can still make her laugh like that . . .

He used to do these wonderful things when we were young too, taking us round art galleries . . . Of course he'd take you round five thousand paintings and by half-way you'd want to kill him. But I know that when he's not here anymore, I will walk into galleries and I will think, 'Why didn't I listen more and take more in?' It's the same thing with reading. I consume history books with a passion now and just think, 'Why didn't I listen to him when I was a child and enjoy this?'

What's interesting about most things my father taught me and I hated him for as a child [is that], as I get older, I've come to realize that in all cases, most cases, he was right. I just hope he'll still be around when my children are old enough, that I will be able to convince them not to be alarmed by his wanting to lecture them, and they will do those wonderful things that we did with him.

*　　*　　*

That leads on to the painful question of how Miller feels about his mortality, about the end being increasingly nigh. Has his childhood terror of death transmuted or intensified? He tells me, in a matter-of-fact way, that he has, of late, been photographing sleeping tramps who look indistinguishable from mortuary corpses. He thinks about death a great deal and remains puzzled by it, even though he has remarked that it is not unlike crossing the Channel. As the years pass, 'you get nearer to the shore, and you can actually, for the first time, not just make out this dim, insubstantial cliff, but you can see little houses and cars moving'.

He admits that an atheist's funeral is a forlorn affair and that he has occasionally indulged in fantasies about very peculiar afterlives: being tenuously present at his own burial, or somehow rematerializing in a bedsit in Derby, unsure of who he is. Obviously, he points out, that is all fearful nonsense. As he puts it:

> Consciousness is contingent upon a particular arrangement of cells . . . I know I'm not going anywhere after death. I can't even make sense of what sort of destination it would be . . . For transmigration, how would whatever it was that survived my death know that it was me while being a cockroach? The cockroach would be working flat out at being itself. I once had a joke about this: Marie Antoinette trying to comfort her maid on the way to the guillotine, saying, 'It's all right, Fifi, I have a feeling that I am going to be Shirley MacLaine – whoever that is.'

When he presented a pair of short Radio 4 programmes in 2009, entitled *The Line Between Life and Death*, a philosophical discussion about brain transplants led on to humorous musings about whether immortality would become intolerably boring (as in Janáček's *The Makropulos Affair*) or whether your personality would keep intelligently evolving.[132]

Miller's old theatre colleague John Wells, a Christian, once called him the most God-haunted atheist he had ever met, and anticipated some belated religious conversion.[133] Frankly, it is hard to envisage that happening. Miller himself thinks that he would have to be afflicted with dementia, and even then it would be improbable. He has popped into the odd Advent service and has even remarked that the atmosphere of pious expectancy there quickens some vestigial sense of the holy in him. Nevertheless, he has mainly attended with the interest of an anthropologist watching ritualistic observances.[134] Such occasions may inspire some kind of outsider's wistfulness in him or a vague nostalgia for his Anglican school assemblies. He, incidentally, disputes that his mother started speaking Hebrew near the end of her life and that any kind of rekindled spirituality led her to wander into the synagogue where she had got married.

He recalls Hume's words to Boswell: 'There are two darknesses, the one from which we came and the other to which we are going. Why should I fear the second more than I have any apprehension of the first?' He associates death, rather poignantly, with early childhood and Christmas parties: '[memories] of being collected slightly early, of there still being musical chairs, and jellies . . . It's being taken into the darkened hall [by Nanny] and . . . half-glimpsed there's a pretty girl crossing a lighted doorway, in an organdie dress, and laughing en route to some festivity that one now can't have.'[135]

He clearly still feels that to die is to be missing out on life, and he is not yet at peace with the notion that 'one's place will close over', that those you loved and who loved you will carry on without you. One afternoon, in a depression, he looks at crowds pouring into the Underground station at Leicester Square and describes it as the mass march to the grave. When he was in Oxford, a few years ago, presenting a literary evening of his favourite writings, he wept as he read the closing lines of Philip Larkin's *Toads Revisited*: 'Give me your arm, old toad;/ Help me down Cemetery Road.'[136] When downbeat, he talks of not wanting to carry on much longer. On another day, he'll say, 'The time will come . . . but right now I feel I've got some more things to do.'

He had a serious scare in early 2010, having to leave the opening night of a production because he felt unwell. Back at home, he collapsed in the small hours and was found by Rachel, prostrate in the hallway, juddering with pain and saying, 'I think I am dying.' Rushed to University College Hospital, where he once trained, he was treated for a kidney stone and hooked up to intravenous drips. Rachel was, understandably, shaken, yet within a week, fighting exhaustion, he was back casting for his next show, popping in to check on a current one, giving a platform talk, mouthing off about Peter Hall. He can't let it lie: life, work, the vexation.

What he really fears, he says, is a slow demise, Alzheimer's disease, or other neurological disorders which might leave him unable to communicate. The idea of long-drawn-out agonies terrifies him, but then 'coming to an end', he says, 'would be a blessing'.[137] He is a patron of the Voluntary Euthanasia Society (aka Dignity in Dying) because, while accepting that the ethical issues are complex, he believes that life ought to be like a bus ride. When you want to get off, you should be able to ring the bell.

What he additionally dreads is dying like his father, feeling he has been a hopeless flop. He confesses:

> I am now frightened of death for that reason – the immediate antecedent of thinking, 'Christ, I've been around for however many years and it's been a complete and utter flop. I have totally fucked up. I haven't done the serious physiology or the serious psychology that I might have done. All I've done is put on *King Lear*, which is about another flop!'

He once fancied that he would, one day, finally feel content with his achievements, but that may never happen. In spite of his laurels and guaranteed place in the history of the performing arts, he persists in feeling underloved.[138] As regards the fields of academic learning and science, an element of acceptance might be incipient in his Newton-inspired image of the sea of knowledge: 'I stand on the beach and look out across this enormous rolling ocean of what is to be known and realize that there is absolutely no chance of knowing it now.'[139] More often he has compared his acute sense of failure and exclusion to Jude the Obscure dying in Oxford, hearing the applause from the Sheldonian where others are being awarded their degrees.[140] On return trips to St John's, he has come close to tears, wandering through the quad as the bell summons the dons to dinner in hall. He has even contended that Cantabrigian intellectual puritanism has been the mainspring of his depressions. Once you have encountered Bloomsbury and Apostolic ideas, he says, 'you will almost inevitably arrive on your deathbed in the knowledge that you have blown it'.[141]

If religion-induced guilt can lead to depression, then this is the intelligentsia's self-chastising equivalent. Maybe it is not surprising that he remains fascinated by J. L. Austin's philosophical *Plea for Excuses* – studying how people deal with their faulty performances in life – or that he still dwells on the Wittgensteinian issue of volition, as in 'My arm goes up' or 'I raise my arm.' After all, he stresses, 'this brings up deep questions about responsibility: "For what things can I be blamed and for what things can I be praised?"'[142]

The root problem is that, as during his confused primary school days, he cannot do the maths. He mistakenly calculates that dozens and dozens of drama productions aren't equal to one scientific paper, thinking that all his directing adds up to nothing.[143] It's a defect of perception, a blind spot. It's a bias toward science bordering, ironically, on the irrational, lumbered with emotional baggage. He too easily denies that his stage and screen work has, if not actually saved lives, valuably enriched many. Going so far as to side with John Carey's polemic *What Good are the Arts?*, he suggests this whole side of our culture probably does not merit any government subsidies.[144] Now that really is depressing.

He acknowledges that his indoctrinated value system is questionable, and a deep ambivalence lingers in his comment: 'I think I shall go to my grave not knowing what was worthwhile.' He can sound pragmatic and resigned, stating: 'We are unsatisfied, I think, unsatisfiable, and life isn't an altogether satisfying business.'[145] Now and then, he attains a delicate balance:

> I suppose it is true, my life does resemble a butterfly's existence, moving around from one flower to the next. But, of course, butterflies do pollinate. There is a point to their activity. I hope there is to mine.[146]

His gloomiest self-image, picturing himself as a poor friend and a flop, is – I find in writing this biography – countered by heartfelt expressions of admiration from scores of people who have crossed paths with him, including some who he has assumed do not care for him. Collectively, they add up to a chorus of approval:

RODNEY MILNES: Is there anyone better to talk to in the world?

CHRISTOPHER PLUMMER: It is wonderful. You pick up 25 years later and . . . Jonathan just goes on finishing the sentence that he was about to finish . . . He has such a rich personality, he somehow stays with you for years. You can't say you miss him because he is, somehow, always there.

GEORGE MELLY: He is the most interested, complicated, funny and at the same time discontented person that I have ever met. I love him dearly.

Oliver Sacks: The aesthetic and the analytic are beautifully combined in him . . . What do I think drives him? Curiosity. He is suddenly fascinated by a glint of light, the way someone walks, something he's read. He seems to me to be essentially, you know, the same sort of unspoilt, curious and, in a way, innocent boy whom I knew 50 years ago.

A. S. Byatt: He was always my idea of an impossible Renaissance man . . . You can see this throughout my novels [in which he has made appearances] . . . There would not be an 'ideal' vision of what television can do in *A Whistling Woman* without Jonathan . . . [and] he has been a benign and hopeful presence in my life, and the life of my mind, from Cambridge until now.[147]

Michael Wood: He was, in his TV work as well [as stage directing], the most scintillating and inspiring teacher. That's what it's about. So bollocks to those who think otherwise. The fact is the guy could do it and, in the main, the people who criticized him couldn't hold a candle to him.

Michael Blakemore: He has made ideas exciting, made people reconsider the classics and brought people to the opera. He's brought a buzz to the cultural scene and that is, actually, one of the most important things you can do.

Thomas Hampson: He was groundbreaking, willing to take risks. His impact upon the opera world has been, without question, one of the most significant of any director in modern times . . . part of all the schools of thought whose developments we are now experiencing.

Karl Miller: He's like ginger. He has gee'd people up.

Nicholas Garland: It astonishes me to hear journalists who rate culture, honesty and good citizenship just traducing this man who has done nothing but benefit this country.

John Fortune: If he'd been born French, there would be streets named after him.

William Donaldson: I love him, I adore him! I wish I knew him better, I simply find him faultless. He's a hero to me and that's the end of it.

You might think that Dr Miller had, after all, discovered the elixir of love, although, from Ancient Greek drama onwards, choruses of approval have, of course, never been the whole story.

*   *   *

Just a handful more snapshots, a few of my own diary notes, fragments of a bio-graphical scrapbook.

January 1995[148]

This is first time I meet Miller. It is the morning after the ROH *Così* press night, and there the great man sits, in his veritable reference library of a living-room, taking a call from Covent Garden. He is sort of strewn on his back like an adolescent, a good half of him casually sloping off the sofa. His gingery suede shoes are jutting out into the middle of the room, looming large on the end of mossy green corduroy legs that stretch away into the distance. It is really as if one were seeing him through a wide-angle lens. Far off in the corner, his arm shoots out, giving a wave. Finishing the call, he swiftly starts talking away, with a softly-spoken authoritativeness, making countless intricate connections between doctors and directors, between theatrical pretending and philosophical questions about how conduct relates to what we think of as someone's underlying personality.

His body is now, seemingly, levitating on the diagonal, toes pointing south-west, head to the north-east. He has moved on to discuss the importance of Erving Goffman and subintentional gestures in his stage productions (unselfconsciously, it seems, pushing one ear out with a forefinger as he speaks). He shifts to the topic of how people listen (at which I hastily confirm eye contact). As a student of non-verbal behaviour, he would, indeed, be his own best thesis. He ruminates with one large hand resting on top of his head, angled in from behind, making him look like the world's most erudite monkey. Maybe this funny low/highbrow combo is the key to his appeal.[149] Intellectually, he has that dragonfly quality, darting at lightning speed and hovering over each question with intense con-centration. He is not without a touch of self-congratulation but – wondering about the *Così* reviews – he has a vulnerability that provokes sympathy. We talk for an hour or so. He is instantly likeable and interestingly complicated. It's an incomplete picture.

On Vision

In his book *Nowhere in Particular*, he points out that his 'pictures of bits' have a natural counterpart in vision itself, because our capacity to see fine detail is con-centrated in that very small area inside the eye, the fovea. He goes on to elucidate:

> The result of this restricted acuity . . . [is that] we are constantly flicking our gaze from one part of the visual field to the next, and by bringing the specialised centre of the retina to bear on one sector of the scene after another we collect an anthology of sporadic snapshots from which we build up an apparently detailed picture of the world.[150]

Summer 2009

Since knocking for a second time on Miller's door, several years ago, I have been slowly working on his biography. Of course, I don't think he is faultless. Those years would have been far less interesting if he were. Actually, one of the great things about him is that, for all his directorial appreciation of the understated minutiae of life, he himself has glaring flaws, almost like a larger-than-life character in some comedy of humours.

He is shockingly bilious at points, acerbic rather than satirically amusing, hyperbolically fuming about his pet hates. He can be a whirlwind of egocentricity and appallingly, hilariously pleased with himself. He gives himself rave reviews, talking of his 'brilliant mind', saying that his directorial insights are 'as deep as you can get'. A self-marketing variation on his ancestors in commerce, he hard-sells his achievements most doggedly when the press has been dismissive. Also when he is unemployed and frustrated, these aspects of his personality appear magnified and distended, like the anamorphic portraits – based on convex mirrors and sensory distortions – which so transfixed him in *The Body in Question* and *On Reflection*.[151]

Various journalists have exclaimed 'Enough already!', recoiling from his distended grumps and from the verbal 'machine gun mow[ing] down a lifetime of enemies'.[152] They have fallen out of love with him and, if this is the final Act, it is a sorry conclusion to the life of a supremely gifted man. He was adored once. His principled refusal to adopt a false grin for PR photos has made him look hangdog. It seems as though the young comic has turned into an aged curmudgeon with a dour glare, if not a self-pitying pout. The child who was tongue-tied by a stammer is now unable to bite his tongue, or else the endlessly reiterated complaints are a kind of embittered stutter. Back in the early Sixties, in Miller's personal notebooks, he inscribed that quotation from Dickens about the rare breed of grown men who 'retain a certain freshness and gentleness and capacity of being pleased, which are an inheritance they have preserved from childhood'. Yet today's world, especially contemporary Britain, strikes him as sterile. His deep despondency is articulated in terms of splenetic dislike. When he grumbles over and over about the hatefulness of theatre critics, one wants to groan. Should I re-entitle the biography *What's with the Long Face?* Just occasionally, Rachel explodes with flushed exasperation.

Still, that's on a bad day. Moreover, in conversation, his flaws often seem more tragicomic than intolerable.[153] They are funny as well as sad. That he wears them on his sleeve is, furthermore, a saving grace. For a man of the theatre with a philosophical interest in pretending, he conceals his feelings remarkably rarely. The lack of self-censorship is touching and disarming. Its childlike naivety is another counterbalance to his potentially intimidating intellectual side. He can be abashed as well, tail between the legs. A quick chiding from Rachel tends to do the trick. He knows that he has led a privileged life. He knows that most people have never had it so good as he has. The phrase 'whirlwind of egocentricity' is his own, apologizing to me on the phone one time after being in a gloomy mood.[154] The bile and bitterness never quite obliterate the man's warmth.

On Heroes

As a national public figure, he might be said to function like a dramatic hero, in several different ways. He is looked up to, by many fans, as a colossal talent. He simultaneously serves as our comic protagonist. People laugh at him banging on, and at points, I suspect, identify with him when he complains about the world's shortcomings with unrestrained irritation. In his outbursts, many people can recognize their own foibles and frustrations. As Tom Sutcliffe jovially said to me the other day: 'He's a bit of a monster, but so are we all.'

On Contradictions

Miller is full of them. He is hyperbolical, except that he is often extremely precise in conversation, carefully qualifying others' postulations, jettisoning crude delineations. Yes, he can sound terribly arrogant. Yet he does not like grandiosity and he is, fundamentally, a very unaffected man. He is highbrow, but he enjoys popular movies, from *Bend it Like Beckham* to *Teenage Mutant Ninja Turtles*. At odds with the impression that he is forever carping, he is friendly, obliging, unbelievably generous with his time and his ideas, remarkably supportive and gentle if he senses you are having a bad day.

The really lasting conflict is the moral psychological battle between his internalized Cavalier and Roundhead, his fun-loving and his academically puritanical selves. He has been at war with himself, in the interior, for most of his life. Famously multi-faceted and professionally capricious, he remains nevertheless very much himself. As Nicholas Garland points out, he does not adjust his behaviour or adapt his vocabulary according to the social context. Like Samuel Johnson, he will converse with anybody, talking to an old crofter about antique looms with the same high-powered engagement as to a history professor – consistently.

On Connections

For all his rhapsodies of self-doubt about his career choices, he and Sacks both observe that everything started slowly coming together in the last decade or so. 'We feel we've all been flitters,' Sacks muses, 'but it becomes clearer and clearer with Jonathan that the apparently centrifugal, unrelated range of his interests has synthesized and integrated in a marvellous way.' Miller concedes that this makes him feel happier at last. 'I increasingly see now I'm really old', he says, 'that there is a world of connective coherence, of vigorously related ideas . . . [resulting] from all the various things I drifted into by happenstance when I was younger.'

Towards the end of *Subsequent Performances*, he is discussing Monteverdi's *L'Orfeo*, and an accompanying illustration shows Poussin's neoclassical painting *A Dance to the Music of Time*. Here the seasons, pastorally personified, tread a measure in a graceful circle, lightly holding hands, all linked up like a daisy chain. A snapshot on the opposite page pictures Miller's performers reproducing that image of conjoined harmony.[155]

On Metaphors

Miller is famous for his metaphors as a conversationalist, helping you to understand something by describing it as something else. See the heart, for example, as a fire pump. When he was a young Footlights comedian, in his globetrotting sketch *Down Under*, his prop was an aeroplane propellor which he inventively turned into a canoe paddle, a scythe, antlers, what you will. He has a gift for conversion and he has applied that to his own professional life, forever turning into something else before your eyes. He's a human Swiss Army knife.

On Repetitions

The fact that he has hobbyhorses has become increasingly apparent with age. He does repeat himself, which makes him seem a far less elastic personality than in his youth, as if time had acted on body and mind like the vulcanization of rubber. He has always scorned received ideas but he seems to have become encrusted with some of his own. Also, many of his favourite reference points – though certainly not all – stem from his intellectually formative years: Wittgenstein, Goffman, J. L. Austin. He is manifestly a mind of his time, in that he still draws on that store. For all that, the ideas recurring through his work are manifold and kaleidoscopic, the elements being shaken up and enticingly rearranged. You might say his mental processes, when he is on top form, are akin to jazz, in blending regular riffs with playful inventiveness. Or, to mix one's metaphors, just when you think he's rattling down a familiar track, you ask another question and find yourself flying down an amazing branch line with new vistas of knowledge opening up. Others have likened him to a fabulous search engine and infinite riches in a little room.

Gloucester Crescent

Serene yet cosy, the house is full of curious gems. It is also another kind of collage of Miller's life. So many bookshelves stand crammed from floor to ceiling that a surveyor tells him the weight of them is pulling the bricks and mortar apart at the seams.[156] Other walls are covered with higgledy-piggledy framed pictures: several from his father's art-collecting days; paintings by Rachel's mother; a fine chalk sketch of a patient, drawn by Emanuel himself; and a bust which he sculpted of Betty. These sit alongside Miller's own works in paper and wood. The mantelpieces are a cornucopia of *objets trouvés*: Balinese puppets, a Nigerian ritual mask, medical models of inner organs next to vases of flowers. A massive, carved, Assyrian bas relief of a lion lies near some old wooden shoe lasts and a cache of glass prisms. On the stairs are prints of architectural sketches by Jan Vredeman de Vreis, which inspired the sets in the *BBC Shakespeare Series' Troilus and Cressida*. In the back garden, the gigantic horse's head from *Timon of Athens* lies propped against the wall. It's among flower pots, under a towering magnolia tree which was just a sapling when Miller and Rachel first saw the place.

The Garden

In later life Miller said he felt that his mind had matured like a garden, mulched and manured with years of experience and reading, and that this process resulted in richer, subtler directing.[157] He remarked in his sixties, at our first meeting, that he felt smarter and more in control of his thinking, in many ways, than when he was in his twenties or thirties. 'I understand things much better: certain problems in philosophy that were really beyond me then, I can tackle now,' he said.

As a realistic medic, he acknowledged that the march of time had some detrimental effects. 'I feel stiff in the mornings,' he admitted during that conversation, 'and my memory is, perhaps, not quite as good as it used to be. I sometimes have to read a book twice to have it all down pat.' In 2009, he confessed to being aghast on discovering how much he'd forgotten from one favourite volume, and he has been reading much less of late, with the mass of material still to get through making him feel bewildered.[158]

It has become increasingly noticeable that names are not always on the tip of his tongue anymore. He seems less agitated than one might expect, given that his personality is so bound up with eloquence, expansive knowledge, the life of the mind. He speaks slightly slower, gets a bit breathless when trekking up and down stairs to fetch books from his study or his latest artwork. He cannot go for long hikes in the country as he used to, sadly for many friends who recall his wonderful botanical commentaries.

One afternoon, he rings me in a humorously spry, albeit cynical mood, suggesting an alternative title for the biography. *The Main Branches of Arithmetic*, he says, would be woefully apt, the allusion being to *Alice in Wonderland*'s mathematical subdivisions: Ambition, Distraction, Uglification and Derision. 'It's the story of my life!' he asserts. He then blithely adds that *Best Before* would do, which he has just seen on a sweet wrapper.

Autumn 2003

I'm watching Miller's rehearsals for his semi-staged revival of Monteverdi's *L'Orfeo* at the Royal Festival Hall. He is ambling about, up on the stage and around the auditorium, in baggy jeans and an old brown jumper. Silver-haired with his half-specs on a string, he is at once casual and gentlemanly, speaking to everyone with a slight stoop and little smile, as if they might share a joke. He keeps wandering back up the aisle to sit with Rachel while, onstage, Mark Tucker's Orfeo is heartrendingly bereft of his beloved wife. What Monteverdi was writing about, Miller remarks, was not nymphs and shepherds. It was the fact that people die and we cannot get them back. Nowadays, he approaches the obituaries pages with apprehension, expecting to have lost someone. Indeed, he bases one scene, where the ensemble are told of Euridice's death, on the hesitant awkwardness of funerals attended at Hoop Lane Cemetery, in Golders Green – 'people gathered in embarrassed knots, not knowing what to say or how to make their departure'. In the closing scene, when Orfeo is visited by his father, Apollo –

who bids him assuage his grief and accept life's transience – the director has no *deus ex machina*. Instead, Orfeo sits desolately on the edge of the stage while Apollo talks softly, seated behind him, 'like Michael Brearley,' says Miller, 'with someone at the Tavistock'. I ask him a week or so later, how he would cope if he lived on after Rachel. It is, I think, the only time he is lost for words. He falls silent before struggling to say that he cannot bear to think about it.

Late December 2005

Now in Vilnius, watching him staging *La Traviata* for the Lithuanian National Opera, I witness one of his professionally rougher rides. This is a production of some prestige, with the country's president and PM due to attend, and the rising star Asmik Grigorian is going to be scintillating as Violetta. Unfortunately, one of the company's regular prima donnas is, against Miller's wishes, taking the part for one performance. It rapidly becomes clear that she cannot act to save her life. During an afternoon rehearsal, word spreads that she is up in the boss' office, furious that she has been given insufficient directorial attention, and threatening to break her contract. In reaction, Miller deliberately starts raising his voice, audibly mouthing off about the management and, it seems, spoiling for a showdown.

The diva fails to realize her threat. When she reappears for a fantastically awkward tech run – with the two Violettas taking turns to climb in and out of the one deathbed – Miller's tactic is to play it very cool. The quiet obstinacy with which he declined to work on his adolescent Hebrew lessons reasserts itself here. He leaves the stroppy star to her own laughably petty devices, which include huffing about allergenic perfume on the pillow, and blatantly getting the orchestra to applaud her rendition. They rattle their bows like bones in the pit.

Outside rehearsals, Miller is agitated by the history of his ancestors' native land. His awareness of the genocidal massacres of modern times has far from dimmed since his first trip to Lithuania with Nicholas Garland. Now, as we wander around the city's former Jewish quarter, in thick snow, he dwells on the locals' participation in the Nazi Holocaust, and on the issue of anti-Semitism swept under the carpet. We had planned to go out to Paneriai, the historic, forested killing grounds. He cannot face it.

Against the odds, even when in the doldrums, he can still be great company. Extremely hospitable, he and Rachel take me along to the restaurants they have discovered, and he always resists going Dutch with old-fashioned good manners. He will not return to Vilnius to direct *Così*, as scheduled, the following year, certainly not when the opera house insists on dictating the casting again.

On Englishness

Is he quintessentially, ineradicably English? Even if the whole idea of national character is questionable, a spectrum of opinions has formed about his natural home. Producer Patrick Uden, from *The Body in Question*, believes: 'Jonathan is really a European. We live in a country where narrow specialization is celebrated, so he fits uneasily here in a way that is ironically what makes him so great.' Nicholas Garland comparably states, 'With his intellectual vigour, he had a continental personality.' Miller himself says that American campuses, with their go-getting entrepreneurial spirit, feel more hospitable to his cross-disciplinary style than the reticent UK. He thinks, if it were not for his family ties, he would now be an academic in the States. David Pountney suggests that '[Jonathan] as the pirouetting outsider . . . presents a very complex and in some senses typically Jewish face to the world – feeling compelled to dazzle constantly in case someone should shoot him down.'

Conversely, Miller has underlined, 'Every part of my memory is saturated with English imagery.'[159] He is, in turn, deeply embedded in the minds of many English people as part of their cultural landscape and their memories. For all that, his sense of disillusioned estrangement remains pervasive. 'I don't live in England, I live in Gloucester Crescent,' he says, mentally creating his own small island. And it gets smaller. Many of the street's old guard have been moving out (Michael Frayn and Claire Tomalin and, more recently, Alan Bennett). Other neighbours from past decades have died (including Freddie Ayer, Dee Wells, Alice Thomas Ellis, George Melly).

NW1 became socially grimmer during the last decade, getting itself compared to Jack the Ripper's East End when the dismembered bodies of vice girls and a trainee rabbi were found strewn around the area in bin bags.[160] Camden Market seemed to be awash with drug dealers, and the shabby-genteel Crescent was daubed with graffiti in delinquent spates of vandalism. When Miller took issue with a loitering gang, for spitting as he passed, they threatened to break his teeth, and his bank card was twice snatched at a nearby cashpoint machine. He became a forthright spokesman in the press, voicing the fears of many when he averred that crime in Britain was reaching appalling levels. Camden Town was no longer what it was, he said, and something had to be done about those 'feral children' roving the streets.[161] Partly because of such bad publicity, the local council and police embarked on a markedly beneficial clean-up crusade. Meanwhile, the toymaker-turned-philanthropist Torquil Norman, a fellow Gloucester Crescent resident, redeveloped and reopened the derelict Roundhouse as an arts venue, with an attached creative centre for adolescents. More broadly speaking, though, some would regard those 'feral children' as the alarming end product of post-World War 2 liberties, of the authority-challenging social revolution in which *Beyond the Fringe* played a celebrated part.

If more is not done, says Miller, to counter the country's civic deterioration, then all you can do is retreat into your shell, shut the front door and stay inside, with your books for company. He is seeing me off, on the threshold, as he expresses this opinion, just peeking out through the closing portal with a teasing smile as he reaches his conclusion.

Ongoing

He talks about holing up, but he has never been the retiring sort. One minute he's quitting, the next he is mentioning a stack of future commissions. He's like some irresolvable Escher staircase. Is he coming or going?

While the media in Britain have categorized Miller as a whinger, he has constantly rolled back from the critical punches. Even today, undefeated, he can get enthused about fresh projects. He has been hypersensitive, all the same. He was never a stoic with a stiff upper lip, and he no longer rallies readily from being winded.[162] Back in his Cambridge days, he warned his fellow Apostles against the Bloomsbury aesthetic. If you are sensitive to everything, he pointed out, ultimately you will destroy yourself. He has only narrowly avoided that fate.

On a particularly bad day, in a lull between jobs, he uses the term 'suicidally depressed' and is, perhaps, panic-stricken about the offers drying up, about no more knocks on the door inviting him to come out and play. I wonder if inactivity strikes him with horror, as a kind of living death. Rather than overwork wearing him out, is it actually his lifeblood? Unemployment seems to age and drain him of vitality. He looks pale and cadaverous.

His voice cracks slightly as he speaks of the multiple strings to his bow snapping, and he admits that he has been damagingly outspoken. His gift of the gab has been the making of him and his undoing. He has used the press to his advantage, to spread the word eloquently about his work, and to 'let things be known' during spats. Yet journalists have never offered guaranteed sympathy or a talking cure, and he has an increasingly short fuse with irritating members of the press. He says, fretfully, that he must put a stop to all interviews and reconcile himself, once and for all, to the end of his career, to winding down, to going quiet.[163] Having reached the second decade of the twenty-first century, he is, I think, just starting genuinely to accept this.

Still, for a biographer trying to round off, there have been points in the past few years when the seemingly endless stream of new schemes has inspired mildly hysterical laughter. It is like trying to pin down mercury, or catch a rabbit – one which keeps morphing into a duck and who knows what else. Indeed, his fabulously fickle career is almost oneiric, leaping all over the place, now here, now there. Having belatedly turned storyteller – reading his old favourite *Emil and the Detectives* on Radio 4 – and having got a taste for poetry reading, he has said he would like to pursue both those strands too . . .[164]

I have a dream about Miller, after we have been discussing the idea of him working at the East End's Arcola Theatre. In the dream, he is busying himself at this converted factory space, directing *The Sound of Music* with slide projections and, most improbably, Sophia Loren. He is sitting in the corner, merrily operating the projector himself, using slides from his holiday in the Tyrol. I wonder, on waking, if I couldn't just slip this into his inexhaustible CV.

I think he will never cease working if he can help it. Perhaps he will, as he envisages, die in harness. 'I shall probably still be saying "I really must stop" as

I make my way to the crematorium,' he says. It is almost Beckettian: 'I can't go on, I'll go on.'[165]

Back in Spring 2002

I have been sitting in on Miller's final day of rehearsals for *Camera Obscura* in the Almeida's off-site rooms in Islington. He and I are standing on Upper Street after a lunchtime sandwich and an extremely enjoyable chat – vintage Miller – all about streamlined fish, the design of postal vans, John Locke, Eadweard Muybridge and zoetropes (those Victorian spinning toys with viewing slits which trick the eye into seeing still pictures in continuous motion).

'What are you going to do now?' he says. I reply that I had intended to come back and watch him carry on. 'What are you doing?' I ask. 'Curtain call. You don't need to watch that, do you?' he replies quizzically. 'Maybe I don't,' I say, and we head off in opposite directions making classic Goffmanesque signs, holding the invisible I-will-call-you telephone to the ear.

There's a little phrase that Jonathan Miller uses in conversation. It is one of his leitmotifs when he is explaining something complicated but has to round off for the time being. 'And so on,' he says, giving the matter some kind of closure yet leaving it open to further speculation. And so on.

Time present and time past
Are both perhaps present in time future,
And time future contained in time past.
If all time is eternally present
All time is unredeemable.
What might have been is an abstraction
Remaining a perpetual possibility
Only in a world of speculation.
What might have been and what has been
Point to one end, which is always present.
Footfalls echo in the memory
Down the passage which we did not take
Towards the door we never opened
Into the rose-garden.

— T. S. Eliot, 'Burnt Norton', *Four Quartets*

NOTES

The direct quotations used in this biography are from interviews that I have conducted (or from emails and letters sent to me) unless otherwise indicated. Miller has been so prolific and met so many celebrated people that I have inserted extra anecdotes and observations among these Notes. I hope that makes them a livelier read.

Introduction
1 Miller saw *A Matter of Life and Death* in 1946.
2 Emanuel Miller had helped establish the Portman Clinic in the 1930s, shortly before his son was born. He co-founded the *British Journal of Delinquency* later, in 1950. That was renamed the *British Journal of Criminology* in 1960. Emanuel worked alongside the psychoanalyst Edward Glover on both these projects.
3 Andrew Billen called him 'the most famous brain in Britain' in the *Evening Standard*, 24 November 1999. Kevin Jackson in the *Independent on Sunday*, 11 July 2004, suggested that Miller – being interested in everything – is actually a pantomath, and is regarded in cartoonish popular mythology as the Cleverest Man in the World. The *Sunday Times*, 16 April 1989, alluded to him as 'homo universalis'.
4 The comment on his planet-sized brain comes from Edward Hall, son of Sir Peter Hall. As Eleanor Wachtel points out in her book – Wachtel, E. (2003), *Original Minds* (Toronto: HarperFlamingo), p. 7 – some have mistakenly assumed there must be several Jonathan Millers because his areas of expertise are so copious. Actual mix-ups have occurred with the journalist who shares his name and who, as the *Sunday Times* media correspondent in 2003, campaigned against the BBC licence fee. The subject of this biography should, likewise, not be confused with Channel 4 News' foreign correspondent; the homonymous former CEO of AOL; the Kentucky politician and former state treasurer; the West Virginian politician/health insurance salesman/substitute teacher; the chief digital officer of News Corp; the president of Icarus Films; the film critic for Chicago Public Radio; the artistic director of Chicago A Cappella (a choir given to Renaissance hymning and Jewish hip-hop); the biographer of Depeche Mode; the bassist in the band DevilDriver; the author-illustrator of *The Adventures of Sammy the Wonder Dachshund*; the Olympic mountain biker; the GP accused of sexual misconduct in Derbyshire in 2009; Dr Jonathan Miller of the Healing Music Organization; or Rabbi Jonathan Miller.
5 PBS's *The Dick Cavett Show* took the extraordinary step, in 1980, of having Miller in conversation for a whole week rather than the normal one night. Michael Parkinson, for BBC TV, had him as a guest on multiple occasions: November 1972, September 1975, January 1977, October 1978, January 1980, October 1980 and February 1982. Miller also appeared on Parkinson's ITV show in June 2007. That interview was chosen as one of the 'classics' for the website michaelparkinson.tv in October 2008. Parkinson's autobiography – Parkinson, M. (2008), *Parky: My Autobiography* (London: Hodder & Stoughton) – specifically ranks Miller as a favourite interviewee, categorizing him as one of the great talkers along with Orson Welles, Peter Ustinov, Jacob Bronowski and Stephen Fry. As mentioned in *Parky*, p. 185, Miller was on board for a technological try-out when Parkinson and Cavett attempted a simultaneous transatlantic broadcast, using a new-fangled satellite. He was also a guest on *The Tonight Show Starring Johnny Carson* in February 1972.
6 See Miller, J. and Pelham, D. (1984), *The Facts of Life* (London: Jonathan Cape), and Miller, J. (ed.) (1972), *Freud: The Man, His World, His Influence* (London: Weidenfeld & Nicolson).
7 The 'Godfather' status was noted by Roger Wilmut in Wilmut, R. (1980), *From Fringe to Flying Circus: Celebrating a Unique Generation of Comedy 1960–1980* (London: Eyre Methuen), p. 2.
8 Quotation from Della Couling's interview, *Opera Now*, July 1991.
9 Miller revived *Don Giovanni* in Valencia in January 2012, *Così fan tutte* for Washington Opera in February, and *Don Pasquale* at La Scala in June, with *Rutherford and Son* opening in February 2013.
10 Miller, J. (1999), *Nowhere in Particular* (London: Mitchell Beazley). This publication, incidentally, does not have numbered pages, hence there are no page references when I allude, hereafter, to this book.

Chapter 1: Birth and Parents

1 The Welbeck Nursing Home is now the private London Welbeck Hospital, specializing in cosmetic surgery. Legend has it that Miller was a miraculous birth, staggering the obstetrician by starting from the womb wearing an impressive red beard, but this is only according to his mock CV in the programme notes for *Beyond the Fringe* (preserved in the V&A Theatre Collections).

2 Both Miller and his sister, Sarah, assured me this was the case though the medical directory of 1934 logs Emanuel's professional address as 28 Wimpole Street. I remain greatly indebted to Sarah Miller whom I interviewed before her death in 2006. She had partially investigated her family history and wrote an illuminating preface for the reprint of Betty's 1945 novel *On the Side of the Angels*. That reprint is the edition that I refer to throughout these Notes, unless otherwise specified: Miller, B. (1986), *On the Side of the Angels* (London: Penguin/Virago Press).

Sarah also generously shared a wealth of facts, photographs and documents with me. Dr Alyson Hall and her colleagues at the Emanuel Miller Centre (now in Gill Street, London E14) have been another invaluable source of information.

3 See Weinreb, B. and Hibbert, C. (eds) (1983), *The London Encyclopaedia* (London: Macmillan), p. 600, on Park Crescent's elegance.

4 Wheatstone had lived at No. 19. The stereoscope was discussed by Miller in his Channel 4 *Equinox* documentary, *Moving Pictures*, in 1989.

5 I am particularly indebted to Michael Parkinson's BBC TV interview, broadcast in January 1977. There Miller reminisced about his childhood, including references to Nanny Hogarth, his Westinghouse stammer and other matters that crop up later, including debutante balls at the Dorchester, the Air Scouts, swimming classes and malignant cricket balls at St Paul's School.

6 The 'I'm doing what I'm doing' riposte resurfaced in Bennett's comedy, *Forty Years On*, where Matron plays Nanny Gibbins. See Bennett, A. (1991), *Forty Years On and Other Plays* (London: Faber), p. 47. Hogarth's successor, Nanny Morgan, also appears thinly disguised on p. 48, making preposterously unscientific claims about the dangers of wearing or not wearing wellington boots.

7 In the *New York Times* of 22 January 1967, William H. Honan mentioned a fan who rated Miller's conversation above hearing Caruso sing. Hugh Hebert, *Guardian*, 18 March 1972, described Miller as a 'veritable living stream of consciousness who bleeds words . . . as thick with ideas as blood with corpuscles'. Cavett's praise for his 'amazing' virtuosity came in programme number five of the 1980 week-long run of shows with Miller, and in the book Cavett, D. (2010), *Talk Show: Confrontations, Pointed Commentary and Off-screen Secrets* (New York, NY: Times Books, Henry Holt and Company), p. 216, Cavett placed Miller alongside Noël Coward and Peter Ustinov in the rare breed of 'instantly publishable' conversationalists. Windy Miller is a character in BBC TV's *Camberwick Green*.

8 Miller managed, on one occasion, to get the right ticket by circumlocution, asking the Underground ticket inspector for 'One to the arch that is made of marble, please'.

9 Elishiva Landman, who became a musician-turned-medic in America, was the foster-daughter of Emanuel's LSE sociologist friend, Morris Ginsberg, part of London's Jewish intelligentsia who formed networks of friendships down the generations. Landman's foster-mother ran a playgroup at their Redington Road home in Hampstead.

10 I am most grateful to Willie Botterill at London's Michael Palin Centre for Stammering Children for all the expert information on the nature of stutters.

11 Miller discussed insufficient parental embraces, 'disorders of attachment' and his 'limited capacity' for friendships in the course of *In the Psychiatrist's Chair*, BBC Radio 4, 12 September 1999.

12 That is the wartime memory of Miller's boyhood friend, Nicholas Garland.

13 Sara and Simon Spiro had four children: Dorothy, Betty, Henry and Julian.

14 The lot of Jews in nineteenth-century Lithuania is discussed in more detail by Don Levin in Levin, D. (2000), *The Litvaks: A Short History of Jews in Lithuania* (Jerusalem: Yad Vashem).

15 I am greatly indebted to Betty's younger brother, Julian, for his reminiscences about the Spiros.

16 Simon Spiro owned five stores in Cork including a cigar shop on Patrick Street and a jeweller's shop on Bridge Street. Betty's family home was the Laurels, Western Road, which later became a boarding house and then a centre for adult education. Sarah had an idea that, before Simon's marriage, he had got one of his shop-girls into trouble and packed her off to America. However, in written correspondence with Sarah, on 1 June 1986, an elderly member of the Jewish Cork community, Esther Hesselberg, cast doubt on that, saying it would have been gossiped about and he was a perfect gentleman. His professional achievements are detailed in Hyman, L. (1972), *The Jews of Ireland* (Shannon: Irish University Press), p. 224.

17 Betty wrote about her mother in 'Notes for an Unwritten Autobiography' in *Modern Reading*, 1945, Vol. XIII, 42. Sam Spiro and Sara Bergson married in Stockholm in 1907, when he was in his mid-forties and she was just over thirty.

18 Henri Bergson's ancestry was complex. He was the son of a Polish Jewish father. His mother, also Jewish, was of Irish and English stock.

19 Thanks are also due to David Roderick who, having staged Wolf Mankowitz's *The Hebrew Lesson* at Richmond's Orange Tree Theatre in 2003, sent me illuminating general background information on Irish history in relation to Jewish immigrants.

20 Adapted from James Joyce's short story in *The Dubliners*, Miller's eerie and menacing, if abstruse film of *Clay* was completed back in the UK. This was a monochrome short, presented by Melvyn Bragg in November 1973, under the aegis of BBC TV's *Full House*.

21 Betty wrote about Cork Gaol, the nursery cries, and the time-bomb in 'Notes for an Unwritten Autobiography', pp. 40–1. There had been a spate of IRA bombs in London during 1939–40, including one left in a suitcase at Leicester Square underground station. Betty also wrote about Ireland in her first novel, *The Mere Living* (which portrayed an immigrant family in Cork), and in her last, *The Death of the Nightingale* (which grappled with the subject of the IRA). In between, only a trace of her Irish roots was apparent in *Farewell Leicester Square*'s title, that phrase being taken from the music hall marching song 'It's a Long Way to Tipperary'.

22 Isaiah Berlin is quoted in Sarah Miller's preface to *On the Side of the Angels*, p. x.

23 For the record, Julian is logged in the St Paul's School register under his official names as 'Albert Emanuel, s. of S Spiro, Merchant, of Holland Park'. Miller does not recall visiting any Crown Film Unit studio with his uncle before he took up film-making himself. However, in a letter to a friend, Betty wrote about going to see the set of *The Secret Agent* and keenly watching John Gielgud and Peter Lorre at work. My attention was drawn to this by the academic and writer Jane Miller who knew Betty and is Jonathan Miller's sister-in-law. In her illuminating preface to the reprint of *Farewell Leicester Square* – Miller, B. (2000), *Farewell Leicester Square* (London: Persephone Books) p. xiii – Jane Miller alludes to that *Secret Agent* letter, and to Julian landing his initial job with Hitchcock thanks to Emanuel Miller's friend, Michael Balcon of Gaumont-British.

24 Miller's medical account of Betty's teenage illness diverges from Sarah's belief that their mother had contracted scarlet fever.

25 St John Ervine's letter, responding to the eighteen-year-old Betty, is referred to in *On the Side of the Angels*' preface, p. vii.

26 *The Mere Living* was published in February 1933, under the name Betty Bergson Spiro. See Spiro, B. B. (1933), *The Mere Living* (London: Victor Gollancz). Betty sent an advance copy to Ervine. As noted in *On the Side of the Angels*' preface, p. x, he judged it 'immensely interesting', though he was sniffy about her wasting her brain as a 'clever-clever girl novelist'. *The Mere Living* was followed by *Sunday*: that is Spiro, B. B. (1934), *Sunday* (London: Victor Gollancz).

27 Rosamond Lehmann's comment on Betty's 'stereoscopically clear' characters appears in *On the Side of the Angels*' preface, p. xiv.

28 St John Ervine's allusion to Betty's 'high, if hysterical sense of language', ibid, p. xi. Praises from *Time and Tide* and other sources appeared on the back pages of the 1945 edition of *On the Side of the Angels*: that is Spiro, B. B. (1945), *On the Side of the Angels* (London: Robert Hale).

29 For reference, the *Twentieth Century* magazine was, for a time, called the *Nineteenth Century and After*.

30 Miller, B. (1952), *Robert Browning: A Portrait* (London: John Murray).

31 It was a Remington according to Miller, an Olivetti according to Sarah.

32 Spiro, B. B. (1935), *Portrait of the Bride* (London: Victor Gollancz), p. 9. Her authorial dedication, 'For him who is nowhere reflected within the pages of fiction; but who is, in life, beloved collaborator', suggests Betty feared Emanuel might be confused with Bernard.

33 Ibid., pp. 247–8.

34 Ibid., pp. 263–4.

35 Ibid., p. 258.

36 Ibid., pp. 242–3.

37 I am indebted to Betty's Swedish cousin Ann Romyn (who became a London-based painter) for this and other observations, and to many others for memories of the Miller family, including Betty's friend, the Bloomsbury author and critic Naomi Lewis, who, in her nineties, kindly granted an interview for this biography.

38 Incidentally, in 2009, London's Jewish Book Festival included a discussion about *Farewell Leicester Square*'s still 'controversial' subject matter.

39 Jane Miller mentions this letter (the same one in which Betty discussed the filming of *The Secret Agent*) in her preface to *Farewell Leicester Square*, p. x.

40 The original publication was Spiro, B. B. (1941), *Farewell Leicester Square* (London: Robert Hale), though my page references allude to the already mentioned Persephone reprint.

41 Park Square Gardens appears under the name of Park Square West in Spiro, B. B. (1942), *A Room in Regent's Park* (London: Robert Hale), pp. 10–14.

> She crossed Marylebone Road. Heavy traffic pounded towards Euston, towards St Pancras, shaking the buildings, sending the fine dust smoking up into the air . . . When she turned into Park Square West,

he [Robert] was there . . . Behind railings, behind neatly clipped hedges, the lawns lay outspread . . . an oasis guarded by privilege . . . [And] she herself had grown up, under lock and key, in this pleasant cage . . . under the auspices of a uniformed nanny, frisking decorously . . . There were various small châlets in the gardens; he drew her into the shadow of one of these, and continued his experiments (begun only recently) in the matter of kissing.

Robert is also, incidentally, a medical student with artistic aspirations, lightly satirised but having, in common with Betty, a keen appreciation of literary fragments and life's small details.

42 *A Room in Regent's Park*, p. 18.

43 *Jonathan Miller's London*, part of the *Cities* series, was made by John McGreevy Productions of Toronto for Nelsen-Ferns International in 1979. Broadcasts have included US cable TV in October 1988.

44 When he made the John McGreevy production, Miller thought that Abram Miller (also known as Abraham) hailed from Russia. His sister Sarah's later research into the family history revealed that he came from Wigrance.

45 One of Sarah Miller's cousins told her that Abram spoke of seeing a 'pogrom' of sorts, although that word is not generally applied to events in pre-1870s Lithuania.

46 Some of Abram's younger siblings later followed him to London.

47 Thanks go to Jeremy Schuman for the healer/dealer point. Those Lithuanian Jews who trained abroad, as scientific medics, are mentioned in *The Litvaks: A Short History of the Jews in Lithuania*, p. 61. Regarding the more 'witchdoctory' sort of healing rituals brought from Eastern Europe, Derek Reid's paper in Aubrey Newman (ed.) (1981), *The Jewish East End 1840–1939* (London: Jewish Historical Society of England), p. 298, records how, for example, troubled sleepers underwent a shamanistic ritual: wax poured over their heads into water, to reveal the image of their bugbears.

48 The Poor Jews Temporary Shelter was not set up in Leman Street until 1885, but the charitable Board of Guardians was established in 1859. The local Jewish associations for religious study, called chevras, provided some social support. There was a steiblech system: small house-based synagogues helping the landsleit (families who had emigrated from the same neighbourhood), and perhaps others from Abram's shtetl were already in London. For information on greeners and sweatshops, I have drawn on Fishman, W. J. (1988), *The Condition of East End Jewry in 1888* (London: West Central Counselling and Community Research), pp. 5–7; also Berrol, S. (1994), *East Side/East End: Eastern European Jews in London and New York 1870–1924* (London: Praeger), pp. 13–15; also Charles Booth, using Booth, C., edited by Fried, A. and Elman, R. (1971), *Charles Booth's London: A Portrait of the Poor at the Turn of the Century Drawn from his Life and Labour of the People in London* (Harmondsworth: Penguin), pp. 169–73, 207–20 etc. That is the edition referred to hereafter.

49 Mayhew visited the East End for the *Morning Chronicle* in 1850, and he published *London Labour and the London Poor* soon after. Charles Booth's research started in the late 1880s, with his final volume of *Life and Labour of the People in London* being completed in 1902.

50 The edition I have used is Zangwill, I. (1972), *Children of the Ghetto* (London: White Lion). See pp. 1 and 21. Zangwill blended his early childhood memories with descriptions of the East End circa 1892 (the year this work was first published).

51 Again, thanks are due to Jeremy Schuman for the information on Rebecca's background. The Jewish inhabitants remaining in Vilkaviškis were killed, en masse in a single day, when the Nazis arrived in the city in 1941.

52 *The Condition of East End Jewry in 1888*, pp. 5–7, also draws attention to the *Spectator*'s 1887 report on every second Jewish funeral in the metropolitan area being a pauper's one. Researcher Beatrice Potter contributed to the description of London Jews in Charles Booth's survey, pp. 173 and 219–20. The money needed to set up as a tiny capitalist was apparently raised by saving or gambling, or with help from supportive Jewish societies.

53 I am indebted to Sarah Miller for her recording of Emanuel's sister, Clara, reminiscing about life in Fournier Street. No. 5 is now an upmarket antique shop called 'Townhouse' with a scenically faded sign reading 'Market Café' over the door.

54 A 1900 map, reproduced in *The Jewish East End 1840–1939*, shows that Fournier Street's residents were between 95 and 100 per cent Jewish.

55 Booth's survey was opposed to mass immigration. It did not champion the Jews becoming tiny capitalists. The 1888 House of Commons Select Committee on Emigration and mmigration was followed by the 1890 House of Lords Select Committee on the Sweating System. Well-to-do Jewish families, long established in British society, weren't unanimously welcoming either. Arthur Sebag Montefiore, Bethnal Green's Anglo-Jewish Conservative candidate, was not keen on the newcomers. The Aliens Act of 1905 declined to place specifically anti-Semitic restrictions on immigration, but that did not stop the notorious Siege of Sidney Street in 1911 rekindling the debate. The siege led to headlines about Jewish criminals shooting British policemen.

56 Annie Chapman's body was discovered in Hanbury Street in September 1888, and Mary Jane Kelly's corpse was found in November at No. 13 Miller's Court (which was between Commercial Street and Crispin Street). Both women had been mutilated. Accounts differ slightly regarding the wording of the graffiti. *The Jewish East End 1840–1939*, p. 114, points out that Ripper-related riots, though overlooked by most commentators, did actually occur and were reported in the *East London Observer*, 15 September 1888.

57 Jack London's account was published in 1903. Here, I am drawing on a recent reprint: London, J. (2001), *The People of the Abyss* (London: Pluto), p. 31 and pp. 28–30. Abram's family business may well have offered better conditions than those witnessed by Jack London. Booth recorded, p. 170, how some sweating masters were on kind and friendly terms with their employees.

58 Late nineteenth-century statistics – alluded to by Jack London, p. 79 – showed that one in four adults in the capital was destined to die a pauper, in the workhouse, infirmary or asylum. The East End percentage was, inevitably, even higher.

59 The statistic quoted by Jack London, p. 135, was 55 per cent (compared to 18 per cent in the West End). Average East End life expectancy was only 30 years (compared to 55 in the West End).

60 Following the migrational trend of those who could afford to leave Spitalfields, Abram later moved on to Hackney's Victoria Park, then – harassed by the forerunners of today's BNP extremists – to the Jewish enclave of Stamford Hill.

61 When writing about the East London Child Guidance Clinic in the *Journal of Child Psychology and Psychiatry*, 1978, Vol. 19, 309–12, George Renton recorded a conversation with the elderly Dr Hugh Gainsborough.

62 Jack London, pp. 20–5, echoing the 1909 Royal Commission on Britain's poor laws.

63 The Whitechapel Art Gallery was founded in 1901. The East End had further establishments encouraging cultural and intellectual interests, including the Jewish Working Men's Club with its lectures and debates, its affiliated Lads' Institute and its Musical Society founded in 1900 (presenting concerts and comic operas).

64 This is discussed by Berrol, p. 102.

65 The father–son rift was hardly improved when Emanuel's mother died in 1918 and Abram married a Polish widow within six months, to the consternation of his children.

66 Special mention is made in *The Jewish East End 1840–1939*, pp. 99–100, of the fêted Spitalfields 'Prodigy from Fashion Street', Selig Brodetsky, who won a place at Cambridge and a Senior Wranglership, in 1908, as a top-class mathematician.

67 Sarah Miller believed that her father married late, after Abram's death, because he felt unable to break wholly free from his father's authority, in spite of heading off to Cambridge and professional success. Incidentally, in terms of clubs and rebelliousness in the East End, it is not thought that Emanuel ever went, as Rosenberg did, to the Anarchists' Club which was attended by Lenin, Stalin, Trotsky and Gorky in 1907.

68 William Bateson coined the term 'genetics' in 1905 and became Cambridge's new professor in the field in 1908.

69 Rivers and Head conducted their nerve-severing experiment between 1903 and 1907. This duo and their influential predecessor John Hughlings Jackson – who all inspired Emanuel – were to receive attention again as Jonathan Miller re-examined their work on several occasions. He did so in his BBC Radio 3 talk, *Man: The Double Animal,* 3 July 1972 (transcribed under the title 'The Dog Beneath the Skin' in the *Listener*, 20 July 1972); in BBC TV's *The Body in Question* in 1978; and in a BBC TV *Horizon* feature entitled *Dr Miller and the Islanders*, 26 February 1998. Pat Barker duly acknowledged Miller as a source of information: Barker, P. (1995), *The Regeneration Trilogy* (London: Viking), p. 220.

70 That department was founded in 1897.

71 Miller recalls his mother sardonically implying that wild oats were sown.

72 Emanuel was based at the RAMC's hospital in Tooting.

73 Historian Juliet Gardiner highlights the 1930s' mix of despair and hope: Gardiner, J. (2011), *The Thirties: An Intimate History* (London: HarperPress), p. 12. She explores, pp. 188–91, the era's idea that scientists might save society, noting that this was discussed by the Tots and Quots, a dining and debating group formed in 1931 by Hugh Gaitskell and the zoologist G. P. Wells (H. G. Wells' son). Members included the socialist and scientist Lancelot Hogben (who later worked with Emanuel), J. Z. Young and J. D. Bernal. Though never an MP, Huxley helped create and headed UNESCO.

74 Pioneering psychiatrists in the UK were inspired by Clifford Beers' mental hygiene movement in the US, but it was not until 1930 that the Mental Treatment Act was passed in Britain, addressing the national need for good mental health. Emanuel may also have been encouraged by the example of Toynbee Hall, founded in Whitechapel in 1884, and committed to undertaking social work in deprived urban areas. The East London Child Guidance Clinic was set up at the London Jewish Hospital in 1927, under the auspices of the Jewish Health Organization.

75 Emanuel described the tough work in the Great Depression and the ideal director in *The Evolution of a Clinic Director*, his address to the 1965 Inter-clinic Conference of the National Association for Mental

Health (referred to by Jack Kahn in his 'Tribute to Emanuel Miller', *Journal of Child Psychology and Psychiatry*, 1978, Vol. 19, 307–8).

76 Colleagues at the East End Child Guidance Clinic included Noel Burke as well as Sibyl Clement Brown. The latter described the East End activities of the team – and Emanuel's youthful dynamism – in her address to the Association of Child Psychology and Psychiatry, given at the Middlesex Hospital on 2 November 1977. The transcript is preserved in the archives of the Emanuel Miller Clinic.

77 This is alluded to in the 1932 minutes of the Portman Clinic, then known as the Psychopathic Clinic. Thanks go to Carlos Fishman at the Portman for background information, and to Dr David Rumney who researched the history of the clinic.

78 W. H. R. Rivers and Henry Head had been among the leading players in the medical section of the British Psychological Society when it was set up in 1919.

79 Emanuel's books included the following. (1) Miller, E. (1926), *Types of Body and Mind* (London: Kegan Paul & Co); (2) Miller, E. (1935) *Insomnia and Other Disturbances of Sleep* (London: J. Bale & Co); (3) Miller, E. (ed.) (1937), *The Growing Child and Its Problems* (London: Kegan Paul & Co); (4) Miller, E. (1938), *The Generations: A Study of the Cycle of Parents and Children* (London: Faber); (5) Miller, E. (ed.) (1940), *The Neuroses in War* (London: Macmillan). *Types of Body and Mind* notably fused questions of physique and psychology with the literary. It linked character types and traits with short, tall, rotund and gangly bodies, with passing reference to various fictional characters (Quixote, Sancho Panza etc).

80 Sybil Clement Brown, as above, addressing the ACPP.

81 Emanuel became a member of the Eugenic Society in 1949 and a fellow in 1957. Gardiner, pp. 212–16, details how leading medics supported eugenics pre-World War 2 (the term having been coined by Darwin's cousin, Francis Galton). She adds that Lancelot Hogben questioned the genetic argument. Jonathan Miller suggests his father would have been more liberal than draconian in his jurisprudential capacity. On the Home Office's advisory council, his job was to flag up any potential transgression of medical ethics in the treatment of offenders.

82 He gained MRCP status in 1939 (when he also appeared in the *Who's Who* of world medicine), then an FRCP in 1946. Jonathan Miller recalls that some of Emanuel's colleagues called his father 'that elongated Israelite', though not without affection.

83 Wolfe had been forced to join his father's furrier business as the eldest son. He is said to have been a Channel swimmer, though such crossings only began to be formally validated in 1927. Wolfe's achievement is thus impossible to confirm. His outstanding talent for natation was to skip two generations. Miller's eldest granddaughter became a championship swimmer as an adolescent.

84 Emanuel had not actually owned No. 23 Park Crescent and Miller (at odds with Sarah) believes No. 35 Queen's Grove was only a leasehold, so a nagging sense of insecurity continued.

85 Emanuel was a member of the Child Guidance Council; the first consultant and director of the child psychiatry department at St George's Hospital (where a unit was named after him); an emeritus physician at the Maudsley and the London Jewish Hospital. He instigated the founding of the multi-disciplinary ACPP (now called the Association for Child and Adolescent Mental Health) in 1956, and he edited the *Journal of Child Psychology and Psychiatry* from 1960.

86 Fond obituaries about Emanuel appeared in publications including *The Times*, 4 August 1970; the *British Medical Journal*, 8 and 15 August 1970; and the *Lancet*, 8 and 15 August 1970. The emphasis placed on his remarkably polymathic interests belies his son's argument that only today's dumbed-down media would deem such a trait extraordinary.

Chapter 2: The War and Post-War Years

1 Emanuel was of the rank of major and then promoted to lieutenant-colonel. Being nearly fifty, he was too old for foreign service. The 'nut-house' quotation (hyphenated thus in the original text) is from an illuminating short memoir: Miller, J., 'Among Chickens', *Granta*, Spring 1988, No. 23, 141–8.

2 This untitled short memoir by Miller appeared in Johnson, B. S. (ed.) (1968), *Evacuees* (London: Victor Gollancz), pp. 199–204. I have drawn on the same piece for Miller's ensuing descriptions of the 'smell of turps'; his renovated parents; the cornfield; the plankton-like convection current; the shunting trains; and the air-raid siren.

3 Miller in the *Evening Standard*, 9 February 1970.

4 'Among Chickens', p. 141. The full-grown Miller would go on to introduce comical chicken impersonations into various productions in which he appeared or which he directed. These range from his 1955 Cambridge performance as Troubleall in *Bartholomew Fair* to his film of *Alice in Wonderland* and his 2008 staging of Chekhov's *Three Sisters* at RADA.

5 In the archives of Thone, now renamed Taunton Preparatory School (and part of Taunton School), there is one fading report card charting Miller's progress from 1940 to 1942. Unfortunately, it is hard to tell if he was doing as poorly in class as he remembers because the card's grading system is not entirely lucid, and the general comments inscribed each term by his form mistress, Miss Lang, may have been his first inaccurate

reviews. They do not closely tally with his ranking in class. Indeed, after a terse mid-1941 note saying 'Has ability, too fussy', her remarks about his two subsequent 'rather better' and 'much better' semesters look as if they are ignoring his grades if, that is, one assumes that his position in class, logged as '3' then '6' then '6' meant third in mid-1941, then sixth then sixth again (with the total number of pupils being eleven at first, and eighteen by the end).

However, assuming Lang was not so contrary, then a higher number (e.g. '6' as opposed to '3') presumably meant the pupil was higher up the class (on the sixth rung up as opposed to third from the bottom). If that is how it goes (and it's a big 'if'), then in his first semester (1940) Miller's maths was not so bad (rated at '8') but in other subjects he really was close to the dunce's cap, coming in third from bottom overall and being on the lowest (rather than top) rung in history, geography and drawing (earning '1' for each of those). In that case, Lang's term summary, 'A good beginning', must have been merely polite.

By the end of his time there, with much veering en route, he had gone from a '2' to a '13' in English, from '3' to '12' in Scripture and from '5' to '10' in music. Also, going by the low-number-equals-low-rank assessment, his maths had slipped (to '3' at one point).

His final overall position was still only a mediocre '6'. His relatively young age within his year (due to his July birthday) couldn't have helped, and the report records many absences, seemingly totalling 87 during the spring and summer terms of 1941 (possibly relating to his mother contracting pneumonia).

6 Betty Miller, 'Notes for an Unwritten Autobiography', p. 45.

7 Miller discussed theories about cognitive problems, without any directly personal allusions, in his article 'The Wild Boy of Aveyron', *New York Review of Books*, 16 September 1976. He also considered the potentially positive effects of unhappy experiences – including enhanced creativity – for the programme *In Praise of Fear: Jonathan Miller on Dickens*, BBC Radio 3, 31 May 1970. That was transcribed in the *Listener*, 28 May 1970.

8 Although Peter is, of course, a fictional and archetypal little boy, Betty confessed in a letter to the author John Verney that this book (written in Bishop's Lydeard as well as in Droitwich) came 'very close to reality' in certain respects. This is noted in *On the Side of the Angels'* preface, p. xiii.

9 *On the Side of the Angels*, p. 206.

10 A plaque commemorating Henry Spiro as one of the fallen can still be seen at St Paul's School today.

11 Julian Crispin went on to become an insurance broker in the City and, latterly, the chairman of a Lloyd's members agency.

12 Sarah recalled this detail about Emanuel's copy of *Alice*.

13 Betty Miller, 'Notes for an Unwritten Autobiography', p. 44.

14 Miller's comment (from an interview with the author referred to Mozart's Don Giovanni and Byron's Don Juan. He explained further: 'What he wants is to take Donna Anna away from her father, away from Don Ottavio; he wants to tormentingly take Zerlina away from Masetto . . . He's not really interested in seducing women. He's not notching up conquests, he's notching up defeats, and I think it's much more interesting.'

15 Retrospectively, Sarah thought her parents were even-handed except for some traditional emphasis on the son having the best education.

16 The Priory was in Kings Langley. 'Led Astray' was originally published in the *Spectator*, then in Inglis, B. (ed.) (1961), *John Bull's Schooldays* (London: Hutchinson), pp. 101–4. I am indebted to this for the descriptions of the Priory (which appears under the pseudonym of the Friar House) regarding the Jungian chant, and the moist art class, *et al.*

17 Miller also describes ludicrous eurhythmics classes in 'Led Astray' and, even if his tone is more consistently comical, a continuity can be discerned between this memoir and his mother's article 'At the Villa Eole: A Fragment of Autobiography', *Cornhill*, Vol. 166, No. 995. Betty's account of her adolescent stay at the convalescent school near Calais includes, on p. 409, a humorous account of the Russian posture instructress:

> White-coated and bounding rhythmically upon the pliant springs of her toes, her mastiff's face gleaming with sweat, Madame Ossipov barked out her commands – 'Ang! Doo! Ang! Doo!' . . . Since all her converse with us was carried out by means of these strange sounds it seemed to us that Madame Ossipov was in fact without human speech.

18 This is a point recalled by Julian Crispin, for Miller joined him at Shirley House after leaving the Priory.

19 More seriously, Emanuel's arthritis would prevent him from driving in later life.

20 Churchill, 5 March 1946. For English Jews, reeling from the Holocaust's fully exposed atrocities, Mosley's renewed attempts to orchestrate London marches were not reassuring either.

21 A longer post-war ban, specifically on colourful neon and floodlights, was sustained until 1949.

22 The squirrel pie recipe was issued in 1946. Miller points out that he never went hungry at Queen's Grove. Still, fluctuating rations saw the cheese allowance pared down to one ounce (per person, per week) as late as 1952 and, at one point, Clement Attlee's government allotted more bread to hard-working labourers than to life-of-the-mind types. Not so much grinning and bearing it, the government's slogans 'Work or want' and 'Export or die' were gloomily compelling.

23 While at prep school, Miller voraciously read pseudo-historical sagas by Bulwer Lytton and Harrison Ainsworth.

24 It seems additionally astonishing that this went on under Betty's nose given that, in 'Notes for an Unwritten Autobiography', pp. 43–5, she described her mean and inattentive nursemaid, Biddy, smacking her knees with a hairbrush and rebuking her for a close shave with a paedophile in the park. 'If you promise me to be a good girl in the future,' said Biddy, 'I won't tell your mother.'

25 Miller wrote about his childhood fear of death and Nanny Morgan in the *Listener*, 19 October 1967.

26 I am indebted to Rosemary Dinnage's book, Dinnage, R. (ed.) (1990), *The Ruffian on the Stair: Reflections on Death* (New York, NY: Viking Penguin Inc.), pp. 223–5. Therein Miller referred to the 'unansweringness' of corpses, his mother envisaged 'at death's door', and the bear's skull.

27 Peter Hennessy discusses fans and opponents of the era's imported American culture, aka Coca-Colonization: Hennessy, P. (2007), *Having It So Good: Britain in the Fifties* (London: Penguin), pp. 15–16. Miller wrote about his passion for the cinema in 'Desert Island Reels', *Punch*, 19 January 1966. There he alluded to the States' cracker-barrel Canaan and billowing abundance of comedy, as well as mentioning the first film he ever saw. It made him literally sick with excitement, and the projectionist's flickering beam initiated his interest in perception. He naively imagined the eye worked similarly with a small screen inside each person's head.

28 Miller attended Arnold House prep school along with his friend John Bingham (Lord Lucan).

29 I am most grateful to Marit Gruson for her memories of the Millers. The daughter of actress Greta Smedderg (a contemporary of Garbo's at the Royal Dramatic Theatre), she married director Göran Gentele who became general manager of the New York Met, although his time there did not overlap with Miller's.

30 Oliver Sacks recalls this, comparing Miller's powers of improvisational mimicry to a subsequent acquaintance, the American comic Robin Williams. The cod-French burbling can also be heard in BBC Radio's pre-*Beyond the Fringe* recording of *Monday Night at Home,* from October 1959, where Miller sends up a gabbling foreign presenter of a classical concert.

31 From 'Among Chickens', p. 147. Miller has also suggested that his mother encouraged his use of metaphors and similes by her own gift for them and by greatly admiring a comparison he drew, in his teens, between a frost-covered lawn and the bloom on lavender leaves. That is recorded by Wachtel, *Original Minds*, p. 14.

32 The Swedish expedition happened shortly after World War 2 and this Hythe holiday was in 1947.

33 *Beside the Seaside: A Holiday with Children* was published in a collection: Smith, S., *Beside the Seaside: A Holiday with Children*, in Blakeston, O. (ed.) (1949), *Holidays and Happy Days* (London: Phoenix House), pp. 147–61. The story has been referred to in features about Miller in the *Guardian*, 12 September 1998, the *Sunday Telegraph*, 28 October 2001, and elsewhere.

34 There was to be a sting in the tail for Stevie Smith when, years later, in August 1963, Miller was to feature in *Life* magazine, as a star comic with a glowing write-up and a big photo spread.

35 Informative sources on Stevie Smith and her set include Frances Spalding, who discusses this poem: Spalding, F. (1988), *Stevie Smith: A Critical Biography* (London: Faber), pp. 187–8. Also Barbera, J. and McBrien, W. (1985), *Stevie: A Biography* (London: Heinemann); and Smith, S., edited by Barbera, J. and McBrien, W. (1981), *Me Again: Uncollected Writings of Stevie Smith Illustrated by Herself* (London: Virago).

36 Olivia Manning's reference to Smith battening is noted in Barbera and McBrien's *Stevie: A Biography*, pp. 161–2.

37 This letter was among Sarah Miller's possessions, and the trouble surrounding it is discussed by Spalding, p. 188.

38 I am indebted to Spalding, p. 186, for the subsequent point about fairy notes. Miller also thought of Smith as a fellow child. She was generally associated with writing children's verses (of a pleasant variety) and with drawing sweetly amusing cartoons – a habit which Miller developed as a teenager.

39 Contrastingly, Miller speaks with unqualified fondness of the Richard sisters, Charlotte and Simone, two of Betty's friends from her days in France, who were artistically well-connected seamstresses with socialist principles.

40 By way of qualification, Betty's Bloomsbury friend Naomi Lewis pointed out that, whatever their differences, Mrs Miller remained very fond of Emanuel and he, in turn, set up a writer's award in her name after she died.

41 This is mentioned in *On the Side of the Angels*' preface, p. xvii.

42 Miller's quip is logged in the *Oxford Dictionary of Modern Quotations*. Using it as a household joke, Nigella Lawson has noted that one of her multi-cultural recipes, 'to borrow from Jonathan Miller, is not quite char sui, it's just char sui-ish'. That is in Lawson, N. (1998), *How to Eat* (London: Chatto & Windus), p. 443. In 2012, the Welsh–Jewish stand-up Bennett Arron ran with the gag, his Soho Theatre show being entitled *Jewelsh*.

43 Miller's metaphor is a variation on *Brideshead Revisited* where Evelyn Waugh's narrator, Charles Ryder,

detects 'a thin bat's squeak of sexuality, inaudible to any but me' in Sebastian Flyte's sister, Julia.

44 The *Daily Mail* cartoon appeared on 15 June 1991. The *Sunday Telegraph* article featured on 28 October 2001. John Osborne's personal remarks are discussed in the light of the playwright's possible anti-Semitism in Chapter 6.

Informative articles and books discussing British anti-Semitism in recent years include 'Does Anti-Semitism Still Linger in Britain', *Daily Telegraph*, 26 January 2005, and a volume of collected essays, Iganski, P. and Kosmin, B. (eds) (2003), *A New Antisemitism?: Debating Judeophobia in 21st-Century Britain* (London: Profile). When interviewed on BBC Radio 4 on 1 January 2006, Britain's chief rabbi, Sir Jonathan Sacks, spoke of a global 'tsunami of anti-Semitism'. In terms of statistics, the Community Security Trust's report on anti-Semitic incidents in the UK, published in 2010, noted an unprecedented surge to 926 reported incidents in 2009 (with the January Gaza conflict being linked to that). Though a sizable drop, the 639 incidents registered in 2010 were the second-highest annual total since the CST's records began in 1984. The Trust suggests the general trend since the late 1990s has been a rise in incidents, after a dip in the mid-1990s. Before that, in the late 1980s and early 1990s, incidents increased (linked to the political right having gained ground).

45 Interview with Lucy Hughes-Hallett, *Vogue*, November 1978. The subsequent comment on 'prophylactic' Jewishness also comes from this article.

46 Miller reminisced about *A Matter of Life and Death* on *The 100 Greatest Films*, Channel 4, 28 December 2002.

47 'Among Chickens', pp. 145–6, where Emanuel's religious reversion and feelings of guilt are also discussed.

48 The 'lungfish' remark was made on the American broadcast *Bill Moyers Journal*, 4 May 2007. Sarah, who was religious, spoke of Emanuel combining science with almost occult mystical interests, but Miller insists his father was, at heart, a Spinoza-style sceptic who just felt guilty about having abandoned his Jewish roots when he became an Oxbridge doctor.

49 Betty wrote about J's shoelaces in 'Notes for an Unwritten Autobiography', pp. 45–6.

50 Emanuel also sent Miller off to St John's Wood Jewish Youth Club, like Alec Bergman in *Farewell Leicester Square*, wanting his son to have Jewish friends.

51 John Hughlings Jackson was an evolutionary neurologist whose work influenced W. H. R. Rivers and Henry Head (as noted later, in Chapter 10). By curious coincidence, he had also once resided at Emanuel's childhood address, No. 5 Fournier Street.

52 Miller was sent very early on, before the war, to Susan Isaacs, the experimental head of child development at London's Institute of Education. He also saw the therapist Gwen E. Chesters who contributed to Emanuel's book, *The Growing Child and Its Problems*.

53 The 'séance' comment first surfaced, in public, when Miller was talking on BBC Radio 3's *The Horror Story*, 23 December 1971. Sarah Miller toyed with the idea of becoming an analyst or counsellor herself after she underwent psychotherapy in middle age.

54 Miller has written of the enabling unconscious in 'Going Unconscious'. This appears in the *New York Review of Books*' volume of collected essays: Silvers, R. B. (ed.) (1995), *Hidden Histories of Science* (New York, NY: NYREV Inc.). Miller further discussed the subject with Kevin Jackson, *Independent*, 26 October 2001.

55 Emanuel Miller, *The Generations*, pp. 20–1, 160–1 and 169–70. Betty Miller concerned herself with the long-term effects of insufficiently loving parents (in contrast with excessively loving ones) in her *Nineteenth Century and After* article of October 1948 entitled 'Two Fathers and their Sons' (a biographical piece about the formative experiences of Samuel Butler and Henry James).

56 With *Insomnia and Other Disturbances of Sleep* being published in 1935, most of Miller's restless nights obviously occurred after Emanuel had written this book.

57 Emanuel Miller's article 'The Rooted Sorrow', *Twentieth Century*, May 1956, 448.

58 *The Generations*, p. 147 (indicating that anti-establishmentarian youths were kicking around well before the Satire Boom of the Sixties).

Chapter 3: 1947–53

1 St Paul's has long been among the exclusive set known as the Clarendon schools. That is to say it is classed as a leading UK educational establishment along with other major public (i.e. fee-paying) schools: Eton, Harrow, Rugby and Westminster.

2 St Paul's School for Boys is now on a modern campus, across the Thames in Barnes. The original edifice in Hammersmith was designed by Waterhouse in the early 1880s.

3 In his BBC Radio 4 memoir *The Strongest Influence in My Life*, Miller spoke of his sense of imprisonment and of exclusion from that Eden glimpsed through the lab's 'aquarium windows'. This was transcribed under the heading 'Before the Fringe' in the *Listener*, 17 July 1975. Incidentally, though his retrospective account of seeing the dogfish dissection and signing up for the Lower Biological Eighth makes it sound as

if he switched sides very neatly and suddenly in 1951, that is a telescoping of time. His engagement with science had clearly begun before 1951. After all, he spoke of his medical ambitions to Danny Kaye in 1948, and Stevie Smith's *Beside the Seaside*, mentioning that same career plan, was penned in 1947. The minutes kept by the Chesterton Society – a St Paul's debating group – also record that Miller hotly defended science, in opposition to anti-scientific classicists, in October 1949.

4 In 1961, Miller himself would write (in a February letter to Oliver Sacks) of his love of the 'daguerreo-typic' world of old-fashioned science (as opposed to modern hospitals). That said, turn-of-the-century science books, to an adolescent reading them in 1950, might not have seemed so very archaic.

5 Christopher Booker discusses, at more length, how the old and the new overlapped for his generation in *The Neophiliacs* (originally published by Collins in 1969). See Booker, C. (1992 edn), *The Neophiliacs: The Revolution in English Life in the Fifties and Sixties* (London: Pimlico), regarding page references hereafter.

6 He spoke of the dancing, lime-coloured disc when talking on the 1977 *Parkinson Show*. I am also indebted in this section to two articles by Miller. 'Men of the Age (II): The Medical Student', published in the *Twentieth Century* magazine, October 1960, 343–8, refers to his ideal of bearded savants and teak benches, to his mildewed tomes, and to his father's office. His piece 'Saying "Ah" (Part 1)' in *Vogue*, 1 January 1967, alludes to 'secular communions' in the 'sanctified annexe'.

7 Miller alluded to his lamp-lit narcissistic romanticism in 'Men of the Age (II)'. His fervid late-night experiments, as described there, echo Mary Shelley's *Frankenstein*.

8 This early friend was Angus McKenzie (later an MBE and audio broadcasting expert). He lived in a Redington Road house, just up the street from Miller's pre-war crèche.

9 Sacks and Korn were truly lifelong friends, having been introduced to one another in their prams in Brondesbury Park (just the other side of Kilburn from Swiss Cottage). Though Miller would not officially join the Lower Biological Eighth until the autumn of 1951, he was friends with Sacks and Korn before that. This is apparent from the school magazine, the *Pauline*, which recorded in May 1951 how Korn and Miller performed as a comic double act (with Sacks in the same revue). Sacks also recalls their Literary Society activities being in progress as early as 1950.

10 Oliver Sacks on the Walker Library encounter: Sacks, O. (2002), *Uncle Tungsten: Memories of a Chemical Boyhood* (New York, NY: Vintage), p. 271. Other quotations, unless stated, are from my interview with Sacks.

11 Miller was quoted on Sacks' Borgesian fantasist traits in the *Guardian*, 5 March 2005. In the *Seattle Times*, 5 March 1991, he also noted that their approaches to neuropsychology differed, saying that he deemed Sacks to be a romantic by inclination, while Sacks thought him too clinically cold.

12 Some BBC Radio listeners will also know Korn as a connector of far-flung facts on *Round Britain Quiz*. Though he has, sadly, suffered from memory loss of late, he was still absolutely brilliant when I interviewed him for this biography in the 'Noughties'.

13 Sacks tells of the Highgate Ponds incident in *Uncle Tungsten*, p. 123, and 'like a demented meteor' is his description.

14 In *Uncle Tungsten*, p. 16, Sacks recalls Miller being somewhat dismissive about his family home in Barnsbury, declaring the decor lacked personal style. Miller now paints an intriguing picture of the house as very grand and dark, 'with all sorts of Jewish scholars lurking in the corridors, like Russian pilgrims in Tolstoy'.

15 I am indebted to Sacks for his splendid description of the pickling fiasco, *Uncle Tungsten*, pp. 273–4. Not put off by the incident in Hythe, Sacks still adores cuttlefish. His personal letterhead is, to this day, decorated with one. One might add here that Miller's love of animal species was not all-embracing. He drew the line at arachnophilia. Describing himself as 'a true spider coward', he confessed (in the *Spectator*, 9 January 1959) that he once spent the best part of a night in the country, 'trying to gas one of these monsters with a beekeeper's smoke-gun'.

16 Miller headed off, more enthusiastically, to watch cricket matches at Lords on Saturdays, accompanied by Sarah.

17 Thanks go to Michael Simmons (a solicitor and one of Miller's contemporaries) for his memories of the Green Cup boxing competition and St Paul's gymnastic classes. I am also most grateful to other Old Paulines for their memories of Miller, including Julian Rees (who went on to become a journalist) and Eric Beck (another Sid Pask pupil and a consultant physician at London's Whittington Hospital).

18 The recycling unit was a business run by Korn's brother. Miller recollects with fierce pride how the nerdy-looking Korn triumphed in a St Paul's cross-country race, 'startling the hell out of the jocks', and he clearly admires the flat-footed Sacks' aquatic transformation. Even late in life, the ex-pat Sacks has apparently been spotted gliding around Manhattan in a wet suit – his morning exercise.

19 The geography master's alleged sneers seem somewhat at odds with the *Guardian*'s feature about Miller, 12 September 1998, which said that the latter recollected no instance of anti-Semitism at his British public school. Today Miller confirms St Paul's was not horrendously draconian or anti-Semitic at the time. Sacks points out that its markedly anti-Semitic phase, which outraged Isaiah Berlin, came later. This was when

the school infamously restricted its Jewish intake. As an alternative to the CCF and athletics, Miller briefly joined the school's Air Scouts, but any notion of becoming a Niven-style heroic pilot was short-lived. Training merely entailed inspecting dismembered Model Ford engines, and staring through aerodrome fences on soggy afternoons.

20 Sacks says nobody laughed at Pask's stammer. They imitated it, but he suggests there was something aspiring in that. A certain desirability was associated with stutters at the time, thanks to Anthony Blanche's luxurious stammer in *Brideshead Revisited*.

21 Sacks' writings on Pask include *Uncle Tungsten* and his earlier memoir, 'Canada: Pause (1960)', published in *Antaeus*, Spring 1989, No. 62. Pask's Bunsen is described there, on p. 196, with Pask's surname encrypted as Kasp.

22 'Canada: Pause (1960)', p. 197.

23 Other outstanding achievers taught by Pask include the professor of surgery and Conservative peer Lord McColl of Dulwich, and UCH's pioneer in neonatal respiration Professor Osmond Reynolds.

24 Miller's reminiscences about Pask, on which I have drawn, again include 'Men of the Age (II)', and 'Before the Fringe' in the *Listener*.

25 I was told this by Dick Quinnell, organizer of St Paul's Sid Pask Reunion.

26 While Miller's passion for Darwin chimed with Emanuel's interest in the science of inheritance, the son was also, maybe, keen to 'proselytize' about evolutionary theory as an alternative to his father's religion.

27 Miller mentions that Pask's weekend Field Club expeditions neatly let him off the hook regarding any notion of attending Saturday synagogue. He adds that when he and Korn were obliged to attend high festival services, they went together, covertly reading biology books and other literature instead of listening to the rabbi. Ultimately, Emanuel could hardly object to his son's morphology-obsessed National History Museum outings, being himself a long-distance member of Paris' Société de Morphologie.

28 Sacks writes in *Uncle Tungsten*, pp. 186–91, and elsewhere, about the periodic table, the emotional uncertainties and the upheavals of his youth. Miller spoke on BBC Radio's *Desert Island Discs*, 2 January 1994, about being unsettled during the war and about his passion for hard science which made everything seem predictable.

29 The Scottish coast plan is recorded in the *Pauline*, 1952, 64–5. The magazine had described the Kew and Byfleet outings in 1951, on pages 118–19. I am most grateful to the archivist, Simon May, and the librarians at St Paul's for their trove of material. Incidentally, there should be no confusion between the two Jonathan Millers at St Paul's between 1947 and 1953. Jonathan A. Miller was the son of actor-director Hugh Lorimer Miller and subsequently became a Stock Exchange council member.

30 The *Pauline*, 1952, 117, refers to Miller's demonstration on the subject of blood, with his whale lecture also written up in that issue (on page 12). The same publication, 1953 (March), 10, describes his impromptu talks and the pile of bones.

31 Julian Rees noted Miller's presentation skills and knowledge.

32 Miller reminisced about Cumbrae in 'Return Tickets', *The Times*, 12 April 1962 (recalling that 'sun-lit fortnight') and again in 'Men of the Age (II)'.

33 The gang's history might be compared with Mary McCarthy's book *The Group*, although her set were bright American girls.

34 Lindenbaum became an eminent doctor while Nathani was to give up medicine in favour of social work in Australia.

35 The Arts Council, established in 1946, followed on from the wartime Council for the Encouragement of Music and the Arts. Cinema ticket sales peaked in 1946, with one-third of the population attending once a week, and 13 per cent going twice weekly. Stratford's Memorial Theatre had been reopened, auspiciously, by Barry Jackson.

36 Joan Bakewell notably discusses the inspiring impact of the Third Programme in her autobiography, Bakewell, J. (2003), *The Centre of the Bed* (London: Hodder & Stoughton), pp. 82–3.

37 Eight million people visited the South Bank over the summer of 1951. Some wags suggested that the soaring Skylon building was only a perfect symbol for Britain in that it had no visible means of support.

38 The minutes book for St Paul's aforementioned debating group, the Chesterton Society, specifically records, on 21 October 1949, how Cutler irreverently informed the society that 'scientists have no culture' and Miller snappily responded that 'even hypocritical cultured classicists like Mr Cutler are willing to receive medical attention when they are ill'. When quoting from the pupils' jottings in the Chesterton minutes books, I have now and then, for the sake of clarity, corrected hasty errors and odd punctuation. As indicated in the *Pauline*, 1952, 113, Miller also participated in the school's more formal debating society, the Union, though not frequently.

39 Sacks mildly recollects Miller's toilet humour. 'Whenever I wanted to go to the lavatory,' he says, 'Jonathan would shout in an enormously loud voice, "Oliver's going to piss!" – which made it difficult and embarrassing.'

40 When it came to plants, Sacks and Miller again had their separate terrain. The former homed in on the

non-flowering ferns or Pteridophyta, while the latter took to the mosses and liverworts, the Hepaticae.

41 Of emigrating, Sacks says: 'Perhaps one of the reasons I came to America was the feeling that it was a sort of classless society, and that neither being middle-class nor being Jewish were categories which would matter here.'

42 Regarding the 'neurotic Jewish' tag, Sacks adds a qualification: 'I think Jonathan was among the first of us to become critical of Freudian thinking, but we probably all used the term, "neurotic".' Another Old Pauline claims Miller anxiously did not reveal he was Jewish for ages, but the Chesterton Society minutes book alludes to his hobbyhorse being anti-Semitism on 12 May 1950.

43 Regarding the pairs within Miller's six-strong gang, Korn and Nathani were close, as were Sacks and Lindenbaum. The benzene ring comparison isn't perfect though, Miller and Cutler not being bosom buddies.

44 *The Hedgehog and the Fox* was passed round just after Miller left St Paul's in 1953, which was its year of publication. Its flyleaf inscription is possibly the only surviving evidence of the full gang, as no one seems to have taken an actual snapshot of them. It is somewhere between a chain letter and a mock incantation. The first line is penned by Miller (thanking Sacks), followed by Cutler, Nathani and Korn, with a cheeky finale by Lindenbaum. It reads as follows:

This was kindly given to me by Oliver when I had glandular fever. Thankyou Oliver!!
This was kindly given to me by Jonathan when I had influenza. Thankyou Jonathan!!
This was kindly given to me by Tony when I was perfectly alright. Thankyou Tony!!
This was kindly given to me by Mish when I had neurasthenia. Thank you Mish!!
This was kindly stolen by me from Erik when I needed it. Thank you Erik!!

45 The Nobel Prize-winning Lagerlöf had trained as a teacher at the same institute as Miller's maternal grandmother, Sara.

46 St Paul's official literary group was the Milton Society. Miller underlines that he was not well versed in literature compared to Korn and played only a minor role in the Lit. Soc. Still, he was its secretary with Korn as treasurer.

47 This exchange with Shaw must have occurred in the early months of 1950.

48 Emerging at around the same time, Shrewsbury School's jokey magazine was the *Salopian*, with contributors including Richard Ingrams and Willie Rushton. It is discussed in Humphrey Carpenter's history of the British Satire Boom (first published by Victor Gollancz in 2000). The edition I have used is Carpenter, H. (2002), *That Was Satire That Was* (London: Phoenix). This work was published under a different title in the US: Carpenter, H. (2000), *A Great, Silly Grin* (New York, NY: Public Affairs).

49 The French police claimed to have foiled the planned London bombing. With the divvying up of Palestine descending into chaotic violence in 1947, Holocaust survivors on the Palestine-bound Jewish refugee ship *Exodus 47* also made headlines, using iron bars to battle desperately with the immigration-controlling British Navy who blocked their way.

50 Sacks discusses the High Master and the Literary Society in *Uncle Tungsten*, pp. 277–8.

51 The 'intersection' phrase is Sacks' own from the preface in Sacks, O. (1986), *The Man Who Mistook His Wife for a Hat* (London: Picador/Pan Books), p. xi. In 2007, he was appointed by Columbia University as a professor of clinical neurology and clinical psychiatry, and as its first 'Columbia artist' – a newly created designation.

52 The Old Vic Company seasons in 1949–50 were presented at the New Theatre (subsequently renamed the Albery and thereafter the Noël Coward Theatre). The ensemble was back in residence at the Old Vic in 1950–1. Michael Benthall directed *She Stoops to Conquer* in 1949, and Hugh Hunt staged *Love's Labour's Lost* in 1950. George Devine directed *Bartholomew Fair* and Glen Byam Shaw staged *Henry V* in 1950–1. Miller would later work with several of the actors whom he saw in those productions: Roger Livesey and Paul Rogers as well as Redgrave, McKern and Clunes. The London theatre scene was also buzzing thanks to Donald Wolfit's 1949 season in Camden Town, and Laurence Olivier's two seasons at St James' in 1950–1. This was considered to be a golden age for classical actors, though the era's performance style would soon be regarded as creakily old-fashioned.

53 This is from Miller in conversation with Eleanor Wachtel, *Original Minds*, p. 27. The comment relates to the 1949–51 Old Vic company seasons and the *Jack and the Beanstalk* which he saw earlier.

54 Michael Romain logged Miller's aquarium analogy and touched on *Jack and the Beanstalk* in his very useful, compact compendium of interviews, Romain, M. (1992), *A Profile of Jonathan Miller* (Cambridge: Cambridge University Press), pp. 24–5. I refer to this henceforth as Romain's *A Profile*.

55 Miller says that his father bought him art materials but they never painted together.

56 The two debates on art are described in the Chesterton Society minutes book, dated 29 June 1951 (on the Royal Academy) and 23 January 1953 (on modern art, where Miller was said to be incomprehensible and pouting). Miller has, incidentally, since taken part in platform discussions and given talks at the RA where he was made an honorary fellow in 1990. The specific allusion to him being 'volcanic' appeared in the *Pauline*, 1951, 117 (in its article about that first debate).

57 I owe this nugget of information to Alan Franks, feature writer for *The Times*.

58 The *Pauline*'s review, 1952, 7–9, noted Miller's extremely spartan set design, though there is no accompanying photograph to compare with, say, his 1974 *Così fan tutte* (two doors, two chairs, one couch). Tony Cutler recalls Miller playing Brutus in *Julius Caesar*. However, Miller says he acted in no school plays and, according to the original programme, Cutler was Metellus Cimber and Korn was Cassius, while Miller only created the decor. Miller played Brutus, later, in a Footlights sketch.

59 The revues raised funds for working-class boys' clubs which were named after the school's founder, John Colet.

60 I am grateful to the BBC producer Piers Plowright, Miller's contemporary at Arnold House, for his personal memories and his article in the school's newsletter, *Assembly*, Spring/Summer 2003.

61 After a dig about no swooners among the visiting female spectators, the *Pauline*, 1949, 97–8, concluded that Kaye fans had found 'an excellent substitute' for their hero in Miller's impersonation.

62 Codron is not mentioned in the programme of the 1949 Colet Clubs revue, so presumably he appeared with Miller on the bill of another sketch show. The Chesterton Society's two debates, on whether Woolworths or Shakespeare had done more for civilization, are logged in its minutes book, 13 February 1948 and 16 October 1952.

63 From the *Pauline*, 1951, 65. Sacks served as the raconteur and played the piano in this same revue. However, he was shy compared to Miller – not destined to be a Dudley Moore – and he did not become a regular fixture. Miller also appeared in a group vignette called 'Bevan's Heaven', set in one of Britain's new National Health hospitals. He did not get to play the consultant or even the registrar, but Char Wallah – serving cups of tea.

64 From the *Pauline*, 1952, 61–2.

65 It was, incidentally, Bacharach who penned the teasing Chesterton minutes about Miller's incomprehensibility in the modern art debate, 23 January 1953.

66 The original programme for the Colet Clubs revue missed the pun, using the correct spelling, 'Paradis'. The *Pauline*, 1953, 5, added that 'J. W. Miller . . . is now nearing the end of his Danny Ustinov [i.e. imitative Danny Kaye/Peter Ustinov] development and finding much that is unique'. While noting that he tended to 'put subtlety to an overstrain and fantasy to underelaboration', the review concluded that his 'exuberance and vitality, and facial and corporal significance' rendered everything screamingly amusing.

67 Miller's physical clowning would later be compared to Marceau's, in 1961, as noted in the *Jewish Chronicle*, 24 August 2006.

68 Henri Bergson's theory about laughter was set out in his 1899 tract entitled *Le Rire* (or *On Laughter*). He discussed *élan vital* in his 1907 book, *Creative Evolution*.

69 The *Pauline*, 1953, 5. Peter Cook, Miller's later co-star in *Beyond the Fringe*, was a few years younger but, while at Radley, he staged school revues, with his roles including a dung beetle – though that may not exactly count as common ground. He also scripted a musical about an evangelical jazz maestro determined to convert African cannibals.

70 Irving Wardle, *Observer*, 28 August 1960, reviewing *Beyond the Fringe*.

71 The conversion of the laboratory bench into the school stage is noted in A. N. G. Richards' book *St Paul's School in West Kensington: 1884–1968* (privately printed in 1968), p. 19. Somewhat ironically given his later job-hopping, Miller appeared in 'Tinker, Tailor . . .', which was a vocation-selecting sketch performed with the careers master in the 1949 revue.

72 The *Under-Twenty Parade* listing was printed under 10 March in the *Radio Times* of 6 March 1953, and Miller and Bacharach featured again on 18 March and 7 April 1953, and 20 April 1954. Their skits for the series included a Bank Holiday special where they interrupted canoeists and trekkers, pretending they were even more sportily dangling off Nelson's Column. Miller has no idea how they got talent-spotted. It could have been the broadcaster Jack Longland (brother of Miller's form master Cecil Longland) or the BBC producer Reggie Smith (Olivia Manning's spouse from Queen's Grove). The contact probably was not Emanuel, though he had broadcast talks for the BBC, such as *Talking it Over: Your State of Mind and Family Life* in 1939. The Light Programme became Radio 2 in 1967.

73 The transcript, dug out for me by the tireless staff at the BBC Written Archives centre in Reading, combines Miller and Bacharach's material from their first and second sessions for *Under-Twenty Parade*.

74 In terms of formative aural environments, a parallel might be drawn with Edward Elgar, whose music so evoked the English countryside where he grew up. The composer once stated that he remained, at heart, the child who used to linger on the River Severn's reedy banks with a sheet of paper, 'trying to fix the sounds'. Ludwig Koch was a possible influence on Miller too. This singer-turned-1940s-broadcaster – a friend of Julian Huxley's – had brought the music of nature to people's attention, recording bird calls, animal cries and street sounds. Miller now recalls Koch's work affectionately, a fact not really at odds with him having parodied the man in his youthful skit 'Radio Page' (as performed for Footlights in 1954).

75 According to Korn, 'Round the World with Radio' developed out of nonsense dialogues which he and Miller improvised at parties, on one occasion wondering how far they could go with sheer gobbledegook and still be considered witty.

76 Bacharach does most of the talking in this extract, with Miller starting off then mainly playing the feed.
77 'Radio Page' (the title of which alludes to the *Radio Times*) was performed by Miller in the 1954 Footlights revue, *Out of the Blue*. The same skit, with further variations, resurfaced in his performance on BBC Radio's *Monday Night at Home*, 21 December 1959, as logged in the BBC Written Archives.
78 As a youngster, Miller enjoyed several BBC Radio comedy series besides ITMA. These included *Much-Binding-In-The-Marsh* (from 1947, starring Kenneth Horne and set in an aerodrome-turned-country-club), and *Take It From Here* (from 1948, with Jimmy Edwards playing a professor with East End roots, and with topical skits and parodies of cinematic cliches, scripted by Frank Muir and Denis Norden).
79 Korn and Miller's performance of 'Round the World with Radio' (which was along the same lines as the Miller-Bacharach version) had been reviewed for the *Pauline* in May 1951, and the Goons' first programme (under the preliminary title *Crazy People*) was only broadcast at the very end of that month (28 May). Still, in the *Twentieth Century* magazine, June 1960, and elsewhere, Miller has discussed how he relished various comedians including the Goons.
80 *La Cantatrice chauve* (*The Bald Soprano*) dates from 1950, but Miller does not recall knowing about any absurdist playwrights at the time.
81 Bacharach reassured one panellist that he was not deranged.
82 The NHS had got rolling in 1948. Women began to land some notable top jobs after the war. The University of London, for example, acquired a woman chancellor for the first time in 1948. The following year peeresses were permitted in the House of Lords, and Simon de Beauvoir published *The Second Sex*. Racial tensions rose in the US in 1948 when the state of Oklahoma refused to admit a black student to law school; South Africa's Afrikaner Nationalists denied coloured (i.e. mixed race) citizens the right to vote in 1951; the Mau Mau swore to drive whites out of Kenya in 1952, etc.
83 The Chesterton Society minutes book recorded this dispute on 26 May 1950. On 21 January 1949, in his maiden speech about BBC standards, Miller called for more plays then furiously dismissed the 'rot' his opponent Harold Organ had talked about outdated television cameras. Organ went on to become an electrical engineer.
84 Chesterton Society minutes book, 27 October 1951. Korn was, of course, on *Dale* and *Choice*.
85 *Ibid.*, 31 October 1951.
86 *Ibid.*, 16 October 1952.
87 On both 25 October 1951 and 24 October 1952, the minutes book noted that Miller's speeches were being expunged from the records. His own 'unwritten minutes' note was jotted down on 12 October 1951. Having been singled out for interrupting constitutional proceedings on 25 October 1951, he proceeded to call the assembled company an unruly mob on 16 October 1952. He stood in one election for an official post in the society but lost by miles, as noted on 3 March 1950.
88 Chesterton minutes, 30 January and 6 February 1953.
89 Miller spoke of how he neither emulated nor competed with Emanuel in 'Relative Values', *Sunday Times Magazine*, 9 July 2006.
90 This letter, from 30 January 1952, is referred to in the *On the Side of the Angels* preface, p. xv.
91 John Gross, who was to become a theatre critic for the *Sunday Telegraph*, was growing up in the East End at the time and he heard on the Jewish grapevine about this hilarious young comic.
92 Judith Taylor, née Mundlak, is now, like Sacks, a US-based neurologist and botanical author.
93 The Chesterton Society minutes book records that Miller, in January 1953, was allotted the topic *Dancing: The First Step to Demoralization*. He 'beamed with pride at the thought of his libido', and had to be restrained from launching into all his jazz moves.
94 Miller says that he showed willing with Penelope Isaacs – the daughter of Emanuel's lifelong friend, Jack – without reaping great rewards either.
95 In spite of his association with the banned Literary Society, Miller had been invited to join the Milton Society. Earlier that term, he had read the main part in, of all things, G. B. Shaw's *The Doctor's Dilemma*. He and Rachel were in the audience listening to Harley Granville-Barker's *The Voysey Inheritance*. Both readings are mentioned in the *Pauline*, 1953, 57.
96 Ruth Collet was taught at the Slade by the artist-doctor Henry Tonks who has become the subject of a Pat Barker novel, Barker, P. (2007), *Life Class* (London: Hamish Hamilton).
97 The gown was later bequeathed to a fellow Pauline, Julian Rees, who passed the locker room just as Miller was clearing out at the end of term. After much clattering, Miller whisked off, waving the said garment at Rees and crying 'Here, take this: it was my mother's!'

Chapter 4: 1953–6

1 To be specific, Miller had won a major scholarship.
2 This is Christopher Foster's recollection. He was at King's College.
3 Bartlett, F. C. (1932), *Remembering: A Study in Experimental and Social Psychology* (Cambridge:

Cambridge University Press). I should probably point out that I have blurred two Johnian stairwells here as it was in Miller's second year that he became Bartlett's neighbour.

4 Meyer Fortes had started out as one of Morris Ginsberg's protégés and joined Emanuel at the East London Child Guidance Clinic when researching exceptionally low and high achievers among firstborn offspring. Fortes would give the commemorative Emanuel Miller Lecture in 1972. Entitled *The First Born*, it was subsequently published as follows. Fortes, M., edited by Goody, J. (1987), *Religion, Morality and the Person: Essays on the Tallensi Religion by Meyer Fortes* (Cambridge: Cambridge University Press), pp. 218–46.

5 Bakewell, pp. 51–2. I also owe the point about 'racy' collar-touching hair to Bakewell, p. 87.

6 Sanger received his Nobel Prize in 1958. Two further Cantabrigian scientists, Richard Synge and Archer Martin, had landed theirs, for chemistry, in 1952, while Bertrand Russell won his, for literature, in 1950. Francis Crick and James Watson, along with Wilkins, were awarded the prize in 1962, having caused the understanding of heredity to advance by leaps and bounds. Miller only found out about their work after his undergraduate years, or that is the way he remembers it. Writing in Pagnamenta, P. (ed.) (2008), *The University of Cambridge: An 800th Anniversary Portrait* (London: Third Millennium), p. 240, Miller says that, curiously, he was 'almost entirely unaware' of the double helix developments. Those developments did not make major headlines at the time, with news of the coronation and *Playboy*'s foundation being more prominent.

7 'Dadie' was George Rylands' popular nickname.

8 Miller's natural sciences degree, as he aimed to become a doctor, focused on anatomy and physiology.

9 'Men of the Age (II)', as before. I have drawn closely on this article and on Miller's feature 'Where is Thy Sting?', *Spectator*, 3 March 1961 (published under the pseudonym John Lydgate). There he wrote about the 'dead house' in Cambridge and his other medical encounters with death.

10 From 'Where is Thy Sting?'

11 E. D. Adrian verified that nerves register the intensity of a stimulus by increasing the frequency (not the magnitude) of their impulses. Adrian had also, like Emanuel, worked with soldiers suffering from shell-shock during World War 1. He was awarded a Nobel Prize, jointly with Sir Charles Sherrington, in 1932.

12 Having found how ionic currents were involved in the transmission of signals, Hodgkin and Huxley were to become Nobel Prize-winners in 1963.

13 Miller mentions, in passing, that Horace Barlow is a Darwin by descent as well as being married to one of Rachel's cousins. He further praises the teaching of the retinal physiology expert William Rushton – not to be confused with the *Private Eye* satirist.

14 There is still an Emanuel Miller Prize awarded by St John's for short theses combining philosophy of science with the behavioural sciences (psychology and social science). This is thanks to a bequest made in Emanuel's will.

15 Hinde ran the field station with W. H. Thorpe, who had set it up in 1950. It expanded and was called the Sub-Department of Animal Behaviour from 1959. Hinde was also the PhD supervisor for Jane Goodall, the subsequently world-famous expert on chimpanzees. There was a Tavistock Clinic connection too. Hinde had started attending seminars there in 1954, discussing parent–child ties – in the light of ethology – with the head of the children's department, John Bowlby.

16 In the autumn of 1986, Miller helped Barlow organize the Royal Society's Rank Prize Funds International Symposium, entitled *Images and Understanding*. His cinema-rel⸻ ⸻ Pictures' printed in the resultant book of essays, Barlow, H. Bl⸻ *Images and Unders⸻ding* (Cambridge ⸻ FT Arts L⸻

23 *Varsity* and Winner's editorship of 1955 is discussed in *The University of Cambridge: An 800th Anniversary Portrait*, pp. 150–2.

24 This is recalled by Bakewell, *The Centre of the Bed*, p. 101, and in Karl Miller's essay about Boxer and Cambridge, entitled 'Rex Grantae', in Miller, K. (1993), *Rebecca's Vest: A Memoir* (London: Hamish Hamilton), p. 129. Boxer was the first undergraduate to face being sent down for such an offence since Percy Bysshe Shelley, though his sentence was quickly reduced to rustication and he rematerialized at a May ball on the stroke of midnight, mocking the authorities. Karl Miller additionally mentions Boxer's stutter, p. 128, pointing out that having a stammer had gained increasingly fashionable associations with the rise of the flamboyant theatre critic Kenneth Tynan. Boxer went on to be not just founding editor of the *Sunday Times'* colour supplement but also editor-in-chief for *Vogue*. He married the newscaster Anna Ford and he became a humorous frequenter of Gloucester Crescent. Another connection backs up the unnerving law of six (or fewer) degrees of separation: Boxer's mother was a Hughlings Jackson, linking back to Emanuel Miller and Fournier Street. Boxer enjoyed mentioning his impressive ancestry to tease Miller.

25 Again, on the wild boy of Aveyron, see Miller's article in the *New York Review of Books*, 16 September 1976.

26 Jack Goody, as a young tutor in the 1950s, socialized with Jane's circle and Miller.

27 Miller helped with the front cover for the December 1953 issue (under the *Gadfly* title), and his 'APRES MOI' cartoon was printed in the same issue. The knotted and competitive cats had featured in the October 1953 issue (*Gadfly*), while his Empson skit was for 23 January 1954 (when the *Granta* title was restored). God sneaked in on 8 June 1954. His cartoons had some competition from other contributors, not least Quentin Blake.

28 Empson, W. (1935), *Seven Types of Ambiguity* (London: Chatto & Windus).

29 This comment is from *Rebecca's Vest*, p. 131.

30 Miller wrote pieces in *Varsity*, as Robert Hinde recalls. *Granta*, 15 October 1955, also mentions him sending up an appalling 'Cambridge Diary' article he himself had written.

31 Miller co-edited the 28 April 1956 issue of *Granta* with, among others, his friends Garry Runciman and Tim Leggatt from King's. He had been logged as an assistant to the editors for the issue of 31 October 1953, in his first term.

32 'Fragment of a Story' was printed in *Granta* on 14 May 1955. Clearly, it connects with Betty's liking for literary fragments. The tunnel Miller writes of is, curiously, right under the tip of Gloucester Crescent.

33 'Servant Couple' appeared in *Granta* on 28 April 1956.

34 It is telling that Miller remembers Betty being amused by the chauffeur's hierarchy-inverting toddler at Queen's Grove. The child was heard, belowstairs, asking: 'Does Daddy drive Dr Miller or does Dr Miller drive Daddy?'

35 When I tried to ascertain from MI5 if any files on Miller were open for public viewing, I was swiftly passed on to the British Home Office press department whose response was wonderfully evasive, at once peremptory and peculiarly vague. 'We don't comment on matters of security', declared the voice at the end of the line, somewhat sweepingly. Did that, I inquired, mean that there was a rule about personal files? Were they closed permanently or while the individual was still around? 'Did I', the voice continued, 'mention the word "rule"'? No, I am just saying I wouldn't have thought that would be available, I mean, yeah.' Would it not, I pressed on, be worth double-checking that it was a no-no? 'Er, No', concluded the voice. That slice of history will, evidently, have to wait.

wary about recruiting from the Apostles in Miller's time. Though ...nt until 1979, it was 1955 when the Foreign Office ...after he had defected to Russia.

Friendship in British Intellectual and Professional Life (Cambridge: Cambridge University Press), p. 33.

40 The Johnian physician Donald MacAlister (cited by Lubenow, p. 27) was speaking at the annual Apostles' dinner, in 1896. Denis Mack Smith, who was in the Apostles at the same time as Miller, points out that, by then, everyone selected had a pronounced sense of humour. Their meetings were, he suggests, highly enjoyable rather than of huge import.

41 Lubenow discusses the Apostles' and the Bloomsbury Group's shared conversational style, p. 240. The intellectual aristocracy, centring on a set of intermarried families including the Darwins and Trevelyans, is described by the Apostle Noel Annan. See Annan, N. (1999), *The Dons: Mentors, Eccentrics and Geniuses* (London: HarperCollins). See Levy, P. (1979), *G. E. Moore and the Cambridge Apostles* (London: Weidenfeld & Nicolson), p. 3, regarding V. S. Pritchett's essay 'Conversations'. That touches on how the Bloomsbury Group discussed G. E. Moore-style brainteasers such as 'What exactly do we mean by red?' It is a question that still engages Miller.

42 Miller confirms that he spoke with Blunt. Apparently, though, no priceless pearls of wisdom or state secrets were exchanged on that occasion. In 1979, Francis Haskell (who had Russian relatives) was hounded by members of the British press. They decided he must be sheltering Blunt who had vanished after being accused of spying.

43 The Apostles' current membership is still, strictly speaking, under wraps, although many older members have proved ready and willing to talk about the group.

44 Although not quite an Arthurian Round Table, Miller is obviously another 'Sir'. Noel Annan should be logged as a provost of King's as well as a baron and life peer. One might add that it is Denis Mack Smith, CBE, and so on. Also, to be strictly accurate, James Cornford (another descendant of Charles Darwin) did not quite overlap with Miller's undergraduate years in the Apostles. They met when Miller returned to Cambridge for a stint at Addenbrooke's Hospital.

45 Eric Hobsbawm's comment comes from his autobiography. Hobsbawm, E. (2002), *Interesting Times: A Twentieth-Century Life* (London: Allen Lane/Penguin), p. 189.

46 It is not quite clear how this tallies with the anti-vivisection poster of a wolf which Miller initially stuck on his wall at St John's, although the cat was apparently not in pain, being rendered unconscious.

47 Ascherson wrote at length about 'Lex Miller' in the *Observer*, 12 June 1988.

48 The creed of friendship, surpassing patriotism if necessary, was famously spelled out in E. M. Forster's *Two Cheers for Democracy*. Regarding candour, Denis Mack Smith ruminates on the Apostles' secrecy, saying: 'It allowed us to let our hair down a bit . . . We could discuss rather odd subjects without bothering.'

49 Henry Sidgwick's memoirs state that the Apostles constituted the 'strongest corporate bond' of his life. Lubenow, pp. 33 and 53, discusses that and how Sidgwick cherished the group's principles.

50 With a mix of idealism and mild irony, a new Apostle's swearing-in ceremony alluded to his student membership as time spent in the 'real' world of ideas, in contrast to the 'phenomenal' world out there beyond academia. Miller points out that, along with Kantian ideas, the Apostles discussed Plato's concept of the ideal or essential forms lying beyond the physical world's merely transient versions of them. 'But that was just a joke . . . self-consciously ironic and "gay" in the old sense of the word,' he says.

51 Miller makes an exception for Karl because he was a salt-of-the-earth, working-class, Scottish intellectual.

52 Apparently, for a whole decade, Miller avoided mentioning to his mentors that he had gone into the theatre. He distinguishes this showbiz world of 'vulgar theatricality' from Dadie Rylands' refined, 'Schlegel-like amateur enterprises', though Christopher Foster says that other Apostles felt ambivalent about the somewhat frivolous Rylands.

53 When quoting from Miller's letters (handwritten and typed), I have left in strikingly idiosyncratic spellings but not every small slip. Also, in this letter (undated), he was obviously using 'REAL LIFE' in the non-apostolic sense of real, and 6' 4" was slightly hyperbolical. In later chapters, Miller's notebook entries are printed with italicized entries, for clarity.

54 Barbara Scott's reply from the television audition department, 6 May 1953.

55 The Poppy Day festivities were described in the *Cambridge Review*, 14 November 1953, 132–3, along with the photograph of Miller. I am most grateful to the archivists of St John's College for this and other cuttings.

56 Miller appeared in cameo roles in both *Out of the Blue* and the 1955 Footlights show, *Between the Lines*.

57 John Gielgud, James Mason and Marlon Brando starred in Hollywood's *Julius Caesar* in 1953.

58 I owe the point about the routing of Footlights' predominantly effete cross-dressing tradition to Trevor Williams. Thanks go to him for sharing not only his memories but also his photograph albums with me.

59 John Pardoe (the Liberal MP), who was in *Out of the Blue*, emphasizes how Miller was an outstandingly fresh and almost separate entity doing his monologues.

60 The script of *Out of the Blue*, preserved in the Lord Chamberlain's papers in the British Library, demonstrates how exceptionally improvisational Miller was, constantly adjusting skits and not even providing a complete written text of his routines for the censors.

RADIO PAGE
by Jonathan Miller
Pips.
Weather forecast: South of England will move in a westerly direction late tonight. Summary of weather since noon day before yesterday.
Police message: woman knocked down by steamroller and suffered injuries from which chief constable of Hampshire has since died; police anxious to interview man with long blue hair. They've never met a man with long blue hair . . .
Country Magazine: yokel's tune . . . Introduction of Ludwig Kock and his bird noises, that of the lesser spotted pillow-wert.
Critics: exhibition of Persian digestive biscuits. The animal noises of the critics during their discussion.
Radio Play: Curtain UP! We present James McKechnie in an unending series of radio plays. He provisions himself at Totnes and cuts across country, cuts himself a stout stick of hickory. Kurt and the boys in the car suddenly appear. No-one but a blind chauffeur could have missed him. It was a blind chauffeur. Runs into a church and makes himself a rude bed, stays the night. Wakes and cuts himself a stout stick of licorice. Meets girl with terrible affliction. They kiss. That was The Blue Mountain with James McKechnie. Here is Inspector Morris from Scotland Yard to say a few words, 'Use the 999 system and you won't get into any scrapes.'
3rd Programme: timid announcer announces Chamber Music concert. After one folk song Bertrand Russell is introduced who talks about Prof. Moore and the apples, Russell is asked to request a tune and, for the Moral Science faculty and Professor Gilbert Ryle, choses Berkeley's theme tune: I hear voices and there's no-one there.
Announcer says good-night.
In the article about Miller's performance in *Illustrated*, 10 July 1954, the write-up refers to 'an exhibition of contemporary digestive biscuits' rather than Persian ones.
61 Miller spoke of wanting to be what he parodied in a humorous interview with himself on BBC Radio's *Woman's Hour* in January 1965.
62 This Russell skit is preserved in the Footlights archive in Cambridge, on a vinyl recording of Miller's early sketches. It resurfaced as 'Portraits from Memory' during the Broadway run of *Beyond the Fringe* and that is transcribed (with small improvisational differences) in the following publication. Bennett, A., Cook, P., Miller, J. and Moore, D., edited by Wilmut, R., (2003), *The Complete Beyond the Fringe: Alan Bennett, Peter Cook, Jonathan Miller and Dudley Moore* (London: Methuen), pp. 129–30. This book was first published in 1987, but my references are to the 2003 edition.
63 *Out of the Blue* opened at the Phoenix on 6 July 1954. The cuttings, all from mid-July, are preserved in the Footlights archive.
64 Harold Hobson, *Sunday Times*, 11 July 1954. Miller's 'Down Under', as drafted for the Lord Chamberlain's office, was again written only in form of jotted notes, not a complete script:
Scenes: forest, waving trees in the high wind; wild life; native reaping spaghetti. Up the river to Michelberg, a town built for the crushing and extraction of bauxite, the machines employed for this purpose. Making aluminium for the modern world, aluminium for a million and one household uses – aluminium riding boots, etc . . . Mention the great promise of the future.
This was the sketch where Miller wielded the aforementioned aeroplane propellor, creatively turning it into a canoe paddle and much else.
65 *In Town Tonight*, 6 July 1954. *Guess My Story*, 11 July 1954.
66 The slot on *Sunday Night at the London Palladium* did not turn up until 1955. This ratings-topping programme was produced by Brian Tesler. The Oxford-educated son of an East European Jewish émigré and a major figure in light entertainment on British TV, he went on to be become a founder-director of both Thames Television and Channel 4.
67 As aforementioned, *Illustrated*, 10 July 1954. Neal Ascherson mentions that Miller was entertainingly obsessed, at this time, with imitating grotesque illustrations in one of Cesare Lombroso's old pseudoscientific publications about criminal physiognomies. 'It was almost pornographic to him,' Ascherson remarks, 'particularly the more mistaken and strange it was. He found it both funny and stimulating . . . He just can't help collecting ludicrous attitudes, accents and appearances.'
68 In the same week as Miller was appearing on the TV game show *Guess My Story*, Emanuel was on BBC Radio delivering his lecture *The World of a Child*.
69 I have drawn here on features written by Derek Monsey for the *Sunday Express* and Peter Senn for the *Oxford Mail*, undated but both filed in the Footlights archive. Miller's dissection sessions were keeping him up with his course work which spilled over into the vacation for medics.
70 Ronald Bergan suggests Miller has 'convinced himself' that he was never truly part of the Cambridge thespian crew. That is in Bergan, R. (1989), *Beyond the Fringe . . . and Beyond: A Critical Biography of Alan Bennett, Peter Cook, Jonathan Miller and Dudley Moore* (London: Virgin), p. 60.

71 Miller is remembered as a Cambridge 'superstar' in Bamber Gascoigne's introduction to Wilmut's *From Fringe to Flying Circus*, p. xiii, and Gascoigne himself went on to script *Share My Lettuce*, a comic 'diversion with music', which transferred to the West End in 1957. Margaret Drabble reminisced in the *Radio Times*, 25 March 1975, that Miller was pointed out to her 'like a landmark' when she visited the city, aged seventeen.

72 Trevor Williams went on to be a solicitor.

73 *Granta*, 15 October 1955 (the retrospective critique being slipped into its *Between the Lines* review), and *Cambridge Daily News*, 8 March 1955.

74 *The Times*, 8 March 1955, suggested that the whole cast had opted for rumbustious comic actions rather than refining the delivery of their lines.

75 As with Footlights, Miller was not officially a member of the Amateur Dramatic Club. *Bartholomew Fair* was directed by Robin Midgley who went on to work for the BBC, became the first artistic director of the Leicester Haymarket and helped redraft Terence Rattigan's radio play *Cause Célèbre* for the stage.

76 This is a retrospective entry from 19 February 1956 (as transcribed from the original manuscripts at Smith College in Massachusetts). That appears in Plath, S., edited by Kukil, K. V. (2000), *The Journals of Sylvia Plath: 1950–1962* (London: Faber), p. 202. Perhaps Miller would have preferred Peter Cook's drag rendition of another Jonsonian prostitute, Doll Common, in Radley's staging of *The Alchemist*.

77 *The Times*, 25 November 1955.

78 *Cambridge Daily News*, 26 November 1955.

79 Miller, *Daily Express*, 25 June 1955.

80 This extract is from Miller's monologue 'The Death of Lord Nelson' as printed in *The Complete Beyond the Fringe*, pp. 149–50. Regarding the skit as it featured in 'Our Island Heritage', the script of *Between the Lines* in the Lord Chamberlain's papers reveals a few differences. It is only logged in the form of a sketchy outline, but the ship's crew chorus 'What shall we do with a drunken sailor?' there (not in *The Complete Beyond the Fringe* version), and it is surmised that Nelson may have gasped, 'Disprin, Hardy.'

Those alert to parallels with Danny Kaye may note a striking visual similarity between Miller in this sketch and the American star's appearance in a bicorne hat in *The Inspector General*.

81 The *Stage*, 30 June 1955, and *Empire News*, 3 July 1955 objected, as well as the *Daily Sketch* (quoted in *The University of Cambridge: An 800th Anniversary Portrait*, p. 308). The Turf Club's destruction occurred in 1952, and significant troubles occurred in Kenya and Cyprus in 1954. The octogenarian Churchill had just been succeeded by Anthony Eden in April 1955. The septuagenarian Labour Party leader Clement Attlee was only replaced by Hugh Gaitskell in December 1955. Young Englishmen (with Miller among them) were also discontented about National Service dragging on into the mid-1950s.

82 Among others, the *London Illustrated News*, 16 July 1955, described this sketch admiringly.

83 An appraisal of Miller as both slicker and more bizarre featured in the *London Evening News*, 8 June 1955. It was Ron Bryden, writing in the *Cambridge Review*, 11 June, who mentioned Carroll. Levin's article appeared on 8 July in the weekly *Truth*. The *Tatler*, on 13 July, also breathlessly hailed 'the world's first surrealist comedian', declaring that 'Danny Kaye and Harpo Marx, in certain moods, are his peers, but Mr Miller's large naked feet dance delicately on a rainbow stretched between Trumpington [on the edge of Cambridge] and Dali-Dali land'. The *Spectator*, 8 July, found his 'hallucinations' more uneven.

84 Sadly, McEwen was to die in middle age, suffering from a brain tumour. His music was mentioned by Van Morrison in the *Irish Times*, 11 April 1998. His father was Sir John McEwen, the politician and Under-Secretary for Scotland.

85 This was reported by the *News of the World* and the *Evening Standard*, 5 July 1955. Around this time, Miller also had a role in *The Man from Paranoia*, a BBC Radio comedy involving a don with a singing goldfish, though Miller himself cannot remember a thing about this.

86 Maybe there was also a hint of Emanuel at his gloomiest in Miller's Gothic send-up (as preserved, in outline, in the Lord Chamberlain's script): 'Wind, rain, thunder, lightning . . . a howl is heard. "What's that?" "Only father".'

87 This is listed in the original programme for *Between the Lines*, though it is not in the Lord Chamberlain's script. The BBC have a record of broadcasting 'Buld Knuk' on *Monday Night at Home*, 22 February 1960. The text turned up in *Granta*, 8 June 1954, as transcribed here (with slight adjustments, removing a hyphen from 'summer-evening', changing the final 'And' to 'and').

88 Sarah herself suggested this was her rebellion. The headmaster of King Alfred's accepted her as a pupil, but was not best pleased about Emanuel having dug tunnels under his playing fields during World War 2. The forking tunnels were for the War Office Selections Board, to test officers' nerves, but they caused the sports pitches to sag.

Chapter 5: The Late Fifties

1 Rachel briefly wanted to join the Jewish Society, a fact that Miller recalls without any sign of minding.

2 Miller's *Granta* friend, the architect Cedric Price, was best man and drew a portrait of Rachel in honour of the occasion.

3 Emanuel may have had short notice about the wedding arrangements because he was considered, within the family, to be antagonistic. Betty had also been annoyed that his work had dictated a move from Queen's Grove to a large, gloomy apartment nearer Harley Street.

4 Miller discussed his holidays in the *Sunday Times*, 10 September 1995, and in another newspaper article, unattributed in the BBC Written Archives, dated 16 April 1962. In fact, going as far back as his boyhood trip to Sweden, one of his cousins recollects him constantly longing to return from there to London. Perhaps he was craving to be settled in at home in St John's Wood as that vacation was right after his peripatetic war years. On one much later occasion – when his own offspring were twenty-somethings – he headed off with Rachel for an uncharacteristic Yuletide break in the Caribbean. After just three days he was so exasperatingly bored that they threw in the towel. 'The children were rather surprised when we turned up on the doorstep on Christmas morning,' he recollects.

5 In managing the household, Rachel was quite unlike her undomesticated artist-mother. She handled the spending, estimating that the £1,500 they had – £500 from each set of parents, plus £500 from Miller's Palladium booking – would last three years.

6 Miller points out that Rachel's sister, Jane Miller, uncovered several of these links while researching her autobiographical book, Miller, J. E. (2003), *Relations* (London: Jonathan Cape).

7 Redcliffe Salaman's country house was in Barley, near Royston. His book on the potato – Salaman, R. (1949), *The History and Social Influence of the Potato* (Cambridge: Cambridge University Press) – is now seen as a forerunner of Kurlansky, M. (1997), *Cod: A Biography of the Fish that Changed the World* (Toronto: Alfred A. Knopf), and the whole genre of so-called microhistories or material histories.

8 Miller won the Goldsmid scholarship to UC with a long essay on the all-or-none law.

9 Claude Bernard's *milieu intérieur* is discussed in *The Body in Question* and elsewhere. See Miller, J. (1978), *The Body in Question* (London: Cape), p. 135

10 Miller's aforementioned *Twentieth Century* article, 'Men of the Age (II)', appreciatively describes the prayer-like orderliness and almost heraldic formality.

11 Some have commented on the medical self-destructiveness of his smoking. He says that cancer had not yet been linked to smoking, but an American study had made the connection in 1954.

12 In this section, I have drawn again on Miller's article 'Where is Thy Sting?' for his analogies with beef, windfalls and the slaughterhouse, death's whispering glissando and its anticlimax.

13 As a teenager, Miller had, briefly, been on the bottom rung of the hierarchy, working during one school vacation as a hospital porter.

14 'The plaint made by a putatively sick person is', Miller notes, 'also comparable to an audition. Being a patient is a role as well as a predicament.'

15 The fellow trainee, who recalls the viva and Miller being much liked was Eric Beck, who had been a biologist at St Paul's as well.

16 Claire Rayner, *Mail on Sunday*, 13 September 1998.

17 Miller mentioned his plan to pursue psychiatry in, for example, his interview with the *New Yorker*, 8 September 1962.

18 As well as being irked by those snobbish consultants, Miller says that he was struck by how hard it was to take psychiatric histories when he first tried it.

19 He states that he chose University College not just because his mother had studied there or because it was historically the 'godless institution of Gower Street' (founded for non-Anglican students). More broadly speaking, the mind was valued at UC and the medics were not just 'rugger buggers'. He was also enticed by the presence of the top immunologist Peter Medawar and J. Z. Young (his old role model and viva examiner at St Paul's). A letter that Miller wrote to Oliver Sacks in early 1956 (undated, but January or February) reveals that Young was encouraging him to use his experimental labs in his spare time when he enrolled at UC. Very much exchanging scientific ideas in this letter – one of many that Sacks has kindly let me peruse – Miller asked Sacks if he wanted to collaborate in his planned experiments concerning frogs' dorsal roots and locomotor patterns. His sources of inspiration were, doubtless, multiple: possibly E. D. Adrian; Alan Hodgkin and Andrew Huxley's work on frogs' sciatic nerves; and maybe Walter Pitt's paper on dorsal root interaction, *Journal of Neurophysiology*, 1955, 18, 1–17. Miller's plan never came to anything. However, he did become a friend of the Nobel Prize-winning Medawar.

20 J. L. Austin's essays were collected in Austin, J. L. (1961), *Philosophical Papers* (Oxford: Clarendon Press), but 'A Plea for Excuses' had first been read in 1956 as Austin's presidential address to the Aristotelian Society, and 'Pretending' was printed by the same society in 1958, following a symposium on the subject at Southampton University, chaired by Stuart Hampshire. Chapter 6 returns to 'Pretending' and Chapters 9 and 16 to 'A Plea for Excuses', with reference to Miller and his stage directing.

21 Ernst Gombrich's TV discussion with Miller, concerning psychological aspects of the visual arts, is transcribed in the book of the TV series, Miller, J. (ed.) (1983), *States of Mind: Conversations with*

Psychological Investigators (London: BBC). Miller referred to Gombrich's ideas in his theatre book, Miller, J. (1986), *Subsequent Performances* (London: Faber), pp. 215 and 228, and in the book which accompanied his *Mirror Image* exhibition, Miller, J. (1998), *On Reflection* (London: National Gallery Publications), p. 26. Wollheim is discussed in *Subsequent Performances*, pp. 33, 61, 205 and 214–15, and in *On Reflection*, p. 80.

22 Sir Thomas Browne was a notably cultured seventeenth-century doctor. Set up in Miller's first term, the TBS was an alternative to the purely medical Sir Thomas Lewis Society. Some TBS articles in the *UCH Magazine* indicate that a fair few UCH medics were disappointingly ill-informed outside their own subject. See Vol. XLI, No. 4, 160, after the TBS launch was announced in issue No. 3, 138.

23 C. P. Snow had not yet given his famed lecture. However, he had written about the Two Cultures in the *New Statesman*, 6 October 1956.

24 Miller's articles appeared in the *Spectator* from 8 August 1958 onwards, and in the *New Statesman* from 21 July 1961. For one issue of the *Spectator* (12 June 1959), he reviewed a selection of children's books, something his mother also did on occasion (as in the *New Statesman*, 15 November 1958).

25 The *New Statesman*, 28 July 1961, printed Miller's apologies for errors.

26 *UCH Magazine*, Vol. XLII, No. 3, 81–2.

27 *Ibid.*, Vol. XLII, No. 4, 113.

28 By 1964, Miller would be operating as a Two Cultures go-between, teaching at Hornsey Art School where he converted two students to medicine. He lectured on the subject of buildings and biological forms at the Architectural Association when his friend Cedric Price was teaching there, and his thoughts on the city as metaphor, given the heading *Metaphoropolis*, were also discussed with John Donat on BBC TV, 14 December 1968. That was pegged to Miller editing an issue of *Architectural Design*.

29 Conceivably, the film may have been the Pathé brothers' vintage documentary of shell-shock victims at Netley who were wracked by distressing 'dancing' gaits. Philip Hoare's history of Netley – Hoare, P. (2001) *Spike Island: The Memory of a Military Hospital* (London: Fourth Estate), pp. 227 and 285–6 – mentions that film and Miller's *Alice in Wonderland*, which was shot at the same location in the 1960s (shortly before the building was demolished).

30 Miller acknowledges that his humorous contributions were influenced by James Thurber. The mirror in the park vignette appeared in the *UCH Magazine*, Vol. XLII, No. 3, 84, with the serious note about the neurological film on p. 83. The Freep letter appeared in Vol. XLII, No. 4, 127, as did Miller's review *Animals in Motion* and *The Human Figure in Motion* (featuring photographs by the fast-shutter pioneer Eadweard Muybridge, and published by Dover Books).

His 'God moves in a mysterious way' cartoon, recycled from *Granta*, slipped through the net again too. However, it was a new drawing which caused a rumpus. He depicted the headline-making Bishop of Woolwich with a speech bubble about the Lord not being an old man with a long white beard. Floating above on a cloud was God, stubbornly fitting the traditional description and muttering, 'How the fuck does he know?' The magazine's printers hotly objected, the Dean was aghast, and the joke was censored. I am indebted to Dr Léon Illis, who preceded Miller as the magazine's editor, for digging out his old proofs of that.

31 'A Brief Exposure', *UCH Magazine*, Vol. XLII, No. 3, 104–5. Miller also recycled 'Servant Couple' from *Granta* in Vol. XLIII, No. 1, 171–2.

32 Miller's 'From a Notebook: Materia Medica' was printed in *UCH Magazine*, Vol. XLIV, No. 2, 53–5. Interestingly, in his collection of his mother's writing is a piece entitled 'From a Notebook'. This had appeared in the *Twentieth Century*, July 1955, 59–65, and included a diary fragment about a couple's sparse conversation on a train.

33 The *UCH Magazine's* next editor, in Vol. XLIII, No. 2, mentioned Miller's radically improved covers but the artistry was not valued by the UCH Medical School library. His covers were, sadly, removed in the binding process.

34 Facetti designed under the company name Snark International as well. Stephen Bayley's column 'Notes and Theories', *Independent on Sunday*, 24 April 2005, discussed his influence on England.

35 Collage also featured markedly in the Whitechapel Art Gallery's cutting-edge 1956 exhibition 'This is Tomorrow', which included work by Richard Hamilton and John McHale.

36 Wolfe, T. (1966), *The Kandy-Kolored Tangerine-Flake Streamline Baby* (London: Jonathan Cape).

37 The incident with Riley undeniably adds some punch to exclamations made by Roger Law, the *Spitting Image* satirist, about Miller popping up everywhere and even teaching paperback design at Hornsey Art School where Law studied for a while. As he heartily puts it: 'What the fuck did Jonathan Miller know about paperbacks!'

38 *Forks and Hopes* was reviewed in the *UCH Magazine*, Vol. XLII, No. 2, 53, with one complaint about prolonged items but high praise for a 'thoroughly well produced' entertainment. Miller additionally directed the Fallopians revue in his final year, with Rachel making her one and only stage appearance. She played a shy milkmaid in a rendition of 'The Twelve Days of Christmas', which concluded dramatically

with the Euston Boys' Brigade marching in through the dock doors, drumming en masse.

39 In the BBC Written Archives' files on Miller, a BBC Press Service document from July 1964 describes him as a founder member of *Tonight*.

40 'The Pied Piper of Hampstead' was broadcast on BBC Radio's *Monday Night at Home* on 25 May 1959. The BBC script is missing, but it appeared in the *UCH Magazine*, Vol. XLIII, No. 2, 200–1. The mini-thriller was based on an actual rat-catcher who had plied his trade in Queen's Grove, complete with the Solomon Grundy-style Five Day Plan, though he did not come to such a sticky end.

41 Miller still remembers this 'Biting of the Generals' sketch and first performing it for Footlights. A review of the Fallopians' 1957 show – in the *UCH Magazine*, Vol. XLII, No. 2, 51–2 – suggests that Miller performed a Dimbleby imitation there. This was along with other sketches including the 'Cerulean Trousers' or 'Heat-Death of the Universe' sketch, which is discussed later in the context of *Beyond the Fringe*.

42 The two letters are in the BBC Written Archives, dated 15 and 19 February 1957. The first was from Holland Bennett, TV Booking Manager, and it regarded contracts. The second (though unsigned) was probably from Baverstock's assistant, Cynthia Judah, concerning the 'STOP QUICK' incident.

43 This letter from Judah was dated 8 May 1957. To clarify, Miller was not sacked outright from the BBC. His radio sketch work for *Saturday Night on the Light* and *Monday Night at Home*, in fact, followed in the wake of the Lord Nelson debacle. That might, notwithstanding, be seen as a relegation.

44 I am indebted here to Alasdair Milne's autobiography, Milne, A. (1988), *DG: The Memoirs of a British Broadcaster* (London: Hodder & Stoughton), p. 20. Ned Sherrin also recounted the incident with the cameras in Sherrin, N. (1991), *Theatrical Anecdotes: A Connoisseur's Collection of Legends, Stories and Gossip* (London: Virgin), p. 180. There he says that Miller misread the cameraman's hand gestures and led the latter a merry dance, ending in a collision with the studio wall. Baverstock patched it up later with Miller, when *Tonight* got wind of *Beyond the Fringe*.

45 Miller was in this social scene mainly because of his earlier Footlights shows and his work at the *Spectator* through which he met the theatre critic Alan Brien, Bernard Levin and others.

46 As a public-school pupil, Tynan had been flamboyantly outré in debates. As a scholar at Oxford, he was the most talked-about young man in town: a witty, brilliant speaker with a fashionable stammer, who also tried his hand at student-journalism and acting. From 1954 to 1963, he was a powerful theatre critic for the *Observer*, with a maxim famously pinned to his desk: 'Rouse tempers, goad and lacerate, raise whirlwinds.' *Oh! Calcutta!* (punning on 'O! Quel cul t'as!', the French for 'Flip! You have one hell of an arse!') debuted in 1969, playing for long runs in both New York and London.

47 Miller's friendship with Tynan can be traced in Kathleen Tynan's edited collection. That is Tynan, Kenneth, edited by Tynan, Kathleen (1994), *Kenneth Tynan: Letters* (London: Weidenfeld & Nicolson). See p. 353 for his 'like-minded' comment, 28 June 1966. See, also, Tynan, Kathleen (1987), *The Life of Kenneth Tynan* (London: Weidenfeld & Nicolson), on Miller feeling the less without Tynan's attention, p. 269.

48 This letter is from 3 March 1960.

49 The UCH surgical unit was led by one of Miller's favourite consultants, Professor Pilcher.

50 From a letter written at the Central Middlesex, 23 May 1960.

Chapter 6: The Start of the Sixties

1 John Bassett (no relation of the author) had known one of Rachel's sisters at school. A jazz musician on the side, he also hooked up with Miller regarding entertainments for the private-party circuit before *Beyond the Fringe* officially got rolling. In an advertisement, placed in the *Observer* on 13 December 1959, Bassett was offering trios, bands and cabaret acts, including Miller and Dudley Moore, for hire.

2 Bennett, also a junior lecturer, had appeared in *Better Late* at the 1959 Edinburgh Fringe Festival. Incidentally, Ponsonby had been nudging the Edinburgh International Festival to include some light entertainment for a few years, programming the comic cabaret singer Anna Russell in 1958, followed by Flanders and Swann.

3 Moore had graduated in 1958. He had already featured as a soloist in Johnny Dankworth's jazz band and performed in a comic cabaret duo with the Cambridge Footlighter Joe Melia.

4 *Pieces of Eight*, which also starred Fenella Fielding, opened at the Apollo in September 1959, commissioned by the ex-Pauline Michael Codron. Apparently, Cook was irked by Pinter's soon-to-be-trademark pauses because sketch-writers were paid royalties by the minute.

5 Wisty's early incarnation was called Grole and I have drawn here on Miller's memories of seeing Cook quoted by Harry Thompson in Thompson, H. (1997), *Peter Cook: A Biography* (London: Hodder & Stoughton), p. 77. Elsewhere, I am indebted to this and other biographies of the *Beyond the Fringe* team: Cook, W. (ed.) (2005), *Goodbye Again: The Definitive Peter Cook and Dudley Moore* (London: Arrow); Games, A. (1999), *Pete and Dud: An Illustrated Biography* (London: Chameleon); Alex Gray's website about *Beyond the Fringe*, entitled *Some Fickle Circumstance*, and other works mentioned below.

6 Miller's diagnosis clearly niggled. In an interview years later (on BBC TV's *Person to Person* in 1979), Cook remarked: 'It came from me. It doesn't make me a schizophrenic. It just means Jonathan's wrong, as he so often is, bless his heart.'

7 The precise location of this restaurant was always disputed by the *Beyond the Fringe* foursome.

8 Bennett's impressions are recorded in Wilmut's *From Fringe to Flying Circus*, p. 11. Moore, Cook and Bennett also wrote reminiscences as postscripts in *The Complete Beyond the Fringe*.

9 The four personalities can be variously configured, compared or contrasted. In spite of the class difference in their roots, Bennett and Miller were akin in prizing intellectual pursuits and also in their capacity to be in two minds (a quality which Paul Taylor noted about Bennett in the *Independent*, 7 May 2004). Alternatively, one might compare Miller's sense of being underloved as a child with Cook (who was raised by nannies and packed off to boarding school) or with Moore (who felt that maternal affection was withheld, being hospitalized as a child for operations on his club foot). That did not mean, of course, that the group would necessarily bond.

10 Miller, quoted in Wilmut's *From Fringe to Flying Circus*, p. 11.

11 Ronald Bergan records Ponsonby's memories, p. 8.

12 *The Complete Beyond the Fringe*, pp. 71–2.

13 'Treatment of Inorganic Mercury Poisoning with N-Acetyl-D L-Penicillamine', the *Lancet*, 25 March 1961, 640–3.

14 Hatter's Shakes was, presumably, the very ailment that troubled Lewis Carroll's teacup-biting Mad Hatter, the character whom Cook would soon be playing in Miller's film of *Alice in Wonderland*.

15 This is recalled by Eric Beck whose path, after St Paul's and UCH, once again crossed with Miller's at the Central Middlesex. Miller's film preceded the psychophysicist Gunnar Johansson's stir-causing 1970s experiments which devised a method of using point-light displays (i.e. lights attached to a man's joints) to analyze complex patterns of biological motion, as described in Johansson's 1973 article 'Visual perception of biological motion and a model for its analysis', *Perception and Psychophysics*, Vol. 14, No. 2, 201–11. However, as Johansson notes in that article, bright or dark spots moving against a contrasting background had been used in earlier, simpler studies of motion, including his own during the 1950s.

16 Cook's alleged timidity, recalled by Miller, is mentioned by Harry Thompson's biography, pp. 93–4. Moore's fear of arrest is mentioned by Barbra Paskin in Paskin, B. (1998), *Dudley Moore: The Authorized Biography* (London: Pan), p. 66.

17 *Daily Mail*, 24 August 1960. Peter Lewis went on to be a scriptwriter for BBC TV's *That Was The Week That Was*.

18 It had actually been the production's tight budget that made elaborate backdrops impossible. Still, Brechtian trends in the theatre were notably being promoted by Joan Littlewood's Theatre Workshop, and Beckett's spartan *Waiting for Godot* had caused a stir, premiered by Peter Hall at the London Arts Theatre in 1955. Cook briefly fancied the idea of Julie Christie making nude cameo appearances. However, he and Miller knew, from their boys' schools, that dancing girls were not a bare necessity in revues.

19 The film executives appeared in the draft submitted to the Lord Chamberlain on 16 August 1960 for the Edinburgh run, in an untitled sketch set in the boardroom of Gala Films.

20 Cook had clearly overcome any early cavils about daring political satire since it was he who imitated Macmillan at length. For the record, Miller assures me that *The Times* review of 27 August 1960 was mistaken in attributing the impersonation of the PM to him rather than to Cook.

21 John Bridges, who produced the BBC's *Monday Night at Home*, says that he had worked individually with the *Beyond the Fringe* boys and had sought to team them up before 1960. Nevertheless, he explains, Miller had shocked another top executive, Clare Lawson Dick. One afternoon, when Bridges had invited her to vet his plan, Miller apparently bounded into the recording studio and launched into a 'fuck fugue' where he impersonated a BBC announcer saying that *Lady Chatterley's Lover* had been cleared of obscenity and celebrating this by enunciating 'fuck' three times, very slowly and clearly. Lawson Dick could by no means be persuaded to see the funny side of this. If that was pre-*Beyond the Fringe*, Miller was anticipating the conclusion of the *Lady Chatterley* trial which was reached in November 1960.

22 The scripts of *Beyond the Fringe* submitted to the Lord Chamberlain's office and preserved in the British Library do not precisely tally with the live performances. The press reviews of the time indicate Miller and co. kept slipping in additional vignettes, adjusting the show. 'Bollard' does not actually feature in the script submitted for the Edinburgh run. It is in the redraft submitted on 21 April 1961 for the London transfer. There is no sign there of the legendary stage direction 'Enter two dreadful queens', famously adjusted to 'Enter two aesthetic young men'. The stage direction of April 1961 merely reads: 'A commercial film studio, Cameraman. Enter JONATHAN & PETER.' Bennett played the director/cameraman.

23 Bennett wrote 'Frank Speaking'.

24 *Edinburgh Evening News*, 25 August 1960.

25 The audience reaction is recorded in Paskin's biography, p. 60.

26 Paskin, p. 63.

27 Letter dated 21 September 1960, from 68a Regent's Park Road. Incidentally, not all the Edinburgh reviews were raves. *The Times*, for example, had been positive but somewhat tepid on 25 August.

28 From Miller's 1977 interview with Michael Parkinson.

29 From Wilmut, *From Fringe to Flying Circus*, p. 11.

30 Though Miller holds that anti-Semitism was less endemic in the medical profession by this time, maybe he saw the entertainment industry as a particularly accessible trade. When interviewed for Shenker, I. (1985), *Coat of Many Colours: Pages from Jewish Life* (Garden City, NY: Doubleday), pp. 278–9, he agreed that large numbers of Jews had gone into showbiz. This was not, he suggested, due to some ingrained talent, 'as if there was a race-linked gene which meant that monotheism went with great tap dancing'. Rather, it was not a respectable profession and 'therefore not heavily guarded at the entrance by white Anglo-Saxon Protestant custodians'.

31 Macmillan made his 'never had it so good' proclamation in July 1957, but Wilson damned the Conservatives' insufficient support for science in the *Scotsman*, 25 November 1957, building up to his 'white heat' speech of October 1963. Dominic Sandbrook highlights the contradictory prizing and misprizing of scientists, including doctors, circa 1960 in Sandbrook, D. (2009 edn), *White Heat: A History of Britain in the Swinging Sixties* (London: Abacus), pp. 50–7.

32 Miller alluded to the proliferating specialist journals in 1957, in the *UCH Magazine*'s editorial column, Vol. XLII, No. 3, 81–2.

33 Again Sandbrook, p. 55, goes into illuminating detail, quoting from Anthony Crosland's 1956 book, *The Future of Socialism*, regarding the cultivation of leisure.

34 'Men of the Age (II)', as before.

35 The UCH associate was Dr Léon Illis.

36 Just to clarify, Miller did complete his pre-registration year on the neurological firm at the Central Middlesex as well as his pathology job at Addenbrooke's (as later underlined in the BBC publicity material for *The Body in Question*).

37 Miller's letter to Sacks, written at the Central Middlesex on 23 May 1960, indicates that he had already been shifting his ground somewhat uneasily as he wrote: 'The prospect of doing clinical psych. now seems less attractive after three months . . . I find that I am sapped by prolonged contact with individual patients. Pathology [with the prospect of specializing in Neuropathology] seems to give one the professional excuse for detachment without binding one to complete separation' – something like the theatrical middle ground of standing in the wings?

38 The Lady of Shalott letter was sent from Cambridge, November 1960.

39 Miller's letter about 'daguerreotypic decor' was written to Sacks from Addenbrooke's on 11 February 1961.

40 Miller had read Edmund Gosse's *Father and Son* on the St Paul's Field Club trip to Cumbrae, along with Darwin's *The Voyage of the Beagle*.

41 The 'literary illusion' missive was written on 3 July 1961, from London's Fortune Theatre.

42 Sacks discussed this period of his life, his LSD sampling and werewolf-like or 'wolf boy' double life in the *Guardian*, 5 March 2005.

43 Sacks had sent this package from the Queen Elizabeth Hospital in Birmingham on 4 July 1960, just before he headed off to North America.

44 Sacks' lesser known book *Migraine* was published in 1970, before *Awakenings*. The migraine clinic supervisor then sacked him for writing it.

45 Miller says he got the first name wrong, alluding to the doctor Tertius Lydgate in *Middlemarch*.

46 The articles by Miller in the *Spectator* were all published within the first five months of 1961.

47 Fazan had previously directed Bamber Gasgoigne's West End-bound show *Share My Lettuce*, starring Kenneth Williams and Maggie Smith. Fazan describes the Fringers, in London and New York, in her autobiography, Fazan, E. (forthcoming 2012), *Fiz: Between the Lines* (Victoria, BC: FriesenPress).

48 From *The Complete Beyond the Fringe*, pp. 77–81.

49 *Ibid*, p. 72.

50 William Donaldson subsequently authored Donaldson, W, (2002), *Brewer's Rogues, Villains and Eccentrics* (London: Cassell) among other books.

51 Donaldson's comments are from an interview with the biographer. He has sadly died since then, in 2005. In the role of young impresario, he took *The Last Laugh* from Cambridge to Oxford, changing its title to *Here is the News* and simultaneously cutting out Cook's outstanding sketches, so it failed to transfer to London.

52 Bennett did not complain either. His scholarly income was even less than Miller earned. As for Moore, his impoverished parents had taken twenty years to save £100 according to Douglas Thompson's biography, Thompson, D. (1996), *Dudley Moore: On the Couch* (London: Little, Brown & Co.), p. 49.

53 This roguery is what happened according to Donaldson's own account, and he added that Bassett was double-crossed en route because he naively had nothing in writing.

54 Donaldson recalled that he and Albery, after the wages meeting, gave each of the Fringers about £25 a week more and never got another squeak out of them. That said, in *The Complete Beyond the Fringe*, p. 180, Bennett records how a mildly impolite letter was sent in 1964, in a last-ditch attempt to gain compensation for the group's early exploitation. Donaldson additionally managed to knock Bennett off his bicycle in Shaftesbury Avenue in the 1990s, as noted in Donaldson, W. (1992), *The Big One, the Black One, the Fat One and the Other One: My Life in Showbiz* (London: Michael O'Mara), p. 13.

55 The reviews mentioned in this paragraph were all printed between 11 and 14 May 1961.

56 The Queen's reaction is discussed by Nicholas de Jongh in de Jongh, N. (2000), *Politics, Prudery and Perversions: The Censoring of the English Stage 1901–1968* (London: Methuen), p. 15.

57 This comment by Frayn comes from his introduction to *The Complete Beyond the Fringe*, p. 1. Of course, British satire had been around for ages prior to *Beyond the Fringe*, in various forms. In Renaissance drama, the splenetic Thersites from Shakespeare's *Troilus and Cressida* springs to mind. Other literary predecessors included Jonathan Swift, George Orwell, Aldous Huxley, Evelyn Waugh. The visual arts had turned notably acerbic with William Hogarth in the eighteenth century, followed by the cartoonist James Gillray. However, the general protocol during Miller's lifetime had been propriety, deference and proud nationalism, all lingering from the Victorian era.

In the late 1950s, scathing critiques had begun to emerge: Richard Hoggart writing on British society in *The Uses of Literacy*; Doris Lessing rebuking the dry rot of conformity in *Declaration*; Harold Wilson calling the Conservatives 'obsolete Edwardians' (in the *Scotsman*, 25 November 1957). The British film *I'm Alright Jack* (1959) has been classed as satire, and *Room at the Top* (also 1959) portrayed Northern, working-class, disaffected cynicism. In the press, there was the vintage magazine *Punch*, and Bernard Levin's 'Taper' column was sharp-tongued. Also, there had been satirical touches in John Bird's 1959 Footlights show, *The Last Laugh*.

In most stage revues, though, daring had been limited to double entendres and the skimpy wardrobe of the dancing girls. *Beyond the Fringe* was extraordinary in its gall and huge popularity, penetrating more social strata than *Punch* ever managed – as Lewis Morley observed in his memoirs, Morley, L. (1992), *Black and White Lies* (Pymble, NSW: Angus & Robertson/London: HarperCollins), p. 49.

58 Parlophone's studios were just yards from the New London Synagogue of Miller's childhood in Abbey Road.

59 Several other big-name photographers took Miller's portrait, including Cecil Beaton. Many of those images are stockpiled in the National Portrait Gallery's archive.

60 Billington chatted with Miller in Edinburgh after the Festival's press conference for *Beyond the Fringe*. He discusses the LP in *That Was Satire That Was*, p. 124, and he is further eloquent about how *Beyond the Fringe* became British youth's unofficial set text and a force for social change in his own book Billington, M. (2007), *State of the Nation: British Theatre Since 1945* (London: Faber), pp. 127–30.

61 Cleese's comment is from an interview with the author. Michael Palin adds – in *The Pythons' Autobiography by the Pythons*, published in 2003 (London: Orion), p. 70 – that the Fringers' satire was laceratingly acute because the parodies were extraordinarily close to the bone, barely exaggerated.

62 Levin, B. (1970), *The Pendulum Years: Britain and the Sixties* (London: Jonathan Cape), p. 318.

63 From Wilmut's *From Fringe to Flying Circus*, pp. 4 and 17.

64 Miller's comment on standstills in the writing process comes from a 1961 cast interview on BBC Radio's *New Names Making the News* (which was replayed to Miller on Radio 4's *Meeting Myself Coming Back*, 21 August 2010).

65 Bennett's memory is alluded to in Frayn's introduction to *The Complete Beyond the Fringe*, p. 3. Miller's article on the opening of The Establishment was 'Can English Satire Draw Blood?', *Observer*, 1 October 1961.

66 Regarding Mort Sahl's impact on Miller, Rachel recalls her husband was thrilled when he first heard an LP of the fast-talking Jewish-American comic, at a party in the late 1950s. He immediately declared he must go to the States. As it happened, that LP belonged to a Cambridge friend, Joe Melia, who would replace Miller in the continuing London run of *Beyond the Fringe* – when the original team headed off to the USA.

Prior to the replacement cast, Sahl himself visited the UK, was introduced to Miller and the others backstage at the Fortune, and proved surprisingly old-fashioned. He expressed outrage at four-letter words being uttered in front of his female companion, Joan Collins. In the *New Yorker*, 8 September 1962, Miller distinguished between Sahl's onstage style and the Fringers' gentler scepticism. He wrote in enthusiastic praise of Sahl in the *Twentieth Century*, June 1960, and in the *New Statesman* of 21 July 1961, as well as interviewing him on television.

67 That is mentioned in Wilmut's *From Fringe to Flying Circus*, p. 54, and according to *Time Out*, 13–19 June 2007, the handbag wielder was the Irish actress Siobhán McKenna objecting to Lenny Bruce's Catholic-baiting in 1961. Recalling his own early comic turns at the club, John Fortune also exclaimed that, 'Jonathan['s article] sort of saddled us with this weight of expectation which you couldn't possibly deliver!'

68 Shore may have discussed science funding, *en passant*, with Miller but the latter certainly was not an adviser in any way when it came to Shore's 1963 policy document 'Labour and the Scientific Revolution', calling for one hundred million pounds extra for scientific researchers – a move discussed in Morgan, K. O. (2001), *Britain Since 1945: The People's Peace* (Oxford: Oxford University Press), pp. 231–2.

69 In the 1960s, Miller also signed an urgent plea for the PM to help lift the Egyptian blockade of the Strait of Tiran.

70 Miller introduced an Amnesty International Conference on torture in 1977, recalling Betty Miller's past commitment to PEN meetings.

71 The *Guardian* published the letter that was sent to the Soviet Embassy on 20 August 1991. Miller's famous face was singled out by BBC TV news cameras amidst the huge crowds of protestors at the anti-war march in Hyde Park, 15 February 2003. In 2007, he and his wife also signed the letter to *The Times*, 8 September, protesting at the British government's denial of visas to Palestine's under-19 football squad. The 2010 letter to the *Guardian*, also signed by Stephen Fry, Richard Dawkins and Philip Pullman, took issue with the Vatican's opposition to condoms, its record on gay rights, and its failure to tackle the issue of clerical sexual abuse.

72 From 'Alien Admissions', *Spectator*, 7 April 1961, and 'Wildcat Headaches', *Spectator*, 28 April 1961.

73 *The Complete Beyond the Fringe* records various sketches turning up in Edinburgh, Cambridge, Brighton, London and New York.

74 Eric Idle supports the notion that Miller was the forefather of modern observational comedy.

75 That classification occurs in Frayn's introduction to *The Complete Beyond the Fringe*, p. 2. He put the columnist Paul Jennings in the whimsical-fantastical camp too.

76 *The Complete Beyond the Fringe*, pp. 28–31 (with corrected spelling here).

77 'A Bit of a Giggle', *Twentieth Century*, July 1961, 40. Miller did not recall any specific dream upon waking.

78 Miller's vicar sketch was entitled 'Man Bites God', with an allusion to *ITMA*. Interestingly, in another skit called 'Wry Twist' (which was dropped before the London run), Miller played Johann, an East European immigrant. Johann was treated condescendingly by Bennett and Moore who both portrayed medical inspectors, doling out charity clothes. This is recorded in the Lord Chamberlain's script of the Lyceum production, 26 August 1960, and reverses the roles of *Beyond the Fringe*'s opening routine where Moore was the suspected East European, surveyed by Miller and Cook as hostile English gents.

79 Miller comments on the connections between Jewishness and comedy, on intellectual liberation and assimilation appear in Israel Shenker's *Coat of Many Colours*, pp. 280 and 289.

80 Miller discussed his guilty feelings with Malcolm Muggeridge on BBC TV's *Intimations*, 30 November 1965.

81 Besides her unstaged script *Shadow on the Window*, Betty's interest in playacting had also been evident in her novels where she used the theatre as a frequent metaphor for life.

82 As before, *The Complete Beyond the Fringe*, pp. 71–2. In terms of Betty being outshone by her son's showbiz fame, she had probably become used to that after *Out of the Blue* when he had grabbed more media attention than her book of edited epistles: Barrett Browning, E., edited by Miller, B. (1954), *Elizabeth Barrett to Miss Mitford: The Unpublished Letters of Elizabeth Barrett Browning to Mary Russell Mitford* (London: John Murray).

83 Miller's line about German music in 'Aftermyth of War' was a direct allusion to *A Diary for Timothy*. That film was, incidentally, scripted by E. M. Forster (of the Cambridge Apostles) as well as being made by the Crown Film Unit. Miller's 'Down Under' sketch had previously sent up the sort of documentaries which Julian made, depicting colonial industrial projects.

84 Miller's comment about his fascination with aircrew was made when reminiscing about *A Matter of Life and Death* on *100 Greatest Films* in 2002.

85 The show was broadcast on BBC TV, in an edited version, on 16 August 1964. Moore was also shortlisted for 'Man of the Year'.

86 *Bridge on the River Wye* was released by Parlophone in 1962, produced by George Martin. Its working title had been *Bridge on the River Kwai* but the film company threatened legal action. Undefeated, Martin edited the recording, excising the 'K' every time 'Kwai' was said.

87 *Oliver!* opened in 1960. Miller never joined the cast.

88 Perhaps Miller was encouraged to take this part by the fact that Cook, while still at Cambridge, had won applause acting alongside Eleanor Bron in John Bird's production of Simpson's *A Resounding Tinkle*, and Moore had composed the music for the Royal Court's 1959 staging of *One Way Pendulum*. Woodfall Film Productions (under Michael Balcon's British Lion banner), presented the 1965 screen adaptation of *One Way Pendulum*. The reviews were appreciative in the main. However, *The Times*, 28 January 1965, had sniffed at Eric Sykes and Miller's self-conscious crankiness, and the *New York Times*, 3 March 1965, scorned the whole thing as British froth. Incidentally, Miller never appeared in *The Avengers* as an uncredited thug or even a highly accredited one. The claim that he did so is a world-wide-web porky. Nor

did he pop up in the 1998 French movie about suicidal schoolgirls hurling themselves through windows, *Terminale*.

89 Eleanor Bron also became the long-term partner of Miller's old Cambridge associate, Cedric Price.

90 Law had also been an art-school student in Cambridge along with Peter Cook's wife-to-be, Wendy.

91 Miller named his vice when conducting an interview of himself for BBC Radio's *Woman's Hour*, recorded in December 1965, but the comment may have sprung from the fact that the programme had also focused on lust. 'A lot of us do' is a quotation from Douglas Thompson's biography of Moore, pp. 72–3.

92 Gerard DeGroot underlines this in DeGroot, G. (2009), *The Sixties Unplugged* (London: Pan), p. 215.

93 Jan Moir in the *Daily Telegraph*, 2 September 1996, quoted both Miller's comments, on the Stock Exchange and on not boasting.

94 Bennett confirmed that Moore's prowess was 'highly enviable' to all his fellow Fringers, as Paskin records, p. 68. Moore's comment is quoted by Douglas Thompson, pp. 72–3. Cook actually married Wendy Snowden in New York in 1963.

95 Miller's note about D. M. is dated 10 February 1962 with the last sentence added in March 1962. Miller was also quoted in Moore's obituary in the *Guardian*, 28 March 2002, describing him as 'libidinous, childlike, goatlike – the embodiment of some peculiar mystical satyr'.

96 I have, strictly speaking, conflated two stage doors here as the Bisto kids and woeful puffer-like lady turned up during *Beyond the Fringe*'s Broadway run. Miller described them in Tristram Powell's 1971 TV documentary, *West Side Stories*, the full unedited transcript of which can be found in the BBC's Written Archives.

97 Geoffrey Bennison's heyday was in the late 1970s and early 1980s when he ran a shop on London's Pimlico Road. Bennison, the English textile company, which was named after him and recreates eighteenth- and nineteenth-century prints, now has outlets in Los Angeles, New York and London. The Millers also used to go to his Christmas parties in Golden Square – 'above Glorex Woollens, dear' – where the door was always opened by an ex-sailor called Babs.

98 In this era there was a marked overlap between those filmgoers who attended porn screenings and those who watched art-house movies.

99 'Alan Bennett's Diary', *London Review of Books*, 5 January 2006.

100 Recounted in Harry Thompson's biography, p. 131.

101 It was syringes and prostitutes. In Miller's article, 'The Sick White Negro', *Partisan Review*, Spring 1963, he likened Bruce's Establishment performances to a mesmerizing séance and, en route, described him as a comic collagist.

102 'I Won't Pay for the Trip', *Vogue*, 1 September 1967, kindly supplied by the library of Condé Nast.

103 Other connections might have been John Bird who had been a young director under Devine; Moore who worked as a Royal Court composer; Miller's thematically related *Porn Shop* sketch; or the fact that he was already connected with the Court through his earlier cabaret performances for Clement Freud.

104 Kenneth Tynan, *Observer*, 22 July 1962. Robert Muller, *Daily Mail*, 20 July 1962.

105 The *Sunday Times*, 24 June 1962, reported Miller jumped at Devine's offer. On BBC Radio 4's *Profile*, 19 November 1978, Cook spoke of Miller scorning his own comic monologues.

106 The Bertrand Russell skit went down so badly that he was not even invited back to complete his two-show contract.

107 Miller swiftly learned to accept the limited narrative fluency of the stage (limited by comparison with the movies, at least), and the thrilling flux and evolution of live performances compensated. He discussed that in the *Listener*, 19 December 1968.

108 Miller boasted in *Subsequent Performances*, p. 79, that Osborne was generally 'delighted to see what it was that he had meant', as that meaning emerged in Miller's production.

109 Osborne's diary entry appears in Osborne, J. (1991), *Almost a Gentleman: An Autobiography, Vol. II* (London: Faber), p. 242. In terms of anti-Semitism, the playwright's poisonous letter to his adolescent daughter, Nolan (dated 16 December 1980 and quoted in the *Guardian*, 22 April 2006), compared her to stiff-necked, cold-hearted Jews. That said, he co-ran Woodfall Film Productions and did not prevent the casting of Miller in *One Way Pendulum* in 1965.

110 This appears, slightly adjusted and interlinked with another rehearsal memo, in *Nowhere in Particular*.

111 This quotation is not from the July 1962 notebook entry, but from Miller in conversation. He further underlines that his directing has been influenced by his philosopher friend John Searle's theory of speech acts, which developed on J. L. Austin's idea of performative utterances (i.e. verbal pronouncements, such as curses or vows, that virtually enact something).

112 The rough drafts were kept by Dennis Bailey, who provided the illustrations. For clarity, the production titles' inconsistent styling has been adjusted here.

113 From Miller's notebook entry dated 5 June 1962. Perhaps there is a faint echo here of *Dombey and Son*, wherein Dickens described the monstrous 1830s excavations which ploughed deep through Camden

Town to create the realm of the railroad. See Dickens, C. (1995 edn), *Dombey and Son* (Ware: Wordsworth Editions), pp. 63-4.

114 'Fuck-off money' was actually a phrase Miller picked up from Stanley Kubrick during the New York run of *Beyond the Fringe*.

115 Airmail letter sent to Sacks at Mount Zion Hospital, San Francisco, October 1961.

116 He featured fairly regularly in the *New Statesman* by this point.

Chapter 7: 1962-4

1 While Miller was replaced, in the London production, by his old Cambridge acquaintance and approximate lookalike, Joe Melia, Cook's place was taken by David Frost. The West End show finally closed in 1966 after a record-breaking run of 2,200 performances.

2 Though Miller alluded to Bundy's number as 'O, star of Alabama' when he mentioned it in the 1971 BBC TV documentary *West Side Stories*, presumably Monsieur Bundy was having a stab at 'O, moon of Alabama' (from the Brecht/Weill opera *Mahagonny*, which Miller would direct many years later in Los Angeles). I am indebted to *West Side Stories* regarding several aspects of the SS *France* voyage and the Fringers' time in America, including the subsequently mentioned angst about muggings and nuclear gales, the high society parties, Miller's alternative Jewish and American identities, and porn cinemas. Also informative were Miller's articles 'Been to America' and 'West Side Stories', published in the *New Statesman*, 19 January 1962 and 8 February 1963.

3 From Cook's reminiscences in *The Complete Beyond the Fringe*, p. 186. Probably to his father's relief, Tom showed no great love of the limelight after his cameo appearance in the philosophers sketch, 'Words . . . and Things'.

4 *Private Eye*, 17 September 1962. The term 'poove' had apparently been coined by Jeremy Geidt, and 'The Hounding of the Pooves' was accompanied by illustrations from a vintage physicians' handbook with adjusted captions.

5 Miller's comments on opera queens and on heterophobia appeared in the *Sunday Telegraph*, 15 November 1987, and in the *Independent*, 12 July 2007.

6 Miller was not averse to joking about his pathology work in press interviews. On 21 October 1962, a month after the *Private Eye* article, the *New York Times* reported his quip: 'My patients can wait. They're all dead anyway.'

7 I am grateful to *Private Eye* for supplying me with a photocopy of the original letter.

8 *The Complete Beyond the Fringe*, pp. 116-18.

9 Most of the reviews were delayed by the crisis until 29 October. Cooke's article appeared on 30 October. Robert Brustein, the *New Republic*'s critic, also loved what he saw as the Brits' purgative alienated attack on the prejudices of the older generation. His notice was reprinted in his book, Brustein, R. (1965), *Seasons of Discontent: Dramatic Opinions 1959-1965* (London: Jonathan Cape), p. 190.

10 *The Jack Paar Show* was on NBC, 1 March 1963. Other appearances included *The Tonight Show Starring Johnny Carson* and Channel 2's 1963 end-of-the-year satirical review.

11 Miller uses the metaphor of an oil well for his Broadway earnings.

12 His *New Statesman* 'Been to America' feature from January 1962 had included an admiring review of the Second City team, with some measured criticisms but particular praise for Nichols.

13 JFK was, in fact, seeing the show for a second time, having already caught it in London.

14 Recorded by Alexander Games in Games, A. (2001), *Backing into the Limelight: The Biography of Alan Bennett* (London: Headline), p. 63.

15 From Bennett's reminiscences, reproduced in Lin Cook's book, Cook, L. (ed.) (1997), *Peter Cook Remembered* (London: Mandarin).

16 Bennett described the celebrity-stuffed parties in 'Seeing Stars', *London Review of Books*, 3 January 2002. They are likewise alluded to in Carpenter's *That Was Satire That Was*, p. 260. Back in London, after New York, the Millers would attend further glamorous parties thrown by the American ambassador David Bruce. There they were introduced to Groucho Marx, who didn't disappoint in reprising oodles of his best gags.

17 Miller talked about that party on the 1977 *Parkinson Show*. Rachel's sister, Jane, adds that some Manhattan socialites may have mistakenly thought her brother-in-law was ultra-decadent when she visited New York. 'Jonathan would just introduce us as Jane and Rachel Miller and never explain [the shared surname], you know!' she says. 'And we looked sort of identical, both being pregnant at the same moment [as Rachel had another child on the way].' In Miller's 2007 *Parkinson* interview (broadcast on 23 June on ITV), he humorously recalled how scruples and sheer embarrassment kept him from participating in another orgy in the Sixties, just abstemiously apologizing as he stumbled upon a rather famous man *in flagrante* – with his artificial leg left in the middle of the room. The leg was allegedly Al Capp's.

18 The other guests at this dinner – held after JFK's assassination in 1963 – were Susan Sontag and Isaiah Berlin.

19 Miller left *Beyond the Fringe* some five months before the other three threw in the towel, and he was replaced by Paxton Whitehead whom the *New York Times*, on 10 January 1964, described as a 'facsimile'.
20 He spoke of this nightmare in the *Sunday Times*, 15 April 1973. The fear caused by his resurgent stammer may partly explain why Miller has taken on no major stage roles since *Beyond the Fringe*, though he has been offered leading parts including the philosopher, George Moore, in Stoppard's *Jumpers*.
21 Miller's view of Moore's musicianship is discussed by Paskin, p. 65. His comment on Bennett as miniaturist is quoted by Wilmut, *From Fringe to Flying Circus*, p. 20, and he discussed Cook's comic genius, for example, on *Q.E.D.: What's So Funny About That?*, BBC TV, 21 March 1989. In terms of admiration and envy, as Paskin notes, Miller claims to have felt 'very inferior' regarding Dudley's enviable musicianship. Meanwhile, Moore believed he was patronizingly viewed as the show's accompanying extra. Yet Miller's interest and personal fondness were certainly apparent when he later reunited with Dudley to discuss pianism (in a neurological context) on BBC TV's *The Body in Question*.
22 Moore described the rift with Bennett in *The Times*, 3 November 1983, and the *Observer*, 29 October 2000.
23 Wilmut, in *From Fringe to Flying Circus*, p. 20, quotes Bennett's comment with the coda that Miller's throwaway habit also annoyed Moore initially.
24 From Stephen Schiff's profile of Bennett, *New Yorker*, 6 September 1993.
25 Miller recalled the high dudgeon and the door in his *Parkinson Show* interview of November 1972.
26 *Life* magazine, 16 August 1963.
27 Bennett on Halliwell in *The Complete Beyond the Fringe*, p. 179. He referred to being in Miller's shadow in Bennett, A. (1994), *Writing Home* (London: Faber), p. 107, as well as mentioning, p. 109, an ironic missive which he sent in the 1980s, responding to *In Britain*'s suggestion that he write a feature for them about Miller. The tourist rag received a telegram back: 'Sorry, already interviewing him for *Racing Pigeon Gazette*.' Still, it is hard to say who should have been the more miffed when a theatrical survey was conducted on the streets of London and the majority of passers-by, on being shown a snapshot of Bennett, confused him with Miller. That was mentioned by Richard Eyre in his 'Director's Diary', *Guardian*, 23 December 2000.
28 Bennett confirmed this, saying that he and Miller 'really got on each other's nerves' in the *Observer*, 28 May 1967.
29 The 'bubonic plagiarist' joke is sometimes misattributed to Cook. Bennett mentioned the long-standing joke about the near-drowning in his contribution to *Peter Cook Remembered*. Apparently, it was assumed for a minute or two that Frost was satirically impersonating a drowning man, before Cook went to the rescue.
30 Cook married three times, Moore four.
31 'Silly paraphernalia' is Bennett's phrase. See *Writing Home*, p. 251.
32 Miller directed *A Poke in the Eye* (aka *Pleasure at Her Majesty's*) in 1976. Dudley was busy in Hollywood. *The Secret Policeman's Ball* was in 1979, and both were filmed for TV by Roger Graef. There were other public reunions including Miller, Bennett and Cook discussing the old days at the 69 Theatre Symposium in Manchester, 1 October 1969, and the foursome chatting with Parkinson on TV in November 1972.
33 Miller's intoxicated love of the US was not completely unqualified. On first seeing New York (when he nipped over by plane in December 1961, before *Beyond the Fringe*'s transfer), his resultant 'Been to America' article for the *New Statesman* ruminated:

> Nearly everyone appears to hold America in special regard. It may be admiration; it may be scorn or even bilious envy. Distant, inaccessible and rare, it hangs like a mirage, like Fournier's Secret Realm, or Alice's garden . . . I also had built and lived in my own imaginary America . . . a very elaborate palimpsest of ideas, a compendium of practically every hopeful or depressing social notion one could conceive.

He went on to describe how, on a grim rainy night, New York's suburbs were nightmarishly indistinguishable from Golders Green, and in midtown everything seemed strangely old, 'a 19th-century modernism, like a futurist city in Wells or Verne, crusted in Byzantine terra-cotta'.
34 Christopher Guest spoke of Miller in the *Guardian*, 10 January 2004.
35 Rachel managed to attend hospital courses on child development and psychiatry in New York.
36 Letter to Sacks dated 29 August 1963.
37 Miller was clearly capable of enjoying non-religious Jewish culture back in London too. At least in 1978, when he was rehearsing his ENO *Marriage of Figaro* near his grandparental home in the East End, he loved having lunch at the nearby Jewish restaurant, Blooms, and cracking jokes with the waiters.
38 Silvers, who had also helped establish the *Paris Review*, was introduced to Miller via UCL's Richard Wollheim.
39 Among *NYRB* colleagues with whom Miller socialized, mention should be made of Jason Epstein (Barbara's husband, and later editorial director of Random House). The *NYRB* also used British writers

from the Karl Miller camp, including Neal Ascherson, Francis Haskell and Noel Annan, not to mention Stevie Smith.

40 This photograph was reprinted in the *New York Times*, 5 October 2003 (Cornell Capa/Magnum Photos). Silvers and Plimpton had neighbouring flats in 540–1 East 72nd Street, where Bennett also took up residence and sometimes fraternized with Silvers.

41 Sontag's son, now himself a writer, is David Reiff.

42 Sontag made that point about unifying interests in the *Sunday Telegraph* magazine, 8 October 1978. She had, when young, wished to become a doctor.

43 Judy Cook (née Huxtable), who married Peter in 1973, relates how Miller wanted to know more about the scene. They took him to a strip club where, supposedly, his eyes were out on stalks. Then afterwards, at dinner, he discussed it very academically and objectively. In her book – Cook, J. (co-written with Levin, A.) (2008), *Loving Peter: My Life with Peter Cook and Dudley Moore* (London: Piatkus), p. 94 – she says that she could not tell what Miller thought and he seemed like a dotty professor.

44 Kazin was the author of Kazin, A. (1948), *A Walker in the City* (New York, NY: Reynal & Hitchcock).

45 Kazin bears a striking tweedy resemblance to Alfred from Rodent Control in Miller's early sketch, 'The Pied Piper of Hampstead'.

46 Notebook entry, 20 January 1964. This appeared, slightly adjusted, in *Nowhere In Particular*, and I have altered a couple of punctuation marks here for clarity.

47 Reviews of *Centaur* and *After the Fall*, *NYRB*, 1 February 1963 and 5 March 1964.

48 Miller wrote on *The Presidential Papers* in *Partisan Review*, Winter 1964, No. 1. The exchange with Trilling is recorded in the *NYRB*, 6 October and 17 November 1966, relating to Miller's suggestion that liberals, by citing Trilling, had encouraged Bruce to run wild.

49 Miller continued to write occasional articles for the *NYRB* in the years after he moved back to the UK. As previously noted, his piece alluding to Harlan Lane's book, *The Wild Boy of Aveyron*, appeared in the issue of 16 September 1976. Therein, he perused the case notes about the feral child and he traced a whole history of related ideas, from medieval myths about wolf-reared juveniles ('dramatiz[ing] a widely shared fantasy about the negligence . . . of our natural parents') up to the latest child therapy and teaching practices.

50 His *New Yorker* film and TV reviews appeared between August and December 1963. He had already reviewed films as a locum in London for the *New Statesman* and, in Manhattan, he stood in for Brendan Gill. Countering the general consensus, he notably exposed the sentimentality creeping into Britain's gritty working-class films (in the issue of 17 August), and he strongly praised Peter Brook's *Lord of the Flies* (on 31 August) as a satire of public schoolboys, rather than a universal allegory. He also spoke about William Golding's novel on American TV in *Books for Our Time*, Channel 13, 16 June 1964, and discussed the art of cinema in another long TV interview applauded in the *New York Times*, 11 October 1963.

51 The critical agenda that Miller was adopting was defined, a few months beforehand, in the *Observer*, 9 June 1963.

52 His piece on JFK's assassination, entitled 'Views of a Death', came out on 28 December 1963.

53 He wrote of the shuddering jelly on 16 November 1963, taking issue with the pious and grandiose tones adopted in history programmes as well.

54 Minow was chairman of the Federal Communications Commission.

55 In terms of improving television, Miller also signed the Campaign for Better Broadcasting's letter to *The Times* in late 1969, alongside George Melly, Sir Adrian Boult, Henry Moore and others.

56 The renaming gave a nod to George Melies' early sci-fi film which had also been entitled *A Trip to the Moon*.

57 *New York Times*, 13 February 1964.

58 Letter to Sacks, 14 November 1963.

59 The *NYT* reported on Roger O. Hirson's comedy *World War Two and a Half*, 10 and 20 February 1964.

60 Paskin, p. 79, records Cohen saying that he found both Miller and Cook aggressive, pretentious and condescending during *Beyond the Fringe*, so he was not solely riled by the Bel Geddes incident.

61 The *NYT*, 13 March 1964, reported on Miller's involvement in the planned *Profiles in Courage* series, though it was not scheduled for broadcast on NBC-TV until November. His choice of Anne Hutchinson was partly inspired by his brother-in-law Karl's research into the history of New England and its thinking, and partly by Robert Lowell's kinship with her. Wendy Hiller evidently had not minded Miller's film review of *Toys in the Attic* (10 August 1963) where he wrote: '[Here] poor Wendy Hiller is crucified on a caricature of ingrowing virtue, which she nevertheless manipulates with a certain lip-trembling conviction.' Hiller was to work with him again, in the UK.

62 *What's Going On Here?* was aired on WNEW TV in May 1963 and appeared on CBS in October, actually just before Miller's *New Yorker* column about TV and his other American television projects. For the making of the show, he and Cook formed the ironically named South Sea Trading Company with co-producers Clay Felker and Jean Vanden Heuvel (daughter of the founder of the Music Corporation of

America). Patrick McCormick was on board as a performer, and the anchormen were the popular comic duo Bob and Ray.

63 Miller appears to have almost entirely obliterated *World War Two and a Half* from his memory, perhaps because William was born on 24 February 1964, just days after the show went into meltdown.

Chapter 8: The Mid-Sixties

1 Confidential memo from Grace Wyndham Goldie, head of talks and current affairs, 22 August 1962, following on from a *détente* in 1961 when Alasdair Milne got Miller back on *Tonight*, discussing revue. The *Sunday Telegraph*, 2 July 1962, had already appreciated Miller's interviewing techniques in the Third Programme's portrait of the Alberts, the eccentric sibling comedians Tony and Douglas Gray who would go on to star in the first programme aired on BBC2 in 1964. Goldie wanted Miller to report from America as a kind of alternative Alistair Cooke. He proved hard to pin down in the bustle of New York. However, he was encouraged to contribute items whenever he had a spare moment. Douglas Cleverdon of the Third Programme particularly liked his idea – inspired by the Victorian London sociologist, Henry Mayhew – of talking to New York workers, so that led to *East-Side Taxi-Driver* being recorded and broadcast in 1963.

2 The *Monitor* announcement appeared in the *Daily Telegraph*, 13 June 1964.

3 Melvyn Bragg described *Monitor* as the mother and father of British TV arts programmes in a 40th anniversary article about the series, *The Times*, 30 March 1998.

4 Miller's brother-in-law, Karl Miller, had also previously worked as one of Burton's team on *Monitor*.

5 This is noted in the producer Nancy Thomas' internal letter, sent from *Monitor*'s offices on 29 June 1964.

6 Wheldon's note of 29 July 1964 alludes to Robert Kee being invited to serve as the alternative anchorman but then being double-booked by *The Late Night Show*. It also explains that Wheldon found Miller's request for the delay in transmission on returning from his own summer holiday.

7 Christopher Booker in the *Spectator*, 26 June 1964. Hugh Carleton Greene had taken over from Sir Ian Jacob in 1960.

8 Miller discussed taking over *Monitor* in his *Radio Times* introductory article (draft version in the BBC Written Archives) and in the *Daily Mail*, 2 July 1964.

9 Miller says that he was, at that point, still unaware of *Beside the Seaside*, but Patrick Garland filmed the item on Smith for *Monitor* and it seems to have been Garland, not Miller, who interviewed her. The BBC Written Archives' notes refer to shots of Smith talking to 'Patrick out of vision'.

10 Wheldon wrote a concerned note to Nancy Thomas, on 1 December 1964, asking for a firm decision on the new cameras and adding, 'I am, of course, not at all sure that we can force whatever it is you finally want through the various authorities here.' In *Monitor*'s broadcast of 9 March 1965, Miller also had to apologize for the 'lurching' camerawork in one item filmed about six months earlier, 'using a handheld camera technique which I've taken the pledge not to use again in quite that way'.

11 Anne James was the producer's assistant on *Monitor*. Encouraged by Miller to become a researcher and then a producer in her own right, she remains a friend to this day, along with Nancy Thomas.

12 Pre-Miller, *Monitor* had featured Jackson Pollock, N. F. Simpson, John Berger, Ronald Searle and others.

13 Harold Macmillan had also talked about the cameras whirring and shown them in a party political broadcast in 1962. Billington discusses the adventurousness of *That Was The Week That Was* in *State of the Nation: British Theatre Since 1945*, p. 131. In *White Heat*, pp. 101–2, Sandbrook points up George Melly's admiration for *Ready, Steady, Go!*, its deliberately unrehearsed style and jerky camerawork. That programme was produced by Associated Rediffusion.

14 *The Times*, 18 and 21 November 1964. In December 1964, a discussion on *The Critics* (the transcript of which is in the BBC Written Archives) included praise of *Monitor*'s coverage of the now legendary Peter Brook season.

15 Miller and Sontag were sent up on *Not So Much a Programme*, 22 November 1964 – just five days after the kick-off debate on kitsch. Levin also discussed *Monitor* with Norman St John-Stevas on this programme.

16 *Not Only . . . But Also* started in January 1965.

17 The 'miner writer' quotation comes from Bennett's sketch, 'The Lonely Pursuit' (the recording of which was recently re-released on the BBC Audiobooks DVD of 2009). *On the Margin* did not begin until 1966, by which point TV documentaries about northern artists had become a cliché, so Bennett was not directly or simply alluding to *Monitor*. He was also, of course, partly sending up his own origins.

Another of his *On the Margin* sketches, entitled 'The Critics', where a bunch of reviewers ludicrously discussed Chekhovian biscuits, may have subconsciously owed something to Miller's old skit, *Radio Page*, wherein an exhibition of contemporary digestive biscuits was appraised.

18 The *Sunday Times*, 20 December 1964.

19 Brien in the *Spectator*, 22 January 1965, and Booker in the same publication, 8 January 1965. Booker looked back on Miller's *Monitor* in *The Neophiliacs*, p. 249, suggesting nothing but dust lay behind the craze for novelty. *Monitor* also received a disparaging letter from William Empson on 23 April 1965,

slating Christopher Burstall's 'very disgusting' item about James Joyce and stating that 'whenever you chaps think that you are particularly high-minded what you produce is sickeningly low-minded'. This did not stop Miller featuring Empson two months later.

20 Obviously 'the last year' was not strictly accurate, Miller's programming having been broadcast for under eight months. This letter, as preserved in the BBC Written Archives, was drafted on 5 July 1965 in response to Priestley's article of 1 July 1965.

21 The last programme of the series, No. 155, was broadcast on 13 July 1965. Miller's letter went to press, appearing in the *Listener* on 15 July.

22 Melvyn Bragg, in *The Times*, 30 March 1998, mentions that Miller attended a 40th anniversary party for *Monitor* and cheerfully confessed he had driven the programme into the ground.

23 Anne James additionally recollects: 'Jonathan was like a bubbling cauldron of fascinating ideas or a barrage balloon with Nancy Thomas holding the cable so that it didn't blow away.' Thomas directed many of *Monitor*'s documentary features. In her view, 'People were simply furious with me and we were all shaken [by the reviews], but I like experiment. I was very cross at the reaction when it made him nervous. He was wonderfully stimulating and always open to our ideas too.'

24 According to Paul Ferris' biography – Ferris, P. (1990), *Sir Huge: The Life of Huw Wheldon* (London: Michael Joseph/Penguin), p. 163 – Miller said comic impersonations of Wheldon were the only means they had of 'pretending that we had control over him, in the form of a working model'. Wheldon greatly liked Miller and gave him a pretty free rein but he was, apparently, a man terrified of losing control.

25 After Beckett's death, years later, Miller reminisced about that dauntingly uneasy weekend in Paris when the great playwright 'would speak of nothing except minor league French football and the Tour de France'. That comment appeared in the *Daily Telegraph*, 27 December 1989.

26 In having cast McKern, Miller was now working with one of the actors whom he had watched, as an adolescent, on stage at the Old Vic.

27 *The Symposium* was itself not without humour, Plato's characters including Aristophanes with hiccups. By the by, an impersonation of the director himself was slipped into *The Drinking Party* with the strikingly Millerish actor Roddy Maude-Roxby instructing Julian Jebb's fussing character on how to act out Plato: 'Don't "do" it, just "be"!'

28 Leo Aylen, with whom Miller worked on *Monitor*, was commissioned to write the adaptation.

29 Miller had thought of filming *The Drinking Party* in Cambridge, until the jazzman and journalist George Melly – who had become a Gloucester Crescent friend – mentioned the Queen's Temple at Stowe. Melly had been a pupil at the school.

30 The neo-classical architecture and evening dress echoed Resnais' movie. *The Drinking Party*'s first scenes, with the guests wandering through sunlit trees, also had a trace of the woodland scenes in Russell's *Debussy Film*, and there would be more sunlit woods at the start of Miller's *Alice*.

31 On 5 July, Miller had sent (via Anne James) an anticipatory message to Bennett, saying that the Rev. Hoskins, at the Old Rectory, ought to provide 'much food for creative thought'. Bennett was, like Miller, a noted satirist of vicars. James recalls that Hoskins duly proved terrifically eccentric and great comic mileage was got out of him, with McKern joining in the fun.

32 The film was broadcast on 14 November 1965 and repeated on 10 July 1966, when these cuttings from the *Sunday Times* and *Daily Mail* were supplied for the *Radio Times* listings.

33 All letters are preserved in the BBC Written Archive's file on *The Drinking Party*. Wheldon was, by this point, BBC TV's controller of programmes. Leo McKern also sent Humphrey Burton a note, 18 November 1965, saying that he hoped to work with Miller again after this first, greatly satisfying experience. Stephen Hearst (whom I interviewed before his death in 2010) remembered showing *The Drinking Party* to American colleagues who were astounded that such high-calibre TV was possible.

34 Bennett described the incident with the down-and-out in his article, 'The Stripped-Pine Wilderness', *Listener*, 28 November 1968, and in *Writing Home*, pp. 390–1. *Backing into the Limelight*, p. 73, indicates that the 'Camden Town Tramp' sketch was made in late 1965 for Ned Sherrin's series *BBC-3*. Bennett received payment for this sketch in December 1965.

35 Marc's *Life and Times in NW1* cartoons were eventually collected in a book – Marc (1968), *The Trendy Ape* (London: Hodder & Stoughton) – with a dedication in the front to Jonathan and others. George Melly worked as Boxer's collaborator, contributing material. Goldblatt's analyses of soccer matches may relate to England winning the World Cup in 1966, or to the amateur football which Miller sometimes went along to watch when, on Sundays, Gloucester Crescent's Nick Tomalin and others used to kick a ball around in Hyde Park. Goldblatt also notably talked about two figures whom Miller knew personally, Ravi Shankar and Marshall McLuhan.

36 Karl Miller was the *Listener*'s editor from 1967, being at the *New Statesman* until then.

37 *The Cres* was recalled by Sophie Radice, who reminisced about growing up at No. 25 in her article entitled 'No Time Like the Crescent', *Evening Standard*, 27 October 1995. Alice Thomas Ellis wrote a

column called 'Home Life' in the *Spectator* describing life in NW1.

38 Miller's letter to Sacks of 29 August 1963.

39 His article 'Living Longer Than We Know How To' appeared in the *Observer*, 12 August 1962.

40 Miller discussed the disease on BBC TV's *Newsnight*, 20 February 1987; *Life File: The Living Dead*, 4 March 1988; Esther Rantzen's *Trouble in Mind*, 9 April 1989; and the BBC's 1989 and 1991 series *Who Cares?* and *Who Cares Now?* Bergan quoted Miller talking about his guilty feelings, p. 148, and it was discussed in Radio 3's *Lebrecht Interview* of 31 August 2009.

41 *Mr Sludge* was recorded in mid-January and broadcast on 6 February 1966. Miller had been planning the filming of it in the very last weeks of his mother's life and, in his *Listener* article of 19 October 1967, he said that, after a good long gap, he had begun to think about death again.

42 Regarding spiritualists, Miller stated, 'I don't believe it. It's all bosh', on the discussion programme *Is Death the End?*, BBC TV, 19 March 1967.

43 *Mr Sludge*'s mix of the sceptical and the eerie was discussed in Miller's *Listener* article, as above.

44 *The Death of Socrates*, broadcast on 3 July 1966, was filmed on the premises of the Camden funeral directors Leverton and Sons and in an ex-laundry in St Charles' Hospital, which served as Socrates' prison cell. Though Humphrey Burton had hoped for something less gloomy, it went on (with *The Drinking Party*) to become a highly rated double bill on American TV's Channel 13. In the UK, the *FT*'s end-of-year round-up called it 'one of the most original contributions to the medium'.

45 Miller's adaptation for BBC1's *Omnibus*, broadcast on 7 May 1968, pared down M. R. James' full title of *Oh, Whistle and I'll Come to You, My Lad*. In its praise for *Whistle and I'll Come to You*, the BFI website underlines Miller's minimal special effects and use of tension-building devices, steeply angled shots and disorienting close-ups. The website contends that the director had learned from Val Lewton's RKO low-budget classics of the 1940s. The influence of Bill Brandt's images would also be evident in Miller's *Alice in Wonderland*.

46 By way of a coda, in 1972, it was suggested that Miller should take over Michael Hordern's role as the comic philosopher in Tom Stoppard's NT play, *Jumpers*. He declined, saying stage appearances no longer appealed and his stammer could be problematic.

47 Hordern's Parkins is not suffering from obvious senility at the start, but he is an increasingly batty professor, a socially bumbling clown, peculiarly slow to process conversational exchanges with the chambermaids and muttering odd phrases to himself like mantras.

48 The *Sunday Times* reviewed the film on 12 May 1968. The *Sunday Telegraph*, 12 May, was contrastingly dismissive, irked by how Miller 'bragged' about his working methods on *Line-Up* afterwards. Still, Billington in the *Guardian*, 8 May, had welcomed it as a splendidly atmospheric and sensitive adaptation, striking a fine balance between the comic and the macabre. The public ranked the film amidst their 100 most scary moments (in film, TV, advertising and music) for Channel 4's survey in 2003.

49 *Whistle and I'll Come to You*'s own introductory commentary (appended by the BBC) alluded to 'how a man's reason can be overthrown when he fails to acknowledge those forces inside himself which he simply cannot understand'. Though using less forthright terms than Melly, the BFI has noted that Hordern's ultimate horror appears to be 'the invasion by night of his bedroom by a spirit that animates and stiffens and makes human the [bed-]sheets'. That comment comes from the sleeve notes of the 2001 video release of the film.

Claims, by some purists, that Miller unjustifiably imposed a psychoanalytic reading on James' ghost story ignore distinct insinuations in the original text. E.g. James' professor quivers and goes pink when a male colleague suggests sharing his double room. See James, M. R. (1994 edn), *Ghost Stories* (Harmondsworth: Penguin), p. 76. Miller's take is, in fact, less obviously about suppressed homosexuality than the original tale (though the other male guest at the hotel perhaps wants to strike up a friendship).

As for the BBC4 adaptation of the same story, broadcast on 24 December 2010, this shared Miller's truncated title and had Parkins as an aged gentleman (played by John Hurt). However, it weirdly invented a whole storyline about the protagonist having a beloved wife whom he puts in a care home because she is suffering from dementia. In 2012, the BFI released both *Whistle and I'll Come to You* adaptations, paired on a DVD, as part of its *Ghost Stories: Classic Adaptations from the BBC* series.

50 The neurologist Macdonald Critchley (who was associated with the National Hospital, Queen's Square) wrote about 'the sense of a presence' in the mid-1950s. His survey of case studies can be found in his book, Critchley, M. (1979), *The Divine Banquet of the Brain and Other Essays* (New York, NY: Raven Press), pp. 1–12.

51 Miller has spoken of being very frightened by the supernatural in Romain, *A Profile*, p. 36. His point about unclassifiable ghosts appeared in *Evening News*, 26 October 1979, and he stressed their paradoxical and marginal nature on Radio 3's *The Horror Story* in 1971. One friend says that Miller's retentive memory played tricks on him once, when he was being shown round a Gothic mansion in Scotland. Increasingly unnerved, he kept knowing what would be in the next room, until eventually his host, with a smirk, conjectured that he might just have read Sir Walter Scott's close description of this ancestral pile.

52 On the subject of learning the long speeches, Robert Gillespie, who played Browning, points out that

Autocue was not readily available in those days.

53 *The Times*, 7 February 1966, gave the programme high marks too, though grumbles about prolix lecturing cropped up in the BBC's feedback from the public.

54 The letter from Samuel Rosenberg to Huw Wheldon (controller of programmes), dated 16 November 1965 and with 'URGENT – what is the situation?' pencilled at the top, is preserved in the BBC Written Archives along with others relating to this complaint.

55 Letter from Miller to the BBC's solicitor, L. P. Roche, 25 November 1965, just the day after Betty's death. In terms of influences, experimental forms of docudrama were encouraged in the 1960s by the emergence of New Journalism (which mixed journalistic research with devices from literary fiction, as in Tom Wolfe's *Kandy-Kolored Tangerine-Flake Streamline Baby*).

56 Roche's response, 2 December 1965, said that Miller was completely within his rights under English law.

57 *Daily Mirror*, 13 May 1966.

58 Letter from the Jolly Hotel, BBC Written Archives.

59 Bennett, A. (2005), *Untold Stories* (London: Faber), pp. 559–61.

60 The *Sunday Times*' Atticus column, written by Nick Tomalin, cited this advertisement, 27 February 1966.

61 Miller says that he first thought of adapting *Alice* during his time in New York, when he somehow got talking about Carroll to the celebrated playwright Lillian Hellman. In his internal BBC memo proposing the project, sent on 9 April 1965 to the head of arts and music, he emphasized the idea of Wonderland's characters reflecting Liddell's home life, and the superlatively dreamlike 'fabulous fickleness' of the story. He was already, at that point, suggesting hints of decay in the settings, though the idea of Victorian attitudes to childhood and its mourned ephemerality were to emerge more markedly later. He ultimately summed up his interpretation, for viewers, in the *Radio Times*' Christmas edition of 1966.

62 'The Child as Swain', William Empson's essay on *Alice in Wonderland*, inspired Miller to frame his adaptation with 'Intimations of Immortality' (which was also alluded to in *Mr Sludge*). The essay appeared in Empson, W. (1935), *Some Versions of Pastoral* (London: Chatto & Windus) – another edition of that being released, in collaboration with Penguin, in 1966. Empson referred to that Wordsworth poem, as well as suggesting that Carroll's fantastical tales related to the Oxford milieu of Christ Church.

63 Here and later I have drawn on Miller's internal BBC memo of 9 April 1965 and the article *Vogue* published about the making of *Alice*, December 1966 (especially regarding England's 'Hapsburg insects', its magical, mossy fecundity, and Mallik as a cold infanta with an air of indifferent hauteur). The Pre-Raphaelite influence is also discussed in *Subsequent Performances*, p. 242, with allusion to Holman Hunt's *The Awakening Conscience* and William Dyce's beach painting, *Pegwell Bay*.

64 The incredulous query was sent to Burton – who was by then Miller's boss in the music and arts department – on 12 May 1966.

65 Both the croquet and the tea party were filmed at Albury Park, Surrey.

66 Alison Leggatt was an aunt of Miller's old university pal, Tim Leggatt. The BBC Written Archives reveal that other big names were approached. In a letter dated 2 March 1966, Miller jovially invited Frankie Howerd to play the Mock Turtle (with Gielgud as the Gryphon). Another, dispatched on 11 March, asked Noel Coward to be the Caterpillar. Miller's aforementioned missive from the Jolly Hotel suggested Dudley Moore for the Dormouse, and he also approached Kenneth Williams and Spike Milligan according to Stephen Hearst's BBC memo of 28 October 1965.

67 Miller has discussed the odd way in which you can see double in dreams. See *Subsequent Performances*, p. 242.

68 The chaperone was Jean Liddiard who, as Eric Idle's postgraduate girlfriend, had helped him get his part in the film.

69 Originally Miller had wanted Pasolini-style, non-professional casting in *The Drinking Party*, offering the role of Socrates to the celebrated classicist Robert Graves, before it was given to McKern.

70 Irate animal-lovers additionally had to be reassured that the hedgehogs were not being clubbed through croquet hoops.

71 Correspondence from Alan Bennett to Kate Bassett, 7 April 2003. The Pool of Tears was an antique tiled bath preserved under the floor of Derbyshire's Castle Donington.

72 In a note to Burton, on 25 July 1966, Palmer suggested colour would be more marketable to American TV networks. Palmer today remembers Miller being amenable to the change, but the latter says he was not and Anne James (who was, once more, Miller's assistant on this production) recalls him being furious. With a remake proving logistically impossible, the black-and-white cameras got rolling again in August. Miller sent everyone a reassuring letter, saying the enterprise was under way again, with its cargo intact, on 2 August 1966.

73 Ravi Shankar first played in the West in 1956. Tracking down his music, George Harrison took up the sitar in 1965 for the Beatles' song 'Norwegian Wood'. Shankar would go on to play, famously, at the 1967 Monterey Pop Festival, at Woodstock in 1969, and with Harrison at the 1971 Concert for Bangladesh.

74 That camera, in turn, caused a hoo-ha as the BBC classified all presents accepted by directors as bribes.

75 The scientist's name was probably inspired by the news headlines at the time, announcing the world's first hovershow, in Hampshire in June 1966, and the Ministry of Defence's million-pound investment in hovercrafts.

76 Jean Liddiard confirms that Miller and Bennett got on very well, in spite of the Pool of Tears.

77 Muggeridge's article, 'Alice, Where Art Thou?', *Centrepiece*, BBC Written Archives' (microfiche files).

78 Miller in *Vogue*, as above. Writing to Miller afterwards, Wilfrid Brambell also said: 'I cannot remember any job I have enjoyed more than "Alice". I miss it.' Letter preserved in the BBC Written Archives, dated 3 August 1966.

79 *Vogue*, as above. It was that article which was accompanied by Lord Snowdon's photographs. The film was the cover story for *Life International*, 26 December 1966.

80 Since Miller states that Satyajit Ray's acclaimed film *Pather Panchali* (with its child-in-woodland scenes) was a cinematic influence on *Alice*, a question mark hangs over whether Palmer, strictly speaking, introduced him to Shankar's music. *Pather Panchali* came out in 1956, with music by Shankar.

81 Tony Palmer went on, of course, to become a renowned film-maker, prestigiously winning many BAFTAs, Emmy Awards and the Prix Italia (twice), not to mention directing theatre and opera, writing books and music reviews and presenting Radio 3's *Night Waves*.

82 Hearst confirmed that Wheldon's criticisms, and his own, were taken in good heart by Miller.

83 Reported in the *New York Times*, 16 October 1966.

84 I have drawn here on Dick Adler's feature in New York's *World Journal Tribune*, 15 January 1967, on *Playbill*, February 1969, and in the *Daily Mail*, 6 January 1967, which reported his departure.

85 William H. Honan's feature, *New York Times*, 22 January 1967.

86 Miller was only credited as 'production associate' by the time *Come Live With Me* was at the Billy Rose Theatre, New York, January 1967.

87 Cook's *Analysis in Wonderland* comment was noted in the *Evening Standard*, 24 November 1966. Soon after, word spread that Miller was quitting the BBC, causing intensified speculation about the film. Still in New York with Soupy Sales at this point, he tried to quell the rumour, emphasizing that he had not resigned. His contract had merely come to an end. That was reported in the *London Evening News*, 14 December 1966 (along with the fact that he was suffering from a stress-related boil on his neck). Today he exclaims, with exasperation, that his *Alice* was scrupulously mid-Victorian, having nothing to do with Freud's theories which were developed later.

88 *Daily Mail*, 24 November 1966. Dance was additionally alluding to Dennis Potter's idea for a BBC rewrite of *Cinderella*, which had not been realized but which apparently involved Prince Charming strangling Cinderella. One might wonder if he and Hamling had merely flicked through Carroll's book looking at Tenniel's pretty illustrations, but the festive season intensified the protectionist drive, combined with the fact that 1965 had been *Alice in Wonderland*'s centenary year. As noted by Rohan McWilliams in his June 2011 article 'Jonathan Miller's *Alice in Wonderland* (1966): A Suitable Case for Treatment', *Historical Journal of Film, Radio and Television*, Vol. 31, No. 2, 229–46, earlier psychoanalytic interpretations of Carroll were extant but had not become widely known in the mid-1960s: for example Lennon, F. B. (1947), *Lewis Carroll* (London: Cassell & Co), also Greenacre, P. (1955), *Swift and Carroll: A Psychoanalytic Study of Two Lives* (New York, NY: International Universities Press).

89 Still in America over the Christmas period, Miller managed to perpetuate the BBC rescheduling furore by joking – at an American private screening, with journalists present – that he had not wanted *Alice* 'wasted on a lot of little bastards at 5 o'clock'. This made it into the *Daily Mail* on 6 January 1967. Other papers coyly reported that the phrase was 'little Batmen' or 'little kids'.

90 In *Subsequent Performances*, p. 247, Miller rather surprisingly reclaimed 'travesty' as a positive term, noting: 'By the time I was editing . . . I realized that if the film succeeded at all it was by avoiding direct adaptation . . . it was an ironic *imitation* of *Alice in Wonderland,* and it is only as a travesty that it has a relationship with the original novel.' Earlier, in his *Radio Times* article of 22 December 1996, he suggested that the film was a knight's move away, as he had been as faithful as possible in many respects but no one could just transpose the entire text straight into imagery. The 'knight's move' seems more like it, for the film manages brilliantly – rather like Orson Welles' Falstaff movie, *Chimes at Midnight* – to remain somehow profoundly true to the original work while being highly inventive.

91 Most reviews came out on 16 December 1966. The *Mail* disliked Mallik's performance while the *Evening Standard* and *The Times* suggested the production was dull. However, *The Times* pointed out its scenes of charming sylvan beauty and its dreamlike quality, free of tricksy special effects, while the *Morning Star* judged the direction outstanding. Nancy Banks-Smith's praise was tempered by mention of longueurs, but in the *Guardian*, 22 August 2003, she resoundingly celebrated both this adaptation and Dennis Potter's drama, *Alice,* saying: 'I didn't realise at the time how interesting they were.' The biographer Roger Lewis – in Lewis, R. (1977), *The Life and Death of Peter Sellers* (New York, NY: Applause), p. 430 – further refers to Miller's film as 'one of the best literary adaptations I know'.

92 *Alice*'s queer yet matter-of-fact jump cuts and subtle use of wide-angle lenses were among the dreamlike filmic techniques employed. The *Observer*, 21 April 2002, referred to the survey conducted by Dr Christopher Evans of the National Physical Laboratory, with the top five films being Resnais' *Last Year at Marienbad*, Kubrick's *2001*, Fellini's *Juliet of the Spirits,* Miller's *Alice*, and Bergman's *Wild Strawberries*. The dinner party on the beach in Peter Greenaway's *Drowning by Numbers* may allude to the Last Supper, but it also, arguably, looks like a cross between the Mad Hatter's tea party and the Camber Sands scenes in *Alice*. Historic still-life paintings evidently influenced both directors, yet a parallel might also be drawn between the grotesque banquets in Greenaway's films and the foreground table, piled high with dead seafood, in the Ugly Duchess's kitchen.

93 Gielgud's letter was written on 11 October 1966, after an early private preview. That was followed, on 3 January 1967, by Hugh Carleton Greene's BBC memo calling *Alice* a 'near masterpiece'. In *Subsequent Performances*, p. 241, Miller emphasized the link with *The Trial*, Orson Welles' take on Kafka, noting how Alice and Joseph K both faced mysterious legal accusations.

94 Also showing there were no hard feelings, Miller was interviewed in 1968 (about his *School for Scandal* at Nottingham Playhouse) for the BBC TV programme *How is It and Why?*, produced by Tony Palmer.

95 Worsley's article appeared in the *Financial Times*, 4 January 1967. As for Dodgson, the son of a parson, he was expected to become an Anglican priest and was, moreover, supposed to take holy orders as a condition of his Christ Church residency. Bending the institution's rules, he did not complete that process, and he apparently had issues with collegiate life.

96 Perhaps there is a little nod to William Empson, regarding the Caterpillar's wispy whiskers. Other in-jokes were Alan Bennett playing the Mouse as a very arid Oxford historian, and Julian Jebb, in a straw boater, looking only fractionally more archaic than a 1950s Footlights sketch.

97 McKern's Duchess additionally looked like some nightmare version of the ward sisters and matrons played by Hattie Jacques in the *Carry On* films.

98 A transcribed BBC interview with Miller, dated 11 November 1966, BBC Written Archives.

99 George Melly may, in turn, have detected a hint of his Gloucester Crescent house which was littered with stuffed animals.

100 Miller talked about drama and psychiatry in an unattributed article entitled 'Mr Miller in Wonderland', BBC Written Archives microfiche files. Sacks appreciatively called it *The Neurologist's Alice*, and the *Lancet* article attracted comment in *The Times* and *Evening Standard*, 16 and 17 February 1967. In 1968, incidentally, Miller wanted to make a TV series about various patients of Sigmund Freud and Russia's A. R. Luria.

101 Emanuel suggested Netley as a location. The crew filmed there just before the building was demolished.

102 Empson had, it should be noted, already linked Alice and madness in his *Child as Swain* essay, suggesting that Carroll's climactic banquet in *Through the Looking-Glass* was akin to high table at Christ Church, with the heroine becoming a grown-up queen but refusing to accept the insane conventions of that world. Miller's post-Pool of Tears scene is really like a dementia ward-cum-Oxbridge common room.

Regarding other possible influences, his cavorting caucus race is reminiscent of the hospital sports day in *On the Side of the Angels*, pp. 100–3: an event watched by the Jonathan-like infant, Peter, and featuring joke-races, mental patients with weird gaits, and quirky prizes. Of course, when writing that, Betty may have had Carroll in the back of her mind, especially if her offspring had been reading it around that time. As a *UCH Magazine* snapshot shows, Vol. XLII, No. 2, p. 55, wacky races featured at a University College Hospital sports day, where Miller fired the starting gun. Then there was the historic footage of neurological patients or shell-shock victims with 'dancing' gaits, as recorded in the aforementioned Pathé brothers' Netley documentary.

103 The Alice–Lear comparison arose in Miller's 1970 conversation with the American radio presenter Studs Terkel whose book, Terkel, S. (1999), *The Spectator: Talk about Movies and Plays with the People Who Make Them* (New York, NY: New Press), contains a transcript, p. 209.

104 In his letter to Sacks, 29 August 1963, Miller also conversely noted how he longed to be old already, 'with wide flappy bottoms to [my] trousers'. Announcing Rachel's due date, he concluded, 'I suppose I had better slip in and wear even flappier trousers and sink deeper into my armchair.'

105 That reading would make *Alice* a variation on the Eurydice myth. However, Miller's initial BBC memo of 9 April 1965 suggested another interpretation, saying that Alice's failure to exit through doors signifies a child trying to escape from a dream that's growing too small for her waking mind.

106 Charles Dodgson was a keen early photographer, of course, though Julia Margaret Cameron is more strongly evoked in *Alice*'s opening shot. Framed by leaves, Mallik echoes Cameron's image *Pomona* from 1872, a portrait of Alice Liddell. Strictly speaking, rather than producing daguerreotypes, Cameron used the wet collodion-on-glass method.

107 The 'trippy' elements in the original book might have as much – or more – to do with medical conditions than magic mushrooms. Dodgson is known to have experienced at least one migraine with aura. As in epilepsy, that can cause sudden perceived distortions in size (known as micropsia and macropsia

or Alice-in-Wonderland syndrome). Dodgson was also a founding member of the Society for Psychical Research, which undertook to do investigative research into hallucinations (as well as mediums, mesmerism and reportedly haunted houses). The idea of Wonderland as asylum was, by the by, arguably seeded by Carroll's Cheshire Cat observing 'We're all mad here'.

108 The dinner party is further described by Peter Nichols, under Spring 1969, in Nichols, P. (2000), *Peter Nichols: Diaries 1969–1977* (London: Nick Hern), pp. 40–1. Nichols says 'Cromwellian spirit'. When Miller relates this dream to me, he says the 'Cromwell stoop'. To put the dream in context, the movie *Cromwell* (with Wymark) was being made in 1969, coming out in 1970. Miller's interest in radical Puritans had also extended, from the Anne Hutchinson TV play, to planning a BBC drama about the Putney Debates and Charles I's execution. Though mentioned in BBC archival correspondence on 21 February 1967 – wherein Humphrey Burton asked Miller to both write and direct – this idea never came to fruition.

Chapter 9: Late Sixties to Early Seventies

1 Miller and Melly had become firm friends on their trip to Belgium where the latter interviewed Magritte for *Monitor*. On the side, Miller spun comic fantasies about the painter's suburban wife being scandalously raunchy behind closed doors.

2 That was in 1965.

3 Melly talked to me about Miller in a wonderfully perceptive and funny interview before he sadly became ill and succumbed to lung cancer in 2007. The incident with Mesens also features in Melly, G. (1997), *Don't Tell Sybil* (London: Heinemann), pp. 190–1.

4 The Black Museum is now called the Crime Museum.

5 The TV producer Roger Graef, who had moved in nearby, tells another party anecdote that could have come straight out of *Life and Times in NW1*. The journalist Dee Wells, Freddie Ayer's wife, apparently crawled over to Graef on her knees and introduced herself with the words: 'I know I should know, but what is it you've written or done?' Now a small legend in its own right, that comment is attributed by Miller to Nick Tomalin.

6 Again, *Peter Nichols: Diaries 1969–1977*, p. 40. I have somewhat blurred two social scenes here as Frayn had not yet moved to Gloucester Crescent at the time of the dinner party. Nevertheless, in my interview with Nichols he spoke of both that dinner with Miller and of being glad he did not live in the Crescent in that era.

7 Sophie Radice, *Evening Standard*, 27 October 1995.

8 Stafford-Clark in Romain, *A Profile*, pp. 179–80. He is said to have been less impressed by Miller's conversation on the day of Princess Diana's death when, apparently, Miller dismissed the news with a wave of his hand in order to carry on with his complaints about feeling professionally undervalued in Britain.

9 The obstruction order was served in April 1970 according to Bennett's diary dates in *The Lady in the Van*, the non-stage version printed in *Writing Home*, p. 63.

10 It seems Miss Shepherd ran this one past Bennett too, because *The Lady in the Van*, p. 61, begins with a similar tête-à-tête. She was not completely mad. A snake had, in fact, escaped from Parkway's pet shop.

11 Alan Bennett was also treated to a bevy of programme proposals in this vein. See *The Lady in the Van*, p. 68.

12 The nicknaming of the Fertile Crescent borrowed the anthropological term for the region of Western Asia known as the cradle of civilization.

13 One of Miller's colleagues from the time says that, on other journeys, he varied the thyroid threat with more laddish salutations directed at perambulating females, apparently not giving a hoot about being recognized.

14 After attending hospital courses on child development and psychiatry in New York, Rachel took about six months off when William was born. After that she spent a year sitting in at London's Whittington Hospital, with a view to specializing in paediatrics. She gained a DCH (Diploma in Child Health) then, happening to contract tonsillitis, she visited her local GP at the Cavendish Centre in Kentish Town. She was offered a post as a trainee there, became a partner in the practice and stayed there for the rest of her working life. In the Seventies, during a GPs' psychiatry-related refresher course, her interest in that subject was renewed and she flirted with the idea of joining a discussion group led by a disciple of the psychoanalyst Michael Balint (who had Tavistock Clinic connections). Miller was opposed to that, feeling that their marriage might be subjected to endless analysis as a consequence.

15 I am indebted, regarding this remark, regarding Tom's later reference to getting rat-arsed and Shirley Conran, and regarding William's school projects, to Richard Rosenfeld's article which combined interviews with Tom and William for the 'Relative Values' column, *Sunday Times*, 3 January 1993. Tom, incidentally, passed four O-levels.

16 Miller discussed that with Dick Cavett in 1980, in the fifth of his aforementioned five-interview sequence.

17 Miller's *St Matthew Passion* was staged at Holy Trinity Church in Chelsea, London, in 1993. It was on

BBC TV in April 1994.

18 There was a tradition of going to Bedales in Rachel's family and she had attended the associated junior school.

19 William is now married to a designer who has worked for Colefax and Fowler among others.

20 His more official godparent was Robert Lowell.

21 After the chase, Miller was driven round the area by the police, treating them to neurological advice on the unreliability of their identification procedures. In Miller, K. (1998), *Dark Horses: An Experience of Literary Journalism* (London: Picador), p. 8, Karl Miller records another striking instance of physical courage, describing how his brother-in-law climbed up onto an icy roof to fix a leak, a feat Karl was loath to perform himself. Even more surprisingly, alongside arachnophobia, the other great dread to which the famed polymath confesses is being subjected to a general knowledge test, in public. Dick Cavett recalled that in his *New York Times* blog, 2 May 2008, as reprinted in his book *Talk Show*, p. 131, with mention of Miller's other haunting fear, being tortured for information that he doesn't possess.

22 Miller remembers this slightly differently from Sue Bond as 'typin', smokin' and gettin' paid for it'.

23 He made the Johnnie Walker docu-advert in 1967. The old manse, which the family no longer owns, was in Archiestown.

24 Rosenfeld's interview recorded this comment on the sibling rivalry. The young Tom pouted despondently at his baby brother's arrival and did his best to hurl him down the stairs, later becoming 'desperately jealous' (by his own confession) when the teenage William acquired lots of girlfriends. The pair had some slanging matches when they crossed paths at work too, hence William's allusion to mutual wind-ups.

25 A downcast stance, echoing the angel in *Melencolia,* was adopted by Kenneth Haigh in *Prometheus Bound*; by Old Hamlet's ghost in Miller's 1970 Oxford and Cambridge Shakespeare Company production; by the central character in his 1980 *Falstaff* for Kent Opera; and by Penelope Wilton's Helena in his *All's Well* at Greenwich. The picture is mentioned in *On Reflection*, p. 179, and Miller adopted something like the posture himself as early as the Footlights revue *Out of the Blue*, when he played a dejected village idiot.

26 Inevitably somewhat simplifying Freud's thesis, I am alluding here to 'Mourning and Melancholia', which features in Freud, S., translated by Whiteside, F. (2005), *On Murder, Mourning and Melancholia* (London: Penguin), pp. 203–18. Freud interestingly connected melancholia with a fear of impoverishment, traits shared by Emanuel and his son. Still, Freud himself stressed that his analysis was far from scientifically proven, and his description of its symptoms (including self-abasement) do not all chime with Miller's depressive behaviour.

27 Miller discussed his depressions in his interview with Lucy Hughes-Hallett, *Vogue*, November 1978, 199–201; in the American publication *People*, 26 March 1979; and on *The Dick Cavett Show*, in programme five of the 1980 sequence, where he drew a white dwarf analogy.

28 Jeannie's only other criticism of her surrogate parents was that, as liberals, they let her choose and thus turn down their suggestion of changing schools. That said, they conveyed that she needed to work harder and she did well, going on to college and socializing with Miller's friends during her twenties. William adds that it was a boy's dream, having an older sister.

29 Tom and William Miller, in turn, worked in McNally's New York restaurants as teenagers.

30 After *Whistle and I'll Come to You*, Miller was asked (in a letter from Graeme McDonald, dated 18 June 1969 and preserved in the BBC Written Archives) to write for the *Wednesday Play* slot. He offered, instead, to direct an already scripted screenplay adapted from *At the Jerusalem*, Paul Bailey's novel set in an old people's home. This idea foundered not just because of Miller's stage-directing schedule but also due to the channel's costly switchover from black-and-white to colour. He did make a brief return in 1973, directing his Joycean short, *Clay*, for *Full House*, and he reworked his Nottingham/Old Vic *King Lear* for the broadcaster's *Play of the Month* series in 1975.

31 Michael Billington, *Guardian*, 6 July 2002.

32 This New York premiere included *My Kinsman, Major Molineux* (adapted from Hawthorne's American Revolution parable), though actually the other part of Lowell's trilogy, *Endecott and the Red Cross*, proved so dramatically intractable that it had to be dropped at the last minute, causing some grief among the cast.

33 This is noted by Ian Hamilton in Hamilton, I. (1983), *Robert Lowell: A Biography* (London: Faber), p. 315.

34 Brustein's review entitled 'We are Two Cultural Nations' was reprinted in his aforementioned book, *Seasons of Discontent*, pp. 256–9.

35 Interview, *The Times*, 13 March 1972.

36 It was recorded for both PBS TV and Columbia Records.

37 Miller's stated aim was recorded in the *Guardian*, 14 February 1967. He similarly stressed that he liked extreme, unnatural theatre when interviewed by Mark Boxer, the *Sunday Times*, 20 March 1966.

38 Romain discusses that chain of influence in *A Profile*, p. 9. The actors were masked and everything was in black and white in *My Kinsman, Major Molineux*. To generate menace, Miller utilized not only a languorous pace but also ominous humming, like swarming flies. While foreshadowing the buzzing insects

in *Alice*, that owed something to Peter Brook who employed humming effects too.

39 Langella in Romain, *A Profile*, p. 164.

40 The *Beyond the Fringe* foursome, during their New York run, had irreverently omitted to show up for a VIP visit to Strasberg's famed Actors Studio.

41 Robert Silvers recalls how Miller was beloved of the Lowells and, as a doctor, coped admirably with the poet's manic depression, being able to talk to him during those periods.

42 Lowell warmly described Miller as a brilliant and bubbling young Englishman and a near-miraculous director of his work in letters to Elizabeth Bishop (10 March 1964) and to Mary McCarthy (19 November 1966). These can be found in Lowell, R., edited by Hamilton, S. (2005), *Letters of Robert Lowell* (London: Faber).

43 Jeremy Kingston in *Punch*, 15 March 1967; the *Sunday Telegraph*, 12 March, on mumbling; and Harold Hobson in the *Sunday Times* on inaction, also 12 March.

44 Miller lodged with Dworkin who was the master of Yale's Trumble College.

45 He would later become more cheeky about both gurus, dismissing Kott's 'more lunatic fancies' and Brook's increasing dedication to 'completely spurious', primitivist, Jungian myths.

46 The American universities where Miller has been a visiting VIP range from small-town campuses, to Berkeley on California's Nobel Riviera, where he met up again with his former UCL pal Richard Wollheim. On the long list of other befriended academics are the experimental psychologist Irvin Rock, the philosophers Donald Davidson and John Searle, and (via a connection with Karl Miller) the Harvard professor of American history, Daniel Aaron.

47 Miller had, of course, identified with Prometheus in the *Twentieth Century* article of July 1961, comparing the naughty spirit of laughter to the Zeus-defying rebel's gift of fire.

48 LBJ's order is discussed by Ian Hamilton, p. 360.

49 Miller waved off the said aspic in his Yale programme note (preserved in the Yale Repertory Theatre archive). The set was a huge brick tower sunk into the bowels of the building, through the stage floor.

50 From the Yale programme note.

51 For instance, Henry Hewes, *Saturday Review*, 27 May 1967, and Francis Fergusson, *New York Review of Books*, 3 August 1967.

52 Appreciative comments came from Richard Gilman, *Newsweek*, 22 May 1967, and Kerr, *New York Times*, 11 May 1967.

53 Undated letter to Oliver Sacks, circa June 1967.

54 Radio 3, January 1971. Miller's Mermaid production was in June 1971, with Thorne as Io.

55 *London Evening News*, 25 June 1971.

56 Spike Milligan was also on the Mermaid's unusually entertaining board. Robin Midgley, who had directed the undergraduate *Bartholomew Fair* at Cambridge, had been working at the Mermaid too in 1967, the year Miller made his debut there.

57 Mannoni, O. (1956), *Prospero and Caliban: The Psychology of Colonization* (New York, NY: Praeger). In *Village Voice*, 1 March 2004, Miller emphasized that social structures are crucial in his productions due to his youthful contact with anthropological ideas (via his father and Rachel's Great Aunt Brenda).

58 Miller discusses Prospero acting like a psychoanalyst in *Subsequent Performances*, pp. 161–2. He additionally observes how Prospero has to surrender an essentially infantine notion that he can magically control the world.

59 Irving Wardle, *The Times*, 16 June 1970. The *Guardian*'s review of the same day was an exception, with Philip Hope-Wallace wanting more magic and spiritual majesty.

60 Tara Arts' touring and West End production, which played at London's Arts Theatre in 2007, presented *The Tempest* as 'Shakespeare's classic exploration of colonialism'. Incidentally, *Umbatha* – the writer Welcome Msomi's acclaimed Zulu adaptation of *Macbeth*, played out as an intertribal conflict in nineteenth-century Africa – premiered in 1971, coming to London's Aldwych Theatre in 1972.

61 Beaton, N. (1986), *Beaton But Unbowed: An Autobiography* (London: Methuen), p. 143. Beaton also noted, p. 144, that those theatre critics who nitpicked did not like the colonial interpretation or the dour grey setting.

62 The ditching of clichés is discussed in *Subsequent Performances*, p. 107, while in Ralph Berry's book – Berry, R. (1977), *On Directing Shakespeare* (London: Croom Helm), p. 32 – Miller emphasizes that, not being a theatre enthusiast, he does not always know the precedents, a possible bonus as regards inhibiting traditions.

63 Erwin Panofsky's studies of Renaissance iconography informed this staging.

64 Later, when Miller was executive producer on the *BBC Shakespeare Series*, the February 1981 broadcast of *The Winter's Tale* was reviewed by Clive James, the *Observer*'s TV critic. He noted the cast were surrounded by cubes and cones such that, 'You can't quell the fear that if one of them sits on a cone instead of a cube, then the blank verse will suffer.' The set was not as close to pure Platonic geometry as that sounds, but James had attended Miller's OCSC rehearsals in Cambridge.

65 D. A. N. Jones, *Listener*, 2 October 1969, followed by letters on 9, 16 and 23 October. Also Simon Gray, *New Statesman*, 3 October 1969. During the subsequent US tour, another dose of scorn was dished out by the *New York Times*. Miller woke on 1 January 1970 to Clive Barnes' review putting the boot into 'arrant amateurism' from Oxbridge.

66 *Review*, BBC2, 21 February 1970.

67 *The Times* and *Daily Telegraph*, 6 and 7 April 1971 respectively.

68 This issue was further discussed by Miller in *Subsequent Performances*, p. 111. He points out that it was Freud's follower and biographer, Ernest Jones, who really developed an analysis of Hamlet.

69 When Miller staged his fourth *Hamlet* at the Tobacco Factory in Bristol in 2008, Benedict Nightingale's *Times* review of 24 March referred to the ghost's conversational manner and observed that 'purgatory might be the Athenaeum' – curiously hitting upon Emanuel's old club. On another occasion, when Miller directed *Hamlet* at London's Warehouse Theatre (now the Donmar), Lucy Hughes-Hallett noted in the *Evening Standard*, 6 August 1982, that he saw the usurped Prince of Denmark as one of Shakespeare's interstitial, satirical malcontents rattling around without a proper niche in society. She concluded that the director sounded as if he felt a special affinity with his protagonist. Nonetheless, Miller suggests that, rather than being any personal trip down Memory Lane, his OCSC *Hamlet* notably recreated the Elizabethan set design known as the Theatre of Memory. The academic historian Frances Yates had just been researching the Theatre of Memory, looking at Robert Fludd's mnemonic theatre sketches where particular alcoves were associated with certain facts or incidents and thus served as an aide-mémoire. See Yates, F. (1969), *Theatre of the World* (London: Routledge & Kegan).

70 It does seem improbable that ghosts smoke. However, the neurologist Macdonald Critchley – in his aforementioned paper on 'the sense of a presence', p. 7 – alludes to a striking case study (written up by William James). The man in question 'sensed' a friend standing close by him and, if he slid his eyes to the side, he could 'recognize' the grey-blue material of his friend's trousers which appeared semi-transparent, like tobacco smoke.

71 Miller publicly championed Brook in a letter to *The Times*, 13 October 1971, defending directors' interpretations against conservative 'mandarin bardolatry'. John Fortune, incidentally, took credit for seeding the de Chirico idea.

72 John Mortimer, *Observer*, 19 March 1972. Miller had, in a similar vein, radically axed the opening exchange on the battlements in *Hamlet*, blithely running counter to the production's programme note by J. C. Trewin, which sang the praises of that very scene.

73 Billington, *Guardian*, 17 April 1974.

74 In his interview with *Music and Musicians*, April 1974, Miller stated: 'The performing arts have been dogged by a sort of hideous pedantic romanticism about the obligation that we owe to the author or to the originator of a work. We owe him nothing at all.'

75 He has rebuked such modernizations. See Ralph Berry, p. 33, and *Subsequent Performances*, p. 119.

76 Miller spoke of this to Hugh Hebert, *Guardian*, 18 March 1972.

77 *Julius Caesar* played at Donald Albery's New Theatre (subsequently renamed the Albery, now the Noël Coward Theatre), the venue where the young Miller had seen the Old Vic company in residence, back in 1949.

78 Miller's letter to Sacks, 10 December 1968. Several Oxbridge students who auditioned for the OCSC remember Miller looking like exhaustion incarnate.

79 Letter to Sacks, as above.

80 With less than the proverbial six degrees of separation, Burge was also John Bird's father-in-law. Miller resided in a Nottingham house owned by the father of the film director Stephen Frears (who married the Millers' NW1 neighbour Mary-Kay Wilmers in 1968).

81 To give a predecessor credit, William Gaskill had staged George Farquhar's *The Recruiting Officer* in 1963, ripping away the dandyish trimmings to expose a grungy world. It would also be an exaggeration to say Miller rediscovered Marston's long-forgotten *Malcontent*, his professional revival having been preceded by Southampton and Oxford student productions in the Sixties.

82 Regarding the date of Miller's *Malcontent*, I have switched the order of his Nottingham productions to group the more stylized and the more naturalistic ones together. His *Malcontent* (while evidently having Gothic-surreal leanings in common with *My Kinsman, Major Molineux* and *Julius Caesar*) came after *The Seagull* and *Lear*, in 1973. Nicholas de Jongh in the *Guardian*, 14 June 1973, was notably critical, crying 'rape' and arguing that a morally serious play had been Goonified by force.

83 *From Chekhov with Love* was produced by David Susskind for Rediffusion, broadcast in the UK on 14 June 1967. Bother with the trade unions and with CBS's scheduled broadcast were reported in the *New York Times*, 25 June 1967. CBS aired it in September the following year.

84 Michael Billington's TV column in *The Times*, 17 June 1968, welcomed the end result as gracefully poignant and high-calibre, though he questioned the accuracy of Gielgud's aloof Chekhov. The *New York Times* was unimpressed, 12 September 1968.

85 High praise from the *Morning Star* and *Sunday Times*, 1 December 1968.

86 *The Times*, 30 November 1968.

87 Among others, Janet Suzman (who starred in Miller's *Three Sisters* in 1976) sees these qualities in him. That said, his blend of humour and philosophizing is really more discernibly Apostolic than Slavic.

88 Robert Stephens, who was to play Trigorin in Miller's later staging of *The Seagull*, clearly sensed medical precision, praising Miller's ability to get to the heart of things and strip Chekhov clean like a skeleton. His comments appears in Romain, *A Profile*, p. 160.

89 Miller critically discussed the 'Keats Grove genteel' school of English Chekhov productions in *Subsequent Performances*, pp. 164–7, putting Peggy Ashcroft in that camp, and not mentioning he had directed her in *From Chekhov with Love*. Although Fenella Fielding is the sister of the Conservative peer, Baron Feldman, she was not of the Ashcroft genteel school and, like Miller, she is of East European Jewish descent.

90 As well as being an amour of Gorky and H. G. Wells, Budberg had written the original script of *From Chekhov with Love*. As regards long-standing collaborators, Patrick Robertson and Rosemary Vercoe became regular set and costume designers for Miller in Nottingham. Having responded admirably to his requirements for *The School for Scandal* (the most detailed brief they had ever been given), the couple went on to work for him at the ENO and around the world.

91 Again, I have not described Miller's productions in chronological order as he was repeatedly shuttling between different companies. *King Lear* was actually his Shakespearean debut with professional actors. It opened in Nottingham in late 1969, prior to his mid-1970 *Tempest* at the Mermaid (thus upping the awe he inspired when he held auditions for *The Tempest*).

92 Miller discussed Lear's savage depression with Peter Ansorge, *Plays and Players*, March 1970. He writes more on the character's paranoia and other matters in *Subsequent Performances*, p. 134, and he spoke about him feeling unloved and abdicating as a crisis gesture to the radio presenter Studs Terkel in 1970 (Terkel, pp. 202–3).

93 Miller was part of an iconoclastic Sixties school of thought which was at work in the opera world too, with Pierre Boulez's 1966 Bayreuth *Parsifal* taking a strikingly anti-grandiose approach to Wagner.

94 Michael Hordern commented on the very real domestic relationships in Romain, *A Profile*, p. 152.

95 In the Eighties, Miller was to write a slim, illustrated book called *Steps and Stairs*. This was a fascinating, concise history of the titular architectural features and their metaphorical significance. His essay bounded nimbly from the physics of leg joints and the psychology of chimps, to how flights of steps have represented life's ups and downs, social ascents and falls from grace. Also featured was the great chain of being. This concept (derived from Aristotle and Plato) envisaged the whole universe as a hierarchical ladder with God on top, followed by angels, kings, nobles, ordinary men and animals. The great chain of being preoccupied Miller when he was working on *Lear* and it was to have a bearing on other projects in his career, including *The Taming of the Shrew* and 'The Dog Beneath the Skin' in 1972. *Steps and Stairs* was a special commission for United Technologies, the industrial conglomerate behind the escalator firm Otis. Incidentally, Julia Trevelyan Oman, Miller's designer on *Alice in Wonderland*, had written her Royal College of Art thesis on steps and stairs in the 1950s, another possible instance of ideas consciously or unconsciously appropriated.

96 The Beatles most famously encapsulated the mixed feelings back in 1968 with the lyrics: 'You say you want a revolution./Well, you know,/We all want to change the world . . . But when you talk about destruction,/Don't you know that you can count me out.'

97 In the terminology of anthropological relativism, the viewpoint which an 'interstitial' character adopts, when analyzing a social group, might be said to hover between an 'emic' account and an 'etic' account (that is, between the perspective of an insider and of an outsider).

98 Miller discusses Hordern and geriatric lunacy in *Subsequent Performances*, p. 134.

99 Erving Goffman's works include Goffman, E. (1956), *The Presentation of the Self in Everyday Life* (Edinburgh: University of Edinburgh); Goffman, E. (1974), *Frame Analysis* (Cambridge, MA: Harvard University Press); and Goffman, E. (1963), *Behaviour in Public Places* (London: Collier-Macmillan).

100 As Miller points out, subintentional actions were incisively described by philosopher Brian O'Shaughnessy.

101 Miller went on to film Hordern as Lear not only for BBC TV's *Play of the Month* in 1975 (produced by Cedric Messina) but also in 1982 for the BBC's Shakespeare series – with Wilton moving on to play the older daughter, Regan. Hordern was replaced by Max von Sydow when the director restaged the play at the Old Vic in 1989, and Christopher Plummer took the title role in Miller's 2004 American production. Hordern's performances as Lear (and as the professor in *Whistle and I'll Come to You*) were scattered with what Goffman called 'escape cries', which are somewhere between noises and words ('Ouch', 'Oops', 'Tsk', 'Hmm' and so on).

102 Martin Esslin in *Plays and Players*, April 1970, and Anthony Curtis in the *Financial Times*, 11 February 1970, both greatly admired *King Lear*, played out, with spartan bleakness, against a black void.

103 Extract from *So That's the Way You Like It* as printed in *The Complete Beyond the Fringe*, pp. 108–10.

104 The Fringers appeared on *Tempo*, which was presented by Tynan, during their West End run. Miller scripted a successful history of cartoons for the programme and the foursome lampooned C. P. Snow.

105 Miller took issue with the sidelining of Iago and with Olivier's portrayal of Othello as a muscular African instead of a sophisticated, Renaissance, Mediterranean Arab.

106 Alec Guinness had initially been invited to play Shylock. However, he turned it down, saying he could not stand the play. He was, incidentally, married to Rachel Miller's cousin Merula Salaman, but it was Alan Bennett who got to work with him, becoming friends with the actor and his wife.

107 The NT board member was, allegedly, Harold Sebag Montefiore. This production's history is a puzzling collage of sometimes divergent memories, with various claimants to its groundbreaking ideas. Olivier claimed that it was he who shunned the hooked nose. See Olivier, L. (1986), *On Acting* (London: Weidenfeld & Nicolson), p. 119. In Joan Plowright's autobiography – Plowright, J. (2001), *And That's Not All* (London: Weidenfeld & Nicolson), p. 155 – she seems more in line with Miller's account, recalling her husband experimented with a nose. Another anomaly arises. Olivier says he thought of the late-Victorian setting, while Miller has said his original inspiration was hearing – or imagining hearing – 'The quality of mercy' speech delivered with a dry, impatiently legalistic emphasis ('The quality of mercy is not *strained*'). That conjured up Victorian judicial chambers, he has stated (Ralph Berry, p. 131). It is, then, curious that Tynan's memo to Miller, two weeks before opening night, suggested a reading of the line with 'strained' underlined. See *Kenneth Tynan: Letters*, p. 467, on that score. Sticklers for originality may further note that a nineteenth-century *Merchant of Venice* had been staged in Regent's Park the previous year.

108 Regarding the viciously stereotyped Jew in *The School for Scandal*, John Shrapnel explains that Miller deliberately did not tone down that character, instead highlighting Sheridan's eighteenth-century anti-Semitism.

109 Plowright, *And That's Not All*, p. 151, recalls Miller alluded to his grandfather. Olivier grafted on aspects of his own noble, Jewish-looking Uncle Sydney, as noted in *On Acting*, p. 124.

110 Arendt, H. (1958), *The Origins of Totalitarianism* (London: George Allen and Unwin). Miller additionally drew on Italo Svevo's novelistic portraits of Adriatic port life; on Henry James' *The Portrait of a Lady* (for the depiction of Portia); and on the homosexual bond between Oscar Wilde and Bosie (regarding the characters Antonio and Bassanio).

111 Miller discussed the term 'kind' (which also features in *King Lear*) with Hugh Hebert, *Guardian*, 10 March 1970. His *Merchant* preceded the publication of Empson, W. (1977), *The Structure of Complex Words* (London: Chatto & Windus), but Empson had been exploring the terrain for many years, in *Some Versions of Pastoral* and elsewhere.

112 D. A. N. Jones, *Listener*, 7 May 1970.

113 Thomas Quinn Curtiss, *International Herald Tribune*, 22 July 1970, noted the anti-father complex.

114 The kaddish was sung, for *The Merchant*, by the choirmaster of the synagogue in Abbey Road which Miller once attended.

115 Undated letter to Sacks, during rehearsals of *The Merchant*, March–April 1970.

116 J. C. Trewin, *Birmingham Post*, 30 April 1970, called it the event of the year. Gielgud sniped in a letter to Irene Worth, 20 June 1970, about Miller's 'flat-footed' *Tempest*, adding he could not face the gimmicks in *The Merchant*. This is recorded in Gielgud, J., edited by Mangan, R. (2004), *Gielgud's Letters* (London: Weidenfeld & Nicolson), p. 356.

117 The film was made by ATV and the video was produced by Artisan Entertainment, in their *Literary Masterpieces* series, 1973. It was shown on ITV, 10 February 1974, and on ABC in America where Jewish groups disagreed in their appraisals. Some protested at the play's anti-Semitism and others welcomed Miller's sympathetic concept.

118 Miller reportedly adjusted Sir Laurence's first idea that Shylock might suffer an attack of incontinence when punished and wretched in the court. Olivier's agonized, offstage scream as the blinded Oedipus – back in 1946 – had become legendary. That cry was driven by the actor envisaging the agony of an ermine with its tongue frozen on the ice by cunning Arctic trappers.

119 Olivier, L. (1982), *Confessions of an Actor* (London: Weidenfeld & Nicolson), p. 235–46. Plowright enjoyed working with Miller too, albeit with the sharp comment that, if he really wanted Portia at Belmont to be Jackie Kennedy with her jet set, then he should have cast the lady herself. See *And That's Not All*, pp. 153–4.

120 The stage fright is described in Anthony Holden's biography, Holden, A. (1988), *Olivier* (London: Weidenfeld & Nicolson), p. 411.

121 Olivier, *On Acting*, p. 120.

122 *On Acting*, p. 122, and Miller quoted, p. 71, in Haill, L. (ed.) (1985), *Olivier at Work: The National Theatre Years* (London: Nick Hern) – a book created in collaboration with Joan Plowright, Richard Olivier and the National Theatre.

Chapter 10: Early to Mid-Seventies

blew up a grainy corner of the frame, with Reed's hand clawing Mills' breast, after the actors and their director refused to film a close-up of that.

85 Those sketches, one called 'Jim's Yard' and the other set in the fictional boardroom of Gala Films, can be found in the Lord Chamberlain's copy of *Beyond the Fringe*'s Edinburgh script at the British Library. The film execs determine to market an arthouse delicacy under the title *Jungle of Lust*, in a double bill with a blue movie. 'Jim's Yard' (aka 'Jim's Inn'), where the dialogue is strewn with product placements, was mainly Cook's satiric conceit – allegedly purloined later, without his permission, by *That Was The Week That Was*.

86 Miller's general comment about working in the movie business is that it's 'like trying to weave a Gobelin tapestry in a gorilla's cage'. Noel Harrison (the actor-singer son of Rex) was in *Take a Girl Like You* and has spoken, in the *Independent on Sunday*, 20 February 2005, of turning his back on England because Miller was mean to him, not letting him go to sing his hit, 'Windmills of Your Mind', at the Oscars ceremony. The director says he was unhappy during this project but had no ill feelings towards Harrison.

87 Miller had been keen to proceed from this debut to film *Bleak House* by Dickens – one of his favourite novelists – but those hopes were dashed. He and Terry Southern (who scripted *Dr Strangelove*) had also intended, in the mid-Sixties, to collaborate on a big-screen adaptation of the dreamlike comic fantasy *Amerika* by Kafka, another of Miller's favourite writers.

88 The mock-historical 'Life of Dr. Jonathan' was, arguably, *Life and Times in NW1* given the *renovatio* treatment, in being superficially translated to a different (in this case, past) era.

89 The 'Dr. Jonathan' columns alluded to include 5 November 1971, 10 March 1972, 20 October 1972, and 3 November 1972.

90 Judging by *Peter Hall's Diaries*, *Private Eye*'s mockery was tormenting Miller during his NT troubles. He referred to the magazine as a major cause of his fraught behaviour in the 'breast-beating scene' of 11 December 1974.

91 I have taken this point from George Melly who made it so incisively in Fantoni, B. and Melly, G. (1980), *The Media Mob* (London: Collins), p. 70–1.

92 A surreal play by Peter Cook, recorded on the band Godley and Creme's concept album *Consequences* in 1977, is also said to caricature the *Beyond the Fringe* team, Miller included. At least, that is what is surmised in Hamilton, P., Gordon, P. and Kieran, D. (eds) (2006), *How Very Interesting: Peter Cook's Universe and All That Surrounds It* (London: Snowbooks), p. 496. Loose parallels may be drawn between the Fringers and four characters (all played by Cook who was, by then, booze-sodden). There is an alcoholic lawyer (Stapleton); a client with a northern, possibly Bennett-like accent who is seeking a divorce; a pianist neighbour with an E. L. Wistyish voice (Blint); and a second lawyer called Pepperman. Maybe glancing digs at Miller lie in the irascible Pepperman's claim that he is never quarrelsome and in his repeated exclamations about his Jewishness. ('I am Jewish and always have been. I'm not ashamed of it and I'm not proud of it. The whole thing is not an issue to me – it's irrelevant . . . The fact that I've been massacred personally for thousands of years is neither here nor there. So can we agree at least on one thing, namely not to waste our time discussing whether I'm Jewish or not?') That said, the whole script is pretty befuddled. Pepperman is fundamentally a caricatured lawyer (always hectoring about legal technicalities) and more of an ironically stereotyped Jew than specifically Millerish. Pepperman cries, during the absurd apocalyptic climax: 'I am to blame for everything. Everything that has ever gone wrong in the world is my fault. I did the crucifixion personally. I bought the nails . . . Hiroshima was my idea . . . I'm willing to atone for my sins' etc.

93 One might wonder if Miller really thought that Wells contributed to the Boswells columns (which got rolling just after the opening of *Danton's Death* in 1971). He used another Wells translation in 1974, for his NT *Figaro*. As for Cook, talking on Radio 4's *Profile* on 10 November 1978, he rebuffed the claim that *Private Eye* was anti-Semitic and said he did not provide information about Miller to the magazine.

94 The appreciative footnote seems to have been left out of Booker, C. (2005), *The Seven Basic Plots: Why We Tell Stories* (London: Continuum International).

95 *Private Eye*, 19 November 1971 and 12 January 1973.

96 Envy may have been in the mix when Cook, ten years later, impishly satirized Miller on TV's *Russell Harty Show*. That was in January 1983 when Miller was flying particularly high, having just been given an Olivier Award for his opera directing and a CBE in the New Year's Honours list. That month, too, there was to be a BBC TV *Omnibus* about his new *Magic Flute* (for Scottish Opera), a Channel 4 broadcast of his ENO *Rigoletto*, and – the very same day – a *Richard III* being aired for the ongoing *BBC Shakespeare Series* which he oversaw.

97 That passage from *Getting On* can be found in *Forty Years On and Other Plays*, p. 128. The speech has, on one level, an air of the autobiographical about it (as well as faint rhythmic echoes of Hamlet's 'this goodly frame . . . quintessence of dust' soliloquy). Of course, if Miller and Bennett conversed about ageing, the latter may have influenced the former's output as well as vice versa – another instance of dialogic memory. Either way, a notable similarity and simultaneity is evident, with *Getting On* opening in the West

End in October 1971 and Miller's *Vogue* diary piece coming out that same month. In BBC TV's *West Side Stories* (broadcast the following month), a curious trace of Hamlet's 'quintessence of dust' also lurked in Miller's depressive view of bodies in porn movies as he remarked, 'one begins to realize what a poor, punctured creature man is'.

98 *Desert Island Discs*, BBC Radio, 24 April 1971. Miller says, now, that he was just being provocative.

99 The unedited transcript of *West Side Stories* is in the BBC Written Archives.

100 *Ghosts* opened on 17 January 1974. *The Seagull* and *Hamlet* followed on 31 January and 14 March.

101 Alan Strachan, in particular, remembers *Ghosts* being riveting. The critics were divided. Harold Hobson, on this occasion, loved Miller's damped-down naturalism (*Sunday Times*, 20 January 1974) though Billington felt deprived of Ibsen's Romantic, heightened drama (*Guardian*, 18 January 1974).

102 Not medically satisfied with Ibsen's portrayal of inherited syphilis, Miller additionally suggested that Eyre's Oswald was akin to Karl Abraham's case study of hysterical blindness. There the son of a philandering father dreamed about a blinding sun, and psychosomatically blinded himself to be free of the oppressive presence of his radiantly successful competitor.

103 I am indebted here to Peter Eyre's review of *Subsequent Performances* in the *Spectator*, 10 May 1986, where he recalled *Ghosts*. The opera singer Valerie Masterson similarly noted Miller's skill in discovering how to marry a performer's personal traits to their stage character. Interviewed in *Classical Music*, 25 November 1978, she remarked that he must have watched her very closely, having cast her as the Countess in his ENO *Marriage of Figaro*, because he found an interpretation of the role that cleaved to her natural mien and vocal style.

104 *Sunday Times*, 24th March 1974, with preceding criticisms from the *Guardian* and *Daily Telegraph* on 20th March.

105 Besides Wardle, who gave Miller great praise in *The Times*, 1 February 1974, those cheering *Family Romances* included Peter Hepple in the *Stage*, 14 February 1974, and Billington, *Guardian*, 17 April 1974.

106 The title *Bed Tricks* referred to the folktale convention where an expected lover is replaced cunningly by another. *All's Well That Ends Well* and *Measure for Measure* opened in July and August 1975. Miller staged *The Importance* earlier, right after leaving the NT, in March 1975. *She Would If She Could* came in April 1979, when Alan Strachan was AD.

107 Nicola Pagett warmly remembers Miller suggesting part-swapping when she was Masha in *The Seagull*.

108 It was put out that Courtenay was unwell, leading to the teasing *Evening Standard* query, 'Isn't there a doctor in the house?', 6 April 1979. Ursula Jones stood in, at very short notice. *She Would* was, incidentally, another example of Miller's liking for trompe l'oeils, with Bernard Culshaw designing an ingeniously deceptive folding set based on an antique Dutch cabinet.

109 According to the *Daily Mail*, 30 August 1995, Eddington regarded *She Would* as a disaster, saying that Miller had seemingly not read the play in detail and was so busy that he could not be there for Ursula Jones or the first night.

110 Jack Tinker hated this Bracknell, *Daily Mail*, 21 March 1975. John Gielgud was critical once again, condemning Handl in his missive to Irene Worth, 6 November 1979. See *Gielgud's Letters*, p. 423. Martin Hoyle in *Time Out*, 11–18 September 1996, recorded Charlotte Cornwell (who played Cecily) saying that the cast struggled not to laugh at Handl's accent in this 'near-improvised' production. Still, de Jongh's praise appeared in the *Guardian*, 21 March 1975, and Morley's in *Punch*, 2 April 1975. Morley added that he saw Handl as the inheritor of some huge clothing emporium, visiting outlying relatives – which sounds a bit like one of Miller's factory-owning aunts from Karlstad. Actually, Miller had wanted Handl to play Bracknell with a trace of East End cockney, like a Gaiety Girl who had married an aristocrat. In other words, he had been planning a radical reading even if it was not the emergency Mittel-European one that the reviewers, understandably, took to be his big idea.

111 Billington, in the *Guardian*, was not overwhelmed but did find *All's Well* oddly compelling with its dry, cool clarity. The *Daily Telegraph*, also on 11 August 1975 and along with other papers, disliked the acting, the 'amateur' blocking and the modern conversational style combined with period costumes. The actor David Horovitch thought the characters he played for Miller, including Bertram, should have been much nicer. He complained that Miller appeared to be a cynical misanthrope. That is in Romain, *A Profile*, p. 171. The idea of coeval school chums was unusual, Parolles often being played older. As with Lear and the Fool, Miller again adjusted the presumed generational relations between characters.

112 Miller discusses tuitional heroines in *Subsequent Performances*, pp. 141–5. Penelope Wilton played Helena at Greenwich Theatre.

113 Perhaps remembering the cricket bat supplied to him by John Barton in *Volpone* at Cambridge, Miller has armed some of his actors with character-defining props, not least Isabella's handbag in *Measure for Measure* and Shylock's attaché case in *The Merchant*, which Olivier clicked open and shut meticulously in the chilling trial scene.

114 *Observer*, 18 August 1975, *Financial Times* and *Daily Telegraph*, 14 August 1975 were very positive.

115 *Evening Standard*, 14 August 1975.

116 John Shrapnel described the cast as a family in Romain, *A Profile*, p. 129.

117 *Three Sisters* began at the Yvonne Arnaud Theatre, Guildford, and toured the UK. Its West End opening was at the Cambridge Theatre, co-produced by Duncan Wheldon, on 23 June 1976.

118 Miller's comments appeared in the *Guardian*, 9 July 1976.

119 In most productions, Chebutykin just washes his hands or splashes his face with water.

120 I have drawn here on Milton Shulman in the *Evening Standard*, Billington in the *Guardian*, Irving Wardle in *The Times*, B. A. Young in the *Financial Times*, all 24 June 1976, plus the *Observer*, 27 June.

121 The NT comment was from Benedict Nightingale, *New Statesman*, 2 July 1976. Only one or two publications dissented, such as the *Tatler*, August 1976, saying the astringent realism was unsympathetic. Peter Eyre, who played Tusenbach, described the production as definitive in Tania Alexander's obituary, *Independent*, 11 December 2004. Incidentally, Miller's production of Chekhov's *The Cherry Orchard* – strangely mentioned in *Subsequent Performances*, p. 164 – really is a legend. He had not staged it when the book was published, though he was to direct it years later, in 2007.

122 The Olivier Awards (initially called the Society of West End Theatre Awards) were inaugurated in 1976, with Wedgwood urns for trophies. Miller was also named Best Director by *Plays and Players* magazine that year. Suzman won an *Evening Standard* Best Actress Award.

123 These are shamelessly scrunched statistics. Miller staged all his Old Vic productions in 24 months, though he was officially AD from January 1988 into 1990. I have made so bold as to count neither *Candide* at the Old Vic nor *The Beggar's Opera* at Wilton's Music Hall. They might be termed music theatre, but they were staged in collaboration with opera companies. Finally, if one were to count Miller's *Long Day's Journey into Night*, one would need all the fingers on Anne Boleyn's hand, but that show was a transfer from Broadway.

124 These negative and positive comments are from a variety of articles including *New Statesman*, 30 November 1973 and 19 July 1974; *The Times*, 25 May 1973; *Guardian*, 17 April 1974; *Daily Express*, 12 May 1972, and *Punch*, 24 June 1970.

125 Rachel quoted in *People*, 26 March 1979.

126 This was recorded in *The Times*, 20 January 1976. One might compare this to the satirist Alexander Pope who exacted bitter verbal revenges on those who slated him, though mostly in verse.

127 *Evening Standard*, 16 May 1975, on venom. The 'shrieking hatred' quotation comes from his comments on BBC TV's *Arena*, 9 November 1977.

128 Miller on testosterone and egos, *Independent*, 14 September 1998.

129 These comments have accumulated over the years, cropping up in articles including the *Guardian*, 13 March 1987; *Telegraph*, 14 June 1991; *The Times*, 15 June 1991; *Independent*, 12 February 1993, and in interviews with the author.

130 Maurice Wigan, *Sunday Times*, 12 May 1968.

Chapter 11: Mid-Seventies Onwards

1 Miller, quoted in the *New York World Journal Tribune*, 15 January 1967.

2 *Noye's Fludde* was at the Roundhouse, 21–23 December 1972. The actor Michael Williams, who lived locally, played God in avuncular mode. The conductor was John Lubbock, who had founded the Orchestra of St John's Smith Square in 1967.

3 *Arden Must Die*, Sadler's Wells, 17–19 April 1974, was also broadcast on BBC Radio 3.

4 Miller landed the job thanks to Stephen Wright (formerly of the OCSC) who was, by that time, running a music agency. The two were to become client and agent, and they remained so for years with Wright as the head of IMG Artists. The NOC was run by Jeremy Caulton, Lord Harewood's ENO assistant, who knew Wright.

5 Associates recall that Miller often managed to rise above his worries with quick-witted jokes. In the technical rehearsal, when his assistant suggested the lighting looked 'a bit Terry Hands', he replied, quick as a flash, 'Ah, but Terry Hands makes light work.'
  Nevertheless, jangled by Goehr's avant-gardism, he would subsequently work with pre-Sixties scores: Britten's from the Fifties, Weill's from the Thirties, Janáček's from the Twenties, and mainly earlier classics. Even if you include Sondheim's *Candide* among his opera productions, that was written in the Fifties, albeit with 1970s alterations.

6 The opera's premiere in West Germany in the late 1960s had been particularly polemical because of Goehr and his librettist's near-Brechtian parody of a Nazi song and because of a (subsequently cut) epilogue which turned aggressively on the audience. Miller had changed the Tudor setting to a more Dickensian one, seeing parallels with the sinister Kent marshes of *Great Expectations*. Dexter took great exception to that.

7 *The Cunning Little Vixen* was to open in mid-1975.

8 Peter Cook on Radio 4's *Profile*, 10 November 1978. Miller continues to compare himself, as an opera director, to a Grand Prix pit mechanic who works under the car but never bothers to watch the race.

9 Michael Blakemore attended one of these home concerts, and Rachel still participates in occasional

381

public concerts, playing the cello at Conway Hall.

10 Sarah's enthusiasm for classical concerts was encouraged by Betty's older sister, Dorothy. Consequently, by the mid-Fifties she was going to the Festival Hall two or three times a week. Miller apparently accompanied her once or twice.

11 The *Pauline*, June 1953, 62, welcomed Miller's presentation. Michael Bacharach was treasurer of the Gramophone Society. According to Korn, Miller had become the most informed in their gang regarding jazz, approaching it systematically, reading voraciously and amassing 78s of Louis Armstrong, Wild Bill Davison and many more. Miller won praise in the *Pauline*, March 1953, 15, for another 'very interesting' Gramophone Society lecture on the origins of, and developments in jazz.

12 Rory Bremner, in the *Sunday Telegraph*, 29 October 2006, said that his instinct for mimicry was 'the product of a musical ear', adding that he lost the ability to read music because playing by ear came so naturally.

13 'Dance of the Blessed Spirits' was still haunting Miller four decades on, floating into his *Camera Obscura* at the Almeida in 2002.

14 In that respect, Miller had introduced structuralist comparisons even before his *Family Romances* trilogy.

15 Ronald Pickup spoke of Saint-Just's semitones in Romain, *A Profile*, p. 148, and Miller discussed the Schoenberg structuring in *Quarto*, September 1980. In *The Times*, 4 March 1967, he talked about Robert Lowell's plays being opera libretti without the music, with stylistically varied arias and recitative.

16 The *Daily Telegraph* and *Sunday Times* reviews, 18 and 21 April 1974 respectively, agreed on that. Miller certainly appreciates the moment, in rehearsals, when the full orchestra first turns up with the conductor, replacing the piano-playing répétiteur. He compares the thrilling surge of power to being the co-pilot of a 747 at take-off.

17 The designer, Bernard Culshaw, says there was an inevitably steep learning curve, adding humorously that Miller may have requested an extra balustrade on the set's wooden jetties to fence the chorus in while he worked out what on earth to do with them.

18 A strip cartoon was the original inspiration for Janáček's tale of the vixen's capture and escape, after which she is tragically shot but leaves cubs behind to continue the life cycle.

19 The production, which opened on 22 May 1975, was designed by Vercoe and Robertson from the Nottingham Playhouse. The animals' colourful vintage folk costumes and *ancien régime* military uniforms contrasted with the human characters' monochrome clothes of the 1920s (the opera's composition date).

20 Patrick Carnegy, writing delightedly in the *Times Educational Supplement*, 30 May 1975, saw the dragoon pun and Miller's wealth of sexual references, 'some of it positively Krafft-Ebing'.

21 Miller seems to have been going through a particularly marked phase of changing his mind on the hoof, for Lubbock jovially recalls that, with *Noye's Fludde*, there was a new concept every week, which left some under-tens discombobulated.

22 The staging for Opera Australia (or Australian Opera as it was then known) opened at Melbourne's Princess Theatre, 17 March 1976, with a transfer to Sydney Opera House in June. The Frankfurt production was in late 1977. Some Britons were becoming more open to the idea of working in continental Europe, especially since the UK had joined the Common Market in 1973. However, the Labour government in the mid-Seventies wavered about EEC membership and the costly Channel Tunnel was put on hold, so the nation's island mentality was not greatly eroded.

23 This was later, in the 1990s. Graham Vick was chosen, instead, to stage *Ermione*.

24 Platt founded Kent Opera in 1969. He had not previously met Miller though he had, years before, taken one of his children for consultations with Emanuel. Initially doubting that the former comic could add more strings to his bow, Platt was completely won over at their first meeting, declaring: 'To turn down that amount of intelligence would be crazy, if not criminal.'

25 Miller only skipped 1978, the year of *The Body in Question*. Norrington additionally explains that their directing and conducting roles merged on occasion as each made suggestions about the musical phrasing and the staging, and as he played the nursemaid, nagging his colleague until even the trickiest bits were polished.

26 *Onegin* opened in September 1977 and *Falstaff* toured to Bath in November 1980.

27 Enid Hartle (who played Mistress Quickly) recollected that evening in Norman Platt's 2001 memoir, *Making Music* (Ashford: Pembles Publications). Jonathan Summers (who was a searingly jealous Ford) spoke to Romain for *A Profile*, p. 196.

28 Miller was not reverential about all the musicians who returned to original instruments and were nicknamed 'vegetarians'. He referred to Christopher Hogwood's Academy of Ancient Music as the Academy of Ancient Muesli. That is according to a blog by Brian Dickie, general director of Chicago Opera Theatre, on briandickie.typepad.com.

29 It should be noted, Miller does not recreate 'museum piece' productions with absolute academic rigour, sometimes giving himself the leeway of a decade or two regarding period settings. Rather than looking back to Rococo styles, his neoclassical *Così* pointed forward from 1790, with what became known as

empire-line dresses. This was partly because he saw parallels with *Mansfield Park* (where Jane Austen's characters also discover themselves via disguises).

30 Some critics, not least Stanley Sadie in *The Times*, 8 November 1974, found the production too sombre and wanted more of an opera buffa, though others appreciated Miller's style.

31 In his much later *Così*, for the Royal Opera House, Miller was to make this scene more of a medical farce in modern dress. Mesmer's methods had been markedly criticized and Mozart had lost touch with him by the time he wrote *Così*.

32 Kent Opera's *Così* started touring three months after Miller's NT *Figaro*, opening at Eastbourne's Congress Theatre, 6 November 1974.

33 Miller has staged eight of Mozart's operatic works, revisiting several of those repeatedly.

34 Miller on Mozart arias in the *Observer*, 21 November 1999. These comments come with the rationalist's proviso that there can be 'soulfulness' without the existence of a soul.

35 The subcategories of 'speech acts' are many and various but include 'indirect' and 'sublocutionary speech acts'. Miller alluded to Searle's theories, in relation to opera, on *The Lebrecht Interview*, BBC Radio 3, 31 August 2009.

36 *L'Orfeo* opened at Bath's Theatre Royal on 3 June 1976 and was revived in 1977, with a London airing at the Collegiate in Camden that March.

37 Miller's *L'Orfeo*, evoking *A Dance to the Music of Time*, was comparable with his OCSC *Twelfth Night*, regarding the latter's allusion to Botticelli's *Primavera* Graces. That said, his craft was maturing. Instead of obstructing the stage with geometric forms this time round, Miller had Poussin-inspired backdrops painted on smoothly revolving periactoids (three-sided columns) for *L'Orfeo*.

38 Rosalind Plowright recalled working on *L'Orfeo* in Romain, *A Profile*, p. 191. Sue Lefton helped choreograph the dances.

39 This was, one might argue, the seventeenth-century's equivalent of structuralism, looking for deep parallels. Poussin and his contemporaries' beliefs were discussed at length in 1995 in Richard Beresford's *A Dance to the Music of Time by Nicolas Poussin* (London: Trustees of the Wallace Collection). Miller adds that Monteverdi and Poussin also shared the same philosophy, both adhering to Stoicism.

One reference book much used in the *L'Orfeo* rehearsals was Anthony Blunt's catalogue raisonné of Poussin's drawings (or his 'catalogue traisonné' as Miller dubbed it after the author was exposed as a spy in 1979).

40 *Musical Opinion* (reviewing the revival at Sadler's Wells, July 1981) described this as the barest ever set for *Così*. The narrow stage echoed the frieze-like foreshortened perspectives of neoclassical painters such as Jacques-Louis David, and Miller pays tribute to the Apostle Francis Haskell for having introduced him to Robert Rosenblum's *Transformations in Late Eighteenth Century Art* and Heinrich Wölfflin's *Principles of Art History* and other writings about the formal organization of space in pictures. Sadly, Haskell had not remained a close friend because, apparently, he scorned the director's more radical Shakespeare productions as unorthodox violations.

41 Miller made Lensky look rather like Schubert, noting that his aria had a touch of that composer's *Die Winterreise* about it.

42 Peter Knapp, who played Onegin, made the small-screen point when talking on *Music Now*, BBC Radio, 18 November 1976. The continuum from theatre to opera was encapsulated by the recurrence of one tiny bit of detailing, as follows. Critics had been struck by Miller's behaviourally authentic yawning fit in *Beyond the Fringe*, when he played a prisoner suddenly facing execution. That yawn had resurfaced, becoming a directorial leitmotif in his *Measure for Measure* and in *Onegin* when Brian Burrows' Lensky was terrified by the prospective duel. The original source of this was, perhaps, Miller's own experience back at Cambridge, noticing the anatomy students' nervous yawns when faced with corpses.

43 *La Traviata* opened on 21 August 1979. As well as seeing certain parallels with Flaubert's *L'Education Sentimentale* (Violetta's beloved, Alfredo, being a provincial in Paris, like Frédéric Moreau), Miller based his staging of Verdi's classic on Nadar's daguerreotypes, with muted brown-black costumes. He declared in *The Times*, 22 November 1978, that his approach was antithetical to the 'flamboyant vulgarity' of Zeffirelli's lavish film version which resembled, he said, 'a mixture of a party at George Weidenfeld's and a reception at the British Embassy in 1968.'

44 Miller acknowledges that this deathbed scene was also informed by his own domestic experience of seeing one of his children, delirious from tonsillitis, unreachable in a paroxysm of distress and panic.

45 This lunch party was hosted by Tania Alexander. Miller adds that Berlin, though knowing nothing of seventeenth-century interiors, let it be known that he considered it vulgar to have a bed on stage in *Falstaff*.

46 Examples of Sutcliffe's criticisms include *Guardian*, 13 November 1979 (on *La Traviata*), 6 November 1980 (on *Falstaff*), and 30 October 1982 (on *Fidelio*).

47 Michael Ratcliffe made the 'cocked hat' comparison in Ratcliffe, M. (ed.) (1983), *Kent Opera in Progress* (Ashford: Kent Opera), pp. 51–7.

48 *Kaleidoscope*, 22 August 1979; *Musical Opinion*, February 1980; *Music and Musicians*, November

1979; *Guardian* and *Edinburgh Evening News*, both 23 August 1979, commented on this.

49 Milnes wrote for various publications including *The Times*, the *Spectator* and *Harpers & Queen* where, in April 1974, he said he was apoplectic about *Cosi*. He referred to Miller's flowering in *Kent Opera in Progress*, p. 25.

50 *Rigoletto* opened at Eastbourne on 4 November 1975.

51 I am indebted here not just to Milnes but also to the critic Alastair Macauley for his memories of the production's almost Dickensian darkness.

52 It was *La Traviata* which played at the Edinburgh International Festival.

53 Miller partly drew on Goya because he was similar to Beethoven in extolling enlightenment and liberty. Bernard Culshaw and the lighting designer Nick Chelton (who says that Miller really taught him to scrutinize paintings) worked with layered gauzes to create the chiaroscuro and ghostly effects of aquatint.

Staging an Opera, the documentary featuring *Fidelio*, was made by TVS in 1982 and shown during April and May 1983. A BBC TV documentary featuring *L'Orfeo* was broadcast on 12 January 1979. So, these Kent Opera programmes piggybacked as *The Body in Question* (from November 1978) upped Miller's profile on television.

54 Patrick Carnegy greatly appreciated *Making an Opera* in the *Times Educational Supplement*, 8 April 1983. Other memorable programmes have included Thames TV's record of Miller's ENO *Mikado* rehearsals in 1986 and the six-part series of workshops, *Opera Works*, made by Patrick Uden in 1997 for BBC2 (as discussed in Chapter 15).

55 *The Times*, 18 June 2001, referred to its closure in those terms. A more recent resurrection of the company as New Kent Opera did not last.

56 A transcript of Miller's speech was very kindly supplied, with much other Kent Opera material, by Norman and Johanna Platt.

57 Miller was on the arts programme *Line Up* every year in the late Sixties, as well as, for instance, on *Canvas* in 1970 and *Kaleidoscope* (talking about *Arden Must Die*) in 1974. He was on *Read All About It* in 1975 and featured in both *Arena* and *Omnibus* in 1976. Besides his chats with Michael Parkinson in 1972, 1975 and 1977, he was a guest on *Just a Nimmo* in 1976 and *André Previn Meets* the following year (alongside his 1971 *Desert Island Discs* and LWT's *Russell Harty Show* appearance in 1973). Discussion shows included *The Question Why* as well as *Any Questions?*, both in 1969, plus the radio phone-in *Whatever You Think* in 1972. *Call My Bluff* had him on (pun intended) in 1977, after *Quote . . . Unquote* and the televising of *A Poke in the Eye with a Sharp Stick*, both 1976.

58 Miller's private notebook, 13 April 1962. The BBC TV children's series *Animal Magic* was first aired that very same day. Miller's old UCH friend Léon Ellis recalls that the two of them used to wander around the zoo on Sunday mornings (when the place was open early to academic scientists), and Miller would fantasize comically about the creatures and keepers.

59 *The Zoo in Winter*, directed by Patrick Garland, was first shown in 1969 then featured in the BBC's anniversary broadcast, *Forty Years*, in August 1976, though it was, of course, David Attenborough who would present the naturalist's megaseries *Life on Earth* in 1979.

60 *Charles Darwin Lived Here*, BBC TV, June 1973.

61 Sabbagh, quoted in America's *Saturday Review*, September 1980 (when *The Body in Question* was to be broadcast by PBS in association with KCET of Los Angeles).

62 *The Body in Question* was first transmitted on BBC2, in weekly instalments, from 6 November 1978.

63 BBC Enterprises described the programmes as neither simply a history of medicine nor a medical partwork, but a non-chronological series of essays on chosen medical topics with Miller looking at each from different perspectives. I am grateful to Patrick Uden for his files of background material on the series.

64 The co-producing TV companies, besides America's PBS/KCET, were ABC in Australia and Canada's CBC and OECA.

65 Postcard to the BBC radio producer Hallam Tennyson, dated 2 May 1977, BBC Written Archives. In his *Evening Standard* feature of 24 November 1999, Andrew Billen recalled working on the magazine serialization of the 1991 BBC TV series *Madness* and being warned, by the producer Udi Eichler, that Miller was 'all but incapable of committing his thoughts to paper'.

66 The crisis meeting was 4 March 1977.

67 Uden had directed for *Tomorrow's World* but had not come up through the normal training procedures where directors started as researchers.

68 In Miller's later BBC TV series *A Brief History of Disbelief*, the producer Richard Denton simply filmed interviews in the presenter's home with, for example, Richard Dawkins chatting about godlessness at the kitchen table. The *Body in Question* set was also, perhaps, a televisual variation on Frances Yates' Theatre of Memory. Miller said it was strewn with the furniture of his imagination to reflect how the brain's stockpiled images can seem half-forgotten, can be glimpsed (as it were) over one's mind's shoulder, then suddenly gain striking new relevance. It was a good plan to make Miller feel completely at home as the filming of the series took months on end, an unheard of amount of time in the studios, says Uden.

69 Miller was thinking associatively when wearing his arts hat too (drawing parallels between Monterverdi and Poussin, or finding an analogy for Rigoletto's scenario in 1950s Little Italy). However, this needs to be distinguished from Edward de Bono's creed of 'lateral thinking', popularized in the 1970s, anti-logical and now used for managerial problem-solving.

70 BBC technicians were on strike during April 1977. Uden recruited his cameraman, Ken Lowe, and started test-shooting in May. Besides becoming good buddies with the electricians, Miller recalls madly befriending Charles Darwin in the BBC canteen. A biodrama was being filmed in another studio, therefore the look-alike actor playing the august evolutionist was frequently to be seen, in full Victorian dress and side-whiskers, queuing for chips. 'So,' Miller exclaims, 'I would be nudging up the line, just to be closer to Charles Darwin and I started to hero-worship this man! I became so enthused, I gave him a very early edition of *The Origin of the Species*. Then a few months later, I bumped into him again and asked him how he'd got on with it. And he said: "I couldn't understand a *word* of it, love!"' The admired serial was *The Voyage of Charles Darwin* starring Malcolm Stoddard.

71 Von Hagens' autopsy programme was shown on Channel 4 in 2002, with the Independent Television Commission being brought into assess if it had broken broadcasting rules.

72 Richard Denton, when working on Miller's 1991 BBC series, *Madness*, had a farcical tussle and developed a different solution, as he humorously recalls:

Jonathan would drive you insane! You would record a conversation and transcribe it, then he would read a new book and change his mind. So we would go backwards and forwards, backwards and forwards . . . But if you just kept focused on corralling him, you would get wonderful stuff . . . I would transcribe, edit, restructure it and take it back to him, then he would spot the words I'd put in, so you do get very good at writing ersatz Miller . . . He has a way of shackling together unlikely adjectives and nouns that's very clever.

73 Miller's book *The Body in Question* in fact expanded on the TV script and it was published just before the series began in 1978, by Jonathan Cape (hence Susannah Clapp's professional help). It was published, in North America by Random House, and they recently remarketed it as an ebook in 2011. In the UK, the series was on the front of the *Radio Times*, 4–10 November 1978, with the TV script additionally serialized in the *Listener*. It was referred to as a 'blockbuster' series by the press. The first programme was watched by 3.7 million viewers (logged as 7.2 per cent of the UK public), and the final post-mortem by 2.8 million.

74 *The Times*, 6 November 1978, made the point about Monday nights. The phrase 'Dissector-General' appeared in Richard Last's *Daily Telegraph* TV column for that week. Marc's cartoons in *The Times* included – on 15 November 1978 – a ward round with a consultant opining: 'Queasiness, hypochondria? The first question, gentlemen, is has he been watching Dr Miller?' The series was immortalized in the mock-nursery rhyme by Roger Woddis, *Radio Times*, 10 February 1979: 'There was a Doctor Miller once/Who lectured on TV./ He probed our hearts and other parts/ Nice people never see.'

75 Clive James in the *Observer*, 12 November 1978, suggested that Miller's mind flitted, but he praised the presenter's energetic brilliance too. J. G. Ballard in the *New Statesman*, 20 October, admitted he was probably envious while growling, surely unfairly, that *The Body in Question* did not contain one arresting idea, and that Miller just mimicked originality. Meanwhile, one exceptionally philistine TV listing reduced the presenter's philosophical stance to '*Je pense donc je suis ponce*', *Observer*, 28 January 1979.

76 Positive specialist reviews from Michael O'Donnell in the *New Scientist*, 16 November 1978, and Mendel, *Observer*, 19 November.

77 The 'lovely spleen' salutation was recorded by the *Evening Standard*, 10 November 1978.

78 Uden says that Fisher Dilke, working on the series, 'really went into orbit' devising illuminating metaphors and illustrative adventures with Miller.

79 Though not life-threatening, there was another alarming moment when the TV crew's plane was confiscated by the Sudanese government. This was when they were filming witch doctors, to contrast their practices with those of British GPs.

80 Miller dislikes the term 'body language' because, he says, it wrongly implies every movement has a specific meaning.

81 Surprisingly, Uden reveals the one thing that Miller did not like was having his hands filmed, holding something, in close-up. This was because he had some malformed fingernails.

82 Clive James, as above, pointed out that Miller's physicality made him a terrific proponent for his own anti-spiritual argument: namely, that *being embodied* is the only way we have of *being*.

83 Although Miller says he has not read his father's books, other shared ideas arise. For example, in *Types of Mind and Body*, p. 14, Emanuel underlined that 'Mind divorced from Body is as incomprehensible as Body divorced from Mind'. Emanuel's obituary in *The Lancet*, 8 August 1970, strikingly said his skill as an enthusiastic teacher tied in with his use of illuminating metaphors.

84 Miller illustrated this issue with the anamorphic diagram of the body which was charted by the neurologist W. G. Penfield on corresponding surface-areas of the brain.

85 The Mesmer sketch was created by Lindsay Kemp. There was also a satirical skit with a pompously

tetchy consultant. This related to Miller's Mannoni-influenced contention that medics could be imperious and even neo-colonial, treating a patient's body as if it were *their* property.

86 *Sunday Times*, 9 November 1979. The TV critics' award was given in March 1979.

87 William became director of talent and brand ventures for BBC Worldwide in August 2009.

88 The ENO *Marriage of Figaro* opened on 23 November 1978. LWT's *South Bank Show*, entitled *Anatomy of an Opera*, was aired on 17 December 1978.

Chapter 12: On into the Eighties

1 For *Figaro*, Miller drew on the artworks of Jacques-Louis David and *les petits maîtres* of the 1780s. Making the setting more French than Spanish, he based the Count's ancestral pile on a small chateau, with shabby grandeur, which he and Rachel had visited in the Loire. A hall of mirrors featured along with a sequence of rooms which gradually led outwards, with ever more windows, to the garden. His cast and production team also watched *Barry Lyndon* because Miller admired the painterly candlelit decadence of this period movie, made by his old associate Stanley Kubrick. As an earl with a job, the ENO's Lord Harewood obviously didn't take the onstage portrayal of idling aristocrats personally.

2 Miller touched on the Shakespearean and Chekhovian spirit of Mozart when talking on BBC Radio's *Kaleidoscope*, 3 November 1978.

3 Masterson has said that, while her character was melancholic, she herself was extremely happy working with Miller on *Figaro*. An internal ENO memo from Lord Harewood to the music director Sir Charles Groves, dated 18 July 1978, indicates some objections had been raised about bringing the Countess' children into the piece. *The Times*, 22 November 1979, records Miller explaining that the children elaborated on the opera's theme of cycles and generations.

4 The director's request was mentioned in staff correspondence, sent from Caroline Loeb to Edmund Tracey on 25 November 1976, now preserved in the ENO's archives. The director also discussed Cherubino on *The South Bank Show* and in *Classical Music*, 25 November 1978.

5 The tune of Figaro's aria 'Non più andrai' (meaning 'No more gallivanting') is played, ironically, to entertain Don Giovanni during the supper which turns out to be his last.

6 *Daily Telegraph*, 19 October 1979. The critic Peter Stadlen was, here, recalling the 1978 premiere, saying some controversial eccentricities were toned down in the revival.

7 This disparity was, indeed, discussed in the *Guardian*, 29 July 1983.

8 That last comment, regarding the 'failed version', actually applies to audience responses to classic plays as well as to operas. It comes from Miller's private notebooks of 1986, at which point he was anticipating sniffy reviews of his production of *Long Day's Journey into Night*.

9 *Sunday Times*, 26 November 1978, and Alan Blyth, *Daily Telegraph*, 9 April 1979.

10 *The Times* waved the production a fond goodbye on 5 May 1990, declaring it was 'going down fighting'. There had been some disagreement about certain revivals, executed by staff directors in Miller's absence. The *Observer* and *Sunday Telegraph* were both markedly negative in their reviews of 7 September 1986.

11 The *Evening News*, 26 October 1979, reported that Miller seemed obsessed. By having the ghosts talking privately to each other, Britten certainly made it hard not to regard them as real.

12 The *Financial Times*, 10 March 1989, said that Miller did not impose an interpretation and this neutrality was the production's strength.

13 The projected images were inspired by Fox Talbot's vintage photographs and pictured Ashridge Park in Hertfordshire. Some critics (such as Desmond Shawe-Taylor, *Sunday Times*, 18 November 1979) mocked the immense scale and airport-style, sliding glass doors of the mansion. Others (including Stephen Walsh, *Observer*, 11 November 1979) noted that Miller maintained all the piece's claustrophobic intimacy, against the odds, in the spacious Coliseum.

14 Macdonald Critchley's paper on 'the sense of a presence', (previously mentioned in connection with the reclusive professor in *Whistle and I'll Come to You*) has further reverberations here. One case which Critchley cited concerned a VIP's lonely secretary, said to be repressing desires, who imagined she was attended by a handsome cavalier, like a glistening shadow. Another patient, prone to epileptic seizures, sensed that someone or something terrifyingly evil was nearby. Betty Miller's work on spiritualism and Elizabeth Barrett Browning may have informed her son's approach as well, Barrett Browning having been categorized as a neurasthenic.

15 Rosalind Plowright played the governess first, in 1980, winning an Olivier Award for her performance. Gomez had previously played the part for the English Opera Group.

16 Joseph Losey's award-winning film of *The Go-Between* had been released in 1970, adapted by Pinter from L. P. Hartley's novel.

17 The suggestive games and a malign streak in the children were mentioned by Stephen Walsh, as above. Pears' letter cannot be found, but it is thought to be preserved among Lord Harewood's papers.

18 This quotation comes from Rodney Milnes' interview with Miller, in the magazine *Opera*, February 1994.

19 *The Turn of the Screw* continued to be revived at the Coliseum until 1993. Miller's production formed

part of the English National Opera's repertoire in their US tour of 1984 (along with his *Rigoletto*). In 1990, when the ENO became the first major foreign opera company to tour the Soviet Union, it was one of the three productions showcased there. It also transferred to LA Opera where it was described – retrospectively, two decades on, in the *LA Times* of 13 March 2011 – as having been 'nightmarishly unnerving' and having shown the characters at their worst (in contrast to an apparently antiseptic, new production by Jonathan Kent).

20 Recorded by Michael Ratcliffe, *Kent Opera in Progress*, p. 55.

21 On one recent occasion, a malfunctioning iPod caused last-minute panic as Miller was due to board a plane for a foreign engagement.

22 Hytner was Miller's assistant on *Arabella*.

23 *Arabella* opened on 16 October 1980 and was revived in 1984. Miller had at least improved on the Coliseum's money-saving idea of borrowing an old set from the Royal Opera House. He brought in his designer Patrick Robertson to double the ballroom's splendour using low-budget mirrors together with a spinning staircase.

24 Miller admires Janáček as well for musically capturing conversational rhythms and intonations.

25 In the ENO's archive, a note from Edmund Tracey to Lord Harewood, 21 February 1979, indicates the post of associate director had been offered to Miller then. A three-year contract was agreed by April 1979.

26 John Higgins retrospectively referred to this great success in *The Times*, 25 February 1984. Rodney Milnes called it a triumph in almost every way in *What's On*, 2 October 1981. Minor critical objections related to the single set (compared unflatteringly to Habitat stripped pine) and to some awkward blocking, especially regarding the chorus.

27 The waving of banknotes was reported in *Opera*, December 1981. *Otello* was broadcast on BBC Radio 3 on 9 October 1981, having opened on 24 September. It was revived, with the ageing Craig, in 1982 and 1983. This was recorded and released on CD by Chandos, 2001.

28 The *Spectator*, 3 October 1981, and other reviews observed how Iago acted as if he were conducting a clinical experiment. That invites comparison with the milder proto-psychoanalytic experiments of Don Alfonso in Miller's *Così* for Kent Opera. While Howlett was horribly plausible, Miller could only suspend his incredulity at the pairing of the pint-sized Craig with the graciously towering Rosalind Plowright by thinking of Sophia Loren's marriage to Carlo Ponti.

29 This series is known by various names including *The BBC Television Shakespeare*.

30 The oeuvre, calculated at 37 plays, excluded *Two Noble Kinsmen* and other texts considered questionable collaborations.

31 Messina alluded to the greatest BBC project ever undertaken in his preface to Shakespeare, W. (1978), *As You Like It: The BBC TV Shakespeare* (New York, NY: Mayflower Books). Not all the productions made under Messina were dull, with acclaim was granted to the series' *Twelfth Night* and *Henry VIII*.

32 Quoted *Sunday Times*, 11 August 1985.

33 Dick Cavett talked to Miller for five programmes in a row at the start of 1980 (with another stint to come in 1981). *The Body in Question* was broadcast by PBS from September 1980. *The Taming of the Shrew*, the first production which he directed for the *BBC Shakespeare Series*, was broadcast in the US in January 1981 (its transmission in the UK being in October 1980).

34 *A Midsummer Night's Dream* was rehearsed in mid-1979.

35 As executive producer, Miller oversaw Jack Gold's *Merchant of Venice*, Elijah Moshinsky's *All's Well* and *A Midsummer Night's Dream*, plus Jane Howell's *The Winter's Tale* and her *Wars of the Roses* tetralogy (that is all three parts of *Henry VI* and *Richard III*).

36 Miller got plenty of media coverage. For example, he was interviewed by Parkinson in January 1980 when his executive appointment had been announced, and in October, the night before *The Taming of the Shrew* was broadcast. A documentary entitled *Jonathan Miller Directs: The Making of Antony and Cleopatra* went out on BBC TV on 7 May 1981.

37 He saw Antony and Cleopatra's tragedy as a story about going to pieces in (or near) the tropics, a little like Graeme Greene's *The Heart of the Matter*.

38 As well as employing young rising talent, Miller happily let the teenage son of his old Footlights pal, Brian Marber, sit in on rehearsals. That was the future comedian, playwright and director Patrick Marber.

39 Regarding the educational material, the BBC drew on its appended *Shakespeare in Perspective* TV programmes to publish Sales, R. (ed.) (Vol. I, 1982 and Vol. II, 1985), *Shakespeare in Perspective* (London: Ariel Books, BBC). There were introductory *Prefaces to Shakespeare*, presented by famous actors, broadcast on BBC Radio. The play texts, as used in the Shakespeare series, were published by the BBC in 1980 and subsequent years, with production material, stills of camera shots and interviews.

In terms of the bureaucracy, Miller apparently did as little of the boring executive paperwork as he could. Sarah Miller, incidentally, never worked directly with her brother although she was a secretary in the BBC music and arts department. One of her colleagues there remembers that she once submitted a commendable programme idea concerning *The Tempest*, but it was not linked with the *BBC Shakespeare*

Series and was not pursued.

40 Gold's previous dramas had, outstandingly, included *The Naked Civil Servant*.

41 The director Will Kerley, likewise appreciated Miller's tutorial instinct and supply of fascinating books when he assisted on *A Midsummer Night's Dream* at the Almeida in the 1990s. Miller provided a fine substitute for an Oxbridge education, says Kerley.

42 The outdoor shoots, under Messina, had not been a great success.

43 *Troilus'* colonnades were based on prints of Jan Vredeman de Vries' architectural exercises, combining classical simplicity with a hint of boarded-up, modern inner city. The street scene in the *Shrew*, also built of raw plywood, was inspired by Serlio's sixteenth-century design for a comic scene.

44 Moshinsky had already directed Britten's operatic *Midsummer Night's Dream*, as well as staging *Troilus and Cressida* at the NT in 1976.

45 Peter Conrad directly compared Miller's *Otello* and his 'sotto voce' *Othello* in the *Times Literary Supplement*, 16 October 1981.

46 Miller prides himself on having promoted a shift away from generally bland studio lighting, instead illuminating from the side or from behind using seemingly real sources, such as windows, lanterns or tapers. For example, he would saw off the back of a jug, beside a candle, to conceal an extra bulb. 'The technical crew were very disturbed by what I wanted,' he says, 'but a few years later they were doing that sort of thing all the time.'

47 Vermeer was not quite a contemporary of Shakespeare's but was working in the mid-seventeenth century. Veronese was active during Shakespeare's lifetime, though the painter died in 1588 and scholars date *Antony and Cleopatra* as 1603–7.

48 The TV series *M.A.S.H.* was broadcast, in both the US and the UK, during the Seventies and Eighties. Miller encouraged Charles Gray and Jack Birkett (aka 'The Incredible Orlando') to camp up the parts of Pandarus and Thersites. Since Shakespeare drew on Chaucer for *Troilus*, the cut of the costumes hovered between medieval and Renaissance.

49 If searching for further moments that may have been informed by Miller's own life, one might discern a trace of the St Paul's School Green Cup competition in *Troilus*, with Ajax versus Hector played out as a ludicrous boxing match. More morbidly, in *Timon*, the self-exiling and bitter hero ended up in what looked like a blitzed city, a seashore and a cemetery rolled into one (rather than in a Shakespearean wood). There he breathed his last in a derelict tomb like the one which had horrified Miller as a child, with knotty roots and corms indistinguishable from bones.

50 According to John Fortune, Miller called for many a run-through of this amusing vignette. Bird relates how improvisation was slipped in as well. 'I ad libbed in one long speech,' he remembers, 'and at the end I said, "Was that all right?" and Jonathan said, "Keep it in [including the closing query]" . . . American school children with the text in front of them must have been baffled!'

51 Walzer, M. (1966), *The Revolution of the Saints: A Study in the Origins of Radical Politics* (London: Weidenfeld and Nicholson). At the end of Miller's production, a version of *Psalm 128* (an orderly vision of God, the pater familias, wife and children) was sung, as it might have been in a Puritan household in Shakespeare's era.

52 In playing this role, Cleese took guidance from both Miller and his own therapist, Robin Skynner, with whom the actor later co-authored Cleese, J. and Skynner, A. C. (1983), *Families, and How to Survive Them* (London: Methuen).

53 Reviews applauding *The Shrew* ranged from *Punch*, 5 November 1980, to *Christian Science Monitor*, 23 January 1981.

54 Bogdanov presented the alternative Channel 4 series *Shakespeare Lives!* in 1983.

55 That was after one month of rehearsals.

56 Both Miller and Jack Gold used sustained single-camera shots deliberately, but Moshinsky says racing against the clock played its part too, as with one very long shot in his *All's Well* which became the subject of academic theses.

57 Miller also argued that whitewashing the victim was no solution to the real problem of anti-Semitism – an issue discussed by Marion D. Perret, 'Shakespeare and Anti-Semitism', *Mosaic*, 16, 1–2, Winter–Spring 1983, 145–63, and in Susan Willis' account, Willis, S. (1991), *The BBC Shakespeare Plays: Making the Televised Canon* (Chapel Hill, NC: University of North Carolina Press), pp. 37–9. Mitchell's Shylock was a sympathetic though flawed personality – less assimilated, incidentally, than Olivier's portrayal.

58 In the *Guardian*, 28 July 2005, Dominic Dromgoole of Shakespeare's Globe alluded to Hopkins as the last blacked-up British Othello, saying it looked way past its sell-by-date. James Earl Jones, in the end, provided the voice-over introduction for the transmission of Howell's *Wars of the Roses* tetralogy in the USA.

59 Some accused Miller's *Othello* of racism, while others thought he robbed the play of its racist issues.

60 Miller's trademark deep-focus shots, with Hopkins in the foreground and Hoskins behind, hinted that the jealousy-inducing Iago was like a malign voice in Othello's head. Hopkins discussed the backstory

concerning the character's mother in the *BBC TV Shakespeare Series* edition of *Othello*, London, 1981, pp. 22–23. Filmed in close-up, the actor amazingly managed to convey all that personal history in the two lines, 'and when I love thee not,/Chaos is come again'.

61 Miller alludes to Klein in *Subsequent Performances*, p. 147.

62 By packing characters into deep-focus shots, creating triangular perspectives, Miller sought to provide the equivalent of a theatre spectator's peripheral vision, an all-encompassing view. Not everyone appreciated that. Insider criticisms are recorded in Willis, pp. 65, 118 and elsewhere.

63 Having not admired the *BBC Shakespeare Series* under Messina's tenure, Cleese had initially feared the production would involve much thigh slapping and unmotivated laughter. This is noted by Michael Brooke on the BFI website, screenonline.org.uk.

64 Hoskins talked about being kidnapped on BBC Radio's *Desert Island Discs*, 13 November 1988, where he chose music from *The Magic Flute* to which Miller introduced him.

65 In Miller's *BBC Shakespeare Series* production, Penelope Wilton switched to play Regan, with Brenda Blethyn as Cordelia.

66 H. R. Coursen's essay, 'The BBC-TV *Antony and Cleopatra*: Far More Harm Than Good', printed in Bulman, J. C. and Coursen, H. R. (eds) (1988), *Shakespeare on Television* (Hanover, NH: University Press of New England).

67 *New York Times*, 14 December 1981; *LA Times*, 18 October 1982; *Washington Post*, 20 April 1981; and Michael Ratcliffe, *The Times*, 8 May 1981.

68 This was Ratcliffe's overview of the series in *Kent Opera in Progress*, p. 53.

69 The DVD box set is entitled *The Shakespeare Collection* (BBC, 2005). When it was announced, in 2007, that Sam Mendes had been signed up to remake all 37 Shakespeare productions for the BBC over twelve years, Miller (in the *Daily Telegraph*, 18 November) condemned the original American sponsors' rules while adding that today's BBC needed to look beyond canonical literary celebs such as the Bard and Jane Austen.

70 The cameraman was Jim Atkinson.

71 Miller was awarded an honorary D.Litt. degree by the University of Leicester in 1981 and was already Visiting Professor of Drama at London's Westfield College.

72 The series broke even, and did so ahead of schedule, in 1982. It was widely bought by schools, in video format, helped by the surge in sales of VCRs during the Eighties.

73 *King Lear* was broadcast on 19 September 1982. Miller's ENO *Rigoletto* opened on 22 September. That same night, *Hamlet* transferred to the Piccadilly Theatre, in association with the producer Ian B. Albery (having opened at the Warehouse on 17 August 1982). It was a hectic month. Miller's Kent Opera *Fidelio* started rehearsals the following day, and his book *Darwin for Beginners* was launched the week after that.

74 Shrapnel was a notably sympathetic and efficient King Claudius.

75 *Subsequent Performances*, p. 111.

76 The main points about *Hamlet* were noted in reviews (all 1982) including *The Times*, 29 November; *Daily Telegraph*, 19 August; *Sunday Telegraph* and *Sunday Times*, 22 August; *Financial Times*, 18 August; *New York Times*, 5 September; and in Robin Stringer's article, 'Dr Miller Escapes to Other Things', *Daily Telegraph*, 21 September.

77 The *Evening Standard*, 23 September 1982, expressed such sentiments.

78 Some bold re-envisaging of classic operas had occurred elsewhere and earlier. Famously, there had been Wieland Wagner's radical approach to his grandfather's work at Bayreuth in the early 1950s, and Patrice Chéreau's *Ring of the Nibelung* at the same address in 1976, with the gods presented as nineteenth-century capitalists.

79 The Swiss opera house in Basle had set *Rigoletto* in 1930s Chicago just before this ENO production. Lord Harewood believed that Miller's idea was leaked while he was delayed by *Otello*. Norman Lebrecht's *Evening Standard* feature, of 7 January 2009, called Miller the inventor of the time-shift opera.

80 Mark Elder was the ENO's music director from 1979 to 1993.

81 Reported *Daily Telegraph*, 25 August 1982.

82 *Time*, 29 November 1982.

83 In Brighton's *Evening Argus*, 23 February 1995, Miller's deputy director, David Ritch, retrospectively alluded to the proverbial colonels in the shires. Having prematurely scorned the Mafia concept, they later wished to see it, but by then they could not get tickets for love or money.

84 The set's detailing was particularly accurate because Miller's designer Patrick Robertson headed off with him to New York, taking hundreds of photographs.

85 Rawnsley's sufferings were staggered: 4 November 1982 and 5 November 1987.

86 The Met row was reported in the *Daily Express*, 10 March 1984, and *Observer*, 18 March. *Rigoletto* played there in June 1984, as part of a triumphant tour that started in May in Texas, going on to Houston, Austin and San Antonio. The box-office record was broken according to *City Limits*, 25 January 1985, in spite of a decidedly cool *New York Times* review, 21 June 1984. When interviewed by *Women's Wear Daily*,

29 May 1985, Miller reckoned that Met audiences, desiring visual opulence, did not love the production.

87 The hiring dispute concerning White was discussed in *The Times* and on BBC TV's *Sixty Minutes*, 21 June 1984, as well as in the States (e.g. *Anchorage Daily News*, 27 June 1984). The GLC temporarily froze the quarterly instalment of its annual (over one-million pound) grant to the ENO.

88 Sammy Davis Jr's association with Sinatra's Rat Pack, who knew Mafia cronies, presumably did not count. There had been some instances of colour-blind casting in the Seventies, notably Carl Anderson as Judas in *Jesus Christ Superstar*. The push against the problems of race-related exclusion on stage and screen gained momentum a couple of years after the Willard White dispute, with the Non-Traditional Casting Project co-founded by Actors Equity in 1986.

89 Hanchard starred in Miller's 1994 production of *L'Incoronazione di Poppea*. White made his Met debut in 2000 in Miller's *Pelléas et Mélisande*, appearing in several revivals thereafter.

90 *Rigoletto* had been seen internationally, on the small screen, by June 1984, following on from the January 1983 broadcast in the UK. The VHS recording came out in 1989 (Warner Home Video), and a DVD was produced (by Kultur for the US) in 2007. Miller's staging was used (in truncated form) on Channel 4's series *Operatunity* in February 2003. Its cult status was alluded to by theartsdesk.com in February 2014.

91 High praise came from *Punch*, 6 October 1982; the *Daily Express*, 25 September; and the *Daily Mail*, 24 September. Some critics alluded to odd incongruities caused by the update, but the *Daily Telegraph*'s Peter Stadlen and *The Lady* were pretty much alone in being appalled (24 September and 7 October).

92 Interview with Peter Lewis, *Mail on Sunday*, 19 September 1982.

93 Miller in the *Sunday Express*, 19 September 1982. He also said, in *Time Out*, 6 August 1982, that science was preferable to the arts: 'You're either right or wrong. I can't bear fighting this endless battle as though I've made some tremendous error.' On the funding front, he was quoted, in the *Mail on Sunday*, 19 September 1982, saying: 'Inflation has changed the whole structure of the English theatre. If you want to do serious work you have to join the large subsidised companies or . . . put it on by the skin of your teeth.'

94 Routledge, who played Mrs Peachum, made this comment when interviewed for *Fame, Set and Match*, BBC TV, 23 November 2002.

95 *The Beggar's Opera* was broadcast on BBC2, 29 October 1983, and reviewed in the *Daily Telegraph* and *The Times*, 31 October. It was aired in the US, on A&E Cable TV, in December 1988.

96 This James MacTaggart Memorial Lecture invites comparison with Newton N. Minow's 1961 'vast wasteland' address to the National Association of Broadcasters in the US, and Miller's warnings were, doubtless, informed by his own past reviews of American TV.

97 Channel 4, a public service station but commercially funded, began broadcasting in November 1982. It started out as a subsidiary of the Independent Broadcasting Authority, the regulatory body for UK commercial television. It was Channel 4 that aired TVS's *Staging an Opera* in April–May 1983, after its January broadcast of Miller's *Rigoletto*.

98 Cable had been legally restricted to public service broadcasting. After the 1982 Hunt Inquiry into the potential of cable expansion, the government granted eleven interim franchises in 1983, and the Cable and Broadcasting Act and Telecommunications Act followed in 1984, allowing for numerous channels.

99 Designed by Philip Prowse, the library was inspired by the architect Étienne-Louis Boullée's neoclassical vision for a Bibliothèque Nationale, with added Egyptian touches including plaster casts of obelisks.

100 Miller additionally saw *The Magic Flute* as exploring, like *Così*, the themes of appetite v. reason and pleasures v. duties. Incidentally, with regard to the ongoing issue of political correctness, the black character Monostatos was based, by the director, on the ground-breaking, Haitian, revolutionary slave-turned-general Toussaint L'Ouverture. The Scottish Opera production originally included a tongue-in-cheek *Black and White Minstrels*-style dance, performed by Monostatos' accomplices. This has been described by Philip Prowse as probably the last racist joke ever allowed in the theatre – albeit that some minstrel-show routines (such as the *Cakewalk*) started as a send-up, by plantation workers, of grandiose white affectations. *The Magic Flute*'s reviewers seemed to find the choreography amusing at the time, but it has since been adjusted with more sensitivity to political correctness.

Miller developed his staging, with a bigger budget and great success, for Zurich Opera in the 1990s. In Zurich Opera's DVD recording, Monostatos is still a blacked-up singer (Volker Vogel) but the dance by him and his white accomplices is now more gently comical and surreal, something like antique mechanical dolls doing funky disco moves.

101 Scottish Opera's *Magic Flute* opened at Glasgow's Theatre Royal in January 1983 and toured to the Dominion, in London, in February. It was revived to tour again in October 1985 and October 1988, as well as being a stopgap production at the Coliseum in 1986, when the ENO was cash-strapped. The *Observer* applauded it there on 2 February.

102 Miller's old Establishment friend, Jeremy Geidt, was a comic wheeze as Sir Oliver Surface until he actually caught a serious respiratory infection during the run. As regards political correctness, there was a minor controversy with exchanges in the *Jewish Advocate*, May–July 1983, about Sheridan's supposed

anti-Semitism. The American Repertory Theatre's archives include a letter from the managing director, Robert Orchard, responding to one personal complaint on that subject. It explains that an emergency cast change made the production less balanced on one evening and that Miller had rushed backstage to order immediate adjustments, 'a swift reaction unprecedented in my experience'. Letter to M. I. Weinberger, 27 May 1983.

103 This is from Peter Lewis' interview, *Mail on Sunday*, 1 May 1983, when Miller was on his way from Harvard to McMaster. He was tying up the loose threads of stage and screen through 1983, before he moved on to his three-year fellowship at the University of Sussex in November. In strictly linear terms, his MacTaggart Lecture was slotted in between McMaster and Sussex.

104 *States of Mind*, BBC TV, 1983. The accompanying book, consisting of the edited dialogues with introductions by Miller, was published in 1983 by the New York publishers Pantheon, as well as by the BBC in the UK. William J. Clancey's review weighed it up, in detail, judging it well-balanced overall, in the *AI Magazine*, Winter 1983, 61–66.

105 Again, Peter Lewis' interview.

106 *New Society*, 14 April 1983.

107 All 1983: Stuart Sutherland, *Times Literary Supplement*, 17 June; Liam Hudson, *Sunday Times*, 10 April; Francis Huxley, *Guardian*, 14 April; Rosemary Dinnage, *New York Review of Books*, 18 August.

108 The philosopher and author Colin McGinn, who did not know Miller at this stage but later became a friend, remembers watching the programmes and being astonished that any frontman knew so much. 'He was able,' McGinn emphasizes, 'not only to handle the discussion at an impressive level, but to make it intelligible.'

109 Miller discussed his philosophy-linked interests in an interview for *Time*, 6 June 1983.

110 The La-Z-boy remark appeared in *Diversion*, July 1992.

111 This refers to the experiments described in 1973 by Gunnar Johansson in *Perception and Psychophysics*, Vol. 14, No. 2, 201–11.

112 The maths left him feeling like an old Russian peasant, as he told to the *Daily Express*, 29 March 1986.

113 Miller alluded to translatable perceptual skills, in theatre and medicine, in the *Radio Times*, 4–10 November 1978.

114 *Cortex*, 1987, No. 23, 655–65. The third co-author was Richard Vincent from Royal Sussex County Hospital's cardiology department.

115 *Ivan*, BBC2, 3 December 1984; *Prisoner of Consciousness*, Channel 4, August 1986.

116 *Observer*, 9 December 1984.

117 *The Times*, 15 August 1986.

118 Sacks, O. (2007), *Musicophilia: Tales of Music and the Brain* (London: Picador).

119 Miller observed that when you see a TV flickering across the road or a drive-in movie from afar – such that you aren't absorbed by dialogue or storyline – it is the cuts, the discontinuities which you register most. Along with his Johansson-style Sussex experiments, the material in Miller's aforementioned 1986 Royal Society paper 'Moving Pictures' clearly fed into his *Moving Pictures* documentary in 1989.

120 Miller, J. and Van Loon, B. (1982), *Darwin for Beginners* (London: Writers and Readers Publishing Cooperative) went on to be reprinted many times, distributed round the world by Unwin and Penguin among other companies, and under different titles. For example, there was Miller, J. and Van Loon, B., edited by Appignanesi, R. (2000 edn), *Introducing Darwin and Evolution* (Cambridge: Icon Books and New York, NY: Totem Books). More recently, it was rebranded as *Introducing Darwin: A Graphic Guide* (London: Icon Books).

121 Richard Lewontin's *New York Review of Books* article of 16 June 1983 is reproduced in his book, Lewontin, R. (2000), *It Ain't Necessarily So: The Dream of the Human Genome and Other Illusions* (New York, NY: New York Review of Books).

122 Miles Kington, *The Times*, 28 September 1983. Perhaps the publication of Miller's first pop-up, shortly before he began his Sussex fellowship, contributed to his feeling that his colleagues there did not rate him as a serious scientist.

123 *Private Eye*, 21 October 1983.

124 Miller, J. and Pelham, D., *The Human Body* (London: Cape), was published in 1983. The *Spectator* commented on 26 November 1983 and 27 October 1984. In America, the *Village Voice*'s review of *The Human Body* was decidedly mixed, 27 December 1983, but the *New York Times* was charmed by *The Facts of Life*, 18 November 1984.

125 The sales of Jonathan Cape's first print run were reported in the *Evening Standard*, 10 October 1983. Viking distributed the book in America.

126 John Gross reviewed the Cooper-Hewitt Museum's exhibition called *Surprise! Surprise!* in the *New York Times*, 17 January 1988.

127 *Body Works* was produced by Genesis in March 1985.

128 *Origins*, BBC2, 18 March 1986. Reviewed in the *Radio Times*, 15 March, *The Times*, 19 March etc. Christopher Reeve was the linkman in the American broadcast of *Origins*.

129 Miller's planned major series on evolution was, it should be pointed out, a project intended for Channel 4, not the BBC. He was not completely foiled, managing to get back into BBC science programming in 1989.

130 Many of Miller's media colleagues voiced support for the concerns he expressed. They believed BBC producers should trust their instincts, that being a creed on which the Corporation's best public service achievements had been based. David Housham expressed this view, with reference to Miller, in the publication *Broadcast*, 18 October 1985.

131 These comments appeared in *Newsday*, 17 June 1984. In fact, Miller had been wary of academic backbiting earlier too, alluding to it in the *Sunday Telegraph*, 21 February 1982.

132 Miller's comments on jerks and Welles appeared in the *Mail on Sunday*, 7 March 1985, and *Women's Wear Daily*, 29 May 1985.

133 Miller admitted to intensely missing these things in the *Sunday Times*, 27 October 1985.

134 In fact, due to opera productions being scheduled far in advance, the Mozart was pencilled in Miller's diary before he even arrived at Sussex. So his tying up of loose ends was barely distinguishable from his return to directing. In that light, *The Beggar's Opera* – with the womanizing Macheath – looks less like a farewell and more like a warm-up for *Don Giovanni*.

135 Miller's designer was, again, Philip Prowse.

136 As with Old Hamlet's ghost, Miller wanted to avoid rigidity, so he based the slain Commendatore's statue on the Maréchal de Saxe's tomb in Strasbourg where the sculptor, Jean-Baptiste Pigalle, depicted the Maréchal in motion, walking down some steps towards Death while being desperately restrained by a woman – like the Commendatore's grief-stricken daughter, Donna Anna.

137 Miller on hell, *Paris Review*, Issue 165, Spring 2003.

138 Miller had, indeed, envisaged an unusually old Don, wearily feeling his age, but Shimmel was a given in the casting.

139 Hall had staged *Don Giovanni* in 1977. Negative reviews of Miller's production (e.g. *Evening Standard*, *Glasgow Herald*, *Observer* and *Sunday Telegraph*, on 6, 7 and 8 December 1985) deemed it unsexy and sombre, with the Commendatore too mundane and the gory finale too distasteful. A minority (e.g. the *Sunday Times*) considered the supper scene enthrallingly intimate, and liked the women's regained power at the close.

140 The ENO *Don Giovanni* was more traditional but perhaps Sellars' Spanish Harlem production, with vintage tunes pumping out of the Don's ghetto blaster, owed something to Miller's Little Italy *Rigoletto*. Sellars' staging premiered, in July 1987, at the Summerfare festival in Purchase, New York.

141 Karen Stone helped Miller restage *Don Giovanni* for the Maggio Musicale in Florence in 1990, then worked on its revival for LA Opera and the Savonlinna Festival 2001. NBR New Zealand Opera took it up in July 2005, with Stanley M. Garner taking on the staging.

142 Idle was to be succeeded by Bill Oddie and then Richard Suart who still plays Ko-Ko and is, celebrated for his constantly updated Little List. Satirizing current politicians and celebrities, Suart has only been censored once, when the production played in Venice. He wanted to send up Berlusconi.

143 Miller says Harewood had initiated the *Mikado* project.

144 Partly laughing at (rather than just along with) English racism, a few Japanese running gags were retained, with Miller's plummy characters pulling their eyes narrow and launching into madly inappropriate bouts of karate.

145 The 1930s setting included elements harking back to the Edwardian era and the Twenties.

146 The choreography was by Anthony Van Laast. Another influence was, surely, Sandy Wilson's pastiche period musical, *The Boy Friend*.

147 Miller's original Mikado was Richard Angas. The *Daily Express*, 10 October 1986, likened the character's appearance to Peter Hall as did the *Jewish Chronicle*, 18 October 1991. Rhoda Koenig's *Independent on Sunday* review of Miller's Bristol *Hamlet*, 30 March 2008, thought Roland Oliver's Polonius – powerfully chilling with mandarin whiskers – was the image of Hall too.

148 One might momentarily wonder if I. E. Snellgrove was a character invented by Peter Cook, given that, during the Eighties, Cook used to adopt a ludicrous persona – 'Sven from Swiss Cottage' – when ringing up Clive Bull's radio phone-in show on LBC. Presumably, Snellgrove (responding in the *Sunday Telegraph*, 14 September 1986, to the 'Entebbe raid' comment in the same publication on 7 September) was not concocted by Miller himself, as a successor to the fictional T. Y. Freep of his *UCH Magazine* letters page.

149 As early as the 1880s, there had been an American parody entitled *The Texas Mikado*.

150 The meringue image was cited by Richard Trubner in the *New York Times*, 23 October 1988. It seemed particularly appropriate that Miller was – on the opening night of this light comedy – supposed to be floating above Cape Canaveral for a TV show about weightlessness. He only got to complete the preliminary tests at Farnborough, feeling his dental fillings go pop in a decompression tank.

151 At *The Mikado*'s premiere, some critics expressed modified rapture, questioning if the setting was

justified, and Alan Blyth in the *Daily Telegraph*, 29 September 1986, thought the show somewhat frenetic and self-consciously clever. Nevertheless, he found David Ritch's subsequent revivals genuinely funny (25 November 1988) and declared himself an enthusiastic convert to the updating (*Opera*, April 1990). In spite of the occasional cry that this show is getting creaky, the revivals continue to be acclaimed, with the 2008 run being applauded as impressively polished and satirically sharp. It received its 25th anniversary production in February 2011, to be followed by a further two month run, over December 2012 and January 2013.

152 The *Guardian* referred to him as still the UK's most famous opera director on 19 November 2004.

153 PBS, 28 October 1988.

154 *Phantom* opened in 1986. Thames TV's film of *The Mikado* was released on VHS in 1987 (with the camerawork directed by John Michael Phillips). The 2005 DVD is formatted for the States and Canada.

155 There had been Miller's Kent Opera trips as well, staying in Eastbourne hotels. Another more immediate influence was the Anglo-American hotel in Florence where Lazaridis and Miller had preliminary discussions about *The Mikado*. Likewise, the surrealist link is only very tangential between the fictional ENO Grand Hotel, with planets hanging from the ceiling, and Miller's wacky juvenile fantasy (in the St Paul's casino-building debate) about Brighton being one of Britain's weird and wonderful mystery towns.

156 The Thirties chic style was also fashionable after *Bluebell*, the 1986 British TV series about Margaret Kelly of the Bluebell Girls dance troupe, choreographed by Van Laast.

Chapter 13: The Mid-Eighties

1 The 'ugly, racist, rancorous little place' quotation comes from the *Sunday Telegraph*, 7 September 1986.

2 The unemployment figures in 1984 peaked at 3.3 million. Other reasons to be less than cheerful about Britain included the jingoism stirred up by the 1982 Falklands War (as evident in the *Sun*'s notorious 'Gotcha' headline); the prevalence of football hooliganism in the mid-Eighties; IRA mainland bombings; and Thatcher refusing to implement full sanctions against South Africa's apartheid regime in 1985. Miller had, personally, found himself subject to sarcastic abuse on the street as well.

3 *Marxism Today*, December 1985.

4 *The Flying Dutchman* opened at Opera Frankfurt in 1979, a springboard for Miller's European work in the 1980s.

5 Interviewed by Mark Lawson, for Jewish Book Week in March 2009, Miller observed that the real problem with Wagner is that his characters are surely from *Harry Potter*. Meanwhile, talking on *The Dick Cavett Show* in 1980 (programme two of the five-interview sequence), he contributed to the stereotyping of Germans, satirically describing the Frankfurt chorus as wanting a dictator-director. 'I couldn't get the goose step,' he said. Countering that, he now remembers his Frankfurt assistant director, Renate Itgenshorst, with unqualified fondness. She became a family friend. Moreover, in the 1980 Cavett interview, he went into self-mocking mode, recounting how he failed to calculate for the Frankfurt chorus being 70-strong. When they first climbed aboard one of the ships in rehearsals, it looked like a refugee boat heaving off Hong Kong, he remarked. With adjustments and less crew, the opening scene proved spectacular. On a billowing ocean of blue-green silk, two vessels sailed into view, initially tiny scale models on the horizon, then larger and larger, until they were vast.

6 Miller again, arguably, had it both ways in terms of the supernatural, since Senta's artworks indicated the whole drama might have been in her imagination.

7 *Così* in St Louis was, in fact, Miller's opera debut in America, for it preceded the US tour of *Rigoletto*.

8 Linda Blandford quoting Miller, *New York Times*, 1 August 1982, and Simmons quoted in the *St Louis Globe-Democrat*, undated cutting, from the archives of Opera Theatre of Saint Louis.

9 Miller's rather surprising taste for copious amounts of quality clothes tends to go undetected because his style is casual. However, Andrew Billen could not help noticing his pioneering, double-layered look in the *Evening Standard*, 24 November 1999. The idiosyncratic habit of wearing two shirts presumably keeps Miller cosy, rather than being a variation on Emanuel's old fear of losing the clothes off his back.

10 I am indebted to the OTSL's administrator Maggie Stearns for all her help and her diary of that summer spent with Miller and Simmons. Incidentally, since this was 1982, maybe Simmons' party pieces actually seeded Miller's idea that the *Mikado*, without the Japanese trappings, might be fun.

11 Despina dressing up as a doctor may have had extra resonance for Miller. His programme note emphasized how *Così* shows that everyone contains a potential alternative identity. This was in the same year as he announced his return to medicine. That said, he points to a different personal connection, suggesting that *On the Side of the Angels*, his mother's novel, was a kind of World War 2 *Così*. The opera's male lovers switch sweethearts when disguised as roving Albanians. As Miller points out, Betty depicted 'how normally decorous [men], once they got into army uniform, began to misbehave as if they thought they were somehow unrecognisable.'

12 Donal Henahan, *New York Times*, 18 and 27 June 1992. He particularly celebrated Miller's balance of thoughtfulness and comedy, rationalism and sensitivity, natural acting and visual symmetries.

13 Calvin Simmons died on 21 August 1982. The news surely fed into Miller's farewell to the performing arts. It was only a month later, in September, that the *Sunday Express* recorded his depressed statement, 'I just feel I've come to the end of it . . . Roger, so to speak, and out.' Renate Itgenshorst, from Frankfurt, was to die tragically young as well, falling down a flight of stairs.

14 The BBC *Così* was filmed in the autumn of 1985, conducted by the ENO's Peter Robinson. It was shown on BBC2 at Easter, 31 March 1986, with a simultaneous stereo broadcast on Radio 3. It was preceded by *Miller on Mozart* on 27 March. Therein the director discussed adapting the opera for the small screen. Co-produced with the American Arts and Entertainment Network, *Così* was on American TV on New Year's Eve 1987.

15 A degree of artificiality was deliberately retained – the distant view of Vesuvius being fashioned in marquetry – but Miller recalls how, ironically, it ended up looking deceptively real, just as if it had been filmed on location. The reviews were mixed. Rodney Milnes in the *Spectator*, 12 April 1986, appreciated the visual references to Joseph Wright of Derby's painting of scientific investigations, *An Experiment on a Bird in the Air Pump*. He liked the unaffected acting, the intimacy and the unfussy still shots, concluding: 'Thank you, and more please.' However, criticisms alluded to static blocking, to patchy comic moments, and to the whole being less daring than Peter Hall's Glyndebourne *Così*. The word on the grapevine was that Alan Yentob in the BBC arts department intended to produce a whole Miller-Mozart series, but that never happened.

16 The Jones-inspired production was for Florence's Maggio Musicale in 1991. There Miller had the house full of Roman antiquities, as if the historic collector Sir William Hamilton had left the place to the girls for the holidays. The director has, moreover, staged *Così* in Scandinavia (Bornholm, 2002) and New York (Mostly Mozart Festival 2004). His modern-dress version was recreated for Seattle Opera (2006).

17 As well as the UK's 1986 Faber edition of *Subsequent Performances*, a US edition came out the same year, published in New York by Viking/Elisabeth Sifton. It was based, in part, on his 1977 T. S. Eliot Memorial Lectures for Kent University and his 1984 Cambridge Clark Lectures.

18 In a similar vein, Miller discussed his interest in the changes that occur when you repeatedly Xerox artworks in *Subsequent Performances,* pp. 189–96 (all page references are to the Faber edition). That was in connection with the set design for his Kent Opera *L'Orfeo* where Poussin's images were not simply reproduced but reworked by the modern artist Daniel Lang (with assistance from Bernard Culshaw and the technical crew).

19 *Subsequent Performances*, p. 35. The point was supported by zoological drawings of shape-changing fish from Miller's vintage biology textbook, D'Arcy Thompson's *On Growth and Form*. In an earlier interview – in *Shakespeare Quarterly*, Vol. 27, 1976, 13–14 – Miller had likened successive productions to botanical histology, to cutting longitudinal then oblique then traverse sections of a plant stem.

20 The Necker Cube, Rubin Vase and Jastrow's duck-rabbit are all repeated leitmotifs in Miller's books. The Necker Cube turns up in *The Body in Question*, p. 337; *States of Mind*, pp. 48–9; and *Subsequent Performances*, pp. 97–8 and 112. The Rubin Vase features in *The Body in Question*, p. 223, and *States of Mind*, p. 50. The duck-rabbit pops up in *Subsequent Performances*, p. 113, and *On Reflection*, p. 113. Kanizsa's trompe l'oeils also appear in *The Body in Question*, pp. 336–7, *States of Mind*, pp. 52–3, and *On Reflection*, pp. 6–6. The photographer André Kertész's portrait, in the style of a funhouse mirror, and other distorted, anamorphic images recur in *The Body in Question*, p. 19; *On Reflection*, pp. 45 and 185; and in *Subsequent Performances*, pp. 36–7.

21 Miller had needed assistance, having to dictate some passages to his editors because of writer's block. The reviewers noted that Miller did not always acknowledge (or, perhaps, know of) his cliché-ditching predecessors. He did unexpectedly give Peter Hall credit as an RSC groundbreaker, before going on to criticize his NT regime. The reviews, all 1986, included Peter Conrad, *Observer*, 27 April; Frederic Raphael, *Sunday Times*, 25 May; Richard Osborne, *Times Literary Supplement*, 5 September; and Sean Day-Lewis, *Daily Telegraph*, 23 May.

22 All 1986: Billington, *Guardian*, 8 May; *Evening Standard*, 12 June; Penelope Mesic in the magazine *Chicago*, November.

23 *Tristan und Isolde*, for LA's Music Center Opera, opened on 6 December 1987 at the Dorothy Chandler Pavilion – where the Oscars ceremony used to be held. This production was set up by the company's Cambridge-educated director, Peter Hemming. It transferred to the Maggio Musicale in Florence, 20 October 1988.

24 The *Independent*, 18 December 1987, reported that the local edition of *Variety* had quoted Miller saying he was just marshalling the stage traffic. Miller had renamed the opera *Tristan und Isolde und David*, according to the *Los Angeles Times*, 6 March 1988.

25 Decidedly mixed *Tristan* reviews, all 1987, included the *San Francisco Chronicle*, 9 December; *Wall Street Journal*, 15 December; and *Los Angeles Herald Examiner*, 8 December. More positive about Miller's contribution were the *Daily Telegraph*, 21 December, and *LA Times*, 12 December.

26 *New York Times*, 14 March 1991, quoted Miller regarding the over-coloured pop-up book.

27 David Hockney's comments are from his book, Hockney, D. (1993), *That's the Way I See It* (London: Thames & Hudson), pp. 168–72, and from a *Los Angeles Times* interview, 13 January 2008.

28 In an interview with *Opera Monthly*, July 1991, Miller said he wanted to do a *Star Wars* version of Wagner's *Ring*, but that came to nothing.

29 *The Mikado* was co-produced by LA's Music Center Opera, Houston Grand Opera and the ENO. It opened on 10 March 1988 at the Wiltern Theater as part of the UK/LA festival of British arts.

30 That lunch was at the Venice Beach restaurant which Moore owned.

31 Paskin, p. 319, recorded Miller's satiric observation that Lane resembled Karen Black in *Five Easy Pieces*, 'as if she'd just tottered out of a trailer in rhinestone-encrusted high-heel shoes'. The same author mentioned, p. 320, that Moore had to be firmly taken in hand by Miller's team, to make him buckle down to work.

32 Recorded *Los Angeles Times*, 6 March 1988.

33 The Houston production was in November 1989.

34 Miller directed *Misura per Misura* in mid-1987, with its Rome performances at the Teatro Ateneo and the tour extending to Sicily. This time, for Shakespeare's seedy city scenes, the design had more than a hint of George Grosz. Miller was enchanted to meet – *en passant*, in Italy – Alida Valli who had played the alluring Anna in *The Third Man*. 'There she was, this person for whom I'd always had, well, this great love: a grey, bubble-haired, very gracious old lady! . . . I loved it in Rome,' he says. Though his cast escaped injury in Verona, tragedy struck when they drove on to their next destination, with one company member being killed in a car crash.

35 *Tosca* opened at the Teatro Comunale, 17 June 1986.

36 In the Tuscan composer's original, the opposing sides were monarchists and republicans, the latter hoping Napoleon's troops would triumph. Miller was not, of course, the first to portray twentieth-century Fascist Italy. He was inspired by Rossellini's gritty, neorealist film from 1945, *Rome, Open City*, although that portrayed the Catholic church positively. There had also been a Tosca-meets-World War 2 movie, *Before Him All Rome Trembled*, directed by Carmine Gallone in 1946.

37 The Christian Democrat Giovanni Pallanti's comments were reported in the *Guardian*, 7 June 1986. Allegations of an anti-papal plot were reported in the *Independent,* 23 August 1990. No stranger to controversy, Mehta had faced down protests about anti-Semitism in 1981 when he included Wagner in a concert in Israel, politely arguing that no music should be banned in a democracy and carrying on in spite of activists alarmingly running on to the stage.

38 The typist, the side room and the chair-straddling execution were all allusions to *Rome, Open City*. Miller worked in less specific cinematic elements, setting up Scarpia's office like a floodlit film set. That served to bring out Puccini's themes of pretending v. reality. It also tallied with Miller's view that the composer's music was not looking back to Napoleonic times, but was, rather, looking ahead to the era of Hollywood movies.

39 Scarpia was played by Romano Emili. I am indebted to Tom Sutcliffe for his detailed description of the Florence production, in the *Guardian*, 23 June 1986.

40 Jonas, Elder and Pountney adopted the Power House nickname themselves for their co-authored book, Jonas, P., Elder, M. and Pountney, D., edited by John, N. (1992), *Power House: The English National Opera Experience* (London: Lime Tree). Harewood had been encouraged by Elder to employ Pountney at the start of the Eighties, then Jonas had replaced Harewood in the mid-Eighties.

41 Anthony Besch's Scottish Opera production had premiered in 1980, with revivals in 1982 and 1986. The British critics were disappointed that Eva Marton was unavailable for the transfer of Miller's *Tosca* from Florence. They found the production dreary and deaf to Puccini's colourful music. Hostile reviews included Bayan Northcott, *Independent*, 30 January 1987; Hugh Canning, *City Limits*, 12–19 February; and John Higgins, *The Times*, 30 January (with Higgins noting that the cast, on the sloping set, looked as if they were struggling to find their sea legs). Actually, Paul Griffiths in *The Times*, 2 July 1986, had not much cared for the Florence premiere either. The writer Penelope Fitzgerald refused even to watch Miller's *Tosca*, saying that he was just 'so silly' as a director, and encouraged to be so. That is recorded in her letters, Fitzgerald, P., edited by Dooley, T. (2008), *So I Have Thought of You: The Letters of Penelope Fitzgerald* (London: Fourth Estate), p. 421.

Positive comments in 1987 included *Punch*, 11 February. Karen Stone, as staff producer, restaged Miller's *Tosca* in 1988, with Janice Cairns, gaining excellent notices from the *Guardian*, 26 August; *Evening Standard*, 30 August; and Anthony Payne in the *Independent*, 1 September. The ENO 1990 revival suffered from bad reviews regarding Jane Eaglen's Tosca comparing her – in the case of the *Daily Express*, 27 August – to a dowdy cleaning lady. When the production transferred to Houston in January 1991, with Eva Marton restored, it was a box-office hit.

42 The geographic slide sideways was, of course, a tactic Miller had used when staging *The Marriage of Figaro* (the play and the opera) in Spanish- then French-style surrounds. The director was, at the same

time, keen to excise the cheesy jocularity of Figaro, the titular Mr Fix-It in *The Barber* (Rossini's prequel to *The Marriage of Figaro*). The West End *Barber* which Miller had seen as a boy was swamped in garish Hispanic trappings, he says. He spoke of such trappings and excessively twinkly Figaros to *Time Out*, 25 November–2 December 1987, and to the *Sunday Express*, 22 November 1987.

43 Miller introduced allusions to pictures by Pietro Longhi and Tiepolo, with his set designed by Tanya McCallin. The cabinet of anatomical curiosities was inspired by eighteenth-century wax models crafted by Bologna's Giovanni Manzolini and his wife, Anna (which are now in the city's Museo delle Cere Anatomiche).

44 Tom Sutcliffe, *Guardian*, 20 November 1987. *The Barber* was further criticized for its lack of stylistic homogeneity and for Mark Elder's slow-paced conducting. In the *Spectator*, 5 December 1987, Rodney Milnes sighed that, without Della Jones' virtuosic Rosina, he would have been near-suicidal. The *Observer*, 22 November, said that Miller should be employed to think up ideas for more competent practitioners. Positive reviews, though in the minority, included *Time Out*, 25 November–2 December, *Sunday Telegraph*, 22 November, and *Independent*, 20 November.

45 Milnes conceded it was great fun in *The Times*, 18 November 1995, and he was warmly alluding to Miller's copper-bottomed gags by 4 June 2001. There was further praise from the *Express*, the *Scotsman* and *Time Out* in 1995. Henry Little staged that revival.

46 *Time Out*, 8 November, and *What's On*, 15 November 1995, both referred to the comedy getting coarsened. Michael Tanner took this line strongly, *Spectator*, 5 December 1998.

47 Miller's comments on avant-gardists, as on opera queens, appeared in the *Sunday Telegraph*, 15 November 1987, just before the first reviews of *The Barber*. His criticisms were to continue into the next millennium, with him alluding (on BBC Radio's *Start the Week*, 2 February 2009) to so-called cutting-edge directors being blunt instruments.

48 In May 1987, it was recorded in the ENO files that Miller remained on a £1000 annual retainer but, by June 1988, a telegram from his agent Stephen Wright to the ENO referred to his name and billing as associate director being removed from the company's material from the end of that season.

49 This is from an email sent to the author by David Pountney in 2003.

50 Harewood would remain a friend for life, with Miller and Rachel continuing to be welcome guests at his historic mansion near Leeds. He died, aged 88, in 2011.

51 When interviewed for *Plays and Players,* January 1988, Miller was taking over the Old Vic as artistic director and he spoke of wanting to bring Pountney in to direct there, which suggests they were not getting on badly.

52 Miller was quoted on the Tory government's philistinism and insufficient funding of the arts by Michael Romain, *What's On*, 18 November 1987. Writing in the *Sunday Telegraph*, 10 January 1988 (and other papers) about the intelligentsia's hatred of Thatcher, Graham Turner quoted Miller's allusions to fingernails on blackboards, suburban gentility, loathsomeness and typhoid. The *New York Times* picked up on this, 21 February 1988. Miller was the *New Statesman*'s high point of the week, 9 September 1988, for mischievously turning a discussion about alternative medicine on Channel 4's *After Dark* into a call for Thatcher's terrible uncaring government to be ousted, adding that he hoped she was watching. Journalists have continued to rebuke Miller's comments. Sarah Sands referred to his 'authentically snobbish voice of the left' in the *Guardian*, 3 July 2007, and David Hughes' and others' comments, posted on the *Daily Telegraph*'s website, 16 February 2009, judged that Miller's splutterings about commuter idiocy had spoken volumes about him.

Chapter 14: Nearing the Nineties

1 *Long Day's Journey* opened on 28 April 1986.

2 Lemmon's comment comes from Romain's *A Profile*, p. 145. The actor was also quoted in Glimmerglass Opera's *Donor and Subscriber Preview*, April 1989, saying every minute with Miller was totally stimulating. The director particularly recalls how Lemmon never fussed about waiting to rehearse his scenes, sitting in a side-room, quietly playing blues chords on a piano 'with his ear close to the keyboard, as if he were a radio operator listening to very faint messages.'

3 Just to clarify, Miller's original casting conversation had been with another producer, Roger Peters.

4 Spacey's profile was relatively low at the time. He had played Oswald in Ibsen's *Ghosts* on Broadway, with Liv Ullman, but his performance was tersely disparaged in the *New York Times,* 31 August 1982.

5 Spacey discussed the production, and Lemmon, on US TV's *Charlie Rose Show,* and he reminisced about his invite-filching escapade when interviewed by Emanuel Azenberg for the video release of the American recording of *Long Day's Journey* (Vestron Video, 1988). He spoke about the show again in New York's *Press and Sun Bulletin*, 29 December 2004.

6 *Arena*, broadcast 31 March 2012.

7 Max Stafford-Clark premiered *Top Girls* in 1982. Miller acknowledges David Mamet as an American theatre artist interested in capturing the texture of real speech. In the wake of Orson Welles' films and

screwball comedies such as *His Girl Friday*, Robert Altman had been using overlapping dialogue on screen as well.

8 Lemmon talked on BBC TV's *Newsnight*, 1 August 1986, about Miller almost conducting the piece. The director was, of course, freer here than when working with a conductor on an opera. Dealing with actual musical scores, he had hardly been able to play around with the positioning and pacing of the performers' words. Still, he had treated Mozart's recitative passages with notable realism and he will occasionally ask a conductor if, say, a dramatically enriching longer pause would be acceptable.

9 He overlapped dialogue in *The School for Scandal* and *The Seagull* at Nottingham.

10 In referring to sonatas, he was particularly alluding to Chekhov's use of repeated and inverted themes.

11 Conversational turn-taking was discussed with Professor Emanuel Schegloff in *States of Mind*.

12 He used that phrase in Ross Wetzsteon's article, 'The Director in Spite of Himself', *American Theatre*, November 1985.

13 Frank Rich, *New York Times*, 29 April 1986. Miller's letter, responding to Dick, was printed on 15 June. When his production was filmed and broadcast, the *NYT*'s TV critic John O'Connor (on 13 April 1987) praised Lemmon's superb performance but judged the simulation of conversation a gimmick. It was shown on pay-cable's *Showtime*, courtesy of public TV's *American Playhouse* productions. The recording was screened again, Channel 13, 4 May 1988.

14 *Telegraph*, 30 July 1986.

15 Black Sunday was 29 June.

16 Rich had said Miller was the third but most daring of three British directors rethinking O'Neill around this time, the others being David Leveaux and Keith Hack. Barnes was cited by Joan Bakewell on BBC TV's *Newsnight* and in Glimmerglass' *Donor and Subscriber Preview*, as above.

17 Olivier had been directed by Michael Blakemore in 1971. Reviewing Stateside for the *Guardian*, 5 April 1986, Billington had largely agreed with Frank Rich. He had additionally praised Spacey's mercurial love-hate relationship with his brother. Interviewed by the *Sunday Telegraph*, 27 July 1986, Miller snapped back: 'I happen to know more about tuberculosis than certain critics.' Billington acknowledged the rebuke in the *Guardian*, 5 August 1986, though he pointed out that the tubercular O'Neill's own stage direction mentioned feverish eyes and sunken cheeks.

18 The London reviews in favour of *Long Day's Journey* included the *Evening Standard* and *Financial Times*, 5 August 1986, plus the *Sunday Times* and *Observer*, 10 August. *The Times* and *Telegraph*, 6 August, the *Sunday Telegraph*, 10 August, and the *Times Literary Supplement*, 15 August, were less impressed. The *Sunday Times* review also celebrated the news of Miller's Old Vic appointment, which had followed the opening of *Long Day's Journey* on Broadway.

19 *The Shrew* opened at the RST, Stratford, 8 September 1987.

20 Besides the trouble with Shaw, rumours were leaked (*Independent*, 25 March 1987) that Miller was also threatening to quit if a set design, not of his choosing, was imposed on this *Shrew*.

21 The admiring comments came from *City Limits*, 10 September 1987; *Punch*, 13 September; *Daily Telegraph*; and *Observer*, 17 and 23 September. *Time Out*, issued on 16 September, thought there were leaden patches. Billington was won round at the London Barbican (*Guardian*, 8 September 1988), finding the production had gained more pensive gravity. Curiously, Miller appears to have forgotten the good reviews and his Tavistock Clinic angle on Kate.

22 Stuart Burge, as the incoming AD at the Royal Court in 1977, made Miller his associate director only to comment later that, once appointed, the man was barely seen again. That observation is also attributed to Max Stafford-Clark who was another associate and, from 1979, Burge's successor. See Little, R. and McLaughlin, E. (2007), *The Royal Court Theatre Inside Out* (London: Oberon), p. 189, and Findlater, R. (1981), *At the Royal Court: 25 Years of the English Stage Company* (Ambergate: Amber Lane).

23 Selassie's world was portrayed as peculiarly hermetic, with the emperor deludedly believing he remained powerful even after his fall. His ivory tower was shattered by rebels and then by Jonathan Dimbleby (or Dimbleeblee, as Miller's cast comically called him), arriving to film an exposé.

24 Trevor Nunn had directed the RSC's *Nicholas Nickleby* with a strong element of physical theatre in 1980, and a new wave of companies working in that vein, including Théâtre de Complicité, were emerging during that decade.

25 This set might be seen as another variation on Frances Yates' Theatre of Memory, with its voices reminiscing from cubbyholes. Indeed, Michael Coveney in the *Financial Times*, 18 March 1987, spotted that parallel.

26 Miller was not altogether happy with Theatre Downstairs' transfer in September 1987. He saw it as a lamentable decompression, a problem he had likewise encountered when his Donmar *Hamlet* moved to the Piccadilly Theatre.

27 The telecast was *Arena: The Emperor*, 5 February 1988.

28 Jones discussed Miller's Old Vic tenure in a platform talk at the NT, 22 October 2003.

29 As well as having worked on the international opera scene, Miller had a stash of all the back numbers of the journal *Théâtre en Europe* which he shared with his Old Vic designers. *Théâtre en Europe* was

edited by Strehler among others, and Hudson's Old Vic sets were compared to Richard Peduzzi's designs for Chéreau.

30 Miller's West End programming was welcomed by Michael Ratcliffe, *Observer*, 24 January 1988, and by others. Irving Wardle had observed in *The Times*, 21 May 1986, how Miller's appointment was part of a promising shift in British theatre, with a 'lost generation' of directors regaining a foothold after a long period of exclusion from the National and the Royal Shakespeare Company. Those directors included Michael Blakemore. John Dexter was trying to establish a quality West End company. Miller and the young Kenneth Branagh's classical Renaissance Company were seen as a pair of Davids challenging the two Goliaths of the NT and the RSC. Peter Hall was also intent on launching his own operation at the commercial Haymarket Theatre Royal in the late Eighties.

31 Miller acknowledged, at the time, that the Glasgow Citz and Manchester's Royal Exchange Theatre were presenting some comparably adventurous productions. It would, certainly, be wrong to suggest foreign works were barely seen in Britain. Under Peter Hall, the London Arts Theatre had, of course, brought in new French plays in the mid-1950s, including Ionesco's work and Beckett's *Godot* (in English). Declan Donnellan and Nick Ormerod's touring company, Cheek by Jowl, had staged British premieres of *Andromache* in 1985 and Corneille's *The Cid* in 1986. The London International Festival of Theatre, now known as LIFT, co-presented the Katona József Theatre in conjunction with Miller's Old Vic in 1989. LIFT got started with biennial imports in 1981, and Lyubimov had won an Evening Standard Award in 1983 for his *Crime and Punishment*. As regards the individual plays which Miller programmed, *Marya* had been glimpsed as BBC TV's *Play of the Month* in 1979 (courtesy of producer Cedric Messina, directed by Jack Gold). *Too Clever by Half* had been staged, not very successfully, at Richmond's Orange Tree Theatre in 1985 (under the title *Diary of a Scoundrel*). *A Flea in Her Ear* (John Mortimer's translation) had been staged by the National Theatre at the Old Vic in the mid-1960s. Impresario Peter Daubeny was, also, at that time presenting the Aldwych's aforementioned World Theatre Seasons (including the Comédie Française, the Moscow Art Theatre, troupes from Poland, Greece, Japan and Africa). Thelma Holt, running Camden's Roundhouse for several years from 1977, imported international companies, particularly from the Edinburgh Festival.

32 Reworking his Mermaid *Tempest*, Miller was particularly interested in the idea of the magus as a Renaissance scientist, in the mould of John Dee or of the physician-philosopher Robert Fludd whose experiments were blurred with occult magic.

33 The casting director Pippa Ailion underlines how Miller, characteristically, created a fantastic educational situation for everyone. She learned about art history and, when her son came to the theatre after school, the AD would help with his homework, humorously illustrating the breathing mechanism of locusts. Her Old Vic post was, Ailion says, probably the happiest of her working life.

34 *The Life of Kenneth Tynan*, p. 398, records Miller's suggestion that Tynan felt exiled.

35 The enterprise literally became a family affair with Tom Miller, by then a professional photographer in his twenties, taking publicity shots for his father's productions.

36 The definition of newcomers is often a little hazy. Alex Jennings was not a total unknown. He had been directed by Nicholas Hytner at the Chichester Festival in 1995 before appearing in Miller's RSC *Shrew*. Alex Kingston only graduated from RADA in 1987, but she had been in *Grange Hill* as a teenager and in the TV mini-series *A Killing on the Exchange*. Ranjit Bolt had been a stockbroker. His translation of *The Liar* landed in Miller's lap out of the blue, going on to win great acclaim. Andrzej Krauze had a substantial track record as a cartoonist in Poland. He fled martial law in 1981 to settle in London.

37 Jones staged *Too Clever by Half*, *A Flea in Her Ear* and *The Illusion*. The Old Vic was an important break for him, although he had directed productions before that, notably the premiere of Judith Weir's *A Night at the Chinese Opera* for Kent Opera in 1987. Michell was a bright young thing, promoted from RSC assistant director to resident director in 1987. He staged *Marya*.

38 Miller was not alone in inclining towards sloping stages. Richard Jones and Tim Albery (especially with his *Billy Budd*) became known for their cantilevered views of the world, as noted in the *New York Times*, 27 August 1989.

39 The hieratic gestures came from baroque paintings.

40 Perhaps the 'lordly' dismissing of the *Andromache* felt like a variation on the High Master at St Paul's crushing Miller and Korn's Literary Society. Korn's version was published, with a preface by Miller, in Korn, E. (trans.) (1988), *Jean Racine's Andromache* (London/New York, NY: Applause). Raine's adaptation was, incidentally, staged at the Almeida many years later, under the title *1953*.

41 In his droll *Times Literary Supplement* piece 'How I Shot J. R.', Korn remarked on his translation, saying: 'How many false notes does it take to spoil a symphony? Not many: go Pa-Pa-Pa-*Oink* in Beethoven's *Fifth*, and you are dead, brother.' This was reprinted in Korn, E. (1989), *Remainders: From the Times Literary Supplement 1980–1989* (Manchester: Carcanet).

42 Paul Taylor, *Independent*, 22 January 1988.

43 Glowing reviews of *Candide* included the *Sunday Times*, 11 December 1988, and Mark Steyn in the

Independent, 8 December 1988. That was in contrast to the *Independent*'s damning critique of the show, 21 May 1988, during its warm-up at Glasgow's Mayfest, prior to tightening, cuts and the recasting that brought in Routledge (as the Old Lady). She ended up winning the Olivier Award for Best Actress in a Musical. Other cast members included Nickolas Grace, Bonaventura Bottone, and Mark Beudert in the title role.

44 Humphrey Burton's BBC video of the production was broadcast on 1 October 1988. Further distribution was, apparently, prevented by Bernstein's managers who disliked one performer.

45 Hudson and Jennings were winners in the Critics' Circle Awards too.

46 *Bussy d'Ambois* was another play that Miller had wanted to stage at the National. In the NT archives, a letter from Peter Hall to Miller, 25 July 1972, alludes to that.

47 'All my fault. I loved it in Vienna ten years ago', said Miller in the *Sunday Times*, 4 December 1988, referring to Angelika Hurwicz's production of *The Tutor*.

48 *One Way Pendulum* was first seen on stage at the Royal Court in 1959. Interviewed by the *Daily Mail*, 27 April 1964, shortly before the film version's release, Miller called it one of the best dramatic examples of absurdism, comparable to Lewis Carroll and the logic of infancy.

49 *The Tempest* sold out regardless of the fact that Max von Sydow, accustomed to longer rehearsals in Sweden, fluffed some lines on press night. He was a big box-office draw, having starred in *The Exorcist* as well as in Ingmar Bergman's *The Seventh Seal* and productions at Sweden's Royal Dramatic Theatre.

50 David Mirvish handled much of the Old Vic business, flying over from Canada, as Ed Mirvish was in his seventies by this point.

51 Steven Pimlott was directing both productions and his comments were reported in the *Sunday Times*, 7 October 1990. He underlined the fact that the budget had not been exceeded and he said it was a shame that Mirvish had not played by the rules. Many other ideas were left on the drawing board, never to be realized by Miller. These included staging studio productions in the neighbouring annexe (now the NT Studio), programming operas, bringing in Nicholas Hytner and premiering Kurt Vonnegut's comedy about a psychoanalyst specializing in indecisiveness. Miller's interest in *Make Up Your Mind* was reported in the *New York Times*, 11 August 1989. He mentioned his plans to try out catwalks, bleachers and the next-door annexe in *Theatre Design and Technology*, Winter 1991. Peter Zadek's *Lulu* had already been regretfully shelved due to his ill health.

52 Rumours about the UCLA chair in television and film studies were reported in the *Evening Standard*, 16 May and 13 September 1989.

53 Miller told David Mirvish, on 22 July 1990, that he wished to resign and his departure date was set for March 1991.

54 Quotation from the *Sunday Telegraph*, 27 July 1986.

55 Miller was writer-presenter for both *My God* and *Four Virtuosos*. *My God* was broadcast (six programmes in all) in April–May 1988 and an *International Herald Tribune* interview, published 18 April 1988, indicates that Miller was heading off to Manchester to conduct interviews for that series in February–March. *Four Virtuosos*, made by Tempo Video, was on Channel 4, July–August 1988. The series was, surely, a source for some private jokes for Miller and Dudley Moore, considering the former's piano-side concert commentaries in *Beyond the Fringe*.

56 Miller nipped out to stage *La Traviata* at Glimmerglass Opera in Upstate New York in July 1989 as well as directing *The Mikado* in Houston for November of that year. LA Opera's *Mahagonny* opened in between those two, in September. It received decidedly mixed reviews, with bemusement apparently caused by the loss of Brecht's traditional placards and by the Hollywood setting. Maybe some punters who remembered *Beyond the Fringe* were particularly confused. Miller and Moore had, back then, taken the mickey with their sketch, *The Ballad of Gangster Joe, from the Weill opera Walnut*.

57 The Maggio Musicale *Don Giovanni*, at the Pergola in June 1990, highlighted the work's dreamlike qualities with a disturbingly skewed set by Robert Israel. That transferred to Los Angeles in the autumn of 1991, revived by Karen Stone. Miller's book about Don Giovanni – Miller, J. (ed.) (1990), *The Don Giovanni Book: Myths of Seduction and Betrayal* (London: Faber) – was also published in the US by Schocken Books that same year. It featured essays from Roy Porter, Marina Warner, Jane Miller and others. These analyzed the restless Don from various historical, philosophical and psychological perspectives, discussing how he related to Enlightenment themes, seeing him as a sexual Faust and an eternally immature Oedipal figure. The *Independent on Sunday*, 29 July 1990, judged this book to be a remarkable dramatization of the interdependence of performance and scholarship. The *New Statesman*, 27 July, found it too academic.

58 *Dialogue in the Dark*, BBC TV, 4 June 1989. Romain in *A Profile*, pp. 210–11, notes that Ignatieff initially envisaged extra scenes with Dr Johnson and Boswell, after dark, on the Thames. Perhaps Miller foresaw more *Private Eye* 'Dr Jonathan' jibes, swiftly ditching the idea with, 'Oh God, not a night shoot!'

59 *Who Cares?*, BBC TV, from 11 May 1989. He, incidentally, presented his aforementioned Channel 4 scientific documentary *Moving Pictures* in July 1989 as well.

60 *Jonathan Miller: A Full Life*, Channel 4, 10 April 1989, made by Television South.

61 The *Daily Telegraph*, 14 March 1989, alluded to the fact that Miller was working on *Born Talking*

at that point. This series consisted of four programmes and was an international co-production by John McGreevy/Primedia Productions, in association with TV Ontario and BBC TV, ABC Australia and the Discovery Channel. It was first broadcast during September 1990 in the UK. It was released on video and distributed far afield by Educational Film Services, Hong Kong.

62 Non-verbal communication was, likewise, the subject of Miller's 1989 Darwin College Lecture, *Communicating Without Words*. This was subsequently published in Mellor, D. H. (ed.) (1990), *Ways of Communicating* (Cambridge: Cambridge University Press).

63 Reviews included the *Guardian*, 24 September 1990, the *Independent on Sunday* and *Observer*, both 30 September 1990.

64 *Madness* was also known as *Museums of Madness*. That Miller was making the series was reported in the *Sunday Times*, 9 October 1988. It was first shown on BBC TV in October 1991, with PBS swiftly following suit in the US. The inserted dramatized scenes were not Miller's handiwork, and he suggests some Wellcome Institute colleagues were rightly critical because the history was rushed (with him zipping to the US, Trieste and elsewhere in the programmes). The reviews that noted how he cast doubt on his father's profession, and on the categoric pigeonholing of aberrant and so-called schizophrenic behaviour, included the *Sunday Telegraph*, 6 October 1991. Emanuel himself dissected the problems of classification in psychiatry. That was in the last paper he wrote (as noted in his obituary, *British Medical Journal*, 8 August 1970). Regarding Miller's condemnations in *Madness*, the *Psychiatric Times* was still nursing its wounds more than a decade later, with Professor Max Fink fighting back in his article, 'A New Appreciation of ECT', April 2004, Vol. XXI, Issue 4.

65 *Q.E.D.: What's So Funny About That?*, BBC TV, 21 March 1989. Miller's theory of comedy clearly linked back to his boyhood fascination with scientific systems of classification. See above, too, regarding Emanuel's last paper. Miller co-edited a book about humour, Durant, J. and Miller, J. (eds) (1988) *Laughing Matters: A Serious Look at Humour* (Harlow: Longman Scientific and Technical).

66 In terms of his high media profile, other programmes where Miller appeared included *Cover to Cover* (discussing new books), *Life File* (on Alzheimer's), *Horizon* (on Parkinson's disease and medical ethics) and *Omnibus* (on the Royal Opera House), all between March and May 1988. At other points during that year, he was on BBC Radio's *Kaleidoscope*, *The Anne Robinson Show* and *The Keys to Creative Genius*. In 1989, he contributed to two more Alzheimer's programmes – *Trouble in Mind* and *Everyman: Just an Illness* (both aired on 9 March) – plus four *Late Show* programmes, *Arena*, *Saturday Night Clive* etc.–

67 The Gillick *Late Show* was broadcast on 9 February 1989, and it cropped up again as a highlight in the BBC programme *TV Hell*, 31 August 1992. Gillick made the 'mouth-on-legs' comment as the credits rolled.

68 Desmond Barrit says that he loved Jonathan's gentle rehearsal process at the Old Vic, keeping the hours short and not giving excessive notes. Alec McCowen, for his part, has underlined that the director was completely focused during *Dialogue in the Dark*. Disproving the notion that Miller cannot get on with living writers, Ignatieff was delighted with their studio shoot in Glasgow. See McCowen and Ignatieff in Romain, *A Profile*, pp. 141 and 212.

69 Frederic Raphael, quoted by Mark Lawson in *Drama*, 1988, Vol. 1.

70 Phil Penfold, *Evening Chronicle*, 20 May 1988, recorded the cast's snipes in rehearsals for *Candide*. Evidently, Wells had clarified that *Private Eye*'s 'Life of Dr. Jonathan' column was nothing to do with him. Nevertheless, his lack of know-how when it came to co-directing had, according to Miller, caused the two of them to fall out over this production.

71 Presented at Miller's old Footlights haunt, *Into the Woods* won an Olivier, a Critics' Circle Award and two Evening Standard Awards.

72 Leigh explains that the shows' huge set was to jut out over part of the stalls, reducing the number of rows and spoiling the sightlines for some circle seats as well. 'We reckoned,' he says, 'that, if it played to 60 or 65 per cent business, it would lose in the region of 484,000 to 500,000 pounds, which was a lot of money.'

73 When Kevin Spacey took over the Old Vic in 2004, he initially echoed his predecessor's continentalism, kicking off with a Dutch play, though not a vintage one. In 2006, he enjoyed a big success there with *A Moon for the Misbegotten*, O'Neill's sequel to *Long Day's Journey*.

74 In the Seventies, Miller had been interested in Hampstead's New End Theatre (a former hospital mortuary).

Chapter 15: The Nineties

1 *Opera Now*, December 1990.

2 The *Sunday Telegraph*, 24 March 1991, quoted Miller's remark: 'We need mortality. It gives us the sort of intensity we require; it gives urgency to life.' With the opera world planning ahead, most of his

1991 productions had been lined up during 1989–90, his fifty-fifth year. Miller's air miles have, obviously, clashed with his late mother's philosophy of staying close to home, to scrutinize what's under your nose. Besides the 'lone ranger' tag, the *Evening Standard* nicknamed him 'the vagabond genius' on 13 August 1993.

3 I have substantially drawn, in this paragraph, from Richard Rosenfeld's *Sunday Times* interview with Tom and William, 3 January 1993. This article also mentioned that Tom, 30, had just bought his own flat in north London.

4 Miller quoted by Jan Moir, *Daily Telegraph*, 2 September 1996.

5 Rachel's imminent retirement was reported in the *Daily Telegraph*, 14 June 1991.

6 Miller had been to Poland with Rachel and Peter Eyre the year before, coinciding with the tour of *The Emperor*.

7 Della Couling's interview appeared in *Opera Now*, July 1991, but was already being leaked and quoted by other publications in mid-June.

8 These comments cropped up in Bruce Johnston's interview, *Daily Telegraph*, 14 June 1991, and in Miller's remarks on the *Today* programme, BBC Radio, broadcast the same day.

9 The *Daily Telgraph* editorial, 14 June 1991, then on impertinence, 17 June.

10 *Daily Mail*, 15 June 1991.

11 Geoffrey Wheatcroft, *Evening Standard*, 14 June 1991. To be fair, some articles were more measured than my selections here suggest, expressing mild sadness as well as weariness regarding Miller's bitter goodbye. Diverse journalists, including Bruce Johnston, expressed continuing fondness, while Wheatcroft suggested the director's farewells were themselves a very British ritual, 'as regular as the Lord's Test or Trooping the Colour'.

12 This Bennett-Miller rift, relating to *Enjoy*, was alluded to in the *Independent*, 7 May 2004.

13 An anonymous associate of Bennett's was quoted in the *Observer*, 12 August 1984, saying that disappearing was his 'nuclear weapon'.

14 From Bennett's correspondence sent to the author, 7 April 2003.

15 *Wind in the Willows* was at the NT and *The Lady in the Van* was adapted for the radio, both in 1990.

16 *The Madness of George III* opened at the National in 1991. Bennett acknowledged in *Writing Home*, p. 230, that both Miller and the medical historian Michael Neve had suggested that George's madness might make a play.

17 'Favourite Uncle' status was bestowed on Bennett by Charles Nevin, *Independent on Sunday*, in November 1991. He was named the nation's 'literary teddy bear' and 'Betjeman II' in the *Independent*, 29 January 1995. By 2008, Watford Palace Theatre's spring brochure was quoting the *Sunday Telegraph*'s description of him: 'Perhaps the best-loved of English writers today'. That said, Miller was shortlisted once, alongside Bennett, for the *Sunday Telegraph* and British Library's 2008 National Treasures poll. Judi Dench landed more votes than either of them, to win the Brontë Award in the arts category. Miller came fifth in the Top 100 British Public Intellectuals poll, run by *Prospect* magazine in 2004 (with Richard Dawkins gaining first place). Miller did not feature in the Global Top 100 in 2005.

18 Bennett's introduction, in Bennett, A. (1998), *Plays 2: Kafka's Dick, The Insurance Man, The Old Country, An Englishman Abroad, A Question of Attribution* (London: Faber), pp. viii–xi. Jingoism was, of course, particularly rampant during the Falklands War.

In 1993, Miller was still being criticized for his comments and protesting in the *Daily Mail*, on 19 August: 'I'm not a traitor. I'm a patriot. And that's why it grieves me to see this country mutilating itself . . . This sceptred isle has become a septic isle.'

19 The difference with Abram Miller and Simon Spiro was, of course, that the trades they learned enabled them to settle after emigration. On a slightly different tack, Miller compares the unglamorous aspects of his international career to *Auf Wiedersehen, Pet*, saying, 'It's like a construction worker who has to go to Germany. You can't pick and choose.'

20 Miller spoke of the *Sprecher* to Penelope Gilliatt, *New Yorker*, 17 April 1989.

21 He discussed proscenium arches in *Theatre Design and Technology*, Winter 1991.

22 The *Daily Mail*, 9 February 1991, reported Miller coming top in a London marriage bureau's survey which apparently questioned 800 of the UK's most influential, thirty-something, high-earning female executives. The effect has not entirely worn off, judging by the blog of 4 October 2008 on blondeshiksel. blogspot.com where an ardent fan reported having swooned over Miller and fancied a 'bunk-up', when they chatted after a platform talk.

23 *Spitting Image* was on ITV from 1984 to 1996, with John Sessions impersonating Miller's voice. A satiric tone had also been prevalent – combined with some praise – in Bergan's 1989 book, *Beyond the Fringe . . . and Beyond*. In 1992, Romain's *A Profile* was more admiring.

24 *Spitting Image*, series 1–4, recently reappeared on DVD (Network, 2008). Obviously, the real-life Miller has little need to talk baloney, but Richard Denton (who directed the BBC *Madness* series) jovially remembers one dispute about a movie:

We didn't argue for long – because you don't argue for long with Jonathan – but I was saying *Cinema Paradiso* was rubbish. Then, about a month later, he said, 'You're right. It's complete rubbish.' I said, 'Well, why did you disagree?' and he said, 'Well, I hadn't seen it and I thought you were probably wrong.' That's the only argument with Jonathan that I ever won, though it took four weeks!

25 Roger Law mirthfully recalls the 'Terry 2' sketch, and those multi-tasking skits undeniably turned the joke on Miller in terms of his own theory of comedy – that laughter is provoked when normal categories are defied.

26 Robert McNab's Degas documentary for *Omnibus* was on BBC1, 20 May 1996, and the exhibition was at the National Gallery.

27 *La Fanciulla del West* opened at La Scala on 29 January 1991 (with Miller's *Tosca*, meanwhile, being revived by Karen Stone in Houston for 24 January). *Katya* played at the Met from 25 February. Co-produced by the Vienna State Opera and the Wiener Festwochen at the Theater an der Wien, *Figaro* played from 12 May. For the Maggio Musicale at the Teatro della Pergola, *Così* ran from 21 June. *The Magic Flute* was at the Mann Auditorium, Tel Aviv, from 16 July (with the Israel Philharmonic Orchestra). After rehearsals that same month, *Fidelio*'s opening night at Glimmerglass was 10 August.

28 *La Fanciulla* transferred to Turin's Teatro Regio on 17 May 1991. Besides being televised by RAI, it was revived at La Scala in January 1995 then transported to Tokyo's Bunka Kaikan in September. *The Times* of London's review, reporting back from La Scala on 15 February 1991, did not wholly favour Miller's unromantic realism, while admitting it added poignancy.

29 The *New York Times*, 27 February 1991, referred to this *Katya* as *Madame Bovary* on the Volga, admiring Miller's understated direction. The action was, other reviews noted, shifted from the 1860s to a more Chekhovian pre-revolutionary 1905 (somewhat nearer Janáček's composition date of 1921).The Met's regained importance was noted by Peter G. Davis, unattributed article, possibly *New York Magazine*, dated 11 March 1991. There was something of a critical backlash later. *Katya* would continue to be revived into the next century, with the Lyric Opera of Chicago importing it in November 2009, with Miller's name still attached.

30 The *Financial Times*, 9 November 1993, called it a landmark production. Miller had exceptionally detailed discussions with the costume designer James Acheson (of *Les Liaisons Dangereuses* fame) about authentic underwear and the uncleanability of eighteenth-century clothes. He brought in another protégé, Peter Davison (originally Richard Hudson's Old Vic assistant), to design the vast dilapidated chateau he required. Davison became a frequent collaborator for a while.

31 Raimondi points up how, '[Jonathan] concentrates always on what happens inside the character, making minimalist choices. Sometimes it is not easy to follow his thought, but suddenly you become aware that a smile, a gesture of the hand, a glance have become of the utmost importance. You realize what he wanted you to express. It is a beautiful world.' The Vienna Staatsoper *Figaro* played at Ferrara's Teatro Comunale in January 1994, with some cast changes, and it went on to Japan's Bunka Kaikan auditorium in September 1995. Its life was perpetuated on video, by Sony, in 1993. Allegedly, however, the Staatsoper's incoming boss Eberhard Wächter was nursing a grudge, having previously run the city's rival Volksoper company for whom Miller had failed to direct a show. 'Consequently,' one insider says, 'Eberhard hated this absolutely perfect production. It was sent on a tour to Japan, and all the sets were left there.'

32 After his *Tosca* in 1986, his *Tristan* (from LA) in 1988, his *Don Giovanni* in 1990 and this 1991 *Così*, Miller's productions at Florence were *Figaro* in June 1992, *La Bohème* in December 1994, *Idomeneo* in May 1996, *Ariadne auf Naxos* in June 1997 and, after a slightly longer gap, *Don Pasquale* in September 2001. His *Figaro* completed a major Mozart tripartite cycle for Florence, and it employed a different team from his staging in Vienna, although Peter Davison remained on board. Thomas Hampson played the Count and Joan Rodgers was Susanna. It was broadcast on Italian TV and was still being revived in Florence in 2003. With *Idomeneo*, Miller began exploring Mozart's somewhat lesser-known opera seria.

33 Miller mentioned Clair and Pagnol as influences when interviewed, in *Opéra International*, December 1995, about updating Puccini's tragic romance by a hundred years. He drew on period photographs by Brassaï and André Kertész and, as with *La Traviata*, he discerned parallels with Flaubert's *L'Education Sentimentale*. When he restaged *La Bohème* for the ENO in 2009, he additionally alluded to Marcel Carné's film *Hôtel du Nord*, as well as stating that he partially based the male would-be artists, slumming it, on *Withnail and I*.

34 Though this chapter deals predominantly with the 1990s, some of the strings of productions mentioned extended on into the Noughties. *Don Pasquale* opened in September 2001, with a transfer to Seville in February 2003, before arriving at Covent Garden in November 2004. Isabella Bywater designed the three-storey set (interestingly comparable to a four-storey apartment block created by director-designer Herbert Werknicke for his staging of J. S. Bach's *Actus Tragicus* at Theater Basel in 2000, and to Russell Craig's smaller-scale, two-storey set for Welsh National Opera's 1986 *Barber of Seville*). Equally stunning, Peter Davison's *Figaro* set had used a revolve which enabled the characters to move through the house, between the grander rooms and the servants' quarters, before the audience's eyes.

35 The festival's then artistic director, Cesare Mazzonis (who was also artistic director of La Scala) supports Mehta's remarks about Miller in Florence, observing: 'Jonathan has his own style. There is a subtlety and always many surprises . . . We always worked without incidents and very happily.'

36 Family friends from the UK visited, not least Lord Harewood and Caroline Garland (who, in terms of social interconnections, was Nicholas Garland's third wife and the daughter of University College's Nobel Prize-winning immunologist, Peter Medawar). She particularly loved the 'magic carpet' of whizzing over to Italy in a light aircraft, flown by William who, by then, had a pilot's licence.

37 Miller points up that his 1920s hotel setting was, visually, inspired by Erich Salomon's photographs of post-World War 1 statesmen. The link with *The Magic Flute* had been made, in 1920, by Goldsworthy Lowes Dickinson, the Cambridge historian and pacifist closely associated with the Bloomsbury Group. Besides his essay on the League of Nations, *The Future of the Convent*, Dickinson had reinterpreted Mozart's opera as a parable for post-World War 1 civilization. See Dickinson, G. L. (1920) *The Future of the Covenant* (London: League of Nations Union), and Dickinson, G. L. (1920) *The Magic Flute: A Fantasia* (London: George Allen & Unwin). In 2006, Kenneth Branagh's film version of *The Magic Flute* would also use World War 1 as its setting.

38 Miller's photographs of clapboard barns in Cooperstown and nearby Cherry Valley had fed into the set of his *Katya Kabanova*. His Glimmerglass productions opened as follows: *La Traviata*, July 1989; *Fidelio*, August 1991; *Il Matrimonio Segreto*, July 1992; *L'Incoronazione di Poppea*, July 1994; *Tamerlano*, July 1995; and Janáček's *Jenufa* in July 2006.

39 With Miller's assistance, Glimmerglass came to rival the Opera Theater of St Louis in its fostering of young American singers. I am indebted for this information to the art dealer-turned-Glimmerglass board member and benefactor Eugene Thaw, who loaned Miller his Cherry Valley cottage. Thaw originally met the director, through Freddie Ayer and Dee Wells in NW1.

40 Rachel was working long-distance, with her laptop, on the studies of Alzheimer's and other illnesses which she conducted for the medical website DIPEx.

41 *La Traviata* won accolades. The *Daily Telegraph*'s Charles Osborne, on 22 August 1989, called it one of the finest stagings he had seen, and its combination of photographically sharp realism with dreamlike tableaux was particularly admired. That oneiric feel was partially created by the set: an almost bare, blue-green chamber. The director points out that a beautiful Musée des Arts Décoratifs exhibition, which he saw in Paris, encouraged his directorial habit of framing gorgeous period costumes in near-abstract spaces – having walls painted with just rough brush strokes or faded washes. His 1991 Glimmerglass *Fidelio* was set in a grimmer, prisoner-surveying, Panopticon-style gaol, as discussed by Foucault in *Discipline and Punish* and first thought up by Jeremy Bentham in 1785. That set was also faintly reminiscent of the brick tower in Miller's *Prometheus Bound,* and it might be compared to the revolving central tower in his later production of *La Clemenza di Tito*.

42 A touch of the director's own youthful performance in John Barton's *Volpone* crept in, for Miller had the English Count repeatedly wielding a cricket bat, though only an imaginary one. His *Mikado* had, by the by, featured batting gags too. The *Manchester Evening News*, 19 July 1993, reviewing a subsequent UK staging of *The Secret Marriage*, observed that the Count's overarm bowling just was not cricket in the composer's era. The surtitles joke was particularly apt at Glimmerglass in 1992, because the company's productions had always been in English until that year.

43 On *Poppea*, Miller teamed up with Jane Glover as his conductor, and with the lawyer-turned-costume designer Judy Levin who was a long-lost American cousin of his.

44 *New York Times*, 2 August 1994. There was high praise almost across the board even though the *Wall Street Journal*, on 1 August, was not keen. *Poppea* transferred to BAM in January 1996, when Harvey Lichtenstein was executive producer.

45 As Rodney Milnes dryly noted in *Opera*, February 1994, this trilogy was not to be confused with the 'disgusting old opera queens' whom Miller had disparaged in his comments on the industry in Britain. *Roberto Devereux* (depicting Elizabeth I's dearly beloved but doomed Earl of Essex) opened at the Opéra de Monte-Carlo in January 1992, *Maria Stuarda* in March 1993, *Anna Bolena* in March 1994.

46 *Maria Stuarda* and *Anna Bolena* were both co-productions with Bologna's Teatro Comunale. *Roberto Devereux* and *Maria Stuarda* transferred to Turin's Teatro Regio in 1997 and 1999 etc.

47 The trilogy was first revived in Monte Carlo, March 1997. The venue received 1,500 ticket requests beyond the capacity. That was reported in *Opera International*, May 1997, No. 213. The opera house's general director, John Mordler, explains why they worked so well, emphasizing: 'Even when it's just "stand up and sing" in bel canto opera, Jonathan has this way of relaxing and getting even the most difficult performers to act.'

48 *Anna Bolena* opened in Munich in October 1995 and *I Puritani* in May 2000.

49 Miller willingly concedes this *Il Matrimonio Segreto* was copied more or less exactly from Glimmerglass. His productions at the Opernhaus Zürich have been *Die Gezeichneten*, December 1992; *Falstaff*, October 1993; *Il Matrimonio Segreto*, July 1996; *Nabucco*, June 1998; *Die Zauberflöte*, December 1999;

Die Schweigsame Frau, December 2001; *Die Entführung aus dem Serail* or *Il Seraglio*, June 2003; *La Clemenza di Tito*, April 2005.

50 Horst Koegler's *Opera News* review, April 2002, admired the 'Swiss precision' in Miller's staging of Richard Strauss' fiancée-swopping Jonsonian comedy, *Die Schweigsame Frau*. That starred the soprano Elena Mosuc. On *Falstaff*, the *Schwäbische Zeitung* of 26 October 1993 referred to the director as 'der britische Psychiater', and the *Neue Zürcher Zeitung*, 1 January 2000, similarly alluded to the psychological nuances in *Die Zauberflöte*.

51 Miller's continental audience seemed more willing than some UK critics to accept that Mozart's *Singspiel* was a European Enlightenment fantasy and that the Queen of the Night – rather than resembling something from Aztec Night at the Copacabana – should be a Hapsburgian battle-axe surrounded by shady bishops, like the Holy Roman Empress Maria Theresa.

52 While aesthetically sharing some common ground with Miller's Vermeer-inspired *Taming of the Shrew*, Peter Davison's sets for *Falstaff* invoked the paintings of Pieter de Hooch, Adriaen van Ostade and Gerard ter Borch. Hints of modernity sneaked into the tavern with its tongue-in-cheek dartboard. Juan Pons (who had been in *La Fanciulla*) played the title role, alternating with Albert Rinaldi, in Zurich in 1993. *Falstaff* was restaged in Berlin, at Daniel Barenboim's Deutsche Staatsoper Unter den Linden, in February 1998 (starring Raimondi, and with Abbado conducting). It also transferred to Ferrara's Teatro Comunale in 1999 and was filmed for television by RAI.

53 Since 1998, *Nabucco* has been repeatedly revived, with runs in 2006 (along with three of Miller's other Zurich productions), 2007 and 2008. Designed by Isabella Bywater, its semi-abstract setting was based on Napoleon's architectural engravings of Egyptian temples. The *NZZ's* review noted how Miller carefully created individuals rather than generalized racial types. That observation was posted on the opera house's website.

54 Before his 2003 *Il Seraglio*, his Mozart repertoire had already augmented – at the Salzburg Festival in July 1997 – to encompass the composer's youthful work *Mitridate, Re di Ponto*, with its tensions involving Rome and a Parthian princess. Miller's Glimmerglass production of Handel's *Tamerlano* preceded that, in 1995, depicting the Tartar emperor Tamburlaine.

55 This portrayal of the lady meant that the normally comedic ending, when she is graciously released from the harem, became more emotionally complex, veined with sadness. In his productions of *Tamerlano* and *Il Seraglio*, Miller drew on Orientalist painters from Handel and Mozart's own eras (such as Jean-Etienne Liotard and Jean Baptiste Vanmour). He was influenced, regarding imperialism and questions of assimilation, by Edward Said and Linda Colley, in particular Said, E. W. (1978), *Orientalism* (London: Routledge & Kegan Paul) and Colley, L. (2002), *Captives: Britain, Empire and the World 1600–1850* (London: Jonathan Cape).

56 Miller has talked about Jurassic Park singers on many occasions, including in his conversation with Graham Sheffield for the International Society for the Performing Arts Foundation, 1998.

57 The veal images echo the actress Coral Browne's celebrated quip about dull co-stars.

58 He commented on the three tenors in *Opera News*, June 2002, and spoke of giving the 'massively inert' Pavarotti a wide berth. In fact, he had scorned celebrity 'plum cakes' dumped in the middle of productions as early as April 1974, in his interview for *Music and Musicians*.

59 *Fedora* opened at the Bregenz Festival in mid-1993, then played at the Vienna Staatsoper in December 1994.

60 *La Bohème* transferred to the Bastille as a co-production with the Opéra National de Paris in December 1995. It was subsequently revived both there and in Florence.

61 Miller's comments on the Bastille productions and Bartoli were reported in the *Evening Standard*, 14 December 1995 and 26 July 1996.

62 Ronald Blum of the Associated Press alluded to the Gheorghiu-Alagna duo dismissing Miller's *La Traviata* as 'awful', 10 April 2002. *The Times*, 4 May 2007, reported Gheorghiu's remark: 'Jonathan Miller? I barely know him. He just used my name to promote himself.' His Bonnie and Clyde tag is oft repeated, as in the *Sunday Times* on 11 June 2006, *The Times* on 4 May 2007 etc. He called her and Alagna 'dangerous juveniles' as well, in the *Sunday Times*, 12 May 2002.

63 Miller discussed deformed stars, *Daily Express*, 16 October 1996.

64 Von Stade's comment appeared in *Newsday*, 21 March 1995.

65 The designer John Conklin and Miller were inspired by Eugène Atget's period photographs and by Deborah Turbeville's book, Turbeville, D. (1981), *Unseen Versailles: Photographs by Deborah Turbeville* (New York, NY: Doubleday). The set overlaid a spinning maze of architectural shards with projected photographs of Versailles and Fontainbleu's parklands.

66 Praise came from the *New York Times*, 25 March 1995; the *Independent*, 31 March; and the *Financial Times* on the same day (making the prism analogy). The Bergmanesque quality was recalled by Eric Myers, writing for *Variety*, 10 October 2006. By contrast, John Simon's interval growl was reported in the *New York Observer*, 10 April 1995, and his *New Criterion* review, in May, was damning. By the time

the *Financial Times* was appraising a revival on 20 December 2010, it had switched to scorning Miller's production for callously ditching the work's natural settings and exotic symbolism, a 'wilful trivialisation' which reduced Debussy to 'a drawing-room tragedy'.

66 Miller eschewed the Hogarthian look on this occasion because that style had been used in David Hockney's celebrated Glyndebourne production. Pre-World War 2 Berlin was where Auden and Isherwood had roved. This staging won appreciative appraisals from the *New York Post*, 23 November 1997, and the *Wall Street Journal*, 1 December.

68 Miller mentioned the 'Marie Celeste' management, *Daily Mail*, 19 August 1993, and mocked the glitz-loving audiences in the *New York Times*, 23 March 1995. An additional quip appeared in the *Wall Street Journal*, 28 May 2008, where Miller observed that a horse and carriage goes unapplauded round Central Park but, if one crosses the Met stage, it is treated as an orthopaedic miracle.

69 Most of the reviews sided with Miller regarding the arias, including the *Guardian* and *New York Observer*, 14 and 16 November 1998. When asked where she stood on the issue, the soprano Renée Fleming (who played the Countess) diplomatically remarks that there is room for musicological variations in such a well-known opera before she adds: 'Jonathan was, in my experience, a collaborative wonderful colleague . . . [with] strong ideas, but they were good, reasonable ideas and he was open to discussion.'

70 The *New York Times* criticized Bartoli's conduct on 9 November 1998, and Volpe's letter to the paper was printed on 14 November, particularly disputing that the singer had turned up late for rehearsals.

71 Miller's comment was quoted in the *Guardian*, 11 November 1998, and in the *Daily Telegraph* on 18 November, where it was joined by Bartoli's riposte about his Brutus-like, ungentlemanly conduct. Perhaps the singer was conflating Caesar and Mark Antony since she underlined how she felt obliged to defend Mozart's honour.

72 The 'wilful, wayward' remark comes from the *Daily Express*, 20 November 1999.

73 Miller suggested there was some kind of cabal and spoke of the jabbing finger in *Opera News*, June 2002.

74 Stephen Moss' *Guardian* feature, 19 November 2004, alluded to the satiric Volpe-Tony Soprano comparison. It also recorded the director anecdotally describing the face-off wherein Volpe, supposedly, underlined that the contract included the arias and Miller riposted that he would only agree in the way France agreed in 1939. 'You could see,' as Miller recalled, 'a cloud of unknowing pass across [Volpe's] eyes, and he just said, "Don't fuck with me."' The director's remark on being 'fired' appeared in *Opera News*, June 2002. He was similarly quoted in the *Paris Review* (Spring 2003), Issue 165 (saying Volpe told his agent he must never dare to think of returning), and in the *Sunday Times*, 28 September 2003 (saying that he had been trampled on, then kicked out). He had returned for a revival of *Pelléas*, but had not been hired to direct any new Met productions after *Figaro*.

75 Volpe in *Opera News*, June 2002. The board members' views were reported in the *Sunday Times*, 19 May 2002. One anonymously snapped that Miller's self-marketing was better than what he produced. Another voiced dismay at the Met alienating this man when it needed his refreshingly original ideas.

76 Concerning this passage on unprofessional conduct and baloney, I have drawn from Joseph Volpe's autobiography, Volpe, J. (written with Charles Michener) (2007), *The Toughest Show on Earth: My Rise and Reign at the Metropolitan Opera* (New York, NY: Vintage), pp. 162–6. Regarding the 'Don't fuck with me' exchange, Volpe phrases his response as follows on p. 166: 'Then [in Miller's *Guardian* interview] his memory got more interesting . . . Miller is an ex-comedy writer. If I'd wanted to play Tony Soprano, I could have come up with a better line than that.'

77 These plaudits came from the *Washington Post* and *Wall Street Journal*, both 4 November 1998, and the *Independent*, 6 November (discussing the queue). Miller's *Figaro* was broadcast by PBS, in the *Metropolitan Opera Presents* series, on 29 December 1999. In the UK, that recording was shown at the Barbican Cinema as part of London's Mostly Mozart Festival in July 2005. The Met revived Miller's *Figaro*, without the director on board, in 2005, 2006, 2007 and 2009. His *Pelléas et Mélisande* was revived there in December 2010, again minus Miller, but with the conductor Simon Rattle making his Met debut. His *Rake's Progress* was briefly resurrected in 2003, along with his *Katya Kabanova* in 2003 and 2004.

78 If one surveys the press coverage of Miller's productions in continental Europe, one finds that, in most countries, he won praise, but not unanimously. For example, regarding his *Falstaff* in Zurich, *Tages-Anzeiger* called it brilliant on 25 October 1993, but *NZZ*'s review, on the same day, considered it too spartan. His *Idomeneo* in Florence left *Il Giorno* underwhelmed, on 5 May 1996. Still, *La Nazione*, *Corriere della Sera* and *La Repubblica* declared the staging an overall success and it transferred, as a co-production, to the Opéra de Lausanne in 1997.

A number of British critics flew out to report on the director's work abroad. Covering the Tudor Queens trilogy in Monte Carlo, the *Guardian* (4 February 1992), loved the stringent economy of *Roberto Devereux*. Nonetheless, the *Financial Times*, reporting on *Maria Stuarda* on 30 March 1993, was appalled by the 'extraordinary inertia' of Miller's tableaux. *La Stampa* and *La Repubblica* (18 and 26 March 1999 respectively) were lukewarm about its Turin transfer. As for the Maggio Musicale production of *La Bohème*, *The*

Times of London (on 24 December 1994) damned the filmic update, saying it did not fit the opera's non-naturalistic conventions. Yet when the piece transferred to Paris' Bastille Opera, the French press picked up on its references to vintage photographs and gave it rave reviews (e.g. *Le Monde*, 15 December 1995).

In America, at Glimmerglass, after the success of *Poppea*, a handful of publications wrote off the baroque *Tamerlano* as woefully low on action. Still, the *New York Times* of 26 July 1995 disagreed, finding its stillness to be poignant. That production was subsequently restaged at Paris' Théâtre des Champs-Ely-sées and Germany's celebrated Handel Festival in Halle, to arrive at Sadler's Wells in London in 2001. On 12 August 1991, the *New York Times* had cheered Miller's Glimmerglass *Fidelio* as superlatively coherent and compelling. By contrast, the *Boston Globe* and *USA Today* (24 and 14 August) found it excessively murky. At the same address, the *New York Times* (on 31 July 1989) had not been bowled over by Miller's generally acclaimed *Traviata*.

79 The *New Yorker*, 18 March 1991.

80 Conrad's piece appeared in *Opera Now*, written for the issue of June 1991 when the 'mean, peevish little country' furore was in the pipeline. When Caroline Garland interviewed Miller for the ROH's magazine, *Opera House*, January 1995, he said that artists quote themselves, just as everyone has their own character or accent. Conrad's philippic further attested that the ex-medic's understanding of character had 'never advanced beyond a facile, mechanistic behaviourism' – simplistically giving protagonists limps or identifying props.

Further condemnations have included Peter G. Davis in *New York*, 17 April 1995 on *Pelléas*. Davis went on to disparage *Figaro*, calling Miller's direction vapid and fudged in *New York*, 16 November 1998. Meanwhile, Andrew Clark in the *Financial Times*, on 9 November 1993, slammed Miller's European productions of 1992 as a string of duds after his previous, marathon year.

81 Miller criticized La Scala in the *Daily Mail*, 19 August 1993. *Manon Lescaut* opened at La Scala in February 1992.

82 Aperçus about Monte Carlo were quoted by Mark Pappenheim, *Independent*, 12 February 1993.

83 The Zyklon B comment appeared in the Italian press: a sting in the tail from Miller after *Mitridate*'s opening night, as Roger Norrington recalls.

84 While Miller admires Peter Stein and Patrice Chéreau as experimental yet essentially classical directors, he condemns most 'Franco-German' theorizing as nonsense. The creed of *konzept regie* is often accompanied by pseudo-academic jargon, he says, recalling how he was warned that, if he didn't have a concept to impose, he would have great problematics with his praxis. When he asked what would be considered an ingenious concept, he was told of an exemplary *Figaro*, staged with inside-out costumes, because that showed the 'seamy side' of life. In the field of philosophy, he also fulminates about many post-modern continental thinkers, including Derrida whom he dismisses as pointlessly abstruse. Most of the current analytic philosophers whom he admires are English or American.

85 Geoffrey Wheatcroft suggested Miller suffered from conceptitis, *Guardian*, 17 January 1995.

86 In the late Eighties and the Nineties, Miller accused top American directors of imposing brash and superficial concepts as well. In the *Seattle Times*, 5 March 1991, he described Peter Sellars as a theatre *schlepper* who just loads an opera in a truck, drives it 200 years up the freeway and dumps it there. He was quoted in *Curtain Call*, January 1987, as saying that Robert Wilson's work resembled window-dressing in Macy's. Whether he has actually seen all the productions he lambastes is another question.

87 Miller's *Capriccio* opened in Berlin, 7 May 1993, and was restaged at Turin's Teatro Reggio, 8 October 2002.

88 In Strauss' aesthetic teaser, a writer and a composer vie over an undecided Countess and co-create an opera featuring themselves as characters. Miller's 2007 Danish National Opera *Fidelio*, set in Pinochet's dictatorship, would additionally invite comparison with his Fascist *Tosca*.

89 Strauss was debating the worth of words and music in the arts while, out in the real world, the Siege of Stalingrad was collapsing. Just days after *Capriccio* opened in Munich in 1942, an allied attack devastated the opera house.

90 Hans-Dieter Roser was artistic administrator in Berlin during the 1990s, having been at Vienna's Burgtheater before. He recollects that the servants were played by soloists with big personalities, not chorus members, in Miller's production.

91 *Maria Stuarda* played at Buxton in July 1993. The Festival was in some disarray after Jane Glover's abrupt departure as AD, and Miller stepped into the breach.

92 The *Observer*, 28 May 1993 and *The Sun*, 9 January 1992.

93 That Opera North co-production of *The Secret Marriage* dispels the myth that Miller never worked for that top UK touring company. Besides playing at Buxton in July 1993, this staging visited the Cheltenham Festival and enjoyed two private performances at Harewood House. The company's 1994 revival, without him on board, was less successful.

94 The *Financial Times*, 12 July 1993, alluded to Miller's rehabilitation.

95 Broomhill was built by Britain's first Jewish MP, Sir David Salomons. His polymathic nephew, David

Lionel Salomons (1851–1925), added the theatre: a fitting auditorium for a doctor-director as it was originally intended for scientific demonstrations. With the house having become an NHS management training base, the theatre had lain dormant – a sleeping beauty, as Miller called it – before being rediscovered by the Broomhill Trust. The trust gave rise to the company called Broomhill Opera.

96 Miller's Broomhill *Ariadne*, with Rachel Sparer in the title role and William Dazeley, opened in the late summer of 1993, with good reviews from *The Times* and *Financial Times*, 25 and 26 August.

97 *Ariadne* was written and rewritten, 1912–16. Miller's silent-movie characters drew on old Keystone Film Company movies. Putting Ariadne in a sanatorium, he was influenced by Thomas Mann's *The Magic Mountain* (1912). The director further developed his vision in his Maggio Musicale production, with the comedy gaining some extra touches from Woody Allen's *Bullets over Broadway*. He discussed that staging in *La Repubblica*, 10 June 1997, and it was greeted as a triumph by *L'Unita* and *La Nazione* on 16 June. It transferred to the Opéra de Lausanne, as a co-production, in November 1998.

98 His Ariadne could almost have been a distant cousin of his Pelléas.

99 Miller on hatching talent, *Evening Standard*, 13 August 1993.

100 His *St Matthew Passion* was first performed in February 1993, conducted by Paul Goodwin and instigated by the concert agent Ron Gonsalves. The *Financial Times*, 20 February, was virtually alone in not caring for it. In this section, I am indebted to Michael White's interview with Miller, *Independent on Sunday*, 14 February 1993; Mark Pappenheim's feature in the *Independent*, 12 February 1993; *Classical Music*, 30 January 1993; and the *Paris Review*, Spring 2003, Issue 165.

101 Milnes in *The Times*, 22 February 1993, noticed how the instrumentalists and singers breathed together.

102 Miller was not implying that the Passion was wholly uncontroversial, for he acknowledged it was curious material for a Jew to embrace, given its connection with two millennia of persecution.

103 Miller's *Passion* was a hybrid in artistic terms too. He overlapped stage drama with narrated storytelling (as he had in *The Emperor*), and he introduced jazz practices to Johann Sebastian, at least in terms of the singers and instrumentalists strolling over to harmonize with one another.

104 Tom Sutcliffe, *Guardian*, 20 February 1993.

105 Katie Mitchell staged Bach's *St Matthew Passion*, as an opera, at Glyndebourne in 2007, while Deborah Warner directed his *St John Passion* for the ENO in 2000, before moving on to *The Messiah* for the same company.

106 Miller's *St Matthew Passion* was restaged in a Camden church and the BBC TV film was broadcast on 1 April 1994. It was additionally recorded on CD by United Records. Other UK dates included Glasgow's Tramway and Bath in May 1994. BAM has presented further revivals at Eastertime in 2001 and 2006, with another in 2009. It would subsequently be staged at London's NT in 2011.

107 *New York Observer*, 31 March 1997.

108 To be fair, *Der Rosenkavalier* had been in the offing for a long time. It was scheduled almost two years earlier, being announced in the *Daily Telegraph* on 5 January 1992, and Peter Jonas mentions that he actually programmed it, much to David Pountney's irritation. Milnes' *Opera* feature, February 1994, suggested that Harewood had left an even earlier memo about the project.

109 Miller says that his unusually serious angle on Strauss was influenced by Karl Kraus' *The Last Days of Mankind* and Joseph Roth's novel *Radetzsky March*. He further envisaged the opera's boorish fool, Baron Ochs, as displaying an all-groping, polymorphous perversity, fitting Freud's Vienna. Ochs was, Miller says, 'the sort who would later support the Anschluss'. On the more romantic side, his own childhood memories of his Swedish uncles, with their factory business and almost aristocratic hunting lodges, may have been somewhere in the back of his mind. Marit Gruson says he fondly refers to her as his 'cousine' with reference to *Der Rosenkavalier*.

110 Highly appreciative remarks came from Milnes in *The Times*, 4 February 1994, and from the *Wall Street Journal*, 11 February. The *Independent on Sunday*, 6 February, noted Miller's forensic scrutiny of the characters' values.

111 The *Evening Standard*, 3 February 1994, declared that Miller's hit countered the ENO's waning popularity. *Der Rosenkavalier* transferred to Madrid and to Houston in 1995 and was staged at New York City Opera in June 2002.

112 Marks' creed was outlined in the *New York Times*, 4 October 1993.

113 There were calls for more romantic comedy in *Der Rosenkavalier*, with neither the *Guardian* nor the *Financial Times* being over-complimentary on 4 February 1994. Doubts were voiced about *Carmen* in the *Observer* and *Spectator* (17 and 23 September 1995), though Simon Jenkins was pretty much alone in accusing Miller (in *The Times*, 16 September) of covert misogyny. While creating a distinctly working-class tragedy, the director's view of Bizet's heroine most obviously invited comparison with his unsultry Cleopatra in the *BBC Shakespeare Series*. His *Carmen* was, in another way, the operatic equivalent of his Old Vic *Andromache*, criticism being directed at its slangy translation (to which the director contributed, according to *The Times*, 3 May 1999).

114 Many bewailed that this staging was tepid, somnambulant and not tear-inducing, and some cried out for less strict naturalism in Violetta's death scene, questioning the doctor's orders that she should stay in bed. Among others, Tom Sutcliffe voiced strong criticisms in the *Evening Standard*, 13 September 1996. In the publication *Coliseum*, Autumn 1996, Miller discussed the interstitial world of the demimonde as a no-man's-land of the unclassifiable, a meeting ground for the well-to-do and the disreputably shabby. Nonetheless, unfavourable comparisons were drawn with Richard Eyre's luxurious Covent Garden production (which starred Gheorghiu). Miller's Lady of the Camellias, when up and dressed, wore trousers like the freethinking boho Georges Sand. This caused further controversy. Her strides loomed large in the *Daily Mail*, 13 September 1996, after the *Independent* of 11 September ran a whole article on them. The *New York Times*, on 3 July 1989, had objected to them at Glimmerglass, though they were based on historic pictures by Paul Gavarni. When Vancouver Opera brought Miller in to restage his Glimmerglass *Traviata* for them in 2011, the *Vancouver Sun*'s critic (on 12 May) celebrated its extraordinarily truthful detailing, countering those punters who found it drab and the *Globe* and *Mail*'s complaint (of 6 May) that it was too static, with singers insufficiently skilled to convey character through small gestures.

115 *Carmen* was admired by the *Evening Standard*, *Independent* and *Daily Telegraph* (on the 14, 15 and 16 September 1995), with praise for the set and detailed crowd choreography.

116 Burgess sang (only slightly disconcertingly in French) in the wings on 10 September 1995, before starring (and switching to English) in the 1998 and 1999 revivals.

117 *Guardian*, 10 September 2001. Milnes in *The Times* of 14 September 1996 had applauded, finding Violetta's last moments heart-rending, with Rosa Mannion simultaneously managing to sing and suggest desperate breathlessness.

118 Miller had grumbled before this point (as noted in *Opera Monthly*, July 1990) about the ROH never employing him. Meanwhile, he had cast aspersions on it as a snobbish and dull place, as an 'ageing dowager trying to do the twist'. (See *Sunday Express*, 22 November 1987; BBC TV's *Newsnight*, 13 January 1987; *Evening Standard*, 16 May 1989.) In truth, the ROH had approached him more than once and been rebuffed. He occasionally recalled (for example when interviewed for *Opera*, February 1994) that Covent Garden had offered him *La Forza del Destino*. He had turned down that Verdi, saying it was balderdash, in the early Eighties. The *Observer*, 12 January 1992, reported him signing a deal to stage an ROH *Oberon*, but nothing came of that.

119 Miller had formerly said that he would not dream of transferring Mozart's scenarios to any century other than the composer's own. He now felt his ideas about *Così* had undergone a sudden evolutionary change, or what biologists would call an acceleration into a completely new form. This shift is recorded in *Opera Monthly*, July 1990, and *Opera House*, January 1995. In 1996, he went on to apply de Chirico's neoclassical-meets-surreal style when staging his *Idomeneo* (a post-Trojan War tale of love triangles and sea monsters) for Maggio Musicale. In his *La Clemenza di Tito* in 2005, the drama was shifted from Ancient Rome to mid-twentieth century Italy. *The Times* review of that, 1 May 2005, suggested the director's setting was close to his Fascist *Tosca*, but a looser fit. The emperor Titus was styled as a 1930s dictator, but did not closely resemble Il Duce.

120 *The Times*, 16 July 2007, celebrated *Così*'s sixth revival at the ROH as a five-star classic. Its 2010 revival additionally enjoyed a live screening in cinemas across Britain and the continent, from Didsbury to Moscow. Incidentally, back in March 1995, a twin production (with a different cast, directed by Miller) had opened at the Teatro dell'Opera di Roma. Washington National Opera subsequently booked in a staging of this production for 2012.

121 Praise came from *Independent* and *Financial Times*, both 20 January 1995; *Independent on Sunday*, 22 January; and *Mail on Sunday*, 29 January. More critical comments (about the the body language and mobile phone gags) came from the *Observer*, 22 January; *Spectator*, 11 February; *Times Literary Supplement*, 10 February. In recent years, the heavy-metal biker outfits, in which the suitors disguise themselves, have been deemed improbable and dated.

122 *Wall Street Journal*, 20 January 1995.

123 Henry Porter, *Evening Standard*, 19 January 1995, advocated the honouring of Miller (though his comments contrasted with Alexander Waugh, in the same issue, calling Miller 'Dr Blubby Genius').

124 Miller alluded to 'plush nonsense' in the *Sunday Times*, 15 January 1995. The subsequent comments come from Stephen Moss' interview, *Guardian*, 19 November 2004, and the *Independent*, 18 October 2004 (including his Harrods quip from a platform talk in Cheltenham). The *Independent on Sunday*, 4 May 2003, logged his derision concerning the ROH's populist ad campaign which aped the Ministry of Sound's nightclub logo. While saying it demonstrated a grotesque lack of confidence in the operatic art form, Miller had not wholly lost his sense of humour. He satirically envisaged the National Gallery, as an equivalent, promoting its nudes with the strapline, 'No need to go to Soho to see porno.'

Apparently due to clashing commitments., Miller had left the ROH in the lurch, pulling out of a *Don Giovanni* scheduled for 2001. It was, incidentally, true that he had co-created the set for *Così*, and he had contributed to the lighting design, adding another string to his bow.

125 Strong criticisms came from the *Financial Times*, *The Times* and the *Telegraph*, all 29 November 2004. On the up side, Anthony Holden defended *Don Pasquale* as witty and inventive in the *Observer*, 5 December 2004. In the *Independent*, 1 December, Edward Seckerson thought that the set's multiple rooms cunningly supported the opera's use of counterpoint, eavesdropping and asides, and Stephen Pettitt in the *Sunday Times*, 5 December, liked the cast's sinister marionette-like movements, saying Miller brought out the characters' unpleasantness. The production was revived in 2005, 2006 and 2010.

126 The tussles with the Armani brigade eventually drove the ROH wardrobe supervisor to shop at Marks & Spencer. Armani declined to let his clothes be used when *Così* was staged in Tel Aviv for Israel Opera.

127 Payne became general director at the ENO in 1998, with Elaine Padmore having taken over as head of the ROH by the time *Don Pasquale* arrived there.

128 That cadre included Phyllida Lloyd and David McVicar.

129 Both operas having premiered in the 1890s, Pietro Mascagni's love-triangle tragedy *Cavalleria Rusticana* is regularly paired with with *Pagliacci*, Ruggero Leoncavallo's darkening portrait of jealousy within a *commedia dell'arte* troupe.

130 If Miller's goatee-bearded Mikado had a satirical hint of Peter Hall, there was surely a touch of Miller in Hall's 2008 Old Vic staging of *Pygmalion*, where Tim Pigott-Smith's Higgins was a dynamic maverick intellectual who never sat straight in a chair, always sprawling at comically casual angles.

131 Filmed with a deliberately informal atmosphere in the dilapidated top floor of what is now Whiteleys shopping mall in Bayswater, *Opera Works* was another Patrick Uden production, first broadcast in September 1997. In a similar vein, Miller had previously worked on *La Traviata* in BBC TV's *Acting in Opera*. That was broadcast in September 1987, prompting Mark Lawson (in *Drama*, 1988) to ask who else could have made Violetta's death such popular consumption. Other work with talented young singers included his production of William Walton's one-act opera, *The Bear* (after Chekhov). That was presented, in the autumn of 1996, at the late composer's island estate near Naples, transferring for a couple of performances to Buxton Opera House that November.

132 The series was repeated more than once on American and Australian TV.

133 Miller was equally inspired by BAM's Harvey Theater. The budget for Wilton's overhaul was a mere £450,000 while Covent Garden was treated to a glittering £214 million refurbishment.

134 Mayhew's interviews with the poor of London, describing their lives, had formed the script for Miller's TV docudrama *Timewatch: Voices of Victorian London*, which featured a rat catcher, hawkers, and a deeply miserable, depressed clown as talking heads. That was produced by Karl Sabbagh in 1996.

135 Miller's other recurrent phrase is 'It's one of the best things I've ever done', which strikingly echoes his mother's epistle, predicting that *Farewell Leicester Square* was going to be 'one of the best novels Victor Gollancz Ltd have ever published'.

Positive reviews of *The Beggar's Opera* (*Independent*, 29 November 1999; *Sunday Times*, 5 December) found it raunchy with a cynical edge, but it was also slated as flat, with its satire proving toothless and a pointless set design of old doors (*Financial Times*, 29 November; *Observer*, 28 November).

Miller's three Broomhill Opera shows, in essence, won diminishing praise as his staging of Handel's *Rodelinda* in Kent, in 1996, divided the critics more deeply than *Ariadne* had done. Ron Gonsalves helped organize that 1996 production which (after a deal with Channel 4 and Hyperion fell through) was recorded by Virgin. In terms of the reviews, the *Sunday Telegraph*, 4 August, cherished Miller's coaxing of real characters from stock scenarios, but the *Independent*, 2 August, called his surprisingly comic finale an arrogant subversion – having the villain rise from the dead. Sundry critics, incidentally, did not like him altering the ending of *Der Rosenkavalier* either. He replaced the black serving-boy who picks up the dropped handkerchief with another child nabbing food.

136 Miller's *Dream* opened at the Almeida Theatre in December 1996, prior to a European tour. This was three years after he had (according to the *Observer*, 23 May 1993) popped into somebody else's Almeida press night, seen the critics, and blithely cried: 'It's like being in a mortuary!' It is not on record if any riposted that he was the theatrical revenant par excellence.

137 Miller preserved snapshots of Vienna's mirror maze in his photographic scrapbooks.

138 The director saw Oberon and Titania as akin to the pukka, ageing ex-pats in Paul Scott's novel *Staying On*, as they argued over their 'Indian boy'. See Scott, P. (1978), *Staying On* (Bombay: Allied Publishers).

139 The production was, for example, admired in the *New York Review of Books*, 6 February 1997.

140 Michael Coveney noted the Millerishness in the *Observer*, 15 December 1996. The other points were made by Robert Butler, *Independent on Sunday*, 15 December; Nicholas de Jongh, *Evening Standard*, 12 December; Georgina Brown, *Mail on Sunday*, 5 January 1997.

141 The Almeida production was, in fact, to be the fourth time *The Dream* was to sour on Miller. Besides the Burgtheater disaster and the Old Vic's axed staging, he had planned to direct the play in the *BBC Shakespeare Series*. On that occasion, finding himself obliged to take over *Timon* from Michael Bogdanov, he had to hand *The Dream* to Elijah Moshinsky – who did a fine job. Negative reviews of his Almeida

production included the *Sunday Telegraph* and *Sunday Times*, both 15 December 1996, the *Independent* and *Financial Times*, both 13 December.

142 Billington, *Guardian*, 14 December 1996.

143 Various critics discerned Miller's ongoing Hogarthian streak in his *Die Schweigsame Frau* and *Don Pasquale* which he set in the eighteenth century (unusually moving backwards in time). *Don Pasquale* could, in turn, be likened to his ENO *Barber of Seville* regarding its doll's house-like aspects. *The Double Dealer* picked up on Miller's previous penchant for Rosenblum-inspired, shallow stages. This time, though, two intersecting corridors were introduced, which played games with the audience's voyeuristic sightlines.

144 Billington, *Guardian*, 14 December 1992. The sharp character studies included Stanley Townsend as an Iago-like Maskwell and John Fortune as a droll, po-faced Lord Froth. Further approbation came from the *Irish Independent* and *Evening Press*, both 2 December, and the *Sunday Independent* and *Sunday Tribune*, 6 December. The *Evening Herald* and *Financial Times*, 2 and 4 December, were underwhelmed with objections being raised about lacklustre patches and wanton ad-libbing.

145 *She Stoops to Conquer* featured Stephen Brennan playing the lead, Marlow, as a writhing stuttering suitor with a wenching flip-side, eighteen months prior to Angus Wright's interestingly comparable Lysander at the Almeida. Among the rave reviews were the *Irish Times*, *Irish Press* and *Evening Herald*, all 17 May 1995, with the *Sunday Independent*, 21 May, discerning a serious undertow on Miller's part. The *Evening Press*, 17 May, and *Public Sector Times*, dated June 1995, felt that Miller could have refined one or two of the broader comic performances.

146 Miller talks engagingly about the anthropological themes – liminality, borders and rites of passage – which link *Twelfth Night*, *The Dream* and this court-to-pastoral comedy. Nonetheless, he started to think *As You Like It* was a silly play when working on it. Seemingly lacking the catalyst of an ingenious concept, his production was in modern dress, with a gangsterish usurping Duke Frederick and his good exiled brother in old-school tweeds and corduroys.

147 Points made in the *Irish Independent*, 20 February 2000, and *Irish Times*, 17 February.

Chapter 16: Into the New Millennium

1 The director didn't greatly enjoy his 2012 stint at La Scala, with one of the star singers only showing up for two or three days of rehearsals.

2 Miller's past years of fostering directorial assistants have paid dividends. Karen Stone and Thomas Novohradsky invited Miller to work for Graz Opera and for the National Opera of Japan when they, respectively, took charge of those institutions. The swapping of posts has also widened Miller's range of venues. Richard Gaddes (who had brought him to St Louis) went on to run Santa Fe Opera, and Paul Kellogg (Glimmerglass' general director) became the head of the New York City Opera from 1996 to 2007. In 1996, the NYCO imported Miller's ENO *Der Rosenkavalier*. They appended his *Mikado* in 2001 (revived in 2003), and then *The Elixir of Love* in 2006 (with Miller restaging the production which he first directed in Stockholm, and would subsequently put on at the ENO). NYCO also co-produced Miller's *Jenufa*, with Glimmerglass, in 2006. They revived *The Elixir of Love* in 2011. Financially pinched and moving out of the Lincoln Center, NYCO presented Miller's Glimmerglass *Traviata* at BAM's Howard Gilman Opera House in February 2012.

As for Toyko, Miller restaged his *Falstaff* there in June 2004, with the National Opera of Japan at the New National Theatre. That production was revived in mid-2007, when he additionally staged his *Rosenkavalier* there. Chinese audiences in Beijing have seen his *L'Orfeo*, in a semi-staged reworking instigated by his former Kent Opera colleague, Philip Pickett, who now runs the New London Consort. *L'Orfeo* has toured widely, playing at London's Queen Elizabeth Hall in late 2003 (as the centrepiece of the South Bank's Inside Monteverdi weekend). It went on to Bergen's Greighallen, May 2004; Beijing Music Festival, October 2004; Cité de la Musique, Paris, September 2005 etc. It toured the world again in 2007. Reviewing the first London performance, the *Daily Telegraph* (4 November 2003) thought it underpowered, though the *Guardian* and *The Times* (both 3 November) and the *Observer* (9 November) found Miller's staging wonderfully seamless and exceptionally moving.

He had a double bill at Graz Opera in February 2003: Cimarosa's rarely seen *Cleopatra* plus Stravinsky and Jean Cocteau's *Oedipus Rex*. Co-produced with Russia's famed Mariinsky Theatre, those two shows transferred to the St Petersburg White Nights festival in June, though the director did not travel to Russia with them. *Cleopatra* was largely dismissed as a hopelessly silly piece, just jokily updated with the heroine as an autograph-signing dumb blonde, with a hint of Princess Di. The director's more statuesque and profoundly mournful *Oedipus Rex* was lauded. Klaus Maria Brandauer made a riveting narrator and Valery Gergiev conducted. Larry Lash's review for Andante.com epitomized how these twinned shows divided opinion.

La Fenice in Venice played host to Miller's Enlightenment Library *Magic Flute* in April 2006. As for the Scandinavian and Baltic network, Miller's 2002 master classes for the Opera Island company in Denmark (culminating in a staging of *Così* on Bornholm), spawned three other productions. After his *L'Elisir d'Amore* or *The Elixir of Love* for the Royal Swedish Opera in Stockholm in 2003, came his 2005 *Traviata* for the National Opera of Lithuania in Vilnius. He then rethought *Fidelio*, his Pinochet production, for the Danish National Opera in Aarhus, in 2007. The documentary *The Opera Island: Bornholm* (made by Nordisk) was shown on DR, SCT, NRK and Polish TV in 2002 and 2003. Miller worked with Opera Island again in 2004 and 2005, for a *Traviata* and a *Don Giovanni* in Kristiansand, Norway, with further master classes during the summer of 2010 in Sandefjord.

3 His first Santa Fe Opera production was his 1920s hotel version of *The Magic Flute*. It was panned as neither enchanting nor funny by the *Dallas Morning News* and *New York Times*, both 6 August 1998. Rossini's *Ermione*, the opera based on Racine's *Andromache*, did not exactly go down a storm either. The *Denver Post*, 7 August 2000, and the November issue of *Opera News* were appreciative but not in the majority. The *Chicago Tribune*, on 15 August, complained that this intensely sombre staging was upstaged by lightning, visible outside the opera house. Miller had, incidentally, directed the US premiere of this neglected work by Rossini for Opera Omaha back in 1992, nipping in before Graham Vick's Glyndebourne production. He had received a fairly encouraging *New York Times* review on 24 September of that year. The same publication, on 7 August 2000, spurned his Santa Fe staging. It overlooked the parallel that he saw with Eugene O'Neill's *Mourning Becomes Electra,* instead suggesting that his shift from the battle-bruised Ancient World to a post-American Civil War setting was just 'picked out of a hat'. Miller sighs: 'Oh, they said it was very gloomy. I thought, "Dear God, it's a tragedy! What do you want!" But then,' he goes on more brightly, 'I had two big successes, the *Falstaff* and the *Eugene Onegin*.' *Falstaff* was, indeed, an SFO box-office hit with Andrew Shore as the Fat Knight. It was a production 'close to perfection' for the *Washington Post*, 6 August 2001. The *New York Times*, the same day, called the directing wonderfully witty and musically sensitive. *Opera News*, November 2001, was less impressed, calling it a pretty straight production on a crooked stage, with the comic business involving Zeffirelli-style shtick. The response from the press, if not from the audience, was again split regarding *Onegin* in 2002. Some reviews judged it flat and underdirected. Others termed it compellingly spare. Miller has worked with Seattle Opera as well. They imported his Santa Fe staging of *Onegin* in 2002, then they asked him to stage his modern-dress *Così* for them in 2006.

4 That is ageism as in penalizing the old (by contrast with the medical establishment's junior-obstructing geriarchy which irked Miller as a young man). He was quoted by the *Independent*, 12 July 2007, accusing British operatic institutions of ageism as well as rampant heterophobia.

5 Barrie Rutter draws a more flattering analogy. He says that Miller's ability to enthral everyone with his wonderful talk reminds him of John Everett Millais' painting *The Boyhood of Raleigh*, where two youngsters sit rapt, listening to an old sailor's tales of the sea.

6 This comes from an unattributed magazine cutting, UK, probably mid-1985, from the BBC Written Archives, in which Miller also spoke – as quoted later in this chapter – of never knowing what was worthwhile.

7 Even at the operatic establishments he likes, Miller may have thrown one or two spanners in the works. Did a brief standoff with Glimmerglass' chief designer stall his run of work there? Did turning down one offer from Munich mean he was not asked again?

8 *Daily Telegraph*, 5 July 2003.

9 Miller on the undeniably macho thing, *Guardian*, 16 September 2003.

10 The framing-up is what interests Miller here. He says he leaves the rest to automatic focus and high street film developing, indicating that he is not controlling the entire process.

11 *Observer* features, 9 January and 20 March 1994.

12 Extracts from *Nowhere In Particular*.

13 *Jonathan Miller: Photographs and Collages*, South Kensington and Chelsea Mental Health Centre, November 2000; *Jonathan Miller: Paper and Metal Works*, Flowers East in Hackney, October 2001; *Jonathan Miller* (including works in wood, metal and paper), Boundary Gallery in St John's Wood, September 2003; *Jonathan Miller: Wood Work*, Daniel Katz Gallery, October 2005.

14 Caro invited Miller out to his workshop, in France, for the clay sculpting.

15 The RCA bestowed an honorary doctorate on Miller in 2008 as well.

16 Miller observes that he and his photographer son share that predilection, even if Tom's commercial work for the press more often entails celebrity portraits.

17 From Miller's article, 'Men of the Age (II)', as previously mentioned. He may equally have had, somewhere at the back of his mind, the psychologist Gaetano Kanisza's trompe l'oeil experiments with overlaid shapes, albeit that his sheet metal involved no translucent colours. He researched Kanisza in the mid-Nineties, as discussed below.

18 Miller's artworks are, as he says, mostly abstract, not depicting scenarios in any way, but human drama is not entirely absent. For instance, some of his shredded-poster collages feature overlaid or torn faces which expressionistically suggest surfacing memories or pain.

19 The *Sunday Telegraph*, 28 October 2001, was linking Miller's comments about his reclaimed materials –

'stuff seized from the edge of the officially visible' – with remarks such as the following: 'I have not been acknowledged or recognised in this country since I began working abroad. People assume that I just dropped off the edge of the English world: you know, "Channel cut off by fog". It's rather like being dead.'

20 *UCH Magazine*, Vol. XLIII, No. 3, 229. It might be argued that Betty Miller, for more than one reason, lies at the root of her son's desire to reclaim 'the negligible or the neglected'. She encouraged Miller to see epiphanies in mundane minutiae even while, as an insufficiently loving mother, she made him feel emotionally neglected.

21 One might observe that Miller has acted as a second-order creative force, both in his artworks and his stage practice: not penning scripts himself but interpreting them; playfully organizing his sculptural *objets trouvés* more readily than starting with a blank canvas. He does draw and paint sometimes, but he has not considered the results worthy of an exhibition.

22 Miller did not exactly advance his cause, commenting in the *Guardian*, 3 December 2001: 'I don't want to malign Charles Saatchi, but his offers [of apparently grisly artworks to Chelsea and Westminster Hospital] seem like crackpot condescension.' He later observed, in the *Daily Telegraph*, 5 July 2003, that his own style of old-fashioned modernism would never be to Saatchi's taste.

23 *The Times* reported on the scrap merchant incident on 4 March 2007. In vain, Miller offered a reward for the return of the purloined works.

24 *Sunday Telegraph*, again 28 October 2001.

25 Kevin Jackson, *Independent*, both 26 November 1999 and 26 October 2001. John Russell Taylor's catalogue essay picked up on the artworks' informed allusions and suggested that they showed a great mind at play, taking a break from formulated thought. Eugene Thaw's art collection includes a Miller assemblage too, in his Santa Fe garden.

26 When *Absolute Rubbish* was shown on Britain's Channel 5, Sam Wollaston condemned Miller's self-congratulatory manner in the *Guardian*. On 10 February 2005, the *Independent*'s TV reviewer, Thomas Sutcliffe (not the opera critic), described the programme as a fiesta of self-satisfaction, but he noted Miller's curiously charming enthusiasm. Giles Smith in the *Sunday Telegraph*'s TV and radio guide, 6–12 February, loved the programme. It was broadcast again in 2006.

27 *Jonathan Miller's London* had previously relished the joys of branch lines, with its titular presenter rattling through the suburbs on the North London line to Kew Gardens and delighting in the ramshackle, rarely observed side of city buildings.

28 Miller's four lectures were given at the National Gallery in 1994. He later repeated these talks for New York's Metropolitan Museum and the Art Institute of Chicago. He, moreover, took up a short research fellowship in 1994 at San Francisco's science museum, the Exploratorium, which culminated in an exhibition on transparency. This clearly harked back to his childhood passion for the translucence of microscope slides and jars brimming with pond life. It connected, too, with his Cambridge-nurtured interest in the physiology and psychology of vision, because his research centred on the experiments of Gaetano Kanisza wherein the brain – faced with certain arrangements of overlapping shapes in different shades – starts to conjecture a 3-D scenario with depth, 'seeing' some of those shapes as transparent films with further layers underneath.

The seed of curating had, arguably, been sown much earlier. Besides the artists on *Monitor*, Miller analyzed Joseph Wright of Derby's painting *Experiment With an Air Pump* for *Canvas* in April 1970. That was the BBC2 series which the ex-Footlighter Julian Jebb produced and to which Bennett contributed. Subsequent articles involving Miller and artworks included the *Sunday Times*, 19 October 1975 (where he studied *Las Meninas* by Velázquez), the *Guardian*, 11 December 1999, and *World of Interiors*, January 2000.

29 *Mirror Image: Jonathan Miller on Reflection* ran at the National Gallery from 16 September 1998 into December. Attracting plenty of 'Miller, Miller, on the wall' headlines, he fronted a BBC2 mini-series, *Jonathan Miller on Reflection*, as a simultaneous tie-in, and his accompanying book, *On Reflection*, was not only printed for National Gallery Publications, but also distributed Stateside by Yale University Press that same year.

30 Sewell's comment on flashing was quoted in the *New Statesman*, 18 December 1998. He added that everyone else's uncritical 'abject genuflecting . . . was quite nauseating', and he elaborated on his point about Miller and art history, stating that the 'nonsense' put forward about Velazquez's *Las Meninas* showed that the curator simply did not understand the iconographic tradition. Disapproving comments from others, notably accusing Miller of rambling, appeared in the *Independent on Sunday*, 27 September 1998, and *Times Literary Supplement*, 23 October.

31 The National Gallery's press officer, Jean Liddiard (formerly the chaperone on Miller's *Alice*) confirms that *Mirror Image* was very successful and the public loved it. Positive press reactions, to the show and the book, included the *Financial Times*, 19 September 1998; Richard Cork in *The Times*, 29 September; and James Fenton in the *New York Review of Books*, 17 December. Fenton thought a couple of Miller's points were wrong, but he commended the mix of material displayed as enlightening and engaging.

32 Lisa Jardine, *The Times*, 3 September 1998; Graham Farmelo, *Independent on Sunday*, 8 November 1998.

33 Collectively, Miller's productions have formed a kind of hall of mirrors, with another arresting instance being *Pelléas*, where the set's spinning maze of architectural shards was embedded with silvered glass. This created dizzying confusions between ghostly reflections and solid reality. Miller's designer, John Conklin, described (in *Vogue*, March 1995) the effect as 'a sense of double exposure' and a strange dreamlike world, 'without an inside or outside, a kind of internalized mental space, a prison of consciousness'. As for *Bussy d'Ambois* and *Poppea*, whole palatial facades were constructed using inverse architectural castings – inside-out and outside-in – while the dramatis personae manifested flip-sides or physically mirrored each other's movements.

34 I am indebted to *Time Out*, 29 October–5 November 1998, for this quotation.

35 *Camouflage* opened in March 2007. The accompanying book was Newark, T. and Miller, J. (2009), *Camouflage* (London: Thames & Hudson). *On the Move* opened in January 2010.

36 Miller's National Gallery lectures have proved productive. His talk on how movement is visualized in a static medium fed into the Estorick exhibition. He wishes to pen a book on the gaze too, leading on from his lecture on that, but writer's block has hindered this. On a smaller scale, he has contributed introductions to *The Paradox Box* (2003) and *The Psychobox* (2004), Redstone Press' publications which contain artistic-scientific optical illusions and verbal teasers, reproducing vintage documents and pictures.

37 His portrait was added to the gallery's collection in 2000.

38 Miller says that the position adopted was the least agonizing option for enforced inactivity, and Conroy underlines that his subject was far from glum when they clocked off. 'I couldn't drive for the tears streaming down my face from the patter', he recollects.

39 Mark Guthrie's picture is on the front cover of Bavister, S. (2001), *Lighting for Portrait Photography* (Hove: RotoVision). The teenage Miller had his portrait painted by George Weissbort, one of Bernard Meninsky's students. That turned up in a Weissbort exhibition at London's Chambers Gallery in May 2006. Another portrait, by Saied Dai, won a Royal Society of Painters prize and was shown at the Mall Galleries in 2014.

40 His Pinochet *Fidelio* opened in August 2007. This was another production inviting comparisons with his Fascist *Tosca*, along with his *Capriccio* and modern-dress *La Clemenza di Tito*.

41 This *Don Giovanni* opened at the Palau de les Arts in December 2006. Miller moved the whole production forwards to the front of the stage, frieze-style, thus coping without the set. He returned in 2012 to restage *Don Giovanni*, with Zubin Mehta conducting.

42 Thomas Novohradsky has recently departed from Tokyo. At the New York Met, Volpe has been replaced by Peter Gelb, yet discussions about Miller returning to redirect *Figaro* have not borne fruit. Since Miller ditched a planned Zurich production of *Aida* in 2006, he suspects that the management there will not re-employ him, even if they have previously been undeterred. They brought him back after his 2003 *Il Seraglio* when, booed at the curtain call, he parried by giving the audience the finger. They likewise encouraged him to return after his modern-dress production of Mozart's opera seria *La Clemenza di Tito* drew mixed boos and cheers on its opening night in 2005. That production particularly split opinion regarding its use of spoken dialogue, for it replaced the work's *secco recitatives* which were not composed by Mozart.

43 *Jenufa* opened in July 2006. Influenced by the novels of Willa Cather and the WPA (Work Projects Administration) photographs of Dorothea Lange, it was enthusiastically reviewed in the *New York Review of Books* by Geoffrey O'Brien, 21 September 2006, and in the *Financial Times*, 9 August 2006.

44 Prior to his modern-dress production for Glimmerglass (with humorous cockney witches in hoodies), Miller's semi-staged version of *Dido and Aeneas* was presented under the aegis of the New London Consort. It premiered at the Cadogan Hall in June 2008, as part of London's Chelsea Festival, with subsequent dates at the Buxton Festival and in Spain then, during March–April 2009, in Amsterdam, Birmingham and Glasgow. In the *New York Review of Books*, 24 September 2009, Geoffrey O'Brien praised the Glimmerglass *Traviata* for its naturalism (making arias more like diary entries); for its simultaneous sense of dreamlike immersion; and for its novelistic detailing combined with spatial austerity (conveying the distance between people and their longing for solitude amid the demands of society). O'Brien further suggested that the fragile vanity of Ryan MacPherson's Alfredo echoed Flaubert's *L'Education Sentimentale*, as the character visibly struggled to live up to an imposing father's expectations. The naturalism occasionally went too far for Anthony Tommasini of the *New York Times*, 4 August 2009, as the singers, almost like Method actors, left pauses stretching the music's shape.

45 BAM has also hosted productions of Miller's modern-dress *Così*, in April 2003, and his *Matrimonio Segreto* in 2008. A Miller mini-season has been discussed, as well as a possible transfer of *Jenufa*. The 2012 *Traviata* at BAM was the production first seen at Glimmerglass, now presented by New York City Opera.

46 John Peter, 25 March 2007, in the *Sunday Times*. Both *The Cherry Orchard* and *Camouflage* then featured in this publication's Critics' Choice listings on 1 April. *The Stage*'s review, 21 March, was in

the minority, finding the piece somehow lethargic. In a *Daily Telegraph* feature, 7 March, Lumley (who also starred in *Sensitive Skin*) described Miller as toxically clever but not didactic. She said that the cast unfolded, 'like Japanese paper flowers' dropped into water. As reported on 11 March in the *Independent on Sunday,* both the actress and her director played it fantastically cool when their café interview with Hermione Eyre was interrupted by a man with a gun in his bag. A West End transfer for the show later fell through, with Lumley declining to be on board for that.

47 As the *Guardian* recorded, 18 November 2002, Miller was involved with the London Shakespeare Workout Prison Project prior to his *Hamlet* for the Shakespeare at the Tobacco Factory company. Allegedly, he became so excited about one inmate's potential, wanting to cast him in an outside production, that he had to be reminded that the man was incarcerated.

48 Cavils aside, admiration was expressed for the clear verse-speaking, for Jay Villiers' performance as the eventually suicidal Claudius, and for Annabel Scholey whose repressed Ophelia madly poked sticks into her dolls' pudenda. Ballard was, incidentally, not entirely unknown, having been in several RSC casts and in *War Horse* at the NT. Praise came from the *Guardian*, 28 March 2008, *Observer*, 30 March and many other newspapers.

49 John Peter reviewed *Hamlet* for the *Sunday Times*, 30 March 2008. Miller spoke of his anti-poetic aesthetic in 2010, when directing *Measure for Measure* at RADA.

50 *The Mikado* was revived on 3 February 2006, with *Rigoletto* following six days later. This prompted Anthony Holden to refer to Miller's drip-feed keeping the ENO alive (*Observer*, 12 February 2006). The ENO's perversity, in not bringing this director back in, was similarly mentioned by Michael Tanner, *Spectator*, 18 February 2006, and the *Evening Standard*'s Norman Lebrecht touched on it, writing for *La scena musica*, 11 January 2006. Miller was not even officially redirecting all his golden oldies, just slipping into rehearsals unpaid to ensure they remained up to scratch. On top of that, his ENO *Carmen* was replaced, in September 2007, with Sally Potter's alternative concept which was panned as bewildering. Rupert Christiansen, *Daily Telegraph*, 26 May 2008, lamented the replacement of Miller's gorgeous and insightful *Der Rosenkavalier* with David McVicar's disappointing one. Reviewing the *Barber of Seville* revival on 24 September 2008, the *Financial Times*'s Andrew Clark additionally highlighted the ENO's failure to bring out many of its classic productions on DVD. In the *Observer* of 5 December 2004, Holden went so far as to suggest that the Royal Opera House should have hired Miller again, either importing his *Pelléas* or giving him Wagner's *Ring* as a fitting climax to his career. Meanwhile, Richard Morrison in *The Times*, 16 July 2007, saluted his great contribution to British culture, saying that the ROH's revival of *Così* was being rightly cheered to the rafters, and that any opera house in need of a boost reliably sent for Doctor Miller.

51 A brand new production of *Die Fledermaus* had been briefly discussed with the AD John Berry, however Miller had not been enticed by Johann Strauss the Younger's operetta. He had, in 2008, been officially rehearsing the ENO's *Barber of Seville* revival. However, he withdrew part-way through, fed up with one of the singers, who greeted polite directorial suggestions with 'Oh, here we go!'

52 In 2011, after Alfie Boe had stated publicly that he rarely went to the opera because he found it boring, the press (e.g. *Independent on Sunday*, 16 October) reported Miller saying that, if that was the case, it was 'odd' that Boe was in the business at all, adding: 'I know he comes from something other than opera: he was a car mechanic, I believe.' The implication is that Miller's tone was disparaging, but that seems very doubtful, given that he more often expresses respect for the manually skilled and readily scorns grandiose opera productions himself.

53 Sky Arts 2 and Sky Arts HD broadcast *La Bohème* on 4 February, with the groundbreaking simulcast of the backstage action being shown on Sky Arts 1. After the weather-related rescheduling, there were only minor technical hitches, with microphones malfunctioning.

54 The reviews in the *Evening Standard* and *Independent*, both 5 February 2009, were mixed, finding Miller's performers exceptional in their naturalistic detailing but too understated for the large-scale sets. Richard Morrison, sorely disappointed in *The Times*, 6 February, wrote the whole staging off as appallingly dreary and unglamorous, with the *Telegraph* of 5 February fundamentally in agreement. The *Ham and High*, on 27 February, thought *La Bohème* had all the makings of a classic, and the *Wall Street Journal*, that same day, was very admiring. MusicalCriticism.com appreciated its understated intelligence, the beautifully acted humour of Rodolfo's boho gang of friends, and the resonances regarding the gloomy 2009 recession. Miller restaged *La Bohème* at Cincinnati Opera in July 2010, and its second ENO run was in October the same year.

55 The 2006 reviews of *L'Elisir* (aka *The Elixir of Love*) at NYCO had been generally quite warm. Some, like Peter G. Davis in *New York Magazine*, 5 May 2003, drew a parallel with Peter Sellars' *Così*, likewise staged in a diner.

56 In a partying mood, Adina and her customers sang their arias like wannabe Marilyn Monroes or rock 'n' roll stars.

Bywater's set had a touch of the sitcom *Happy Days* mixed with Wim Wenders' photographs of the

American West. With the glass-fronted diner, she was also knowingly making a neat pairing with the Edward Hopper-style bar in *Rigoletto* – Miller's other US 1950s update. Reminded of *Rigoletto*, the satirical website www.newsbiscuit.com (on 26 February 2010) imagined the director just going into reverse for his next production and backdating *West Side Story*. 'Dr Jonathan Miller', it announced, 'has wowed audiences and critics alike by setting his new production of Leonard Bernstein's classic . . . in 14th century Verona. Dr Miller told a gathering . . . "I felt I was getting lazy and needed a new challenge . . . It's uncanny how well it works."'

57 Rupert Christiansen, *Daily Telegraph*, 15 February 2010, was not overly impressed but others, including Edward Seckerson in the *Independent*, 13 February, and Fiona Maddocks in the *Observer*, 21 February, greatly enjoyed *The Elixir*.

58 This story broke in *The Times*, 9 June 2008. The ripostes went on for months, e.g. *Independent*, 9 October 2008, *Guardian*, 10 October 2008.

59 Billington's *Guardian* blog, 9 June 2008.

60 Tennant, quoted in *The Times*, 23 December 2008.

61 Miller's comments (except on Gilbert and Sullivan) were noted in the *Independent*, 3 August 2010, being criticized in David Lister's opinion piece the same day, by Terence Blacker on 6 August, and in the *Independent on Sunday* on 8 August. The negative effect was alleviated only by his praise of the Arcola Theatre, on the London fringe, and for recent films including Michael Haneke's *The White Ribbon* (noted separately in the *Independent*, 6 August). The *Telegraph* commented on his theatre attendance, 3 August, and highlighted his scorn for Gilbert and Sullivan on 10 August.

62 The director can overplay his exclusion from the West End. Not so long ago, for instance, he turned down a suggestion from Duncan Weldon (the producer of his *Three Sisters*) that they should collaborate again.

63 In opera, Miller still toys with the idea of directing Janáček's *The Makropulos Affair* or Berg's *Wozzeck* or *Lulu*.

64 He has started directing at RADA where he is now an associate. He staged Chekhov's *Three Sisters* once more, with their student-actors in October 2008, and *Measure for Measure* in March 2010. He adds another *Lear* to his total, directing that for CityLit in late 2012.

65 Miller was first invited back to the National to lead an *Acting in Opera* master class in June 2009. This was for the NT's *The Acting Series Revisited*, investigating if those who appeared in the BBC series in the 1980s had changed or maintained their views. The reviews of his *St Matthew Passion* were mixed. Some were underwhelmed, including the *Guardian* and the *Stage*, both on 20 September 2011, but it was given four-star ratings by the *Telegraph* on 21 September and the *Evening Standard* on 22 September.

66 Though the ENO's AD apparently did not bother with any anniversary cork-popping, the critics of the *Daily Telegraph*, *Independent* and *Guardian* hailed the February 2011 revival of *The Mikado* as miraculously fresh and probably destined to see out *The Mousetrap*.

67 *Rutherford and Son* is due to open at Halifax's Viaduct Theatre on 8 February 2013.

68 The Plummer *Lear* was the centrepiece of the fiftieth festival in Stratford, Ontario, in August 2002, going on to the Lincoln Center's Vivian Beaumont Theater in March 2004.

69 *New York Times* quotations from both Ben Brantley's reviews, 12 September 2002 and 5 March 2004. Canada's *Globe & Mail*, 26 August 2002, did not like such subtlety and was not moved to tears.

70 Geoffrey O'Brien on *Lear*, *New York Review of Books*, 25 March 2004. He additionally pointed out how narrowing lighting made the heath feel like a dark alley with Lear muttering at the storm like a mad tramp. The *National Post*, 26 August 2002 was positive and *Variety* admired much in the production, 5 March 2004.

Geoffrey O'Brien's aforementioned *New York Review of Books'* review of *Jenufa* observed the dextrous use of space there too, particularly how Miller evoked the flatness of the prairie within a mural-like frame and had his singers moving in fluid designs, fleetingly configured into pairs and triads with rapid displacements offering 'constant counter-rhymes to the always startling transitions of the music'.

71 *New York Newsday*, *New York Daily News*, *New York Post*, all 5 March 2004, *Entertainment Weekly*, 12 March 2004.

72 *Observer*, 25 April 2004.

73 Hon. D.Litt., Cambridge, and FRCP, London, both 1997, then FRCP, Edinburgh, 1998. Miller is a foreign member of the American Academy of Arts and Sciences.

74 He referred to the impudence of pipsqueak critics in the *Daily Telegraph*, 26 March 1994, saying that it had been acceptable when he was a novice but not at 60. Andrew Clark has, in the *Financial Times*, 29 November 2004, described him as 'talk[ing] like an ecclesiastical potentate of the ancien régime . . . arrogant and conceited'. Some of Miller's staunchly left-wing associates, in fact, disapproved more of his CBE, accepted in Thatcher's 1980s, than of his knighthood under Labour.

75 Though he has not been made a lord, Miller once dreamed, in the 1960s, of his lace-ruffed hand signing his name, 'Stungalung', on parliamentary notepaper and adding in brackets 'Life Peer – Extension

Pending'. It only goes to show, he says, how comical and snobbish the subconscious can be. In terms of dreams reshuffling elements from daily life, Stungalung sounds like a variation on the Stringalongs from *Life and Times in NW1*. Disembodied lace-ruffed hands featured in the accounts of séances used in the making of *Mr Sludge the Medium*.

76 The band was at the CBE bash. Thatcher was at the Lunch of the Century. The West End producer, Michael Codron, attended an earlier Ivy restaurant lunch where he and his old St Paul's schoolmate were seated at the Queen's right and left hands. As he dryly recalls: '[Jonathan] certainly behaved in a way which attracted her attention so I was left somewhat off the hook and now he has got his K.'

77 When Bobby Robson greeted his new fellow knight, the salutation returned was, 'Delighted . . . and what do you do?' As reported in the *Independent*, 30 November 2002, the former England manager thought this was fantastically refreshing. Miller confessed to ignorance, explaining he had no interest in sport, 'but it is marvellous to meet you!', he declared.

78 By way of qualification, Miller has pointed out that, while he is a coward regarding physical violence, being ill (or potentially ill) can be interesting. When interviewed by Dick Cavett, in the first of their five chats in 1980, he recalled asking to see his own interior when being fluoroscoped for a suspected gastric ulcer. From that, he learned how to wink his duodenum. Nor was he scared of having his tonsils out, aged twelve, regarding the ether as a terrific experiment with consciousness.

79 *Sensitive Skin*, BBC2 mini-series, 23 and 27 November 2005.

80 In 2003 he was part of a high-powered series of scientific talks at London's ICA, organized by Dr Daniel Glaser, the cognitive neuroscientist and popularizer of brain science. Glaser recalls Miller chipping into Ramachandran's Reith Lectures (2003) with 'a brilliant point' about phantom limbs.

81 *The Nation's Health* was a six-parter, starting 6 September 2002.

82 The veterans interviewed included Richard Doll, who established the link between tobacco and lung cancer. The series took a strong sociological line, stressing the link between poverty and illness, looking at 1930s reports on slum children, and going all the way back to the Battle of Trafalgar. It recalled the fraught doubts and hopes surrounding the NHS' foundation in 1948 (in which Emanuel was involved). It also explained how the London blitz had unexpected benefits, inspiring the establishment of blood banks.

83 *Guardian* 'Pick of the Day' on 5, 12 and 19 September 2002 etc.

84 *Flu: A Medical Mystery*, Radio 4, 2 February 2004.

85 Marr interviewed Miller on *Start the Week*, 18 July 2005, by way of an introduction, then *Self-Made Things* ran from 27 July to 24 August.

86 Extended phenotypes genetically determine how, for example, termites build their nests but, as Miller discussed, they do not explain the 'ratcheting effect' which human beings introduce by improving their artefacts from one generation to the next.

87 *Self-Made Things* additionally featured Miller's old friend and sparring partner, Lewis Wolpert of UCL.

88 This series, broadcast from 11 October 2004 and produced by Richard Denton, was occasionally referred to by the BBC as *Jonathan Miller's Brief History of Disbelief*. It is alluded to as *Atheism: A Rough History of Disbelief* as well.

89 The history of atheism had not been told on television prior to this.

90 In the first programme, he returned to the New London Synagogue in St John's Wood to explain why he personally rejected Judaism.

91 Miller had befriended McGinn by sending him an admiring postcard after reading his books. Turner ended up featuring, at length, in *The Atheism Tapes*. That was an affiliated series, compiled because Miller's dialogues were too good to be edited down to sound bites for *A Brief History*. The bonus programmes showed extended extracts from six interviews. They were broadcast on BBC4 from 18 October 2004.

92 The Arthur Miller *Atheism Tapes* interview was repeated, as a tribute to the playwright, on 29 February 2005.

93 This expanded on Miller's back catalogue of unforgettable digs. In the *Sunday Telegraph*, 19 June 1994, he dismissed the Christian row over women priests with, 'I wouldn't mind if the job was done by marmosets.' In the *Evening Standard*, 26 July 1996, he rounded on the Catholic Church's pro-life campaign. Underlining that their leaders kept mum regarding Rwanda's genocidal massacres only to hold forth about 'some two-cell form of pre-life', he suggested that the logical conclusion of their argument was that 'every time someone masturbates they should hold a requiem mass'.

94 *Behzti* was cancelled in December 2004.

95 Groups demonstrated over *Jerry Springer: The Opera* in January 2005. By September that year, the National Theatre had also received hundreds of letters protesting (in advance) about Howard Brenton's drama *Paul*, which linked the apostle with hallucinatory temporal lobe epilepsy.

96 The Danish cartoon furore began in September 2005, intensifying in February 2006, with more trouble arising from Mohammed-mocking French cartoons and the anti-Islam film *Made in America* in 2012.

97 *Private Eye*, 15–28 October 2004.

98 Miles Kington, *Independent*, 14 October 2004.

99 Regarding satirical digs, Gill's *Sunday Times* article, 17 October 2004, complained about the ex-Fringer's conspicuous tendency to apply ridicule to religion, in contrast with the *New York Sun's* review, 13 July 2007, which called for more unchecked jokes. Gill was not alone in pointing out that some gimmicky visuals had been slipped into *A Brief History*, at odds with the frontman's claim that the series was above such rot.

100 *A Brief History of Disbelief* (aka *A Rough History of Disbelief*) was broadcast on PBS TV from 4 May 2007, accompanied by a promotional video on YouTube. Bill Moyers interviewed Miller, on *Bill Moyers Journal*, as a trailer for the series in that same week. Randy Hall, of Cybercast News Service, reported on 30 April 2007 that the American Humanist Association was in favour of Miller's approach, while Janice Crouse (director of the Beverly LaHaye Institute for the conservative group Concerned Women for America) called it 'demagogic and propagandist' and Peter Sprigg (of the Family Research Council) criticized it as a biased 'evangelistic piece for atheism'. Questions were raised on the progressive website BlueOregon, in early May 2007, about Oregon Public Broadcasting 'burying' the series in a graveyard slot (2 a.m.–5 a.m.). OPB replied that they would try to give the programmes a more prominent position later.

101 Miller became president of the Rationalist Association in 2006. He had become an honorary associate of the National Secular Society before *A Brief History*. When he gave a talk on disbelief at north London's Belsize Library in February 2005, so many punters congregated that the doors had to be barred. Those left outside hammered, kept ringing the internal telephone, and ironically hollered: 'It is as hard to get into this library as it will be for Jonathan Miller to get into heaven.' That was reported in the *Camden New Journal*, 10 February 2005.

102 Viewers' comments appeared on the *Have Your Say's* BBC website page regarding *A Brief History*. Radio 4 listeners had also praised *The Nation's Health* for raising the BBC's IQ.

103 Charlie Brooker in the *Guardian*, 18 October 2004, described the programmes as incredibly watchable and clever, 'not just a breath of fresh air . . . as bracing as sticking your head out of the window of a speeding, solar-powered car'. The 'urgent and timely' comment appeared in the same publication, 16 October. Howard Jacobson's 'wall to wall' comment, *Independent*, 16 October. Thomas Sutcliffe, again in the *Independent,* on 8 October, concluded that, '[even] if Miller occasionally reminds you of an [old-school] intellectual diplodocus . . . browsing unhurriedly on philosophical cruxes . . . he certainly won a cheer from me'.

104 The *Guardian* asked 'where is his [i.e. Miller's] successor?', 2 February 2002, and its feature of 8 November 2003 reminisced about the BBC's golden era with paragraphs on *Monitor* and on Miller's *The Drinking Party*, *The Death of Socrates* and *The Body in Question*. The BBC's own *Today Programme*, 12 July 2005, discussed the death of public intellectuals, and Giles Smith portrayed Miller as a beacon in the gathering gloom, *Sunday Telegraph*, 6 February 2005.

105 Jeremy Clarkson, *Sunday Times*, 11 October 2009.

106 Miller's public condemnations of the dumbed-down BBC have included comments in the *Sunday Telegraph*, 3 November 2002; at a Hampstead Theatre platform talk on 12 October 2003; and at a Cheltenham Festival discussion on 14 October 2004. Nigella Lawson has not, to the best of my knowledge, riposted regarding BBC vegetables. Miller went on to define *Big Brother* as 'electronic excrement' and modern television as artistically 'completely impoverished' in the *Independent on Sunday*, 29 May 2005.

107 *What the World Thinks of God*, BBC2, 26 February 2004.

108 *A Brief History* was on BBC2 in October–November 2005.

109 The DVDs, and now Blu-ray discs, featuring Miller or his productions continue to grow in number. They include: *Whistle and I'll Come to You* (BFI, 2001); *Alice in Wonderland* (BFI, 2003, plus Homevision in the USA the same year); *The Shakespeare Collection*, which is the entire *BBC Shakespeare Series* (BBC, 2005); *The Beggar's Opera* (BBC TV in association with RM Arts and NOS, Metrodome Distribution, 2005); *The Secret Policeman's Ball – 25th Anniversary Silver Box Set* (4digitalMedia, 2004); and *Take a Girl Like You* (SPHE, 2008). *Long Day's Journey into Night* is on DVD in America (Image Entertainment, 2005, © the Miles Company, 1987). So is the BBC recording of *Beyond the Fringe* (Acorn Media, 2005). A stack of Miller's international operas is available for home viewing, though not all in the UK: *Tamerlano*, recorded in Halle (Arthaus Musik et al., 2001); *La Fanciulla del West* (Image Entertainment in 1998, then Opus Arte in 2004, and on VHS via Homevision in 2000); *Figaro*, from Maggio Musicale, conducted by Zubin Mehta with Lucio Gallo (TDK, 2005); Zurich Opera's *Die Zauberflöte/The Magic Flute* (TDK, 2002, and Kultur Films Inc., 2004); *Nabucco*, filmed in Genoa (Qualiton Imports Ltd, 2004); *Die Entführung auf dem Serail* (Bel Air Classiques, 2006); *La Clemenza di Tito* (EMI Classics, 2007); *The Mikado* (A&E Home Entertainment, 2005, including Thames TV's *A Source of Innocent Merriment*); *Rigoletto* (as aforementioned, Kultur, 2007); his 2009 ENO *La Bohème* (released by Kultur, on BD, June 2010); *Jonathan Miller's Acting in Opera* in the *BBC Acting Series* (DVD box set, Hal Leonard Corporation/The Working Arts Library/Applause, 2007); and the *BBC Great Composers Series* (Warner Music Vision, 2001–2002).

Alice, *Whistle and I'll Come to You*, *Long Day's Journey*, *Rigoletto* and the *BBC Shakespeare* productions have recently become available for downloading too (via websites including themoviedownloads.com and movielink.com). His *St Matthew Passion* is only on audio CD (Cala, 2000).

There have, naturally, been many TV repeats of Miller's work, including *Whistle and I'll Come to You* (BBC4, 22 December 2004); Roger Graef's *Arena* programme revisiting *The Secret Policeman's Ball* (BBC4 on 9 December 2004 and BBC2 on 20 December 2004); *Timewatch: Voices of Victorian London* on the UK's History Channel, September 2005, May 2006 etc. Miller has additionally featured in the acclaimed documentary *In Search of Mozart* which came out on DVD in 2006 (Vital Distribution). The *Boston Globe*, 4 May 2007, said his contributions provided most of the film's colour and zest. Among those contributions, he observed that Mozart's prodigious talent, like Shakespeare's, seemed to be combined with a perfectly normal psychological existence.

Finally, the BFI website has featured Miller's *Alice* as an educational resource, offering ideas for its incorporation into curriculum subjects as varied as art, history, science, geography, music and GCSE media studies (with a suggestion that students might like to produce a biography of Jonathan Miller).

110 In the *Have Your Say* feedback on the BBC's website, fans begged for a *Brief History* video or DVD release and asked to see more of Miller, loving his natural style. Only *The Atheism Tapes* have become available on DVD (courtesy of Alive Mind in 2007). *A Brief History* has now been posted by fans on YouTube. Meanwhile, those opposed to more of Miller feel that younger faces and new voices are needed. As the *Independent on Sunday*'s radio reviewer Nicholas Lezard complained about an overdose more than once (e.g. on 28 July 2002).

111 Among other suggestions, Miller proposed a new series on imitation with the working title *Doing Likewise*. As regards the 70th birthday TV celebration, Kevin Jackson argued for that in the *Independent*, 26 October 2001. He and the BBC producer David Thompson then pursued the idea for 2004 only to have it turned down. It seems equally bizarre that various histories of the Corporation do not so much as mention *The Body in Question*: for example, the Beeb's own publication Cain, J. (1992), *The BBC: Seventy Years of Broadcasting* (London: BBC), and Vahimagi, T. (ed.) (1994), *British Television: An Illustrated Guide* (Oxford: Oxford University Press, in association with the BFI).

112 The Sky Arts retrospective season, on 19 and 26 July 2009, programmed Miller's *Rigoletto* and *Merchant of Venice* alongside his ENO *La Bohème* and *Absolute Rubbish*. The original plans had been for every Sunday that month and had incorporated *Ivan, The Emperor* and other recordings, but that was scaled down. *The Zoo in Winter* followed on from *Arena*, both 31 March 2012.

113 Miller has featured in person, too, as a reminiscing veteran in Joan Bakewell's BBC2 series *My Generation: Blinded by Light*, on 18 June 2000, and in Sue MacGregor's *Fifty Years On* for Radio 4, 24 July 2002 (eliciting fan mail from Max Bygraves).

114 *Not Only But Always*, Channel 4, 30 December 2004. Readily acknowledging that he imagined rather than met the man for this thumbnail sketch, Johnson says: 'Jonathan [Miller] was the toughest [of the foursome] to cast . . . The key is how he thinks, which is to do with his capacity for language and what we called his constant "visits to the library".'

115 *Pete and Dud: Come Again* opened at The Venue in Leicester Square in March 2006, written by Chris Bartlett and Nick Awde. The comedian Colin Hoult looked bemusingly less like Miller than did the sandy-haired Tom Goodman-Hill who was playing Cook. Another biodrama, called *Goodbye – The (After)life of Cook and Moore*, opened at the Edinburgh Fringe Festival in August 2007. There the titular duo were joined by their fellow comics in a bar in Limbo, facing divine judgement. The writer Roy Smiles' playful piece about the *Beyond the Fringe* team, entitled *Good Evening*, was staged in the style of a revue at Pieter Toerien's Montecasino Theatre in Fourways, South Africa, in July 2007 (with Smiles having to rework some of the classic sketches due to copyright complications). Diane de Beer of www.tonight.co.za reported that David Clatworthy had the hardest part as the 'inscrutable' Jonathan Miller. *Good Evening* went on to be broadcast on BBC Radio 4, on 14 April 2008. There Miller (once again played by Aris) finished up in the beyond, planning a satire of the social fabric of heaven with Cook.

116 Raphael, F. (1984), *The Glittering Prizes* (London: Inner Circle), pp. 97–8.

117 The Folio Society debate was reported in the *Evening Standard*, 10 February 1989 and elsewhere. Miller's arguments later fed into a lecture which he gave at the National Gallery on the difference between pictures and mental images. Some of his ideas were seeded earlier. Many fans of his BBC *Alice in Wonderland* had been taken aback by the final chapter in *Subsequent Performances*, where he found fault with novel-to-screen adaptations in general. However, he persuasively identified several cinematically untranslatable features of prose (such as the iterative tense, which concisely describes oft-repeated actions). He drew distinctions between ways of 'seeing' (the mise-en-scène differing from the reader's 'mind's eye' which does not have to fill in all the details). In his James MacTaggart Lecture, Miller had also criticized the excessive literalism attempted in many British TV adaptations of classic and non-naturalistic plays. That argument chimed with MacTaggart's own opinions because, as a TV producer and director, he had opposed totally naturalistic television dramas.

118 That is the film producer, Paul Raphael. The cinema rage incident was reported at length in the *Sunday Times*, 15 September 1996.

119 Frederic Raphael's account in *Prospect*, October 1996, sardonically alluded to Miller as the 'Man of Culture'.

120 *Son of Enoch* (named after Max Beerbohm's 1912 story, *Enoch Soames*) appeared in *Prospect*, June 1997, 42–5.

121 Margaret married Antony Armstrong-Jones in May 1960. Their divorce was formalized in 1978. She was – some have alleged – having an affair with the wine producer Anthony Barton by 1966. Question marks have also been raised over her relations with Mick Jagger, Peter Sellers, David Niven and others.

122 Bartoli, *Daily Telegraph*, 26 May 2005. Miller and David Hockney rubbed along fine as well, without any rows, at a house party in 2008. A warm friendship was more actively reforged with the elderly Irene Worth. Miller reminisces about her 'hanging on the strap in the [New York] subway and going around galleries groaning with excitement'. She gamely played the mad wandering Io once more, like a crazy bag lady rather than a dazzling beauty, in a 30th anniversary reunion and reading of *Prometheus Bound*. That was at Manhattan's 92nd Street Y in 1997, three years after the 30-years-on reunion of Miller, Frank Langella and Roscoe Lee Browne for a rereading of *Benito Cereno* at the same venue (organized by Karl Kirchwey).

123 *Camera Obscura* was staged in the Almeida's rehearsal room in Islington in May 2002. The edited script was described as Miller's new adaptation of Lorenzo DeStefano's play, *Inman*. DeStefano was inspired by Inman, A. C., edited by Aaron, D. (1996), *From a Darkened Room: The Inman Diary* (Cambridge MA and London: Harvard University Press). The play was criticized for lacking dramatic momentum, but Miller's production was described as superbly acted, disquieting and atmospheric by Suzi Feay, *Independent on Sunday*, 26 May 2002; Kate Kellaway, *Observer*, 26 May; and Billington, *Guardian*, 21 May. Benedict Nightingale was not grabbed in *The Times*, 21 May.

124 Eyre pays further tribute to Miller as the man who saved him from despairingly throwing in the towel in the mid-1960s. The director met the actor at a party, told him not to give up, and soon afterwards cast him in *The Drinking Party*. That led on to *The Death of Socrates*, *Alice* and *The Seagull* in Nottingham which Eyre says marked the first time he personally discovered artistic freedom as a performer.

125 *The South Bank Show*, 9 October 2005.

126 Bennett, A. (2009), *The Habit of Art* (London: Faber), p. 70 on the torrent of words, and pp. 47–8 on the same groove. An element of Dudley Moore might also be discerned in Britten, the piano-player unable to match Auden's conversational prowess, p. 51. As the TV documentary *Alan Bennett and The Habit of Art* (More4, 27 November 2010) mentioned, Bennett's original (soon ditched) title *A/B* indicated the play's protagonists might be two sides of the author himself.

127 Introduction to *The Habit of Art*, pp. viii–x.

128 Miller's talk was given in the Sherrington Building at Liverpool University in January 2008.

129 I am again indebted to Andrew Billen's feature, *Evening Standard*, 24 November 1999, for this quotation, and for the later comment about Miller being his own best thesis regarding non-verbal behaviour.

130 As is doubtless apparent from this biography, Miller's offspring differ as regards being directly interviewed by journalists, with Kate not keen on media exposure and with William being more like his father, happy to talk in spite of being taught, from an early age, 'that invertebrates don't only live in Scottish bogs, they also work on newspapers'.

131 William Miller, *Sunday Times*, 8 February 2009. The *Sunday Times*, 5 August 2012, reheated the private schools issue, declaring the socialist Miller had compromised.

132 BBC Radio 4, *The Line Between Life and Death*, 8 and 15 January 2009.

133 John Wells was quoted in Bergan, p. 286. A. A. Gill appeared to be willing a Pauline conversion on Miller too in his *Sunday Times* piece on *A Brief History*.

134 He commented on Advent services in the *Listener*, 19 December 1968.

135 Miller's allusions to Channel-crossing, his burial, the Derby bedsit and musical chairs featured in Rosemary Dinnage's *The Ruffian on the Stair*, pp. 229–34. 'Nanny' is inserted from an interview with me where Miller again drew the musical chairs and party-leaving analogy and brought his nanny into the picture in the hall, once more associating her with death. In his discussion with Dinnage, he also pictured the dead as a rankled, impoverished multitude, rather like Hans Andersen's little match girl, hankering for life with their noses pressed to the glass. This strikingly echoes his early feelings of exclusion from Christmas festivities.

136 A literary evening arranged by the Friends of the Bodleian, 26 October 2005.

137 Miller interviewed on the BBC's *Five Minutes With* series, October 2009.

138 Norman Lebrecht emphasized this point in his *Evening Standard* feature, 7 January 2009.

139 Quoted by Henrietta Bredin, *Spectator*, 17 November 2007. The image echoes Isaac Newton who felt that he had been 'only like a boy playing on the sea-shore . . . diverting myself in now and then finding a smoother pebble or a prettier shell than ordinary, while the great ocean of truth lay all undiscovered before me'.

140 Miller is now slightly more resigned about not being a medical scientist than he was in previous decades. However, his mixed feelings about his failures and achievements continue to crop up in conversation today. *Jude the Obscure* remains a reference point, having been alluded to for many years (at least from Mark Pappenheim's aforementioned interview, *Independent*, 12 February 1993).

141 Miller on *The Dick Cavett Show,* in their fifth 1980 conversation.

142 He argues that his philosophical concerns feed more directly into his stage work, because he is constantly questioning the characters' intentions (conscious or otherwise) and because the job entails getting performers to 'act', to move and mean it convincingly.

143 He spoke of an irrational forty-to-one ratio, regarding the worth of drama productions and science papers, in conversation with Dick Cavett in their second conversation, 1980. While insignificance can be variously defined, Miller seems paradoxical in prizing the 'trivial details' of life and yet scorning the theatre as a 'trivial business'.

144 Conversely, Miller supported Bristol's Tobacco Factory as an excellent regional theatre, when they were threatened with Arts Council funding cuts in 2008.

145 Comment made with reference to Chekhov's *Three Sisters* in the *Guardian*, 9 July 1976.

146 Quotation from the *Independent*, 14 September 1998.

147 Extract from an email sent to Kate Bassett by A. S. Byatt, March 2003. Byatt is referring to her novel: Byatt, A. S. (2002), *A Whistling Woman* (London: Chatto & Windus).

148 I have drawn here on my diary notes and the article which I wrote about Miller for *Cam Magazine*, January 1995.

149 Even if he is categorized as a great mind, the amiable impression of Miller's lanky physique should never be underestimated. Michael Colgan, of Dublin's Gate Theatre, recalls being on a visit to London and spotting this world-renowned figure loping along a street, 'looking like a confused giraffe, in this yellow coat, scratching the top of his head as if something had gone a bit wrong. He looked decidedly approachable', Colgan explains. That was when he determined to get Miller on board.

150 Miller in the *Independent on Sunday*, 5 September 1999, relating to *Nowhere in Particular*.

151 *The Body in Question*, pp. 17–21, *On Reflection*, pp. 45, 56–7 etc.

152 Journalists focusing on Miller's vociferous complaints have included Stephen Moss, *Guardian*, 19 November 2004 and 25 April 2008 (whence the machine gun analogy); Rupert Christiansen, *Telegraph*, 29 November 2004; Brian Logan, *Times*, 17 March 2007.

153 Moss, 19 November 2004, commented that he did not know whether to laugh or cry at his interviewee's bitterness because it was expressed with such comic brio. While agreeing that Miller's opinions inspired some sympathy, Logan suggested that the director needed to pull himself together.

154 Moss, again 19 November, also extracted a 'sorry' from his interviewee, with Miller calling himself 'a bad-tempered bastard'.

155 *Subsequent Performances*, pp. 192–3. Poussin's dancers might, similarly, be compared to Botticelli's *Primavera*, evoked by Miller in his early *Twelfth Night*.

156 The *Seattle Times*, on 5 March 1991, reported that he owned an estimated 11,000 books. Though not so weighty, he became a deltiologist, a collector of postcards, and had amassed 15,000 of them, mostly of artworks, by the 1980s.

157 The mulching image comes from *The Times*, 13 November 2001, and he continued to underline that age and experience were enriching his directing in the *Independent*, 23 October 2009, countering the suggestion that his talent might have wilted.

158 He discussed reading less and forgetting chunks in that *Independent* article of October 2009.

159 This comment is from Bergan, p. 282.

160 Anthony John Hardy and Thomas McDowell, two Camden residents with severe psychological problems, were found (separately) guilty of those gruesome 2002 murders.

161 Miller in the *Evening Standard*, 15 May 2002 and 8 November 2004. He was also interviewed by Francis Gilbert for Gilbert, F. (2006), *Yob Nation* (London: Portrait).

162 Miller observed this about himself in the *Guardian*, 16 September 2003.

163 In the *Wall Street Journal*, 28 May 2008, he admitted to saying things out loud that he shouldn't, particularly alluding to how he had been considered uncollegial for likening Anthony Minghella's *Madame Butterfly* to a maple-syrup enema (in the *New York Sun*, 3 October 2006).

164 *Emil and the Detectives*, Radio 4, during August 2001.

165 The close of Samuel Beckett's *The Unnamable*.

JONATHAN MILLER:
SELECTIVE CHRONOLOGY

Born 1934. Eldest child of Dr Emanuel Miller and Betty Miller (née Spiro, also known as Betty Bergson Spiro). One sister, Sarah, b. 1937, d. 2006. Married Rachel Collet in 1956. Three children: Tom, b. 1962; William, b. 1964; and Kate, b. 1967.

EDUCATION, CAREER IN SCIENCE AND RELATED RESEARCH POSTS

1939–45: Various schools during World War 2, including Thone School in Taunton; The Priory in Kings Langley (a Rudolf Steiner school); and Shirley House in Watford (prep school).

1945–7: Arnold House, London (prep school).

1947–53: St Paul's School for Boys, London.

1953–6: St John's College, Cambridge.

1956–9: University College Hospital, London.

1959: Qualifies as a doctor.

1959–60: His pre-registration year, doing house jobs, starts in the professorial unit of surgery at UCH, then he is a house physician on the neurological firm at the Central Middlesex Hospital in Harrow, north-west London.

1960–1: Resident assistant pathologist at Addenbrooke's Hospital, Cambridge.

1961–2: More pathology at the Royal Marsden Hospital in Chelsea, and doing autopsies at the London Hospital in Whitechapel. However, simultaneous success, starring in *Beyond the Fringe* in the West End, stymies his career in medicine. Hereafter, he occasionally tries to return permanently to medical research.

1967: Joins a Royal Society study group, for a stint, looking into non-verbal communication.

1970: Takes up an honorary research fellowship at University College London, studying the history of medicine, especially mesmerism, the spiritualist movement and the associated development of neuropsychological theories.

1983: Is briefly a visiting professor of medicine at Ontario's McMaster University, in Canada.

1983–4: Attempts to start out again as a research fellow in neuropsychology at the University of Sussex, with a Leverhulme Trust grant.

1994: A short research fellowship at San Francisco's science museum, the Exploratorium, culminates in an exhibition on transparency.

2005: Organizes a seminar on the subject of imitation, a subject spanning science and the arts, during a residency at New York University.

STAGE AND SCREEN APPEARANCES AS A COMEDIAN, ACTOR, CHAT-SHOW GUEST, PUNDIT and PRESENTER

1949–53: Performs comic turns in the Colet Clubs revues at St Paul's School.

1953–4: Various slots, as a young entertainer, on *Under-Twenty Parade*, BBC Radio.

1954: The Footlights show *Out of the Blue* transfers from Cambridge to the Phoenix Theatre in London's West End.

Is a participant on *In Town Tonight* and *Guess My Story*, both BBC TV, and on *Take the Mike* for BBC Radio.

1955: Plays Sir Politic Would-Be in Ben Jonson's *Volpone* for the Marlowe Society at the Arts Theatre, Cambridge, directed by John Barton.

The Footlights show *Between the Lines* transfers from Cambridge to the West End's Scala Theatre.

He and Rory McEwen (from Footlights) perform cabaret comedy at Clement Freud's Chelsea dining club in what is, today, the Royal Court Theatre Upstairs.

Appears on ITV's *Sunday Night at the London Palladium*.

Small role in *The Man from Paranoia*, BBC radio comedy.

Plays Troubleall in Ben Jonson's *Bartholomew Fair* for the ADC (Cambridge University's Amateur Dramatic Club), directed by Robin Midgley.

1956–9: Performs as a comedian at debutante balls around London, and in the medics' revues at University College Hospital.

1957: Founder member of the magazine programme *Tonight*, BBC TV, doing entertaining routines.

1957–60: Features on BBC Radio's *Saturday Night on the Light* and *Monday Night at Home*.

1960: Co-writes and co-stars in the satirical sketch show *Beyond the Fringe* at the Edinburgh Festival, alongside Peter Cook, Dudley Moore and Alan Bennett.

1961: *Beyond the Fringe* tours the UK then comes into the West End, becoming a groundbreaking hit at the Fortune Theatre. It is recorded as an LP, and filmed by the BBC (broadcast in 1964).

1961–2: Performs at Cook's satirical club The Establishment, albeit not frequently.

1961: The *Beyond the Fringe* foursome, aka the Fringers, are given slots on *Tempo*, Kenneth Tynan's ITV arts magazine programme. Miller's contributions include a history of cartoons and caricatures.

1962: He co-stars with Peter Sellers in Spike Milligan's lampoon *Bridge on the River Wye*, released as an LP.

Presenter/interviewer for *The Alberts*, a BBC radio profile of the eccentric comedians, aka Tony and Douglas Gray.

Beyond the Fringe transfers to Broadway, playing at the John Golden Theater after a short tour to Toronto, Washington and Boston. Miller is the first to quit the show in 1963.

1962–4: With *Beyond the Fringe* making a splash in America, he appears on TV programmes including *The Jack Paar Show*, *The Tonight Show Starring Johnny Carson*, and *Talk of the Town* (the antecedent of *The Ed Sullivan Show*). He is also the subject of a major feature in *Life* magazine.

1963: *East-Side Taxi-Driver*, a documentary piece interviewing a cabbie, is recorded by him for BBC Radio.

1964–5: Back in the UK, he appears on many British TV programmes including *Tonight*; *Not So Much a Programme, More a Way of Life*; the quiz show *Call My Bluff*; Ned Sherrin's humorous series *BBC3*; and more seriously discussing his life and influences with Malcolm Muggeridge on *Intimations*. He pops up on BBC Radio's *Woman's Hour* as well.

Takes over as the presenter and content-determining editor of *Monitor*, BBC TV's seminal arts magazine programme.

1965: The British film of N. F. Simpson's *One Way Pendulum* is released, with Miller cast as the mad genius Kirby Groomkirby, co-starring with Eric Sykes.

1966–71: Makes fairly frequent appearances on the BBC TV arts programme *Line Up*, discussing diverse subjects from the human face to Salvador Dali. Also features on TV and radio's *Any Questions?*, *The Question Why*, *Canvas* (discussing paintings), *The Arts This Week*, and *Desert Island Discs*.

1969: Fronts *The Zoo in Winter*, BBC TV, filmed at London Zoo.

1970: In the States, he appears on *The Dick Cavett Show* and on Studs Terkel's celebrated radio show.

1971: The documentary *West Side Stories*, BBC TV, follows him on a return visit to New York.

1972–7: Reunites with the other Fringers on *Parkinson*, BBC TV, and appears on several *Parkinson* shows. Also on *Russell Harty Plus* on ITV, as well as the BBC's *Just a Nimmo*; *André Previn Meets*; *Arena* (discussing theatre history); *Omnibus* (talking about portraits); *The Book Programme*; and Ned Sherrin's quiz show *Who Said That?*

1973: Presents the documentary *Charles Darwin Lived Here*, BBC TV.

1976: Performs along with Peter Cook, Alan Bennett, the Pythons and other star comics in the televised West End Amnesty International benefit show *A Poke in the Eye with a Sharp Stick* (aka *Pleasure at Her Majesty's*). Miller also directs. This was filmed for TV.

1977: Performs in *The Mermaid Frolics* or *An Evening without Bernard Miles*, another Amnesty benefit show, filmed for TV, with Terry Jones, John Cleese and others, at London's Mermaid Theatre.

To Dinner with the President, a televised Royal Academy dinner, sees Miller giving one of the speeches alongside Shirley Williams and Princess Anne.

1978–9: He presents *The Body in Question*, BBC TV's 13-part history of medicine, also shown in Canada in 1970, in the USA in 1980, and around the world.

1978: Miller's English National Opera debut, *The Marriage of Figaro*, is the focus of a special on ITV's arts programme, *The South Bank Show*.

1979: *Jonathan Miller's London*, with him as frontman and televisual travel guide, is filmed by Toronto's John McGreevy Productions, for Nelsen-Ferns International's *Cities* series. Appears in – as well as directing – *The Secret Policeman's Ball*, another major televised West End comedy gig in aid of Amnesty International. For this, he joins in a reprise of the Shakespeare skit from *Beyond the Fringe*.

1980–2: BBC documentary *Jonathan Miller Directs: The Making of Antony and Cleopatra* complements the *BBC Shakespeare Series* which he is overseeing.

He features in four *Parkinson* programmes. Starts appearing on the TV review programme *Did You See . . . ?*

1980: Stateside, he talks on *The Dick Cavett Show* for five nights running in 1980, with another stint the following year.

1983–4: Other guest appearances include TV's *Breakfast Time*; *Nationwide*; *Sixty Minutes*; *In at the Deep End* (with Chris Serle training to be an opera singer); and BBC Radio's *Kaleidoscope*.

1983: Presenter of *States of Mind*, BBC TV's fifteen-part series about how the brain works, interviewing high-powered experts.

Channel 4 broadcasts the six-part series *Staging an Opera*, following his rehearsals for his Kent Opera production of *Fidelio*. This is shown on American TV in 1985.

1984: He presents *Ivan*, a BBC *Horizon* documentary about the symptoms of Parkinson's disease.

1986: Fronts the one-off programme *Origins: Where We and Our World Came From*, BBC TV.

Discusses directing *Così fan tutte* for the small screen in the BBC documentary *Miller on Mozart*.

Presents *Prisoner of Consciousness*, a Channel 4 *Equinox* documentary about a musicologist and musician devastated by memory loss.

Discusses jokes and laughter with Michael Ignatieff and fellow guest Ben Elton on *Thinking Aloud*, BBC TV.

1987: *A Source of Innocent Merriment*, an ITV documentary, follows Miller's rehearsals for his ENO *Mikado*. This accompanies a television broadcast of the production. BBC TV's *Acting* series features him in its second programme, *Acting in Opera*.

1988: He hosts an interview series about religious beliefs, *My God,* for ITV.

Presents the Channel 4 mini-series *Four Virtuosos*, interviewing Murray Perahia and other musicians.

In his BBC guest appearances, he is to be found discussing Alzheimer's disease (on *Life File*), new novels (on *Cover to Cover*), Royal Opera House regime changes (on *Omnibus*), and theatre-going dolts (on *The Anne Robinson Show*), as well as calling for Margaret Thatcher to be ousted (on *After Dark*).

1989: Is profiled on Channel 4 in *A Full Life: Jonathan Miller*.

He fronts BBC TV's five-part series *Who Cares?* about home-care for the ill, the disabled and dementia-sufferers.

Presents the documentary *Moving Pictures* for Channel 4's *Equinox* strand.

Has a spat with anti-abortionist Victoria Gillick on *The Late Show* (later selected as a highlight for *TV Hell*, BBC TV, 2008).

1990: *Born Talking*, an international BBC/Canadian production, is his four-part series looking into the complexities of acquiring and producing language.

In *What's So Funny About That*, for BBC TV's *Q.E.D.* strand, Miller analyses jokes and laughter.

1991: Fronts a second series about home care, *Who Cares Now?*

Presents the five-part BBC TV series *Madness* (aka *Museums of Madness*). It investigates issues including asylums and therapies. PBS shows this in the USA.

He narrates *Teaching Today*, BBC TV, an educational programme about the National Curriculum and the environment.

1994: Is on *Desert Island Discs* again.

Various one-off contributions to TV and radio series include *Kaleidoscope, Start the Week*, observations about steps and stairs in an episode of *White Heat* (Patrick Uden's BBC/international series about technology). On Channel 4, Miller comments on the history of swearing in a *Without Walls* special about expletives (to which Sir Peter Hall also contributes).

1995: *South Bank Show* profiles Miller.

1996–7: He appears, several times, on the discussion show *The Brains Trust*, along with Edward de Bono, Lewis Wolpert, A. S. Byatt and others. As well as being interviewed on *Ruby Wax Meets . . .* , he contributes to the Corporation's *Great Composers* series.

1997: Workshop sessions, with him directing young singers, are filmed for the six-part BBC series *Opera Works*.

1998: Writes and presents the BBC television mini-series *Jonathan Miller on Reflection*, to tie in with his National Gallery exhibition, *Mirror Image*.

Presents *Dr Miller and the Islanders*, for *Horizon*.

Features on BBC TV's *The Darwin Debate*.

1999: Tête-à-tête with Dr Anthony Clare, *In the Psychiatrist's Chair*, BBC Radio.

2000: Discusses Thatcher and the 1980s with Ken Loach, Claire Tomalin and others on Joan Bakewell's TV series *My Generation*.

2001: Reads *Emil and the Detectives*, for family listening, on BBC Radio 4.

Selects his favourite pieces of prose and poetry for Radio 4's *With Great Pleasure*.

2002: Reminisces on Sue MacGregor's radio series *Fifty Years On*.

Presents a six-part Radio 4 series, *The Nation's Health*, about developments in medicine and health care.

2004: Talks about his latest staging of *King Lear* on American TV's *Charlie Rose Show*.

Presents *Flu: A Medical Mystery*, BBC Radio.

Storms out of a discussion on BBC2's *What the World Thinks of God*.

Features on Radio 3's *My Kind of Song*, and discusses Janáček on the same station.

Presents the BBC4 series *A Brief History of Disbelief*, which is repeated on BBC2 in 2005, and shown by PBS in America in 2007. Longer versions of the interviews conducted with philosophers, theologians and others for this series are released under the title *The Atheism Tapes*.

2004: Interviewed by Kirsty Walk, *One to One with Jonathan Miller*, BBC4.

2005: *Desert Island Discs* again.

Presents a series of programmes about genes and inheritance, *Self-Made Things*, on Radio 4.

Returns to comic acting, playing a Harley Street consultant, in the BBC TV drama *Sensitive Skin*.

Features in the Channel 5 documentary *In Search of Mozart*.

Another Channel 5 documentary, *Absolute Rubbish*, films him making sculptures.

2007: Interviewed for *Bill Moyers' Journal* on American TV, and for *Parkinson* on ITV in the UK.

2008: Writes a letter to Darwin for the *Dear Darwin* series on Radio 4.

2009: Presents a pair of medical/philosophical Radio 4 programmes called *The Line Between Life and Death*.

Sky Arts runs a mini-season celebrating Miller's 75th birthday, with broadcasts of *Absolute Rubbish*, *Rigoletto* and *La Bohème* live, plus *The Merchant of Venice*.

Five Minutes with Jonathan Miller, on the BBC News Channel's high-speed interview strand.

2012: *Arena* profiles Miller on BBC2.

DRAMA AND OPERA DIRECTED SPECIFICALLY FOR THE SCREEN

1963: Though not overseeing the camerawork, he directs the performances of *What's Going on Here?* Satirizing news stories in a sketch format, this was tried out on the American broadcasting network NBC and then taken up to feature in *The Ed Sullivan Show* on CBS, but Sullivan thought it dangerously anarchic.

1965: Directs *The Drinking Party*, for BBC TV's *Sunday Night* film strand.

1966: Scripts and directs *Mr Sludge the Medium*, for the *Sunday Night* slot.

Directs *The Death of Socrates*, a third *Sunday Night* drama.

Adapts and directs *Alice in Wonderland*, for BBC TV's *Wednesday Play* strand. (Released on DVD in 2003.)

1967: *From Chekhov with Love*, made for commercial TV in the UK. Also broadcast, in 1968, on CBS in the USA.

Makes a documentary film, called *Scotch*, for whisky-makers Johnnie Walker.

1968: *Whistle and I'll Come to You*, an *Omnibus* drama, BBC TV. (Released on DVD in 2005.)

1970: *Take a Girl Like You*, the only big-screen film of his directing career.

1973: *Clay*, short drama for BBC TV.

1975: *King Lear* for BBC TV's *Play of the Month* strand.

1980–82: Executive producer on the epic, televised *BBC Shakespeare Series*. He directs six of the plays himself, namely *The Taming of the Shrew*; *Timon of Athens*; *Antony and Cleopatra*; *Othello, Troilus and Cressida*; and *King Lear*. This series is also broadcast in America from 1981. (DVD releases from 2004.)

1983: *The Beggar's Opera*, BBC TV.

1985: The National Film Theatre runs a Jonathan Miller retrospective, showing his screen dramas.

1986: His new BBC TV production of *Così fan tutte* is accompanied by a simultaneous radio broadcast.

1989: *Dialogue in the Dark*, a biodrama about the philosopher David Hume and James Boswell, BBC TV.

1996: His docudrama *Voices of Victorian London* is made for the BBC series *Timewatch*. Miller directs and narrates.

THEATRE PRODUCTIONS AND RELATED POSTS

1957: Directs *Forks and Hopes*, a medley of verse, sketches and songs (rather than a straight drama) in University College Hospital's Foundation Play slot.

1962: Professional directing debut at London's Royal Court Theatre, premiering John Osborne's *Under Plain Cover*.

1964: Invited to direct a Broadway-bound comic drama, *World War Two and a Half*. He quits over 'artistic differences'.

Stages Robert Lowell's *The Old Glory*, inaugurating the American Place Theater, off-Broadway. The production transfers to the Theater de Lys (now the Lucille Lortel Theatre) in New York's Greenwich Village. It wins five Obie Awards and is recorded for TV.

1966: Quits another Broadway-bound comedy drama, *Come Live with Me*, which he is contracted to direct.

1967: *Benito Cereno*, from the *Old Glory* trilogy, at London's Mermaid Theatre.

Miller is soon appointed to the Mermaid's board of governors, and he remains a member into the 1970s.

1967: Robert Lowell's adaptation of *Prometheus Bound*, for Yale Repertory Theatre, New Haven.

1968: *The School for Scandal*, Nottingham Playhouse.

The Seagull, Nottingham Playhouse.

1969: *Twelfth Night*, for the Oxford and Cambridge Shakespeare Company at the Cambridge Arts Theatre. This tours and plays at London's Middle Temple Hall.

King Lear, Nottingham Playhouse.

1970: *King Lear* transfers to London's Old Vic at the invitation of Laurence Olivier, who is based there with the National Theatre Company, awaiting the construction of a dedicated NT building.

Directs Olivier in *The Merchant of Venice* for the NT Company. The production is subsequently filmed for TV (though not by Miller).

The Tempest at the Mermaid.

Hamlet for the OCSC.

1971: *Julius Caesar* for the OCSC.

Prometheus Bound for the Mermaid.

Danton's Death, under the National Theatre banner, at London's New Theatre (now the Noël Coward Theatre).

1972: *Richard II*, at Los Angeles' Ahmanson Theater, and transferring to Washington.

The School for Scandal, staged this time at the Old Vic for the NT.

The Taming of the Shrew, Chichester Festival Theatre.

1973: *The Malcontent* at Nottingham Playhouse, with a London transfer to Sam Wanamaker's festival tent on the site of Shakespeare's Globe (not yet reconstructed).

Associate director, National Theatre.

The Seagull for Chichester Festival Theatre.

Measure for Measure, NT touring production, opens in Harlow.

1974: *Family Romances* – i.e. *The Seagull*, *Ghosts* and *Hamlet* – in rep at Greenwich Theatre.

The Marriage of Figaro, for the NT, at the Old Vic.

The Freeway, for the NT, at the Old Vic.

1974–6: Member of the Arts Council.

1975: Resigns from his post at Peter Hall's National Theatre.

The Importance of Being Earnest at Greenwich Theatre.

Bedtricks – i.e. *All's Well That Ends Well* and *Measure for Measure* – at Greenwich Theatre, where he has been made an associate.

1976: *Three Sisters* tours from Guildford and comes into London's West End (the Cambridge Theatre).

Directs *A Poke in the Eye with a Sharp Stick* (aka *Pleasure at Her Majesty's*).

1977: Made associate director at the Royal Court.

426

1979: *She Would If She Could* at Greenwich Theatre.

A Midsummer Night's Dream at Vienna's Burgtheater.

He gains another directing credit for *The Secret Policeman's Ball*.

1982: *Hamlet* at London's Warehouse Theatre (now the Donmar).

1983: *The School for Scandal* at Harvard's American Repertory Theatre (going on to LA's Olympic Arts Festival in 1984).

1984: Becomes chairman of the Edinburgh Fringe Festival, a post he holds for a decade, serving as a public figurehead.

1986: *Long Day's Journey into Night* opens at the Broadhurst Theatre on Broadway, and transfers to London's Haymarket Theatre Royal. This is filmed, broadcast on American TV in 1987, and is on video by 1988.

1987: *The Emperor* at the Royal Court Upstairs. This transfers to the main house – the Royal Court Downstairs – and is filmed for television, being shown on the BBC's *Arena* strand in 1988.

Misura per Misura (aka *Measure for Measure*) in an Italian production that tours to Rome and Verona.

1988: His RSC debut, directing *The Taming of the Shrew*.

1988–90: Artistic director of the Old Vic, notably introducing British audiences to forgotten historic gems and continental classics, nurturing talent and playing host to leading foreign companies. He himself directs Racine's *Andromaque*, N. F. Simpson's *One Way Pendulum* (with a try-out run at the Royal Alexandra in Toronto), George Chapman's *Bussy D'Ambois*, *The Tempest*, Leonard Bernstein's *Candide* (in a co-production with Scottish Opera), Corneille's *The Liar*, and *King Lear*.

1992: *The Double Dealer*, Dublin's Gate Theatre.

1994: Manhattan's 92nd Street Y hosts a 30th-anniversary reunion of Miller, Frank Langella and Roscoe Lee Browne for a reading of *Benito Cereno*.

Joins Peter Brook and Oliver Sacks for a platform talk in Manchester, relating to Brook's stage adaptation of Sacks' *The Man Who Mistook His Wife for a Hat*.

1995: *She Stoops to Conquer*, Dublin's Gate Theatre.

1996: *A Midsummer Night's Dream*, Almeida Theatre, north London.

1997: Reunion and reading of *Prometheus Bound*, 92nd Street Y.

2000: *As You Like It*, Dublin's Gate Theatre.

2002: *Camera Obscura*, Almeida Rehearsal Rooms, then tours to Bath, Winchester and Oxford.

King Lear at Canada's Stratford Shakespeare Festival in Ontario.

2004: *King Lear* transfers to New York's Lincoln Center.

2007: *The Cherry Orchard*, Sheffield Crucible.

2008: *Hamlet*, Bristol's Tobacco Factory.

Three Sisters, Royal Academy of Dramatic Art, London. Miller becomes an associate member of RADA.

2009: He features in *The Acting Series, Revisited*, the National Theatre's clutch of platform talks recalling and appraising the 1980s BBC *Acting* series.

2010: *Measure for Measure*, RADA.

2012: *King Lear*, City Lit, London.

2013: *Rutherford and Son*, Viaduct Theatre, Halifax and tour for Northern Broadsides.

2014: She Stoops to Conquer, RADA.

2015: King Lear (with Barrie Rutter as Lear) for Northern Broadsides.

OPERA PRODUCTIONS STAGED AND RELATED POSTS

1972: *Noyes Fludde* at the Roundhouse, Camden.

1974: *Arden Must Die* at Sadler's Wells.

Così fan tutte for the small touring company Kent Opera, opens at Eastbourne.

1975: *The Cunning Little Vixen* at Glyndebourne.

Rigoletto, Kent Opera (Dickensian setting).

1976: *L'Orfeo, favola in musica* for Kent Opera, at Bath Festival and other festivals round the UK.

The Cunning Little Vixen staged for Opera Australia, with transfer from Melbourne to Sydney Opera House.

1977: *Eugene Onegin,* Kent Opera.

The Cunning Little Vixen staged for Frankfurt Opera.

1978: *The Marriage of Figaro*, English National Opera, at London's Coliseum.

1979: Miller becomes an ENO associate director.

The Flying Dutchman, Frankfurt Opera.

La Traviata, Kent Opera.

The Turn of the Screw, ENO.

His Kent Opera *L'Orfeo, favola in musica*, or *Orfeo* for short, is also shown on BBC TV.

1980: *Arabella*, ENO.

Falstaff, Kent Opera.

1981: *Otello*, ENO.

1982: Another *Così fan tutte*, this one for Opera Theatre of St Louis, Missouri.

Fidelio, Kent Opera (also broadcast as the culmination of Channel 4's 1983 documentary series *Staging an Opera*).

Rigoletto for the ENO (1950s Mafia setting). Televised on Channel 4 in 1983, and internationally in 1984. This Mafia *Rigoletto* becomes a celebrated and long-standing hit, repeatedly revived for the ENO until it was replaced in 2014.

1983: *The Magic Flute* for Scottish Opera (Age of Reason library setting) opens in Glasgow and features on BBC TV's *Omnibus*. It transfers to the Dominion in London during 1984, and plays at the Coliseum two years later.

1984: Miller's ENO *Rigoletto* tours the USA (together with his *Turn of the Screw*), and it plays at the New York Met.

1985: *Don Giovanni*, ENO.

1986: *The Mikado*, ENO. This is additionally filmed, broadcast on ITV in 1987, and released on video. It becomes another famed, long-standing hit for the Coliseum, frequently revived.

Tosca for Maggio Musicale, in Florence (as a co-production with the ENO).

1987: *Tosca* transfers to the Coliseum (and it is staged for Houston Grand Opera too, in 1991).

The Barber of Seville, ENO.

Tristan und Isolde, for LA Opera at the Dorothy Chandler Pavilion, Los Angeles.

1988: Miller ceases to be an ENO associate.

As an ENO co-production, his *Mikado* is recreated in Los Angeles (plus a PBS TV broadcast), and for Houston Grand Opera in 1989.

Tristan und Isolde transfers from LA to the Maggio Musicale.

1989: *La Traviata* for Glimmerglass Opera in Cooperstown, Upstate New York.

Rise and Fall of the City of Mahagonny, LA Opera.

1990: *Don Giovanni*, for Maggio Musicale (transfers to LA in 1991 and to Finland's Savonlinna Opera Festival in 2001).

The ENO, as the first foreign opera company to tour the post-Cold War Soviet Union, takes Miller's *Turn of the Screw* as one of three productions.

1991: *La Fanciulla del West* for La Scala, Milan (and this plays at the Teatro Regio, Turin as well). It is recorded for video release.

Katya Kabanova for the New York Met (also subsequently staged by the Lyric Opera of Chicago, in 2009).

The Turn of the Screw, now staged in LA.

The Marriage of Figaro, this staging being for Vienna Staatsoper.

Così fan tutte, this staging being for Maggio Musicale.

The Magic Flute (League of Nations hotel setting), Mann Auditorium, Tel Aviv.

Fidelio for Glimmerglass.

1992: *Roberto Devereux*, Opéra de Monte-Carlo.

Manon Lescaut, La Scala.

The Marriage of Figaro, for Maggio Musicale (creating a Miller Mozart cycle for Florence, together with his *Don Giovanni* and *Così* there).

1992: *Il Matrimonio Segreto* or *The Secret Marriage*, Glimmerglass (later at Brooklyn Academy of Music, aka BAM, 2008).

Ermione for Opera Omaha.

Die Gezeichneten, Zurich Opera.

1993: Bach's *St Matthew Passion* at Holy Trinity Church, Sloane Street, London. Also filmed for telecast in 1994. This goes on to be performed at Glasgow's Tramway, in Bath etc. There are international productions too, for example in Barcelona, in the Catalan city of Lleida, and at BAM.

Maria Stuarda for Opéra de Monte-Carlo (also at Bologna's Teatro Comunale in 1994).

Capriccio for Berlin State Opera, aka Staatsoper Unter den Linden.

The Secret Marriage, now at Buxton Opera House for the Buxton Festival, in a co-production by Opera North (which is revived, at Leeds' Grand Theatre, in 1994). He stages *Maria Stuarda* for the Buxton Festival as well.

Fedora at the Bregenz Festival (co-production with Vienna Staatsoper, and transferring there the following year).

Ariadne auf Naxos, Broomhill Opera, at Broomhill in Kent.

Falstaff, now for Zurich Opera.

1994: *The Marriage of Figaro* (from Vienna Staatsoper), now at the Teatro Comunale in Ferrara.

Der Rosenkavalier, ENO (also staged in LA, Houston, Madrid).

Anna Bolena, Opéra de Monte-Carlo (co-production with Bologna's Teatro Comunale).

L'Incoronazione di Poppea, Glimmerglass.

La Bohème, Maggio Musicale.

1995: *Così fan tutte* (modern dress Armani version), Miller's Royal Opera House debut. This becomes a major and long-standing hit at Covent Garden, revived frequently. It is staged, as a co-production, at Teatro dell'Opera di Roma in 1995, with subsequent stagings in the USA.

Pelléas et Mélisande, New York Met. Also broadcast.

Tamerlano, Glimmerglass. Miller gives master classes for young singers at Glimmerglass as well.

Carmen, ENO.

Anna Bolena, large-scale production for Munich's Bayerische Staatsoper (aka the Bavarian State Opera).

La Bohème (as a Maggio Musicale co-production) transfers to Paris' Bastille Opera.

The Marriage of Figaro (from Vienna Staatsoper) is taken to Japan, playing at the Tokyo Bunka Kaikan.

1996: *L'Incoronazione di Poppea* (from Glimmerglass), now at BAM.

Der Rosenkavalier staged for New York City Opera (a recreation of the ENO production).

Idomeneo, Maggio Musicale (additionally staged for Opéra de Lausanne, Switzerland, in 1997).

Il Matrimonio Segreto, large-scale production for Zurich Opera.

Works with young opera singers on the Italian island of Ischia, staging *The Bear*, which goes on to play at Buxton Opera House.

Rodelinda, Broomhill Opera, at Broomhill in Kent.

La Traviata, ENO.

1997: The Donizetti trilogy (*Roberto Devereux*, *Maria Stuarda*, *Anna Bolena*) revived at Opéra de Monte-Carlo.

Miller's staging of Bach's *St Matthew Passion* now arrives at BAM (where it will be repeatedly revived).

Roberto Devereux now at Teatro Regio, Turin.

Ariadne auf Naxos, now staged for Maggio Musicale (a co-production with Opéra de Lausanne, where it plays in 1998).

1997: *Mitridate, re di Ponto* at the Salzburg Festival.

The Rake's Progress, New York Met.

La Traviata, now staged at Paris' Bastille Opera.

1998: *The Marriage of Figaro,* New York Met. Telecast by PBS in 1999, and screened at the Barbican's Mostly Mozart Festival in London in 2005 as a *Live from the Met* broadcast. BBC TV shows documentary footage of the making of this *Figaro* in 2001.

Falstaff, now staged for the Berlin State Opera (recreating the Zurich production). This transfers to Ferrara in 1999.

Nabucco, Zurich Opera. Also staged in Genoa in 2004, and released on DVD that same year.

The Magic Flute, Santa Fe Opera (League of Nations hotel setting).

1999: *The Beggar's Opera,* for Broomhill Opera, at Wilton's Music Hall, London.

Maria Stuarda, now staged at Theatro Regio, Turin.

The Magic Flute (large-scale Age of Reason library staging), Zurich Opera. (Recorded and released on DVD in 2002, and staged at Venice's Teatro La Fenice in 2006).

2000: *Ermione,* Santa Fe Opera.

I Puritani, Munich's Bayerische Staatsoper.

2001: *Don Pasquale,* Maggio Musicale (this being the production subsequently staged at London's Royal Opera House).

Tamerlano (as staged at Glimmerglass), now at Paris' Théâtre des Champs Élysées; at the Handel Festival in Halle, Germany (where is it recorded for subsequent DVD release); and at Sadler's Wells in London (plus a BBC Radio broadcast).

Falstaff, now for Santa Fe Opera.

Die Schweigsame Frau, Zurich Opera.

Miller stages his *Mikado* for New York City Opera.

2002: *Eugene Onegin,* now staged for Santa Fe Opera (and transferring to Seattle Opera in 2006).

Small-scale *Così fan tutte* (modern dress) for a young singers' summer academy on the Danish island of Bornholm. Miller's directing is filmed for a TV documentary, *The Opera Island: Bornholm.* That is aired by various broadcasters, DR in Denmark, SVT in Sweden and NRK in Norway, as well as in Poland.

Capriccio, now staged at Teatro Regio, Turin.

2003: Miller's *Rigoletto* is chosen to feature in Channel 4's talent show, *Operatunity.*

Così fan tutte (modern-dress version) plays at BAM.

Die Entführung aus dem Serail or *Il Seraglio,* Zurich Opera.

For Graz Opera in Austria, he stages Cimarosa's *Cleopatra* and Stravinsky's *Oedipus Rex* (which goes on to the White Nights Festival in St Petersburg, co-produced by the Mariinsky Theatre).

A semi-staged reworking of *L'Orfeo* is performed at London's Queen Elizabeth Hall, with Philip Pickett's New London Consort. This tours internationally over the next few years (to Bergen, Beijing, Paris and elsewhere)

L'Elisir d'Amore or *The Elixir of Love,* Royal Swedish Opera, Stockholm.

2004: *Falstaff,* National Opera of Japan at the New National Theatre, Toyko.

Così fan tutte (modern-dress version) at the Lincoln Center's Mostly Mozart Festival.

Don Pasquale now at the Royal Opera House.

With the Opera Island team, who were behind the Bornholm summer academy, Miller workshops and stages *La Traviata* in Kristiansand, Norway.

2005: *La Clemenza di Tito,* Zurich Opera.

Workshops and stages *Don Giovanni* for the Opera Island team in Kristiansand.

La Fanciulla del West (from La Scala) is seen at the Tokyo Bunka Kaikan.

2006: *Jenufa,* Glimmerglass.

The Elixir of Love, now for New York City Opera.

Don Giovanni at the Palau de les Arts Reina Sofia, Valencia.

2006: *Così fan tutte* (modern-dress version), now for Seattle Opera.

2007: *La Traviata* for the National Opera of Lithuania in Vilnius.

2007: *Der Rosenkavalier* at the New National Theatre, Tokyo.

Fidelio (updated to Pinochet's era), Danish National Opera, in Aarhus.

2008: *Dido and Aeneas*, at London's Cadogan Hall for the Chelsea Festival, with Philip Pickett's New London Consort. This tours the UK, Spain and the Netherlands.

2009: Glimmerglass celebrates its 20-year association with Miller, presenting two productions directed by him, *La Traviata* (newly designed by Isabella Bywater) and *Dido and Aeneas*.

La Bohème, ENO. This production is broadcast with a Sky Arts simulcast, showing the performance and backstage, on two channels.

2010: His ROH *Così fan tutte* enjoys a live screening in cinemas worldwide (courtesy of Opus Arte).

La Bohème for Cincinnati Opera (as an ENO co-production).

The Elixir of Love, now for the ENO.

2011: *La Traviata* (the Glimmerglass, Bywater version) for Vancouver Opera.

Bach's *St Matthew Passion*, now at London's National Theatre.

2012: New York City Opera performs *La Traviata* (as previously staged at Glimmerglass).

Don Pasquale, now at La Scala.

Così fan tutte (the modern dress version) staged for Washington National Opera.

Miller revives his ever-buoyant *Mikado*, which has been a popular hit at the ENO for over quarter of a century.

2014: Carmen for Mid Wales Opera (translated by Rory Bremner).

LECTURES, PLATFORM TALKS AND CLASSES

1948–53: At St Paul's School, the Chesterton Society (a debating club) has Miller and fellow pupils discoursing on multifarious topics. He lectures on music to the Gramophone Society. The school's biology students are, moreover, encouraged to present scientific talks and demonstrations (for fellow pupils and parents).

1953–6: At Cambridge University, membership of the Apostles entails reading out papers for collective, high-powered discussion. He lectures, to town and gown, under the aegis of the Philosophy of Science Club as well.

1970s: He presents his theories about buildings and biological forms to the Architectural Association.

1971: For the British Academy, he delivers his Thank Offering to Britain Fund Lecture, entitled *Censorship and the Limits of Permission*.

His talk at the Royal Institution, about science fiction's prophecies, is filmed for BBC TV's *Writers in Society* series.

1972: He lectures at Nash House on science and the arts for a series of talks co-ordinated by the Institute of Contemporary Arts and the *TES*. He joins the ICA's council to bring the sciences into that arena.

Delivers a BBC Radio lecture, *Man: The Double Animal*, about how early neurologists' hypotheses were influenced by social hierarchies.

1973: He tours Italy, for the British Council, with *Censorship and the Limits of Permission*.

1974: A British Council tour to Denmark with the *Censorship* lecture, plus lectures about Shakespeare and how the interpretation of plays is always, inevitably, changing.

The Uses of Pain, his talk at Conway Hall.

Addressing the Victorian Society at London's V&A Museum, his latest lecture springs from his historical research into Franz Mesmer and other unorthodox physicians.

1977: Giving the T. S. Eliot Memorial Lectures for Kent University, he speaks of 'The Afterlife of Plays', further expounding his notion of '*renovatio*' regarding the interpretation of plays.

1978: He is made visiting professor in drama at London's Westfield College.

431

1982: His Samuel Gee Lecture, *A Gower Street Scandal*, dwells on Mesmer and co.

1983: Summer tour of America with lectures spanning medicine and theatre.
MacTaggart Lecture at the Edinburgh International Television Festival, on the state of broadcasting.

1983: His Ernest Jones Lecture for the British Psychoanalytical Society is about mob behaviour.
Also gives the Happiness Lecture at the University of Birmingham.

1984: In his Cambridge Clark Lectures, he discusses the mind's eye and how, for example, we 'visualize' when reading novels.

1985: Opines on theatre, laughter and other subjects at New York's Juilliard School and Mount Sinai School of Medicine, and embarks on another lecture tour round the States in 1986.

1986: He helps to organize the Royal Society's Rank Prize Funds International Symposium, entitled *Images and Understanding*, and delivers a cinema-related paper 'Moving Pictures', which forms the basis of his FT Arts Lecture that year too.

1987: Orchestrates a conference on comedy, as president of the interdisciplinary wing of the British Association for the Advancement of Science at Queen's University, Belfast. Contributors include neuropsychologists, medical historians, philosophers, sociologists and a circus specialist.

1989: Folio Society debate in London, Miller versus Frederic Raphael, on adapting novels for the screen.
Along with Noam Chomsky, Miller participates in the annual Darwin Lectures in Cambridge. The chosen theme being 'ways of communicating', his lecture is 'Communicating without Words'.
Speaks at the 92nd Street Y, in New York, discussing the human mind.

1991: Lecture tour of American colleges, Penn, Portland, Seattle, Ohio etc.
He is visiting professor at the University of California, Berkeley. The Avenali Chair in the Humanities is a chance for a distinguished figure to lecture and debate. He is distinctly cross-disciplinary.

1994: Delivers a lecture at the New York Public Library, which is published in 1995 and entitled 'Going Unconscious'. This appears in the book *Hidden Histories of Science*, edited by Robert Silvers.
At London's National Gallery, Miller gives a series of talks on the gaze, seeing and reflections, collectively called 'From the Look of Things'. He subsequently tours to New York's Metropolitan Museum and the Art Institute of Chicago with these.

1995: Miller's *Sunday Times* Lecture, 'On Apologising', is inspired by the sociologist Erving Goffman.

1997: Rivers Lecture, given at Cambridge, on imitation.

2000: Discourses on 'the negligible' at New York Public Library.

2001: Takes part in Jewish Book Week's platform talks in London (and again in 2009).

2002: Delivers a lecture, 'The Gaze: Looking as it Appears in Pictures' at the Getty Center, LA.

2003: Discusses freedom and evolution with philosopher Daniel Dennett at the ICA.

2005: Reads favourite literary extracts for a platform event at the Bodleian Library in Oxford.

2005–7: Lectures at London's Royal Society of Medicine; also in Malvern, Chester and Ludlow; and at the University of Texas (talking about model and metaphors).

2007: Master class in directing, Theatre Royal Haymarket, London.

2009: He talks at the Harveian Society of London on philosophical distinctions between actions and events.

2000–14: Miller regularly delivers lectures around Britain.

2010: He gives summer master classes in Sandefjord, Norway, for the Opera Island team.

2012: Morley College, the south London centre for adult education, revives its tradition of Penny Lectures (started in the nineteenth century), with Miller discussing the importance of such public talks. He discovers that his father gave a Penny Lecture there almost fifty years earlier.

2014: Platform talks at the Hay Festival, Hay on Wye, and at the West Cork Literary Festival. Masterclasses at Glimmerglass.

NOTABLE ARTICLES, BOOKS AND SCRIPTS

1953–6: Dabbles in journalism at Cambridge University, notably contributing cartoons and short stories to *Granta* (which was temporarily re-entitled the *Gadfly*). He co-edits one edition, in April 1956.

1957: Starts editing as well as contributing to the *UCH Magazine*.

1958: Begins writing reviews (about medical, zoological, and children's books) for the *Spectator*.

1960–1: In the *Twentieth Century* magazine, his articles cover topics including his St Paul's teacher Sid Pask, the medical profession and comedy.

1961: Co-authors article in the *Lancet* with A. D. M. Smith, entitled 'Treatment of Inorganic Mercury Poisoning with N-Acetyl-D L-Penicillamine'.

His childhood memoir 'Led Astray' is published in *John Bull's Schooldays*, edited by Brian Inglis.

Writes pseudonymous medical articles in the *New Statesman*, followed by articles about America and visiting the States in 1962–3.

'Can English Satire Draw Blood?', in the *Observer*.

1962: 'Living Longer Than We Know How To', *Observer*.

His satirical article 'The Hounding of the Pooves' appears in *Private Eye*. He is outraged to see the byline 'DR J Miller' appended and putting his professional good name at risk.

1963: Contributes to the first issue – and various subsequent issues – of the *New York Review of Books*.

1963–4: Also writes, while in the USA, for the magazine *Commentary*, *Partisan Review* and is employed as a film critic and TV columnist at the *New Yorker*.

1964: Pens a script for the American TV series *Profiles in Courage*, with his episode dramatizing the life of the seventeenth-century puritan Anne Hutchinson. Broadcast in 1965.

Co-writes *A Trip to the Moon*, for American TV, with the CBS producer Robert Goldman. Adapted from Jules Verne, this stars Miller and his fellow Fringers.

1967: In the *Listener*, he muses on his childhood obsession with death.

1967–9: Writes in *Vogue* about the medical profession, superstitions thespians, and the wonders of close observation (as opposed to psychedelic trips).

1968: Compiles the Jackdaw educational folder *Harvey and the Circulation of the Blood*, published by Jonathan Cape.

Adapts as well as directs *Whistle and I'll Come to You* for BBC TV, based on M. R. James' ghost story.

Contributes to a collection of wartime memoirs, *Evacuees*, edited by Bryan S. Johnson.

Editorial on the historic changing nature of cities, published in *Architectural Design*.

1971: His biography *McLuhan* offers a trenchant analysis of Marshall McLuhan.

'My Day' in *Vogue*, on ageing.

1972: Edits *Freud: The Man, His World, His Influence*.

His talk *Man: The Double Animal* is transcribed as 'The Dog Beneath the Skin' in the *Listener*.

His paper 'Plays and Players' (originally for the Royal Society study group in 1967) forms a chapter in *Non-Verbal Communication*, edited by Robert Hinde.

1976: 'The Wild Boy of Aveyron', *New York Review of Books*.

1978: *The Body in Question*, his book accompanying the TV series.

1983: Edits *States of Mind: Conversations with Psychological Investigators*, the book to complement his TV series.

'A Gower Street Scandal', about Mesmer and others, is published in the *Journal of the Royal College of Physicians of London*.

Co-creates the pop-up book *The Human Body* with David Pelham, which becomes a best seller.

1984: Co-creates *The Facts of Life*, another pop-up book, with David Pelham.

Circa 1984: Writes *Steps and Stairs* for United Technologies/Otis.

1985: Contributes to a computer program, *Bodyworks*.

1986: His key book about directing and '*renovatio*', *Subsequent Performances*, is published.

1987: Publication of the script of *Beyond the Fringe*, as co-written by Bennett, Cook, Miller and Moore.

1987: Co-authors an article in *Cortex*, with A. Parkin and R. Vincent, entitled 'Multiple Neuropsychological Deficits Due to Anoxic Encephalopathy: A Case Study'.

1988: His short memoir 'Among Chickens' appears in *Granta*.

Co-edits, with John Durant, the book *Laughing Matters: A Serious Look at Humour*.

1990: His cinema-related paper 'Moving Pictures' is published in Horace Barlow's co-edited book *Images and Understanding*.

Miller's Darwin Lecture, 'Communicating without Words', is published in *Ways of Communicating*, edited by D. H. Mellor.

Contributes to the book *Acting in Opera*, published in America. That is followed, in 2001, by 'Doing Opera', his chapter in *Doing It: Five Performing Arts*, edited by Robert Silvers.

Edits *The Don Giovanni Book: Myths of Seduction and Betrayal*.

1998: *On Reflection*, his book to accompany his National Gallery exhibition, *Mirror Image*.

1999: His book *Nowhere in Particular* has ruminations recorded in a notebook style, interspersed with a selection of his photographs.

2014: An anthology of Miller's writing, entitled On Further Reflection, is produced by Karl Sabbagh's company, Skyscraper Publications.

ARTWORK: CARTOONS, COLLAGE, PHOTOGRAPHY, SCULPTURE, SET DESIGN, EXHIBITIONS

1952: Spartan set design for *Julius Caesar* at St Paul's School.

1957: Having contributed cartoons to *Granta* at Cambridge, he edits the *UCH Magazine* for University College Hospital and revamps its front covers, inspired by Russian constructivism and by the cartoonist and magazine editor Mark Boxer (also formerly of *Granta*).

Late 1950s: Meets Germano Facetti, the designer of Penguin books, who teaches him about typography and collage techniques.

1962–4: Learns about photography from Sam Rosenberg, who knew Betty Miller.

1964: Teaches at Hornsey Art School, including classes that touch on paperback design.

1966: Designs the book jacket for Tom Wolfe's *The Kandy-Kolored Tangerine-Flake Streamline Baby*, published by Jonathan Cape. Is nearly sued by Bridget Riley.

1970s: Joins local classes in screen-printing.

1990s: Starts creating paper collages, from fragments stripped from old posters, in Florence.

1994: The *Observer* features his art, especially his photographs and paper collages.

1998: His photographs are published in *Nowhere in Particular*.

His National Gallery exhibition *Mirror Image: Jonathan Miller on Reflection* arises out of his previous National Gallery lectures and, in part, his 1994 Exploratorium exhibition on transparency.

Circa 2000: Learns to arc-weld in Santa Fe and starts to create found-object sculptures there.

2000: The National Portrait Gallery displays its portrait of Miller, painted by Stephen Conroy (in the same year as the satirical *Spitting Image* puppet depicting Miller is sold in a Sotheby's fund-raising auction).

Writes about his interest in abstract geometric forms, regarding art and everyday objects, in *World of Interiors* magazine.

His photographs and collages are exhibited under the auspices of the Nightingale Project at the South Kensington and Chelsea Mental Health Centre.

2001: The Flowers East Gallery, in Hackney, presents *Jonathan Miller: Paper and Metal Works*.

2003: The set for his Graz Opera production of *Oedipus Rex* is an enlarged version of one of his own welded, rusty, metal sculptures.

The exhibition, simply entitled *Jonathan Miller*, at the Boundary Gallery in St John's Wood, north London, includes works in wood, metal and paper. He gives a platform talk about his art at the nearby Hampstead Theatre.

2005: Channel 5 airs *Absolute Rubbish*, the documentary about his sculptures.

Jonathan Miller: Wood Work is at the Daniel Katz Gallery, Old Bond Street.

2007: He acts as specialist adviser on the Imperial War Museum's major exhibition, *Camouflage*.

2010: Curates *On the Move*, an exhibition about fast-shutter photography, futurism and the depiction of movement, at Islington's Estorick Collection.

The National Theatre hosts a foyer exhibition of his art, to coincide with his NT staging of Bach's *St Matthew Passion*. It is called *One Thing and Another*.

2008–12: The sculptor Anthony Caro is a neighbour and encourages Miller's work in clay. He unofficially sculpts at the Royal College of Art.

MEMBERSHIP OF SOCIETIES, PATRONAGE OF INSTITUTIONS, POLITICAL CAMPAIGNS

1948–53: At St Paul's, besides participating in the Chesterton Society debates and the Colet Clubs revues, he eagerly joins the extracurricular Field Club for biologists. He co-founds, with Oliver Sacks and Eric Korn, the Literary Society (soon banned by the headmaster). Later he attends play readings by the school's Milton Society.

Mid-1950s: At Cambridge University, as well as being a member of the Apostles, he acts as the secretary for both the Humanist Society and the Philosophy of Science Club.

1956: He founds the Thomas Browne Society at University College Hospital, to discuss a broad range of subjects, countering the arts–science divide.

1958–63: Takes part in one or two of the Aldermaston marches, opposing nuclear weapons.

1965: Signs the British Artists' Protest against the continuing Vietnam War.

1967: Signs a plea for the Prime Minister to help lift the Egyptian blockade of the Strait of Tiran.

1969: Takes part in the Campaign for Better Broadcasting, criticizing proposed BBC cuts.

1970s: Is a member of the Athenaeum, the London club, for a while.

Late 1970s: Introduces an Amnesty International Conference on torture. Also appears in and directs charity comedy shows to fundraise for Amnesty International, not least the aforementioned *Secret Policeman's Ball*.

1979: Takes part in the campaign calling for the legalization of cannabis.

1980s: Publicly and repeatedly reviles Margaret Thatcher and her policies.

1987: He supports the establishment of a medical section within the Voluntary Euthanasia Society. He is a patron of this campaigning organization, now called Dignity in Dying.

Signs the British Artists' Protest against Kenya's repressive regime.

1991: Co-signs a letter to the Soviet Embassy protesting at the coup in Moscow and supporting the right to free speech.

2003: Joins a march in London, opposing the Iraq War.

2006 onwards: President of the Rationalist Association.

2010: Signs a letter of protest at the Pope's state visit to Britain.

Also: Vice-president of Sussex Opera and Ballet Society;

Artistic patron of the Little Opera House at the King's Head Theatre, London;

Patron of Norwich Playhouse;

Vice-president of the Campaign for Homosexual Equality;

Patron of the British Stammering Association;

President emeritus of the Alzheimer's Society;

Distinguished supporter of the British Humanist Association.

AWARDS AND HONOURS

1961: *Beyond the Fringe* wins an *Evening Standard* Award, and Miller is a nominee for the title of Man of the Year.

1963: A Tony Award for Miller, Bennett, Cook and Moore, 'for their brilliance which has shattered all the old concepts of comedy' in *Beyond the Fringe.*

1963: Also a Special Citation for *Beyond the Fringe* in the New York Drama Critics' Circle Awards. Miller is shortlisted for the Variety Awards.

1976: For his *Three Sisters,* he is named Director of the Year in the Olivier Awards (or the Society of West End Theatre Awards as they are called in this, their inaugural year). Miller wins the *Plays and Players* Best Director Award as well.

1979: *The Body in Question* is nominated for two BAFTAs: Best Factual Television Series and Most Original Programme/Series. Meanwhile, in the Broadcasting Press Guild Awards, Miller is prized for the Best On-Screen Performance.

1981: Silver Medal awarded by the Royal Television Society as he continues to oversee the *BBC Shakespeare Series.*
Honorary doctor of literature, University of Leicester.
Honorary fellow, University College London.

1982: Honorary fellow, St John's College, Cambridge.
His *Rigoletto* wins an Olivier Award for Outstanding Achievement in Opera, and the *Evening Standard* Opera Award.

1983: CBE.

1986: Nominated for a Tony Award, in the Best Director category, for *Long Day's Journey into Night.*

1988: *Candide* wins the Olivier Award for Best Musical, and Miller's first year of programming at the Old Vic lands five Oliviers in all.

1990: Albert Medal from the Royal Society of Arts, for his outstanding contribution to the arts and science, and for introducing a larger audience to both.

1991: Honorary fellow of the Royal Academy of Art.
Voted Britain's sexiest man by high-earning executive women in their thirties, responding to a marriage-bureau survey.
Wins Florence's Lion's Club Award for directing, after his Maggio Musicale *Così fan tutte.*

1997: Honorary doctor of literature, Cambridge University.
Honorary fellow of the Royal College of Physicians, London.

1998: Honorary FRCP, Edinburgh.

1999: Attends the Queen's Lunch of the Century, for Britain's top achievers.

2002: Knighted for services to music and the arts.

2003: Honorary degree from the University of Sussex.
Nominated artist of honour at Bornholm, for his work there with the company Opera Island.

2004: Tony Award nomination for Best Revival of a Play, for his American staging of *King Lear.*

Also: Honorary fellow, Royal College of Art;

Honorary associate of the National Secular Society;

Foreign member of the American Academy of Arts and Sciences.

BIBLIOGRAPHY

Ainsworth, W. H. (1934 edn), *Old St. Paul's*. London: Readers Library Publishing Co.

Aitken, J. (1967), *The Young Meteors*. London: Secker & Warburg.

Allen D., 'Jonathan Miller Directs Shakespeare', *New Theatre Quarterly*, Vol. V, No. 17 (February 1989), 52–66.

Amis, K. (1954), *Lucky Jim*. London: Victor Gollancz.

—— (1960), *Take a Girl Like You*. London: Victor Gollancz.

Andrews, J. F. (ed.), with contribution by Miller, J. (1985), *William Shakespeare: His World, His Work, His Influences*. New York, NY: Scribner.

Annan, N. (1990), *Our Age: The Generation that Made Post-war Britain*. London: Fontana.

—— (1999), *The Dons: Mentors, Eccentrics and Geniuses*. London: HarperCollins.

Arendt, H. (1958), *The Origins of Totalitarianism*. London: George Allen & Unwin.

Attenborough, D. (2002), *Life on Air: Memoirs of a Broadcaster*. London: British Broadcasting Corporation.

Austen, J. (1979 edn), *Mansfield Park*. Harmondsworth: Penguin.

Austin, J. L. (1961), *Philosophical Papers*. Oxford: Clarendon Press.

Austin, J. L., edited by Urmson, J. O. (1962), *How to Do Things with Words: The William James Lectures Delivered at Harvard University in 1955*. London: Clarendon Press.

Bailey, J. (1994), *A Theatre for All Seasons: Nottingham Playhouse, the First Thirty Years, 1948–1978*. Stroud: Alan Sutton in association with Nottingham Playhouse.

Bakewell, J. (2003), *The Centre of the Bed*. London: Hodder & Stoughton.

Bakewell, M. (1999), *Fitzrovia: London's Bohemia*. London: National Portrait Gallery.

Barbellion, W. N. P. (1991), *The Journal of a Disappointed Man*. London: Chatto & Windus.

Barbera, J. and McBrien, W. (1985), *Stevie: A Biography*. London: Heinemann.

Barker, P. (1995), *The Regeneration Trilogy*. London: Viking.

—— (2007), *Life Class*. London: Hamish Hamilton.

Barlow, H. and Blakemore, C. and Weston-Smith, M. (eds) (1990), *Images and Understanding*. Cambridge: Cambridge University Press.

Barrett Browning, E., edited by Miller, B. (1954), *Elizabeth Barrett to Miss Mitford: The Unpublished Letters of Elizabeth Barrett Browning to Mary Russell Mitford*. London: John Murray.

Bartlett, C. and Awde, N. (2006), *Pete and Dud: Come Again*. London: Methuen Drama.

Bartlett, F. C. (1932), *Remembering: A Study in Experimental and Social Psychology*. Cambridge: Cambridge University Press.

Bavister, S. (2001), *Lighting for Portrait Photography*. Hove: RotoVision.

Beaton, N. (1986), *Beaton but Unbowed: An Autobiography*. London: Methuen.

437

Beckett, A. (2009), *When the Lights Went Out: Britain in the Seventies*. London: Faber.

Beerbohm, M. (1923), *The Works of Max Beerbohm*. London: John Lane.

Bennett, A., 'The Stripped-Pine Wilderness', Listener, 28 November 1968.

—— (1991), *Forty Years On and Other Plays*. London: Faber.

—— (1994), *Writing Home*. London: Faber.

—— (1998), *Plays 2: Kafka's Dick, The Insurance Man, The Old Country, An Englishman Abroad, A Question of Attribution*. London: Faber.

—— (2005), *Untold Stories*. London: Faber.

—— (2009), *The Habit of Art*. London: Faber.

Bennett, A., Cook, P., Miller, J. and Moore, D. (1960) *Beyond the Fringe* (script for Lyceum, Edinburgh), Lord Chamberlain's Papers at the British Library.

—— (1961) *Beyond the Fringe* (script for Arts Theatre, Cambridge etc.), Lord Chamberlain's Papers at the British Library.

—— (1964) *Beyond the Fringe* (script for Fortune Theatre, London in 1964), Lord Chamberlain's Papers at the British Library.

Bennett, A., Cook, P., Miller, J. and Moore, D, edited by Wilmut, R., (2003), *The Complete Beyond the Fringe: Alan Bennett, Peter Cook, Jonathan Miller and Dudley Moore*. London: Methuen.

Bentham, G., revised by Hooker, J. D. (1947), *Handbook of the British Flora*. Ashford: L. Reeve.

Beresford, R. (1995), *A Dance to the Music of Time by Nicolas Poussin*. London: Trustees of the Wallace Collection.

Bergan, R. (1989), *Beyond the Fringe . . . and Beyond: A Critical Biography of Alan Bennett, Peter Cook, Jonathan Miller and Dudley Moore*. London: Virgin.

Bergson, H., translated by Mitchell, A. (1911), *Creative Evolution*. London: Macmillan & Co.

——, translated by Brereton, C. and Rothwell, F. (1911), *Laughter: An Essay on the Meaning of the Comic*. London: Macmillan & Co.

Berrol, S. (1994), *East Side/East End: Eastern European Jews in London and New York 1870–1924*. London: Praeger.

Berry, R. (1977), *On Directing Shakespeare*. London: Croom Helm.

Billington, M. (2007), *State of the Nation: British Theatre Since 1945*. London: Faber.

Biz, J. (1999), *More Viz Crap Jokes*. London: John Brown Publishing.

Blacker, T. (2007), *You Cannot Live as I Have Lived and Not End Up Like This: The Thoroughly Disgraceful Life and Times of Willie Donaldson*. London: Ebury.

Blakemore, M. (2004), *Arguments with England: A Memoir*. London: Faber.

Blunt, A. (1958), *Nicolas Poussin*. London: Phaidon Press.

Booker, C. (1980), *The Seventies: Portrait of a Decade*. Harmondsworth: Penguin.

—— (1992 edn), *The Neophiliacs: The Revolution in English Life in the Fifties and Sixties*. London: Pimlico.

—— (2005), *The Seven Basic Plots: Why We Tell Stories*. London: Continuum International.

Booth, C., edited by Fried, A. and Elman, R. (1971), *Charles Booth's London: A Portrait of the Poor at the Turn of the Century Drawn from his Life and Labour of the People in London*. Harmondsworth: Penguin.

Bowles, J. (1980), *A Thousand Sundays: The Story of The Ed Sullivan Show*. New York, NY: Putnam.

Bron, E. (1978), *Life and Other Punctures*. London: Deutsch.

—— (1996), *Double Take*. London: Weidenfeld & Nicolson.

Brustein, R. (1965), *Seasons of Discontent: Dramatic Opinions 1959–1965*. London: Jonathan Cape.

—— (1981), *Making Scenes: A Personal History of the Turbulent Years at Yale 1966–1979*. New York, NY: Random House.

Buchsbaum, R. M. (1948), *Animals Without Backbones: An Introduction to the Invertebrates*. Chicago, IL: University of Chicago Press.

438

Bulman, J. C. and Coursen, H. R. (eds) (1988), *Shakespeare on Television*. Hanover, NH: University Press of New England.

Burt, C. L. (ed.), with contribution by Miller, E. (1933), *How the Mind Works*. London: Allen & Unwin.

Burton, H. (1994), *Leonard Bernstein*. London: Faber.

Byatt, A. S. (1964), *The Shadow of the Sun*. London: Chatto & Windus.

—— (1985), *Still Life*. London: Chatto & Windus.

—— (2002), *A Whistling Woman*. London: Chatto & Windus.

Cain, J. (1992), *The BBC: Seventy Years of Broadcasting*. London: British Broadcasting Corporation.

Caldwell, L. (ed.) (2007), *Winnicott and the Psychoanalytic Tradition: Interpretation and Other Psychoanalytic Issues*. London: Karnac Books.

Carey, J. (2005), *What Good are the Arts?* London: Faber.

Carpenter, H. (2000), *A Great, Silly Grin*. New York, NY: Public Affairs.

—— (2002), *The Angry Young Men: A Literary Comedy of the 1950s*. London: Allen Lane.

—— (2002), *That Was Satire That Was*. London: Phoenix.

Cavett, D. (2010), *Talk Show: Confrontations, Pointed Commentary and Off-screen Secrets*. New York, NY: Times Books, Henry Holt and Company.

Cavett, D. and Porterfield, C. (1983), *Eye on Cavett*. New York, NY: Arbor House

Chambers, C. (2004), *Inside the Royal Shakespeare Company: Creativity and the Institution*. London: Routledge.

Chinoy, H. K., 'The Director as Mythagog: Jonathan Miller Talks about Directing Shakespeare', *Shakespeare Quarterly*, 27 (1976), 7–14.

Chomsky, N. (1968), *Language and Mind*. New York, NY: Harcourt, Brace & World.

Christmas, L. (1989), *Chopping Down the Cherry Trees: A Portrait of Britain in the Eighties*. London: Viking.

Cleese, J. and Skynner, A. C. (1983), *Families, and How to Survive Them*. London: Methuen.

Cliff, S. (2006), *Home*. London: Quadrille.

Cohn, N. (1970 edn), *The Pursuit of the Millennium: Revolutionary Millenarians and Mystical Anarchists in the Middle Ages*. London: Temple Smith.

Coleman, T. (2005), *Olivier: The Authorised Biography*. London: Bloomsbury.

Colley, L. (2002), *Captives: Britain, Empire and the World 1600–1850*. London: Jonathan Cape.

Cook, J., co-written with Levin, A. (2008), *Loving Peter: My Life with Peter Cook and Dudley Moore*. London: Piatkus.

Cook, L. (ed.) (1997), *Peter Cook Remembered*. London: Mandarin.

Cook, W. (ed.) (2005), *Goodbye Again: The Definitive Peter Cook and Dudley Moore*. London: Arrow.

Cook, W. E. (2006), *So Farewell Then: The Untold Life of Peter Cook*. London: HarperCollins.

Critchley, M. (1979), *The Divine Banquet of the Brain and Other Essays*. New York, NY: Raven Press.

Crosland, A. (1956), *The Future of Socialism*. London: Jonathan Cape.

Davies, C. (1975), *Permissive Britain: Social Change in the Sixties and Seventies*. London: Pitman.

DeGroot, G. (2009), *The Sixties Unplugged*. London: Pan.

—— (2010), *The Seventies Unplugged: A Kaleidoscopic Look at a Violent Decade*. London: Macmillan.

de Jongh, N. (2000), *Politics, Prudery and Perversions: The Censoring of the English Stage 1901–1968*. London: Methuen.

Delgado, M. and Heritage, P. (eds) (1996), *In Contact with the Gods: Directors Talk Theatre*. Manchester: Manchester University Press.

Denny, W. B. (1988), *Court and Conquest: Ottoman Origins and the Design for Handel's Tamerlano at the Glimmerglass Opera*. Kent, OH: Kent State University Museum.

Dickens, C. (1995 edn), *Dombey and Son*. Ware: Wordsworth Editions.

Dickinson, G. L. (1920), *The Future of the Covenant*. London: League of Nations Union.

—— (1920), *The Magic Flute: A Fantasia*. London: George Allen & Unwin.

Dicks, H. V. (1970), *Fifty Years of the Tavistock Clinic*. London: Routledge & Kegan Paul.

Dinnage, R. (ed.) (1990), *The Ruffian on the Stair: Reflections on Death*. New York, NY: Viking Penguin.

Donaldson, W. (1992), *The Big One, the Black One, the Fat One and the Other One: My Life in Showbiz*. London: Michael O'Mara.

—— (2002), *Brewer's Rogues, Villains and Eccentrics* (London: Cassell).

Drabble, M., Hoggart, R., Miller, J. et al. (1969), *The Permissive Society: The Guardian Inquiry*. London: Panther.

Durant, J. and Miller, J. (eds) (1988) *Laughing Matters: A Serious Look at Humour*. Harlow: Longman Scientific and Technical.

Elsom, J. (1979), *Post-war British Theatre*. London: Routledge & Kegan Paul.

Elsom, J. and Tomalin, N. (1978), *The History of the National Theatre*. London: Jonathan Cape.

Empson, W. (1930), *Seven Types of Ambiguity*. London: Chatto & Windus.

—— (1935), *Some Versions of Pastoral*. London: Chatto & Windus.

—— (1966 edn), *Some Versions of Pastoral*. Harmondsworth: Penguin, in association with Chatto & Windus.

—— (1977), *The Structure of Complex Words*. London: Chatto & Windus.

Epstein, L. J. (2002), *The Haunted Smile: The Story of Jewish Comedians*. Oxford: PublicAffairs.

Fantoni, B. and Melly, G. (1980), *The Media Mob*. London: Collins.

Fay, S. (1995), *Power Play: The Life and Times of Peter Hall*. London: Hodder & Stoughton.

Fazan, E. (forthcoming 2012), *Fiz: Between the Lines*. Victoria, BC: FriesenPress.

Ferris, P. (1990), *Sir Huge: The Life of Huw Wheldon*. London: Michael Joseph/Penguin.

Filmer, R., Sommerville, J. P. (ed.) (1991 edn), *Patriarcha and Other Writings*. Cambridge: Cambridge University Press.

Findlater, R. (1981), *At the Royal Court: 25 Years of the English Stage Company*. Ambergate: Amber Lane.

Fishman, W. J. (1986), *The Condition of East End Jewry in 1888*. London: West Central Counselling and Community Research.

FitzGerald, F. (1972), *Fire in the Lake: The Vietnamese and the Americans in Vietnam*. London: Macmillan.

Fitzgerald, P., edited by Dooley, T. (2008), *So I Have Thought of You: The Letters of Penelope Fitzgerald*. London: Fourth Estate.

Flaubert, G. (1969 edn), *L'Éducation Sentimentale*. Paris: Garnier-Flammarion.

Flaubert, G. (1979 edn), *Madame Bovary*. Paris: Garnier-Flammarion.

Footlights, including Miller, J. (1954) *Out of the Blue*, Lord Chamberlain's Papers at the British Library.

—— (1955) *Between the Lines*, Lord Chamberlain's Papers at the British Library.

Ford, B. (ed.) (1989), *The Cambridge Guide to the Arts in Britain, Vol. 8*. Cambridge: Cambridge University Press.

—— (ed.) (1992), *The Cambridge Cultural History of Britain, Vol. 9, Modern Britain*. Cambridge: Cambridge University Press.

Forster, E. M. (1924 edn), *The Longest Journey*. London: E. Arnold & Co.

Fortes, M, edited by Goody, J. (1987), *Religion, Morality and the Person: Essays on the Tallensi Religion by Meyer Fortes*. Cambridge: Cambridge University Press.

Foucault, M. (1995), *Discipline and Punish: The Birth of the Prison*. New York, NY: Vintage.

Foucault, M., translated by Howard, R. (1965), *Madness and Civilization: A History of Insanity in the Age of Reason*. New York, NY: Pantheon Books.

Fowler, J. (2005), *Unleashing Britain: Theatre Gets Real 1955–64*. London: V&A Publications.

Freud, S., translated by Whiteside, F. (2005), *On Murder, Mourning and Melancholia*. London: Penguin.

Fruchter, R. (2004), *Dudley Moore: An Intimate Portrait*. London: Ebury.

Games, A. (1999), *Pete and Dud: An Illustrated Biography*. London: Chameleon.

—— (2001), *Backing into the Limelight: The Biography of Alan Bennett*. London: Headline.

Gardiner, J. (2011), *The Thirties: An Intimate History*. London: HarperPress.

Gennep, A. van (1960), *Rites of Passage*. London: Routledge & Kegan Paul.

Gielgud, J., edited by Mangan, R. (2004), *Gielgud's Letters*. London: Weidenfeld & Nicolson.

Gilbert, F. (2006), *Yob Nation: The Truth about Britain's Yob Culture*. London: Portrait.

Gilbert, S. (2009), *Opera for Everybody: The Story of English National Opera*. London: Faber.

Goffman, E. (1956), *The Presentation of the Self in Everyday Life*. Edinburgh: University of Edinburgh.

—— (1963), *Behaviour in Public Places*. London: Collier-Macmillan.

—— (1974), *Frame Analysis*. Cambridge, MA: Harvard University Press.

Gombrich, E. H. (1960), *Art and Illusion: A Study in the Psychology of Pictorial Representation*. London: Phaidon Press.

Gooding, M. (ed.), with preface by Miller, J. (2004), *The Psychobox*. London: Redstone Press.

Goodwin, T. (1988), *Britain's Royal National Theatre: The First 25 Years*. London: National Theatre in association with Nick Hern.

Gourlay, L. (ed.) (1973), *Olivier*. London: Weidenfeld & Nicolson.

Graham, P. J. (2009), *Susan Isaacs: A Life Freeing the Minds of Children*. London: Karnac Books.

Green, J. and Herman, D. (1991), *Madness: A Study Guide*. London: BBC Education.

Greenacre, P. (1955), *Swift and Carroll: A Psychoanalytic Study of Two Lives*. New York, NY: International Universities Press.

Greene, G. (1968 edn), *The Heart of the Matter*. London: Heinemann Educational.

Greene, H. C. (1969), *The Third Floor Front: A View of Broadcasting in the Sixties*. London: Bodley Head.

Greer, G. (1971), *The Female Eunuch*. London: Paladin.

Gross, J. (1969), *The Rise and Fall of the Man of Letters: Aspects of English Literary Life Since 1800*. London: Weidenfeld & Nicolson.

—— (2001), *A Double Thread: A Childhood in Mile End – and Beyond*. London: Chatto & Windus.

Haill, L. (ed.) (1985), *Olivier at Work: The National Theatre Years*. London: Nick Hern (in association with the Royal National Theatre).

Haill, L. and Wood, S. (1998), *Stage by Stage: The Development of the National Theatre 1848–1997*. London: Royal National Theatre.

Hall, P. (1993), *Making an Exhibition of Myself: The Autobiography of Peter Hall*. London: Sinclair-Stevenson.

——, edited by Goodwin, J. (1983), *Peter Hall's Diaries: The Story of a Dramatic Battle*. London: Hamish Hamilton.

Hallinan, T., 'Jonathan Miller on the Shakespeare Plays', *Shakespeare Quarterly*, 32 (1981), 134–43.

Hamilton, I. (1983), *Robert Lowell: A Biography*. London: Faber.

Hamilton, P. and Gordon, P. and Kieran, D. (eds) (2006), *How Very Interesting: Peter Cook's Universe and All That Surrounds It*. London: Snowbooks.

Hanson, N. R. (1958), *Patterns of Discovery: An Inquiry into the Conceptual Foundations of Science*. Cambridge: Cambridge University Press.

Hardwick, E. (1979), *Sleepless Nights*. London: Weidenfeld & Nicolson.

Hartigan, K. V. (1995), *Greek Tragedy on the American Stage: Ancient Drama in the Commercial Theater, 1882–1994*. Westport, CT and London: Greenwood.

Hartley, L. P. (1958), *The Go-Between*. Harmondsworth: Penguin.

Haskell, F. (1963), *Patrons and Painters: A Study in the Relations Between Italian Art and Society in the Age of the Baroque*. London: Chatto & Windus.

Hastings, M., (1990), *Three Political Plays* (including Hastings, M., with Miller, J., *The Emperor*). London: Penguin.

Hennessy, P. (2007), *Having It So Good: Britain in the Fifties*. London: Penguin.

Hewison, R. (1981), *In Anger: Culture in the Cold War, 1945–60*. London: Weidenfeld & Nicolson.

—— (1983), *Footlights!: A Hundred Years of Cambridge Comedy*. London: Methuen.

—— (1986), *Too Much: Art and Society in the Sixties 1960–75*. London: Methuen.

—— (1995), *Culture and Consensus: England, Art and Politics since 1940*. London: Methuen.

Hinde, R. (ed.) (1972), *Non-Verbal Communication*. Cambridge: Cambridge University Press.

Hoare, P. (2001), *Spike Island: The Memory of a Military Hospital*. London: Fourth Estate.

Hobbes, T. (1651), *Leviathan, or the Matter, Forme, and Power of a Common-wealth, Ecclesiasticall and Civil*. London: Andrew Crooke.

Hobsbawn, E. J. (1994), *Age of Extremes: The Short Twentieth Century 1914–1991*. London: Michael Joseph.

—— (2002), *Interesting Times: A Twentieth-Century Life*. London: Allen Lane/Penguin.

Hockney, D. (1993), *That's the Way I See It*. London: Thames & Hudson.

Hoggart, R. (1957), *The Uses of Literacy: Aspects of Working-Class Life, with Special Reference to Publications and Entertainments*. London: Chatto & Windus.

Holden, A. (1988), *Olivier*. London: Weidenfeld & Nicolson.

Holderness, G. (ed.) (1988), *The Shakespeare Myth*. Manchester: Manchester University Press.

Homberger, E. and Janeway, W. and Schama, S. (eds) (1970), *The Cambridge Mind: Ninety Years of the Cambridge Review, 1879–1969*. London: Jonathan Cape.

Hopkins, H. (1963), *The New Look: A Social History of the Forties and Fifties in Britain*. London: Secker & Warburg.

Hordern, M., with England, P. (1993), *A World Elsewhere: The Autobiography of Sir Michael Hordern*. London: Michael O'Mara.

Hughes, P. (ed.), with foreword by Miller, J. (2003), *The Paradox Box*. London: Redstone Press.

Hughes, R. (1980), *The Shock of the New: Art and the Century of Change*. London: British Broadcasting Corporation.

Hyman, L. (1972), *The Jews of Ireland from Earliest Times to the Year 1910*. Shannon: Irish University Press.

Iganski, P. and Kosmin, B. (eds) (2003), *A New Antisemitism?: Debating Judeophobia in 21st-Century Britain*. London: Profile.

Ignatieff, M. (1988), *Isaiah Berlin: A Life*. London: Chatto & Windus.

Inglis, B. (ed.) (1961), *John Bull's Schooldays*. London: Hutchinson.

Ingrams, R. (ed.) (1971), *The Life and Times of Private Eye, 1961–1971*. London: Penguin/Allen Lane.

Inman, A. C., edited by Aaron, D. (1996), *From a Darkened Room: The Inman Diary*. Cambridge MA and London: Harvard University Press.

Jackson, K. (2004), *Humphrey Jennings*. London: Picador.

James, C. (1990), *May Week Was in June*. London: Jonathan Cape.

James, H. (1984 edn), *The Portrait of a Lady*. Harmondsworth: Penguin.

James, H. (1992 edn), *The Turn of the Screw and Other Stories*. Oxford: Oxford University Press.

James, M. R. (1994 edn), *Ghost Stories*. Harmondsworth: Penguin.

Johansson, G., 'Visual perception of biological motion and a model for its analysis', *Perception and Psychophyics*, Vol. 14, No. 2, 201–11.

Johnson, B. S. (ed.) (1968), *Evacuees*. London: Victor Gollancz.

Jonas, P. and Elder, M. and Pountney, D., edited by John, N. (1992), *Power House: The English National Opera Experience*. London: Lime Tree.

Kantorowicz, E. H. (1957), *The King's Two Bodies: A Study in Mediaeval Political Theology*. Princeton, NJ: Princeton University Press.

Kapuściński, R. (1984) *The Emperor*. London: Picador/Pan.

Kazin, A. (1996), *A Life Burning in Every Moment*. New York, NY: HarperCollins.

—— (1948), *A Walker in the City*. New York, NY: Reynal & Hitchcock.

Kerner, A. translated and edited by Oliver, F. W. (1896), *The Natural History of Plants*. London: Blackie & Son.

Kercher, S. E. (2006), *Revel With a Cause: Liberal Satire in Postwar America*. Chicago, IL and London: University of Chicago Press.

Kipling, R. (1930 edn), *The Jungle Book*. London: Macmillan.

Korn, E. (translator) (1988), *Jean Racine's Andromache*. New York, NY and London: Applause.

—— (1989), *Remainders: From the Times Literary Supplement 1980–1989*. Manchester: Carcanet.

Kurlansky, M. (1997), *Cod: A Biography of the Fish that Changed the World*. Toronto: Alfred A. Knopf.

Kynaston, D. (2007), *Austerity Britain, 1945–1951*. London: Bloomsbury.

—— (2009), *Family Britain, 1951–1957*. New York, NY: Walker & Co.

Lawson, N. (1998), *How to Eat*. London: Chatto & Windus.

Leedham-Green, E. S. (1996), *A Concise History of the University of Cambridge*. Cambridge: Cambridge University Press.

Lennon, F. B. (1947), *Lewis Carroll*. London: Cassell & Co.

Levin, B. (1970), *The Pendulum Years: Britain and the Sixties*. London: Jonathan Cape.

Levin, D. (2000), *The Litvaks: A Short History of Jews in Lithuania*. Jerusalem: Yad Vashem.

Levine, G. (1998), *Memories: with Photographs by Gemma Levine*. London: Ebury.

Levy, P. (1979), *G. E. Moore and the Cambridge Apostles*. London: Weidenfeld & Nicolson.

Lewis, P. (1978), *The Fifties*. London: Heinemann.

—— (1990), *The National: A Dream Made Concrete*. London: Methuen Drama.

Lewis, R. (1977), *The Life and Death of Peter Sellers*. New York, NY.: Applause.

Lewontin, R. (2000), *It Ain't Necessarily So: The Dream of the Human Genome and Other Illusions*. New York, NY: New York Review of Books.

Little, R. and McLaughlin, E. (2007), *The Royal Court Theatre Inside Out*. London: Oberon.

Lombroso, C., and Lombroso Ferrero, G. (1911), *Criminal Man According to the Classification of Cesare Lombroso*. New York, NY: Putnam.

London, J. (2001 edn), *The People of the Abyss*. London: Pluto.

Lovejoy, A. O. (1936), *The Great Chain of Being: A Study of the History of an Idea*. Cambridge, MA: Harvard University Press.

Lowell, R., with Brustein, R. and Miller, J. (1965), *The Old Glory: Endecott and the Red Cross; My Kinsman, Major Molineux; and Benito Cereno*. New York, NY: Farrar, Straus & Giroux.

——, edited by Hamilton, S. (2005), *Letters of Robert Lowell*. London: Faber.

Lubenow, W. C. (1998), *The Cambridge Apostles 1820–1914: Liberalism, Imagination and Friendship in British Intellectual and Professional Life*. Cambridge: Cambridge University Press.

Lytton, E. B., (1907), *The Last Days of Pompeii*. London: G. J. Howell & Co.

MacInnes, C. (1957), *City of Spades*. London: MacGibbon & Kee.

—— (1964), *Absolute Beginners*. Harmondsworth: Penguin.

MacLaren-Ross, J. (1965), *Memoirs of the Forties*. London: Alan Ross.

McWilliam, R., 'Jonathan Miller's *Alice in Wonderland* (1966): A Suitable Case for Treatment', *Historical Journal of Film, Radio and Television*, Vol. 31, No. 2 (June 2011), 229–46.

Maher, M. (1992), *Modern Hamlets and Their Soliloquies*. Iowa City, IA: University of Iowa Press.

Mander, J. (1963), *Great Britain or Little England?* Harmondsworth: Penguin.

Mankowitz, W. (1953), *A Kid for Two Farthings*. London: Andre Deutsch.

—— (1976), *The Hebrew Lesson: A Play*. London: Evans Brothers.

Mann, W. J. (2004), *Edge of Midnight: The Life of John Schlesinger*. London: Hutchinson.

Mannoni, O. (1956), *Prospero and Caliban: The Psychology of Colonization*. New York, NY: Praeger.

Marc (pseudonym for Boxer, M.) (1968), *The Trendy Ape*. London: Hodder & Stoughton.

Marcan, P. (1992), *An East London Album*. High Wycombe: Peter Marcan Publications.

Mariani, P. L. (1994), *Lost Puritan: A Life of Robert Lowell*. New York, NY and London: W. W. Norton.

Marnham, P. (1982), *The Private Eye Story: The First 21 Years*. London: Deutsch.

Marr, A. (2007), *A History of Modern Britain*. London: Macmillan.

—— (2009), *The Making of Modern Britain*. London: Macmillan.

Marwick, A. (1991), *Culture in Britain Since 1945*. Oxford: Basil Blackwell.

—— (1999), *The Sixties: Social and Cultural Transformation in Britain, France, Italy and the United States, 1958–74*. Oxford: Oxford University Press.

Maschler, T. (ed.) (1957), *Declaration*. London: MacGibbon & Lee.

Masters, B. (1985), *The Swinging Sixties*. London: Constable.

Mayhew, H., edited by Quennell, P. (1949 edn), *Mayhew's London: Being Selections from 'London Labour and the London Poor' etc*. London: Pilot Press.

McCarthy, M. (1963), *The Group*. London: Weidenfeld & Nicolson.

McDonnell, M. F. J. (1909), *A History of St Paul's School*. London: Chapman and Hall.

McGinn, C. (2003), *The Making of a Philosopher: My Journey Through Twentieth-Century Philosophy*. London: Scribner.

McSmith, A. (2010), *No Such Thing as Society: A History of Britain in the 1980s*. London: Constable.

Mellor, D. H. (ed.) (1990), *Ways of Communicating*. Cambridge: Cambridge University Press.

Melly, D. (2005), *Take a Girl Like Me: Life with George*. London: Chatto & Windus.

Melly, G. (1970), *Revolt into Style: The Pop Arts in Britain*. London: Penguin/Allen Lane.

—— (1997), *Don't Tell Sybil*. London: Heinemann.

Miles, P. (ed.) (1993), *Chekhov on the British Stage*. Cambridge: Cambridge University Press.

Miller, B. – see also Spiro, B. B.

—— (1952), *Robert Browning: A Portrait*. London: John Murray.

—— (1986), *On the Side of the Angels*. London: Penguin/Virago Press.

—— (2000), *Farewell Leicester Square*. London: Persephone Books.

——, 'At the Villa Éole: A Fragment of Autobiography', *Cornhill*, Vol. 166, No. 995, 406–13.

——, 'Camelot at Cambridge', *Twentieth Century*, February 1958, 133–47.

——, 'Notes for an Unwritten Autobiography', *Modern Reading*, 1945, Vol XIII, 39–46.

——, '"This Happy Evening": The Story of Ion', *Twentieth Century*, July 1953, 53–61.

——, 'Two Fathers and Their Sons', *Nineteenth Century and After*, October 1948, 251–60.

Miller, E. (1926), *Types of Body and Mind*. London: Kegan Paul & Co.

—— (1935), *Insomnia and Other Disturbances of Sleep*. London: J. Bale & Co.

—— (ed.) (1937), *The Growing Child and Its Problems*. London: Kegan Paul & Co.

—— (1938), *The Generations: A Study of the Cycle of Parents and Children*. London: Faber.

—— (ed.) (1940), *The Neuroses in War*. London: Macmillan.

——, 'Medico-legal Aspects of the Aberrations of Adolescence', *Medico-Legal and Criminological Review*, 1935, 3, 181–210.

——, 'The Rooted Sorrow', *Twentieth Century*, May 1956, 448.

Miller, J. – see also Andrews, J. F.; Bennett, A.; Drabble, M.; Durant, J.; Footlights; Johnson, B. S.; Gooding, M.; Hastings, M.; Hughes, P.; Inglis, B.; Lowell, R.; Newark, T.; Peto, J.; Silvers, R.; Sokol, B. J.

—— (1968), *Harvey and the Circulation of the Blood*. London: Jonathan Cape.

—— (1971), *McLuhan*. London: Fontana/Collins.

—— (ed.) (1972), *Freud: The Man, His World, His Influence*. London: Weidenfeld & Nicolson.

—— (1974), *The Uses of Pain*. London: South Place Ethical Society.

—— (1978), *The Body in Question*. London: Jonathan Cape.

—— (ed.) (1983), *States of Mind: Conversations with Psychological Investigators*. London: British Broadcasting Corporation.

444

—— (undated, circa 1984), *Steps and Stairs*. Hartford, CT: United Technologies/Otis.

—— (1986), *Subsequent Performances*. London: Faber.

—— (1986), *Subsequent Performances*. New York, NY: Viking/Elisabeth Sifton.

—— 'Among Chickens', *Granta*, 23, Spring 1988, 141–148.

—— (1990), *Acting in Opera*. New York, NY: Applause.

—— (ed.) (1990), *The Don Giovanni Book: Myths of Seduction and Betrayal*. London: Faber; and New York, NY: Schocken Books.

—— (1998), *On Reflection*. New Haven, CT: Yale University Press.

—— (1998), *On Reflection*. London: National Gallery Publications.

—— (1999), *Nowhere in Particular*. London: Mitchell Beazley.

——, 'Doing Opera' in Silvers R. (ed.) (2001), *Doing It: Five Performing Arts*. New York, NY: NYREV Inc.

—— (under the pseudonym Lydgate, J.), 'Alien Admissions', *Spectator*, 7 April 1961.

——, 'A Bit of a Giggle', *Twentieth Century*, July 1961.

——, 'Been to America', *New Statesman*, 19 January 1962.

——, 'Can English Satire Draw Blood?', *Observer*, 1 October 1961.

——, 'The Dog Beneath the Skin', *Listener*, 20 July 1972.

——, 'Going Unconscious', see Silvers, R. B.

——, 'A Gower Street Scandal', *Journal of the Royal College of Physicians of London*, Vol. 17, No. 4, October 1983, 181–91.

——, 'The Hounding of the Pooves', *Private Eye*, 17 September 1962.

——, 'I Won't Pay for the Trip', *Vogue*, 1 September 1967.

——, 'Led Astray', see Inglis, B.

——, 'Living Longer Than We Know How To', *Observer*, 12 August 1962.

——, 'Men of the Age (II): The Medical Student', *Twentieth Century*, October 1960, 343–8.

——, 'Saying "Ah", Part 1', *Vogue*, 1 January 1967, and 'Saying "Ah", Part 2', *Vogue*, 15 March 1967.

——, 'The Sick White Negro', *Partisan Review*, Spring 1963.

——, 'Throw Away Line: Towards a Definition of Rubbish', *UCH Magazine*, Vol. XLIII, No. 3, 229.

——, 'Unhappy Mediums', *Vogue*, May 1968.

——, 'West Side Stories', *New Statesman*, 8 February 1963.

—— (under the pseudonym Lydgate, J.), 'Where is Thy Sting?', *Spectator*, 3 March 1961.

——, 'The Wild Boy of Aveyron', *New York Review of Books*, 16 September 1976.

—— (under the pseudonym Lydgate, J.), 'Wildcat Headaches', *Spectator*, 28 April 1961.

Miller, J., Parkin, A. and Vincent, R., 'Multiple Neuropsychological Deficits Due to Anoxic Encephalopathy: A Case Study', *Cortex*, 1987, No. 23, 655–65.

Miller, J. and Pelham, D. (1983), *The Human Body: Three-dimensional Study*. London: Cape.

—— (1984), *The Facts of Life*. London: Jonathan Cape.

Miller, J. and Smith, A. D. M, 'Treatment of Inorganic Mercury Poisoning with N-Acetyl-D L-Penicillamine', *Lancet*, 25 March 1961, 640–3.

Miller, J. and Van Loon, B. (1982), *Darwin for Beginners*. London: Writers and Readers Publishing Cooperative (subsequently retitled *Introducing Darwin*).

——, edited by Appignanesi, R. (2000 edn), *Introducing Darwin and Evolution*. Cambridge: Icon Books and New York, NY: Totem Books.

—— (2012 edn), *Introducing Darwin: A Graphic Guide*. London: Icon Books.

Miller, J. E. (2003), *Relations*. London: Jonathan Cape.

Miller, K. (1985), *Doubles: Studies in Literary History*. Oxford: Oxford University Press.

—— (1993), *Rebecca's Vest: A Memoir*. London: Hamish Hamilton.

—— (1998), *Dark Horses: An Experience of Literary Journalism*. London: Picador.

Milne, A. (1988), *DG: The Memoirs of a British Broadcaster*. London: Hodder & Stoughton.

Morgan, K. O. (2000), *Twentieth-Century Britain: A Very Short Introduction*. Oxford: Oxford University Press.

—— (2001), *Britain Since 1945: The People's Peace*. Oxford: Oxford University Press.

Morley, L. (1992), *Black and White Lies*. Pymble, NSW: Angus & Robertson/London: HarperCollins.

Morley, S. (2002), *Asking for Trouble*. London: Hodder & Stoughton.

Muggeridge, M. (1940), *The Thirties, 1930–1940, in Great Britain*. London: Hamish Hamilton.

Muirhead, L. R. (1958), *Oxford and Cambridge*. London: Macmillan, Blue Guide series.

Munby, L. M. (1963), *The History of Kings Langley by the Members of the Local History Group of Kings Langley Workers' Educational Association*. Kings Langley: Kings Langley Branch of the Workers' Educational Association.

Muybridge, E., edited by Brown, L. S. (1955), *The Human Figure in Motion*. New York, NY: Dover Publications.

——, edited by Brown, L. S. (1957), *Animals in Motion*. New York, NY: Dover Publications.

Newark, T. and Miller, J. (2009), *Camouflage*. London: Thames & Hudson.

Newman, A. (ed.) (1981), *The Jewish East End 1840–1939*. London: Jewish Historical Society of England.

Nichols, P. (1975), *The Freeway*. London: Faber.

—— (1984), *Feeling You're Behind: An Autobiography*. London: Weidenfeld & Nicolson.

—— (2000), *Peter Nichols: Diaries 1969–1977*. London: Nick Hern.

Olivier, L. (1982), *Confessions of an Actor*. London: Weidenfeld & Nicolson.

—— (1986), *On Acting*. London: Weidenfeld & Nicolson.

Osborne, J. (1972), *Under Plain Cover: A Play in One Act*. London: Faber.

—— (1991), *Almost a Gentleman: An Autobiography, Vol. II*. London: Faber.

O'Shaughnessy, B. (1980), *The Will: A Dual Aspect Theory*. Cambridge: Cambridge University Press.

Oshiry, E. (1995), *The Annihilation of Lithuanian Jewry*. New York, NY: Judaica Press.

Owens, P. (ed.) (1979), *Kent Opera 1969–79*. Ashford: Pembles Publications.

Pagnamenta, P. (ed.) (2008), *The University of Cambridge: An 800th Anniversary Portrait*. London: Third Millennium.

Panofsky, E. (1955), *Meaning in the Visual Arts: Papers in and on Art History*. Garden City, NY: Doubleday.

—— (1972), *Studies in Iconology: Humanistic Themes in the Art of the Renaissance*. New York, NY/London: Harper & Row.

Parkinson, M. (2008), *Parky: My Autobiography*. London: Hodder & Stoughton.

Paskin, B. (1998), *Dudley Moore: The Authorized Biography*. London: Pan.

Paxman, J. (1999), *The English: A Portrait of a People*. London: Penguin.

Peto, J. (ed.), with a contribution from Miller, J. (2007), *The Heart*. London: Yale University Press.

Philip, J. and Simpson, J. and Snowman, N. (eds) (1967), *The Best of Granta*. London: Secker & Warburg.

Plath, S., edited by Kukil, K. V. (2000), *The Journals of Sylvia Plath: 1950–1962*. London: Faber.

Platt, N. (2001), *Making Music*. Ashford: Pembles Publications.

Plowright, J. (2001), *And That's Not All*. London: Weidenfeld & Nicolson.

Powell, G. and Powell, T. (eds) (1993), *A Dedicated Fan: Julian Jebb 1934–84*. London: Peralta Press.

Proceedings of the British Academy, Vol. LVII, 1971 (published Oxford: Oxford University Press, 1973).

Propp, V. (1958), *Morphology of the Folktale*. Philadelphia, PA: American Folklore Society.

Pythons, the (Chapman, G. et al.) (2003), *The Pythons Autobiography by the Pythons*. London: Orion.

Raphael, F. (1984), *The Glittering Prizes*. London: Inner Circle.

Raphael, F., 'Son of Enoch', *Prospect*, June 1997.

Ratcliffe, M. (ed.) (1983), *Kent Opera in Progress*. Ashford: Kent Opera.

Rebellato, D. (1999), *1956 and All That*. London: Routledge.

Redgrave, M. (1983), *In My Mind's Eye: An Autobiography*, London: Weidenfeld & Nicolson.

Rogers, B. (1999), *A.J. Ayer: A Life*. London: Chatto & Windus.

Rollyson, C. and Paddock, L. (2000), *Susan Sontag: The Making of an Icon*. New York, NY: W. W. Norton.

Romain, M. (1992), *A Profile of Jonathan Miller*. Cambridge: Cambridge University Press.

Rosenblum, R. (1967), *Transformations in Late Eighteenth Century Art*. Princeton, NJ: Princeton University Press.

Roth, J., translated by Dunlop, G. (1934), *Radetzky March*. London: William Heinemann.

Rumney, D. (1981), *The History of the Portman Clinic*. Unpublished monograph.

Russell, B. (1912), *The Problems of Philosophy*. London: Thornton Butterworth.

—— (1914), *The Philosophy of Bergson, by the Hon. Bertrand Russell, with a reply by Mr H. Wildon Carr and a rejoinder by Mr Russell*. Cambridge: The Heretics, University of Cambridge.

—— (1914), *Scientific Method in Philosophy: The Herbert Spencer Lecture 1914*. Oxford: Clarendon Press.

—— (1919), *Roads to Freedom: Socialism, Anarchism and Syndicalism*. London: George Allen & Unwin.

—— (1922), *Our Knowledge of the External World, as a Field for Scientific Method in Philosophy*. London: George Allen & Unwin Ltd.

Russell, B. and Whitehead, A. N. (1925 edn), *Principia Mathematica*. Cambridge: Cambridge University Press.

Sacks, O. (1970), *Migraine: The Evolution of a Common Disorder*. Berkeley, CA: University of California Press.

—— (1973), *Awakenings*. London: Duckworth.

—— (1986 edn), *The Man Who Mistook His Wife for a Hat*. London: Picador/Pan Books.

—— (2002), *Uncle Tungsten: Memories of a Chemical Boyhood*. New York, NY: Vintage.

—— (2007), *Musicophilia: Tales of Music and the Brain*. London: Picador.

Said, E. W. (1978), *Orientalism*. London: Routledge & Kegan Paul.

Salaman, R. (1949), *The History and Social Influence of the Potato*. Cambridge: Cambridge University Press.

Sales, R. (ed.) (Vol. I, 1982 and Vol. II, 1985), *Shakespeare in Perspective*. London: Ariel Books, British Broadcasting Corporation.

Sampson, A. (1962), *Anatomy of Britain*. London: Hodder & Stoughton.

Sandbrook, D. (2005), *Never Had It So Good: A History of Britain from Suez to the Beatles*. London: Little, Brown.

—— (2009 edn), *White Heat: A History of Britain in the Swinging Sixties*. London: Abacus.

—— (2010), *State of Emergency: The Way We Were: Britain, 1970–1974*. London: Allen Lane.

Scotson, L., with foreward by Miller. J. (1985), *Doran: Child of Courage*. London: Collins.

Scott, P. (1978), *Staying On*. Bombay: Allied Publishers.

Searle, J. R. (1969), *Speech Acts: An Essay in the Philosophy of Language*. Cambridge: Cambridge University Press.

—— (1979), *Expression and Meaning: Studies in the Theory of Speech Acts*. Cambridge: Cambridge University Press.

Senelick, L. (1997), *The Chekhov Theatre: A Century of Plays in Performance*. Cambridge: Cambridge University Press.

Shakespeare, W., with preface by Messina, C., (1978), *As You Like It: The BBC TV Shakespeare*. New York, NY: Mayflower Books.

Shanks, M. (1961), *The Stagnant Society: A Warning*. Harmondsworth: Penguin.

Shattuck, R. (1964), *Proust's Binoculars: A Study of Memory, Time and Recognition*. London: Chatto & Windus.

Shellard, D. (1999), *British Theatre Since the War*. New Haven, CT and London: Yale University Press.

—— (2003), *Kenneth Tynan: A Life*. New Haven, CT and London: Yale University Press.

Shenker, I. (1985), *Coat of Many Colours: Pages from Jewish Life*. Garden City, NY: Doubleday.

Sherrin, N. (1991), *Theatrical Anecdotes: A Connoisseur's Collection of Legends, Stories and Gossip*. London: Virgin.

Sikov, E. (2002), *Mr Strangelove: A Biography of Peter Sellers*. London: Sidgwick & Jackson.

Silvers, R. B. (ed.) (1995), *Hidden Histories of Science*. New York, NY: NYREV Inc.

Sissona, M. and French, P. (eds) (1986), *Age of Austerity*. Oxford: Oxford University Press.

Slater, A. P. 'An Interview with Jonathan Miller', *Quarto*, September 1980.

Slater, A. P. (1982), *Shakespeare the Director*. Brighton: Harvester.

Smith, S., *Beside the Seaside: A Holiday with Children*, in Blakeston, O. (ed.) (1949), *Holidays and Happy Days*. London: Phoenix House.

—— (1958), *Some are More Human Than Others: Sketch-book by Stevie Smith*. London: Gaberbocchus.

—— (1975), *The Collected Poems of Stevie Smith*. London: Allen Lane.

——, edited by Barbera, J. and McBrien, W. (1981), *Me Again: Uncollected Writings of Stevie Smith Illustrated by Herself*. London: Virago.

Snow, C. P. (1959), *The Two Cultures and the Scientific Revolution: The Rede Lecture, 1959*. Cambridge: Cambridge University Press.

Sokol, B. J. (ed.), with a contribution by Miller, J. (1993), *The Undiscover'd Country: New Essays on Psychoanalysis and Shakespeare*. London: Free Association Books.

Spalding, F. (1988), *Stevie Smith: A Critical Biography*. London: Faber.

—— (1997), *The Bloomsbury Group*. London: National Portrait Gallery, Insights series.

Spiro, B. B. (1933), *The Mere Living*. London: Victor Gollancz.

—— (1934), *Sunday*. London: Victor Gollancz.

—— (1935), *Portrait of the Bride*. London: Victor Gollancz.

—— (1941), *Farewell Leicester Square*. London: Robert Hale.

—— (1942), *A Room in Regent's Park*. London: Robert Hale.

—— (1945), *On the Side of the Angels*. London: Robert Hale.

—— (1948), *The Death of the Nightingale*. London: Robert Hale.

Stern, J. and Stern, M. (1990), *Sixties People*. London: Macmillan.

Stone, L. (1977), *The Family, Sex and Marriage in England 1500–1800*. London: Weidenfeld & Nicolson.

Strasburger, E. (1930), *Strasburger's Text-Book of Botany*. London: Macmillan.

Suart, R. and Smyth, A. S. H. (2008), *They'd None of 'em be Missed*. London: Pallas Athene Arts.

Sullivan, E. (2001), *Under Pressure and on Time*. Redmond, WA: Microsoft Press.

Sutcliffe, T. (1996), *Believing in Opera*. London: Faber.

Sutton, S. (1982), *The Largest Theatre in the World: Thirty Years of Television Drama*. London: British Broadcasting Corporation.

Svevo, I., translated by De Zoete, B. (1962), *As a Man Grows Older*. London: Secker & Warburg.

Tennyson, A. (1907), *The Complete Poetical Works of Alfred Lord Tennyson*. Toronto: Macmillan Co.

Terkel, S. (1999), *The Spectator: Talk About Movies and Plays With the People Who Make Them*. New York, NY: New Press.

Thompson, D. (1996), *Dudley Moore: On the Couch*. London: Little, Brown & Co.

Thompson, D. W. (1917), *On Growth and Form*. Cambridge: Cambridge University Press.

Thompson, H. (1997), *Peter Cook: A Biography*. London: Hodder & Stoughton.

Tinbergen, N. (1951), *The Study of Instinct*. Oxford: Clarendon Press.

Tiratsoo, N. (ed.) (1997), *From Blitz to Blair: A New History of Britain since 1939*. London: Weidenfeld & Nicolson.

Tomalin, C. (1999), *Several Strangers: Writing from Three Decades*. London, Viking.

Turbeville, D. (1981), *Unseen Versailles: Photographs by Deborah Turbeville*. New York, NY: Doubleday.

Turner, A. W. (2008), *Crisis? What Crisis?: Britain in the 1970s*. London: Aurum.

—— (2010), *Rejoice, Rejoice!: Britain in the 1980s*. London: Aurum.

Tyack, G. (1995), *Oxford and Cambridge*. London: A & C Black, Blue Guide series.

Tynan, Kathleen (1987), *The Life of Kenneth Tynan*. London: Weidenfeld & Nicolson.

Tynan, Kenneth (1964), *Tynan on Theatre*. London: Penguin.

——, edited by Tynan, Kathleen (1994), *Kenneth Tynan: Letters*. London: Weidenfeld & Nicolson.

——, edited by Tynan, Kathleen (1994), *Kenneth Tynan: Letters*. London: Weidenfeld & Nicolson.

——, edited by Lahr, J. (2002), *The Diaries of Kenneth Tynan*. London: Bloomsbury.

Vahimagi, T. (ed.) (1994), *British Television: An Illustrated Guide*. Oxford: Oxford University Press (in association with the BFI).

Vinen, R. (2010 edn), *Thatcher's Britain: The Politics and Social Upheaval of the 1980s*. London: Pocket Books.

Volpe, J., written with Charles Michener (2007), *The Toughest Show on Earth: My Rise and Reign at the Metropolitan Opera*. New York, NY: Vintage.

Wachtel, E. (2003), *Original Minds*. Toronto: HarperFlamingo.

Walker, A. (1981), *Peter Sellers: The Authorized Biography*. London: Weidenfeld & Nicolson.

Walker, J. A. (1993), *Arts TV: A History of Arts Television in Britain*. London: John Libbey.

Walzer, M. (1966), *The Revolution of the Saints: A Study in the Origins of Radical Politics*. London: Weidenfeld & Nicholson.

Webb, P. (1988), *Portrait of David Hockney*. London: Chatto & Windus.

Weinreb, B. and Hibbert, C. (eds) (1983), *The London Encyclopaedia*. London: Macmillan.

Wetzsteon, R., 'The Director in Spite of Himself', *American Theatre*, November 1985.

Wheldon, H. (ed.) (1962), *Monitor: An Anthology*. London: Macdonald.

Whitehead, P. (1985), *The Writing on the Wall: Britain in the Seventies*. London: Joseph.

Willis, S. (1991), *The BBC Shakespeare Plays: Making the Televised Canon*. Chapel Hill, NC: University of North Carolina Press.

Wilmut, R. (1980), *From Fringe to Flying Circus: Celebrating a Unique Generation of Comedy 1960–1980*. London: Eyre Methuen.

Wilson, A. (1964), *Tempo: The Impact of Television on the Arts*. London: Studio Vista.

Wilson, E. (1993), *The Sixties: The Last Journal, 1960–1972*. New York, NY: Farrar Straus & Giroux.

Winder, R. (2004), *Bloody Foreigners: The Story of Immigration to Britain*. London: Little, Brown.

Winnicott, D. W. (1971), *Playing and Reality*. London: Tavistock Publications.

Wittgenstein, L. (1953), *Blue and Brown Books*. New York, NY: Macmillan.

——, translated by Anscombe, G. E. M. (1958), *Philosophical Investigations*. Oxford: Blackwell.

Wolfe, T. (1966), *The Kandy-Kolored Tangerine-Flake Streamline Baby*. London: Jonathan Cape.

Wölfflin, H., translated by Hottinger, M. D. (1950), *Principles of Art History: The Problem of the Development of Style in Later Art*. New York, NY: Dover Publications.

——, translated by Simon, K. (1984 edn), *Renaissance and Baroque*. London: Collins.

Yates, F. (1966), *The Art of Memory*. London: Routledge & Kegan Paul.

—— (1969), *Theatre of the World*. London: Routledge & Kegan Paul.

Young, J. Z. (1962), *The Life of Vertebrates*. Oxford: Clarendon Press.

Zangwill, I. (1972 edn), *Children of the Ghetto*. London: White Lion.

INDEX OF NAMES